*The bucolic Rose Hill campus
of Fordham University in the
early twentieth century*

FORDHAM

A HISTORY OF THE

JESUIT UNIVERSITY

OF NEW YORK

SAINT IGNATIUS LOYOLA

Founder of the Society of Jesus

FORDHAM

A History of the Jesuit University of New York: 1841–2003

THOMAS J. SHELLEY

FORDHAM UNIVERSITY PRESS New York 2016

Visit us online at www.fordhampress.com.

Library of Congress Cataloging-in-Publication Data
Names: Shelley, Thomas J., author.
Title: Fordham, a history of the Jesuit university of New York : 1841–2003 / Thomas J. Shelley.
Description: New York : Fordham University Press, 2016. |
Includes bibliographical references and index.
Identifiers: LCCN 2016000653 (print) | LCCN 2016004526 (ebook) |
ISBN 9780823271511 (cloth : alk. paper) | ISBN 9780823271528 (ePub) |
ISBN 9780823271535 (uPDF)
Subjects: LCSH: Fordham University—History.
Classification: LCC LD1811.F52 S54 2016 (print) | LCC LD1811.F52 (ebook) |
DDC 378.747/1—dc23
LC record available at http://lccn.loc.gov/2016000653

Printed in the United States of America

18 17 16   5 4 3 2 1

First edition

CONTENTS

Color plates follow pages 212 and 340

ABBREVIATIONS

AAB	Archives of the Archdiocese of Baltimore
AAIHS	Archives of the American Irish Historical Society
AANY	Archives of the Archdiocese of New York
AASL	Archives of the Archdiocese of St. Louis
ACGM	Archives of the Curia Generalizia della Missione (Vincentians)
ACSFX	Archives of the College of St. Francis Xavier
ACUA	Archives of the Catholic University of America
AER	*American Ecclesiastical Review*
AMSM	Archives of Mount St. Mary's College and Seminary, Emmitsburg
ANYPSJ	Archives of the New York Province of the Society of Jesus
ARSJ	Archivum Romanum Societatis Jesu
ASJSD	Archives of St. Joseph's Seminary, Dunwoodie
AUND	Archives of the University of Notre Dame
CFU	Catalogue of Fordham University
CH	*Church History*
CHR	*Catholic Historical Review*
FLR	*Fordham Law Review*
FM	*Fordham Monthly*
FOHP	Fordham Oral History Project
FUA	Fordham University Archives
HR&S	*Historical Records and Studies*
RACHSP	*Records of the American Catholic Historical Society of Philadelphia*
WL	*Woodstock Letters*

PREFACE

In 1838 a young Irish immigrant named John Hughes, who had been a priest for only twelve years, was consecrated the coadjutor (assistant) bishop of New York. The following year the Holy See appointed him the administrator of the diocese because of the failing health of Bishop John Dubois. Once he was in charge of the diocese, one of the first decisions Hughes made was to purchase 106 acres in the Fordham section of what was then southern Westchester County as the site for a seminary and college. The cost of the property was $29,750, but Hughes could raise only $10,000 from the impoverished New York Catholic community. He then departed on a ten-month begging trip through Europe to collect the additional $20,000.

The seminary opened at Rose Hill in 1840, and the college opened one year later with six students. The faculty of St. John's College was larger than the original student body. Bishop Hughes made education his first priority because he believed that it was the indispensable means for the poor immigrants who composed most of his flock to break free from the cycle of poverty and to better themselves economically and socially in their adopted land. For four years Hughes struggled to maintain his little diocesan college despite the meager resources available to him in money and personnel. In 1845 he was happy to sell St. John's College to the Society of Jesus, a religious order with an international reputation as professional educators. For their part, the Jesuits were eager to establish a foothold in the largest city in the United States.

The Jesuits arrived at Rose Hill in 1846. The first Jesuit community numbered twenty-nine, exactly the same size as the present-day Jesuit community at Fordham. Despite their diminishing numbers over the past fifty years, the Jesuits have been inextricably connected with the development of St. John's College and later Fordham University to the present day. The name was changed to Fordham University in 1907 after the establishment of the first two graduate schools in medicine and law in 1905. Expansion followed rapidly thereafter. In 1941, when Fordham University celebrated its centennial, the president, Father Robert I. Gannon, S.J., predicted that in the future only two classes of universities would continue to survive in the United States, those that were "very rich" and those that were "indispensable." Father Gannon did not define the precise nature of either term.

As Fordham University celebrates its 175th anniversary, it still does not qualify as "very rich" in comparison with Ivy League institutions that possess multi-billion-dollar endowments. However, Fordham can make a convincing claim to have become an indispensable presence in the American university world, both on the national and local levels. Nationally Fordham has established itself as a leading Catholic and Jesuit university with three undergraduate schools and seven professional and graduate schools with an enrollment of more than 15,000 students drawn from 48 states and 65 countries. Locally Fordham has remained true to John Hughes's vision of an institution that enables the children and grandchildren of immigrants and minorities to equip themselves with the education they need to scale the ladder of success and participate in the American dream.

One measure of Fordham's achievement is the success of the recent fundraising campaign that raised more than a half-billion dollars, $540,000,000 to be precise, a sum beyond the wildest dreams of Fordham's Founding Father, who was hard pressed to raise $40,000. Another measure of Fordham's success and its academic indispensability is what has not changed. While Fordham today welcomes faculty and students of all faiths and none, it still seeks to offer its students a distinctive vision of higher education that draws its inspiration from the Christian humanism of its Catholic and Jesuit heritage. I hope the following chapters will help to explain both Fordham's receptivity to the winds of change in American society and also its commitment to maintaining the fundamental values that have informed Jesuit education since the Society of Jesus opened its first college in 1548 in Messina.

FORDHAM

A HISTORY OF THE
JESUIT UNIVERSITY
OF NEW YORK

COMMENCEMENT DAY, 1845

I

In 1845 the academic year at St. John's College, Fordham, came to a close on Tuesday, July 15, with the usual "exhibition" or commencement ceremonies. It was a hot summer day, but the heat did not prevent several thousand people from descending upon the Rose Hill campus for the ceremonies. The New York and Harlem Railroad added two special trains that transported the guests from the Prince Street station in Manhattan near City Hall up Fourth Avenue through the Yorkville tunnel and across the Harlem River drawbridge to Fordham in one hour, almost as quickly as one could cover the distance today by public transportation. Eight new classrooms had recently been added to the campus, and the buildings were described as forming a perfect square with interior corridors and neatly finished steeples (more accurately cupolas).[1] A large canvas tent had been erected on the front lawn to shield the participants from the scorching sun. However, the crowd was so large that many people spilled out from under the cover of the tent and found places to sit on the lawn.

On the stage were the assembled clerical and academic dignitaries, headed, of course, by the founding father, Bishop John Hughes, who presided in his capacity as *praeses emeritus*. At least on that day New York's embattled bishop was among friends, a representative sampling of the Irish Catholics who had cheered him on during the previous five years through all his battles with the lay trustees, the Public School Society, obnoxious newspaper editors, and most recently the Nativists. Amid such surroundings Hughes could relax for a few hours and savor the victories he had won among admirers who appreciated them as much as he did.

Not the least of his accomplishments was the scene that unfolded before him. In the front rows sat 145 students, compared with the six students with whom he had opened his college four years earlier. On Hughes's left and right were two New York priests whom he had recently consecrated bishops: William Quarter, the first bishop of Chicago, and Andrew Byrne, the first bishop of Little Rock. Present also were Father Constantine Pise

---

1. *Truth Teller*, August 24, 1844.

of St. Joseph's parish in Greenwich Village, the first priest to serve as chaplain to the U.S. Senate; Father Felix Varela, the Cuban political exile who had worked so hard in 1839 and 1840 to raise funds for Hughes's seminary and college at Rose Hill; and Father John Harley, the twenty-nine-year-old college president, who gave an address on the value of Catholic education.

Despite the heat, the ceremonies lasted several hours as students delivered prepared speeches and a brass band played such popular Irish American tunes as "Exile of Erin" and "The Last Rose of Summer." There were no diplomas to be awarded, because St. John's College did not yet possess a charter, but the distribution of "premiums" (a.k.a. prizes) must have been interminable, for the printed list of recipients filled two whole columns of the *Freeman's Journal* the following week. No one went home unhappy, for virtually every student received several prizes, which were for accomplishments that ran the gamut from proficiency in Greek and Latin to "improvement on bugle." Almost all the names were Irish except for those of a sprinkling of Hispanic students from Mexico and Cuba. At the end of the long day Hughes as usual had the final word, telling the audience how pleased he was with the progress of the college.[2]

Unknown to the guests on the festive occasion, a source of intense concern to Hughes that summer afternoon was the deteriorating health of Harley, which would force him to resign as president later that summer. Harley's ill health called into question the whole future of St. John's College, because Hughes had no one of comparable ability among his own clergy to replace him. It also placed an added burden on Hughes himself. "Whilst the college is otherwise prosperous," he told his friend Bishop John Purcell of Cincinnati at the beginning of the new academic year in September 1845, "[Harley's] associates are all without experience, and the superintendence of the institution with its one hundred and sixty boys requires my daily inspection in a quiet and unostentatious way." As was often the case, Hughes was exaggerating, in this instance because he was looking for an excuse to avoid a trip to Cincinnati for the dedication of Purcell's new cathedral. It is as difficult to imagine John Hughes traveling to Fordham every day by train as it is to imagine him intervening anywhere in a quiet and unostentatious way. Nonetheless, his comments to Purcell reveal both his own deep commitment to St. John's College and his increasing weariness at trying to maintain the college with the slender resources of his diocesan clergy.[3]

2. *New York Freeman's Journal,* July 19, 1845; *Truth Teller,* July 12, 19, 1845.
3. AUND, Hughes to Purcell, September 23, 1845.

One possible solution was to persuade the Society of Jesus to assume the responsibility of administering both his college and seminary at Rose Hill. It was a solution that Hughes had been seeking to arrange since 1839, but the Jesuits had always turned down his requests because they did not have the manpower to accept his offer. However, circumstances changed abruptly in 1845 when a farsighted Jesuit superior, Father Clément Boulanger, the former provincial of the province of France, arrived in the United States and stopped briefly in New York on his way to Kentucky to inspect a college sponsored by his province. He was eager to extricate his men from this languishing rural college and transplant them to New York, if he could work out a mutually satisfactory arrangement with Hughes.

Both sides had a vested interest in reaching an agreement. For the Jesuits it would mean securing a foothold for the Society in the leading metropolis of the United States; for Hughes it would mean obtaining the services of a religious order with an established reputation as professional educators. Hughes and Boulanger had met once before, in Paris in the summer of 1843, when Boulanger, at that time the provincial of the province of France, had been ready to abandon the college in Kentucky and transfer his men to New York, but he could not obtain the permission of the father general, Jan Roothaan.

Hughes and Boulanger met twice again in New York City in the spring of 1845, but neither of them mentioned the possibility of the Jesuits' coming to Rose Hill. Both men were experienced negotiators, the equivalent of seasoned poker players who held their cards close to their chest, waiting for the right moment to show their hands. It was the Irishman, not the Frenchman, who blinked first, perhaps because of Harley's failing health. On October 8, 1845, Hughes sent word to Boulanger in Kentucky that he was ready to make a deal. Boulanger hurried east before Hughes sailed for Europe and signed an agreement with him on November 24, 1845, buying St. John's College for $40,000.[4]

The offer would not have seemed so attractive to Père Boulanger and the Jesuits if John Hughes had not worked long and hard during the previous half-dozen years to establish St. John's College on a solid foundation despite severe local obstacles and numerous demands upon his time by

4. ANYPSJ, Canada-New York Mission, Extrait des conventions faites à New-york . . . entre Monseigneur John Hughes évêque de New-york et le Rd. P. Clément Boulanger, S.J., Visiteur. November 24, 1845. Thomas C. Hennessy, S.J, "The First Jesuits at St. John's College (Fordham), 1846," in Thomas C. Hennessy, S.J., ed., *Fordham: The Early Years* (New York: Something More Publications, 1998), 81.

issues of national importance. Any history of Fordham University must begin with him and his tenacious efforts to give New York its first permanent Catholic college.

FOUNDING FATHER

2

John Hughes

John Hughes was born in Annalogan, County Tyrone, Ireland, on June 24, 1797. The son of a poor Ulster farmer, he had to abandon school early in life in order to support his family. "They told me when I was a boy," he said, "that for the first five days I was on a social and civil equality with the most favored subject of the British Empire. These five days would be the interval between my birth and my baptism."[1] Once he was baptized a Catholic, like every eighteenth-century Irish Catholic, John Hughes became a second-class citizen in the land of his birth. Hughes emigrated to America in 1817 and found work as a quarryman and day laborer. When he applied for admission to a seminary in 1819, his educational background was so deficient that he had to spend a year in remedial studies before he was accepted as a candidate for the priesthood.

Ordained a priest for the diocese of Philadelphia on October 15, 1826, Hughes was made a bishop only twelve years later. On January 7, 1838, he was consecrated the coadjutor, or assistant bishop, of New York to assist the ailing Bishop John Dubois, the former seminary rector who had rejected his original application to Mount St. Mary's College and Seminary in Emmitsburg, Maryland. Hughes succeeded Dubois as the fourth bishop of New York on the latter's death on December 20, 1842, and was appointed the first archbishop of New York on July 19, 1850.

John Hughes believed passionately in the necessity of Catholic higher education, as did another founding father, John Carroll, first bishop and archbishop of Baltimore, who, more than any other individual, was responsible for the establishment of Georgetown College between 1786 and 1791. As far back as 1783 Carroll had said that "the object nearest my heart is to establish a college on this continent for the education of youth which might at the same time be a seminary for future clergymen." He called

---

1. John Hassard, *Life of the Most Reverend John Hughes, First Archbishop of New York* (New York: D. Appleton and Company, 1866), 17–18. Hassard was a graduate of St. John's College, Fordham, class of 1855.

The Most Reverend John Hughes, fourth bishop of New York and first archbishop, founder of St. John's College at Fordham in 1841.

Georgetown, the first Catholic college in the United States, "our main sheet anchor for religion."[2] Hughes's lay secretary and future biographer, John Hassard, expressed Hughes's commitment to Catholic education in almost exactly the same words that Carroll used when he wrote that "the subject that of all others [Hughes] had nearest his heart was education."[3] Hughes's recognition of the importance of Catholic college education was

2. Carroll to Charles Plowden, September 26, 1783; Carroll to Plowden, October 23, 1789, *The John Carroll Papers*, ed. Thomas O'Brien Hanley, S.J. (Notre Dame, Ind.: University of Notre Dame Press, 1976), I, 78, 390, cit. in Philip Gleason, "The Main Sheet Anchor: John Carroll and Catholic Higher Education," *The Review of Politics* 38:4 (October 1976): 576–613. "A sheet anchor," explained Robert Emmett Curran, "was the large spare anchor carried amidships to be cast overboard in emergencies. It was in other words the rock bottom support of a ship in crisis." Robert Emmett Curran, *The Bicentennial History of Georgetown University* (Washington: Georgetown University Press, 1993), I, 13.

3. Hassard, *Hughes*, 189.

Founding Father

all the more remarkable because, unlike Carroll, who had received a splendid education in elite Jesuit schools in Europe, his own education had been limited to "patchwork seminary" courses, as William Gordon Bennett, the acerbic editor of the *New York Herald*, frequently reminded him.

Like Carroll, Hughes wanted to give his diocese both a seminary and a college. The property he purchased at Rose Hill in 1839 was intended to house both institutions. Hughes opened the seminary in 1840, but a shortage of funds forced him to delay the opening of the college until the following year. Like Carroll, Hughes looked to the Society of Jesus to supply the teaching staff. Georgetown College was modeled after Carroll's own alma mater, St. Omers, in French Flanders. As early as 1839 Hughes tried to persuade the Jesuits to assume the direction of his projected college at Rose Hill, but it was not until 1845 that he was successful in enlisting their services. Still another common feature of the educational endeavors of John Carroll and John Hughes was the difficulties they both experienced in raising funds to finance their new colleges. Carroll's efforts to attract contributions for Georgetown from wealthy American and English Catholics, including his fabulously rich cousin Charles Carroll of Carrollton, yielded only modest results. John Hughes said bluntly, "I had not, when I purchased the site of this new college, St. John's, Fordham, so much as a penny wherewith to commence the payment for it."[4]

Fordham Manor

In August 1839 John Hughes purchased 106 acres at Rose Hill in the still-rural Fordham area of Westchester County. Located twelve miles from New York City (which at the time consisted only of Manhattan), it was only a ninety-minute carriage ride from the metropolis by the Third Avenue Road, and when the New York and Harlem Railroad reached Fordham in October 1841, the travel time was cut to forty minutes. In 1839 Hughes was still only the coadjutor bishop to Dubois, but in June of that year Rome appointed him the administrator of the diocese after Dubois suffered a series of debilitating strokes. It is indicative of the importance that Hughes attached to education that only two months later he made the first major decision of his administration when he bought the property at Rose Hill.

4. Curran, *Georgetown University* I, 16–19; AANY, A-7, Hughes to Abbot Bernard Smith, July 9, 1858. The letter was edited and published by Henry Browne as "The Archdiocese of New York a Century Ago: A Memoir of Archbishop Hughes, 1838–1858," *HR&S* 39–40 (1952): 129–87.

This purchase represented the third attempt in seven years by the diocese of New York to establish a combination seminary and college, both previous efforts having ended in failure. The first attempt was the work of the French-born Dubois, an experienced educator who had founded Mount St. Mary's College and Seminary in Emmitsburg, Maryland, in 1808. Dubois painstakingly tried to erect a similar seminary and college in Upper Nyack, New York, between 1832 and 1837. As the building neared completion in April 1837, however, it burned to the ground as the result of an accident caused by a careless workman. Dubois said that the fire "swallowed up in two hours $25,000." There was no insurance, and he did not have the money to rebuild the lost structure.[5]

When Hughes, the newly arrived coadjutor bishop, inspected the remains of the building, he pronounced it "a splendid folly." A month later he himself was guilty of an even bigger folly. He bought 467 acres at Lafargeville, near Watertown in northern New York state, in the Thousand Islands, and persuaded Dubois to make this institution, which was at least three days' journey from Manhattan, New York's second venture into higher education. After two years the student body consisted of nine seminarians and "a handful of children." Even Hughes admitted that the faculty was woefully inadequate. "You can have no idea of the set whom Bishop Dubois sent to Lafargeville," he told the rector of Mount St. Mary's, "good pious men, if you wish, but utterly incapable of teaching." After repeated requests from the rector of Lafargeville to close the institution, Hughes did so quietly in 1840 after he had acquired the real estate at Rose Hill.[6]

The property at Rose Hill formed a small residual part of the seventeenth-century Manor of Fordham, a tract of about 3,900 acres that once extended through southern Westchester County from the Harlem River to the Bronx River. Governor John Lovelace had granted the manor to John Archer in 1671, only seven years after the English conquered the Dutch and took possession of the colony. It was the first manorial patent issued in the colony of New York. One result of successive subdivisions of the original Fordham Manor and numerous changes of ownership over the course of a century-and-a-half was the creation in 1827 of the 106-acre farm that John Hughes purchased in 1839. The name Rose Hill dates from 1787, when Robert Watts acquired property in Fordham and named it after his family's ancestral Scottish estate near Edinburgh. After 1827 the property changed hands no fewer than seven times before it was purchased in July

5. AASL, Dubois to Bishop Joseph Rosati, April 18, 1837.
6. AMSM, Hughes to John McCaffrey, June 2, 1841.

1839 by Andrew Carrigan, a prominent New York Catholic layman and merchant, who was acting on behalf of Hughes.[7] Carrigan sold it to the bishop one month later, on August 29, 1839, for $29,750. The property was identified in the indenture as "distinguished by the name of Rose Hill and situate [*sic*] in the Manor of Fordham." Hughes was identified as "Minister of the Gospels."[8]

Seminary and College

What Hughes had in mind for Rose Hill was an institution similar to his own alma mater, Mount St. Mary's College and Seminary in Emmitsburg, which was a combined liberal arts college and theological seminary. At the "Mountain," as it was affectionately called by students and alumni, the tuition of the college students helped to defray the expenses of the seminary while the seminarians subsidized the college by serving as unpaid teachers and tutors. Hughes wanted to create a comparable institution in New York, but it was the seminary that mattered most to him. From the beginning of the college in 1841 until the closing of the seminary in 1860 the fate of the two institutions was closely linked, often resulting in clashes between Hughes and either the college or seminary authorities or both.

The college-seminary model was not unique to Emmitsburg or New York; it was the most common form of Catholic higher education in the United States during the first half of the nineteenth century. Bishop Ben-

7. Carrigan later served as chairman of the finance committee of the Emigrant Savings Bank, president of the Irish Emigrant Society, and as a New York State Commissioner of Emigration. At his death the *New York Times* remarked, "During the whole period of the late Archbishop Hughes' residence in this city no man enjoyed more of his affectionate regard and confidence than Andrew Carrigan, nor was any man more worthy of such distinction." *New York Times*, September 6, 1872, in Marion R. Casey, "Refractive History: Memory and the Founders of the Emigrant Savings Bank," *Making the Irish American: History and Heritage of the Irish in America*, ed. J. J. Lee and Marion R. Casey (New York: New York University Press, 2006), 313.

8. AANY, B, Indenture between Andrew and Catherine Carrigan and John Hughes, Minister of the Gospels, August 29, 1839. For the most detailed and authoritative description of the Rose Hill property and the early days of the college, see Allan S. Gilbert and Roger Wines, two Fordham University professors who used their detailed archaeological excavations at Rose Hill over the course of twelve years to complement their original research into the deeds, wills, and records pertaining to the founding of the college. Allan S. Gilbert and Roger Wines, "From Earliest to Latest Fordham: Background History and Ongoing Archaeology," in Thomas C. Hennessy, S.J., *Fordham: The Early Years* (New York: Something More Publications, 1998), 139–76.

edict Fenwick of Boston anticipated John Hughes by a decade when he said, "The thing I want most (and I am persuaded that until I attain it nothing permanent can or ever will be effected in this quarter) is a seminary and a college. And for my part," he added, "I have not one cent to build them with." As Philip Gleason has pointed out, "the college-seminary relationship was a symbiotic affair" that had great appeal to financially hard-pressed bishops because each of the two institutions helped to support the other. Mount St. Mary's, which may be said to have initiated the system in the United States, continued the practice well into the twentieth century and was the last to abandon it.[9]

Hughes told Bishop John Purcell of Cincinnati in February 1838 that "the idea that most engages my mind at this moment is the establishment of a seminary for ecclesiastics. There is also a prospect of realizing it now, and in no place at any time was it more wanted." He explained to Purcell that New York required its own seminary to improve the unsatisfactory quality of the local clergy. "Clergymen, some of doubtful character and some of whom there is no doubt, have found easy admission into the diocese," he said, "and religion suffers in consequence."[10]

Although the seminary was the apple of his eye, Hughes appreciated the need for a liberal arts college for the sons of New York's growing Catholic middle class. Reflecting perhaps on his own experience as a priest in Philadelphia, where many children of the colonial Catholic elite such as the Careys and the Meades had drifted away from the Church, he told some would-be Austrian benefactors in 1840 that the absence of a Catholic college in New York meant that "the youth of wealthier families are exposed to lose their faith by being educated in dangerous intercourse with Protestantism."[11] If he had been aware of it, he might have cited the case of Dominick Lynch, a wealthy Irish-born New York Catholic businessman, who was one of three laymen who joined Bishop John Carroll in offering George Washington the congratulations of American Catholics upon his election as the first president of the United States. Not one of Lynch's thirteen children remained a Catholic.

9. Benedict Fenwick to Edward Fenwick, July 19, 1830, in Robert Lord, John Sexton, and Edward Harrington, *The History of the Archdiocese of Boston* (Boston: Boston Pilot Publishing Company, 1944), II, 320. Philip Gleason, "From an Indefinite Homogeneity: Catholic Colleges in Antebellum America," *CHR* 94:1 (2008): 58, 66.

10. AUND, Hughes to Purcell, February 24, 1838.

11. Hughes to the Leopoldine Society, April 16, 1840, in Lawrence Kehoe, ed., *Complete Works of the Most Reverend John Hughes, D.D., First Archbishop of New York* (New York: Lawrence Kehoe, 1866), II, 463.

Hughes hoped that a Catholic college in New York would not only protect the faith of young Catholics but also attract Protestant students and help to break down their suspicions of Catholicism. It was an argument that he used with the Jesuit father general, Jan Philip Roothaan, in 1843 (on the feast of St. Ignatius Loyola, no less), when for the second time he was trying to induce the Jesuits to take charge of his college. "[I]t is not the Catholics alone that would profit by it," he told Roothaan. "The Protestants would send their children and the prejudices which they have entertained through ignorance would be dissipated."[12]

Only two buildings were on the Rose Hill property when Hughes purchased it in 1839. One was an unfinished three-story stone manor house with one-story colonnaded wings on both sides. It had been erected recently by Dr. Horatio Shepheard Moat, an English-born physician from Brooklyn, who owned the property from 1836 until 1838. The stone building survives today as the central part of Cunniffe House, the former Administration Building, but the original one-story wings were replaced with the present two-story brick wings in 1869.[13] The other building was the old Rose Hill Manor, a wood frame farmhouse that dated from around 1694 and was to serve many purposes at the college until it was demolished in 1896.[14] Both buildings required extensive renovations before they could be used as college facilities. Hughes estimated that the cost of the renovations would amount to $10,000 in addition to the $30,000 that he had spent to buy the property. It was money that he did not have, and he immediately began a quest for donors to finance his second venture into the field of Catholic higher education.

Finances and Faculty

On September 1, 1839, Hughes launched a subscription drive, speaking at St. Patrick's Cathedral (today's Basilica of Old St. Patrick's Cathedral) and at a different parish church every evening that week. However, he knew that he could never get the $40,000 he needed solely from

12. Hughes to Roothaan, July 31, 1843, cit. in Gilbert J. Garraghan, S.J., "Fordham's Jesuit Beginnings," *Thought* 16 (March 1941): 21.

13. In December 2014 the Administration Building was renamed Cunniffe House in recognition of the generosity of Maurice J. Cunniffe, FCRH '54, a trustee emeritus of the university. The graceful new classical fountain in the rear of Cunniffe House between Hughes Hall and Dealy Hall was erected at the same time and was named the Carolyn Dursi Cunniffe fountain in recognition of the services to Fordham of Maurice Cunniffe's wife, Carolyn Dursi Cunniffe, GSAS '71.

14. Gilbert and Wines, "From Earliest to Latest Fordham," 142–46.

New York's impoverished Catholics. Therefore, the second part of his plan was to conduct a begging tour of Europe. He left New York on October 16, 1839, and spent the next ten months trying to raise abroad the money that he could not get at home.

The bishop's trip took him to Rome (where he spent three months), England, Ireland, and also to Munich, Vienna, and Paris, where he visited the headquarters of the Bavarian, Austrian, and French Catholic missionary aid societies. According to Hassard, in Vienna the Leopoldine Society gave Hughes a "liberal donation" for his college and seminary. There is no indication that he received anything from the Ludwig-Missionsverein in Munich, where the king, Ludwig I, was increasingly insistent that the Bavarian society's funds go exclusively to German Catholic parishes and institutions in America. However, Hughes had better luck when he called upon the Society for the Propagation of the Faith in Paris. He later told the Society that it had provided the principal financial support for the seminary.[15]

Fundraising was not the only purpose of Bishop Hughes's European trip. He was also hoping to recruit faculty for his college and seminary. When he was in Paris in 1839, Hughes met Bishop Charles-Auguste de Forbin-Janson of Toul and Nancy, an ultra-royalist prelate who had been exiled from his diocese by the government of King Louis Philippe after the Revolution of 1830. As a favor to Hughes, Bishop Forbin-Janson wrote to the Jesuit general, Father Jan Roothaan, asking that Jesuits take charge of the two institutions at Rose Hill. Reluctantly Roothaan declined the request because of the lack of personnel.[16]

The Dutch-born Roothaan had entered the Society of Jesus in 1804 in Russia. Only the second general after the full restoration of the Society in 1814 following its suppression by Pope Clement XIV in 1773, Roothaan was eventually to play a crucial role in the coming of the Jesuits to Rose Hill. He spent much of his twenty-four years as general fending off requests for Jesuits from bishops all over the world. A decade after he turned down Hughes's request, he explained to another American bishop why he could not accede to his request. "The great plague of the Society in your part

15. Hughes to Leopoldine Society, April 16, 1840, in Kehoe, *Complete Works*, II, 463. AANY, A-6, Hughes to Society for the Propagation of the Faith, January 22, 1845. Hassard, *Hughes*, 212.

16. Garraghan, "Fordham's Jesuit Beginnings," 18. Bishop Forbin-Janson later donated $6,000 for the establishment of the first French church in New York City, St. Vincent de Paul. Henry Binsse, "The Church of St. Vincent de Paul (The French Church)," *HR&S* 12 (1918), 103–5.

Founding Father

of the world is this," he told Bishop Martin Spalding of Louisville, "that we undertake too many things and do not have the time for the training of subjects." He added candidly, "I understand quite well how urgent are the needs, but if things go on there at this pace, I cannot help entertaining very great fears for the future of that portion of the Society where the harvest is gathered before it is ripe and where one must look for grass instead of grain."[17]

Meanwhile, in New York, the fundraising drive had gotten off to a good start and then quickly ground to a halt. Two days before he sailed for Europe, Hughes issued a pastoral letter in which he barely mentioned the college at all, stressing instead the necessity of building the seminary to overcome the shortage of priests. He reminded New York Catholics how difficult it was for many of them to attend Mass on Sunday or even to find a priest to anoint the dying. He ordered every pastor to open a subscription list in his parish and to submit a report every two weeks to a Committee of Accounts and Collection headed by Father John Power, the pastor of St. Peter's Church and one of New York's two vicars general.[18]

During its first two months the campaign brought in slightly more than $7,000, but then contributions slowed to a trickle and less than $3,000 was raised during the following seven months. Many who made pledges never came through with the cash. While Father Power served as the chairman of the campaign, New York's other vicar general, the Cuban-born Father Felix Varela, the pastor of Transfiguration Church, kept up a steady drumbeat of appeals in the pages of his newly founded weekly newspaper, the *New York Catholic Register*. In November he was still sounding an optimistic note, predicting that "the subscriptions thus far augur so favorably as to leave no doubt of ultimate success." By the following February he was not so sanguine, and later that month he was reporting that one-third of the pledges had not been paid. In March he raised the possibility that the renovations at Rose Hill might have to be suspended, and in April he speculated that Bishop Hughes would not be happy when he returned from Europe.[19]

Shortly thereafter, New York's Catholics heard directly from Hughes himself. Writing an open letter to Varela from Dublin on June 1, 1840,

17. Roothaan to Spalding, n.d., cit. in Gilbert J. Garraghan, S.J., *The Jesuits of the Middle United States* (New York: America Press, 1938), III, 274.

18. *New York Catholic Register*, October 24, 1839. Anyone unable to contribute $1 was excused as "too straitened in circumstances to contribute at all."

19. The final sums reported by Father Varela were $14,672.55 in pledges, of which $9,905.95 had been paid. *New York Catholic Register*, June 10, 1840.

Hughes said that his greatest concern had been the progress of his new seminary and college. "I perceive that but little has been done since I left," he said ominously. However, he added, "This does not discourage me because I think it is owing to causes different from any want of real zeal on the part of the Catholics of the city and the diocese. The only effect it will have will be to delay the commencement, for as we have to begin once only, we must wait until we can begin well—and this cannot be before we have the buildings and the ground paid for."[20]

Distractions

During the formative years of St. John's College, Hughes never had the opportunity to give his undivided attention to its founding. From 1839 until 1844 he was preoccupied with three other major issues: lay trusteeism, public education in New York City, and the rising tide of Nativism throughout the country. His vigorous response to all three issues was to define the nature and tone of his episcopacy and to make him a national figure, admired by some but feared and hated by many others.

In the 1830s every parish church in New York City had a board of lay trustees who often clashed with the pastor or bishop over the administration of the parish. At the cathedral parish a series of confrontations led to an ugly scene on February 10, 1839, when the trustees forcibly removed a Sunday school teacher who had been appointed by Bishop Dubois. Hughes reacted at once because he feared that the civil law invoked by the trustees "gives them the same right to send a constable into the sanctuary to remove a priest from the altar." The trustees were theoretically accountable to the pewholders who had elected them, and so Hughes summoned a meeting of all the pewholders. More than 600 people showed up for the meeting two weeks later.

Hughes knew how to appeal to an Irish American crowd. Rather than discuss the niceties of canon law, he went straight for the jugular and compared the trustees to the British authorities in Ireland. It was pure demagoguery, but it worked. According to Hughes, many in the congregation wept like children. And he added (after listening to his own rhetoric), "I was not far from it myself." The pewholders disavowed the trustees and sided with Hughes. It was the beginning of the end of trusteeism in New York. "*Te Deum laudamus, Te Dominum confitemur*," Hughes told the archbishop of Baltimore the next day. "We killed the trustees, as I told you, but it came so suddenly that they could not believe they were dead."

20. *New York Catholic Register*, June 25, 1840.

Hughes was so pleased with the outcome that he told Bishop Joseph Rosati of St. Louis, "It is a revolution, and I trust a happy one in its consequences for religion."[21]

Trusteeism was essentially an internal ecclesiastical issue, but one year later Hughes became involved in a dispute that was of vital concern to virtually all New Yorkers. Upon his return to New York from his begging trip to Europe on July 18, 1840, he quickly discovered that the biggest concern of the city's Catholics was not the projected seminary and college at Rose Hill but another educational matter, the condition of the public schools. Since 1826 these schools had been administered by the Public School Society, a private charitable organization designated by the Common Council to be the sole recipient of the educational funds allocated by the state legislature every year for the city's public schools.

For fourteen years the city's Catholics had chafed under the monopoly of the Public School Society, which, according to Hughes, was dominated by Presbyterians. The Society suffused its schools with a bland, nondenominational form of Christianity that was quite acceptable to most Protestants, but not to Catholics. As one of the trustees of the Public School Society noted with frustration in 1840, "[The Catholics] do not class themselves among 'sectararians' or 'denominations of Christians' but claim emphatically to be 'The Church.'"[22] Moreover, the atmosphere in the schools was often aggressively anti-Catholic. Hassard commented tartly that "instead of teaching religion without sectarianism, they may almost be said to have taught sectarianism without religion." Catholics objected especially to the mandatory use of the King James version of the Bible and textbooks that ridiculed such Catholic practices as the sacrament of penance. Hughes himself estimated that half of the city's Catholic children received no education at all because their parents would not send them to the public schools and there was no room for them in the overcrowded Catholic schools.

Catholics were not the only New Yorkers who deplored this situation. Governor William H. Seward mentioned it specifically in his message to

21. AAB, Hughes to Samuel Eccleston, March 10, 1839; AASL, Hughes to Rosati, May 7, 1839. Trusteeism was a national problem for the Catholic Church in the United States during the first half of the nineteenth century. The most authoritative and balanced study of the phenomenon is Patrick W. Carey, *People, Priests and Prelates: Ecclesiastical Democracy and the Tensions of Trusteeism* (Notre Dame, Ind.: University of Notre Dame Press, 1987).

22. New-York Historical Society, Minutes of the Meetings of the Board of Trustees of the Public School Society of New York, August 27, 1840.

the state legislature on January 7, 1840. "The children of foreigners," he said, "are too often deprived of the advantages of our system of public education in consequence of prejudices arising from differences of language or religion." He added, "I do not hesitate, therefore, to recommend the establishment of schools in which they may be instructed by teachers speaking the same language and professing the same faith."[23]

Not unreasonably, Catholics interpreted the governor's remarks as an invitation to seek public funds for their own schools. Bishop Hughes was still in Europe, but Catholics quickly formed an association, headed by Father John Power, to contest the monopoly of the Public School Society. Power's role as chairman of this association soon overshadowed his other responsibilities as the chairman of the fundraising drive for the seminary and college. During the spring and summer of 1840 the association met every two weeks in the basement of St. James Church. One meeting was scheduled for July 20, two days after Hughes's return from Europe. "On my return," said Hughes, "I found my diocese, and especially the city of New York, in a ferment." He showed up at the meeting and promptly took command of the Catholic forces.[24]

John Hughes's epic battle with the Public School Society lasted for twenty-one months, from July 1840 to April 1842. It absorbed so much of his time and energy that his friends noticed the toll that it took on his health and even his appearance. In the course of the struggle Hughes argued his case to no avail for eight hours before the Common Council of the City of New York without the benefit of legal counsel, then formed his own short-lived political party and carried the fight to Albany, where the state legislature finally broke the monopoly of the Public School Society with the passage of the McClay bill on April 9, 1842. It was an impressive achievement for him to "knead up" (his words) the Catholic immigrants under his leadership and turn them into a potent political force, obliging a reluctant Democratic party to vote for the educational reforms of a Whig governor who was unable to get his own party to support them. However, it was a pyrrhic victory because the state Senate amended the McClay bill to exclude any sectarian religious instruction in the public schools. "It is paradoxical," said Vincent Lannie, the historian of the controversy, "that the father of American Catholic education

23. George E. Baker, ed., *The Works of William Seward* (New York: J. S. Redfield, 1853), II, 215.

24. Hughes, "Memoir," 149.

should also have acted as catalyst in the eventual secularization of American public education."[25]

The third issue that tested Hughes's leadership qualities was Nativism, which was the name given to the backlash against the large numbers of Catholic immigrants who were pouring into the port cities along the Atlantic coast. In Philadelphia in May 1844 riots had led to the death of thirteen people and the torching of two Catholic churches. When the Nativist leaders announced their intention to stage similar demonstrations in New York City, Hughes threatened to turn New York City into a second Moscow, if any harm came to his churches, a reference to the Russian resistance to Napoleon only thirty years earlier. He also posted armed guards around his churches. As a result the Nativists called off their demonstration and New York City escaped the mob violence that had engulfed Philadelphia.[26]

Getting Started

Despite these bitter and emotionally draining battles over a period of five years, Hughes pushed ahead with his plans to open his seminary and college at Rose Hill. However, lack of funds forced him to choose between the college and the seminary. As a result he decided to delay the opening of the college for a year so that he could inaugurate the seminary at Rose Hill in the fall of 1840. It was a modest beginning indeed for the seminary, with about twenty students and a single faculty member who taught all the subjects, Father Felix Vilanis, apparently an Italian diocesan priest whom Hughes had recruited in Europe. Vilanis did not stay at Rose Hill very long. In 1842 he founded St. Raymond's Church, the oldest parish in what today is Bronx County, and the following year he established St. Patrick's Church in Verplanck, the oldest parish in Westchester County.

In September 1841 Bishop Purcell of Cincinnati apologized for even writing to Hughes. "You are so constantly engaged in fighting &, of course, winning the battles of Faith," he said, "that I scruple intruding a moment longer on yr time." Yet, it was precisely during that hectic summer and autumn that Bishop Hughes also found the time to launch his long-awaited new college, which opened its doors on June 24, 1841, the feast of St. John

25. Vincent P. Lannie, *Public Money and Parochial Education: Bishop Hughes, Governor Seward, and the New York School Controversy* (Cleveland: The Press of Case Western Reserve University, 1968), 258.

26. Ray Allen Billington, *The Protestant Crusade: A Study of the Origins of American Nativism* (New York: Macmillan, 1938), 231–32. Billington said that "Bishop Hughes deserves credit for saving New York from a period of mob rule as that which had racked Philadelphia." Ibid.

the Baptist, Hughes's own patron saint. It is not clear whether there was any formal dedication or inaugural ceremony. At the time, there were ten parish churches in New York City with a combined debt of approximately $300,000. The annual interest on this debt was $20,000, "almost enough to build a new church every year," Hassard remarked. The fundraising drive for the seminary and college the previous year had raised only $10,000, or less than half the amount that Hughes needed to find every year merely to service the debt on his churches. It was a bold venture to start St. John's College under such circumstances.[27]

Lack of money was not the only problem—Hughes also had to find a suitable president and faculty. In the five years that the college was in the hands of the New York diocesan clergy, there were no fewer than four rectors or presidents. The first was a young priest in whom Hughes had great confidence, John McCloskey, a native of Brooklyn, who was the first native-born priest of the diocese. He had served as a professor at Bishop Dubois's ill-starred seminary at Upper Nyack eight years earlier and then spent three years studying in Rome, although he never finished the none-too-rigorous requirements for the doctorate because, as he admitted candidly in his old age, "I did not want to take the trouble." McCloskey served as president of St. John's College as well as professor of rhetoric and *belles lettres* for only two years while retaining his position as pastor of St. Joseph's Church in Greenwich Village.[28]

The vice president was Father Ambrose Manahan, a recent graduate of the Propaganda College in Rome, who also taught Greek and mathematics. Orestes Brownson, the well-known Catholic author, thought well of him as a scholar, but, when he succeeded McCloskey as president in 1843, he proved to be a disaster. The rest of the original faculty consisted of three priests, two lay professors, six tutors, and two seminarians whom Hughes had hurriedly recalled from Mount St. Mary's College and Seminary in Emmitsburg, John Harley and John Conroy, in 1841.[29]

27. AUND, Purcell to Hughes, September 30, 1841. The author of the fiftieth-anniversary history of St. John's College, writing in 1891, could find no trace of any ceremony that occurred on June 24, 1841, but he insisted that "the ceremonies took place." Thomas Gaffney Taaffe, *A History of St. John's College, Fordham, N.Y.* (New York: The Catholic Publication Society, 1891), 51. Hassard, *Hughes*, 254.

28. He was appointed coadjutor bishop to Hughes in 1844, named the first bishop of Albany in 1847, succeeded Hughes as the second archbishop of New York in 1864, and was made the first American cardinal in 1875. John Cardinal Farley, *The Life of John Cardinal McCloskey* (New York: Longmans, Green and Company, 1918), 120.

29. Hassard, *Hughes*, 252. Bayley said that the college was commonly referred to

Hughes had been particularly eager to add Harley and Conroy to the faculty because they already had teaching experience at Emmitsburg. At the same time he was embarrassed to raid the Emmitsburg faculty and he encountered strong resistance from the rector, his old friend John McCaffrey. A month before the planned opening of the college at Rose Hill, he explained to McCaffrey that he was desperate for professors because some of the faculty whom he had recruited in Europe had never arrived. "We must commence next month," he insisted, "and the commencement under the eyes, you may say of this city, must be such as not to fall far short of the anticipations that have been created."[30]

Shortly after the opening of St. John's College, Hughes tried to assuage McCaffrey's wounded feelings. "You know or ought to know," he said, "that I would be the last bishop in the country to do or wish done anything that would materially injure Mount St. Mary's." Again he explained how hard-pressed he was for faculty members in New York. "You know the abortions that have preceded this effort to get up a house of education in this diocese, and that I am not the one to add to the number, if I can help it. To avoid this, two things are necessary, pupils and teachers. It appears that the pupils will not be wanting, if there are teachers. Am I not bound to provide teachers—otherwise what is the object of the undertaking?"[31]

In launching St. John's College, the cruelest blow for Hughes may have been something that he perhaps had never anticipated. After begging for money at home and abroad and scraping together professors wherever he could find them, he must have been disappointed to discover that St. John's College would begin its first academic year with a grand total of six students.[32] The faculty was larger than the student body.

In 1841 Catholic colleges, or male literary institutions, as they were frequently called, were still something of a rarity in the United States. There

as Rose Hill College. James Roosevelt Bayley, *A Brief Sketch of the Early History of the Catholic Church on the Island of Manhattan* (New York: The Catholic Publication Society, 1870), 134.

30. AMSM, Hughes to McCaffrey, May 6, 1841. Hughes originally asked for Harley and another New Yorker named John McCloskey. For some reason McCloskey did not come, and in the middle of September, William Starrs, Hughes's secretary, told McCaffrey that it was "absolutely necessary" that Conroy replace him at Rose Hill. AMSM, Starrs to McCaffrey, September 16, 1841. Conroy later became the second bishop of Albany. Both Harley and Conroy were ordained priests by Hughes on May 21, 1842. *Truth Teller*, June 4, 1842.

31. AMSM, Hughes to McCaffrey, October 2, 1841.

32. Hughes, "Memoir," 144.

were only thirteen in the entire country, four of them in the archdiocese of Baltimore, and most were located in isolated rural areas. Significantly, neither Boston nor Philadelphia as yet had a full-fledged Catholic college. A few Catholic institutions like Georgetown College were well established, but others were ephemeral schools such as St. Thomas of Aquin in Kentucky, which lasted only from 1809 to 1828. Admission standards were rudimentary and flexible. Another short-lived Catholic college, the Jesuit-run St. John's Literary Institute near Frederick, Maryland, advertised that "no scholar [would be] received unless he knows how to read and bears a good moral character."[33]

Ten of the American Catholic colleges established before 1850 have survived to the present day. Chronologically St. John's College, Fordham, ranks sixth in this list, preceded by Georgetown University (1791), Mount St. Mary's College and Seminary (1808), St. Louis University (1829), Spring Hill College (1830), and Xavier University, Cincinnati (1831). The four other Catholic colleges established in the 1840s were the University of Notre Dame (1842), Villanova University (1842), College of the Holy Cross (1843), and St. Vincent's College, Latrobe, Pennsylvania (1846). Six of the universities and colleges are Jesuit institutions today, but, three of them—Fordham University, Spring Hill College, and Xavier University (until 1930 St. Xavier University)—began life as diocesan colleges. Like John Hughes in New York, Edward Fenwick, the first bishop of Cincinnati, wanted to entrust his college to the Jesuits from the very beginning of the school, but the Society of Jesus did not have sufficient personnel to accept his offer.[34]

Among colleges and universities in New York City today, Fordham University can claim to be the third-oldest, if one does not quibble over the fact that Rose Hill did not become part of New York City until 1874. Only Columbia University, founded as King's College under Anglican auspices with eight students in 1754, and New York University, founded in 1834, are older than St. John's College. The City College of New York, the oldest component in the City University of New York, dates from 1847. The seminary at Rose Hill (which folded in 1860) can also claim to be the third-oldest theological seminary within the present confines of New York City, preceded by General Theological Seminary (1817) and Union Theological Seminary (1836).

33. *The Metropolitan Catholic Almanac and Laity's Directory for the Year of Our Lord 1841* (Baltimore: Fielding Lucas Jr., 1841), passim.

34. Edward J. Power, "The Formative Years of Catholic Colleges Founded Before 1850 and Still in Existence as Colleges and Universities," *RACHSP*, 65:1 (1954): 24–39; 65:4 (1954): 230–39; 66:1 (1955): 19–34.

From the beginning, St. John's College capitalized on a location that combined a healthy rural environment with proximity to New York City. In the overstated promotional style of the day, an advertisement assured parents in 1842 that "the utmost attention will be paid not only to the intellectual, but also to the *moral* education of the pupils. Their general deportment and manners will be watched over with scrupulous care." With considerable exaggeration the physical facilities were described as "large, elegant and commodious." As to the students' domestic comfort, the college promised that "everything which parental affection can desire will be found and supplied in assiduous attentions and skillful management of the Sisters of Charity."

In fact the rules of the college were hardly different from those of a seminary. Students were forbidden to leave the campus unless accompanied by a faculty member. Visits to parents in the city were limited to one every three months. All books in the students' possession had to be approved by the president of the college or the prefect of studies. Pocket money was to be deposited with the treasurer and doled out as he saw fit. The core curriculum consisted of Hebrew, Greek, Latin, English, French, poetry, rhetoric, history, mythology, geography, bookkeeping, arithmetic, algebra, mathematics, and moral and natural philosophy. Instruction in German, Italian, and Spanish was available at extra cost, as was instruction in music and drawing. The school year began on the first Monday of September and did not end until July 15. The tuition was $200 per year, the same as at Georgetown College and St. Mary's College in Baltimore. Among the personal items that each student was expected to bring with him were "a silver spoon and silver drinking cup marked with his name."[35]

Growing Pains

The first major crisis in the history of St. John's College occurred in 1843 after John McCloskey had returned to St. Joseph's Church in Greenwich Village and was replaced as president by Ambrose Manahan. John Harley, the vice president, complained that Manahan was an autocrat who insisted on running everything himself. "What was before the home of harmony and happiness is now the abode of discord and unhappiness," Harley told Hughes in February 1843. "Mr. Manahan has come among us, full to overflowing of wild and useless schemes, schemes that are not at all suited to the character and wants of this institution." As a result Harley

35. *The Metropolitan Catholic Almanac and Laity's Directory for the Year of Our Lord 1842* (Baltimore: Fielding Lucas Jr., 1842), 151–53.

feared that the seminarians might leave *en masse* and seek admission to other dioceses. As for the college students, said Harley, "[They] are almost in a state of rebellion, and nothing but the paucity of their number restrains them from open eruption." In view of the situation Harley offered Hughes his resignation.[36]

Instead of accepting Harley's resignation, Hughes fired Manahan and replaced him with Harley. He was only twenty-seven years old but clearly a favorite of Hughes's and a very capable man. Under Harley's leadership the students were pacified, good order was restored, and the college surmounted its first crisis. Unfortunately in 1845 Harley became seriously ill. Hughes took him to Europe with him to consult doctors in London, Dublin, and Paris, but his condition was beyond nineteenth-century medical help. He died at Hughes's residence in New York City on December 8, 1846, at the age of thirty. He seems to have been the most capable and effective of the four diocesan priests who served as presidents of St. John's College. Hughes replaced him with James Roosevelt Bayley, who was to be the last diocesan priest to serve as president of St. John's. Bayley credited Harley with devising the academic and disciplinary system that placed the college on a sound foundation.[37]

Meanwhile, Hughes found some relief from his problems at Rose Hill in 1842 when he persuaded the Vincentians to assume the direction of the seminary. However, there was a fatal flaw in the arrangement that Hughes made with the Vincentians; he had in mind a model of seminary education that was unacceptable to the Vincentians because they wanted the seminary to be totally separate from the college. Hughes and Harley, however, were still committed to the Emmitsburg model of using the seminarians as tutors in the college. Hughes told Father John Timon, the American superior of the Vincentians, "Everything in my power will be done to meet your

36. AANY, A-14, Harley to Hughes, February 28, 1842 [*sic*], 1843. Manahan had a checkered career. Two years later Hughes dismissed him as the pastor of St. Joseph's Church, Greenwich Village, with a stinging rebuke. "Not wishing to have the pain of inflicting any public censure on your character," Hughes wrote, "I advise you to resign, to ask [for] your *exeat*, in the almost extinguished hope that on a new scene where your future character will be determined by your future conduct, you may disappoint the melancholy anticipations which the past is too well calculated to inspire." AANY, A-5, Hughes to Manahan, September 4, 1845. Later in life, Manahan described Hughes as "a tyrant, but with feeling." AANY, Burtsell Diary, I, July 24, 1865.

37. Bayley, *Brief Sketch*, 134–35. On Harley, see the obituary notice in the *New York Freeman's Journal*, December 12, 1846. Hughes attributed Harley's death to diabetes. AUND, Hughes to Purcell, September 23, 1845.

wishes, and, as far as possible, to make things harmonize with the spirit of your Society."[38]

Hughes gave himself an escape clause with the phrase "as far as possible." Harley continued to claim the services of the seminarians who did not pay full tuition (the great majority), much to the annoyance of the seminary rector, Father Anthony Penco, C.M., who claimed that Hughes was not living up to his agreement with the Vincentians. Within eighteen months Penco was threatening to resign as rector. He told Timon, "I have already lost almost completely my peace of mind and heart on this account, viz., seeing . . . the terms of our agreement almost completely forgotten."[39]

Early in 1844 Hughes moved the seminary from Fordham to the Lylburn mansion at 50th Street and Fifth Avenue in Manhattan, the site today of St. Patrick's Cathedral.[40] It was only a temporary move until a permanent seminary building was erected at Rose Hill. However, only sixteen of the seminarians made the move to New York City; the other twelve remained at Rose Hill, to the consternation of Penco, who said, "I cannot take the idea of being in a seminary, the members of which will be constantly at the disposal of another institution." By the summer of 1844 John Hughes and the Vincentians had come to a parting of the ways. Upon the advice of both Penco and Timon, they terminated their contract with the diocese and gladly relinquished control of the seminary. Once again the faculty was reduced to a single person, an *oiseau de passage* named Rainaldi, apparently an Italian secular priest who came and went without leaving a trace.[41]

Elusive Blackrobes

While the Vincentians were still in charge of the seminary, Hughes made a second attempt to obtain the Jesuits for the college during a trip that he made to Europe in the summer of 1843. It amounted to a full-court

38. AUND, Hughes to Timon, August 20, 1842.

39. AUND, Penco to Timon, January 12, July 18, November 20, December 9, 1843.

40. Erected as a private dwelling around 1800, the Lylburn mansion served as the second home of New York's first Catholic "college," the New York Literary Institution, from 1810 to 1814. In 1844 the seminarians were warned not to go to the city on their weekly walks, which meant not to venture south of 27th Street. "Notes and Comments: New York's Great Cathedral," *HR&S* 31 (1940): 157–62.

41. ACGM, Penco to Jean Baptiste Etienne, C.M. (Superior General of the Vincentians), June 29, 1844; Timon to Etienne, June 1, 1844. There is a brief account of the Vincentians' administration of the seminary in John E. Rybolt, C.M., ed., *The American Vincentians: A Popular History of the Congregation of the Mission in the United States, 1815–1987* (Brooklyn: New City Press, 1988), 115–17.

press. A fellow passenger on the ship was Father Peter De Smet, the celebrated Jesuit Indian missionary, who was on his way to Rome. De Smet agreed to deliver a personal letter from Hughes to the general, Father Roothaan, pleading with him to take over St. John's College.

Hughes pulled out all the stops in his letter, cleverly appealing to the Jesuits' self-interest but also trying to place the blame on Roothaan, if he failed to accede to his request. He assured the general that his diocese "resembles an empire rather than a diocese of Europe." "It contains five other large cities," Hughes added, "each of which will become an episcopal see before twenty years, and each division will be larger than all Belgium." Then came Hughes's effort to place the blame on Roothaan for the consequences if he again turned down his request. "Unless something be done in time to multiply a priesthood and provide Catholic education for the youth, thousands of souls must perish for want of the bread of life," he predicted. Then he warned Roothaan not to let slip a golden opportunity for the Society of Jesus. "This is the critical period for the Church in America," he said; "this is the important period for laying the foundations in every kind of religious establishments which will grow with the growth of this young American Empire."[42]

In Paris, Hughes also persuaded Bishop Joseph Rosati of St. Louis and Cardinal Raffaele Fornari, the papal nuncio, to write to the general in support of his request. From St. Louis, Father Peter Verhaegen, S.J., the superior of the Missouri Vice-Province, added his voice to the chorus, urging Roothaan to accept Hughes's offer. "I am of the opinion," he told the general, "that it would be one of the finest of the enterprises taken in hand under your administration."[43] In Paris, Hughes met for the first time with Father Clément Boulanger, the provincial of the French Province, with whom he raised the possibility of sending French Jesuits to Rose Hill.

Both Roothaan and Boulanger recognized the value of a Jesuit presence in New York, but the Jesuits were already stretched thin trying to meet existing commitments. "I will see. I will see. I will do everything possible," the harried Roothaan assured the nuncio in Paris. He also wrote directly to Hughes to explain his dilemma. "Maryland and Missouri can do nothing at all, at least for the present. How can Belgium do any more? France alone has come forward, but asking at the same time for the transfer from Kentucky to the diocese of New York of all those engaged there." Roothaan

42. Hughes to Roothaan, July 31, 1843, in Garraghan, "Fordham's Jesuit Beginnings," 21.

43. Verhaegen to Roothaan, June 6, 1843, in Garraghan, *Jesuits of the Middle United States*, III, 113.

was referring to St. Mary's College in Kentucky, which Boulanger was willing to abandon, but Roothaan was reluctant to do so. Three years later he would change his mind, paving the way for the Jesuits to come to Rose Hill. In 1843, however, Roothaan's response offered little solace to John Hughes. "I should now think of the negotiations no more," Hughes wrote in the fall of 1843, "but take my measures to organize the college on a permanent basis without reference to any religious order."[44]

Although Hughes at various times had offered St. John's College to the French, Belgian, and Missouri Jesuits, he never made any overtures to the Jesuits in Maryland, only 200 miles away, who had opened New York's first Catholic quasi-college in 1808, the short-lived New York Literary Institution. According to the well-documented explanation of Father Francis X. Curran, S.J., the reason was that Hughes feared that Maryland Jesuits would make St. John's College a feeder school for Georgetown College, and he believed that the Maryland Jesuits were overly influenced by some lay Maryland Catholics.[45]

St. John's College made slow but steady progress under the diocesan clergy. "But what else could we expect?" asked the sycophantic editor of the *Truth Teller*. "Our highly gifted and energetic bishop is its founder and patron."[46] The curriculum remained basically that of a classical college with a heavy emphasis on Latin and Greek. Interestingly, however, the course offerings were broadened in September 1842 with the addition to the faculty of two businessmen who were to provide practical instruction "for such as only desire a mercantile education." There were as yet, of course, no graduates who had completed the four-year course, but each school year ended with a commencement ceremony that included speeches and poems by the students and the distribution of prizes.

A reporter for the *Freeman's Journal*, perhaps the editor, Eugene A. Casserly, witnessed the exhibition of 1843 and noted that every passing allusion to the grievances of Ireland drew appreciative applause from the crowd. One wonders what to make of the applause that greeted a recital

44. As a concession to Hughes, Roothaan offered to open a Jesuit residence in New York City, but Hughes rejected the offer out of hand. Roothaan to Fornari, August 21, 1843; Roothan to Hughes, January 16, 1843; Hughes to Father Anthony Rey, S.J., November 18, 1843, cit. in Garraghan, "Fordham's Jesuit Beginnings," 18–28.

45. Francis X. Curran, S.J., "The Founding of Fordham University and the New York Mission, 1846–1850," *Archivum Historicum Societatis Jesu* 26 (1957): 287. Only thirty years earlier the Jesuits had abandoned the New York Literary Institution under orders from their superiors to assure the continuation of Georgetown College.

46. *Truth Teller*, August 27, 1842.

of a Greek ode in the original language. The anonymous writer was impressed with what he witnessed. He always wondered, he confessed, why a city with so many Catholics lacked either a college or a seminary. "What was two years ago an experiment," he wrote, "is now a cheering certainty, and the Diocese of New York has within itself all the means necessary to advance the momentum and kindred interests of education and religion."[47]

In a promotional pitch for the college that the *Freeman's Journal* made at the beginning of the next school year, however, there was a hint that perhaps not all of New York's wealthier Catholics shared the newspaper's enthusiasm for the new college. "We only wish that all would endeavor to avail themselves of its advantages," the paper said and expressed the hope that no Catholic boy would be found at a Protestant college "imbibing with their learning that insidious poison [which results] in the eternal loss of the ill-fated victim of most mischievous parental indiscretion."[48]

The End of the Beginning

The commencement ceremonies held at Rose Hill on July 15, 1846, were the last conducted under the administration of the diocesan clergy. Bishop Hughes was in an especially expansive mood. As was now the custom, a large tent had once again been erected on the front lawn with room for 3,000 people. Hughes was flanked by his new coadjutor, John McCloskey, and the college president, James Roosevelt Bayley. One reason for the bishop's good humor was that his new seminary and chapel on the campus were almost completed, and, unlike the financial debacle in 1839 and 1840, the fundraising drive had been oversubscribed. He had hoped to raise $12,000 or $13,000, but the campaign brought in almost double that amount, more than $24,000.

The ceremonies that year constituted the first real graduation, for in April the state legislature had granted a charter to St. John's College, empowering it to confer "such literary, honors, degrees and diplomas as are usually granted by any University, College or Seminary of learning in the United States." In his concluding remarks that day, Hughes emphasized that the vote in the state legislature had been unanimous, winning the support of even the erstwhile Nativists. He then used that development to argue that the anti-Catholic bigotry of recent years had been an aberration and that most Americans harbored no ill feelings toward the Catholic Church.

47. *New York Freeman's Journal*, July 15, 1843.
48. *New York Freeman's Journal*, August 26, 1843.

Founding Father

Another reason for the bishop's high spirits was that he had finally secured the approval of Father Roothaan for the French Jesuits in Kentucky to take charge of St. John's College the following September. He mentioned the impending change at the graduation, comparing it to the voluntary retirement of one dynasty in favor of another and graciously expressed the hope that, under the direction of the Society of Jesus, "the usefulness, the reputation and the prosperity of St. John's College may be consolidated and extended in perpetuity."[49]

There can be no doubt that John Hughes deserves to be remembered as the founding father of St. John's College and Fordham University. He purchased the property, raised the funds to pay for it, hired the faculty, obtained the state charter, and handed over to the Jesuits a flourishing little college whose direction they were glad to assume. Most remarkably of all, Hughes established almost singlehandedly New York's first permanent Catholic college at the same time that he was coping with the pervasive poverty of a raw new diocese and waging an exhaustive battle with lay trustees, public school officials, state and local politicians, acerbic journalists, and Nativist bigots. It was no mean achievement even for John Joseph Hughes.

49. *New York Freeman's Journal*, October 11, November 22, 1845; April 25, July 18, 1846.

3

A FEW LONELY FRENCHMEN
IN A STRANGE LAND

Prologue

When the Society of Jesus finally put down permanent roots in New York in 1846, there was already a long if slender and discontinuous Jesuit presence in the Empire State. The first priest to set foot in New York City was a French Jesuit missionary, St. Isaac Jogues, who stopped briefly in the city in 1643 (when it was still New Amsterdam) on his way home to France after escaping from his Iroquois captors in the Mohawk Valley with the help of the Protestant Dutch. He reported that there were already eighteen languages spoken and a half-dozen religious groups in the cosmopolitan little settlement. In addition to Isaac Jogues, other French Jesuits labored in northern New York among the Iroquois from 1642 to 1709 in an effort that was more notable for the extraordinary valor of the missionaries than for the number of converts they made.

English Jesuits arrived in Maryland in 1634 with the first settlers, only fourteen years after the Pilgrims landed in Plymouth. The Jesuits made their first appearance in New York in 1683 when the newly appointed Governor William Dongan, an Irish Catholic, brought with him Father Thomas Harvey. Dongan intended eventually to deploy English Jesuits in northern New York to counteract the influence of their French confrères. Meanwhile, perhaps as early as 1684, the Jesuits opened a Latin school in New York City after the arrival of Father Henry Harrison and later Father William Gage and two Jesuit brothers. It was located at the corner of Broadway and Wall Street, today the site of Trinity Church. However, neither the Jesuits nor the Latin school survived the anti-Catholic backlash following the Glorious Revolution in England in 1688, which replaced the Catholic James II with the Protestant William of Orange. In 1701 the New York Provincial Assembly passed an Act Against Jesuits and Popish Priests that remained in effect until 1784, after the Revolution.

Around that time, if not earlier, another Jesuit, Father Ferdinand Steinmeyer, better known as Father Farmer, made flying visits to New York from his home base in Pennsylvania, where Catholics were the beneficiaries of Quaker toleration. Two decades later, in 1808, Father Anthony Kohlmann, a native of Alsace, was appointed the vicar general of the new diocese of New York in the absence of the first bishop, Richard Luke Concanen, O.P. With good reason, Kohlmann has often been regarded as the real founder of the diocese. He did not come to New York alone but brought with him Father Benedict Fenwick, the descendant of an old Maryland Catholic family, and four Jesuit scholastics or seminarians.

Kohlmann not only erected the first St. Patrick's Cathedral (since 2010 the Basilica of Old St. Patrick's Cathedral), but he also established New York's first Catholic "college," the New York Literary Institution. Located first at 347 Broadway and later at Fifth Avenue and 50th Street on the present site of St. Patrick's Cathedral, it offered both a classical and a business course.[1] "The most respectable families—among them the Governor of New York—send their children to us," Kohlmann reported proudly in the fall of 1810.[2] The school was forced to close in April 1814 after Kohlmann and most of the other Jesuits had been recalled to Maryland to assure the success of Georgetown College. Kohlmann regarded the decision as shortsighted and unwise even though it had the support of Archbishop John Carroll, who took a close interest in the welfare of the college he had founded. Generations of New York Jesuits have delighted in quoting Kohlmann's warning to his superior that Maryland "would always be a poor beggarly place" in comparison with the Empire State. With the departure of Benedict Fenwick in 1817, the Jesuits were once again gone from New York, except for the madcap Belgian Peter Malou, who was expelled from the Society in 1821.[3]

French Connections

The year 1846 marks the return of the Society of Jesus to New York after an absence of twenty-nine years and seven years after Bishop

---

1. *New York Mercantile Advertiser*, November 22, 1808; *New York Evening Post*, April 25, 1810. I am indebted to Father Robert G. Grimes, S.J., for providing me with copies of these newspaper advertisements.

2. Kohlmann to unknown, September 13, 1810, in *WL* 31 (1902), 33.

3. Father Francis X. Curran, S.J., insisted that the New York Literary Institution could not properly be called a college because it neither offered courses in philosophy nor granted degrees. Francis X. Curran, S.J., *The Return of the Jesuits* (Chicago: Loyola University Press, 1966), 27. Kohlmann has been widely praised for his role as vicar general in New York and as the founder of the New York Literary Institution, but Robert Emmett Curran gives an unflattering portrait of him as the tenth president of Georgetown College from 1817 to 1820. "By any measure," said Emmett Curran, "Kohlmann's administration was a disaster." Robert Emmett Curran, *The Bicentennial History of Georgetown University* (Washington: Georgetown University Press, 1993), I, 85.

John Hughes had first asked the Society to assume the direction of his college and seminary at Rose Hill. New York's good fortune may be attributed at least indirectly to the travails of the Society of Jesus in early-nineteenth-century France. During the Bourbon Restoration (1814–30) the resourceful Jesuits were able to establish eight colleges even though they were technically illegal under the Concordat of 1801, which governed church–state relations in France. The subterfuge was that the colleges were *petits séminaires*, minor semnaries, even though everyone knew that most of the students had no intention of becoming priests. However, the Jesuits quickly became the object of nightmarish fears on the part of both anticlerical liberals and ultra-conservative royalists because of their supposedly occult political influence, even though they numbered no more than one hundred priests in the 1820s. It was the same combination of enemies on the extreme left and the extreme right that had led to the suppression of the Society in France and in the French Empire under Louis XV in 1764. In 1826 the Count de Montlosier, a slightly unhinged aristocrat and ardent Gallican, launched an inflammatory pamphlet attack on them that led the government to close the eight Jesuit schools two years later in a vain attempt to appease public opinion.[4]

It is indicative of how easy it was to incite suspicion of the Jesuits that these schools were closed by order of King Charles X, the last of the senior line of the Bourbons. At this point in his life he was a devout and even bigoted Catholic who was often accused by his political enemies of capitulating to clerical influence. Worse was to follow for the Jesuits after the July Revolution of 1830, which replaced Charles X with the anticlerical regime of King Louis Philippe. The new monarch was a reassuringly bourgeois version of a Bourbon king selected from the cadet branch of the family at a time when the upper bourgeoisie was the most powerful political class in France. Louis Philippe preferred an umbrella to a sword and was said to have neither a confessor nor a mistress. Under Louis Philippe the Jesuits continued to be barred from teaching in France and were forced to look elsewhere to continue the missionary and educational work they could no longer do at home. They received strong encouragement to cast a wide net for their apostolic activities in 1833 from their general, Father Jan Roothaan, who urged the Jesuits to resume the worldwide missionary work that had been interrupted by the suppression of the Society in 1773. As a result, French Jesuits were soon to be found not only in neighbor-

4. Adrien Dansette, *Histoire Religieuse de la France Contemporaine* (Paris: Flammarion, 1948), I, 280–82.

A Few Lonely Frenchmen in a Strange Land

ing Belgium, Spain, and Switzerland but also in Africa, the Middle East, China, even in the wilderness of Kentucky and eventually at Rose Hill and once again in New York City.[5]

The French Jesuits who came to Kentucky as missionaries in 1831 were following in the footsteps of other French priests who had sought refuge in the United States forty years earlier during the first French Revolution. One of these émigré priests was Benedict Joseph Flaget, a Sulpician, who came to America in 1792 and was named the first bishop of Bardstown, Kentucky, in 1808. His diocese comprised the vast territory between the Allegheny Mountains and the Mississippi River from the Great Lakes to the Deep South, an area larger than France in which ten states and some thirty additional dioceses have since been created. Despite the rigors of forty years of frontier life, Flaget defied the actuarial tables, outlasted two coadjutors, and died peacefully in his bed in 1850 at the ripe old age of eighty-seven. The original center of the Catholic population in his diocese was two rural counties in central Kentucky—Nelson and Washington— where there was a concentration of Anglo American Catholics who had emigrated across the Alleghenies from Maryland shortly after the American Revolution.[6] Kentucky Catholics still refer to the area as the "American Holy Land." Within a dozen years of the arrival of Flaget in Bardstown in 1811, the diocese could boast of three communities of women religious, a cathedral, a seminary, and two colleges. One of these colleges, St. Joseph's College in Bardstown, founded in 1819, was the destination of a group of four French Jesuits who left their homeland for America in 1830 at the invitation of Flaget, but a series of miscommunications prevented them from ever taking charge of St. Joseph's College.[7]

Flaget had first sought Jesuits for his diocese as far back as 1815, when he appealed for help from their American superior, John Anthony Grassi. Grassi had just recalled Anthony Kohlmann and the other Jesuits to

5. John W. Padberg, S.J., "The Restored Society of Jesus in France, 1814–1830: Why the French Jesuits Came to America in 1831," in Thomas C. Hennessy, S.J., *Fordham: The Early Years* (New York: Something More Publications, 1998), 25–28.

6. Nelson and Washington counties date from 1784 and 1792 respectively; a third county, Marion, was formed from Washington County in 1834.

7. Clyde F. Crews, *The Encyclopedia of American Catholicism*, ed. Michael Glazier and Thomas J. Shelley (Collegeville, Minn.: The Liturgical Press, 1983), 760. The establishment of the two colleges twenty miles apart was an impressive achievement in one respect, but it was also an early indication of a trend that would be the bane of American Catholic higher education for the next century: the proliferation of small academically and financially weak colleges.

Georgetown from the New York Literary Institution and was in no position to help Flaget.[8] Flaget tried again in 1830 to get Jesuits to come to Kentucky, this time appealing not only to the Maryland Jesuits but also to the French, English, and Irish Jesuits, and directly to the general of the Society. He still got no results, except a reply from the French provincial, Julian Druilhet, that he was forwarding Flaget's request to the general in Rome.[9]

What finally seemed to work was an invitation from Flaget to the French Jesuits in 1827, an invitation that was extended to them personally by a Kentucky priest, Robert A. Abell, who had received his seminary training in France. At the time, however, the Jesuit colleges were flourishing in France and the Society felt little incentive to dispatch badly needed teachers to America. The situation changed abruptly shortly thereafter with the forced closure of their eight colleges in 1828 and then, after the Revolution of 1830, the general prohibition against Jesuits' operating schools in France. Flaget's invitation suddenly seemed more attractive, and four Jesuits left France for Kentucky in November 1830 without checking to see if the bishop's invitation was still on the table. Two of the Jesuits, Father Peter Lavadière and Brother Philip Corne, prudently remained in New Orleans while the other two, Father Peter Chazelle, the superior, and Father Nicholas Petit, traveled north from New Orleans to Bardstown the following spring.[10]

Contretemps in Kentucky

When the two Jesuits reached Bardstown on May 14, 1831, they were disappointed to discover that the diocesan clergy who were in charge of St. Joseph's College showed no disposition to surrender it to them. Moreover, control of the college was vested not in the bishop but in the board of trustees, whom Flaget apparently had never consulted about the transfer of the college to the Jesuits. To the bishop's surprise and consternation, the trustees resisted his decision to hand over the college to the Jesuits. "Could you believe that some of my clergy highly oppose the measure?" a shocked Flaget wrote to one of his seminarians in Rome.

8. Thomas J. Hughes, *History of the Society of Jesus in North America* (New York: Longmans Green and Company, 1910), Vol. I, Part II, 982.

9. Francis X. Curran, S.J., "The Jesuits in Kentucky, 1831–1846," *Mid-America* 35 (1953): 223.

10. Cornelius M. Buckley, S.J., "French Jesuits at St. Mary's College, Marion County, Kentucky, 1831–1846," in Hennessy, *Fordham: The Early Years*, 31–33.

A Few Lonely Frenchmen in a Strange Land

If Flaget was disappointed, so were the two Jesuits. On closer inspection St. Joseph's College did not appear as attractive to them as it had from the other side of the Atlantic. Not only were the diocesan clergy of Bardstown resentful of a prospective Jesuit takeover of the institution, but the first two presidents of the college had been forced to resign because of financial and disciplinary problems. Flaget himself had described the college as being in a "ruinous state" in a report the previous year to Propaganda Fide, the Roman missionary congregation. Moreover, he made no secret of the fact that he had a low opinion of the faculty. "Self will, a desire to make money, a foolish ambition of acquiring a name, are fast sweeping into the hearts of the young professors at St. Joseph's College," Flaget told this same seminarian, "and the spirit of piety, disinterestedness and humility disappear [*sic*] in the same proportion."[11]

A scene then ensued that was worthy of one of those improbable accounts from the lives of the saints that once enlivened the lessons in the Roman breviary. The bishop proposed that he and the two Jesuits make a novena to St. Ignatius Loyola seeking divine guidance. In the received version of the story, on the last day of the novena, July 31, the feast of St. Ignatius, Flaget unexpectedly received word that Father William Byrne, a diocesan priest, was eager to hand over to the Jesuits the other college in the diocese, Mount St. Mary's Seminary, as he called it. It was an institution that he had founded in an abandoned moonshine distillery in 1821 about five or six miles from Lebanon, Kentucky, in what was then Washington County. Father Byrne was himself an improbable character who could have existed only in the rough-and-tumble clerical world of the American frontier. An Irish immigrant who was in turn briefly a Jesuit novice at Georgetown and then a seminarian at St. Mary's Seminary in Baltimore, Byrne abruptly left the seminary as a subdeacon in 1819 and went west to Kentucky, where Flaget enrolled him in his own seminary and was happy to ordain him for his priest-starved diocese. The following year Flaget appointed Byrne the pastor of St. Charles Church in Loretto, Kentucky, to take the place of Father Charles Nerinckx, a pioneer missionary priest in Kentucky who was returning for a visit to his native Belgium.

Before his departure Nerinckx had purchased a farm where he intended to start a vocational school for boys. Nerinckx returned to Kentucky the

---

11. AAB, Flaget to Martin J. Spalding, n.d., cit. in Thomas W. Spalding, *Martin John Spalding: American Churchman* (Washington: The Catholic University of America Press, 1973), 16. The seminarian later became the bishop of Louisville and the archbishop of Baltimore.

following year to discover that Byrne had established a rudimentary college on the site of his projected vocational school. Rather than contest Byrne's decision, the often prickly Nerinckx was uncharacteristically accommodating and decided to move elsewhere, eventually establishing fourteen churches during his nineteen years in Kentucky before deciding that the diocese was too small for him and Flaget to coexist peaceably within its ample borders.

Mount St. Mary's Seminary suffered at least two major fires during the first decade of its existence, but both times Byrne rebuilt it and expanded it with the help of the local Catholic farmers. The campus included a 500-acre working farm that supplied most of the food for the students. Until 1837 they were required to spend one day a week cultivating the crops, tending to the hogs and cattle, and cutting the firewood to heat the buildings. Byrne found it easier to recruit a labor force for his farm than to find suitable faculty for his classrooms, and so he resorted to the widely practiced Lancastrian method of using the more talented students as mentors and teachers for the other pupils.

One of them was Martin Spalding, a local boy whose grandfather had been part of the Maryland Catholic exodus to Kentucky and whose English ancestors had settled in Maryland in 1657. At the tender age of fourteen Spalding was appointed the professor of mathematics at St. Mary's, where he attracted curious onlookers who wanted to see the boy professor at work in the classroom. Ben Webb, an alumnus of the school and later a journalist and pioneer historian of Kentucky Catholicism, quoted with approval Spalding's description of Byrne as "president of the institution, sole disciplinarian, sole prefect and almost sole professor." Webb also accepted as accurate Spalding's estimate that 1,200 youngsters were educated at Mount St. Mary's during the 12 years that Byrne was in charge of the institution. Teachers of the caliber of Spalding were hard to find in early-nineteenth-century Kentucky, and Byrne, unlike the diocesan priests at St. Joseph's College, was happy to entrust his fledging college to a religious community of professional teachers in 1831.[12]

Byrne and Father Peter Chazelle were as different in personality and background as John Hughes and John Carroll, but they respected each other's dedication to Catholic education and recognized each other's limitations. Chazelle, the polished and charming Frenchman, had only a limited command of English, whereas Byrne, the stern and taciturn Irish

12. Ben J. Webb, *The Centenary of Catholicity in Kentucky* (Louisville, Ky.: Charles A. Rogers, 1884), 284.

A Few Lonely Frenchmen in a Strange Land

immigrant "who rarely smiled and never laughed" according to Webb, had only a barebones undergraduate education. Byrne agreed to surrender the deed to St. Mary's Seminary to the Jesuits, provided that he could remain as president for a year to assist with the transition from diocesan control to the Jesuits, especially in view of their uneven progress in learning English. One year stretched into two and Byrne died of cholera, still president, on June 5, 1833, just as he was about to leave St. Mary's. Unfortunately he died intestate, leading to a long legal wrangle between his nephew and the Jesuits before they could secure title to the property and buildings.

A year earlier, on July 7, 1832, Father Jan Roothaan, the Jesuit general, gave formal approval to Chazelle's decision to accept the ownership of St. Mary's Seminary. Father Julian Druilhet, the provincial of the province of France, had already sent three additional priests to Kentucky: Vitalis (or Guy) Gilles and Thomas Legoüais, both French, and a young Irishman, Eugene Maguire. They arrived together at Mount St. Mary's on May 13, 1832. Legoüais had taught philosophy and theology at the college of Saint-Acheul near Amiens; Gilles had been the spiritual director at the scholasticate in Brigue. Druilhet decribed Gilles as a person of "perfect simplicity of heart and proven virtue." Maguire was an especially welcome addition to the community because he was the only one whose native tongue was English. Unfortunately he died the following year during the same cholera epidemic that carried off Father Byrne.[13]

However, Chazelle had an unexpected windfall when two French-born diocesan priests at St. Joseph's College in Bardstown—Simon Fouché and Evermond Harissart—applied for admission to the Society of Jesus and were allowed to complete their novitiates at St. Mary's with Father Chazelle as director of novices. Fouché's was a name to send shivers down the spine of any French Catholic. Far from being a relative of Joseph Fouché, the infamous regicide and dechristianizer, however, Simon Fouché was the nephew of the confessor of Queen Marie Antoinette. With the arrival of the musically gifted Brother Philippe Corne from New Orleans, there were seven Jesuits at St. Mary's by the end of 1833.

The new provincial, Father François Renault, excused himself from making the customary visitation of St. Mary's on the grounds that it was too far away, but he sent detailed instructions to Kentucky in the spring of 1836. He ordered Chazelle to be sure that the Catholic boys went to confession every month and told him not to neglect the religious instruction of the slaves. He asked Chazelle to consider whether it would be wise for

13. ANYPSJ, Druilhet to Chazelle, September 29, 1832.

some of the Jesuits to become naturalized American citizens in order to assure them of the protection of American law. Roothaan enthusiastically endorsed the suggestion, but he was hesitant to give the Kentucky Jesuits permission to wear their religious habits unless wise and prudent Kentucky Catholics thought that doing so was expedient.[14]

St. Mary's College

In September 1833 the academic year at St. Mary's began for the first time under the full management of the Jesuits. By 1836, if not earlier, the curriculum consisted of both a four-year classical course and a three-year English or commercial course that did not require the study of Greek or Latin. There was also a three-year preparatory course in reading, spelling, and arithmetic for those students who could not qualify for either of the college-level courses. By that date the students were no longer obliged to spend one day a week working on the farm, and the tuition was increased from $64 to $90 per year. The Jesuits also subsidized the college from the annual contribution of the Society of the Propagation of the Faith to the Society of Jesus in France.[15]

The college placed advertisements not only in the local press but also in newspapers as far away as New Orleans, Mexico City, and Havana, with the result that St. Mary's attracted a considerable number of students from Mississippi and especially Louisiana, but none from Mexico or Cuba. The bulk of the students came from Kentucky and included the descendants of many famous Maryland Catholic families such as the Abells, Spaldings, Youngs, Mattinglys, Mudds, and Elders and even one Calvert.[16]

When the Jesuits took over St. Mary's they inherited three substantial brick buildings, including a small chapel, and they added several other buildings in subsequent years, including a residence for themselves and a

14. FUA, Memorialia R.P. Provincialium, Renault to Chazelle, April 18, 1836. ANYPSJ, Roothaan to Chazelle, April 12, 1836. In October of that year Father Roothaan gave permission to the Maryland Jesuits to sell their slaves provided that the slaves' families were not broken up. The Maryland provincial, Father Thomas Mulledy, ignored that stipulation when he sold some 300 slaves to a plantation in Louisiana two years later. It caused such scandal that Roothaan removed him from office. Robert Emmett Curran, "Splendid Poverty: Jesuit Slaveholding in Maryland, 1805–1838," in Randall M. Miller and Jon L. Wakelyn, eds., *Catholics in the Old South* (Macon, Ga.: Mercer University Press, 1983), 142–45.

15. *The Catholic Advocate*, August 6, 1836. I am grateful to Father Robert G. Grimes, S.J., for providing me with a copy of this newspaper advertisement. ANYPSJ, Roothaan to William Stack Murphy, November 25, 1839.

16. FUA. Catalogue of St. Mary's College, 1838, 1841, 1843, 1844.

novitiate located some distance from the other buildings. Chazelle quickly doubled the size of the campus by buying 550 additional acres, and the Jesuits advertised that the college was "situated in the center of a large and well cultivated farm." In Byrne's time the average age of the students was about 14, which perhaps is why he hesitated to call it a college, and the enrollment hovered between 50 and 75 students.

The college had a capacity of 200 boarders, but the enrollment varied from 154 in 1838 to a peak of 177 in 1841 and declined to 136 in 1843 and 123 in 1844. Chazelle claimed that by 1838 St. Mary's was the largest college in Kentucky, a boast that may not have been quite accurate, because St. Joseph's College in Bardstown had 194 students in 1837 and 196 students ten years later. The great majority of the students at St. Mary's were boarders, but there were always a few day students as well.[17]

Surprisingly at least until the 1840s and perhaps even after that date the majority of the students were Protestants. Walter Hill, who entered the college as a student in 1835 and later became a Jesuit, recalled that "in 1836, and indeed till [sic] several years later, the spirit and tone of the college were much influenced by a predominant Protestant element." One reason for the strong Protestant presence was the educational reputation of Jesuit schools, which led a number of prominent Kentucky Protestants to send their sons to St. Mary's. Father Augustus Thébaud, who taught at St. Mary's and was the last Jesuit president, said that only twice in his nine years at the school did a Protestant student become a Catholic. Roothaan expressed his unhappiness with the situation and urged the Jesuits to show more zeal in fostering conversions. Nonetheless, Thébaud thought the experience of a Jesuit education did much to break down anti-Catholic prejudice among the Protestant students and their families.[18]

In 1837 the school received a charter, transforming it into a bona fide college. The initiative for obtaining the charter did not come from the Jesuits, who hesitated to seek it for fear of provoking a Protestant back-lash in an era of rising Nativist sentiment. It was the work of a layman, the Irish-born John Finn, whose son was a student at St. Mary's and who

17. Ibid.

18. Walter H. Hill, "Some Reminiscences of St. Mary's College, Kentucky," *WL* 20 (1891): 30; "Some Facts and Incidents Relating to St. Joseph's College, Bardstown," *WL* 26 (1897): 91. ANYPSJ, Roothaan to Murphy, October 3, 1844. Augustus J. Thébaud, *Forty Years in the United States of America* (New York: U.S. Catholic Historical Society, 1904), 360. At Georgetown the Jesuits were much more successful in attracting converts. Of an estimated 893 non-Catholic students in the 1830s and 1840s, at least 46 (5 percent) became Catholics. Emmett Curran, *Bicentennial History of Georgetown*, I, 173.

represented Marion County in the Kentucky legislature. Finn took it upon himself to petition the legislature to grant the school a charter and skillfully guided the petition through both houses of the state legislature, where it was approved with only one dissenting vote. Governor James Clark, a Protestant whose son was also a student at St. Mary's, signed the bill on January 21, 1837, empowering the school to issue both bachelor's and master's degrees. At the commencement ceremonies later that year a grateful St. Mary's College awarded Finn its first master's degree *honoris causa*.

That same year the Jesuits added to the classical course two courses in scholastic philosophy, transforming it into a four-year collegiate program leading to an A.B. degree. The three-year commercial course apparently allowed students to take whatever courses they wished, but it did not lead to a degree. The small number of A.B. degrees granted, only four or five annually, indicates either how few students enrolled in the liberal arts program or, more likely, how few students remained for the full four years in the collegiate program in order to complete the requirements for the degree.[19]

When Michael Nash, a sixteen-year-old Irish immigrant, arrived as a student at St. Mary's in September 1841, the campus consisted of five or six substantial brick buildings, including a chapel, located around a large terrace or esplanade. The students slept two in a bed "feet to feet" separated by a board in the middle and another board on the side of the bed to prevent them from falling out. Candles or tapers floating in jars of oil supplied the only light and posed a permanent fire hazard. There was no indoor plumbing. Both for a toilet and bathing the boys used a nearby spring. St. Mary's was definitely a country college where hog-killing time was one of the highlights of the year. "*Porcis plurimis fatalis dies*" is the entry in the House Diary for November 20, 1833. The students marveled at the ingenuity of the black cooks in preparing an endless variety of pork dishes and "corn-dodger."[20]

St. Mary's was located not only in rural Kentucky but also in frontier Kentucky, as quickly became evident to Père Clément Boulanger, the former provincial of the province of France, when he made an official visitation to the college in October 1845. He was upset to discover that the boys

19. F. X. Curran, "Jesuits in Kentucky," 234. The faculty seems to have been flexible in enforcing the four-year residence requirement for a degree. "When I left in 1846," said Thébaud, "it is a solemn fact that none of our graduates had spent more than three years in the college." Thébaud, *Forty Years*, 332.

20. "Reminiscences of Father Michael Nash," *WL* 26 (1897): 262–63. Thomas J. Campbell, S.J., "Fordham University," *WL* 45 (1916): 354.

A Few Lonely Frenchmen in a Strange Land

routinely chewed tobacco in the chapel and spat on the floor and the wall. Realizing the futility of forbidding the practice, he ordered the rector to install *crachoirs* (spittoons) in the chapel. He also urged the rector to persuade the boys to give up hunting during the school year. Aware that this admonition was likely to have little effect either, he forbade the boys from keeping their hunting dogs in the dormitories and told the rector to set aside a designated area on the campus for target practice at a safe distance from the buildings.[21]

There is no indication whether the black cooks whose culinary skill the students so much admired were slaves or free people of color, but the Missouri Jesuits, who retained slaves at their novitiate at Florrisant, Missouri, until the eve of the Civil War, euphemistically referred to their slaves as servants or negroes. In Kentucky the Jesuits employed slaves as laborers on the college farm, a common practice among religious communities in the state, where slavery was legal until 1865.[22] Boulanger ordered the rector to be sure that the slaves received religious instruction and to appoint a brother to lead them in morning prayer. On one occasion a conscientious slave owner in Tennessee asked the Jesuits to accept a Catholic slave and his wife so that their children could be raised as Catholics. "Father," said the slave owner to the president of the college, "take the family for nothing. I know that you will treat them well. When the boys and girls know their religion and have received the sacrament, then I shall reclaim them, not before."[23]

Personnel

The province of France, which retained jurisdiction over the Kentucky mission, sent four more Jesuits to Kentucky in 1836, Brother Michael Jarry and Brother Philip Ledoré, and two priests, Father Nicholas Point and Father William Stack Murphy. Both Point and Murphy were to become prominent in the annals of American Jesuit history, but for different reasons. Point remained at St. Mary's for only a year before moving to Louisiana, where he founded St. Charles College at Grand Coteau, but he

21. FUA, Memorialia R. P. Provincialium, Boulanger to Thébaud, October 30, 1845.

22. Gilbert J. Garraghan, S.J., *The Jesuits of the Middle United States* (New York: America Press, 1938), I, 612–14. Kentucky was the only state that refused to ratify all three Civil War amendments. James M. McPherson, *New York Review of Books*, November 25, 2010, 10.

23. FUA, Memorialia R.P. Provincialium, Boulanger to Thébaud, October 30, 1845. Thébaud, *Forty Years*, 70. Flaget owned seventeen slaves as bishop of Louisville and bequeathed them to his successor. Spalding, *Martin John Spalding*, 129n27.

is best remembered for his decision in 1841 to join Father Pierre De Smet as a missionary among the Rocky Mountain Indians. One of the founders of the Catholic Church in Montana and Idaho, Point was also a talented artist who became famous for his paintings and sketches of the Native Americans.[24]

Murphy, who spoke five languages fluently, including Irish (and English without a brogue), was born in 1803 in Cork, where his father was a prosperous lawyer and businessman and his uncle was the bishop. One of his brothers became the first Catholic M.P. to represent Cork in Parliament after the passage of the Catholic Emancipation Act in 1829. Educated at Saint-Acheul, he was a witty and charming conversationalist with an Irishman's endless supply of stories. Murphy was to make a major contribution to American Jesuit education not only in Kentucky but also in New York and in St. Louis. However, one of his first duties at St. Mary's was to prepare boys for their first communion. They ranged in age from fourteen to twenty years.

The province of France sent four more Jesuits to the Kentucky mission in 1839: two brothers, James Séné and Philip Constance; and two priests, Augustus Thébaud and Peter Lebreton. The following year Chazelle was recalled from Kentucky to France, where he was assigned the task of reintroducing the Society of Jesus to Canada after an absence of three-quarters of a century. William Stack Murphy replaced Chazelle both as the president of St. Mary's and as the superior of the Jesuit community, filling both of these roles until September 1845, when he relinquished them to Augustus Thébaud. Murphy also taught English literature; Legoüais, natural philosophy, chemistry, and Spanish; Fouché, mathematics; and Gilles had the unenviable distinction of being designated the Professor of Dead Languages.[25]

---

24. During his brief stay in Kentucky, Point was appalled by the table manners of Kentuckians but edified by the custom of devout Catholics, both men and women, of genuflecting whenever they met a priest. Cornelius M. Buckley, S.J., *Nicolas Point, S.J.: His Life and Northwest Indian Chronicles* (Chicago: Loyola University Press, 1989), 104.

25. Between 1830 and 1839 the province of France sent fifteen Jesuits to Kentucky: Fr. Peter Ladavière, Fr. Peter Chazelle, Fr. Nicolas Petit, and Br. Philip Corne in 1830; Fr. Vitalis Gilles, Fr. Thomas Legoüais, and Fr. Eugene Maguire in 1832; Fr. William Stack Murphy, Fr. Nicholas Point, Br. Michael Jarry, and Br. Philip Ledoré in 1836; Fr. Augustus Thébaud, Fr. Peter Lebreton, Br. James Séné, and Br. Philip Constance in 1839. Ladavière remained in Louisiana and never came to Kentucky; Maguire died of cholera in 1833; Nicholas Point left Kentucky for Louisiana and then for the Rocky Mountain Mis-

In addition to the fifteen Jesuits sent to Kentucky by the province of France between 1830 and 1839, the Jesuits in Kentucky accepted twenty applicants to the Society of Jesus as novices. It would appear that sixteen of them persevered to pronounce vows as either brothers or priests. However, only three of them were native Kentuckians: Fathers Walter Hill, Joseph Adams, and James Graves. The others were French, Irish, German, English, or Canadian.[26] The most famous of them was Father John Larkin. Ben Webb, who knew virtually all of the Jesuits in Kentucky, regarded him as probably their most impressive figure. A Jesuit who succeeded Larkin as rector of a short-lived Jesuit college in Louisville agreed and said that in the space of four years Larkin had made himself "the idol in the city on the Falls."[27]

Like many an English Catholic whose parents were Irish immigrants, Larkin insisted on identifying himself as an Englishman, but he remained a staunch Irish patriot. Born in Ravensworth, County Durham, on February 2, 1801, Larkin had a varied career before joining the Society of Jesus in Kentucky in 1840. A tall, commanding figure who weighed more than 300 pounds in later life, he was educated at Ushaw College near Durham, traveled to India after college, served as a lay volunteer to the missionary bishop of St. Mauritius, entered the Sulpicians at their seminary in Issy near Paris, and transferred to St. Mary's Seminary in Baltimore, where he was ordained a priest in 1827. He spent the next dozen years in Montréal, where he taught at the Grand Séminaire, wrote Latin and Greek grammars, and acquired a reputation as a popular preacher. After attending a retreat given by Father Chazelle at the Grand Séminaire in 1840, Larkin and a seminarian who was a close friend, Frederick William Gockeln, applied for admission to the Society in Kentucky. The local superiors quickly recognized Larkin's abilities. He later served as dean and vice president and president of St. John's College, Rose Hill, and founded the college in New York City that became the College of

---

sion in 1837; Chazelle returned to France in 1840. In addition, Henri Hudon was sent from Canada as a scholastic in 1845. F. X. Curran, "Jesuits in Kentucky," 224, 226, 232.

26. They were Fr. Evremond Harissart, Fr. Simon Fouché, Fr. Michael Driscol, Fr. Michael Nash, Fr. Hippolyte Charles de Luynes, Fr. John Ryan, Fr. Frederick William Gockeln, Br. William Hennen, Br. John Roy, Br. Patrick Crowe, Br. Jeremiah Garvey, and Br. John Callaghan. F. X. Curran, "Jesuits in Kentucky," 227, 232–33. Hennessy, "The First Fordham Jesuits," in Hennessy, *Fordham: The Early Years*, 77–137.

27. Webb, *Centenary of Catholicity*, 395; Garraghan, *Jesuits of the Middle United States*, III, 269.

St. Francis Xavier. He twice turned down an appointment as bishop of a Canadian diocese.[28]

Trouble in Arcadia

July 20, 1834, proved to be an inauspicious day for the Society of Jesus in Kentucky. It was the day that Flaget consecrated Guy Chabrat as his second coadjutor to replace the aged Bishop John Baptist David. The new coadjutor made no secret of his antipathy to the Jesuits, and his hostile attitude was one of the major reasons why they decided to withdraw from Kentucky a dozen years later. The Jesuits were not the only ones who were dissatisfied with the selection of Chabrat, a personal favorite of Flaget's and the first priest he ordained. Seventeen diocesan priests, including Martin Spalding, sent a letter to the pope pointing out Chabrat's unsuitability for the office. Fourteen of the priests were natives of Kentucky and descendants of Maryland Catholics who were unhappy with the appointment of the third French prelate in twenty-six years. In a separate letter to Propaganda Fide, Spalding criticized Chabrat as undignified, impulsive, imprudent, suspicious, and irascible. It was a judgment shared by another future archbishop of Baltimore, Francis Patrick Kenrick, the coadjutor bishop of Philadelphia, who had spent nine years in Kentucky as a newly ordained priest. Kenrick endorsed the criticism of the seventeen Kentucky priests when he forwarded their letter to Rome.[29]

One of the first clashes between Chabrat and the Jesuits occurred when the Jesuits agreed to educate the junior seminarians of the diocese at St. Mary's College after Flaget closed his minor seminary in 1839. Chabrat abruptly terminated the arrangement in 1841 eleven days after the beginning of the fall semester on the specious grounds that the annual tuition of $100 a year was exorbitant. He offered Murphy a tepid apology, assuring him that "you will find me ready and more than willing to do you any favors in my power." Significantly, he felt the need to add: "This may surprise you, but it is the truth."[30]

A more serious issue arose the following year, when Flaget and Chabrat (who more and more was the *de facto* ruler of the diocese) forced the Je-

28. In 1832 Larkin refused the offer from the bishop of Kingston to be his coadjutor; on February 14, 1849, he was actually appointed the second bishop of Toronto by Pope Pius IX, but he succeeded in having the pope cancel the appointment. Francis J. Nelligan, S.J., "Father John Larkin, S.J., 1801–1858," *The Canadian Messenger of the Sacred Heart*, 1957, 33–41, 105–10.

29. Spalding, *Martin John Spalding*, 21, 30–31.

30. ANYPSJ, Chabrat to Murphy, n.d.

suits to open a day school in Louisville, where the seat of the diocese was relocated in 1841. The school was a classical academy for boys between the ages of ten and fourteen that was called the St. Ignatius Literary Institution. From Paris, Chazelle urged the general to refuse permission for the new school, but his warning came too late.

John Larkin got his first experience as a Jesuit educator when he was told to interrupt the second year of his novitiate to help staff the school. He then served as the headmaster from 1843 until its closure in 1846. The number of students increased from seven to eighty, but many were not Catholics and others were unable to pay the tuition, leaving the school in precarious financial straits. However, the biggest obstacle to the success of the school came from the two people who had forced the Jesuits to open it, Flaget and Chabrat. Flaget never gave up hope that the Jesuits would finally accept his offer to take over St. Joseph's College in Bardstown, and he repeated the offer no fewer than seven times between 1834 and 1843. He apparently feared that the success of St. Ignatius Literary Institution in Louisville and its possible development into a college would jeopardize the survival of St. Joseph's College in Bardstown. Earlier Roothaan had politely declined Flaget's requests to take over St. Joseph's College on the grounds that he did not have sufficient manpower to do so but assured him that the Jesuits were praying daily for the Lord to send more laborers to the vineyard in Kentucky. In 1843 he authorized Murphy to give Flaget an absolute refusal. He feared that the Bardstown college could not survive and that the Jesuits would be blamed for its demise.[31]

When the Jesuits purchased property in Louisville and began construction of a new building for the school in 1845, neither Flaget nor Chabrat gave support to the fundraising campaign. In fact, Chabrat did his best to sabotage the campaign by opening his own fundraising drive to construct a new cathedral, forcing the Jesuits to discontinue their campaign. As soon as the Jesuits did so, Chabrat canceled his fundraising drive. Moreover, Chabrat even tried to persuade the Society for the Propagation of the Faith to discontinue its financial aid to the Jesuits in Kentucky. He told the Central Committee of the Society that St. Mary's College would not need a subsidy if the Jesuits lived more frugally and eliminated their supposedly superfluous expenses.[32]

On January 1, 1846, the Jesuits informed the two bishops of their inten-

31. ANYPSJ, Roothaan to Chazelle, July 5, 1838; Roothaan to Murphy, March 15, 1843.
32. ANYPSJ, Roothan to Murphy, September 17, 1843.

tion to close their Louisville school and they packed up and left the city by the end of February. A group of citizens in Louisville asked the Jesuits to reconsider their decision, but not the two bishops, who did not express the slightest regret. By the end of the year the Jesuits would be gone from Kentucky entirely. Ironically, many of the difficulties these French Jesuits experienced in the course of their fifteen years in Kentucky can be traced to the two French prelates in charge of the diocese of Bardstown. In the case of Flaget, who was eighty-three in 1846, one may excuse him partially on the grounds of chronic ineptitude aggravated by advancing senility. In the case of Chabrat, the motivation seems to have been sheer malevolence toward the Society of Jesus for unexplained reasons.[33]

William Stack Murphy was so incensed at the treatment the Jesuits received from Flaget and Chabrat that he told the general more than once that he found it particularly difficult as an Irishman to tolerate the antics of these two French prelates. In response Roothaan scolded Murphy for interjecting an ethnic dimension into the conflict. "You often remind me that you are Irish," the Dutch general told the Irish superior of this mission of the province of France in the United States, "but what confidence can subjects have in a superior who is imbued with prejudices against their country?" Roothaan also reminded Murphy that he was dealing with two bishops and that he should show more respect for the episcopal office, as St. Francis Xavier had done under similar circumstances three centuries earlier.[34]

The deviousness of Flaget and especially Chabrat with regard to the Louisville school was not the only reason for the increasing unhappiness of the Jesuits in Kentucky. The enrollment at St. Mary's College was falling and the financial situation was deteriorating; there were few vocations to the Society among native Kentuckians; and the possibilities for expansion beyond the narrow confines of rural Kentucky were limited. What eventually clinched the decision to leave Kentucky was an attractive offer from Bishop John Hughes in New York to take over his thriving college at Rose Hill. As mentioned earlier, as far back as 1839, Bishop Hughes had tried to obtain the Jesuits for his college and he had tried again in 1843. The provincial of the province of France at that time, Father Clément Boulanger,

33. F. X. Curran, "Jesuits in Kentucky," 231, 237–41. For this entire chapter I have relied heavily on Father Curran's account of the Jesuits in Kentucky, which is based on meticulous research in the Roman Archives of the Society of Jesus. His article was reprinted as "The French Blackrobes Return to America," in *The Return of the Jesuits* (Chicago: Loyola University Press, 1966), 56–80.

34. ANYPSJ, Roothaan to Murphy, April 27, 1844.

had been receptive to Hughes's offer but was unable to accept it because the general would not allow the province of France to give up the Kentucky mission. As late as 1842 Roothaan still envisioned Kentucky and Canada as the two centers for the development of Jesuit missions and colleges in North America. As the general who had authorized the Kentucky mission, he was loath to give it up for fear that the Society would be accused of failure to honor a commitment.[35]

Shortly thereafter, however, Roothaan relented to some extent. He left it to Murphy and Boulanger to decide whether to accept Hughes's offer, but he still refused permission for the Jesuits to withdraw from St. Mary's College. Quoting Luke 10:7 (the Gospel for the feast of St. Ignatius Loyola), he told Murphy: "*Nolite transire de domo in domum*" [Don't move from one house to another]. He ordered him not even to think of abandoning Kentucky and suggested that perhaps St. Mary's College could be reduced to the size that it was when the Jesuits took charge of it in 1831. At the same time he assured Murphy that he would love to see a Jesuit presence in New York. "*Courage et confiance, mon chèr père*" were his closing words to Murphy. Later that year Roothaan told Murphy that "if the Lord wishes to make use of the ministry of the Society in that vast diocese [of New York], He will bring about some favorable occasion to renew the negotiations."[36]

Boulanger was more eager than ever to accept Hughes's offer after listening to the stream of complaints from Kentucky for much of his tenure as provincial. Upon completing his term as provincial, Boulanger was appointed visitor of the province of France to the Kentucky mission with authority to determine the future of the Jesuits at St. Mary's College. Accompanied by Father John Baptist Hus as his *socius* (assistant), Boulanger arrived in Kentucky on June 11, 1845. His on-site inspection and conversations with the local Jesuits confirmed him in his opinion that the future of the Society was in New York, not Kentucky. Once again Flaget asked the Jesuits to take over St. Joseph's College in Bardstown, and in their name Boulanger once again refused the request on the grounds that the Jesuits would be plunging into a "bottomless morass." The following February Boulanger informed Flaget of the decision to leave St. Mary's. The bishop voiced no opposition except to hope that the Jesuits would continue the preparatory program at St. Mary's as a feeder for St. Joseph's College in Bardstown, a request that Boulanger understandably declined.

35. ANYPSJ, Roothaan to Murphy, April 30, 1842.

36. ANYPSJ, Roothaan to Murphy, April 27, 1844; Roothaan to Murphy, October 3, 1844.

Even though the Kentucky Jesuits unanimously supported Boulanger's decision, at the last minute the general hesitated to give his approval. He relented only when the Kentucky Jesuits reaffirmed their unanimous decision, and Flaget made no effort to dissuade them from leaving.

In the meantime, late in 1845, Boulanger had traveled to New York, where he signed an agreement with Bishop Hughes on November 24, 1845, in which Hughes agreed to sell St. John's College at Rose Hill to the Jesuits for $40,000 except for the property occupied by the diocesan seminary.[37] Roothaan had predicted that, if the Lord wanted the Jesuits in New York, He would bring about some favorable occasion that would lead Bishop Hughes to renew his negotiations with them. In fact the occasion that induced Hughes to reach out to the Jesuits could hardly be described as favorable. It was the mortal illness of Father John Harley, the president of St. John's College at Rose Hill. Hughes had no one among his diocesan clergy to replace him and turned to the Jesuits in desperation.[38]

The imprecise wording of some of the provisions of the agreement of November 1845, and the Jesuits' contention that Hughes failed to live up to some of the other provisions, led to an acrimonious dispute between them and Hughes a decade later, but in 1845 the agreement offered the Jesuits a welcome release from their increasingly untenable situation in Kentucky. The circumstances surrounding their departure were not pleasant. They were able to sell the additional property that Chazelle had bought to pay off their debts, but the diocese offered them only a nominal sum for St. Mary's College, and Chabrat was negotiating with another religious order to replace them at the college before they were out the door. They salvaged some books, laboratory equipment, and chalices, but little else.

Twenty-nine Jesuits left Kentucky for Fordham in the spring and summer of 1846, most of them in four groups of five or six.[39] Michael Nash (by

37. ANYPSJ, Extrait des conventions faites à New-york, . . . entre Monseigneur John Hughes évêque de New-york et le Rd. P. Clément Boulanger, S.J., Visiteur, novembre 24, 1845. The Jesuits agreed to assume responsibility for both the administration and teaching at the seminary, but Hughes retained ownership of the seminary building and adjacent property.

38. AUND, Hughes to Purcell, September 2, 1845.

39. Frs. Murphy, Thébaud, and Larkin left earlier. The others were Frs. Clément Boulanger, Michael Driscol, Peter Lebreton, Nicholas Petit, Vitalis Gilles, Hipployte Charles de Luynes, Henri du Merle, and John Ryan, and Brs. Alexander Chauvet, Patrick Crowe, James Séné, William Gockeln, Philip Corne, Michael Jarry, Philip Ledoré, James Graves, Xavier Maréchal, Peter Constance, Adrian Lacoste, Henri Hudon, Michael Nash, John Callaghan, Jeremiah Garvey, and Willian Hennen. Frs. Simon

this time a Jesuit scholastic) was in the last group, which left St. Mary's on July 31, the feast of St. Ignatius Loyola. They traveled north by stagecoach to Louisville, where they boarded a steamboat for Pittsburgh that took them only as far east as Wheeling because of low water in the Ohio River. At Wheeling they switched again to a stagecoach that brought them over the Alleghenies to Cumberland, Maryland, where they were introduced to the marvels of modern technology and boarded "the cars" of the Baltimore and Ohio Railroad for the beginning of a rail trip to Jersey City, where they took a ferry across the Hudson to New York City.

The last leg of their journey was a short ride on the New York and Harlem Railroad from downtown Manhattan to Rose Hill, where they arrived on the evening of August 9, ten days after they had left St. Mary's. Between Mott Haven and Fordham Nash noticed only one building from the window of the train, a farmhouse said to have belonged to Gouverneur Morris. Nash was not impressed with the village of Fordham. "Fordham then was nothing," he wrote a half-century later; "it lived on the college."[40]

Sequel

Back in Kentucky, public opinion blamed Chabrat for the departure of the Jesuits, although the Jesuits carefully refrained from any public criticism of the bishop and attributed their move solely to the offer they had received from Bishop Hughes.[41] An editorial in the *Catholic Advocate* on February 7, 1846, possibly written by Ben Webb, seemed to place the blame on the Jesuits. "Together with all the Catholics of the diocese," declared the editorial writer, "we disapprove [of] as well as regret the change and are very sorry that the Reverend Fathers judged it proper, advisable or *ad majorem Dei gloriam.*"[42]

Almost blind, Chabrat resigned in 1847 shortly after the departure of the Jesuits and retired to his native France, where he died in 1868. The aged

---

Fouché and Thomas Legoüais remained to wind up affairs in Kentucky. Diary of St. John's College, Fordham, July 20, 1846, in Thomas C. Hennessy, S.J., *How the Jesuits Settled in New York: A Documentary Account* (New York: Something More Publications, 2003), 10. It is not clear when or how Du Merle, Chauvet, Maréchal, and Lacoste came to Kentucky. The scholastics were included among the brothers in this list.

40. "Reminiscences of Nash," 266–67.

41. Webb, *Centenary of Catholicity*, 398. Campbell, Garraghan, and Thomas Spalding all minimize the role of Chabrat in the decision of the Jesuits to leave Kentucky. Curran was the first one to call attention to it and to document it. "Jesuits in Kentucky," 237–46.

42. Garraghan, *Jesuits of the Middle United States*, III, 261.

Flaget earned a dubious distinction in the history of the American hierarchy when he became the only bishop ever to receive a third coadjutor. Pope Pius IX signed the bulls on May 9, 1848, appointing Martin Spalding to the position. Spalding was not the choice of Flaget but succeeded him at his death on February 11, 1850, and at last placed the diocese on a sound basis.

Shortly before his death in 1848, Flaget finally succeeded in his long quest to obtain the Jesuits for his beloved St. Joseph's College in Bardstown. Jesuits from the vice-province of Missouri agreed to take charge of the institution.[43] In retrospect they must have regretted their decision because their experience at St. Joseph's was to replicate that of the French Jesuits at St. Mary's a decade earlier. They had no firm legal title to the college, which was deeded to them only in trust as long as they continued to operate an educational institution on the premises, and the diocese resisted all efforts to amend the deed. The Jesuits soon discovered that Bishop Spalding was no fan of religious orders. Anticipating the Americanist attitude of Archbishop John Ireland by several decades, Spalding criticized religious orders for "too much esprit de corps and too little Catholic spirit." He was especially annoyed at the Jesuits in Bardstown for their alleged refusal to staff several poor rural missions, which, if true, was a sharp contrast to the practice of the French Jesuits at St. Mary's, who had been active in the pastoral ministry.[44]

As far as the Jesuits were concerned, St. Mary's was a bad penny that would not go away. In 1851 Bishop Spalding tried to persuade the Missouri Jesuits at Bardstown to take it off his hands. Even the usually pliable Missouri vice provincial, Father John Elet, who had recently been censured by the general for opening a new college without permission, had enough sense to turn down the offer and so informed Father Roothaan. He did not get the pat on the head from the general that he may have expected. "I am astonished that you would even have given this matter serious consideration," Roothaan replied. "For those well-meaning bishops who make demands on us, we have a ready excuse, *hominem non habeo*."[45]

---

43. The Missouri Jesuits also opened a free school and St. Aloysius College in Louisville, the latter without the permission of the general. The college lasted only three years, 1849–52, and the free school survived slightly longer, from 1848 to 1858. Garraghan, *Jesuits of the Middle United States*, III, 253–90.

44. Spalding, *Martin John Spalding*, 82.

45. Roothaan to Elet, April 9, 1851, in Garraghan, *Jesuits of the Middle United States*, III, 306.

A Few Lonely Frenchmen in a Strange Land

St. Joseph's College was one of the casualties of the Civil War. In 1861 all but 14 of the 280 students were from southern or border states. Classes were suspended at the outbreak of hostilities when the southerners left for home and never returned. Both the Union army and the Confederates requisitioned the college for a military hospital at various times during the war. Bishop Spalding predicted a bright future for the college after the war, but the Jesuits were skeptical and gave notice in 1862 of their intention to leave the diocese, which they did six years later, bringing to a close the second unsuccessful attempt of the Society of Jesus to establish a college in Kentucky.[46]

After the departure of the Jesuits from St. Mary's College in 1846, the college passed into the hands of the diocesan clergy and was closed in 1869. In 1871 the Congregation of the Resurrection, a Polish religious community, bought the property and reopened the college the following year. St. Mary's was consolidated with St. Joseph's in Bardstown in 1893, turned into a seminary in 1929, and sold in 1971. Since 1984 it has been a minimum-security prison. None of the buildings from the Jesuit era still exist.[47]

Father Thomas Campbell, S.J., who was twice president of St. John's College, Fordham, and the provincial of the New York Province of the Society of Jesus, was an early chronicler of the Jesuit mission in Kentucky. He gave a memorable description of the history of the community at St. Mary's College when he characterized it as "the recital of a heroic struggle of a few lonely Frenchmen directing an English college in a strange land."[48] Initially at least, New York City would also be a strange land for these Frenchmen, but it would offer them possibilities for growth and expansion unimaginable in rural Kentucky. By sheer coincidence they happened to arrive in New York City, or at least within easy access of it, during the

46. In 1870 Bishop William McCloskey, Spalding's successor, asked the Jesuits to open a college and a church in Louisville. Father Felix Sopranis, an Italian who had been appointed visitor to the Missouri vice province, was open to accepting the offer, but not to returning to Bardstown. He told the new general, Father Peter Beckx, in lapidary Latin, "*Ludovicopoli igitur Nostri immorentur et fructificent; Bardipoli vero nullo modo*" [And so let Ours reside and prosper in Louisville, but under no circumstances in Bardstown]. The Jesuits turned down the offer when McCloskey offered them only an unsuitable site on the outskirts of the city. Garraghan, *Jesuits of the Middle United States*, III, 290, 345.

47. Buckley, "French Jesuits at St. Mary's College," in Hennessy, *Fordham: The Early Years*, 49–50.

48. Campbell, "Fordham University," 354.

decade when the city was pulling ahead of its East Coast rivals to become the undisputed commercial and financial capital of the nation. The move from Kentucky to New York also gave the French Jesuits the opportunity to reconnect with their centuries-old European tradition of establishing their colleges not in the boondocks, but *centre ville*.

RETURN OF THE BLACKROBES 4

The New Metropolis

The New York and Harlem Railroad, which whisked the Kentucky Jesuits from downtown Manhattan to Fordham in an hour in August 1846, was their first introduction to the changes that were transforming New York City. At the beginning of the decade the population of the city (which was then coterminous with the twenty-two acres of Manhattan island) was 312,710. Only 33,000 people lived north of 14th Street, with perhaps as many as a third of them making their living from agriculture. When St. John's College, Fordham, celebrated its twenty-fifth anniversary in 1866, the population of the city had grown to more than 813,669, creating a whole new city between 14th Street and 42nd Street. "The New Metropolis" was the name that the historian Edward Spann gave to New York City in that era.[1]

Thanks partially at least to the Erie Canal, New York City outstripped all its maritime rivals on the East Coast in the thirty-five years before the Civil War. By 1828 the import duties collected at the New York Customs House practically financed the operations of the federal government, defraying all the expenses in Washington except the interest on the national debt. New York also became the financial capital of and the largest manufacturing center in the United States. By the 1840s it was one of the fastest-growing large industrial areas in the world. Between 1800 and 1850 the rate of growth was 750 percent, higher than that of Manchester or Liverpool or, in Sean Wilentz's memorable words, "higher than that of all the jerry-built catastrophes of Dickensian lore." By 1860 the population of New York City was larger than that of twenty of the thirty-three states.[2]

---

1. Edward K. Spann, *The New Metropolis* (New York: Columbia University Press, 1981), 103; Ira Rosenwaike, *Population History of New York City* (Syracuse, N.Y.: Syracuse University Press, 1972), 36. The census of 1860 included seven Native Americans in the population of New York City.

2. Spann, *New Metropolis*, 121; Sean Wilentz, *Chants Democratic: New York City and the Rise of the American Working Class, 1788–1850* (New York: Oxford University Press,

When Father Augustus Thébaud arrived in New York City from France in December 1838, he walked up Broadway from Bowling Green to Prince Street before leaving for Kentucky. He said, "I almost imagined that I was again strolling along the Rue St. Honoré or the Chaussée d'Antin." He was especially impressed with the shops. "On entering any store," he noticed, "you soon begin to perceive that New York was already a great emporium in communication with the whole world, where you could find at short notice any goods, however costly . . . such as you had thought only London or Paris could procure." His impression was confirmed by a walk along the wharves lining the North (Hudson) and East Rivers, where for several miles the docks were crowded with "stately or graceful barks and ships lately arrived from the farthest ends of the globe."[3]

Perhaps even more remarkable than the growth of the city itself was the growth of the Catholic community. Bishop Bernard McQuaid of Rochester said that in 1822, the year before he was born, there were eight priests in the state of New York; when he died in 1909 there were seven dioceses.[4] In 1825 New York was still an overwhelmingly Protestant city with ninety-six Protestant churches and only three Catholic churches. Most of the newcomers who were swelling the city's population were Protestants from rural New England or upstate New York, supplemented by a substantial number of Protestant immigrants from the British Isles and Ireland. A major change in the pattern of European immigration took place in the 1830s. In that decade, for the first time the city experienced the arrival of large numbers of Irish and German Catholic immigrants. In the 1840s the stream of Irish Catholic immigrants became a flood as the result of the Great Hunger in their homeland. "The utter destitution in which they reached these shores," said Bishop John Hughes, "is almost inconceivable." He called them "the scattered debris of the Irish nation."

By 1865 one of every four New Yorkers had been born in Ireland and one of every seven New Yorkers had been born in Germany.[5] Not all of them were Catholics by any means, but many of them were Catholics, and the majority of the population may have been Catholic by that date. As yet

---

1984), 109; Robert G. Albion, *The Rise of New York Port, 1815–1860* (New York: Scribner's, 1939), reprint 1984, 224.

3. Augustus J. Thébaud, S.J., *Forty Years in the United States of America* (New York: United States Catholic Historical Society, 1904), 94–95.

4. The *Laity's Directory to the Church Services for the Year of Our Lord MDCCC, XXII* (New York: William H. Creagh, 1822), 106.

5. Rosenwaike, *Population History*, 41, 43.

Return of the Blackrobes

few of them had the means to give their sons a college education, but there was a growing middle-class Catholic population for the Jesuits to draw upon, as was evidenced by the number of students already at Rose Hill, and the fact that the Religious of the Sacred Heart had begun a successful academy in New York City for "young ladies of the higher class" the same year that St. John's College opened its doors. The Religious of the Sacred Heart charged the same steep annual tuition of $200.

As the Jesuits arrived at Rose Hill during the summer of 1846, they had numerous reasons to be optimistic about the future of the college they had just purchased. At the very least Father Nicolas Petit did not have to count the number of sheep and pigs that went with the transaction as he had done when the Jesuits bought St. Mary's in Kentucky fifteen years earlier. With a railroad at the gates of the college, the diminutive Father Thomas Legoüais, who was practically a dwarf (but "a well proportioned dwarf," according to Michael Nash), no longer had to seek help to hoist him onto his horse so that he could leave the campus. Nor did the Jesuits at Rose Hill have to bargain any longer with local farmers' pestering them to buy their produce. They could wipe the manure off their boots and get down to the business for which they had come to America by concentrating on operating a Jesuit college in New York.

The first two Jesuits to reach Rose Hill were Fathers Thébaud and Murphy, who arrived on April 19 and received a warm welcome from the faculty. Thébaud reported to the general that not only the faculty of the college but also the local clergy in general and the laity were delighted with the return of the Jesuits to New York. "There is a demand for us from all sides," he said proudly. Thébaud was impressed with the size of the college, which he thought had been planned on a grand scale, but he quickly came to the conclusion that the seminary had been neglected. The easy access to the city by rail was a startling contrast to the isolation of St. Mary's College in Kentucky. He estimated the Catholic population of New York City at 90,000 and said that Hughes had promised the Jesuits one of his fifteen city churches if they would open a day school in Manhattan. Commencement that year took place on July 15. For the first time since the college's obtaining the state charter, diplomas were awarded to the graduates. That evening, Father Legoüais noted in the minister's diary, "The Fathers of the Society of Jesus took charge and became owners of this college."[6]

6. ARSJ, Thébaud to Roothaan, May 15, 1846; FUA, Notanda Collegii, April 19, July 15, 1846.

Rose Hill Campus

The Rose Hill campus as it appeared in 1846 has been preserved in a drawing made by William Rodrigue, the brother-in-law of Bishop Hughes and the professor of drawing, penmanship, and civil engineering at the college. Reproduced many times since, it shows four buildings facing a lawn on an oval path leading to and from the college gate adjacent to the railroad station. The scene is instantly recognizable today except for the absence of Fordham's venerable elm trees that were yet to be planted by Father Thébaud. Three of the four buildings still exist, although in much altered form.

The focal point of the drawing is the Moat mansion, today's administration building. As mentioned earlier, the mansion consisted of the present two-and-a-half-story stone building at the center with one-story wings on either side. The northern wing housed the student dining hall while the southern wing was used first as a study hall and later as a student chapel. By 1846 three additional extensions had been erected at right angles in the rear; Thébaud expanded and modified them, giving the building the appearance, from above, of a giant letter *E*.

The labyrinthine rear extensions were apparently added as circumstances required without any overall plan, and they included both three-story brick structures and one-story connecting wooden sheds containing the interior corridors so much admired by the writer for the *Truth Teller* in 1845. In the few surviving sketches and photos they appear as drab and mean-looking utilitarian structures. The center extension led to the college dormitory and was later enlarged to house the secondary school students as well. The southern extension contained classrooms and the "Castle," a three-story brick building that later provided a home for such student activities as the newspaper and the literary magazine. The northern extension was the most substantial, with classrooms and dormitories for the youngest students and a separate study hall for the day students. To the east of these three extensions was a series of wooden sheds containing such practical facilities as washrooms that led the reporter for the *Truth Teller* to describe the buildings as forming a perfect square.

Because the students ranged in age from seven to seventeen or older, the layout of the Moat mansion and its extensions reflected the effort to segregate the college (first division) from the secondary school (second division) and the elementary school (third division) by providing each division with separate dormitories, washrooms, and even separate swimming holes in the Bronx River. An effort was also made to separate the boarders from the more worldly wise day students by confining them to a separate

study hall in the north extension. In 1859 the one-story wings flanking the central portion of the Moat mansion were replaced with the present two-story brick extensions. After the erection of Thebaud, Dealy, and Hughes Halls in the later nineteenth century, the rear extensions to the Moat mansion became superfluous, and most had been demolished by the time St. John's celebrated its fiftieth anniversary in 1891.

To the left of the Moat mansion in Rodrigue's drawing is the old frame Fordham Manor house, which was old even in 1846. Originally a Dutch farmhouse dating back perhaps as far as 1694, it was the infirmary and the residence of the Sisters of Charity in 1846 and was to serve many other purposes before being demolished in 1896 by Father Thomas Campbell during his second term as president of Fordham. "A strange historian with no veneration for relics," Father Robert I. Gannon called him. To the left of the Manor house in the sketch is the parish church of Our Lady of Mercy, today the University Church. It was designed by Rodrigue and completed

The Old Manor House, originally a Dutch farmhouse and the oldest building on the Rose Hill campus in 1841, was constructed c. 1694 and demolished in 1896.

in 1846; only the nave existed at that time, but it already contained the six magnificent stained-glass windows that supposedly were a gift from King Louis Philippe to Bishop Dubois for St. Patrick's Old Cathedral. According to a hoary legend, Dubois sent them to Fordham when he discovered that they would not fit the window frames in the cathedral. If that is true, the French Jesuits arriving at Rose Hill must have had mixed feelings when they looked at them, because Louis Philippe was the king who had barred them from teaching in France after 1830 or even living a community life in France in 1845.[7]

The final building that appears in Rodrigue's drawing is the new St. Joseph's Seminary, completed in 1845. It too was designed by Rodrigue and served as the New York diocesan seminary until Hughes was forced to close it in 1860. The name, like the name of the college, was selected by Hughes, which did not surprise one savvy New York Jesuit historian, Father Francis X. Curran, who pointed out that the bishop's full name was John Joseph Hughes. After Hughes sold the seminary to the Jesuits, it also served many other purposes on the campus until it eventually became St. John's Hall, a residence for undergraduates. There is one building missing from Rodrigue's sketch of the campus in 1846 and that is his own stone cottage, where he and his family resided while he was a member of the St. John's faculty. Also missing from the sketch is the pond that was located between the railroad tracks and the ellipse.

Rodrigue's drawing did not include the rest of the campus, which extended as far east as the Bronx River and must have amounted to about ninety acres even after Hughes had retained some eight acres for the seminary and sold a sliver of land on the western edge of the campus for the right-of-way of the New York and Harlem Railroad. The price he charged the railroad was one dollar and two passes in perpetuity for the president of St. John's College, a legal obligation that has been honored to the present day by the railroad's corporate successors, including today's Metro North Railroad. In one respect the rural Kentucky experience of the French Jesuits followed them northward. They were not able to shake all the manure off their boots until the twentieth century, because the college maintained a farm, orchard, vineyard, and pasture for thirty or forty cows at least until 1893, when Father Thomas Campbell, at that time the provincial of the Maryland–New York Province, ordered them discontinued. Located north and west of the buildings in Rodrigue's drawing, and supervised by the Jesuit brothers, the farm reduced expenses by supplying

7. Dansette, *Histoire Religieuse*, I, 330–31.

a good percentage of the food and milk for the college. It is not recorded what the French Jesuits thought of the bouquet of a Bronx vineyard.[8]

Farther east of the farm was the cemetery located on a hilly slope that is now part of the New York Botanical Garden. The first burial took place on July 11, 1847, one day after the death of Joseph Creedan, a twenty-six-year-old Irish-born novice brother who had entered the Society only two months earlier. New York City acquired the cemetery and some twenty-six surrounding acres by eminent domain in 1888 for $9,300. However, the Jesuits did not abandon their dead and were determined to keep them *apud nos*, in the words of Father Isidore Daubresse. The following year they rejected the suggestion to establish a Jesuit plot in St. Raymond's Cemetery and transferred the bodies of sixty-one Jesuits, nine students, three diocesan seminarians, and two workmen to the new cemetery adjacent to the church.[9]

Father Augustus Thébaud, S.J.

Augustus Thébaud was both the last Jesuit president of St. Mary's College in Kentucky and the first Jesuit president of St. John's College at Rose Hill. A short, stout man with a dark complexion, he was a Breton by birth and had served as a parish priest in his native diocese of Nantes for four years before entering the Society of Jesus in Rome in 1835. Educated both in Rome and in Paris, where he studied science for a year under André-Marie Ampère, the renowned physicist and mathematician, he had been a Jesuit for only eleven years when he was made president of St. John's College. During his six years as president he expanded the boundaries of the campus, but his most important contribution was a thorough revision of the curriculum.

Upon taking charge of St. John's College, Father Thébaud advertised that the Jesuits would continue to maintain the college on the same basis on which it had been operated by the diocesan clergy, but he carefully refrained from indicating how long he intended that to be the case. In fact Thébaud told the general that the system of education at Rose Hill resulted in "a confusion worthy of Babel." Thébaud had been appalled by

8. Gilbert and Wines, "From Earliest to Latest Fordham," in Thomas C. Hennessy, S.J., ed., *Fordham: The Early Years* (New York: Something More Publications, 1998), 140–48. FUA, Memorialia R. P. Provincialium, Campbell, February 10, 1893. Not until the early twentieth century was the farm completely shut down.

9. FUA, Acta Consultorum, October 3, 1888. Thomas C. Hennessy, S.J., "The Fordham Cemetery," in *How the Jesuits Settled in New York: A Documentary Account* (New York: Something More Publications, 2003), 155.

his introduction to Catholic education in America during his eight years in Kentucky, where, he said candidly, St. Mary's College hardly qualified as a grammar school. A "wretched little college" he called it and laughed at the state legislature for allowing it to confer degrees. In Kentucky he had had little opportunity to change the situation, but he had no intention of allowing St. John's to become another St. Mary's, especially after he realized that the former was modeled after another rural college of questionable academic caliber, Mount St. Mary's in Emmitsburg. Thébaud never visited Mount St. Mary's, but his experience of the Emmitsburg system at Rose Hill left him wondering how Bishop Dubois could ever have devised such an unsatisfactory system. "Nothing certainly that Bishop Dubois had seen in France could give him the idea of such a system," he commented. Thébaud was well aware that he was treading on dangerous ground with his criticism of Mount St. Mary's, and he voiced his comments publicly only after the death of its most prominent alumnus in New York, John Hughes.[10]

In 1848 Thébaud unexpectedly had the opportunity to broaden his horizons of American higher education when he visited Harvard and Yale. The occasion was the arrival at Fordham of Father Francisco de Vico, a world-famous Jesuit astronomer who had had fled Italy in the wake of the revolutions of that year. When Vico expressed a wish to visit Harvard and Yale, Thébaud offered to accompany him. They received a cordial reception at both institutions and even got a personal tour of Harvard by the president, Edward Everett, who was to be embalmed forever in later life as the loquacious and eminently forgettable speaker who preceded Lincoln for two hours at the podium in Gettysburg in November 1863.

Thébaud was impressed with his first-hand experience of Harvard or Yale, although he did not think either college measured up to the level of the best European universities and he was skeptical of the innovations they were introducing into their curriculum, such as science courses and modern languages. More important, his visits to Cambridge and New Haven gave him a standard beyond the narrow world of American and French Catholic colleges by which to measure the progress of his own institution. Thébaud noted that students at Harvard and Yale could expect to find "a more aristocratic class of companions, a larger library, perhaps more experienced teachers in the ordinary branches, and undoubtedly more flashy

10. ARSJ, Thébaud to Roothaan, May 15, 1846. *Freeman's Journal*, December 19, 1846; Thébaud, *Forty Years*, 325, 347. Thébaud was also highly critical of the poor quality of Catholic education in early-nineteenth-century France, which he attributed to the devastating impact of the French Revolution.

lecturers on what is called 'modern science.'" He also sounded a prophetic note when he called attention to the inestimable advantage of a hefty endowment. "Owing to the number of its students," he said, "many belonging to rich families, and the generous legacies, bequests, and gifts made to it by men of note, most of them its graduates, Harvard College has grown so as to leave all other educational institutions of the country far behind."[11]

In 1846 St. John's College could boast of neither an endowment nor an aristocratic class of students, but, as Father Thébaud noted in his advertisement in the *Freeman's Journal*, it did have a much-enlarged faculty. Twenty-nine Jesuits, including Father Boulanger, made the trek from Kentucky to New York in the summer of 1846. One of them, Father Vitalis Gilles, was reassigned to Spring Hill College in Mobile, Alabama, in November, but another twenty Jesuits joined the community by the end of the year, bringing the total number to forty-eight; however, it is not clear how many were actually engaged in teaching.[12] Ten different nationalities were represented among them; more than half were native French speakers, nineteen from France, six from Québec, and one from Haiti. Many of the others had been educated in France, but the House Rule required them to follow the standard Jesuit practice of conversing, even among themselves, in the language of the country in which they resided.

In addition to the Jesuits five laymen were also on the faculty, including Bishop Hughes's brother-in-law, William Rodrigue. Still another unexpected addition to the faculty was Father Boulanger, who had negotiated the sale of the college to the Jesuits in his capacity as visitor to the mission in Kentucky, a temporary appointment that was about to expire. However, on March 26, 1846, Boulanger was made the superior of the Kentucky–Canada Mission, which was renamed shortly thereafter the New York–Canada Mission. Until November 17, 1855, he made his residence at Fordham, where he also taught moral theology in the college.

11. Thébaud, *Forty Years*, 326, 340. Thébaud also familiarized himself with the curriculum at Columbia and Princeton. He especially admired the preparatory school operated by Columbia College.

12. For the list of the twenty-nine Jesuits who came to Rose Hill from Kentucky, see Chapter 3, footnote 39. The other twenty Jesuits were Fathers Isidore Daubresse, Arsenius Havequez, and Charles Maldonado; the scholastics Edward Doucet, Martin Férard, Charles Schiansky, Augustin Régnier, Martin Desjacques, August Kohler, Thomas Ouellet, Claude Pernot, Peter Tissot, John Hampston, Thomas Bidwell, Patrick Dealy, and Anthony Hollinger; and Brothers Damasus Gauthier, John Roy, Francis Vachon, and Felix McParland. *Catalogus Provinciae Franciae*, 1847, 39–42. See also Hennessy, *Fordham: The Early Years* and *How the Jesuits Settled in New York*, passim.

Curriculum and Pedagogy

From Thébaud's perspective the increase in the size of the faculty did not alter the problem of the Emmitsburg system at Rose Hill, which, he said, resulted in mass confusion. Students had little personal contact with the faculty, received no advice from them about their studies, and crowded the corridors during the day, shuffling between study halls and classrooms when they bothered to go to class at all. The system also had serious drawbacks for the faculty, because they were required to teach several different groups of students every day.

Thébaud turned for help to Georgetown College, where the Maryland Jesuits had modified the traditional Jesuit *ratio studiorum* of 1599 and adapted it to American circumstances in 1839. At Georgetown the Jesuits devised a seven-year program of studies that consisted of four years of preparatory or secondary school and three years of college. As early as February 1847 the Jesuit board of consultors at Rose Hill voted unanimously to adopt the Georgetown system with minor modifications. In the 1850s Georgetown reversed the time frame to four years of college and three years of secondary school to bring the curriculum into conformity with standard American academic practice. The Jesuits in New York immediately followed suit, because effecting the change meant merely transposing the senior year of secondary school to the first year of college.[13]

The three years of the grammar classes or the Second Division, as the secondary-school program was called, placed heavy emphasis on English and Latin grammar with Greek being introduced in the third year. There were also courses in arithmetic, history, geography, and religion, the last of which was little more than the exposition of the catechism. By their third year, students were reading Caesar and Cicero, Xenophon and Plutarch. An integral feature of the curriculum was the time allotted to composition and public speaking in keeping with the traditional Jesuit practice of promoting *eloquentia perfecta*, the art of clear and persuasive oral and written communication.

At Rose Hill the four years of the college or First Division were labeled (in ascending sequence) Classics, Belles-Lettres, Rhetoric, and Philosophy. The reading of Latin and Greek classics formed the backbone of the curriculum for the first three years of college as the students were introduced to Virgil, Horace, Juvenal, Livy, Tacitus, and Quintillian, as well

13. FUA, Acta Consultorum, February 15, March 8, March 15, 1847. Christa Klein, "The Jesuits and Catholic Boyhood in Nineteenth-Century New York City: A Study of St. John's College and the College of St. Francis Xavier, 1846–1912," Ph.D. diss., University of Pennsylvania, 1976, 131–34.

as Homer, Thucydides, Euripides, Sophocles, Aeschylus, Plato, and Demosthenes. There were also three years of French. Needless to say, the students read Fénélon, Bossuet, and Boileau, not Voltaire or Rousseau (or Pascal). A four-year sequence of mathematics courses began with algebra and led to geometry, trigonometry, and calculus. There were also four years of history and religion with lectures on Evidences of Religion replacing the catechism during the last two years. Science did not make an appearance until the last two years, when there were courses in chemistry, physics, astronomy, botany, and geology.

In junior year the focus was on rhetoric, which entailed critical reading of the classics of English literature accompanied by weekly compositions and debates. Finally in senior year the students reached the culmination of their liberal arts education when they were introduced to philosophy in the form of logic and metaphysics The classroom lectures in senior year were delivered in Latin and were supposed to be supplemented by weekly debates and semi-public philosophical disputations. Successful completion of the four-year program led to the A.B. degree, and students could earn an M.A. degree by taking a second year of philosophy that included not only ethics but also international law, religion, history, and French literature.[14]

Like many college catalogues, the list of the course of studies may have promised more than it delivered. There is no way to measure how fluent most students became in the mastery of Latin and Greek or even in French. Father Raymond A. Schroth, S.J., the most recent historian of Fordham University, is skeptical about how well students understood classroom lectures in Latin, because few of them completed the full seven-year program of secondary school and college courses. He also wondered whether the weekly debates took place as advertised, especially given that some of the students from Latin America and even some of the French-born faculty had only an imperfect grasp of English. In fact, few students ever qualified for a degree.[15]

Formal religious instruction occupied relatively little space in the curric-

14. FUA, Course of Studies, St. John's College, 1862, 33–36.

15. Raymond A. Schroth, S.J., *Fordham: A History and Memoir* (Chicago: Loyola University Press, 2002), 31. The Jesuits were puzzled by the inability or unwillingness of the students to read or speak French despite the amount of time devoted to the subject. "*Quare non major fructus?*" they asked. Perhaps it was a passive-aggressive expression of student Gallophobia. The Jesuits also decided that it was necessary to provide Spanish-language catechism lessons for the Hispanic students. FUA, Acta Consultorum, February 1, 1847; September 7, 1861.

ulum even though the spiritual and moral formation of the young men was the primary objective of Jesuit education in every one of their educational institutions. However, the whole atmosphere of the school was designed to inculcate Christian beliefs and practices with mandatory daily Mass and yearly retreats, religious devotions (especially to the Virgin Mary), enrollment in the sodality, frequent confession, opportunities for spiritual direction, and in the classroom the Christian interpretation of classical texts. The example of the religious dedication of the Jesuits themselves had a profound and lasting impact in shaping the character of the students, as many of them testified in later life.

Father Thébaud criticized Harvard for introducing science courses and modern languages into the curriculum, because he thought that such studies detracted from the all-important emphasis on a classical education. Nonetheless, St. John's College did the same, although to a lesser degree. Thébaud himself taught botany. "He led us frequently on long excursions through the fields," recalled one student, who said that there was "never a weed, flower, shrub or herb that he could not name, classify and describe its properties."[16]

Thébaud's particular academic *bête noire* was the commercial course, the predecessor of today's business school, which he dismissed as an "ugly feature of our institutions." However, theory ceded to the reality of financial exigencies at Rose Hill and the needs of the local Catholic community with the result that St. John's College continued to offer the two-year commercial course that had been introduced by the diocesan clergy. It required neither Latin nor Greek but offered a basic curriculum of religion, English, French, arithmetic, history, and bookkeeping. There was also a two-year elementary program for young boys, the Third Division, that provided instruction in spelling, reading, writing, grammar, geography, catechism, French, and arithmetic. The curriculum left no room for elective courses, but instruction in Spanish, German, Italian, drawing, painting, and music was available at extra cost.

Student Life

The daily schedule subjected teenage American boys to the rigors of a medieval monastic regime with few of its benefits. At least medieval monks could always retreat to the sanctuary of their cells. The young students at St. John's College had no such option. They lived in a fish bowl without a shred of privacy, separated from the outside world for al-

16. Henry Hobart Dodge, "Reminiscences of a Forty-Niner," *FM* (October 1888): 11.

most eleven months of the year, segregated among themselves by age, and closely watched and monitored every hour of the day by prefects, usually Jesuit scholastics (seminarians), who in some cases were only a few years older than they.[17]

Perhaps the most irksome aspect of the regulations for the youngsters was the emphasis on silence, which was imposed on them for twenty hours of the day. They were required to be silent in the chapel at Mass and at morning and evening prayers; in the refectory at breakfast, dinner, and supper; and in the classrooms, study halls, dormitory, wardrobe room, and even in the washrooms. They were officially permitted to speak to one another only during the scattered recreation periods that amounted to four hours a day and the longest of which was only seventy-five minutes.

Meals must have been a particularly trying experience. Three times a day the students filed into the refectory in silence, stood at their places until the prefect led them in grace, and ate in silence while listening to the reading of a devotional book. They were expected to stop eating promptly at the ringing of a bell, to rise on signal for grace after meals, and then to proceed silently single-file with folded arms to their respective recreation areas when they were finally allowed to speak to one another. Like college students everywhere, they complained about the quality of the food and quoted the adage that "God sent food; the devil sent cooks." On one occasion a delegation of college seniors (philosophers, as they were called) brought what they thought was a sample of rancid butter to the procurator. On closer inspection it proved to be perfectly good, and so they first went to the chemistry laboratory where they doctored it with nitric acid and other drugs, before showing it to the procurator, who never suspected that he was being duped.[18]

A new student was surprised to discover at his first meal in the refectory that the spiritual reading had been suspended in honor of his arrival. He noticed that there were fourteen students at each table, with the most coveted places at the head and foot of each table where two lucky students distributed the food to the rest of the table. "They were in a position to do justice to the sons of their mothers, which they did with filial piety," he observed. As soon as grace was concluded, there was an enormous din from the rattle of dishes and cutlery and the shouting of the boys. As the newcomer prepared to settle in for a leisurely meal, the bell was rung again

17. The description of the following rules is taken from Rules and Customs Book, FUA. This was a handwritten guide for the use of the prefects.

18. "Fordham in the Sixties," *FM*, May 1901, 454–55.

for the grace after meals. He left the refectory as hungry as he had arrived. A friendly classmate told him the secret of survival at meals was "to get away at the drop of the flag and keep running to the wire."[19]

Sleeping accommodations were no better than conditions in the refectory. The boys slept in open dormitories within reach of one another's beds (that they were specifically forbidden to touch) without curtains or partitions, under the watchful eye of a prefect. They did not even have access to their own clothes, which were kept in a locked wardrobe room that was open for only a half-hour on Sunday mornings. Twice a week the Jesuit brothers left a change of clothes for them on their beds. The only personal items the students could keep with them were two combs, a toothbrush, and one clean towel each week. On Sunday mornings they were lined up for inspection to be sure that their boots had been properly blackened. They were warned to observe "the most scrupulous modesty" in the dormitories, wardrobe room, and the washrooms. Even the most vigilant prefect in the dormitories sometimes fell asleep, which was the occasion for minor mischief like switching the clothes of the sleeping students or tying their clothes in such tight knots that unraveling them in the morning was virtually impossible.

In 1854, in the first student newspaper, *The Goose-Quill*, an anonymous author wrote a fictional account of the experiences of an alumnus who missed the last train from Fordham and was forced to spend the night in one of the dormitories. "I had not been between the sheets five minutes," he wrote,

> before I heard far off at the other end of the room a loud and most horrifying snort. I sprang up instantly and was about to get out of bed to assist the sufferer (for such I took the author of the sound to be), when a neighbor whispered me to lie still: it was only one of their best snorers, who always sounded the alarm just before commencing operations. "Wait one second," said he, "and you will hear him." And in fact, before he had finished speaking, the snore began, not rising gradually from a low, confused murmur, but bursting suddenly forth into maturity and shaking the very walls, it seemed, with its fierce roar. In a minute more I heard coming from the bed of my neighbor a very doubtful sound, which grew by degrees louder and louder and more distinct until there was no disguising the fact any longer: he was actually snoring. A third soon followed, then a fourth, a fifth, a sixth, until enumeration became impossible; the dormitory was in one promiscuous snore.

19. Ibid., 389.

Soon a long, slim, bony-legged student who was lying opposite to me, his feet projecting nearly a yard beyond the foot of his bed, sprang up and[,] throwing a pair of pantaloons over his shoulders, stalked in a towering passion toward the leader of this nocturnal choir. He certainly presented a most comical appearance. An immense red flannel night-cap surmounted his cadaverous countenance and over a white garment that reached below his knees was thrown the article of dress before mentioned, the seat coming just under his chin and the legs falling down his back. Thus attired, he pulled by the leg the snoring object of his wrath, who forthwith started up and on beholding this frightful figure before him gave a shout of terror which awakened every soul in the room. The grotesque-looking cause of such confusion sneaked back to bed amidst the general laughter.

Quiet was restored and the visitor eventually fell asleep only to be awakened in the morning by a frightful sound.

I awoke and found a prefect telling me it was time to arise while at the same instant my ears were saluted by a sound like that of a regiment of cavalry galloping over oaken floors. I imagined that part of the house was falling and began to dress myself with the utmost speed, but soon discovered that I was mistaken: it was merely the students going downstairs.[20]

The primitive washrooms did not meet even the minimal standards of Victorian bathrooms. "They were wash rooms, not lavatories," insisted one former student, who said that only a rugged Anglo-Saxon term, not a soft Latin euphemism, could describe them accurately. There were large tubs of water in the middle of the room from which the students filled their individual tin cups. At 5:30 on a cold winter morning with the thermometer hovering around zero, it was often necessary to break the ice in the tubs in order to scoop up a tin of water. The janitor of the washroom in the 1850s was a grizzled Irishman named Jimmie Leady, who anticipated

20. "A Night at St. John's," *The Goose-Quill*, December 17, 1854. *The Goose-Quill* was a handwritten newspaper that produced fourteen issues between November 1854 and May 1855. The editors and contributors were anonymous but were known to both the faculty and the students. They were Arthur Francis, John Hassard, and Martin T. McMahon, who said that the newspaper "was rather ignored than permitted by the college authorities. We never, however, could obtain permission to print it." "Reminiscences," *FM*, February 1887, 72. Thomas Gaffney Taaffe, *A History of St. John's College, Fordham, N.Y.* (New York: The Catholic Publication Society, 1891), 93.

complaints from the students by announcing that "only those complain who have not as good at home."[21]

Communication with the outside world was severely limited. Students were forbidden to bring on campus tobacco, wine, or whiskey, and in the early days, it was considered prudent to extend the ban to include gunpowder, firearms, and other weapons. Student letters were subject to inspection except in the case of their correspondence with their parents or guardians. In 1870 the college authorities eliminated even that exception when they discovered that some students were making uncomplimentary remarks about the college in the letters they sent home. At least two students were apprehended and accused of indecent behavior because of intercepted letters. Even when the students went swimming in the Bronx River in the summer or ice skating in the winter, the students had to wait for a signal from the ubiquitous prefect to begin and end their recreation. Leaving the campus without permission was grounds for dismissal; all books and other reading material had to be approved by the vice president; pocket money had to be deposited with the treasurer for safekeeping. On their off-campus walks on free days (or "play days," as they were charmingly called), students were marched through the village of Fordham in "bands" of twelve or fifteen escorted by a prefect who was to ensure that they did not visit taverns or stores or buy newspapers or periodicals. On one of the longer excursions to Highbridge, the prefect was the diminutive Father Legoüais, who by one estimate was only "nine inches taller than a walking stick." Amused at the sight, a country bumpkin hailed him as Tom Thumb, whereupon one of the Fordham students, presumably not a member of the sodality, decked him and knocked him unconscious with one blow. The pious Father Legoüais spent fifteen minutes apologizing to the young tough who had insulted him.[22]

21. Joseph F. Marrin, '57, "St. John's Thirty Years Ago," *FM*, December 1887, 56; Richard S. Treacy, '59, "Reminiscences: The Early Sixties," *FM*, Anniversary Edition, 1916, 69–70. The student living accommodations and washing facilities were equally spartan at the future Georgetown College. One student, James Ryder Randall, the author of "Maryland, My Maryland," who came to Georgetown at the age of nine, said, "I thought of my mother and my home, wondering how such affectionate parents as mine were had condemned their little boy to such torture." Cited in Emmett Curran, *The Bicentennial History of Georgetown University* (Washington: Georgetown University Press, 1993), I, 171.

22. FUA, Acta Consultorum, April 18, 1849; April 7, 1870.

Discipline

Although the use of corporal punishment is never mentioned in the directions for the prefects, it was an integral part of the disciplinary system. David Merrick, a student in the 1850s who later became president of the College of St. Francis Xavier, remarked that as First Prefect Father Henri DuMerle "licked the boys well and was beloved by all." When alumni referred to professors or prefects as strict disciplinarians, they almost invariably but not always meant it as a compliment. Even Father John Larkin, who was no fan of corporal punishment, was known to say that "a boy was like beefsteak, which, when beaten, was made tender." In the early twentieth century corporal punishment was still in vogue, much to the distress of the president, Father John J. Collins. "The only feature of discipline that I strongly object to is the flogging," he said. "[It] has been too frequent and too unreasonable. Occasionally a boy may be corrected or reclaimed by a good flogging, but such occasions occur only very rarely."[23]

This elaborate apparatus of control and surveillance was the opposite of an American honor system and sent a clear message to the students that they were not to be trusted under any circumstances. It was an importation to America of the system that had prevailed in the Jesuit colleges in early-nineteenth-century France, especially at Saint-Acheul, which was their flagship institution and the alma mater of several of the Fordham Jesuits. "The pupils are never to be left to themselves; the vigilance of the masters is to be exercised in every place and at every instant of the day and night," declared the prospectus of Saint-Acheul, whose list of rules constituted a small book according to one French Jesuit historian. In 1824 at Saint-Acheul ten scholastics and fifteen auxiliaries were assigned to the all important task of surveillance.[24]

To be fair, however, this repressive system was not limited to the Jesuits but was standard practice in much of nineteenth-century French clerical education. The idealistic young Ernest Dimnet entered the major seminary in Cambrai in 1890. Forty-five years later he could not shake off the depressing memories of his seminary experience. "We were under con-

23. David A. Merrick, S.J., "Some Recollections of the Fordham Fathers in the Forties," *FM*, November 1887, 29; "Reminiscences of General James R. O'Beirne," *FM*, March 1887, 88; FUA, Diary of Presidents, 1885–1906, John J. Collins, December 21, 1906.

24. Joseph Burnichon, S.J., *La Compagnie de Jésus en France: Histoire d'un Siècle* (Paris: Beauchesne, 1914), I, 265–66. Only 10 percent of the graduates of Saint-Acheul remained practicing Catholics, an achievement that was considered remarkably good at that time. Dansette, *Histoire Religieuse*, I, 278.

stant surveillance," he said, "and surrounded by minute rules which told their own tale." As the French Jesuits were settling in at Rose Hill with their basketful of rules and regulations, on the other side of the Atlantic an enlightened canon of the cathedral of Périgueux wondered "to what degree the uniformity of a detailed set of rules and a cloistered education may be damaging to the soaring of the spirit and the free development of character."[25]

With regard to sports and recreation, there were no indoor recreational facilities with the exception of a billiards room. Backgammon was tolerated, but card playing was strictly forbidden even for the priests in the Jesuit community, and chess was discouraged for the students on the curious grounds that it was an extension of studies rather than a form of recreation. The students were urged to take their recreation outdoors even in the most inclement weather in the belief that doing so was good for their health. Handball was the most popular sport, with teams of six. "Prisoners' Base," a form of tag, was also popular, as was "shinny" or "shinty," a form of hockey of Canadian or Scottish origin, that was played on the frozen pond during the winter. Boxing was also popular to a lesser extent, but not the more aristocratic fencing. The Cadet Corps with its regular military exercises did not make its appearance at Rose Hill until 1885.

Baseball and football would later become the most popular sports at Fordham as at most American men's colleges. Both sports were still in their infancy in the 1850s, and they were played on the Rose Hill campus with scratch teams, makeshift equipment, and improvised rules. Before the introduction of the "dead ball" in the 1870s, some baseball games ended in ludicrously high scores. On one occasion St. John's beat the College of St. Francis Xavier 70 to 3, and in 1865 St. John's beat the semi-pro Enterprise Club of Morrisania 40 to 17 with seventeen runs scored in the last two innings. "We knew all the baseball then known," explained one alumnus of the class of 1857, "and more could not be expected from us. . . . The same could be said of football," he added. "We had no half-backs or snap-backs (at least not technically), but we did not break each other's bones, and our scrimmages gave us as much wind and muscle probably as is derived from the game of today."[26]

When Michael Nash, newly arrived from Kentucky, tried to enforce the

25. Ernest Dimnet, *My Old World* (New York: Simon & Schuster, 1935), 185; Ralph Gibson, *A Social History of French Catholicism, 1789–1914* (London: Routledge, 1989), 90.

26. Joseph J. Marrin, "St. John's Thirty Years Ago," *FM*, December 1887, 57; "Memories of '68," *FM*, May 1898, 421; "Fordham in the Sixties, *FM*, June 1901, 517–18.

regulations at Rose Hill, he complained about the opposition he met from the students, especially the New Yorkers, who were not as docile as Kentucky farm boys. "Without exception," he said, "they were the worst boys I had ever met" without "the remotest instinct of gentlemen." Evidently Nash was not the only one who was shocked at the behavior of the students. In 1850 Father Boulanger appointed Father William Stack Murphy to give the students lessons in "Christian civilization and good manners." The following year the new rector, Father John Larkin, complained privately to a fellow Jesuit about the "rough and coarse tone of language, action and feeling" that he found among the students. Many years later a former student recalled with embarrassment the boorish behavior of his classmates in an algebra class taught by an ailing and infirm Jesuit, Father Duranquet. As soon as Durnaquet turned his back on them to write on the blackboard, they stomped their feet on the floor and threw spitballs at the blackboard.[27]

It has been suggested that the uncouth behavior of the students at St. John's may have reflected their background as the spoiled sons of *nouveau riche* Irish immigrants whose own manners sometimes left much to be desired. On graduation day in 1849, 3,000 people descended on the campus. When a rumor spread that free refreshments were available for everyone, a scene ensued that was reminiscent of Andrew Jackson's inaugural reception at the White House in 1829. Mobs rampaged over the campus, breaking into private rooms, trampling through the garden, and leaving little food or drink for the graduates or their parents.[28]

However, the friction between the students and the faculty may also have reflected the cultural clash between American youngsters and their French teachers. One of the people who came to the rescue of the befuddled Michael Nash and taught him how to handle his obstreperous young charges was a slightly older diocesan seminarian at Rose Hill named Bernard McQuaid. A native New Yorker, McQuaid was a student at Rose Hill from November 1842 until January 1848, where, he said, "I helped rock the cradle of the new institution."

27. Nash, "Reminiscences," 267–68; FUA, Memorialia R. P. Provincialium, Boulanger to Thébaud, March 26, 1850; ACSFX, Larkin to William Gockeln, September 24, 1851; Thomas B. Connery, "Fordham in the Fifties," *FM* 20 (1900): 163.

28. Klein, "Jesuits and Catholic Boyhood," 279. FUA, Minister's Diary, 1840–1860, July 16, 1849. At Georgetown high-spirited southerners resented "shaming punishments" such as kneeling in the refectory as tantamount to being treated as slaves. There were student riots at the college in 1833 and 1850. Curran, *Bicentennial History*, I, 183–86.

As the bishop of Rochester, Bernard McQuaid later became one of the leading figures in the conservative bloc in the American hierarchy, but his approach to American youth differed considerably from that of French Jesuits. He believed that young Americans were quite amenable to discipline, provided they were persuaded that it was reasonable and did not impugn their honor. "The American boy dislikes coercion," said McQuaid in later life, "except the coercion of a manly compliance with rule and order. He cannot abide, nor should he, the faintest suspicion of espionage. His best feelings revolt at the thought. It puts him on a par with a convict or a schemer." James Hennessy described McQuaid as "that most progressive of conservatives," and McQuaid practiced what he preached at the model seminary that he built in Rochester in the 1890s. When a French priest, the Abbé Félix Klein of Americanism fame, visited the seminary in 1903, he was astonished at the free and open atmosphere that prevailed in the institution. "I have confidence in my seminarians," explained McQuaid. "If I have not, I ought not to ordain them."[29]

When it came to the attention of the Fordham Jesuits in 1851 that there was widespread discontent among the students, it never occurred to them to reexamine the rules and regulations under which the students lived. Instead, the shocked fathers decided to begin a novena to the Sacred Heart. However harsh and petty the rules may seem in retrospect, it should be remembered that the Jesuits were the victims of a similar system of training in their own novitiates and houses of formation. Even as fully professed religious at Rose Hill, they could not leave the campus without permission. They had to ask their superiors to replace their worn-out clothes, to allow them to take a bath once a week, and to give them permission to smoke, permission that was to be given only "for reasons of health."[30]

The ban on smoking did not prevent the president, Father Thébaud, from chain-smoking cigars. His medical excuse was that doing so alleviated his chronic asthma. Theory ceded to reality in the Jesuit community at Rose Hill when the superior of the New York–Canada Mission, Father Remigius LeTellier, relaxed the rules so that the fathers could smoke in their rooms but not in public. Even that stipulation was not enforced *ad apicem litterae*. The French Jesuits seem to have been particularly fond of snuff. The students noticed that both Father Doucet and Father Legoüais

29. Bernard J. McQuaid, "Our American Seminaries," *American Ecclesiastical Review* 16 (1897): 472–73. Félix Klein, *In the Land of the Strenuous Life* (Chicago: A. C. McClurg & Co., 1905), 104–5.

30. FUA, Acta Consultorum, May 19, 1851; FUA, Memorialia R. P. Provincialium, Boulanger to Thébaud, April 30, 1849; Boulanger to Thébaud, March 26, 1850.

used it. Father Henri DuMerle, the prefect of discipline, took snuff "not only into his nose, but all along his front," whatever that may mean. Father Henri Régnier, a jovial French Canadian who was the first Jesuit ordained from Fordham, did not even make a pretense of observing the rule. He not only "snuffed" while presiding in the study hall but also gladly shared his snuff box with any student who asked for it. Unknown to the Jesuits, their fondness for snuff was a habit that they shared with Archbishop John Hughes.[31]

The Jesuits formulated the rules at St. John's College as an adaptation of the only rules they had ever known in a laudable effort to provide paternal care and protection for their students. In halting English, Father LeTellier explained that "the discipline of the college ought to be such as to secure as far as possible the Catholic practical feelings, the morality, the progress of the students and the reasonable expectations of their parents." There is abundant evidence that many students responded positively and in later life remembered the dedication of their former teachers with respect and affection. One of the French Jesuits at the College of St. Francis Xavier, Father Theodore Thiry, spent 35 years in the classroom. When he died in 1889, 3,000 people attended his funeral and the pews on both sides of the main aisle in the huge parish church were filled with former members of the sodalities he had directed. Eight carriages accompanied the hearse to the burial at Rose Hill. At the fiftieth anniversary of St. John's College in 1891, speaking on behalf of the alumni, Judge Morgan J. O'Brien said, "Here many a noble life has been sacrificed to education, to duty and to religion. . . . Many of our old professors have passed away. We, the old students of St. John's, come back today to pay our tribute of love and affection to the memory of those whom we knew and loved so well."[32]

31. FUA, Memorialia R. P. Provincialium, LeTellier to Thébaud, March 5, 1862; William Seton, "Memories of an Old Boy," *FM*, November 1895; David A. Merrick, S.J., "Some Recollections of the Fordham Fathers in the Forties," *FM*, November 1887, 29.

32. FUA, Memorialia R. P. Provincialium, LeTellier to Thébaud, May 22, 1861; ACSFX, Minister's Diary, March 15, 1889; *The Illustrated American*, June 24, 1891.

5

UNEASY NEIGHBORS
Jesuit College and Diocesan Seminary

St. John's College: Enrollment and Pedagogy

There were 145 students at St. John's College in 1845, the last year the college was under diocesan administration. By 1850 there were 212 students, but the numbers varied widely thereafter from year to year for reasons that are not always easy to explain. Enrollment dipped to 164 students in 1854, shot up to 203 in 1856, declined again with the outbreak of the Civil War to 152 in 1861 and sank to a low of 110 in 1862, but then almost tripled the next year to 306 students, leading the Jesuits to discuss whether to erect a new building, "since there is scarcely space now for students." Because of the war they deferred a decision until the following year, when they engaged Patrick Keely to be the architect.[1]

Unfortunately the carefully recorded enrollment statistics are of limited value because they do not distinguish the college students from the high school or grammar school students until the 1880s. It is clear, however, that, as at St. Mary's College in Kentucky, few students stayed for the full seven years of high school and college. In 1857, for example, there were 203 students at Rose Hill, but only four received the A.B. degree and another ten received the M.A. degree. This remained the norm until the early twentieth century. Only a few students who completed the undergraduate requirements remained for an additional year or two to qualify for the master's degree. In 1857 for the first time St. John's College awarded an A.B. degree to a graduate of New York's other Jesuit college, the College of St. Francis Xavier.[2] He was Henry Brann, later the pastor of St. Agnes Church in Manhattan. In 1867 there were 567 students at the College of St. Francis Xavier, but at graduation only ten students received the A.B. degree and seven received the M.A. degree. The following year at Rose Hill 12 students received the A.B. degree and seven received the M.A. degree. Only

---

1. FUA, Acta Consultorum, June 15, 1863, March 8, 1864. The statistics on enrollment are taken from the annual *Catalogue of the Officers and Students of St. John's College*.

2. See Chapter 6 for a fuller treatment of the College of St. Francis Xavier.

one graduate had completed the full ten-year course of elementary school, high school, and college.[3]

The high percentage of master's degrees to bachelor's degrees was not limited to St. John's College or the College of St. Francis Xavier. It was a common phenomenon in American Catholic colleges in the nineteenth century partly because, as Philip Gleason has explained, master's degrees were "thought of as reinforced bachelor's degrees" that often did not require even the continued presence of the student on campus. The practice at non-Catholic colleges was no different. One authority on American higher education said of the master's degree, "Almost any college graduate who remained alive and kept out of jail could have it."[4]

The wide geographical distribution of the students is surprising, especially in view of the fact that in the late nineteenth century St. John's College would draw three-quarters of its students from the New York metropolitan area. In 1849, however, almost half of the 184 students were from outside New York, with thirty from the Deep South (nine from New Orleans alone) and twenty-one from Mexico, Cuba, and Puerto Rico. Even more surprising was the presence of twelve students from Martinique and Guadalupe. In addition to the students from the French West Indies, there were three other distinct groups of students whose mother tongue was French, those from France, Québec, and Louisiana. According to one contemporary witness, the members of the French-speaking group did not get on well with one another. As late as 1861 New Yorkers accounted for little more than half the student body (95 out of 176). Even during the Civil War there were always some students from the South, although their number dipped to four in 1863 but rebounded to eighteen the following year.

As procurator of St. John's College from 1850 to 1853, Father Xavier Maréchal was accustomed to sending dunning letters to delinquent parents in three languages—English, Spanish, and French. He anglicized his name to the Reverend J. Marshall, S.J., and often included friendly advice in his requests to parents for payment of overdue tuition. He told one Mexican mother not to worry that her son had difficulty in mastering English, "*la lengua inglesa siendo muy dura, al contrario la lengua española siendo muy dulce.*" The young man and his brother remained at Rose Hill for only

---

3. ACSFX, Historia Domus, 1867; "Memories of '68," *FM* 16 (May 1899): 417–18.

4. George P. Schmidt, *The Liberal Arts College* (New Brunswick, N.J.: Rutgers University Press, 1957), 368–69, cit. in Philip Gleason, *Contending with Modernity: Catholic Higher Education in the Twentieth Century* (New York: Oxford University Press, 1995), 169.

two years, long enough presumably for them to acquire a working knowledge of English.[5]

As was mentioned earlier, in February 1847, one year after assuming control of St. John's College, the Jesuits revised the curriculum and based it on the version of the *ratio studiorum* that had been adopted at Georgetown College in 1839. As Father John W. Padberg has explained, the distinctive pedagogy of the *ratio studiorum* was especially employed in teaching grammar and rhetoric or literature, but it could be adapted to other subjects as well. It consisted of three steps:

> [T]he teacher would first state a precept or rule or proposition of grammar, for instance, or of rhetoric. Then he would explain, elaborate upon, illustrate it by examples from the particular literary author who was being studied at that time, this step usually involving a Socratic questioning of the students' grasp of rule and example. Finally the students were set to applying the rule in written and oral exercises.

The inclusion of the authors who were being studied served two purposes. They were the sources for illustrating the basic elements of grammar and composition in the lower grades and were also the sources for imparting an appreciation of literature and literary criticism in the upper grades. The key element in this pedagogy on both levels was the "prelection," or explanation of the lesson, by the teacher before the student began to study it himself.

As Padberg describes it, the "prelection" involved three steps:

> First, there was a short summary of the content of the section or passage to be studied, plus an attempt to relate it to the material studied immediately previously. Then, the grammatical and syntactical difficulties of the passage were pointed out and solved. Next, the teacher would comment on style, explain difficult allusions, and introduce material from other disciplines such as history or geography which had a bearing on the subject. Finally, at least in the early stages of learning, he would translate the passage, in whole or part.

As Padberg admits, the potential shortcomings of this pedagogy were numerous and serious because it could result in stultifyingly dull classes that locked the teacher into a rote presentation of the material that left the students completely passive. On the other hand, the genius of the *ratio*

5. "Fordham in the Sixties," *FM*, May 1901, 456; FUA, Treasurer's Letter Book, 1851–1852, Marshall to Dona Serrano Mesa, July 12, 1852.

studiorum was that it provided the all-important element of order, which could be a lifesaver for a poor teacher. By combining imagination with order, Padberg observed, a good teacher could become a better teacher, and "a brilliant teacher had ample opportunity to make of his class a vivid experience in learning and a means of true intellectual activity on the part of the students."[6]

The Jesuit Faculty

According to Thomas Gaffney Taaffe, an alumnus of the class of 1890 and the first historian of Fordham, the two most popular and influential members of the faculty at St. John's College during its first half-century were John Larkin and William Stack Murphy, despite the fact that neither of them spent more than a few years at Rose Hill. Near-contemporaries, born in 1801 and 1803 respectively, both men had already made their mark as teachers, superiors, and administrators in Kentucky before coming to Fordham.

When Father Murphy left Europe for America, in imitation of St. Francis Xavier, he turned down the opportunity to pay a farewell visit to his mother in Ireland, an act of mortification that is said to have elicited admiration from everyone (except perhaps his mother). Murphy was only forty-three when he arrived at Rose Hill from Kentucky in the spring of 1846, but his hair had already turned completely white. His thin and spare physique was the result of chronic dyspepsia, a generic term for a wide variety of painful abdominal problems that in the nineteenth century defied more precise medical diagnosis. Murphy's original assignment at Fordham was to be professor of Greek and Hebrew, but he made his deepest impression on the students by teaching eighteenth-century English literature.

After only one year in the classroom, he replaced Father Larkin as dean and vice president. Although not a gifted orator himself, Murphy earned the gratitude of St. John's students by carefully preparing them for debates and literary presentations. More than one of them recalled practicing his lines in Murphy's room while Murphy was shaving and frightening them by gesticulating wildly with a straight razor in his hand. The session often ended with Murphy's spending a half-hour regaling the student with his endless repertoire of stories. When Murphy was interviewing the parents

6. John W. Padberg, S.J., *Colleges in Controversy: The Jesuit Schools in France from Revival to Suppression, 1815–1880* (Cambridge, Mass.: Harvard University Press, 1969), 160–62. See also Christa Klein, "The Jesuits and Catholic Boyhood in Nineteenth-Century New York City: A Study of St. John's College and the College of St. Francis Xavier, 1846–1912." Ph.D. diss., University of Pennsylvania, 1976, 124–28.

of a prospective student, the boy's mother inquired about the quality of the food. "Madam," Murphy replied, "we feed them like princes. Potatoes and molasses for breakfast, molasses and potatoes for dinner, and both for supper. What more could be desired?"[7]

However effective Murphy's pedagogy may have been, contemporaries had difficulty in defining it or relating it to the *ratio studiorum*. "There may have been a method in it," said a friendly critic, "as there is said to be in some people's madness, but it would puzzle anyone to find it out." Like Cardinal James Gibbons, the legendary archbishop of Baltimore, and many others who developed an incurable disease early in life, Murphy lived to a ripe old age. In addition to his service at Fordham from 1846 to 1851 and again from 1857 to 1860, Murphy served as visitor to the Missouri Vice-Province and later as vice provincial of the province, and briefly as the superior of the New York Mission before retiring to New Orleans, where he died in 1875 at the age of seventy-two. As a Yankee priest in New Orleans during the Civil War, he proved invaluable as an intermediary with the commander of the Union army of occupation. Murphy claimed that drinking large quantities of Mississippi mud and water in New Orleans relieved his dyspepsia.[8]

John Larkin served as a member of the Fordham faculty on two separate occasions. The first was in 1846, when at the age of forty-five he was appointed the first Jesuit dean and vice president of St. John's College. A year later he was given the task of establishing a Jesuit college in Manhattan, the College of the Holy Name of Jesus, which was renamed the College of St. Francis Xavier in 1850. In 1851 Larkin returned to Rose Hill, where he succeeded Father Thébaud as the second Jesuit president for the next three years. Unlike the ascetic-looking Murphy, Larkin tipped the scales at more than 300 pounds. One of his students, John Hassard, recalled the first impression that Larkin made on him and his younger brother as students in 1846. "'Isn't he fat,' we both exclaimed, and we both added, 'but how handsome he is.'" It was an impression that was shared by many others. When Larkin was in Paris a few years later, seeking the intervention of the papal nuncio to prevent his appointment as the second bishop of Toronto, the nuncio warned Larkin not to go to Rome to plead his case in person

7. David Merrick, S.J., "Some Recollections of the Fordham Fathers in the Forties," *FM*, 1887, 29; Thomas B. Connery, "Fordham in the Fifties," *FM*, October 1901, 6.

8. Thomas Gaffney Taaffe, *A History of St. John's College, Fordham, N.Y.* (New York: The Catholic Publication Society, 1891), 77–79; Thomas C. Hennessy, S.J., ed., *Fordham: The Early Years* (New York: Something More Publications, 1998), 85–88.

before the pope because, he said, he was "the very kind of man we wish to wear the miter."[9]

Like Murphy, Larkin had his own unique pedagogical style that owed little to the *ratio studiorum* or "prelections" and required a minimum of preparation on his part. He never brought a book or paper to class. Instead he would launch into an hour-long monologue that was often precipitated by some incident in the classroom or a question from one of the students. The students quickly caught on to the technique and tried to stump him by raising the most esoteric topics. Larkin never failed to satisfy their curiosity. He would conclude the class by saying, "Yes, just as usual, you boys have taken advantage of a garrulous old man to waste the whole time of the class." He would then assign them to write a synopsis of his remarks. He cajoled them all. Martin T. McMahon, the future Civil War general, thought he learned more from one hour with Larkin than from a week with any of his other teachers.[10]

One famous outbreak of student misbehavior at Rose Hill has dogged Larkin's reputation as the president of St. John's College and left him unfairly depicted in later life as both anti-Irish and as an overbearing disciplinarian. The incident occurred on the Sunday before St. Patrick's Day in 1852 when a food fight broke out in the refectory. Taking advantage of the absence of most of the prefects, the students began to hurl bread and potatoes across the table in the refectory after a new cook had failed to provide enough meat for supper. The younger boys complained that they were unfairly singled out for punishment by being deprived of butter. During the evening recreation period they shattered some of the window panes by shooting marbles at them. As a result Father Larkin canceled the annual St. Patrick's Day celebration. This in turn provoked a rumor that the cancelation was due to anti-Irish prejudice on the part of the English-born Larkin and led to another round of window smashing.

Larkin quieted the students by addressing them directly. To one alleged perpetrator he said, "Master George, have the good sense to take your hat and leave on the next Rail Road train that passes." However, he did not expel him. Later the ringleaders were identified and dismissed, but Larkin offered an amnesty to the other students if they came forward to acknowledge their guilt and agreed to pay for the damage they had caused. The combination of the stick and carrot was effective in quelling the dis-

9. Thomas C. Hennessy, S.J., "The First Jesuits at St. John's College, Fordham, 1846," in Hennessy, *Fordham: The Early Years*, 84.

10. Martin T. McMahon, "Reminiscences," *FM*, June 1891, 52.

turbance with a minimum of resentment on the part of the students. It was a tactic that was typical of Larkin's approach to discipline. While he recognized the need to enforce standards of civilized behavior among the rambunctious and sometimes unruly student body, he also had misgivings about the French penchant for surveillance and wondered if it was sometimes counterproductive. Larkin had his own streak of Celtic rebelliousness. He said to the boys in the study hall on one occasion that "rules were meant to be kept but expected to be broken." "We fulfilled the expectation pretty consistently and steadily," one of the students confessed.[11]

Shortly after Larkin became president at Rose Hill, the college seniors tested him by claiming that it had become customary for them to be exempted from certain rules and regulations. Larkin called them together and informed them that he "recognized no customs incompatible with good order and discipline." He was pleased to hear later that they reacted to his talk by saying among themselves that "he is mighty civil and polite, but he is mighty tight." At the same time Larkin did away with the practice of expelling students from class and punishing them on the spot. He wanted no harsh words or scolding. "I insist," he said, "upon cool, calm, undisturbed, and polite and friendly remonstrance, particularly with boys above thirteen." The prefects did not challenge Larkin's directives, but they sometimes found it difficult to put them into practice. Several told him that "we have to watch more over ourselves than over the students." "Precisely," Larkin replied, "and you will be the gainers." In 1852 Larkin replaced Father Thomas Ouellet, the French Canadian prefect of discipline who had a reputation as a martinet, with Father Frederick William Gockeln, an old friend from their days together at the Grand Séminaire in Montréal. Gockeln shared his own more enlightened views about student discipline.[12]

The allegation that Larkin was anti-Irish is ludicrously inaccurate. In fact he was an ardent supporter of the radical Young Ireland movement, which represented the leading edge of Irish nationalism in the late 1840s. James McMaster, the ultra-conservative editor of the *New York Freeman's Journal*, was shocked and outraged to discover that St. John's College Li-

11. ANYPSJ, Larkin to Gockeln, April 17, 1852. Taaffe, *History of St. John's College*, 85–88. Taaffe gives a highly colorful account of the incident claiming that there was hardly a pane of glass left in any building on the campus. Thomas B. Connery, "Fordham in the Fifties," *FM* 20 (1901), 157.

12. ANYPSJ, Larkin to Gockeln, September 24, 1851. Even General Martin T. McMahon thought that Father Ouellet was overly severe as a disciplinarian. "Reminiscences," *FM*, June 1891, 53.

brary subscribed to *The Nation*, the leading journal of the Young Ireland movement.[13] One of Father Larkin's proudest moments as president of St. John's College occurred in 1852 when he had the pleasure of welcoming to the campus Thomas Francis Meagher, one of the leaders of the Young Ireland movement, who had just escaped from imprisonment in Australia. Meagher was an alumnus of both Clongowes, the Jesuit school in County Kildare, and Stonyhurst College in Lancashire, the Jesuits' flagship school in England. He used his visit to Rose Hill to deliver a rousing address on behalf of Irish freedom on St. John's Day, June 24. Larkin invited Meagher to return to receive an honorary doctorate at graduation, but he failed to show up without notice, much to Larkin's disappointment and embarrassment.[14]

Thomas Gaffney Taaffe thought that, even more than William Stack Murphy, John Larkin was the outstanding figure during the first fifty years of Fordham's history. He excelled not only as a teacher and administrator but also as a preacher and orator. John Hassard said that "for me, ever since I first saw him thirty-five years ago, the college has been filled with his majestic presence. . . . Neither his preaching nor his conversation gave you the idea of labored precision," explained Hassard; "it was fluent, easy, direct, natural, but every word had its just emphasis and exact pronunciation, and every sentence its sure balance." Hassard noted that "there is a certain tone of speech rarely acquired except by persons of thorough education and breeding: it indicates familiarity with the best usages, refined taste, self-possession, composure." "Father Larkin had more of that," said Hassard, "than any man I ever met except James Russell Lowell." "With him," said another student, Thomas Connery, "the refinement was inborn." Connery remembered especially the effect on the students of Larkin's talks on gentlemanly conduct and good manners. "It was clear," said Connery in words that Bishop McQuaid would have heartily seconded, "that he understood that the American boy was to be most surely reached through the sense of honor."[15]

In his brief span of eighteen years as a member of the Society of Jesus, Larkin served as the president of no fewer than three Jesuit schools, including the short-lived St. Ignatius Literary Institution in Louisville. He

13. McMaster's informant was Bernard McQuaid, then a newly ordained priest in Madison, New Jersey. It was a role that McQuaid would outgrow in later years. *New York Freeman's Journal*, January 20, February 3, 1849.

14. ANYPSJ, Larkin to Gockeln, November 15, 1852.

15. John Hassard, *FM*, December 1886; Thomas B. Connery, "Fordham in the Fifties," *FM* 20 (1901): 228.

also was active in parish ministry and retreat work both in the United States and in England, and he received a special assignment from the Jesuit general as visitor to the Irish Vice-Province. He spent the last two years of his life at St. Francis Xavier in Manhattan, where he was deeply involved in the pastoral ministry and traveled up and down the East Coast conducting retreats. He died at St. Francis Xavier on December 13, 1858, at the age of fifty-seven.

Still another professor who tempered his adherence to the *ratio studiorum* with a generous dollop of common sense was Father Hector Glackmeyer, the talented director of music who also taught Greek. On a gloomy winter day or a drowsy June afternoon, Father "Glack" would begin class by saying, "Boys, we'll skip Demosthenes and have a little of Pickwick." He would then whip out a copy of *The Pickwick Papers* and regale the students with his reading of some amusing passage in his rich musical voice until he had them all laughing. Eventually he would slip Dickens into his desk and say, "After all, boys, we must do *some* work." The result, said one of his students, was that they accomplished three times as much work with Demosthenes as they would have done without the help of Mr. Pickwick.[16]

A favorite of the students was Father Thomas Legoüais, the longtime director of the senior sodality. Whenever Jesuits established a new college, one of the first things they did was organize a sodality of the Virgin Mary. When they arrived at Rose Hill, they discovered that the diocesan clergy had already established a Marian sodality. They promptly combined it with the Parthenian Society, the sodality that Father Legoüais had founded at St. Mary's College in Kentucky. Membership in the sodality was by invitation only and was limited to the brightest and most religious students in the hope that they would form an elite who would set an example for others. Like the religious orders on which they were modeled, there were three stages of membership in the sodality: postulants, probationers, and full members.

The sodalists had their own chapel, and they were expected to recite the rosary daily, receive Communion once a month (unlike the rest of the students, who received Communion only five times a year), attend the weekly sodality meetings, and take part in the triduum (three days of prayer) in preparation for the annual celebration of the patronal feast on February 2, the feast of the Purification of Mary. As in Kentucky, the Jesuits separated the younger sodalists from the older sodalists, and by the

16. Joseph J. Marrin, "St. John's Thirty Years Ago," *FM*, December 1887, 58–59.

Uneasy Neighbors: Jesuit College and Diocesan Seminary

mid-1850s there were three separate sodalities for the First, Second, and Third divisions.[17]

Father Legoüais took a more relaxed approach to the rules than some of his confrères. It was understood that a student could always request permission to leave the study hall to go to confession or seek spiritual direction from one of his professors. Students often took advantage of the rule to visit Father Legoüais not only for spiritual ministrations but also for help with the translation of a particularly difficult Latin or Greek assignment. On a cold winter night they were likely to be rewarded not only with a flawless translation that dumbfounded their teacher in class the next morning but also with one of the hot apples that Father Legoüais was roasting on the stove in his room.[18]

One of the few occasions when the Jesuits appeared in mufti is when they donned secular clothes for a visit to the city. Not until the Third Plenary Council of Baltimore in 1884 did it become mandatory for American priests to wear the Roman collar. Like many clerics accustomed to wearing only a religious habit, the Fordham Jesuits were not well versed in the art of haberdashery. "A Jesuit dressed in worldly clothing was always a cause of joy to the students," commented one of them mischievously. The devout Father Legoüais was the "capsheaf—the worldliest of the worldly" according to this same student. He cut a less-than-dashing figure dressed in an old long coat, a moth-eaten "dicer" of a hat, shoes several sizes two big, great large eyeglasses, and a walking stick as high as his chin that he carried a foot in front of him.[19]

Early Alumni

In the 1850s there was an unhappy young Boston Brahmin named Robert Gould Shaw in the secondary school. His parents were Unitarians, but they sent him to Fordham at the urging of his uncle, a convert to Catholicism and a Jesuit. Young Shaw ran away, only to be brought back by his father. Later he found college at Harvard more congenial, although he did not stay long enough to take a degree. During the Civil War he won fame as the commanding officer of the African American 54th Massachusetts Infantry Regiment and died on July 18, 1863, leading his troops in an attack on a Confederate fort protecting Charleston harbor. He was twenty-five years old.

17. Klein, "Jesuits and Catholic Boyhood," 230–34; FUA, Acta Consultorum, November 27, 1849; Parthenian Sodality, 1837–1884.

18. William Seton, "Memories of an Old Boy," *FM*, November 1895, 19.

19. "Fordham in the Sixties," *FM*, June 1901, 520.

William Rodrigue, Archbishop Hughes's brother-in-law and a professor at St. John's College, sent three sons to the college. They gave their home address as Fordham, New York. One wonders if their father got a discount as a member of the faculty. There was a fourth Rodrigue at Rose Hill, the son of William Rodrigue's brother Aristides. The father moved to Kansas, where he became a leader in the pro-slavery movement in that territory. Andrew Carrigan, who had bought the Rose Hill property on behalf of Bishop Hughes, sent his son of the same name to Fordham. Louis Binsse, one of the leaders of the small New York French Catholic community, had two sons at St. John's. Their father became the commercial consul of the Papal States in New York and incurred the wrath of John Hughes, who suspected him of urging Rome to appoint a coadjutor when the archbishop's health began to fail in the later 1850s.

Several journalists were alumni of St. John's College, an indication perhaps of the impact of the Jesuit emphasis on *eloquentia perfecta*. William Denman Jr. succeeded his father as the proprietor and editor of the *Truth Teller*, one of New York's two Catholic newspapers. Another future journalist was John Rose Greene Hassard, who received his A.B. degree in 1855 and his M.A. in 1857. A convert to the Catholic Church at the age of fifteen, he had a distinguished career as a music critic, book reviewer, and editorial writer first for the *New York Sun* and then for the *New York Tribune*. He also served briefly as secretary to Archbishop Hughes and in 1866 published the first and last substantial biography of Hughes. Still another future journalist was James Gordon Bennett Jr., the spoiled son of the flamboyant founding editor of the *New York Herald*. The younger Bennett makes a fleeting appearance in the college records as a nine-year-old student in 1850. "He was not readily amenable to discipline," said a fellow student dryly. The younger Bennett's presence for even a year is most surprising because Hughes and his father were bitter enemies. Six years earlier, in an open letter to Mayor James Harper, Hughes had called the senior Bennett "the most dangerous man to the peace and safety of a community that I have ever known."[20]

As one might expect, the clergy were well represented among the alumni of St. John's. It is an understatement to say that they were a varied group. Sylvester Rosecrans, the brother of Civil War general William

20. Thomas B. Connery, "Fordham in the Fifties," *FM* 20 (1901): 304. Lawrence Kehoe, ed., *Complete Works of the Most Reverend John Hughes* (New York: Lawrence Kehoe, 1866), I, 456–57. Bennett routinely referred to Hughes as the bishop of Blarneyopolis, a play on his formal title of coadjutor to Bishop Dubois as the titular bishop of Basileopolis in *partibus infidelium*.

Starke Rosecrans, was a convert who became the first bishop of Columbus, Ohio. David Merrick entered the Society of Jesus and became the president of the College of St. Francis Xavier. William Plowden Morrogh, an Irish-born New York diocesan priest, became the rector of St. Joseph's Seminary at Rose Hill and later the pastor of the Church of the Immaculate Conception on East 14th Street in Manhattan. He was the uncle of Father Richard Burtsell, the indefatigable diarist of the New York clergy and his own family. Dr. Burtsell, as he insisted on being addressed in recognition of his Roman doctorate, left a memorable account of his tipsy uncle's leaning over the banister on the second floor of his rectory, losing his balance, and landing in the middle of a group of pious women reciting the rosary. Three of them pinned him to the floor until the curate could be summoned to carry him back upstairs to his room.[21]

A less fortunate but more exotic alumnus was George Rimsal, who received his M.A. in 1856 and was ordained a diocesan priest a few years

St. Joseph's Diocesan Seminary, 1845–60. After the Jesuits purchased it in 1860, they renamed it St. John's Hall and it served many purposes before becoming part of Our Lady's Court (today's Queen's Court) in 1940.

21. AANY, Burtsell Diary, July 23, 1865.

Uneasy Neighbors: Jesuit College and Diocesan Seminary

later. Assigned to teach dogmatic theology in St. Joseph's Seminary at Rose Hill, he left the priesthood shortly thereafter, married, and joined the professional anti-Catholic lecture circuit. He was reconciled to the Church in 1872 in England, joined the Mill Hill Missionaries, and served as Catholic chaplain with the British military expedition to Afghanistan in 1879, where he was decorated for bravery in the capture of Kabul and Kandahar. Apparently miffed that he was not made a bishop for his services, he left the Church again and last surfaced as a minister of the Church of Scotland, functioning under the name of Dr. A. M. R. Browne.[22]

In 1864 a young immigrant from County Armagh named John Murphy Farrelly entered St. John's College and the following July won the silver medal for rhetoric and prizes for Latin discourse and poetry, history, trigonometry, and chemistry. He left the college that summer after only one year to enroll in the newly established St. Joseph's Provincial Seminary in Troy, New York, and a year later was sent to the North American College in Rome. Somewhere along the way he changed his name from Farrelly to Farley (presumably so that the spelling would match the pronunciation) and became the fourth archbishop of New York in 1902 and New York's second cardinal in 1911. Although Farley did not receive a degree, the Fordham Jesuits later lionized him as a graduate and boasted of the "years" he had spent at Rose Hill. Farley never corrected them.[23]

The First St. Joseph's Seminary

As Father Raymond Schroth has emphasized in his history of Fordham, the Jesuits at Rose Hill in the 1840s and 1850s faced the daunting challenge of running four different institutions on the same campus: a college (which itself included an elementary school and a secondary school), a Jesuit novitiate, a Jesuit scholasticate, and a diocesan seminary.[24] At least in the case of the college, novitiate, and scholasticate (which were houses of formation and education for their own aspirants and seminarians), the Jesuits were free to formulate their own rules and regulations according to the norms of the Society of Jesus. This was not true with regard to the diocesan seminary. Hughes had handed over to the Jesuits the administration and teaching in the seminary, but he retained the legal title to the seminary building and the surrounding eight or nine acres and

---

22. There is an extensive file on Rimsal in the archives of the Archdiocese of New York. AANY, G-60, Papers in the Case of Dr. Browne.

23. See "The Archbishop of New York," *FM* 21 (1902), 1–3.

24. Raymond A. Schroth, *Fordham: A History and Memoir* (Chicago: Loyola University Press, 2002), 19–20.

took a close interest in how the Jesuits operated the seminary, which was emphatically *his* seminary.

During the previous six years before the arrival of the Jesuits, the seminary had already experienced a troubled existence under both diocesan and Vincentian administration. The arrangement with the Jesuits worked reasonably well during the first four or five years, but by 1850 it was beginning to break down. There were repeated complaints that the poor living conditions in the seminary were impairing the health of the seminarians. One of the professors, Father Isidore Daubresse, admitted that the cold and dampness had led to the death of at least one student, but he claimed that the Jesuits had appealed to the diocese in vain for three years to rectify the situation. Moreover, said Daubresse, many of the seminarians came to them in poor health. "At vacations outside the seminary during the past several years," he explained to his own superior, "some of them contracted cholera and other diseases. Should one be surprised then," he asked, "that they return to the seminary in poor health?"[25]

There were other complaints as well about the Jesuits at the seminary. Neither Daubresse nor Father Seraphin Schemmel, professors of moral theology and dogmatic theology, respectively, ever became fluent in English. According to Burtsell their English was atrocious. As royalists scarred by the excesses of the French Revolution, they had little sympathy for democratic government. "Whilst I was in school with the Jesuits," Dr. Burtsell confided to his diary, "I thought that they were the leaders of the age. But now I found them wishing to familiarize us with the habits of the middle ages. Especially in the New York Province, the superiors are Frenchmen of very cramped minds, who denounce our [political] institutions as they would denounce the [Jacobin] revolution of 1793." When an alumnus told Father Thébaud that the Church was partially responsible for the French Revolution, he stormed out of the man's house in anger. When Burtsell complained to Father Daubresse that the Church was failing to promote social reform, Daubresse blithely replied that the Church was always the leader in social reform.

The French Jesuit penchant for surveillance must have been as irritating for the seminarians as it was for the college students. Nor were the extravagances of nineteenth-century French piety likely to commend themselves to young American males. Daubresse allowed that he could not have saved his soul if he had not become a Jesuit. Fearful that young diocesan priests would acquire bad habits from their older colleagues (perhaps he had Dr.

25. ANYPSJ, Daubresse to Boulanger, May 11, 1855.

The campus at Rose Hill as it appeared in a photograph taken in 1863.

Morrogh in mind), he told Burtsell that they should be placed in rectories where their mother and sisters could serve as chaperones. Even the strait-laced Burtsell laughed at this suggestion. In 1861 Hughes told the Jesuit superior that he did not want Daubresse to conduct the annual clergy retreat because so many priests had unpleasant memories of him from their seminary days.[26]

In 1855 Hughes decided to get rid of the Jesuits at the seminary after persuading an Irish diocesan priest, James Donnelly, to accept the post of rector. However, at the last moment Donnelly had to decline the offer because his bishop would not release him. "I cannot express to you the extent and magnitude of my disappointment," Hughes replied. It left the archbishop in an embarrassing position, because the Jesuits had heard rumors that he intended to dismiss them. Father Boulanger, the superior of the New York–Canada Mission, threatened to remove his men from the seminary if any diocesan priests were added to the faculty. Moreover, Boulanger demanded that the Jesuits be given more authority at the seminary and a larger stipend. Above all, he insisted on an end to the rumors that Hughes was unhappy with their administration of the seminary.[27]

Hughes tried to mollify the Jesuits by denying that he was displeased with their conduct of the seminary. He assured the rector, Father John Blettner, that he had always regarded the Jesuit control of the seminary as

26. AANY, Burtsell Diary, July 11, August 19, 20, September 1, 1865; Thomas B. Connery, "Fordham in the Fifties," *FM*, November 1901, 98; AANY, A-5, Hughes to John McElroy, S.J., May 20, 1861.

27. AANY, A-2, Hughes to Donnelly, October 2, 1855; ANYPSJ, Boulanger to Blettner, June 19, 1855.

a temporary measure until he had enough diocesan priests to take charge of the institution. The Jesuits were not impressed with Hughes's explanation. That same day Daubresse and Schemmel resigned from the faculty, bringing to an end the brief Jesuit era at the diocesan seminary. For the next five years an increasingly frustrated John Hughes tried to operate the seminary with his own diocesan clergy.[28]

The operation of the seminary was not the only source of friction between Hughes and the Jesuits. Hughes demanded an adjustment of the boundary line between the college and the seminary. The Jesuits objected when Hughes made the seminary chapel the parish church of Our Lady of Mercy, because the only means of access to the church was through the college campus. There was the more personal boundary problem that involved Mrs. William Rodrigue, the archbishop's sister. If she took the wrong exit from her house on campus, she trespassed on college property. There was also conflict over the legal title to the Jesuit Church of St. Francis Xavier on West 16th Street in Manhattan. Another irritant was the provision ("a cramping clause," the Jesuits called it) in the agreement of November 24, 1845, whereby they were obliged to restore St. John's College to the bishop if they withdrew from the diocese.[29]

In addition to these specific grievances, Hughes became convinced that three or four unnamed Jesuits at Rose Hill were conducting a clandestine campaign to undermine his reputation with the laity and to call into question his "honor, veracity, honesty and candor." In these disputes the Jesuits generally adopted a conciliatory stance toward Hughes, but they were quite candid in voicing their complaints to the Jesuit authorities in Rome. "*Monseigneur nous a trompé*" [Monseigneur has deceived us], the Fordham Jesuits told the general and claimed that Hughes had assured them that the Rose Hill property was worth $130,000 in 1844 when it was not worth that much fourteen years later.[30]

In New York, Hughes became more and more inflexible and irascible. When Father Remigius LeTellier, the president of St. John's College, sought advice from Charles O'Conor, Hughes's lawyer and close friend, the archbishop exploded and interpreted the contact as an attempt to appeal to the laity against him. "This, Reverend Fathers, will not do!" he told LeTellier and accused him of attempting to make laymen "umpires" between him and the Society of Jesus. "This appeal to the laity is a new

28. ANYPSJ, Blettner to Boulanger, July 16, 1855.
29. Curran, "Hughes and the Jesuits," 16–17.
30. ARSJ, Plaintes des Pères de la Compagnie de Jésus contre Monseigneur John Hughes évêque, n.d. [1858].

feature in our ecclesiastical discipline," he commented sarcastically. "I recognize no tribunal among the laity of my diocese to whom any priest, secular or religious, has a right to appeal for redress of wrong!" Two years later, when the Jesuits again consulted O'Conor for advice about improving relations between the seminary and the college, O'Conor replied curtly, "Good fences, dogs, etc."[31]

By 1859 the seminary was in dire financial straits. "This cannot be allowed to go on," Hughes warned the pastors of the archdiocese in pleading with them to increase the returns from the annual seminary collection. Ironically the parish that sent in the largest contribution ($606) was the Jesuit church of St. Francis Xavier. Finances were not the only problem. Hughes did not have enough trained diocesan priests to staff the seminary, especially after the defection of George Rimsal and the resignation of the rector, William Morrogh, because of ill health. Hughes admitted defeat and closed the seminary in 1860. "It was the pride of my early episcopacy," he told Cardinal Alessandro Barnabò, the prefect of the Propaganda in Rome.[32]

By this time the relations between Hughes and the Jesuits had improved considerably. One of the most influential figures in the Jesuit community at Rose Hill, Father Legoüais, admitted to the Jesuit general, Father Peter Beckx, that many of the archbishop's complaints about the Jesuit management of the seminary had been justified. The Jesuits were more anxious than ever for a reconciliation with Hughes, and the person whom the general had selected to orchestrate it was Father John McElroy, S.J., an old and trusted friend of the archbishop's. Some preliminary sparring led to a dramatic scene at the archbishop's residence on March 1, 1859, when McElroy and two other Jesuits went down on their knees to apologize to him.[33] Hughes assured the general that McElroy had handled the situation with great finesse and that he had no further complaints against the Society of Jesus in New York.[34]

Hughes was now ready to dispose of New York's first St. Joseph's Seminary, and he sold it to the Jesuits on July 16, 1860, for $45,000.[35] "I shall

31. ANYPSJ, Hughes to LeTellier, June 20, 1857; O'Conor to LeTellier, December 16, 1859.

32. AANY, A-3, Hughes to Rev. Dear Sir; ASJSD, Seminary Collection for the Year 1859; AANY, A-1, Hughes to Barnabò, May 8, 1860, copy.

33. Legoüais to Beckx, October 13, 1858, in Curran, "Hughes and the Jesuits," 38, 43.

34. ANYPSJ, Hughes to Beckx, April 30, 1859.

35. AANY, Indenture between St. John's College, Fordham, and Most Reverend John Hughes, Archbishop of New York, July 16, 1860.

The graduating class of 1865 on the steps of the Administration Building.

build another seminary on a smaller scale," he had told Barnabò a month earlier. During the seminary's 20-year existence the student body averaged between 25 and 40, and the faculty usually consisted of the rector and two professors, never more than three. The total number of alumni ordained was 107, little better than five priests a year, hardly sufficient to provide for the needs of a rapidly growing Catholic population. It would appear that the formation program left much to be desired, at least in the later years under diocesan control. Father William McCloskey, a New York priest who was the first rector of the Pontifical North American College in Rome, complained of the unruly behavior of the Fordham seminarians who were sent to Rome, offending Hughes by telling him that the seminary was "not only a wretched but a dangerous place for our young men."[36]

36. AANY, A-4, McCloskey to Hughes, September 9, 1861. When Hughes accused McCloskey of prejudice against the Fordham seminary, he tried to soften his criticism by admitting that "no better priests have entered on their labor than some who were educated at Fordham, and that, at least, ought to be a consolation to you." AANY, A-4, McCloskey to Hughes, December 7, 1861.

The purchase of the seminary property rounded off the campus and gave the college an additional building that was called St. John's Hall. It was used in subsequent years sometimes as the home of the grammar school and sometimes as accommodation for the college seniors where the private rooms were a vast improvement over the open dormitories. Most of all, the closure of the diocesan seminary removed a major irritant between the Society of Jesus and the founding father of St. John's College.

The Civil War

In the years prior to the outbreak of hostilities in 1861, there may have been less antagonism than one might expect between the southern and the northern students at St. John's College, because most of the New York Irish shared the anti-abolitionist sentiments of their southern brethren. Many abolitionist leaders were anti-Catholic bigots who regarded the Catholic hierarchy in the North and the slave-owning oligarchy in the South as the two biggest threats to American democracy. As former slave owners in Kentucky, the Jesuits at Rose Hill might also have been expected to be ardent anti-abolitionists, but such conjecture may be inaccurate. When Father Maréchal, a French-born veteran of the Kentucky mission, cast his ballot for president of the United States in 1860 at the voting booth in West Farms, he announced publicly that he had voted for the "abolitionist candidate." An unhappy fellow voter threatened him with physical harm, but the feisty Maréchal raised his cane and challenged him to a fight. His critic turned tail and ran away.[37]

New York City was a Democratic stronghold where many wealthy businessmen, especially the cotton brokers, feared that Abraham Lincoln's resistance to southern demands would jeopardize their lucrative commercial ties to the South. Mayor Fernando Wood even floated the idea that New York City should secede from the state to protect its economic interests. However, at a huge rally in Manhattan's Union Square on February 20, 1861, perhaps as many as 250,000 people gathered to demonstrate their support for the preservation of the Union. During the course of the war, the Empire State contributed more than a half-million men to the Union army, more than any other state, and 50,000 New Yorkers died on the battlefields.[38]

37. William Seton, "Memories of an Old Boy," *FM*, November 1895.

38. Union Square was named long before the Civil War because it was the intersection of the city's two major thoroughfares, Broadway and the Bowery Road, now Fourth Avenue.

In October 1861 John Hughes warned the Secretary of War, Simon Cameron, that his people would support the war if the objective was to preserve the Union, but not if it was to abolish slavery. Hughes himself offered strong backing for the war, flying the Stars and Stripes from the cathedral, blessing the colors of the New York 69th Regiment as they marched off to war, and even traveling to France at the request of his friend William Seward, now the secretary of state, to enlist the support of Emperor Napoleon III. "I cannot do much for the war," he told General Winfield Scott, the commanding general of the Union army, in May 1861, "but I am willing to do all in my power for humanity and the alleviation of the horrors of war." He offered him the services of a dozen chaplains and fifty to one hundred Sisters of Charity and Sisters of Mercy "like those who toiled in the Crimea." With his typical impetuosity, and without consulting either the priests or the sisters, Hughes assured General Scott that the priests and sisters would be ready to leave within two hours.[39]

Fordham alumni fought on both sides in the war, but precise statistics about their numbers are hard to ascertain. Two became generals in the Union army and won the Congressional Medal of Honor. Dr. William Seton, the grandson of St. Elizabeth Anne Seton, the founder of the American Sisters of Charity, was a captain in the Fourth New York Volunteers and was wounded twice during the battle of Antietam, the single bloodiest day of the war. Lieutenant Colonel Alcee Atocha was provost marshal in New Orleans during the Union occupation of the city. Louis Binsee became a captain in the Garde Lafayette. Peter Hargous enlisted as a private in the 7th New York Regiment and later became a lieutenant colonel in the 69th New York Regiment. As was already mentioned, Robert Gould Shaw, who had been an unhappy high school student at Rose Hill, died on July 18, 1863, leading his all-black 54th Massachusetts Regiment in an attack on the Confederate defenses guarding Charleston harbor. Among the Rebels Hippolyte Feugas and his brother Clement, both natives of Louisiana, became officers in the Confederate army, as did two other brothers, John and Charles O'Neil of Charleston. Patrick K. Molony, '52, was killed in action on August 21, 1864, with the First Regiment South Carolina Infantry.[40]

Three McMahon brothers served in the Union army. The eldest brother, Captain John E. McMahon, was on the staff of the Army of the Potomac

39. John Hassard, *Life of the Most Reverend John Hughes, D.D., First Archbishop of New York* (New York: D. Appleton and Company, 1866), 437; AANY, A-6, Hughes to Scott, May 7, 1861.

40. "Our Soldier Dead," *FM*, 1902, 22–23; "Patrick K. Molony," *FM*, June 1897, 169–70.

General Martin T. McMahon, 1855, was awarded the Congressional Medal of Honor for bravery at the Civil War battle of Glendale, Virginia, on June 30, 1862.

during the opening months of the war but was forced to retire because of ill health and died shortly thereafter. The youngest brother, Colonel James McMahon of the 163rd New York Volunteers, died at the battle of Cold Harbor while leading a charge against the enemy fortifications. When the regimental color-bearer was killed, Colonel McMahon grabbed the Stars and Stripes from him and planted the flag on the crest of the enemy's fortifications before being killed himself. The third brother, Martin T. McMahon, '55, recovered the bullet-ridden body under a flag of truce. Martin served throughout the war with the Army of the Potomac, rising to the rank of lieutenant colonel and assistant adjutant general. At the end of the war, on March 13, 1865, he was named a brevet brigadier general and on the same day a brevet major general, United States Volunteers. A quarter-century later, on March 10, 1891, he was awarded the Congressional Medal of Honor for bravery in the fighting around White Oaks Swamp, Virginia, on June 30, 1862, at the battle of Glendale during the Seven Days of the Peninsula Campaign.[41]

James Rowan O'Beirne, '54, a native of County Roscommon, served in three different regiments. He rose from private to captain in the 37th New York Volunteers, the Irish Rifles, and was wounded four times at the battle

41. James R. O'Beirne, "Reminiscences in War Times, *FM*, Diamond Jubilee issue, June 1916, 55–57; William A. Ferguson, "General McMahon, *FM* 24 (April 1906): 317–19. I am indebted to Professor Curran for correcting my hazy knowledge of Civil War geography.

General James Rowan O'Beirne, 1854, was awarded the Congressional Medal of Honor for gallantry at the Civil War battle of Fair Oaks, Virginia, in May and June 1862.

of Chancellorsville on May 3, 1863. His last military service was with the U.S. Veteran Reserve Corps, where he was made a major. At the end of the war, on September 26, 1865, he was promoted to brevet lieutenant colonel, colonel, and brevet brigadier general. He was the provost marshal of Washington, D.C, at the time of Lincoln's assassination and claimed credit for organizing the search that led to the capture of John Wilkes Booth. On January 20, 1891, he was awarded the Congressional Medal of Honor for gallantry at the battle of Fair Oaks, Virginia, in May and June 1862.[42]

After the battle of Malvern Hill in June 1862 O'Beirne heard that two of the Confederate soldiers who had been captured were Fordham alumni and at considerable risk to himself rode off to locate them. He identified them only by their last names as Dillon from Georgia and Pinckney from South Carolina, but he remembered both of them as fine athletes at Rose Hill. It was a rainy day and O'Beirne found Dillon with some other prisoners cold and wet, shivering under a tree. O'Beirne brought them a bucket of

42. "General James R. O'Beirne," *Journal of the American-Irish Historical Society* 16 (1917): 145–46.

Irish stew and hot coffee. "Dillon stared at me with a blank look," O'Beirne said, "without a word of reply and looked as haughty and unconscious of my presence as he could. He turned his fine and fiery red head aside to contemplate the cheerless scene from some other angle and dismissed me from his thoughts."[43] Both General McMahon and General O'Beirne remained loyal and active members of the Fordham alumni after the war.

The three Fordham Jesuits who answered Archbishop Hughes's call for chaplains were all foreign-born. Thomas Ouellet was a French Canadian; Michael Nash was Irish; and Peter Tissot was French. Of the three, Father Ouellet may have found military life the most congenial even though he was forty-two years old, because he had earlier acquired the reputation of a stern disciplinarian at Fordham, which led Father John Larkin to ease him out of his position as the dean of discipline. Even in the Jesuit official obituary Ouellet was respectfully described as "a perfect martinet in all that pertained to his sacred duties." Ouellet was assigned to the 69th New York Regiment, one of the five regiments that formed the Irish Brigade.

On one occasion it is a wonder that he was not shot by his own men. During General George McClellan's seven-day retreat from the outskirts of Richmond to Harrison's Landing in June 1862, many of the exhausted troops failed to show up for Mass the following Sunday. In retaliation Ouellet went through the camp kicking over the pots of coffee and canteens of food that had been prepared for them. However, his obsession with military discipline was matched by his bravery on the field of battle. The following year he distinguished himself at Antietam.[44]

At the outbreak of the war Father Peter Tissot was assigned to the 37th New York Regiment, the Irish Rifles, the same regiment as General O'Beirne, who said that Tissot was regarded as the model chaplain of the Army of the Potomac. A modest, self-effacing man, Tissot was rather embarrassed by such praise and discounted tales of chaplains' flying about on the battlefield from one wounded man to another. "I doubt if it was ever done," he said. "At all events it should never be done." He believed that the chaplain should station himself with the surgeons at the field hospital where he could be of service to the greatest number of the wounded and dying.

He did not follow his own advice. When the regiment went into battle, Tissot would station himself astride his horse at the side of the road, tell the troops to make an act of contrition, and give them general absolution in groups as they passed by. Once the battle began, said O'Beirne, Tissot

43. O'Beirne, "Reminiscences," 60.
44. "Father Thomas Ouellet," *WL* 24 (1895): 375–80.

was always "at the front on the line of battle [and] administered the last sacraments amid shot and shell as well as heavy rifle-firing as though it was of no moment to him."

Tissot was pious as well as brave and modest. Out of necessity he sometimes kept the Eucharist on his person for several days. "But instead of being a consolation," he said, "it was a martyrdom. I felt that I was not treating our Lord properly. I was necessarily engaged the greater part of the time with things that had no reference to Him." Tissot was captured by the Confederates during the Seven Days of the Peninsula Campaign in June 1862. His captors treated him kindly, allowed him to live at the residence of the bishop of Richmond, permitted him to visit the Union prisoners of war at the military prison outside Richmond, and released him and two other Catholic chaplains unconditionally after a few weeks. Tissot sold his horse to one of the other chaplains, a fellow Jesuit, Father Joseph O'Hagan, for $200. O'Hagan gave Tissot a promissory note and promised to send him cash within two years. Tissot never heard from him again.[45]

Fordham's third Civil War chaplain, Father Michael Nash, had the most difficult introduction to military life. He was assigned to the 6th New York Volunteers, better known as Wilson's Zouaves, after the name of their commanding officer. Most of them were nominally Catholics, as was Colonel Wilson, who insisted that Nash should always be addressed as "Father," not "Chaplain." The 6th New York were a rowdy, undisciplined, heavy-drinking bunch of New York Irishmen. Collecting them from the saloons in New York City and depositing them on the ship that was to take them to their destination required the help of the police. "They were mad with liquor," Father Nash reported as they came aboard the ship. "There was one continued fight in which pistols, knives and bayonets were freely used. Many jumped overboard during the night, others were thrown into the water." During the first night at sea five men, suffering from delirium tremens, jumped overboard and were drowned.

It was under these unpromising circumstances that Father Nash began his career as a chaplain. However, the combination of Nash's own winning personality and the innate Irish Catholic respect for the priesthood worked wonders during the nine-day trip from New York to Fort Pick-

45. Thomas Gaffney Taaffe, "Rev. Peter Tissot, S.J.," *HR&S* 3:1 (1903): 40–41; Peter Tissot, "A Year with the Army of the Potomac: Diary of the Reverend Peter Tissot, S.J.," *HR&S,* 3:1 (1903): 55–56, 68–69; "A Year with the Army of the Potomac," *FM,* July 1901, 645–46; "Chaplains in the Civil War: Father Peter Tissot, S.J.," *FM,* April 1896, 103–5; James R. O'Beirne, "Reminiscences in War Times," *FM,* Diamond Jubilee issue, May 1916, 52; James Boyle, "An Interesting Letter," *FM* 20 (1901): 277.

ens on Santa Rosa Island off the coast of Rebel-held Pensacola. General McMahon suggested half-facetiously that the 6th New York were sent to Santa Rosa Island so that they could not get near "the personal moveable property of friend or foe."[46]

As the reality of the dangers of war sank in, however, many of the men sought out Nash for confession. McMahon credited Nash with doing more to discipline the regiment than all their officers. When they arrived at Santa Rosa Island, their large transport had to anchor two miles offshore. The captain placed his personal launch at Nash's disposal and several burly volunteers carried Nash and his Mass kit on their shoulders safely through the surf to the shore. During the Confederate shelling of the island, Nash tried to reach a solider who had been mortally wounded and was lying in an open field. When the soldiers could not persuade Nash from risking his life, they dug a trench so that he could reach the dying man safely.[47]

At Rose Hill the war was hardly ever mentioned in the monthly meetings of the board of consultors. The Jesuits briefly considered forming a corps of cadets but quickly scrapped the idea for fear that it would interfere with student discipline, and they limited themselves to offering academic courses in map reading. Despite the need for more classrooms and dormitory space, they considered it prudent to delay the plans to erect a new building, the present Dealy Hall, until after the war. Richard S. Treacy, who entered St. John's College in 1863, recalled a half-century later that Father Tissot, on his return from military service, would entertain the students in the evening with his war stories. Treacy's memory was playing tricks on him, however, when he claimed that there were a large number of southern students at Rose Hill throughout the war. According to the college catalogues, there were only a handful, but Treacy remembered vividly how in deference to them the northern boys refrained from celebrating when General Robert E. Lee surrendered to General Ulysses S. Grant at Appomattox Court House on April 9, 1865, and how the southerners reciprocated the courtesy a week later by refraining from gloating when gloom fell over the campus at the news of the assassination of President Lincoln on April 15.[48]

46. Martin T. McMahon, "Reminiscences," *FM*, June 1891, 53–54.

47. Michael Nash, "Letters from a Chaplain in the War," *WL* 16 (1887): 147–49; "Rev. M. Nash, S.J.," *FM*, November 1895, 31–32. Nash wrote eleven long letters about his first year of military service that were published *seriatim* in the *Woodstock Letters* between 1887 and 1889.

48. FUA, Acta Consultorum, February 6, 1862, September 28, 186; Richard S. Treacy, "Reminiscences: The Early Sixties," *FM*, Diamond Jubilee issue, 1916, 70.

6

NEW YORK CITY'S OTHER JESUIT COLLEGE

Fifty Cents and a New College

In 1847, only a year after their arrival at Rose Hill, the Jesuits opened a second school, in the heart of Manhattan. Four years earlier Bishop Hughes had specifically forbidden the Jesuits to do this, because he feared that a second school would threaten the success of St. John's College, Rose Hill, which at that time was still a diocesan college. Now, however, he urged the Jesuits to establish a city school and even offered them the Church of St. Andrew on Duane Street in the poverty-stricken Sixth Ward (the "Bloody Auld Sixth"), not far from the notorious Five Points. Father Boulanger prudently declined the bishop's offer of the parish and appointed Father John Larkin to take charge of the project.[1]

According to Larkin's often-told tale (which he did not tell under oath), he left Rose Hill in July 1847 immediately after the close of the school year with fifty cents in his pocket. He spent twenty-five cents for his railroad ticket from Fordham to New York City, paid another twenty cents for a carriage to transport his trunk to the residence of a friend, and was left with five cents in his pocket to establish a Jesuit church and college in the metropolis. He was befriended by Father Annet Lafont, the pastor of the French church of St. Vincent de Paul, which was then located on Canal Street. Shortly thereafter a nearby Protestant church on Elizabeth Street just north of Walker Street became available after the congregation split into two antagonistic factions. The asking price was $18,000, with $5,000 to be paid in cash.

With the help of several wealthy New York Catholics, including Bishop McCloskey's brother-in-law, Larkin was able to raise the $5,000 and took out a mortgage on the rest. He renamed it the Church of the Holy Name of Jesus. He also rented a small house at 180 Walker Street adjacent to church to serve as a residence for the Jesuit community. When Michael Nash ar-

---

1. Gilbert J. Garraghan, S.J., "Fordham's Jesuit Beginnings," *Thought* 16 (March 1941): 26; "An Historical Sketch of the Mission of New York and Canada," *WL* 4 (1875): 135.

rived in September 1847, he found the other six members of the community living in extreme poverty without furniture or even cooking utensils. The summer and autumn were spent redecorating the church and erecting partitions in the basement of the church for classrooms, study halls, and private rooms. Classes began around the beginning of October with 120 students while carpenters, masons, and painters continued working until Christmas finishing the renovations.

Less than a month later, on Saturday, January 22, 1848, six priests were busy in the church all day and late into the evening hearing confessions. Around 9:00 they discovered a fire in the basement that was due to a faulty heating system. It quickly spread upstairs to the church, and by 9:30 the whole building was engulfed in flames. At midnight the roof collapsed, leaving only a burned-out shell. The firemen were able to salvage the school furniture, and Father Peter Verheyden rescued the Blessed Sacrament from the tabernacle, but everything else was lost. Michael Nash estimated that 8,000 people gathered in the street to watch the blaze. Some Catholics arrived armed with guns, suspecting that the fire was the work of Nativist arsonists, but in fact the Protestant bystanders were as sympathetic as the Catholics and vied with them in trying to rescue the church furnishings.[2]

Undaunted by the tragedy that destroyed the work of six months in three hours, Larkin announced that classes would resume the following Tuesday in St. James Church on James Street (today Oliver Street) where the pastor, Father John N. Smith, a former Jesuit, placed the basement of the church at his disposal. Smith had been antagonistic to the Jesuits ever since leaving the Society, but now, said Nash, he "proved to be the greatest friend we had in the whole city." The same could not be said of Bishop Hughes. Larkin was furious at his reaction to the fire. "Not one solitary word of episcopal sympathy" came from him, Larkin noted, and he compared his attitude to the treatment the Jesuits had received in Louisville from Bishops Flaget and Chabrat. When Larkin asked Hughes for permission to take up a collection to replace the church and school, Hughes initially refused on the grounds that he did not allow collections in the diocese for "private purposes and petty local interests." However, Hughes met his match in Larkin, who was not intimidated by him. He asked Hughes point-blank why, if the establishment of a Catholic college in the heart of

2. The most detailed description of the fire at the Church of the Holy Name is to be found in "Reminiscences of Father Michael Nash," *WL* 26 (1897): 267–82. Catholic fears of arson were not unfounded. On November 9, 1831, Nativist bigots set fire to St. Mary's Church on Sheriff Street and even stuffed the bell in the steeple to prevent parishioners from summoning help. *Truth Teller*, November 12, 1831.

Manhattan was not a matter of public interest, "pray, tell me what [do] you call a matter of public interest?" Hughes made no reply. Thanks to the intervention of Father Smith, the bishop relented and grudgingly allowed the Jesuits to take up a collection. Larkin insisted on getting Hughes's permission in writing. When Hughes heard that Larkin was also seeking contributions from private donors, he ordered him to stop and "to explain a proceeding so much at variance with my judgment of ecclesiastical order."

Larkin's jousting with Hughes was the first serious disagreement the Jesuits had with him in New York and a harbinger of the more serious difficulties that were to arise later. It confirmed to Larkin the suspicions about the bishop's character that he had expressed to his superior, Father Boulanger, eighteen months earlier in Kentucky. At the time Boulanger had paid little attention to Larkin's warnings. "He sees it now," Larkin told his good friend Frederick William Gockeln, "and suffers greatly from it."[3]

John Hughes was a born autocrat. The historian Jay Dolan said famously that Hughes presided over his diocese like an Irish chieftain. John Larkin came to the same conclusion a century earlier, although he used a different metaphor to express it. "'*La France, c'est moi*,' said Louis XIV. Here the *c'est moi* is everything," Larkin told Gockeln. He believed that Hughes was jealous of the popularity of the Society of Jesus in New York. "Until we came," he told Gockeln, "every eye turned to him; he was alone. The coadjutor [John McCloskey] attracted considerable attention; he was made Bishop of Albany. The Society attracts many; this too is inconsistent with centralization. I have to manage matters with some dexterity," he explained, "for he is a violent man and a stubborn one, and neither reason nor law have any weight against his will."[4]

Larkin was one of the few priests in New York with the gumption to stand up to Hughes. When two Irish-born diocesan priests protested that Hughes had violated their rights in canon law, he replied that he would teach them County Monaghan canon law and send them back to the bogs whence they'd come. Larkin reported that at the annual retreat for the diocesan priests in 1849 Hughes told them that, if they wanted canon law, they were welcome to go to Italy or Spain or any other country where it existed because in New York he was the "lord and master." It is little wonder that Hughes was eager to be rid of Larkin. When Hughes heard that Larkin had been selected as the new bishop of Toronto, he told Larkin that

3. ANYPSJ, Larkin to Gockeln, January 2, 1849; Hughes to Larkin, n.d.; Larkin to Gockeln, March 6, 1849.

4. ANYPSJ, Larkin to Gockeln, May 8, 1848, January 2, 1849.

he was bound in conscience to accept the appointment, a conclusion that Larkin found unconvincing.[5]

After five months in the basement of St. James Church, the College of the Holy Name found a third home in May 1848 when Larkin rented two private houses on the east side of Third Avenue between 11th and 12th streets. It was a better neighborhood than the area around Canal Street, but attendance dropped from 120 to 60 students partly because many parents complained that it was too far uptown. Richard Burtsell, who entered the school in 1847 at the age of eight, recalled a half-century later that there were many vacant lots surrounding the school. Larkin was annoyed at Catholic parents who demanded a Catholic school for their children and then balked at letting them walk a mile to 11th Street. Another reason for the decline in enrollment was the rumors that Larkin was about to be appointed the bishop of Toronto. "They imagine that my absence would break up the school," he explained.[6]

In any event the Third Avenue location was intended to be only temporary. The Jesuits wanted both a church and a school in Manhattan, but the chapel they set up in a parlor of the Third Avenue buildings was too small to accommodate the crowds who came to Mass there. The Jesuits' desire for a church led to another row with Hughes because they wished to confine their pastoral work to preaching and hearing confessions. Hughes insisted that a Jesuit church would have to accept all the pastoral responsibilities of diocesan parishes and provide a full range of sacramental services such as baptisms, weddings, and funerals. It was a condition that Larkin refused to accept.

However, in the fall of 1848 Larkin resigned as the president of the College of the Holy Name with the permission of his superiors and left for Europe to try to prevent his appointment as the bishop of Toronto. He was succeeded by Father John Ryan, S.J., who became the second president on October 25, 1849. Ryan's first priority was to build a permanent church and school, and he purchased several lots on West 15th and 16th streets between Fifth and Sixth avenues.[7] When the former owner of the property saw the poverty of the Jesuit community on Third Avenue, he wanted to rescind the purchase for fear that the presence of the Jesuits would drive

5. AANY, Burtsell Diary, July 26, 1865. ANYPSJ, Larkin to Gockeln, March 6, 1849. Larkin also thought that Hughes was trying to improve his strained relations with his priests by stirring up their jealousy of the Jesuits.

6. ANYPSJ, Larkin to Gockeln, October 17, 1848.

7. A native of Galway and a veteran of the Kentucky Mission, Father Ryan founded the first Catholic church in Yonkers while at Fordham. In 1847 he began celebrating

down the value of the remaining lots on the two blocks. As another sop to the archbishop, the Jesuits hired his brother-in-law William Rodrigue as the architect. Ground was broken for the new college in the beginning of July 1850, and on November 25 of that year the Jesuits and their students moved into the still-unfinished building.[8]

In the meantime, when the Jesuits asked Hughes for permission to take up a collection throughout the diocese for their new college and chapel, they received a curt refusal from the bishop. At first he denied permission on the grounds that the college was not a diocesan institution and did not serve the needs of poor. He told them to operate the college on a self-sustaining basis as the Religious of the Sacred Heart and the Sisters of Charity did at their girls' academies. However, he left open the possibility that he might allow a collection if the property and buildings were surrendered to the diocese. Even if the Jesuits agreed to this condition, Hughes told them ungraciously, he would prefer a collection for the Christian Brothers because they "teach gratuitously the poor children of our communion." Caught between a rock and a hard place, Father Ryan capitulated to Hughes's demand and handed over to him the deed to the college in the agreement that he concluded with him on October 31, 1850, three months after Hughes had been appointed the first archbishop of New York.[9]

Hughes was not finished with the Jesuits. He also told Ryan that he wanted a new name for the church and college. According to Michael Nash, who accompanied him on his visit to the archbishop, he said to Ryan, "Your old church was the Holy Name, that is, the Gesù. Now let me tell you that I shall have no Gesù here. You have your Gesù in Rome outshining St. Peter's. It must not be so here. You have many great and glorious saints of your society. Call the new church after one of these, St. Francis Xavier, for instance. No Holy Name."[10]

Mass in private homes for the Irish workers who were constructing the New York and Hudson River Railroad through the city and erected the first Church of the Immaculate Conception (St. Mary's) before his appointment to Xavier. Thomas C. Cornell, "Catholic Beginnings in Yonkers," *HR&S* 36 (1947): 71–75.

8. Nash, "Reminiscences," 281–82.

9. ANYPSJ, Hughes to Boulanger, April 11, 1850; "Evidence of the understanding between the most R. Archbishop of N. York and the Superior of the Jesuits," October 31, 1850, cit. in Christa Klein, "The Jesuits and Catholic Boyhood in Nineteenth-Century New York City: A Study of St. John's College and the College of St. Francis Xavier, 1846–1912." Ph.D. diss., University of Pennsylvania, 1976," 72. Hughes was appointed the archbishop of New York on July 19, 1850.

10. Nash, "Reminiscences," 281.

When John Larkin visited what was now the College of St. Francis Xavier in its new quarters on West 15th Street after his return from Europe in September 1851, he was disappointed at what he found. He noted without comment that Father Ryan had deeded the buildings and property to Hughes, something that he had steadfastly refused to do. "What a pitiful concern this New York establishment is," he told Gockeln, "but it is best to say nothing about it." The original plans called for a three-story brick building on 15th Street with two wings surrounding a central courtyard. Only the central structure and the west wing were built. An undeveloped lot on 16th Street was transformed into a garden for the Jesuits with trees and bushes brought from Rose Hill. The empty lots east of the building on 15th Street became a playground for students from ages seven to seventeen. Two hundred feet long and one hundred feet wide, it was the sorry equivalent of an urban campus. On a happier note, Larkin estimated that the enrollment had risen to about 170 students, with the result that the college authorities were already running out of space for both the students and the faculty. In 1851 Ryan also secured the services of the Christian Brothers and the Religious of the Sacred Heart for the boys and girls in the parish school. That same year Fathers Charles de Luynes and Charles Maldonado went to Mexico, where they conducted a successful fundraising drive for Xavier. Father Ryan left the Society of Jesus in 1855, became a New York diocesan priest, and was appointed pastor of the Church of the Immaculate Conception on East 14th Street, where he died in 1861.[11]

New York's Premier Jesuit College

"By 1865," said Christa Klein, "it was apparent that Xavier was more truly the school of the metropolitan Catholic community than Fordham." A number of reasons explain why Xavier was able to overshadow its rival at Rose Hill less than 20 years after its establishment. Throughout the latter half of the nineteenth century Xavier was the larger of the two schools. Accurate measurement of the number of college students before 1881 is impossible because the Jesuits did not keep separate statistics for the college departments prior to that date. However, in 1875–76, Xavier had more than twice as many students (elementary school, high school, and college) as Rose Hill, 464 compared with 178. In 1900 Xavier had the largest total enrollment (639) of the 30 Jesuit colleges in the United States

11. ANYPSJ, Larkin to Gockeln, September 24, 1851; *The College of St. Francis Xavier: A Memorial and a Retrospect* (New York: The Meany Printing Company, 1897), 32–33; Edward I. Devitt, S.J., "History of the Maryland–New York Province," *WL* 65 (1936): 194; Cornell, "Catholic Beginnings in Yonkers," 75.

and Canada, and the third-largest number of college students (147). Only the College of the Holy Cross and Boston College had more college students than Xavier. In 1896 Archbishop Francesco Satolii, the first Apostolic Delegate to the United States, indicated that he would like to visit St. John's College at Rose Hill, but he canceled his plans at the last minute. "Thank God," said the president of St. John's, Father Thomas J. Campbell. "I would have been ashamed of the small number of students." Not until 1905–6 did the number of college students at Rose Hill temporarily exceed the number at Xavier, 109 to 104.[12]

Perhaps the important factor in the success of Xavier was the modest cost. Unlike St. John's College, Xavier was a day school with a tuition of only $50 a year that was soon raised to $60, but even that figure compared favorably with the cost of tuition and room-and-board at Rose Hill, which was originally $200 and rose to $330 by the end of the nineteenth century. St. John's College was primarily a boarding school that drew its student body from a much wider area than Xavier. In 1862–63, 45.9 percent of the students at Rose Hill came from the vicinity of New York City; in 1880–81, 43.6 percent; and in 1903–4, 72.3 percent. The comparable figures for Xavier were that 80 percent of the students came from New York City in 1862–63; a whopping 96.4 percent in 1880–81; and 93.3 percent in 1903.[13]

Like Xavier, St. John's also charged only $60 a year for day students, but it failed to attract as many commuters as Xavier because of geography and transportation. Although one old alumnus described the area around West 15th Street as almost rustic in 1851, Xavier was located in the "New City" between 14th Street and 42nd Street that grew rapidly in the two decades before the Civil War. The school was a short distance from the New York and Harlem Railroad on Fourth Avenue and less than a block from the horse-drawn streetcar line that began operations on Sixth Avenue between Vesey Street and 42nd Street in 1851. Six other north–south streetcar lines were operating on Manhattan's main avenues by 1864 as well as numerous crosstown lines. According to one authority, "by the 1880s lower Manhattan was a gridiron of street railways." The construction of four north–south elevated lines in the late 1870s further expedited travel within Manhattan, and after 1883 cable cars on the Brooklyn Bridge provided direct access to

12. Klein, "Jesuits and Catholic Boyhood," 81, 353, 354; *WL* 29 (1900): 550; FUA, Diary of Presidents, 1885–1906, October 17, 1896. When the *Woodstock Letters* mentions the Jesuit college in New York City, it always refers to Xavier, not St. John's.

13. ACSFX, Historia Domus, 1880–1881; Klein, "Jesuits and Catholic Boyhood," 79, 356, 361. In 1900 there were 170 boarders and 76 day students at Rose Hill. FUA, Diary of Presidents, 1885–1906, October 2, 1900.

downtown Brooklyn and the numerous elevated lines in that city. There was frequent ferry service across the Hudson from downtown Manhattan to both Jersey City and Hoboken. By contrast, the only access to Rose Hill by public transportation was the New York and Harlem Railroad until the Third Avenue El reached Fordham in 1901.[14]

Christa Klein suggested still another reason for the popularity of Xavier with New York's Catholic families that is more difficult to substantiate. She believed that Xavier Americanized more rapidly than its sister school at Rose Hill, which was also the residence of the first two superiors of the New York–Canada Mission, Clément Boulanger (1846–56) and Jean-Baptiste Hus (1856–59), who were both French. However, by 1880 only three of the twenty-seven Jesuits at Rose Hill were French. A more plausible explanation for the popularity of Xavier may be that, because it was a day school, there was less emphasis at Xavier than at Rose Hill on the French penchant for surveillance and consequently less resentment among the students. There were six to nine prefects at Rose Hill but only one prefect at Xavier. The Jesuits themselves attributed the good behavior of the students at Xavier to the fact that it was a day school and also to the fact that most of the parents were Irish with a great reverence for priests, an attitude that they inculcated in their children.[15]

Although there was frequent rotation of the professors and administrators between Xavier and Rose Hill, each college developed its own distinctive ethos, and each faculty developed a fiercely protective attitude toward its own institution. In 1857 the Jesuits at Rose Hill complained that Xavier had admitted a number of students who had left St. John's College, and they feared that this would lead to further loss of students at Rose Hill. The Jesuits at Xavier considered the complaints of their confrères seven miles to the north and rejected them. "The College of St. Francis Xavier is altogether independent of St. John's," they declared, and they decided that they had not only the right to accept these students but also a moral obligation to do so, because otherwise the students might be forced to attend public or private colleges. In 1866 Xavier displayed the same independent streak when St. John's College asked it for a loan that it promised to repay on three months' notice. The board of consultors at Xavier (all Jesuits) turned down the request because they doubted that St. John's could repay

14. Kenneth T. Jackson, ed., *The Encyclopedia of New York City*, Second Edition (New Haven and New York: Yale University Press and the New-York Historical Society, 2010), 405–6, 1249–50.

15. Klein, "Jesuits and Catholic Boyhood," 91; FUA, Catalogue of St. John's College, 1880–1881; ACSFX, Litterae Annuae, Letter of 1862–1863.

The College of St. Francis Xavier, New York City, as it appeared in the late nineteenth century.

the loan on such short notice and they wanted to save their money to buy additional property for their own college.[16]

The Jesuits at Xavier were exaggerating when they boasted in 1857 that their school was completely independent of St. John's College. There was one major difference between the two institutions that kept Xavier dependent on its older rival. St. John's College possessed a charter from New York state (obtained by Bishop Hughes before he sold the college to the Jesuits) that enabled it to confer degrees. By 1854 Xavier had gradually added the full four years of college courses to the curriculum, but it still lacked a state charter, with the result that the graduating seniors had to receive their degrees from St. John's College. Philosophy was taught in the senior year of college at Xavier as well at Rose Hill and in other Jesuit colleges, but it was taught only unofficially at Xavier because the Jesuit

16. ACSFX, Acta Consultorum, February 7, 1857, May 30, 1866.

general had not given the school formal permission to teach that subject. Without a full-fledged philosophy component in the curriculum, the Jesuits at Xavier saw little hope of their obtaining a state charter for their school.[17]

Disaster struck in 1859 when the general, Father Peter Beckx, decided that philosophy in New York should be taught only at Rose Hill, not at Xavier. When Father William Stack Murphy, the newly appointed superior of the New York–Canada Mission, informed the Jesuits at Xavier of the general's decision, the consultors described it as "the death blow of this college" and complained that the general had made his decision without consulting any of the Jesuits in New York. The decision was a particularly cruel disappointment because it came at a time when the Jesuits at Xavier were in the process of acquiring additional property in the hope that one day in New York they could have "something like a university."[18]

Murphy tried to soften the blow by telling the Jesuits at Xavier to continue teaching philosophy surreptitiously while he appealed the general's decision. Fortunately for Xavier, Father Félix Sopranis, the visitor to the New York–Canada Mission, sided with Murphy and the New York Jesuits. He obviously did not have the authority to countermand Beckx's decision, but he promised to do his best to get Beckx to reverse it. In the meantime he told the Jesuits at Xavier to proceed slowly with their plans to expand the school. "Do not build, do not buy, wait [for] the question about philosophy [to] be decided," he advised them and gave permission for them to "draw [up] a plan of a large and magnificent college or university."[19]

Sopranis was as good as his word. He prevailed in Rome and persuaded Beckx to allow Xavier to continue teaching philosophy, which assured its continuation as a college, not as a mere literary academy. A state charter followed shortly thereafter on January 10, 1861, and for the first time in June of that year Xavier issued its own degrees after having relied on St. John's College for the previous five years. Xavier could finally boast that it really was completely independent of St. John's College.[20]

As for constructing a new home for Xavier that would be worthy of a college or university, the Jesuits hired Patrick Keely, the well-known church architect, to come up with suitable plans. He designed a structure consisting of twin four-story buildings 120 feet long by 60 feet wide connected

17. Klein, "Jesuits and Catholic Boyhood," 134–36.
18. ACSFX, Acta Consultorum, September 19, 1859.
19. ACSFX, Acta Consultorum, April 15, 1860.
20. *College of St. Francis Xavier*, 208–10.

by a one-story building 80 feet in length. If it had been built as planned, the total frontage on 15th Street would have come to 200 feet. Ground was broken on August 13, 1861, only four months after the outbreak of the Civil War. However, shortage of funds forced the Jesuits to scale down their plans as they had been forced to do once before in 1850. Only the eastern wing of the college was built, at a cost of $45,000.[21]

The erection of the massive new Baroque parish church on 16th Street in 1878 (also designed by Patrick Keely, who was better known for his Gothic churches) led to a flurry of reorganization and rebuilding of the college facilities. By 1894 a large four-story grammar school and a new entrance to the college were built on 15th Street west of the building erected in 1861. A Jesuit residence, library, and theater were constructed in another new large four-story building east of the new church on 16th Street. Progress came at a price. Even the semblance of a campus disappeared as the Jesuits' garden on 16th Street was expropriated to make space for the new buildings.

One of the major innovators at Xavier was Father Samuel H. Frisbee, a convert to the Catholic Church and a graduate of Yale, who became the seventh president in 1880. Frisbee offered a scholarship to the classical course to the brightest student in every parochial school in New York City, not only to implement the Jesuit tradition of free education but also to raise the academic standards at Xavier, which were already higher than at Rose Hill. At Xavier the full course (elementary school, high school, and college) was twelve years in length, compared with ten years at Rose Hill. The difference was that both the elementary and high school programs at Xavier were four years in length instead of three. An admirer of Frisbee's said that his aim was to change nothing, but to improve everything, which was not quite accurate.

In 1882 he completely eliminated the commercial course, which enrolled only 17 percent of the students in 1880. The college catalogue defended the change on the same grounds that Oxford dons once invoked to insist that they were preparing their students to run the British Empire. "The details of business life can be learned only by practice," the Xavier catalogue declared, "and these once mastered, superior training makes itself felt from the outset." At the same time Frisbee adapted the *ratio studiorum* to the needs of nineteenth-century American college education by modernizing the classical course with additional classes in science and math. At the time only 60 percent of the students at Rose Hill were enrolled in the classi-

21. Ibid., 68.

cal course. While not all of Frisbee's innovations were retained after he stepped down as president in 1885, the 1880s and 1890s were widely regarded as the golden age of Xavier.[22]

The Jesuits at the College of St. Francis Xavier successfully accommodated their educational apostolate to the needs of the local Catholic community by placing a classical college education within reach of lower-middle-class Catholics who did not have the financial resources to send their sons to Rose Hill. In 1896, one alumnus, Charles H. Colton, who later became the bishop of Buffalo, described most of the student body as the sons of "the progressive middle class and the industrious and honest working people of the noblest and loftiest principles, who wished to give their sons a liberal education to make their lot and station better than their own." During its first fifty years Xavier graduated 649 students, many of whom became priests, lawyers, doctors, and businessmen and constituted the Catholic elite of New York City. The overwhelming majority were Irish Americans with a sprinkling of German, English, Scottish, French, and Dutch names. Judging by the surnames, it would appear that only one student was Italian and only one was Hispanic.[23]

Far and away the most popular vocational choice of the graduates was the clergy, who numbered 204, or 31.43 percent of the graduates in 1897. If one adds the 43 seminarians, the percentage rises to 38.06 percent of the graduates. Of that number 19 of the priests and 20 of the seminarians were Jesuits; there were one Benedictine monk and four Paulist priests; the rest were diocesan priests and seminarians, the great majority of them belonging to the archdiocese of New York and the diocese of Brooklyn. The law was the second most popular choice of the graduates, 14.33 percent, with 93 lawyers and law students. Medicine was a distant third, 6.32 percent, with 41 physicians and medical students. There were also 18 professors, principals, or teachers; 14 merchants; six journalists; five contractors; two bankers; and two brokers. The profession of many of the alumni is unknown, although one proudly described himself as U.S. weighman at the New York Custom House. St. Francis Xavier was definitely a local college. Not only were most of the graduates natives of New York City, but only 12

22. *College of St. Francis Xavier*, 143–44, 148, 154; Klein, "Jesuits and Catholic Boyhood," 140, 153, 175.

23. Charles H. Colton, "Reminiscences: A Quarter of a Century Ago," *The Xavier*, April 1896, in David E. Nolan, "The Catholic Club of New York City: A Study of Lay Involvement in New York City, 1888–1960," M.A. thesis, St. Joseph's Seminary, Dunwoodie, 1995, 2. *College of St. Francis Xavier*, 240–58.

of the 220 lay alumni whose addresses are known resided outside the New York metropolitan area in 1897.

Among the Jesuit alumni William O'Brien Pardow had a celebrated career as a preacher and president of Xavier. Thomas J. Campbell served as acting president of Xavier; president of St. John's, Rose Hill, on two separate occasions; and as provincial of the Maryland–New York Province from 1888 to 1893. John Wynne was a key member of the editorial board of the *Catholic Encyclopedia*, the founding editor of *America*, and a thorn in the side of every Jesuit superior. One of the Paulists, John J. Burke, was editor of the *Catholic World*, helped to found the Catholic Press Association, organized the Chaplains' Aid Association during World War I, gave the U.S. hierarchy its first national organization when he founded the National Catholic War Council in 1917, and served as the first general secretary of the National Catholic Welfare Conference from 1919 to his death in 1936.

Six graduates of Xavier became bishops: Winand Wigger, bishop of Newark, 1881–1901; Charles E. McDonnell, bishop of Brooklyn, 1892–1921; John A. McFaul, bishop of Trenton, 1894–1917; Michael J. Hoban, coadjutor of Scranton, 1896–99, and bishop of Scranton, 1899–1926; Charles H. Colton, bishop of Buffalo, 1903–15; and Thomas F. Cusack, auxiliary of New York, 1904–15, and bishop of Albany, 1915–18.

Several of the alumni who became priests rose to important positions in the archdiocese of New York. John Edwards was a vicar general under Cardinal Farley; James McGean was a member of the board of diocesan consultors, the most important advisory body to the archbishop. He and Henry Brann, the pastor of St. Agnes Church, were frequent guests at celebrations at Xavier; John E. Burke was the first pastor of St. Benedict the Moor Church on Bleecker Street, the first black Catholic parish north of the Mason-Dixon line, and in 1907 he was named the executive director of the Catholic Board for Mission Work among the Colored People. His successor at St. Benedict the Moor, Thomas O'Keefe, was also an alumnus of Xavier. Francis P. Duffy was one of the founders of the *New York Review* in 1905 while a professor at St. Joseph's Seminary, Dunwoodie, and became a national hero as a chaplain in World War I.

One of the most distinguished lay alumni of Xavier was Charles George Herbermann, who taught the classics at Xavier from 1860 to 1869 and at the City College of New York from 1869 to 1915. Together with John Gilmary Shea, he was instrumental in founding the U.S. Catholic Historical Society in 1884 and served as president from 1898 until his death in 1916. Herbermann was also the editor-in-chief of the *Catholic Encyclopedia*, was made a papal knight by Pope Pius X, and was awarded the Laetare medal by the

University of Notre Dame. A close associate of Herbermann's was another Xavier alumnus, Thomas J. Meehan, who was the managing editor of the *Irish-American* from 1874 to 1904, assistant managing editor and prolific contributor to the *Catholic Encyclopedia*, and editor of the publications of the U.S. Catholic Historical Society from 1916 to his death in 1942.

The most respected Catholic jurist in New York City in the late nineteenth century was Morgan J. O'Brien, who received his A.B. degree from St. John's College in 1872 and his M.A. from Xavier a year later. Elected to the New York State Supreme Court in 1887, he was appointed to the appellate division in 1896 and named presiding judge in 1905. Throughout his life O'Brien was an exemplary Catholic layman, chairman of innumerable committees, and a speaker at virtually every major Catholic event in New York for fifty years. Alfred J. Talley was another alumnus who became a municipal judge in New York and, like Morgan O'Brien, served as the chairman of the influential Committee on Catholic Interests of the Catholic Club of the City of New York. Francis X. Donoghue became a judge in Yonkers. The home of Donoghue's parents was one of the places where Father John Ryan and other Jesuits from Fordham celebrated Mass before the erection of the first Catholic church in Yonkers.

In addition to the graduates who received B.A. and M.A. degrees at Xavier, several hundred other students were enrolled in the commercial or business course, which did not require Greek or Latin and did not lead to a degree. Although the commercial course was discontinued in 1882, it produced two of the wealthiest Catholics in New York City, John Crimmins and Hugh Grant. Crimmins was a contractor and one of a handful of Catholics identified as a millionaire by the *New York Tribune* in 1892. Grant was a successful real estate speculator and Tammany Hall stalwart. In 1888 he was the second Catholic to be elected mayor of New York City.[24]

Both Crimmins and Grant were devout and dedicated Catholics. Crimmins, the father of fourteen, was a close friend of Archbishop Michael Augustine Corrigan and was a generous supporter of Catholic charities. More than anyone except the archbishop himself, Crimmins was responsible for the construction and financing of the new diocesan seminary at Dunwoodie in 1896 at a cost of $1 million. Grant and his wife were generous donors to Jesuit causes; after his death, she endowed Regis High School in Manhattan, the only tuition-free Jesuit high school in the United States.[25]

Pastoral Ministry

Both at St. John's College and at Xavier the Jesuits were active in the pastoral ministry. The Jesuits at Rose Hill staffed the parish church of Our Lady of Mercy at Fordham (originally the seminary chapel) from 1860 until 1892, and they ministered to scattered Catholic communities along the Hudson River in Spuyten Duyvil, Yonkers, and Dobbs Ferry and in the upper Harlem Valley as far north as Croton Falls and Brewster.[26]

However, the Jesuit involvement in the pastoral ministry in Manhattan was much more extensive than at Rose Hill. Their Church of St. Francis Xavier was the center of a large urban parish with a crowded schedule of Masses, devotional services, and sacramental ministrations, especially confessions, which drew penitents from all over the city. Between August

24. "American Millionaires," *Tribune Monthly* (June 1892), in Sidney Ratner, ed., *New Light on the History of Great American Fortunes: American Millionaires of 1892 and 1902* (New York: Augustus M. Kelly Inc., 1953), 57–85. On the Grant family, see Anthony D. Andreassi, C.O., *Teach Me to Be Generous: The First Century of Regis High School in New York* (New York: Fordham University Press, 2014), 15–37.

25. On the role of Crimmins in the construction of Dunwoodie, see Thomas J. Shelley, *Dunwoodie: The History of St. Joseph's Seminary* (Westminster, Md.: Christian Classics, 1993), 53–59, 79–81.

26. Arthur A. Weiss, S.J., "Jesuit Mission Years in New York State, 1654 to 1879," *WL*, 75: 131.

1862 and 1863 the priests at St. Francis Xavier baptized 142 adults and 573 infants, prepared 243 youngsters for First Communion, distributed Holy Communion to 67,760 people, witnessed 146 marriages, gave the last rites to 300 individuals, conducted 14 parish missions in their own church and elsewhere, preached 701 sermons, and made 2,400 sick calls and 160 visits to prisons. They heard 108,728 confessions in the parish church where it was not uncommon to have 15 or 20 priests hearing confessions on special occasions such as parish missions. In addition there were 3,400 members in the parish temperance society, and 1,600 new members were added to the scapular society that year. As for the distribution of alms, they simply listed it as *multa quotidie*, "many daily."[27]

As early as 1852 the Jesuits at Xavier expanded their pastoral ministry to include the Tombs, the main prison in New York City, which was within walking distance of the the church. Once or twice a month they also traveled by train to Sing Sing, the large prison located some twenty miles north of the city. They also served as chaplains at St. Vincent's Hospital and New York Hospital, two of the largest hospitals in New York City. A major expansion of this pastoral ministry occurred when Archbishop John Hughes asked the Jesuits to replace the Redemptorists as chaplains in the public institutions on three islands in the East River, Blackwell's Island (now Roosevelt Island), Wards Island, and Randalls Island, and later also on Hart's Island in Long Island Sound. There were a total of fourteen institutions on the four islands, which included an orphanage, reformatory, two mental institutions, several prisons and workhouses, and several hospitals, including a smallpox hospital at the southern tip of Blackwell's Island. The 9,100 inmates and patients included some of the most wretched and destitute residents of the city.[28]

The first Jesuit who volunteered for the work as a chaplain on the islands, Father John Jaffré, died shortly thereafter. He was replaced by two other priests in May 1861. The following year the Jesuit chaplains baptized 253 adults and 279 infants, prepared 108 people for Confirmation, gave the last rites to 1,245 people, and distributed Communion to 9,000 people. Most of the Catholics were Irish. The Jesuits found it relatively easy to persuade even those who were not regular churchgoers to return to the practice of their faith because of the same phenomenon that they had noticed among the Irish parents of the students at Xavier—their respect and reverence for the priesthood. During the first six years of the Jesuit ministry

27. ACSFX, Litterae Annuae, Letter of 1862–1863.
28. Weiss, "Jesuit Missions," 135.

on the islands, in addition to Father Jaffré, three other priests also died in the line of duty: Philip Chopin, George Laufhuber, and Joseph Pavarelli.[29]

Despite the loss of these *victimae caritatis*, as the Jesuits characterized them, or perhaps because of their deaths, the Jesuit mission on the islands flourished. Initially a major obstacle had been the hostility of the Protestant officials in charge of the institutions, but the dedication and fortitude of the Jesuit chaplains toned down at least the open manifestations of this hostility and led to a grudging respect for their efforts. Nonetheless, one Jesuit chaplain observed that even the best-intentioned Protestant doctors and nurses had only the vaguest understanding of the sacramental ministry of Catholic priests.[30]

By the 1880s five Jesuit chaplains were assigned full time to this difficult and dangerous ministry. In addition to those who "have died from infectious diseases or excessive labor," the provincial, Thomas J. Campbell, told the vicar general, Monsignor Thomas Preston, others "have been ruined in health by innutritious food or the insanitary conditions in which they have been forced to live." One Jesuit chaplain on Blackwell's Island said that the first requisite for this ministry was good health. "The life is a very laborious and exhausting one," he explained. "Once on duty means always on duty," he said. He began his day with private prayer at 5:00 A.M. and made the last round of the hospital wards at 7:00 P.M.[31]

In 1866 Archbishop John McCloskey gave the Jesuits the Church of St. Lawrence O'Toole on East 84th Street to assist their ministry on the islands. "No doubt," the Jesuits recorded presciently, "it will soon be one of the leading city parishes, but it pleases us most of all because it is midway between our two colleges and close to the three islands that are the most fruitful fields of our apostolic works." For the Jesuits, McCloskey was a welcome change from his predecessor, John Hughes. Shortly after he became the archbishop of New York in 1864, McCloskey returned to the Jesuits the deeds to the Church and College of St. Francis Xavier that Hughes had forced them to surrender to the diocese.[32] In 1876, when the Jesuits at St. Francis Xavier were thinking of building a new church, Father Charles Charaux, the superior of the New York Mission, urged them to do

29. ACSFX, Litterae Annuae, Letter of 1862–1863; ACSFX, Liber continens nomina defunctorum.

30. ACSFX, Historia Domus, 1863–1864: Charaux to Father Rector, February 26, 1876.

31. AANY, Campbell to Preston, n.d.; J.P.M. Schleuter, S.J., "Requisites for Missionary Work on Blackwell's Island," *WL* 26 (1897): 382–86.

32. ARSJ, Loyzance to the general, December 9, 1864.

so immediately while McCloskey was still the archbishop. "We can hardly expect that his successor, whoever he be," he explained, "will be as kind and favorable to our Soc[iety] as he has always shown himself to be."[33]

Despite the gift of the Church of St. Lawrence O'Toole, the Jesuit community at Xavier continued to be responsible for the ministry to the islands, perhaps because after 1879 Xavier was also the headquarters of the Maryland–New York Province. By the end of the century the Jesuits had replaced the original Church of St. Lawrence O'Toole with a large new church on Park Avenue and renamed the upper church in honor of St. Ignatius Loyola. When the pastor, Father Neil McKinnon, objected to the archdiocese's demand that the Jesuits continue to provide a chaplain for Hart's Island, Archbishop Michael Corrigan told him that Bishop Farley often heard Cardinal McCloskey and Monsignor William Quinn (the vicar general) say that the Jesuits agreed to take care of the islands in return for the parish of St. Lawrence. "I am determined that this agreement with the diocese will be lived up to," Corrigan told McKinnon.[34]

Xavier Union and the Catholic Club

In 1863 Father Joseph Loyzance, the president of Xavier, formed an alumni sodality, a standard practice in many Jesuit schools. In 1870, the moderator of the sodality, Father Patrick Francis Dealy, persuaded his superiors at Xavier to give the sodality a permanent home in one of the buildings on West 15th Street. He then proposed to expand the scope of the sodality to include both social and cultural activities.[35] He encountered considerable resistance from members of the sodality who feared that this expansion would alter the spiritual character of the sodality. However, an enthusiastic minority supported Father Dealy's proposal. With his encouragement, in March 1871 they organized the Xavier Union and obtained a charter of incorporation from the state legislature on May 12, 1873.[36]

33. ACSFX, Historia Domus, 1864; Charaux to Father Rector [Henri Hudon], February 26, 1876. I am grateful to the late Father Henry Bertels, S.J., for bringing this letter to my attention.

34. AANY, G-16, Corrigan to McKinnon. At the insistence of the Holy See, the lower church of St. Ignatius Loyola remained the church of St. Lawrence O'Toole.

35. The Irish-born Dealy was the first Fordham student to become a Jesuit. He entered the Society in 1846 after three years at St. John's College when it was still a diocesan institution. He was educated at Jesuit colleges in Canada, France, Austria, Belgium, and Rome and was president of St. John's College from 1882 to 1885. Thomas C. Hennessy, S.J., *How the Jesuits Settled in New York: A Documentary Account* (New York: Something More Publications, 2003), 178–79.

36. AAIHS, Register of the Xavier Union, Charter of the Xavier Union, May 12, 1873,

"The Xavier Union has been formed [from the sodality]," the founders of the new society declared in the charter, to promote objectives "not strictly within the scope of a religious body." Specifically they announced their intention of establishing a reference and circulating library with the best reviews and journals; sponsoring literary, religious, historical, and scientific lectures; and providing musical entertainments and social activities.

Father Dealy was the guiding force behind the Xavier Union even after he left Xavier to become president of St. John's College, Rose Hill, but he deliberately remained in the background, allowing the lay officers to assume responsibility for the direction of the society. Active membership in the Xavier Union was originally limited to full members of the Xavier Alumni Sodality. Anyone who ceased to be a full member of the Sodality was immediately excluded from membership in the Xavier Union. However, there was a provision for other "Catholic gentlemen" to be admitted to associate membership without the right to hold office or vote for officeholders.

The Xavier Union began with 65 members in 1871, only a small proportion of the 300 members of the Xavier Alumni Sodality, which continued to exist as a separate organization. By 1888 membership in the Xavier Union had increased to 398, and it moved out of its cramped quarters on 15th Street to its own clubhouse on West 27th Street, where it began to assemble a library. As the popularity of the society increased, more and more applications for membership were received from those who had never attended the College of St. Francis Xavier. In 1882 the by-laws were changed to allow associate members to become active members simply by expressing their desire to do so. It was also decided to admit to full membership not only alumni of Xavier but also all Catholic laymen who were of "undoubted fidelity to the church and devotion to the Holy Father."[37]

Six years later, in 1888, as the ties with Xavier grew more tenuous, the name of the society was changed from the Xavier Union to the Catholic

---

pp. 1–4: Register of the Xavier Union, Preamble to the Constitution and By-Laws, May 12, 1873, pp. 7–8.

37. AAIHS, Register of the Xavier Union, Amendment to the Constitution, June 2, 1882, pp. 45–46; Amendment to Constitution, April 4, 1884, p. 49; *Bulletin of the Catholic Club of the City of New York*, January 1888, n.p. For the opposition to the formation of the Xavier Union, see Nolan, "Catholic Club," 3–5. The most recent study of the Catholic Club is Patrick J. Hayes, "Catholic Action in the Archdiocese of New York: The Case of the Catholic Club of New York City," in Jeremy Bonner, Christopher D. Denny, and Mary Beth Fraser Connelly, eds., *Empowering the People of God: Catholic Action before and after Vatican II* (New York: Fordham University Press, 2014), 21–45.

Club of New York City. Another tie with Xavier was broken that year when Father Dealy reluctantly resigned as the moderator of the Xavier Union upon his reassignment to Boston. For some reason the Jesuits declined the request from the club to replace him as moderator with another Jesuit. The officers of the club appealed to Archbishop Corrigan, who replaced Dealy with Father Arthur Donnelly, the vicar general, and later with his secretary, Father Charles McDonnell, an alumnus of Xavier and the future bishop of Brooklyn. At his first appearance before the Catholic Club, Donnelly told the members, "Next to the priesthood, I consider such an organization as this the backbone of the Catholic Church."[38]

In the 1890s membership in the Catholic Club became both more inclusive and more exclusive. The numbers swelled to almost 1,000, but the new members were increasingly drawn from the ranks of upper-middle-class Catholics. In the early days grocers and shopkeepers and even one ship chandler rubbed shoulders with lawyers and physicians. In 1892 the by-laws were amended to limit admission to those who were "members of liberal professions or graduates of colleges or who have passed at least two years at a collegiate institution." There were no more ship chandlers in the Catholic Club. That same year the club moved to a new five-story clubhouse at 120 Central Park South, overlooking the park. It became the favorite site for hosting elegant receptions for visiting Catholic dignitaries like Archbishop Francesco Satolli, the apostolic delegate. Expenses did not seem to be a problem. In 1893 the budget was $85,000, and expenditures for cigars ($4,058.28) exceeded the combined gas and electric bill ($3,289.97).[39]

The Catholic Club proved its value to the Catholic community during the state constitutional convention of 1894 when an attempt was made to eliminate government aid to "sectarian" child-caring institutions. Working closely with Archbishop Corrigan, the Committee on Catholic Interests of the Catholic Club, under the chairmanship of Judge Morgan J. O'Brien, led a successful effort to defeat this proposal and preserve government assistance to 20,000 youngsters in 58 Catholic institutions.

In 1916 Patrick J. Hayes, the auxiliary bishop of New York, called the

38. AAIHS, *Bulletin of the Catholic Club of the City of New York*, January, February, March 1888, n.p.

39. AAIHS, Register of the Xavier Union, Amendment to the Constitution, November 3, 1892, p.61; Annual Reports of the Officers and Standing Committees, June 16, 1893, pp. 9, 12. There were 977 members of the Catholic Club in 1893. AAIHS, Annual Reports of the Officers and Standing Committees, Report of the Committee on Admissions, June 16, 1893, p. 12.

Catholic Club "the greatest achievement of the Catholic laity in this city." The club reached the peak of its influence in the 1920s when membership grew to 1,600 and there was a long list of applications. Once again the club's Committee on Catholic Interests demonstrated its value by playing an active role in combating the anti-Catholic xenophobia of that decade. William D. Guthrie, a constitutional lawyer and a member of the club, successfully challenged the Oregon School Law of 1922, which would have effectively outlawed private and parochial elementary schools in that state. In a unanimous decision the U.S. Supreme Court declared the law unconstitutional.[40]

The Catholic Club never recovered from the Great Depression, despite a generous donation and loan from the usually parsimonious Patrick Cardinal Hayes, and gradually faded into oblivion during the 1960s. However, for fifty years, first as the Xavier Union and later as the Catholic Club, it was the most prominent lay Catholic organization in New York and gave the lay Catholic elite a focal point where they could strengthen their bonds with one another and coordinate their services to the Catholic Church in New York City. It remained a legacy to the Catholics of New York from the College of St. Francis Xavier even after the college itself had disappeared from the scene.

Finis

In 1900 the College of St. Francis Xavier was the third-largest Jesuit college in the United States and Canada. Twelve years later it graduated its last class, and the college department was transferred to Rose Hill. Throughout the first decade of the twentieth century the college enrollment at Xavier remained approximately the same as at St. John's College, Rose Hill. Only in 1910 and 1911 was there a dramatic shift in numbers, with twice as many students at Rose Hill as at Xavier (174 to 74 in 1910, 165 to 76 in 1911). However, the consolidation of the two colleges had been under consideration for some time.

The Xavier house history explains that "the reason for the change was greater efficiency and progress since there was an urgent necessity in broadening the scope and methodology on the college level and introducing more and diverse courses into the curriculum." Academically it made sense for the Jesuits to concentrate their limited financial and personnel resources in one college. After the opening of Brooklyn College in 1908 there were four Jesuit colleges within twenty miles of one another in the

---

40. Nolan, "Catholic Club," 19, 40.

New York metropolitan area: St. John's, Xavier, Brooklyn College, and St. Peter's College in Jersey City. In 1909 the total enrollment in the four colleges was 296.[41] There was little room for expansion at Xavier, but plenty of space on the Rose Hill campus.

The shifting demographics of the Catholic population also hurt Xavier as Catholics left lower Manhattan for the outer boroughs. Father James H. McGean, the pastor of St. Peter's Church on Barclay Street, complained in 1896 that "Brooklyn and [New] Jersey have taken away our industrious middle class." An alumnus of Xavier, McGean estimated that 500 families had left the parish since 1882. Access to mass transit, with its sacrosanct five-cent fare, which had once worked in favor of Xavier, now benefited St. John's with the completion of the Third Avenue El to Fordham in 1901 and the extension of the IRT subway lines to the Bronx in the following decade. Another factor in the decision to close the College of St. Francis Xavier may have been competition with another day school, Cathedral College, the six-year minor seminary (high school and junior college) that was opened by the archdiocese of New York in 1903 and had 327 students in 1912.[42]

Another factor in the decision to discontinue the college at Xavier was the changing nature of the neighborhood, which had become more and more commercial and industrial. "In several years Xavier will be surrounded by business houses and not suitable for a good college site," the provincial, Joseph Hanselman, told the general, Father Franz Xavier Wernz, in 1906. New York University had already moved its undergraduate department from Washington Square in Manhattan to University Heights in the Bronx in 1894, and Columbia University had moved from midtown Manhattan to Morningside Heights in 1897. "If we move north," said the president of Xavier in 1907, "we will be at the gates of Fordham and amalgamation would be the only sensible solution."[43]

At a meeting at Fordham on January 18, 1912, with the approval and encouragement of Hanselman, the New York Jesuits decided to retain only one college in the New York area, St. John's, Rose Hill, which Hanselman envisioned as "the great university center," which fit in nicely with Wernz's dream of transforming Fordham into the American equivalent

41. *WL* 38 (1909): 457.

42. AANY, Minutes of the Meetings of the Diocesan Consultors, December 2, 1896. Archbishop Farley heard that the Jesuits at Xavier had criticized him for opening Cathedral College. FUA, Diary of Presidents, 1885–1906, John J. Collins, S.J., June 26, 1905.

43. ARSJ, Hanselman to Wernz, October 4, 1906; David Hearn to Wernz, May 15, 1907.

of the Catholic University of Louvain, which was widely regarded as the best Catholic university in the world.[44] Only the high school departments were to be retained at Xavier, Brooklyn College, and St. Peter's College. Hanselman had already taken the precaution of moving the assertive Father Thomas J. McCluskey from Xavier, where he was likely to defend Xavier's interests vigorously, and made him president of St. John's College. He then appointed the more pliable Father Joseph Rockwell as president of Xavier.[45]

The plan had to be modified when the president of Brooklyn College, Father John H. O'Rourke, made an impassioned plea to save his institution because of the large Catholic population in the borough; the strong support of the bishop, Charles McDonnell, a Jesuit alumnus; and his fear that the high school would not be financially viable without the college. O'Rourke carried the day and the Jesuits agreed to keep open Brooklyn College, a decision that they would almost immediately regret.[46]

The marriage between Xavier and St. John's, which took effect in September 1912, was not a happy one on the part of either partner. Father Thomas J. Campbell, a former provincial who had been president of both institutions (Fordham twice), said candidly in print that the scheme was "impossible" to begin with and the result was "chaos." By March 1913 the board of trustees at both Rose Hill and Xavier had voted to rescind the agreement signed by representatives of their two colleges on September 10, 1912. Unfortunately, as the Jesuit historian Francis X. Curran noticed fifty years ago, the text of the agreement has been ripped out of the minutes of the meetings of board of trustees of Xavier. As a result one can only surmise the reasons for the bitter recriminations that followed the merger.[47]

The academic year at St. John's began in September 1912 with 290 students, a record enrollment that reflected the transfer to Rose Hill of many of the students from Xavier. Since Fordham had become a university in 1905, some Jesuits at Rose Hill considered renaming the college department the College of St. Francis Xavier of Fordham University, which seems to have been the understanding of the Jesuits at Xavier when they voted

44. I am grateful to Professor Emmett Curran for bringing to my attention Father Wernz's dream of making Fordham the American Louvain.

45. ARSJ, Hanselman to Wernz, Septemeber 8, 1911.

46. ARSJ, Hanselmann to Wernz, January 28, 1912.

47. FUA, Minutes of the Meetings of the Board of Trustees, March 27, 1913. Campbell, "Fordham University," *WL* 45 (1916): 369–70. One of the Jesuits at Xavier blamed the confusion on the failure of the Jesuits at Rose Hill "to meet the issue honestly and straightforwardly." ACSFX, Acta Consultorum, January 17, 1913.

to merge with St. John's. As graduation day approached in 1913, rumors circulated that the graduates would receive their diplomas from the College of St. Francis Xavier, which led to protests from seniors and alumni. The trustees of Xavier insisted that the graduates should have the option of receiving their degrees in the name of either institution. Other disputes revolved around money, specifically whether the burses and legacies that had been donated to Xavier should be transferred to St. John's College and whether Xavier should continue to pay the tuition of its former scholarship students who were now at Rose Hill.[48]

A further complication arose over the future of Brooklyn College. It had failed to qualify for a permanent charter from the state because of financial difficulties and consequently was unable to confer degrees. The new Jesuit general, Wlodimir Ledóchowski, solved that problem by ordering it merged with the now-defunct College of St. Francis Xavier. As a result, New York's once-premier Jesuit college experienced a brief afterlife as Brooklyn College–College of St. Francis Xavier and conferred degrees on the graduates in the name of the College of St. Francis Xavier. However, that did not solve the financial problems. In 1918 O'Rourke was unable even to meet the interest on the debt and said that "it would be better to leave Brooklyn and not pile debt upon debt which there is no hope of paying." The Jesuits heeded his advice and closed Brooklyn College in 1921.[49]

Sequel

The College of St Francis Xavier was neither the oldest nor the wealthiest nor the most prestigious Jesuit college in the United States. It can stake a modest claim to have been briefly one of the largest Jesuit colleges in late-nineteenth-century America, but perhaps its real significance is best captured by a phrase that Sir Richard Southern used to describe the Austin canons in medieval England. Like the Austin canons, the Jesuit fathers at Xavier were "ubiquitously useful" to a broad spectrum of the Catholic community of New York City. They conducted a classical college for middle-class Catholics of limited means; maintained a busy parish church that drew worshipers from all across the city; served as chap-

48. FUA, Acta Consultorum, October 1, 14, November 18, 25, December 18, 1912; February 17, March 10, April 17, 1913; ACSFX, Minutes of the Board of Trustees, September 13, 1912, March 31, 1913.

49. FUA, Acta Consultorum, April 7, 1913; Joseph H. Rockwell, S.J., to Alumni of St. Francis Xavier College, June 1913, *WL* 42 (1913): 401–2. ARSJ, O'Rourke to Ledóchowski, August 26, 1918. St. Peter's College was closed in 1918 and was reopened in 1930.

lains to the most disadvantaged members of the Catholic population in the city's hospitals, prisons, and asylums; and inspired the creation of the most important and exclusive lay Catholic organization in late-nineteenth-century New York City. By any standard that may be considered ubiquitous usefulness.

"And one poor man has to be in charge of it all," complained Father David Hearn, the president of the College of St. Francis Xavier, in 1907. "Really it is rather too much," he told the general, "it is almost beyond human power." One may sympathize with Father Hearn, but Father John Larkin's mythical fifty cents paid handsome dividends for New York Catholics during the course of the following sixty-five years.[50]

50. ARSJ, Hearn to Wernz, May 15, 1907.

7

ET IN ARCADIA EGO
The Gilded Age at Rose Hill

The Growth of Gotham

The four decades between the Civil War and the turn of the twentieth century were boom years in New York City, as they were throughout much of the rest of the country with the exception of the South. The population of the city almost quadrupled from 813,000 to 3,473,000, culminating in the creation of Greater New York in 1898, a metropolis that included not only Manhattan, but also the Bronx, Queens, Brooklyn, and Staten Island. By 1900 New York City had more people than all but six states, was twice as large as Chicago, and was home to one-quarter of the nation's millionaires. It was also the headquarters of two-thirds of America's largest corporations. In the 1870s and 1880s New York City acquired some of its most prominent public buildings, such as Commodore Cornelius Vanderbilt's Grand Central Station with its ninety-foot-high train shed, the first Madison Square Garden, Boss Tweed's scandal-ridden Court House (which cost twice as much as the acquisition of Alaska), the American Museum of Natural History, the Metropolitan Museum of Art, and the Metropolitan Opera House.

On May 24, 1883, proud New Yorkers celebrated the opening of the Brooklyn Bridge, the longest suspension bridge in the world at that time and one of the engineering marvels of the age. Unfortunately the city fathers chose Queen Victoria's birthday for the ribbon-cutting ceremonies, a coincidence that was not appreciated by the city's Irish Catholics, who nearly rioted to show their displeasure. Three years later New York harbor received its most famous landmark, the Statue of Liberty, a gift of the French Republic that was to be a beacon of hope for millions of immigrants arriving in America.

Catholics made their own contribution to the city's architectural splendor on May 25, 1879, with the dedication of St. Patrick's Cathedral, a potent symbol of the Irish Catholic presence in New York City. Another symbol of the Irish Catholic presence was their domination of local politics. "Honest John" Kelly, who was married to a niece of Cardinal McCloskey, replaced Boss Tweed as the head of Tammany Hall. As early as 1871 the

New York Times noted with alarm that "there is an established church and a ruling class in New York, but the church is not Protestant and the ruling class is not American." Nine years later New York elected its first Catholic mayor, William Grace, and would elect two other Catholic mayors before the end of the century. John Talbot Smith, a pioneer historian of New York Catholicism, estimated that New York was a predominantly Catholic city for about a dozen years, from 1885 until the creation of Greater New York in 1898.[1]

During the Gilded Age the Catholic population of the archdiocese of New York (which included Manhattan, the Bronx, and Staten Island as well as seven upstate counties) probably tripled from about 350,000 to 1,200,000. Across the East River in the diocese of Brooklyn, which was created in 1853 for Brooklyn and the rest of Long Island, there were approximately 1 million Catholics by 1900. In both dioceses the bulk of the Catholic population was concentrated in New York City, and in both dioceses the bishops continued Archbishop Hughes's policy of aggressively promoting the expansion of Catholic education.

However, the growth of Catholic higher education lagged far behind the impressive expansion of the parochial school system on the elementary level, reflecting the reality that, although the Irish had succeeded in gaining control of local politics, the Catholic community in New York City was still overwhelmingly a community of poor immigrants and their children. In 1900 there were five Catholic men's colleges in the city, but all were small and undistinguished academically: St. John's at Rose Hill, the College of St. Francis Xavier on West 16th Street, Manhattan College in Manhattanville, St. John's College, and St. Francis College in Brooklyn. Their combined enrollment was less than a thousand at a time when the total Catholic school population in the two dioceses exceeded 78,000 students.[2]

The area of the archdiocese of New York that experienced the greatest proportionate increase in the number of parishes (if not Catholic popu-

---

1. For a detailed description of the dedication of the cathedral, see Charles R. Morris, *American Catholic* (New York: Times Books / Random House, 1997), 3–25; *New York Times*, January 7, 1871; John Talbot Smith, *The Catholic Church in New York* (New York: Hall and Locke, 1908), II, 446.

2. *WL* 29 (1900): 550; *The Catholic Directory, Almanac* (Milwaukee: M. H. Wiltzius and Co., 1901); Manhattan College dates from the establishment of Manhattan Academy by the Christian Brothers in 1863; St. Francis College was founded by the Franciscan Brothers of Brooklyn in 1858; and St. John's College, Brooklyn, was established by the Vincentian Fathers in 1870.

lation) was the Bronx, which did not even exist as a separate political entity in the nineteenth century. It was a collection of towns and villages in the southern part of Westchester County that was annexed by the city of New York in two stages with the approval of the state legislature. First the city annexed the area of the Bronx west of the Bronx River in 1874 ("the Annexed District," it was called briefly) and then the rest of the Bronx in 1895. Three years later, with the creation of Greater New York, the whole area became the Borough of the Bronx and a separate county in 1914. It is at least roughly indicative of the growth of the Catholic population in the Bronx between 1865 and 1900 that the number of parishes increased from four to twenty-five, but one would never guess the momentous changes that were taking place in New York City and the Bronx from the perspective of the closed confines of St. John's College, Rose Hill.

An Ideal Rural Scene

While New York City and even the Bronx experienced unprecedented growth during the Gilded Age, St. John's College emphasized the advantages of its isolation from the bustling metropolis that was expanding practically to its front gates. "The country for miles around is most picturesque," declared the college catalogue in 1900. "Vast reaches of lawns, rows of noble trees and rich farm lands surrounding the college buildings present an ideal rural scene and afford the seclusion necessary for a seat of learning." It was a hyperbolic description of the rural character of Fordham even by the florid standards of contemporary advertising and would have been more accurate in 1846 when Father Edward Doucet said that only one house, the Powell mansion, was visible from the campus.

In 1890 the Grand Concourse was laid out through the central spine of the Bronx, and in 1901 the Third Avenue El reached Fordham. In 1887 the railroad (now the mighty New York Central) had already relocated its right-of-way from the surface to an open cut below street level because of the increased pedestrian traffic, and a map published in the *Fordham Monthly* in 1906 showed that the neighborhood surrounding the campus had already been surveyed and graded into city streets. Thomas Gaffney Taaffe, an alumnus and Fordham's first historian, marveled that the campus still remained an oasis of peace and quiet only a dozen miles from Gotham, but even he admitted that the rural character of the area was fast disappearing, especially on Fordham Heights, where the little cottage of Edgar Allan Poe was now surrounded by tall buildings. "That vandal, Modern Improvement, has seized upon that charming bit of Arcadia,"

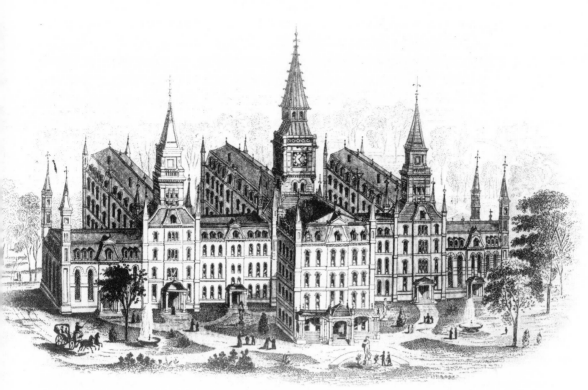

Sketch of projected plan in 1864 for the completion of St. John's College. The only section that was built was the east wing of present-day Dealy Hall, completed in 1867.

Taaffe lamented, "and now the sounds of hammer and trowel drown the last sweet plaint of Poe's poor heartbroken muse."[3]

Although the description of the bucolic nature of the neighborhood in the college catalogue was a gross exaggeration, it was a telling indication of the approach to higher education favored by some, but by no means all, of the Jesuits at Fordham. For the more conservative Jesuits, their model was still the protective environment of a rural seminary that, they thought, promoted character formation by segregating the students from the temptations of the outside world. They seemed to think that it was a model that would also be favored by many Catholic parents. However, there were always other Jesuits at Rose Hill during the Gilded Age who took a more innovative and sophisticated approach to Catholic higher education. At least occasionally these Jesuits had the opportunity to make their voices heard and to nudge the college ever so gently and tentatively into the mainstream of the American academic world.[4]

In 1858 Archbishop Hughes commented churlishly that St. John's College had "retrograded" after he sold it to the Jesuits in 1845. If he was

3. Thomas Gaffney Taaffe, "St. John's College," *FM*, June 1894, 145.
4. *Catalogue of St. John's College, 1900–1901*, 4–5.

speaking about a decline in enrollment, he was in error. However, in the four decades after Hughes's death in 1864, St. John's College presented a curious combination of continuity and change, progress, and stagnation that led to unfavorable comparisons with its vibrant younger sibling, the College of St. Francis Xavier in Manhattan. What changed the least at Rose Hill in those years were the curriculum and the precarious financial condition of the college.

The catalogue of St. John's College for 1900 showed little difference in content from the catalogues of the Civil War period, except for some minor changes in terminology. The standard European Jesuit nomenclature of First Division, Second Division, Third Division was changed to the more recognizable American designations of college department, academic department (high school), and grammar department (the last two years of grade school). Likewise the four years of college were now called freshman, sophomore, junior, and senior year instead of classics, *belles lettres*, rhetoric, and philosophy. More substantively, the academic department or high school course was lengthened from three to four years. The two years of the grammar department were called rudiments A and B. A commercial department rounded off the course of studies.

Despite the change in nomenclature and the popularity of the commercial department, a traditional classical education remained the ideal. In the college department in both freshman and sophomore years each week there were five hour-long classes of Latin and four of Greek. The class load was reduced to two hours of each subject in junior and senior years when philosophy came to dominate the curriculum with five hours allotted to it each week in junior year and ten hours in senior year. There were four classes in English each week in both freshman and sophomore years, but only two classes in junior year and none at all in senior year, although there was a class in elocution for one hour a week in senior year.

It was explained that the main reason for the emphasis on Latin and Greek was "their efficiency for training the mind." Admission requirements placed heavy emphasis on a classical background in high school. Applicants who could not furnish proof of proficiency in Latin and Greek had to take an examination that required them not only to translate into English passages from Cicero, Virgil, Lucian, and Homer but also to translate into Latin and Greek an English text based on Cicero's *De Senectute* and Xenophon's *Anabasis* (complete with accents). The Latin composition was described as the most important element in the language examinations.

One wonders how rigidly these admission requirements were enforced. When Francis J. Spellman, a graduate of a public grammar school and high school in Whitman, Massachusetts, applied for admission to St. John's College in the fall of 1907, he was interviewed personally by the president, Father Daniel J. Quinn, as were all the applicants. Father Quinn asked young Mr. Spellman a few questions about the second aorist of an irregular Greek verb. Satisfied with Spellman's answer, he welcomed the future cardinal archbishop of New York to the college and introduced him to the prefect of studies.[5]

The other constant factor at St. John's College during the Gilded Age was the precarious state of the finances, a situation that lasted well beyond the turn of the twentieth century. In an address to the alumni in 1883 John Hassard scolded them for their stinginess in comparison with the alumni of Mount St. Mary's in Emmitsburg, Maryland, who had saved their alma mater from bankruptcy, and the alumni of Seton Hall, who had raised the funds for a new student residence. He drew howls of laughter when he said, "I know for a positive fact that the alumni of St. John's have so far strained themselves for the past two years as to have given their college fifty dollars." However, he softened his criticism by expressing confidence that in the not-too-distant future Catholic colleges would be as successful in raising funds as their secular counterparts.[6]

That happy day had not yet arrived at Rose Hill by the turn of the twentieth century. In 1889 the student publication complained that "St. John's . . . has been less favored than even her sister colleges in donations from friends." In 1900 the college catalogue stated bluntly, almost proudly, that the "entire lack of financial resources has been characteristic of the college all through the years of its existence. It has never had any endowment fund and the donations have been rare and small." The lean and candid prose suggests that the author of this combination confession and boast was Father Thomas J. Campbell, Fordham's equivalent of Grover Cleveland, who completed the second of his two discontinuous terms as president late in August 1900.[7]

The following year Father Campbell's successor as president of St. John's College, Father John A. Petit, told the alumni that "our family skel-

5. *Catalogue of St. John's College*, 1865, 1868, 1900–1901; Robert I. Gannon, S.J., *The Cardinal Spellman Story* (Garden City, N.Y.: Doubleday and Company, 1962), 8.

6. *FM*, November 1883, 122–23.

7. *FM*, December 1889, 53. *Catalogue 1900–1901*, 3. Campbell was president 1885–88 and 1896–1900. The quip about Campbell as Fordham's Grover Cleveland is attributed to Paul Levack, a longtime professor of history at Fordham University. I am grateful to Father Patrick J. Ryan, S.J., for the reference. Father Augustus J. Thébaud, S.J., also had nonconsecutive terms as president, 1846–51 and 1859–63.

eton is our list of scholarship endowments." Only two scholarships had been established in the course of the previous sixty years, compared with 300 scholarships at Cornell and 215 at Harvard. Even the College of St. Francis Xavier could boast of 29 burses. He noted also that the previous year New York University had received $300,000 in gifts and Columbia University had received $460,000. Only a month earlier Petit had been hard-pressed to find the money to admit two poor but promising students to St. John's at the request of one of the professors.[8]

The Rose Hill Campus

In contrast to the rigidity of the curriculum and the habitual fiscal uncertainty, there was an extensive transformation in the physical appearance of the campus with the erection of three or four new large stone buildings. (The arithmetical ambiguity depends on whether one considers the present Dealy Hall to be originally one or two buildings.) The boundaries of the campus also underwent considerable alteration. The property purchased by Archbishop Hughes and sold to the Jesuits in 1845 and 1860 amounted to approximately 106 acres. The state of New York acquired some twenty-six acres for the New York Botanical Garden by eminent domain in 1889 for $93,966.28, but the college authorities were able to compensate for this loss by purchasing some of the Powell Farm, located just south of the campus. This addition enabled them to extend the southern boundary of the college to Pelham Avenue (Fordham Road) from Third Avenue to present-day Bathgate Avenue. Fifty years earlier under Father Thébaud the college could have acquired even more extensive frontage on Pelham Avenue except that the skittish Jesuit authorities in Rome feared that the purchase of additional property would drive the college too deeply into debt. The size of the campus was approximately 75 acres in 1900.[9]

The new buildings were the first substantial physical additions to the campus since the construction of the diocesan seminary and the college church in the mid-1840s, and they were a vast improvement over the extensions to the administration building and the "sheds" built by Archbishop Hughes and Father Thébaud. The new buildings were constructed of blue granite quarried on the campus, and they were ornamented with marble from a local quarry that the college had acquired in Tremont. The model

8. George A. Petit, S.J., "Alma Mater and the Present," February 18, 1901, *FM*, March 1901, 319–20.

9. Thomas Gaffney Taaffe, *A History of St. John's College, Fordham* (New York: The Catholic Publication Society, 1891), 118.

for the granite-and-marble design was the picturesque little gatehouse erected by Father Thébaud in 1852.

The first of the new buildings was Senior or Seniors' Hall, a five-story building located to the east of the Administration Building for the college students that eventually contained dormitories, classrooms, study halls, reading rooms, a billiard room, and a gym complete with a batting-net for baseball practice during the winter. Proposed during the Civil War with the Tipperary-born Patrick Keely as the architect, construction was delayed until after the end of the conflict and it was finished only in the summer of 1867 during the presidency of Father William Moylan. It remained the principal campus building for several decades thereafter. The west wall of the building was deliberately left unfinished to facilitate the addition of an extension at a later date.[10]

Dealy Hall as it appeared in the late 1890s after the completion of the west wing and before the advent of the architectural vandals who disfigured it in the mid–twentieth century.

10. FUA, Acta Consultorum, June 15, September 28, 1863. Today's Seniors' Hall is the east wing of Dealy Hall.

The fundraising drive for Seniors' Hall was a disappointment and indicated the difficulty of interesting New York Catholics in the value of Catholic higher education. A total of fifty-five donors contributed $8,247, less than the $9,905 raised in 1839–40 by Bishop Hughes for the purchase of the Rose Hill property at a time when the Catholic community in New York City was much smaller and poorer than it was twenty-five years later. The contributions ranged from $1,000 from Father Edward Lynch, a Fordham alumnus, to several people who gave $25. Charles O'Conor, Andrew Carrigan, and James Olwell, all prominent local Catholic laymen, contributed $500 each. The banker Eugene Kelly, one of the wealthiest Catholics in New York, sent $250 with the promise of $250 more, while Catherine Collins, a servant girl in the rectory of the Church of St. Francis Xavier, almost matched him with a contribution of $245. An anonymous donor pledged the princely sum of $5,000 through Mother Aloysia Hardey, R.S.C.J., the superior of the Convent of the Sacred Heart. Unfortunately the donor never came through with the cash.[11]

Reform Manqué

Father Moylan's successor, Father Joseph Shea, made his contribution to the renovation and modernization of the campus in 1869 when he pulled down the one-story wooden extensions of the Administration Building and replaced them with the two-story brick additions that still exist almost a century and a half later. Father Schroth has pointed out that there is hardly a square inch of space in any campus building that has not been recycled and reused for different purposes many times over since it was first constructed. That is particularly true of the Administration Building and its two wings. Today the main corridor on the first floor of the north wing contains the formal portraits of Fordham's forty-three presidents. If these solemn-looking gentlemen could engage one another in conversation, it is likely that even they would have difficulty in rehearsing the history of the interior arrangements of the buildings that they erected.

Father Shea was also responsible for the first major attempts to modernize the curriculum, discipline, and student housing during his presidency between 1868 and 1874. Shea was under pressure to initiate these changes because of mounting student discontent, but his efforts met with only limited success. "No boy ever found a judge in him," one alumnus said affectionately about Shea, but Shea made the tactical mistake of agreeing to serve as the spiritual director and confessor of any student who asked

11. FUA, Notanda Collegii.

him to do so. The result, said Father Thomas Campbell, was that "it tied his hands in the matter of exterior discipline and in the government of the students."[12]

Shortly before the Christmas vacation in 1868, the college authorities learned of a "conspiracy" to induce some twenty or thirty students not to return to Rose Hill after the vacation but to apply instead for admission to the College of St. Francis Xavier. For good measure the departing students were prepped to smash the windows of the college buildings as they made their exit. The conspiracy was nipped in the bud, the ringleaders were expelled, and a "wholesome fear of authority" was said to have descended upon the campus.[13]

However, student restlessness did not disappear but only went underground. In response, the college authorities tightened the censorship of student mail. Henceforth even the letters of students to their parents were subject to inspection after several students had expressed dissatisfaction with the management of the college and some parents had removed their sons from Rose Hill and sent them elsewhere. Resentment of the disciplinary regime was paralleled by unhappiness with the curriculum. A classical education was the ideal that was fostered in Jesuit colleges throughout the world, but Father Shea noted with alarm in the fall of 1869 that "the students [are] losing all taste for classical studies and . . . some of the smartest boys . . . asked leave to follow the commercial course."[14]

Shea responded to this crisis on several different levels. He attempted to relax the strict rules by little concessions such as proposing to give the students a smoking room, but he was voted down unanimously by his board of consultors. Even the kindly Father Legoüais, an inveterate snuffer, objected to the proposal. Shea learned his lesson. When he attempted to undertake the far more serious change of allowing some of the college students to live in private rooms in the upper floors of the former seminary building rather than in the dormitories, he circumvented local Jesuit opposition by informing the consultors that he had obtained "the full permission and consent" of the superior of the New York Mission.[15]

Unfortunately Shea's disciplinary reforms did not work, reflecting per-

12. "More About the Good Old Days," *FM*, December 1899, 148; Thomas J. Campbell, S.J., "Fordham University," *FM*, Diamond Jubilee Edition, June 1916, 32.

13. FUA, Acta Consultorum, December 11, 14, 1868.

14. FUA, Acta Consultorum, October 5, 1869, April 7, 1870. Father Charles Charaux opposed opening the letters of students to their parents on the grounds that doing so violated "the natural rights of parents."

15. FUA, Acta Consultorum, February 24, 1869; October 26, 1870.

haps Alexis de Tocqueville's dictum that the most dangerous time for a bad government is when it begins to make reforms. The Jesuit faculty complained of a loss of control over student behavior. According to them at least, the students showed that they were incapable of dealing responsibly with their newfound freedom. Father Patrick A. Halpin accused Shea of introducing the "latitudinarian regime of secular establishments of learning." Ironically the person who was brought in to replace Shea and restore law and order in the summer of 1874 was Father Frederick William Gockeln. Father John Larkin had originally brought Gockeln to Rose Hill in 1852 as the dean of discipline to replace the excessively severe Father Thomas Ouellet. As president Gockeln restored the old disciplinary regime and abandoned Shea's "latitudinarian" attempt to replace the student dormitories with individual rooms.[16]

The growing popularity of the commercial or English course at the expense of the classical course was a more difficult problem to solve. Between 1863 and 1881 the percentage of students enrolled in the commercial course rose from 23 percent to 38 percent of the student body. In 1870 Father Shea initiated still another reform when he endeavored to construct a six-year commercial course that would parallel the classical course, but the experiment lasted only one year. For the next two decades, the commercial course, the unwanted but money-making black sheep of the curriculum, went through many variations in length and content until it was dropped in 1892 but restored again in 1897.[17]

Meanwhile, at Xavier the classical course was so popular that the commercial course was completely abandoned in 1882. Thus Xavier could boast that it was more faithful to the principles of the *ratio studiorum* than Fordham. Christa Klein makes the shrewd observation that the difference may have been due to the attitude that the students imbibed from their parents. She speculates that at Xavier lower-middle-class parents who were struggling for social acceptance may have placed a higher value on the prestige of a classical education than the parents of Fordham students, who were often pragmatic and self-made businessmen who had prospered without the benefit of Greek and Latin.[18]

16. Patrick A. Halpin, S.J., "Father Gockeln," *FM*, January 1887, 52.

17. Monsignor John M. Farley, the vicar general and future cardinal archbishop, may have ruffled some Jesuit feathers at the commencement ceremonies in 1893 when he told the graduates that "if you have no taste for books or study, leave the learned professions alone. Go straight to business at once. With character and cultivated talents such as yours, you will succeed." *FM*, October 1893, 2.

18. Christa Klein, "The Jesuits and Catholic Boyhood in Nineteenth-Century New

Another milestone in Fordham's history occurred during the presidency of Father Shea with the arrival on campus during the summer of 1872 of Father Thomas J. A. Freeman, a native of Nova Scotia, who as a boy had worked on coastal schooners in the New England trade. After a year of preparation at Columbia's School of Mines, Freeman was assigned the unenviable task of teaching science in a college that was committed to the primacy of a classical education. Father Augustus Thébaud, Fordham's first Jesuit president and another scholar with a scientific background, had downplayed the importance of science in the curriculum at Rose Hill. That was not true with Father Freeman, who vigorously championed the role of science and sought space for modern chemistry and physics laboratories. He was offered room for his embryonic science department on the first floor of the old diocesan seminary, which had been neglected for years. Although the new facilities were barely adequate, they were a considerable improvement over the cramped quarters previously occupied by the Science Department in one of the wings of the Administration Building. One of Father Freeman's first tasks was to repair the laboratory equipment that the Jesuits had brought with them from Kentucky almost thirty years earlier.[19]

Several farsighted Fordham presidents came to Father Freeman's aid. Father Patrick Dealy began construction of a separate Science Hall in the spring of 1885, and it was completed with its distinctive tapered chimney in September 1886 during the first presidency of Father Thomas J. Campbell. It contained not only chemistry and physics laboratories and classrooms but also philosophy classrooms, a student library with school banners and athletic trophies, a museum, and meeting rooms for the Debating Society and the Historical Society. Renamed Thébaud Hall, it serves today as the Office of the Campion Institute and the Center for Enrollment Services. Once the Science Department was relocated to its new quarters in this building, the former diocesan seminary was renovated as the residence of the youngsters in the two-year preparatory course and it was renamed St. John's Hall. Today it forms the oldest part of Queen's Court, one of the student residences.

The practical benefits of modern science were introduced to the campus when electric lights and steam heat were installed in all the buildings

York City: A Study of St. John's College and the College of St. Francis Xavier, 1846–1912." Ph.D. diss., University of Pennsylvania, 1976," 147–53.

19. Taaffe, *History of St. John's College*, 106; "Rev. Thomas J.A. Freeman, S.J.," *FM*, December 1907, 128–29.

in 1888 and 1889. A dynamo in the basement of Science Hall supplied electricity and steam heat to the other building through underground conduits.[20]

Some students wondered how beneficial the electric lights would be. "There are some who hold that there is a virtue in electric light which makes even the study of Greek endurable and pleasant," the editors of the *Fordham Monthly* declared. "This is a very bold opinion to carry about." However, they added, "considering that the causes of electricity are as yet unknown, there may be something in the wonderful fluid (?) powerful enough to soften Greek and Mathematics." If the students poked good-natured fun at the benefits of electric light, the Jesuits were deadly serious about the limitations of the telephone and refused to have one on campus "both on account of expense and delays in sending messages."[21]

20. For a detailed and well-documented account of the coming of electric light to Rose Hill, see Roger Wines and Allan S. Gilbert, "St. John's College at Fordham and Its Pioneering Electrification in the Bronx," *The Bronx County Historical Journal* 51: 1&2 (Spring & Fall 2014): 28–46.

21. FM, April 1888, 122; FUA, Acta Consultorum, March 19, September 17 1889.

Et in Arcadia Ego: *The Gilded Age at Rose Hill*

Change and continuity often existed uneasily side by side. The same year that St. John's College began to equip its buildings with steam heat and electric light, and the railroad suppressed its right-of-way below street level, the college bought a stagecoach to transport day students back and forth from Yonkers to Rose Hill. Sometime prior to that date a horsecar line began operations between Fordham and West Farms. It was still in operation in 1888 when a student asked the aged Father Edward Doucet why it was affectionately known as the Huckleberry Line. Doucet explained that the name was due to the proclivity of the horsecars to jump the tracks; while the driver and conductor busied themselves putting the car back on the rails, the passengers passed the time picking huckleberries from the adjacent fields.[22]

Father John Scully, a native of Brooklyn, who was president of St. John's College from 1888 to 1891, made two major additions to the campus. First, in the fall of 1889 he broke ground for the construction of Junior or Juniors' Hall for the high school students. Architecturally it was a carbon copy of Seniors' Hall erected twenty years earlier, a five-story blue granite-and-marble building with limestone trim that contained classrooms, a dormitory, study halls, a gym, a reading room, and a billiard room. Located east of the Administration Building and north of Seniors' Hall, it cost $85,000 and was in use by the middle of October 1890. The money came from the grant of $93,966.28 that the city gave to St. John's College for the acquisition of twenty-six acres of college property for the Botanical Garden. The building served for many years as the home of the Fordham Preparatory School and more recently as Hughes Hall, a student residence. In 2012 it was renovated to become the home of the Gabelli School of Business.[23]

Father Scully's second addition to the campus was the erection of the Faculty Building, which was really a wing that was added to the west side of Seniors' Hall. The west wall of Seniors' Hall was an eyesore for twenty years because it had deliberately been left unfinished to facilitate the addition of an extension. The cornerstone of the Faculty Building was blessed on August 16, 1890, just as Juniors' Hall was nearing completion. The north side of the Faculty Building contained a two-story student chapel (whose tall window openings are clearly visible today) and the south side contained the faculty and student refectories on the first and second floors. The upper floors were reserved for the rooms of the professors, and a hall-

22. FUA, Acta Consultorum, October 3, 1888; *FM*, November 1888, 29.
23. FUA, Litterae Annuae, Letter of August 1, 1890, to January 1, 1891.

way connected the new building with Seniors' Hall. A dome or cupola with a twelve-foot cross added an elegant finishing touch to the mansard roof. The cost was $40,000.[24]

Both Seniors' Hall and the Faculty Building have long since been consolidated into one building as Dealy Hall, which has suffered from the depredations of unenlightened architects more than any other building on campus. When additional space was needed for faculty offices after World War II, the mansard roof and dome were replaced by an ugly two-story concrete bunker that has all the charm and character of the sheds that were added to the Administration Building in the 1840s and 1850s.

The flurry of new construction in the later nineteenth century made possible and necessary the elimination of virtually all the utilitarian additions to the Administration Building except for one brick three-story rear extension in the center of the building that housed the library. Another survivor, but not for long, was the venerable Rose Hill Manor House, which dated from the seventeenth century, but it had deteriorated to the point that it was demolished at the order of Father Campbell in 1896.

The construction of Juniors' Hall with its spacious dormer attic revived interest in whether the college seniors should have their own rooms, a topic that had first been raised in the 1860s. The faculty was still divided. Father Doucet opposed the idea on the grounds that it would create divisiveness among the students and make it easier for them to hide contraband. Father Dealy favored individual rooms but only for sleeping, not for studying or for use during the day. Father Halpin, who had been critical of Father Joseph Shea's attempt to introduce private rooms twenty years earlier, now favored it as a reward and privilege that would motivate the younger students. It was noted that the College of the Holy Cross had already made the transition from dormitories to individual rooms as had Stonyhurst College in England. The innovators prevailed, and the top floor of Juniors' Hall was partitioned into individual rooms for the college seniors. By 1900 rooms were available at extra cost for all the college students.[25]

Student Activities

As has been mentioned several times already, an integral element in the spiritual formation of students at all Jesuit colleges was the student

24. Taaffe, "St. John's College," *FM*, June 1894, 113–14; Campbell, "Fordham University," *FM*, Diamond Jubilee Edition, June 1916, 33.

25. FUA, Acta Consultorum, August 27, 1860, October 14, 1889; Litterae Annuae, Letter of August 1, 1890, to January 1, 1891; *Catalogue of St. John's College, 1900–1901*, 12.

Et in Arcadia Ego: *The Gilded Age at Rose Hill*

The Fordham Cadets in the late nineteenth century.

organizations known as the sodalities, whose members committed them-selves to a regular pattern of devotional practices such as the daily recita-tion of the rosary, visits to the Blessed Sacrament, and frequent reception of Holy Communion. The spirituality of the sodalities placed heavy em-phasis on devotion to the Blessed Virgin, especially during the months of October and May, and on the traditional Jesuit devotion to the Sacred Heart of Jesus, especially during the month of June.

The sodalities reached their fullest development at Fordham in the late nineteenth century. Only the best and the brightest young men were in-vited to join the sodalities in the expectation that they would set a stan-dard of behavior for the rest of the student body. The Jesuits founded the oldest Fordham sodality, the Parthenian Sodality, at St. Mary's College in Kentucky in 1837 and introduced it to Rose Hill upon their arrival in 1846. A bronze statue of the Virgin Mary was erected in the quadrangle behind the Administration Building in 1887 to commemorate the fiftieth anniver-sary of the establishment of the Parthenian Sodality in Kentucky. Father Thomas Freeman, the director of the Parthenian Sodality, presided at the blessing of the statue on May 1, 1887. All the members of the sodality were present as well as the cadet corps in full military array. "After the blessing, the sweet strains of the *Magnificat* arose," one student observed with unconscious irony, "and then the cadets fired several volleys."[26]

During May every year the students gathered in front of the statue for the special Marian devotions. By 1900 there were four separate sodalities in operation, one each for the college, high school, elementary school, and the day students.[27] Each sodality was affiliated with the head sodality in Rome, the *Prima Primaria*, and each had its own Jesuit spiritual director and a full complement of student officers. In 1900 the combined membership of the four sodalities was 107, only one-third of the total enrollment of 315, but the aim of the sodalities was not quantity but quality. The following year the sodality chapel in the south wing of the Administration Building was renovated and refurbished.[28]

In 1889 one enthusiastic sodalist declared that "with all due reverence to the good old days, St. John's Present has gone more out of its way to show its devotion and loyalty than St. John's Past." The reason for his boast was that the sodalities at Fordham had recently affiliated themselves with the St. Vincent de Paul Society, the principal Catholic charitable organization in New York City, in what a later age would call a religious outreach program. The sodalists assisted the Jesuit chaplains at Randalls Island in providing religious instruction and spiritual comfort to the patients and prisoners in the institutions on the island. It was not easy work. "Often the loathing sights in the wards of those suffering from some of the more horrible incurable diseases would find them returning from their work heartsick and wearied in body," one sodalist reported, "but their spirits were always buoyant." After their experience on Randalls Island, the sodalities at Fordham were seeking permission from the city to extend their apostolate to the even bigger challenge of the inmates in the institutions on Blackwell's Island.[29]

In addition to erecting the new science building, Father Dealy also authorized and encouraged the creation of Fordham's first permanent student publication, the *Fordham Monthly*, which appeared in November

26. "May Devotions," *FM*, May 1913.

27. They were, respectively, the Parthenian Sodality, the Sodality of the Immaculate Conception, the Sodality of the Annunciation, and the Sodality of the Immaculate Conception under the patronage of St. John Berchmans.

28. *Catalogue of St. John's College, 1900–1901*, 53–56. "The Sodality Chapel," *FM*, June 1891, 8.

29. *FM*, June 1889, 172.

1882, almost thirty years after the demise of the *Goose-Quill*. Three years later Dealy took advantage of a program sponsored by the federal government and made the preliminary arrangements to introduce a cadet corps to Rose Hill. Father Campbell had succeeded Father Dealy as president by the fall of 1885 when the first commandant arrived, Lieutenant Herbert G. Squires, who had served with the U.S. Seventh Calvary in the Indian Wars in the Dakotas. During his four years as commandant Squires overcame the initial skepticism of the students and increased the cadet corps from a dozen to 150 students who were divided into four companies. He also designed the flashy gray military uniforms, which were based on the uniforms worn by the cadets at West Point. By 1890 all students were required to participate (in uniform) in military drills three hours each week, later reduced to two hours.

The cadet corps was particularly popular with the youngsters in the preparatory program, and a separate company was organized for them with their own distinctive uniforms. It took considerable ingenuity to satisfy adolescent enthusiasm by finding mini-rifles for them that were shorter than they were. Some were as young as seven years. The faculty was as enthusiastic about the cadets as the youngsters and voted to purchase two surplus cannons from the federal government to ornament the campus and enliven drill practice. Only the ever-practical Father Dealy raised the question of the danger posed to the students by novice artillerymen.[30]

By 1890 the cadet corps was so well established at Rose Hill that a military tattoo by them became a regular and expected feature of the commencement exercises. "Energy and snap" were said to be the secret of their success. They frequently took part in the productions of the Dramatic Society, where their appearance on stage was greeted with sustained applause. The cadets also gave St. John's College widespread publicity by performing at major public events in the archdiocese. As the cadets became better known, the college became more selective about accepting invitations and more demanding about receiving proper recognition. For example, the Jesuits initially hesitated to allow the cadets to attend the gala ceremonies that were planned for the laying of the cornerstone of St. Joseph's Seminary, Dunwoodie, on May 17, 1891. The reason for their hesitation was that Archbishop Corrigan had also invited the marching band from Father John Drumgoole's orphan asylum on Staten Island and the marching band from the Catholic Protectory, a reform school in the Bronx. "We ought not to let our boys parade with orphans and Protectory boys"

---

30. FUA, Acta Consultorum, October 14, 1889.

they said, "because the parents would object, especially on account of the Protectory boys who are quasi-prisoners."[31]

If the cadets did attend the festivities at Dunwoodie, the Jesuits wanted assurance that they would get top billing as representatives of the oldest Catholic college in New York. Whether or not they received that assurance, the cadets were present at the blessing of the cornerstone, and it must have been an experience that they long remembered. On that occasion upward of 40,000 people descended upon Yonkers, a city of 30,000 people, creating a chaotic and dangerous situation that overwhelmed the resources of both the railroad company and the Yonkers police. Even Archbishop Corrigan arrived three hours late after abandoning his stalled train and walking the last two miles to the seminary.

The cadets were unexpectedly called upon not only to furnish a ceremonial presence but also to preserve law and order, which they did with considerable expertise and finesse in the judgment of their commandant, Lieutenant Clarence Edwards. If one can believe the account in the student magazine, at one point the youngest cadets pushed back an unruly crowd with fixed bayonets while an older cadet grabbed the bridle of a runway horse, bit the horse, and wrestled him into a ditch.

At the end of the festivities 20,000 people descended upon the Dunwoodie depot of the New York and Northern Railroad (later the Putnam Division of the New York Central) for the return trip home. Trains left Dunwoodie for the city with men and boys perched on the roof of the coaches, clinging to the sides of the locomotive, spread out on top of the tender, and even sitting on the cowcatcher. Lieutenant Edwards and the cadets took one look the chaotic scene and decided to march two miles east to Mount Vernon, where they boarded a special train of the Harlem division of the New York Central that had been dispatched for them from White Plains. They arrived back at Fordham that evening at 9:30.[32]

The two oldest college societies, the Debating Society and the Dramatic Society, date from 1854 and 1855 respectively. Like those of the Parthenian Sodality, the roots of the Dramatic Society go back to the Jesuits' sojourn in Kentucky, where they had continued their traditional encouragement of dramatics by sponsoring student productions in the midst of the wilder-

31. FUA, Acta Consultorum, April 13, 1891.

32. "The Day at Dunwoodie," *FM*, May 1891, 132; *New York Times*, May 18, 1891. By the turn of the twentieth century enthusiasm for the cadet corps had waned among the college students, and membership was restricted to the high school and grammar school students. *FM*, October 1905, 34. See also Thomas J. Shelley, *Dunwoodie: The History of St. Joseph's Seminary* (Westminster, Md.: Christian Classics, 1993), 1–11.

ness. One play, "Benedict Arnold the Traitor," featured the (mock) hanging on stage of Major André, the English spy, to prolonged and patriotic applause from an enthusiastic audience of backwoodsmen. Both student societies were well established and thriving at Rose Hill by the beginning of the twentieth century. A play by the Dramatic Society at Thanksgiving became an annual event, but Father Campbell was dissatisfied with the stodgy performances of the St. John's Debating Society. In one of his less successful innovations, in 1886 he changed the name from the St. John's Debating Society to the House of Commons in the hope of emulating the British Parliament by promoting more extemporaneous debates. In 1888 the name was changed once more, this time to the more acceptably republican St. John's Senate. Two years later the name was changed again, this time back to the St. John's Debating Society. *Plus ça change* . . . Political sympathies among the debaters were evenly divided between Democrats and Republicans, but the southern students were quick to howl and protest whenever the Republican debaters attempted to employ their party's usual tactic of invoking the legacy of the Civil War by waving "the bloody shirt."[33]

Fiftieth Anniversary

The commencement ceremonies on St. John's Day, June 24, 1891, were combined with the celebration of the fiftieth anniversary of the founding of the college. The focus of the celebration was not the Society of Jesus but the founding father, John Hughes. To their credit, on this day (Hughes's birthday), the Jesuits magnanimously overlooked their often-stormy relationship with him. Clusters of American flags were hung from the stately elms in recognition of his patriotism during the Civil War. As usual a large tent was erected on the front lawn for the commencement exercises, but this year there was an altar in the center of the platform where Archbishop Michael Augustine Corrigan celebrated what was called a "Pontifical Military Mass" accompanied by the ubiquitous cadets. One participant noticed that the fragrance of the incense mingled with the smell of the newly mowed hay. That was not the only unusual combination of circumstances. Some curious liturgical incongruities ensued in the course of this military Mass. When the archbishop solemnly intoned, "*Gloria in excelsis Deo et in terra pax hominibus*," the drill sergeant of the cadets bellowed, "Company, attention! Present arms!"

There was the usual round of interminable speeches, including one by

33. *FM*, June 1889, 168.

the loquacious Archbishop Patrick Ryan of Philadelphia, who had spoken for almost two hours at the dedication of St. Patrick's Cathedral in 1879. There were two equally interminable poems, one an original composition of thirty stanzas by James N. Butler, '84, later the first dean of Fordham Medical School. It unintentionally mimicked doggerel, as may be gleaned from the following sample verse:

> Ye elm-trees old, ye fields of green,
> Ye halls of work and play,
> And every dear familiar scene,
> Be glad with us today.

The highlight of the festivities was the unveiling of the statue of Archbishop Hughes that now stands in front of the Administration Building. It was the work of the sculptor William Rudolf O'Donnell and was presented to St. John's College by Judge Morgan J. O'Brien, the chair of the committee that had raised the funds for the statue from the alumni and friends of the college. Judge O'Brien also announced that, for the English inscription on the monument, the committee had decided upon Hughes's memorable declaration that

> I have always preached that every denomination, Jews, Christians, Catholics, Protestants—of every shade and sex—were all entitled to entire freedom of conscience, without let or hindrance from any sect or number of sects, no matter how small their number or how unpopular the doctrine that they profess.

Father John Scully, the president of St. John's College, responded to Judge O'Brien's address, and then Archbishop Corrigan pulled the cord that unveiled the statue of Archbishop Hughes, which had been wrapped in American flags. The day concluded with a dinner for 322 invited guests and donors.[34]

In connection with the fiftieth anniversary of the college, the editors of the *Fordham Monthly* compiled a list of 518 graduates that, they said, was "as correct as it is within our power to make it." They documented the fact that, unlike the College of St. Francis Xavier, which was essentially a local New York college, St. John's College had a national and even an international reputation. Almost one-third of the alumni lived as far afield as California, Texas, and Louisiana as well as in Canada and Mexico. At

---

34. *FM*, October 1891, 1–12. For some unexplained reason the proposed inscription was not used, perhaps because the length made it impractical.

both Xavier and at St. John's the two leading vocational choices of the graduates were the priesthood and the law, but the proportions were significantly different. At St. John's 130 (25.1 percent) of the graduates chose the priesthood and almost as many, 124 (23.9 percent), chose the law. At Xavier the comparable figures were more lopsided with 247 (38.06 percent) of the graduates choosing the priesthood and only 93 (14.33 percent) choosing the law. At both colleges medicine was a distant third, attracting 41 (6.32 percent) graduates of Xavier and 48 (9.27 percent) graduates at Fordham.[35]

At Fordham between 1846 and 1891 there were only four years when the

35. *FM*, September–October 1890, 15–19. The statistics for St. John's College are for 1846–90; the statistics for Xavier are for 1847–97. *College of St. Francis Xavier*, 240–58.

college failed to produce vocations to the priesthood, and it produced as many as seven candidates in 1876 and eight candidates in 1886. Moreover, the graduates who entered the seminary included some of the brightest students. They included one-quarter of those who graduated *summa cum laude* and nearly half of those who won the two most prestigious awards, the Biographical Medal, which dates from 1859, and the Hughes Medal, which dates from 1878.[36]

Fin de Siècle

With respect to the enrollment at St. John's College, Archbishop John Hughes proved to be a better prophet than an analyst when he claimed that the college had retrograded after he sold it to the Jesuits in 1845. In the year of his death in 1864, the enrollment stood at 306, more than double the enrollment in 1845, but (except for brief spikes in 1865–66 and again in 1889–92) it did not exceed that number again on a permanent basis until 1900. The enrollment figures include not only the college but also the high school and the grammar school. As was mentioned earlier, Father Campbell was relieved when Archbishop Francesco Satolli, the first apostolic delegate to the United States, canceled a scheduled visit to Rose Hill in 1896 because as the president of St. John's College, he was embarrassed at the small number of college students. In 1903, when the total enrollment at Fordham had grown to 377, only 133 were in the college (98 in the classical course), 204 were in the high school, and 40 were in the grammar school. By that date, 72.3 percent of the students were from the New York area, compared with 45.9 percent in 1862.[37]

Campbell was not alone in deploring the slow growth of the enrollment at Fordham. Father Robert Fulton, the prickly, pompous, and punctilious provincial of the Maryland–New York Province, complained in 1886 in embarrassingly poor English to the local Jesuit superiors that "it would seem that the number of pupils has decreased in no College, has increased in nearly all. But the increase is slight and the numbers are not satisfactory." "Why are not our pupils [*sic*] overflowing," he asked, "and our teaching famous as in some countries?" He offered no solution except to order closer supervision of the schools. "I call for aid," he said, "upon all those who have at heart the greater glory of God."[38]

36. *FM*, June 1892, 188.

37. FUA, Diary of Presidents, 1885–1906, October 17, 1896; FUA, Notanda Collegii; *WL* 32 (1903): addendum; Klein, "Jesuits and Catholic Boyhood," 356, 361.

38. FUA, Provincial Letters, Fulton to Rev. Dear Father, September 27, 1886. Three years after assuming the office of provincial, the insufferably stuffy Fulton told the local

A dozen years later another provincial and former president of St. John's College, Father Thomas J. Gannon, sounded a different note when he expressed his satisfaction with the growth of the nine Jesuit colleges in the Maryland–New York Province, which, according to his calculations, had graduated 6,000 of the 7,500 graduates of the Jesuit colleges in the United States.[39] Of that number Gannon claimed that Fordham could take credit for 669 graduates by 1895 and 777 graduates by 1902. Gannon's concern was that Fordham's relative prosperity might lead to the neglect of the Jesuit vow of poverty. He warned the president, Father George A. Petit, who was also the rector of the Jesuit community, not to allow a well-intentioned minister (the assistant in charge of the Jesuit residence) or others to introduce luxuries that were incompatible with the Jesuit lifestyle as a community of poor men. "The rector is God's champion," he told him, "and chosen guardian of the law in its integrity."[40]

The commercial course had been reinstated at Fordham by Father Campbell in 1897 after it had been dropped in 1892 by Father Gannon, who characterized it as "a demoralizing course which was generally rated as the 'Refuge of Idlers.'" The restored commercial course was a cause of concern to Gannon because it was absorbing so much of the energy of the Jesuit faculty. He urged Father Petit to find a way to limit the Jesuit involvement with the course so that the faculty could give more attention to the classical course. He also urged Father Petit to increase the library budget, and, ever mindful of the old French Jesuit penchant for surveillance, he warned Petit not to increase the number of private rooms until he had a much larger staff to supervise the students properly. When Petit indicated that he wanted to raise the tuition of the day students above the $60 fee

Jesuit superiors that "it may possibly be within your recollection that shortly after entering upon the duties of my present office, I addressed a letter to the superiors of the province" about better observance of the rule. "I do not remember any general direction that was carried out satisfactorily," he said. FUA, Provincial Letters, Fulton to Dear Rev. Father, October 1, 1885. Campbell said that Fulton's "sharp and cutting manner" alienated many Jesuits, including himself. ARSJ, Campbell to Anton Anderledy, the Father General of the Society of Jesus, April 15, 1891.

39. The nine Jesuit colleges were Georgetown, Gonzaga College, Washington, D.C.; St. John's College, Rose Hill; College of St. Francis Xavier; College of the Holy Cross; St. Joseph's College, Philadelphia; Loyola College, Baltimore; Boston College; and St. Peter's College, Jersey City.

40. FUA, Provincial Letters, Gannon to Rev. Dear Father, April 5, 1901; Gannon to Petit, September 16, 1902. Gannon's total of 669 graduates by 1895 is at considerable variance with the total of 518 graduates in 1890 compiled by the editors of the *Fordham Monthly* only five years earlier.

that had been established in 1865, Gannon not only approved the proposal but encouraged him to implement it, noting that the College of St. Francis Xavier had raised its tuition to $100. He feared that parents would think that St. John's College offered an inferior education if it charged less than Xavier. "Boys leave us and go to Columbia, N.Y. University, Harvard, etc. and pay $150 for tuition without a murmur," he observed, "and this higher charge only means for them that they are getting a better article because they are paying more for it."[41]

Although Gannon was more optimistic than the dyspeptic Fulton about the progress of the Jesuit colleges in the northeastern United States, he was disappointed that the five Jesuit colleges in New York and New England had produced so few vocations to the Society of Jesus in comparison with more than 900 vocations to the diocesan clergy. Fordham had a particularly poor track record with only 11 Jesuits compared with 116 diocesan priests among its more than 600 graduates. At the College of the Holy Cross in Worcester the statistics were even more discouraging, with only six Jesuits among the 349 graduates who became priests. Gannon pointed out that Holy Cross had produced not only most of the diocesan clergy but nearly all of the hierarchy of New England as an indication that there had been very little personal advantage for the Jesuits in their educational apostolate.[42]

Gannon oscillated between cheerleader and crèpe hanger. "Courage in the matter of law and medicine," he told Father John J. Collins as Collins launched Fordham's new law school and medical school in the summer of 1905 and transformed St. John's College into a university. "God is with us!" At the same time, Gannon presented such a depressingly bleak picture of the prospects of the Society of Jesus in the Maryland–New York Province that he made Father Fulton seem like an incurable optimist. "Every year the status becomes more exacting and difficult on account of the increasing number of old and sick and partially incapacitated men," he said. "We must have more and better vocations in order that the supply may meet the demand year by year. I possess only a certain number whom I distribute as most equable and best." Like old men everywhere, Gannon was inclined

41. FUA, Notanda Collegii; FUA, Provincial Letters, Gannon to Petit, February 24, 1902; Gannon to Petit, June 4, 1902. The editors of the *Fordham Monthly* counted 130 alumni who were priests or seminarians in 1890. *FM*, September–October 1890, 15–19. Gannon, "St. John's, Fordham, A Classical College," *WL* 23 (1894): 126.

42. FUA, Provincial Letters, Gannon to Rev. Dear Fathers, April 5, 1901. At the time, Gannon was trying to raise funds for a new Jesuit novitiate in New York to replace the one in Frederick, Maryland.

to indulge in fanciful recollections of the good old days. "Sometimes," he confessed, "we older men think that our younger men of today are not quite so ready to tackle a difficulty and work hard to surmount obstacles for God's glory as was commonly done in former days."[43]

Despite the impressive improvements in the physical plant that took place during the later nineteenth century, in 1900 St. John's College remained essentially the small classical college that John Hughes had founded in 1841 and sold to the Society of Jesus four years later. The faculty was composed almost entirely of Jesuits, and, while the living quarters of the college students had been vastly improved with the transition from dormitories to individual rooms, the spiritual atmosphere on campus remained largely intact. The pervasive presence of the Jesuits, the structure and content of the curriculum, the obligation of daily Mass and the annual student retreat, the influence of the sodalities and the disciplinary code of the college all combined to foster an intensely religious culture. While presidents like Thomas Campbell expressed impatience about lagging enrollment, the modest size of the college was a potent factor in helping to preserve its traditional Catholic ethos, as Thomas Gannon implicitly recognized.[44]

During the first dozen years of the twentieth century, St. John's College experienced two major developments that ultimately produced more significant changes than during the previous sixty years. First was the establishment of the first two graduate schools, the Medical School and the Law School in 1905, under Father John J. Collins. This marked the beginning of the transformation of St. John's College to Fordham University. The second major development was the consolidation of St. John's College with the College of St. Francis Xavier in 1912. Despite the chaotic way in which the consolidation took place, it paved the way for the Society of Jesus to concentrate its educational resources on creating one strong Jesuit undergraduate college in the New York metropolitan area.

Expansion brought new luster and prestige to Fordham, but it also presented the double challenge of maintaining Fordham's academic standards as well as its distinctively Jesuit and Catholic identity. Lurking in the background was still another fundamental question about the proper response to the changing nature of higher education in America. Sooner or later Fordham had to decide whether its traditional insistence on the primacy of

43. FUA, Provincial Letters, Gannon to Collins, August 16, 1904.

44. Even in the 1890s the lay professors could not leave the campus without the permission of the prefect of discipline, and they were forbidden to frequent taverns within three miles of the college.

a classical education was adequate to meet the needs of its students when so many of the best colleges in America had decided otherwise. Father John Wynne, ever the irrepressible gadfly, raised an even more basic issue when he questioned whether the education that Jesuit scholastics received in the United States prepared them adequately to be productive scholars and effective teachers in their own colleges and universities.[45]

45. ARSJ, Wynne to Wernz, April 14, 1911.

Et in Arcadia Ego: *The Gilded Age at Rose Hill*

THE END OF THE LITTLE
LIBERAL ARTS COLLEGE

8

Harvard and the Jesuits

Writing in 1941 to commemorate the centennial of Fordham University, Professor Francis X. Connolly, a layman who was a legendary and much-beloved professor of English literature, singled out the otherwise unremarkable presidency of Father George Petit (1900–4) for special mention.[1] He characterized Petit's four years as president at the turn of the twentieth century as the apex of St. John's golden age as a small liberal arts college. He credited him with perfecting a superb classical curriculum based on the *ratio studiorum* that the Jesuits at Fordham had devised and refined during the 1890s. The result, claimed Connolly, was an "educational Utopia" that stood in marked contrast to the elective system that prevailed at Harvard and some of the other more prestigious secular colleges in America. The ratio of students to faculty at Fordham was six to one, almost all of whom were Jesuits. Three-quarters of the students were boarders who lived under a set of rules that had changed little during the previous fifty years and regulated every facet of their life from rising at 6:00 A.M. until lights out at 9:00 P.M.

Connolly waxed eloquent about the esprit de corps that this highly regimented regime promoted. "Students slept in the same dormitory," he noted approvingly, "prayed together, ate together, sat in the same classrooms, shared the same simple recreations, read and discussed the same works, aspired for [*sic*] the same honors and aimed almost universally at the same ideals." Connolly's nostalgic recollections of turn-of-the-century Fordham give a misleading impression of the college's popularity among New York's growing middle-class Catholic population. Many of them hesitated to send their sons to Fordham, or their sons were reluctant to go there, precisely for some of the reasons that Connolly singled out for praise.

1. In a perceptive tribute to Connolly, Father Raymond Schroth, a former student, said that "Connolly looked at literature in the way that Jesuits viewed philosophy, as a guide to life." Raymond A. Schroth, S.J., *Fordham: A History and Memoir* (Chicago: Loyola University Press, 2002), 360.

Two years before Father Petit's appointment as vice president of St. John's College in 1897, Father William Pardow, the provincial of the Maryland–New York Province, wondered why the college could attract only 150 students in a city of 600,000, many of whom were Catholic.[2] The answer was that many Catholic families preferred to send their sons to non-Catholic colleges because those colleges offered better opportunities for professional and social advancement. It came as a great shock to the American Jesuits in 1893 when Harvard Law School published a list of 112 colleges whose graduates they were willing to accept as "regular students" after the academic year 1895–96. Only three Catholic colleges made the list, all of them Jesuit institutions: Georgetown University, Boston College, and the College of the Holy Cross. The University of Notre Dame was added to the list in 1894–95, but Boston College and Holy Cross were dropped in 1897–98. Apparently St. John's College, Fordham, was never even in the running for inclusion, but the cruelest blow for the Jesuits at Rose Hill may have been that Manhattan College, a rival institution conducted by the Christian Brothers in New York City, was added to the list in 1900–1.[3]

The exclusion of Boston College and Holy Cross from the list led to howls of protests from their alumni and complaints from American Jesuits. Charles W. Eliot, the president of Harvard University from 1869 to 1909, disclaimed any anti-Catholic bias and said that the list was based on purely educational criteria. The controversy took another turn when Eliot published an article in the *Atlantic Monthly* in October 1899 in which he criticized Jesuit education. His reference to the Jesuits was brief but pointed and caused great offense. He compared it to the obscurantism of the Moslem system of education based on the Koran and complained that Jesuit education had not changed in 400 years except for some "trifling concessions to natural science." "Nothing but an unhesitating belief in the divine wisdom of such prescriptions can justify them," Eliot declared, "for no human wisdom is equal to contriving a prescribed course of study equally good for even two children of the same family between the ages of eight and eighteen."

Eliot mounted a full-blown explanation and defense of the elective system at Harvard. Citing the immense expansion of knowledge in the nineteenth century and "the increasing sense of the sanctity of the individual's gifts and will-power," Eliot asserted that "we must absolutely give up

2. Pardow to Luis Martín, S.J., November 24, 1895, cit. in Kathleen A. Mahoney, *Catholic Higher Education in Protestant America: The Jesuits and Harvard in the Age of the University* (Baltimore: Johns Hopkins University Press, 2003), 149.

3. Ibid., 251–56.

the notion that any set of human beings, however wise and learned, can ever again construct and enforce on school children one uniform course of study." An earlier generation of American Catholic leaders had feared the influence of dogmatic Protestantism at America's premier colleges and universities. They now considered the liberal Protestantism that Eliot combined with an optimistic Enlightenment faith in science to be an even graver threat to Catholic students on such campuses. As Kathleen Mahoney has remarked, "for Eliot, a Unitarian in religion and a scientist by profession, there was no need to reconcile religion and science. Science itself was religious."[4]

The most effective Jesuit response to Eliot's criticism came from Father Timothy Brosnahan, a former president of Boston College, who published it in the *Sacred Heart Review*, a Jesuit weekly, after the *Atlantic Monthly* refused to accept it on the grounds that it was too controversial. Brosnahan's rebuttal was polite but forceful and witty, laced with ironic comments that gave Eliot a lesson in what the Jesuits meant by *eloquentia perfecta*. He called attention to a number of elementary factual errors that revealed Eliot's superficial knowledge of Jesuit education, such as his misdating of the *ratio studiorum*. He demolished Eliot's contention about the rigidity of Jesuit education by pointing to the fact that, in contrast to seventeenth-century Jesuit colleges where Greek and Latin constituted 100 percent of the curriculum, at Georgetown University nearly half of the class time was devoted to modern studies. As for the primacy of science in the curriculum, Georgetown required a specific number of science courses for a degree whereas at Harvard a student could graduate without ever taking a single science course.[5]

Brosnahan's main argument was the need for a unified and balanced college education and the inability of inexperienced undergraduates to formulate such an educational program for themselves. He sounded like Jonathan Swift when he asked whether "we shall yet witness the exhilarating spectacle of 'tots' of eight or ten years of age gravely electing their courses under the guidance, or rather with the approval[,] of their nurses." He complained that within the previous fifteen years, the elective system

4. Charles W. Eliot, "Recent Changes in Secondary Education," *The Atlantic Monthly* 89 (October 1899), 443. The article was originally a paper read before the American Institute of Instruction on July 10, 1899. Mahoney, *Catholic Higher Education*, 84.

5. For a detailed critique of the *ratio studiorum* and its modifications over the past four centuries, see Allan P. Farrell, S.J., *The Jesuit Code of Liberal Education: The Development and Scope of the "Ratio Studiorum"* (Milwaukee: Bruce Publishing Company, 1938).

had become an educational fetish, but he strengthened his credibility by not rejecting it completely. "There may be a medium," he said hopefully, "between the alternatives of rigid uniformity and extreme 'electivism.'" As a parting shot at Eliot, he opined that he might find it possible to discover this medium "without the immediate and direct interposition of Divine wisdom."[6]

At Fordham, Father Thomas Campbell was more outspoken and less measured than Brosnahan in his reaction to Eliot's criticism. Brosnahan had pointed with pride to the introduction of "modern" subjects at Georgetown, but Campbell mocked the emphasis on science in secular universities and predicted that it would soon reduce them to the level of workshops and destroy all genuine culture. Addressing the alumni of Holy Cross College in 1898, Campbell condemned parents who abandoned Catholic colleges for such institutions and called them "cowards" and "traitors." He gave no indication that he thought there was any need for improvement in Jesuit education. For him a genuine college education was still a classical education, and he bristled at the suggestion that the Jesuits were not even capable of doing that well. "Inability to teach the classics?" he roared. "Why the language of the greater part of the classics is our mother tongue," he assured the Fordham alumni in 1900. "We use it at table, we employ it in conversation, we write our letters in it; it is our official medium for the transaction of business." Campbell failed to mention that, unlike some American Jesuits, when he wrote to the general in Rome he usually wrote in English, not in Latin. As he might have said, *non est mendacium sed mysterium*.[7]

Father George A. Petit, the president of Fordham, boasted the following year that "our curriculum enforces the fundamental studies and forbids the students' energies to be dissipated by needless options. Nor may our boys follow a will-o'-the-wisp electivism with its easier paths and shorter cuts." In the narrow little world of Catholic higher education, Father Henry Brann, an alumnus of the College of St. Francis Xavier and the pastor of St. Agnes Church in Manhattan, went unchallenged when he told the 1900 graduating class at St. Peter's College in Jersey City that a freshman in a Jesuit college was better educated than the average senior at Harvard. Austin O'Malley, a Fordham graduate, class of 1878, and professor at the University of Notre Dame, ascribed the predilection of Catholic students

6. Timothy Brosnahan, S.J., "President Eliot and Jesuit Colleges," in Mahoney, *Catholic Higher Education*, 257–70.

7. *FM*, December 1898, 155; *FM*, February 1897, 88; *FM*, May 1900, 399.

and their parents for secular colleges to three motives, none of them especially altruistic: the lure of wealth, snobbery, and the desire to escape the more rigorous discipline of Catholic colleges.[8]

Some of the harshest criticism of Catholic students at secular colleges came from undergraduates at Fordham, who reflected the views of their Jesuit mentors and perhaps their own suspicions that their education was not all that it was cracked up to be. The editor of the student literary magazine claimed that there was no longer any reason for Catholics to attend non-Catholic schools in view of the large number and high academic quality of Catholic colleges. He undermined his own argument, however, when he conceded that Catholic graduates of prestigious secular colleges were more likely to become leaders in the Catholic community than the graduates of Catholic colleges. He feared that they would "corrupt" the Catholic community because of their "acquired aptitude for presenting fallacies in their most specious garb."[9]

In view of the large number of Catholic students on secular campuses, some American bishops attempted to provide pastoral care for them by establishing Catholic campus centers or Catholic Halls, the forerunners of the Newman Clubs. One bishop said that he reluctantly assigned chaplains to secular colleges for the same reason that he assigned chaplains to prisons—to care for Catholics who were in places where they should not be in the first place. At least one Jesuit educator, Father Francis B. Cassilly, the vice president of St. Ignatius College in Chicago, reluctantly endorsed this initiative to provide Catholic centers at secular colleges, but his fellow Jesuits generally opposed this effort for fear that it would undermine their own colleges. When Bishop Bernard McQuaid of Rochester, one of the most conservative prelates in the United States, considered establishing a Catholic Hall at Cornell, which was located in his diocese, one of the editors of the *Fordham Monthly* expressed his opposition and flaunted his classical learning by saying, "No, we want no Catholic Hall on any alien soil. It is a sop to Cerberus." At the time the college with

8. George A. Petit, "Alma Mater and the Present," *FM*, March 1901, 318; Henry A. Brann, "The Jesuit Colleges and Harvard University," *FM*, July 1900, 546; Austin O'Malley, "Catholic Colleges," *FM*, October 1898, 31–36. Between 1891 and 1896 forty-two students were expelled from Fordham for serious violations of the rules, which Father Schroth considers "evidence of strong resistance to Jesuit education." Schroth, *Fordham: A History and Memoir*, 116.

9. Francis B. Cassilly, S.J., "Catholic Students at State Universities," *The Ecclesiastical Review* 34 (1906): 118; "The Catholic Movement in Non-Catholic Universities," *FM*, January–February 1907, 149.

the largest number of Catholic undergraduates in the United States was Harvard University.[10]

Dissenting Catholic Voices

While the American Jesuits were aggressively defending their colleges and promoting Catholic higher education in a hostile academic environment, some friendly Catholic critics were calling upon them to take a more critical look at the kind of education they were offering to young American Catholics. One of them was a distinguished alumnus of St. John's College, Fordham: John Murphy Farley, the archbishop of New York from 1902 to 1918. Addressing the Catholic Educational Association in New York City in 1905, Farley mentioned with pride the progress that parochial schools had made since the Third Plenary Council of Baltimore in 1884 when the U.S. bishops mandated the establishment of a parochial school in every parish. Farley noted that, in the subsequent two decades, parochial schools had gradually earned the confidence of Catholic parents by constantly improving their academic standards.

However, Farley complained that Catholic colleges had not made similar progress and did not command the same respect as parochial schools in the Catholic community, with the result that many Catholic parents sent their sons to non-Catholic colleges. (They were less likely to send their daughters to non-Catholic colleges.) He looked to the bishops to intervene and to force Catholic educators to make the needed changes. "If the episcopate could legislate," he said, "and could insist on the raising of standards all along the line, we believe the colleges would win the confidence of the people as the [parochial] schools have succeeded in doing."

Years earlier, presiding at a Fordham graduation, Farley risked the ire of his Jesuit hosts by assuring the students in the commercial course that they should not feel one bit inferior to their classmates in the classical course. He probably antagonized the Jesuits even more when he declared, "Our only possible course is to be honest and candid, to sacrifice tradition and prejudice as long as Catholic principle is not infringed." It must have been a shock for a dyed-in-the-wool traditionalist like Father Thomas Campbell to hear the archbishop of New York sound like the president of Harvard when he said, "We are in an age of transition, and we must alter our ways of doing things."[11]

10. "The Greater Universities," *FM*, June 1907, 369. Mahoney, *Catholic Higher Education*, 103.

11. *New York Times*, July 12, 1905. In that same year Farley sanctioned the establishment at his diocesan seminary of *The New York Review*, the most scholarly and progres-

Professor Austin O'Malley, an ardent defender of Catholic higher education, anticipated by almost sixty years Monsignor John Tracy Ellis's famous criticism of the proliferation of small and weak American Catholic colleges. O'Malley thought that, of the eighty Catholic colleges listed in the *Catholic Directory*, only a handful were first-class and another twenty were "good." The only three that he singled out for favorable attention were the Catholic University of America, Georgetown, and Notre Dame. "We spend enough money to pay the running expenses of a good college in every state of the Republic," he complained, "and what are we getting for this money? We might have and should have universities like the [*sic*] Pennsylvania or Harvard or Yale." O'Malley had little sympathy with those who cited the poverty of the American Catholic community as a reason for the poor performance of American Catholic colleges. "We complain about the scantiness of our resources," he said, "while we are throwing millions of dollars into holes in the ground."[12]

Another friendly critic of American Catholic and especially Jesuit higher education was one of their own—one of "Ours," they would have called him—Father John Wynne. A born maverick who was a thorn in the side of every superior he ever had, Wynne exemplified the mystifying Jesuit paradox of being able to produce, tolerate, and sometimes profit from nonconformists within their own supposedly monolithic ranks thanks to superiors who recognized the fundamental loyalty of these critics to the Society of Jesus and to the Catholic Church.

Father Wynne was one of these classic and talented Jesuit mavericks. A native New Yorker, born in 1859 and a graduate of the College of St. Francis Xavier, Wynne was the editor of the *Messenger of the Sacred Heart* from 1892 until 1909, when he founded *America*, the national Jesuit weekly. He was eased out of that position within a year because of alleged financial incompetence, but he played an indispensable role as one of the editors of the *Catholic Encyclopedia*, a massive sixteen-volume work that appeared between 1907 and 1914 and was a major scholarly achievement for Ameri-

---

sive Catholic theological journal in the United States, although he dropped it like a hot potato three years later after complaints from Rome. Thomas J. Shelley, "John Cardinal Farley and Modernism in New York," *CH* 61 (1992): 350–61. A dozen years earlier, as provincial Father Campbell forbade Jesuits at Fordham even to mention the Americanist controversy that was dividing the leaders of the American Catholic Church. FUA, Memoriale Visitationum Provincialis, February 10, 1893.

12. Austin O'Malley, "Catholic Collegiate Education in the United States," *Catholic World* 67 (1898): 293, 304.

Father John Wynne, S.J., wore many hats in the Society of Jesus, including this Indian headdress, a gift from the Mohawk Nation for his efforts to promote the canonization of Kateri Tekakwitha. (Courtesy Archives of the Archdiocese of New York)

can Catholics at a time when they were still largely a working-class immigrant community.

As an editor of the *Catholic Encyclopedia*, Wynne complained that he could find only two American Jesuits who were qualified to contribute articles to the *Encyclopedia*, Father Anthony Maas and Father Walter Drum, both Scripture scholars.[13] Wynne attributed the poor showing of his fellow Jesuits not to any inferior intellectual ability but to the educational system in which they were trained, at least in the Maryland–New York Province. At Woodstock, the Jesuit theological seminary in Maryland, Wynne claimed, inexperienced professors were appointed to the faculty without any op-

13. Maas emigrated from Germany to America in 1877 at the age of nineteen; Drum grew up at U.S. Army posts all across the country. *WL* 58 (1929): 408–23; 51 (1922); 122–31. Both were theological troglodytes. "Maas carried his typology to absurdity," said Gerald Fogarty. Drum was an avid heresy hunter during the Modernist Crisis and may even have been a member of the Sodalitium Pianum, the notorious Integralist secret society. Gerald P. Fogarty, S.J., *American Catholic Biblical Scholarship* (San Francisco: Harper & Row, 1989), 42, 181.

portunity to improve their mastery of the subjects they taught. "Like begets like," said Wynne, with the result that in Jesuit colleges the members of the faculty were shifted from teaching one subject to another at the whim of rectors and prefects of studies who were not scholars themselves and had no appreciation of scholarship. "We have no high or fixed standard of studies," Wynne lamented.

Even when it came to employing editorial and clerical help for the *Catholic Encyclopedia*, Wynne preferred to hire young women from the schools of Religious of the Sacred Heart rather than the graduates of Jesuit colleges because he found that the young women were better educated. He heard similar complaints from the rectors of diocesan seminaries about the alleged shortcomings of graduates of Jesuit colleges who had applied for admission to their institutions. "It is no wonder," Wynne told the general, "that parents send their sons to secular colleges." He cited the example of two of his fellow editors of the *Catholic Encyclopedia*, Charles Herbermann and Condé Pallen, whom he described as "the pride of Xavier and Georgetown." "[They] have lost faith in our education," Wynne said. "Each has a son at Columbia."[14] Although Father Wynne gave heartburn to more than one superior, he was a well-informed and well-intentioned gadfly who urged his superiors and confrères to take a more critical look at the caliber of the colleges they were operating and at the educational standards in their own seminaries.[15]

Fordham During the Great War

When St. John's College, Fordham, celebrated its seventy-fifth anniversary in September 1916, most of Europe had been engulfed in war for a full two years with a loss of life on a scale unprecedented in the history of modern warfare. On the western front millions of soldiers faced one an-

14. ARSJ, Wynne to Wernz, April 14, 1911. "The local superiors told me there was no way of managing Fr. Wynne," the frustrated provincial of the Maryland–New York province told the general shortly after Wynne sent his bombshell letter to Rome. ARSJ, Joseph Hanselman to Wernz, August 13, 1911. Father Albert J. Loomie, S.J., professor of history at Fordham for many years, said: "The biography of John Wynne must inevitably be written if American ecclesiastic history is to record a true picture of the Church during his lifetime." *WL* 80 (1951): 66.

15. Wynne was especially critical of Father Thomas Gannon for failure to encourage scholarship when he was the provincial of the Maryland–New York province. The criticism was unfair. Gannon actually shared Wynne's views about the shortcomings of American Jesuit scholarship and urged the establishment of a single scholasticate for the whole United States. "No men of eminence are found among the professors in our scholasticates," he lamented. ARSJ, Gannon to Wernz, n.d. [1906–?].

other across trenches that stretched for more than 300 miles from the North Sea to Switzerland. In those days, St. John's Day, June 24, was always the occasion for a major celebration at Fordham. In 1916 the wide Atlantic still isolated America from the carnage in Europe, and that year the festivities at Rose Hill took place as usual. A week later, on July 1, the British army launched a major offensive against the Germans on the Somme River that cost them 60,000 casualties in the space of a few hours. In November President Woodrow Wilson won reelection with a pledge to keep America out of the war, but the German decision to resume their policy of unrestricted submarine warfare at the beginning of 1917 pulled the United States into the conflict and resulted in America's declaration of war on April 6, 1917.

The entry of the United States into the conflict unleashed a wave of patriotic fervor and hysterical fear of German Americans who hitherto had been regarded as the ideal immigrants. The pulpits of Protestant America rang with denunciations of the *boche* and stirring endorsements of the war as a divinely sanctioned crusade. Not since the Civil War had clergymen been so sure that they knew the mind of the Almighty and that God was on their side. Few had the humility to say, as President Abraham Lincoln once did, that they hoped they were on God's side. Both conservative and liberal Protestant clergy outdid one another in blessing the war and calling for wholehearted support of President Wilson.[16]

One curious and unexpected side effect of America's entry into the war for American Catholics was that Nativist fear of the pope, which had enjoyed one of its periodic revivals in the first decade of the twentieth century, suddenly abated and switched to fear of the kaiser. Prior to April 1917, for obvious reasons, neither of the two largest ethnic groups in the American Catholic community, the Irish and the Germans, showed much enthusiasm for abandoning a policy of neutrality. However, America's entry into the war led to an abrupt change in attitude on the part of American Catholics as they rallied to their country's call. Conscious that many Americans still doubted the loyalty of their Catholic fellow citizens, the U.S. bishops made strenuous efforts to voice support for the war and vied with American Protestant leaders in attributing divine approval to America's intervention in the conflict.

Cardinal Farley (he received the red hat in 1911) was relatively restrained.

16. "The simple fact is," wrote Sydney E. Ahlstrom, "that religious leaders—lay and clerical, Jewish, Catholic and Protestant—through corporate as well as personal expressions lifted their voices in a chorus of support for the war." Sydney A. Ahlstrom, *A Religious History of the American People* (New Haven, Conn.: Yale University Press, 1972), 884.

The End of the Little Liberal Arts College

He said, "We have never been found wanting in any crisis in our history." Characteristically, William Cardinal O'Connell of Boston went further. Without revealing his sources, he declared that "the spirit of God is working through Woodrow Wilson." James Cardinal Gibbons of Baltimore, the ranking American Catholic prelate, broadened the divine mandate to include the legislative branch of the federal government. "The members of both Houses of Congress are the instruments of God in guiding us in our civic duties," he declared.[17]

At Fordham both faculty and students were outspoken in professing their patriotism. The editors of the *Fordham Monthly*, in an open letter to President Wilson, declared that "in this dark hour of trial the sons of Fordham, past and present, are enlisted in your support to the last man." With a naïveté that evokes incomprehension among young people a century later, they told Wilson, "Command us. We are absolutely yours, for we hear in your voice the command of the Almighty." The students were only echoing the sentiments of the president of the university, Father Joseph A. Mulry, who traveled throughout the country urging American Catholics to support the war. He outdid even Cardinal O'Connell in ascribing divine guidance to the White House. "When the call came from Washington for men and arms," said Mulry, "it was as though God Himself stood in my presence and said: 'I, Myself, call you to war.'"[18]

In the Cathedral of Saints Peter and Paul in Philadelphia, Mulry prayed to the "God of Battles" and assured a congregation of several thousand people that "this war will purify the soul of the nation." Mulry was very much the priest as well as the patriot. One of the best preachers in the Maryland–New York Province, he conducted a retreat for 2,000 recruits at Fort Dix in New Jersey at which he warned them in fire-and-brimstone sermons to avoid profanity, drunkenness, and sexual misbehavior.

He returned to Fort Dix in May 1918 to preach at a military Mass celebrated by auxiliary bishop Patrick Hayes of New York, the newly appointed bishop for the armed forces. On this occasion, in the presence of 15,000 soldiers and their families and friends, the patriot swamped the priest in the pulpit. "I have no patience with the pacifists and conscientious objectors who too often throw over their selfish cowardice the cloak of religious principles," he said. He need not have worried. Only

17. Elizabeth McKeown, *War and Welfare: American Catholics and World War I* (New York and London: Garland Publishing Company, 1988), 48–49; James Hennesey, S.J., *American Catholics: A History of the Roman Catholic Community in the United States* (New York: Oxford University Press, 1981), 225.

18. *FM*, April 1917, 363–64, February, 1918, 4.

four Catholics were among the 3,989 conscientious objectors in World War I. Mulry told the newly minted soldiers, "Go over there and take the trenches that your brothers are holding for you. Victory will come." At a time when Pope Benedict XV was urging the war-weary nations of Europe to negotiate a compromise peace, Mulry preferred to quote the words of another pontiff, Urban II, on the occasion of launching the First Crusade. "God wills it," Mulry thundered. At least one young soldier got the historical allusion from Mulry's preaching at Fort Dix. "He makes us feel like the Crusaders of old," he said.[19]

One Fordham alumnus who appreciated Mulry's rhetoric was Dr. James J. Walsh, the former dean of the Medical School. He told Mulry that, when he first came to Fordham as a student forty years earlier, the memory of the Fordham alumni who served in the Civil War was very much alive. Even before the entry of the United States into the Great War, Walsh expressed confidence that Fordham students and alumni "shall nobly follow in the footsteps of old Fordham men and place new standards of bravery and patriotic heroism for the generations to come."[20]

Mulry himself could never be accused of being an armchair patriot. With the encouragement of Bishop Hayes, he requested permission from the Jesuit general to visit the Fordham alumni in France but apparently failed to receive an answer. One of the reasons for Mulry's request was to refute allegations that American Catholics, and especially American Jesuits, were not genuine patriots. That same concern may explain some of his more bellicose statements in promoting American participation in the war and his scathing comments about those who did not share his views.[21]

Fordham's most impressive collective contribution to the war effort was the formation of the Fordham University Overseas Ambulance Company, which consisted of 127 volunteers who were sworn into the army on June 14, 1917, under the command of Captain Joseph E. Donnelly, a professor at the Medical School. When the Red Cross ran short of funds, two Fordham alumni, Joseph and Arthur McAleenan, stepped in and donated $13,000

19. *Ram*, February 7, April 25, May 17, 1918. Hennesey, *American Catholics*, 225. Professor Shailer Mathews of the Divinity School of the University of Chicago, a leading liberal American Protestant theologian, echoed Mulry's sentiments when he said that "for an American to refuse to share in the present war . . . is not Christian." Ahlstrom, *Religious History of the American People*, 885.

20. FUA, Mulry Papers, Walsh to Mulry, December 21, 1917. Five years after he resigned as dean, Walsh was still using the stationery of the Medical School in his personal correspondence.

21. ARSJ, Mulry to Ledóchowski, January 18, 1918.

to equip four ambulances. The Fordham Ambulance Company, or the Fordham Ambulance Corps, as it was usually called, sailed for France on August 23 and was assigned to assist the French army in the evacuation of their wounded troops. The following April, from "somewhere in France," Donnelly assured Father Mulry that the Fordham Ambulance Corps had acquired a sterling reputation. At the end of the war, 46 members of the unit received the *Croix de Guerre* from a grateful French government.[22]

After a visit to Washington in August 1918, Mulry said that the War Department intended to have every able-bodied young man between the ages of eighteen and twenty-one in France by July 1919. As a result, it was clear to him that Fordham would have to suspend its B.A. program for the duration of the war.[23] In the summer of 1918 Congress passed legislation creating the Students' Army Training Corps (SATC), which established military training programs on participating college campuses. Fordham was one of the first colleges to volunteer. On October 1, students over eighteen years of age were inducted into the U.S. army as privates at a salary of $30 per month. Fordham received $1 a day for each student in compensation for room and board. The War Department practically took control of the campus and redesigned the curriculum to fit its needs. Greek and Latin were dropped in favor of more practical courses such as War Aims, Military English, navigation, surveying, radio theory, and code practice. When not in class, the students were expected to devote their time to calisthenics, drill practice, and bayonet practice. Two residential buildings were converted into barracks and the old gym became a mess hall.

On All Souls' Day in 1918, Bishop Patrick Hayes presided and preached at a military Mass that was attended by two French prelates, Bishop Eugene Julien of Arras and Monsignor Alfred Baudrillart, the rector of the Institut Catholique in Paris. Both received honorary doctorates at the academic convocation that followed the Mass. Nine days later, "at the eleventh hour of the eleventh day of the eleventh month of the year," in the often-quoted phrase, the armistice was signed in France and the guns fell silent after the final German offensive ground to a halt. On December 1, only two months after it began, the SATC program was terminated at Fordham and the campus returned to more peaceful pursuits.

A century later it is impossible to establish with certainty the total number of Fordham students and alumni who served in the "Great War,"

22. Donnelly to Mulry, April 4, 1918, *FM*, May 1918, 481; Robert I. Gannon, *Up to the Present: The Story of Fordham* (Garden City, N.Y.: Doubleday and Company, 1967), 150–51.

23. FUA, Acta Consultorum, August 1918.

as it was called until 1939, although Mulry tried to compile a comprehensive list. According to Father Robert I. Gannon, 1,529 alumni were in the service of their country by June 1918, when the first American troops arrived in France. Thirty-six of them made the supreme sacrifice. They were commemorated after the war with the Memorial Gateway at the Third Avenue entrance to the university. It was designed by Major William F. Deegan, an alumnus who was also an architect. Thousands turned out for the dedication of the Memorial on Armistice Sunday in 1920 at an outdoor ceremony that blended both religious and military elements. Father Joseph A. McCaffrey, an alumnus of the class of 1911 and chaplain of the Second Division of the American Expeditionary Force, delivered the principal address, to which Father Edward P. Tivnan, S.J., the president of Fordham, responded. Another Fordham alumnus, Monsignor Joseph J. Mooney, the vicar general of the archdiocese of New York, blessed the Memorial in the absence of Archbishop Hayes. Among the military dignitaries who were present was Colonel John J. Phelan of the New York 69th Regiment of the 165th Rainbow Division, in which many of the Fordham alumni had served during the war.[24]

Memories of the war lingered on the Rose Hill campus long after the end of the conflict, as they did throughout the country as Americans continued to celebrate their heroes and honor their dead. In June 1919 Fordham awarded an honorary degree to Father Francis P. Duffy, a New York diocesan priest and an alumnus of the College of St. Francis Xavier, who became the best-known American chaplain in World War I through his service with the New York 69th Regiment. On October 8, Fordham received a visit from the heroic primate of Belgium, Désiré Joseph Cardinal Mercier, who had won worldwide fame for his courageous leadership during the German occupation of his country and his vigorous protests against the forcible deportation of Belgian workers to Germany.[25]

On November 20, 1921, Fordham pulled out all the stops to honor Marshal Ferdinand Foch, the Supreme Allied Commander in the final months of World War I, and to confer on him an honorary degree of Doctor of

24. FUA, Mulry Papers, Mulry to Dear Friend, November 1, 1917; Gannon, *Up to the Present*, 151, 155; *Ram*, November 22, 1920; http://armyrotc.com/edu/fordham/history .htm. The *Ram* published the names and units of the deceased on November 8, 1920. Father Robert I. Gannon's tally of Fordham's contribution to the U.S. Army included three major generals, two colonels, one lieutenant colonel, four majors, twenty captains, about 140 lieutenants, and ten chaplains, but unfortunately he provided no documentation. Gannon, *Up to the Present*, 155.

25. *FM*, June 1919, 347, October, 1919.

Laws. Admission to the campus was by ticket only. Children from parochial schools and Jesuit high schools lined the path from the Memorial
Gateway to the auditorium where the formal ceremony took place. Numer-
ous military units and veterans' organizations were present, including the
band of the 69th Regiment; representatives of the Fordham Ambulance
Corps; the American Legion; the Veterans of Foreign Wars; and even griz-
zled Civil War veterans from two posts of the Grand Army of the Republic.
The degree was conferred in a ceremony presided over by Archbishop
Hayes, who had succeeded Cardinal Farley as the fifth archbishop of New
York on March 10, 1919.

Foch was a devout Catholic, the brother of a Jesuit priest and an alumnus of the Jesuit college of St. Clément in Metz. He rose to the top of his
profession despite the rabid anticlericalism of many of the leaders of the
French Third Republic, including the wartime premier Georges Clem-
enceau, who once said that "the only thing worse than a bad priest is a
good priest." Father Tivnan greeted Marshal Foch as "one of our own
boys" from a sister college. In a brief address in French at the end of the
ceremony, Foch expressed his gratitude to Fordham and his debt to his
Jesuit professors at St. Clément. "I did not come here to speak my own
praises," he said, "but to pay a tribute of praise to those who have been my
teachers and to tell them my gratitude." The final words of the seventy-

On November 20, 1921, Marshal Ferdinand Foch, the Supreme Allied Commander at the end of World War I, received an honorary Fordham doctorate from Father Edward P. Tivnan, S.J., in an elaborate ceremony presided over by Archbishop Patrick J. Hayes.

year-old marshal, who was the most famous soldier in the world at the time, were directed at the students. "There is much that I might say in detail as I call to memory the past," he added, "but my hope for the future is in you young men."[26]

The Greater Fordham Campaign

Father Robert I. Gannon added one other person to the honor roll of Fordham's World War I dead. He believed that Father Joseph Mulry deserved to be included in that list because his patriotic activities during the war had contributed to the deterioration of his health and forced him to

26. "Reception to Marshal Foch," *FM*, December 1921, 172–78. When Foch returned to St. Clément's for a reception after the war, he said modestly about his own contribution to the Allied victory, "I did what I could."

resign as president in January 1919. He died on August 31, 1921, just three months before the reception for Marshal Foch at Rose Hill, an event that he would have attended with unbounded enthusiasm. Mulry's successor was Father Edward P. Tivnan, a thirty-seven-year-old New Englander (a native of Salem, Massachusetts) with a doctorate in chemistry from Georgetown University. Tivnan was the youngest Jesuit president of Fordham since the appointment of Father Thomas J. Campbell in 1885 and the first Jesuit president with a background in science since the appointment of Father Augustus Thébaud in 1846. Unlike Thébaud, however, Tivnan regarded science as a positive and indispensable component in the curriculum of a Jesuit college.

For better or for worse, by 1919 Fordham was no longer the little residential liberal arts college that Professor Connolly remembered with affection. It was now a university with a College of Pharmacy and Graduate Schools of Medicine and Law as well as three other embryonic graduate schools that would quickly develop into Schools of Arts and Sciences, Social Service, and Education. However, the undergraduate school, St. John's College, remained the heart of the Jesuit enterprise at Rose Hill, and Tivnan gave top priority to expanding and enhancing the physical facilities of the college.

Tivnan proposed a joint fundraising campaign with Georgetown and Holy Cross with a goal of $10 million. When that proved to be impracticable, he scaled back his plans and decided that Fordham would conduct its own fundraising campaign with a goal of $1,900,000. In 1905 Father Collins had called upon the alumni to raise $1 million, but his appeal quickly fizzled with few tangible results. Conscious of both Collins's abortive effort and the notoriously stingy financial support from the alumni over the previous fifty years, Tivnan hired a professional fundraising firm to conduct the first systematically organized campaign in Fordham's history.[27]

Perhaps Tivnan's hopes were buoyed by the success of the New York Catholic War Fund in the archdiocese of New York in the spring of 1918. Cardinal Farley hoped to collect $2,500,000 from this campaign, and he received almost double that amount, $4,962,424, the equivalent of $6.50 from each Catholic, although a quarter of the contributions came from non-Catholics. Tivnan's optimism for the success of the Fordham fund drive was also based on the fact that Canisius College in Buffalo, a Jesuit

27. FUA, Acta Consultorum, May 3, June 5, 1920. The consultors agreed unanimously that none of the funds should be used to prolong the life of the faltering Medical School.

college in a smaller city with fewer alumni, had recently conducted a successful fundraising campaign that brought in a million dollars.[28]

Tivnan worked closely with the archdiocese in launching the campaign, which began with a dinner (they were still called banquets) at the Waldorf Astoria in honor of Archbishop Hayes on November 27, 1920. The centerpiece of the campaign, and the bait for the archdiocese's participation, was the erection of a new building to be called the Cardinal Farley Memorial Hall in honor of Hayes's predecessor and Fordham alumnus. The notoriously parsimonious Hayes poked fun at himself, perhaps unconsciously, when he declared at the dinner, "I know that I am picking my own pocket in coming here, but I am willing for them to take all that I have and more if I have it." He issued an open letter to the priests and laity of the archdiocese urging them to support the campaign. It was read from the pulpit of every parish church at Mass on Sunday. Governor Alfred E. Smith, whose own education was limited to the St. James parochial school on the Lower East Side of Manhattan, wondered why the wealthy archdiocese of New York could not support a single Catholic university and asked whether Catholic higher education "was to be the privilege of the few or the opportunity of the many."[29]

The general chairman of the campaign was the ever-faithful Morgan J. O'Brien, now a retired presiding justice of the New York Court of Appeals. The General Sponsoring Committee, which consisted of more than one hundred members, included virtually every prominent Catholic in New York City. The local Irish Catholic political establishment was well represented. Both Governor Smith and New York City Mayor John Hylan lent their endorsement to the campaign, as did former Governor Martin H. Glynn, a Fordham alumnus (and the first Catholic governor of New York since Thomas Dongan in the 1680s), who served as the chair of the upstate committee. Congressman W. Bourke Cockran and Charles F. Murphy, the leader of Tammany Hall, added their names to the list.

The two wealthiest Catholics in New York, Thomas Fortune Ryan and Nicholas F. Brady, agreed to serve on the Sponsoring Committee, as did Brady's brother-in-law, Francis P. Garvan. Adrian Iselin, James Butler, Henry Heide Jr., William D. Guthrie, Major General John F. O'Ryan, Peter Doelger, Louis J. Ehert, and John G. Agar, who had been the lay

28. ACUA, National Catholic War Council, Committee on Special Activities, Report of John C. Agar, April 2, 1918; Report to Cardinal Farley, May 1918. FUA, Tivnan Papers, Meeting of the Executive Committee of the Greater Fordham Campaign, October 14, 1920.

29. *Ram*, December 20, 1920.

chairman of the New York Catholic War Fund, were also members of the committee. Among the prominent non-Catholics were Nicholas Murray Butler, the president of Columbia University; Bird S. Coler; Otto H. Kahn; and Charles W. Schwab. The committee singled out John D. Rockefeller Jr., J. P. Morgan, Mrs. Andrew Carnegie, and Alfred H. Smith, the president of the New York Central Railroad, as "special prospects," but it is not clear if they received anything from them. In the immediate postwar years recommendations from generals were highly prized, and Brigadier General Clarence R. Edwards, once the commandant of the Fordham cadets, provided a glowing tribute. "The Jesuits know how to make men, real men," he said. "Their contribution to America is a great one and deserves the commendation of every citizen regardless of his religious beliefs."[30]

Fordham appealed to its alumni not only for money but also for 2,000 volunteers to collect the anticipated avalanche of contributions. In the campaign literature Father Tivnan emphasized the need for Fordham to expand its undergraduate facilities to meet the increasing number of applicants. The previous year he had been forced to turn away 225 applicants because of lack of space. He also mentioned that the success of the campaign was crucial to the survival of the fledgling graduate schools. Morgan O'Brien claimed that every year 4,000 young Catholic men and women in New York City applied for admission to graduate schools. "Shall they be forced to go to non-Catholic schools?" he asked. The goal of the campaign was $1,900,000, which was to be used for a new dormitory, new science building, library, administration building, gymnasium, and the creation of an endowment.[31]

The Greater Fordham Campaign began on January 15, 1921, and was to close on January 31. The expectation was that Fordham would raise $1 million in those two weeks and that the rest of the contributions would follow in subsequent months. The campaign got off to a flying start, with pledges of $163,000 on the first day, but it quickly ground to a halt. Nine months later Tivnan reported total pledges of $393,000 but only $197,000 in cash. Expenses amounted to $75,000. In February 1922, a year after the beginning of the campaign, a shaken Father Tivnan reported to the alumni that the net result after deducting expenses was a disappointing total of $157,000. Edward P. Gilleran, an alumnus of the class of 1913, took charge of the campaign after the professional fundraisers were fired. He too was

30. FUA, Greater Fordham Campaign, General Sponsoring Committee, press release.

31. FUA, Greater Fordham Campaign, O'Brien to Reverend Dear Father, December 20, 1920.

quickly disappointed with the results. "Some fellows seem to think," he reported to the alumni, "that they will be relieved of their valuables if they attend a Fordham function." One alumnus, Father Francis J. Spellman of class of 1911, a priest of the archdiocese of Boston, who was busy climbing the greasy pole of ecclesiastical preferment, pledged $100, but he had come through with only $25 in cash by May.[32]

It was a bitter blow to Tivnan that not only Canisius but also Holy Cross and Georgetown conducted successful fundraising campaigns while Fordham's campaign was an embarrassing failure. He was particularly disappointed in the poor response from wealthy New York Catholics. Fewer than twenty of them pledged $1,000 or more. John Hassard, a loyal alumnus and an inveterate critic of the stinginess of his fellow alumni, would not have been surprised. Neither was Father Joseph O'Hare, Fordham's president, sixty years later. Reflecting on Tivnan's experience, he thought that Fordham's poor showing in comparison with other Jesuit institutions in the 1920s had a "familiar ring."[33]

A major factor in the failure of the campaign may well have been the unhappiness of many of the alumni with the languishing state of varsity football at Fordham. Despite its modest size, Fordham had become a powerhouse on the local scene and had developed a loyal and enthusiastic following among the alumni. However, in 1910 Fordham dropped varsity football for a full two years after the most successful season in its history, and it dropped varsity football again in 1919 over a dispute about hiring a new head coach. "It is not merely the absence of a team for the present year that causes disappointment," declared the student editors of the *Fordham Monthly*. "The prospect of lean years to follow is perhaps an even more serious consideration."[34]

The Roaring Twenties

Despite the failure of the Greater Fordham Campaign, the 1920s were boom years for Fordham. The university could boast of a rapidly expanding enrollment on both the undergraduate and graduate levels and an impressive building program at Rose Hill. There was still no endowment, and the money came from tuition and from judicious investments by

32. FUA, Greater Fordham Campaign, Tivnan and O'Brien, Confidential Report, January 1921; Gilleran to Dear Fellow Fordhamites, December 1, 1920; unidentified author to Tivnan, May 25, 1921; Gannon, *Up to the Present*, 166.

33. FUA, Greater Fordham Campaign, Tivnan to Daniel G. Reid, August 18, 1921; Joseph O'Hare to John C. Walton, April 2, 2001.

34. *FM*, October 1919; Gannon, *Up to the Present*, 167–68.

the treasurer, Father Joseph Keating, whose luck did not run out until the end of the decade. Like much of the prosperity of that decade, however, Fordham's success rested on fragile foundations, especially in the graduate schools, where (with the exception of the Law School) all the members of faculty were part-time teachers. Their salaries were determined by the number of courses they taught, and administrators quickly dropped courses that did not generate a profit "Where classes are large, student fees adequate, salaries reasonable, and administration competent," said Father Robert Gannon years later, "tuition goes a long, long way."

No one knew better than Gannon that Fordham was flirting with disaster in the 1920s by expanding the graduate schools at breakneck speed without adequate physical facilities or the necessary financial resources. In an age when American higher education was becoming more professional than ever before, regional academic accrediting agencies were looking with increasing skepticism on mushrooming universities like Fordham. Disaster was to strike in 1935, when the Association of American Universities dropped Fordham from its list of approved institutions. Father Gannon, who was recruited from St. Peter's College in Jersey City to repair the damage and rebuild Fordham's shattered reputation, opined years later that he never regarded an expanding enrollment as evidence of success.[35]

By the late twenties Fordham included not only the campus at Rose Hill but also a Downtown Division located in the Woolworth Building in lower Manhattan that contained an undergraduate college as well as the graduate schools. For a brief period there were also satellite centers located in Manhattan, Westchester County, and New Jersey. However, the major changes in the infrastructure of Fordham University during the interwar years occurred at the Rose Hill campus, where no fewer than eight new buildings of various sizes, shapes, and purposes were erected between 1922 and 1930. All were designed in a handsome collegiate Gothic style that represented a mellowing and refinement of the rather stark style of the blue granite and marble Gothic buildings erected in the later nineteenth century.

The first two new buildings had no direct connection with the university. The first was located at the corner of Fordham Road and Bathgate Avenue and housed the printing plant of the popular Jesuit magazine the *Messenger of the Sacred Heart.* Shortly thereafter an adjacent residence was built for the Jesuit staff of the magazine with an entrance on Fordham Road. The connection between the printing plant and the university was strengthened when it became the site of Fordham University Press after

---

35. Gannon, *Up to the Present*, 173, 174, 214.

James J. Walsh, M.D., graciously surrendered his ownership of the title to the university in 1907, when the Press was established. Today the building, much altered and expanded, is Murray-Weigel Hall, an infirmary for Jesuits of the Northeast Province. The former staff house of the *Messenger*, Kohlmann Hall, is a residence for the Fordham Jesuit faculty.[36]

For most of the twentieth century Fordham University Press led a precarious existence, sustained by periodic but short-lived revivals. A major change occurred with the appointment of Helen Tartar as editorial director in 2003. Under her leadership the Press published more than 650 books before her tragic death in an automobile accident in 2014. She also expanded the scope of the Press's publications from its traditional emphasis on philosophy and theology to include interdisciplinary studies, especially in such areas such as anthropology, literary studies, and political theory. "Helen was one of the most passionate and dedicated editors in the academic publishing field," said Fredric Nachbaur, who became director of the Press in 2009 and has continued, with new editorial director Richard W. Morrison, Tartar's commitment to quality academic publishing. In 2015 Fordham University Press published some 100 books and could boast of a backlist of approximately 700 titles.

If Father Tivnan had been able to follow his heart's desire, the first new collegiate building at Rose Hill would have been a badly needed new library. He opted instead for a gymnasium in response to student demands and for fear that, without an adequate gymnasium, Fordham would lose many promising applicants to other colleges, both Catholic and non-Catholic. "One of our greatest needs is a thoroughly equipped gymnasium," Tivnan told the alumni in December 1920 as he was launching the Greater Fordham Campaign, "and I am not going to rest until I see a building of that kind erected at Fordham."[37]

Construction of the gymnasium began during the summer of 1923 and the building was dedicated on January 16, 1925. No fewer than 2,500 people turned out for the dedication, which was followed by a basketball game at which 1,600 fans saw Fordham defeat Boston College (Tivnan's alma mater) by 46 to 16. The new gymnasium was one of the largest college gymnasiums in the country, with 24,000 square feet of unobstructed floor space, larger than the gyms at Princeton, the University of Pennsylvania, or the Catholic University of America. The track team was able to run ten laps to the mile, and there was even a separate boxing room and a wrestling

36. Ibid., 172.
37. *FM*, December 1920, 173.

The "new"
gymnasium,
dedicated on
January 16,
1925. At the
time it was
one of the
largest college
gymnasiums
in the United
States.

room. The spectators' gallery had room for 1,100 people. The basement contained a swimming pool, 70 feet long by 30 feet wide, with its own spectators' gallery.[38]

Excavation for the new library was begun shortly after the gym was dedicated, and six months later, on June 11, 1925, the cornerstone was blessed. It was the first of five buildings erected by Father William Duane, although for the library he adhered closely to the plans designed by Father Tivnan. It replaced a cramped wing at the center of the Administration Building that was one of the last remaining nineteenth-century additions to that building. Constructed in the collegiate Gothic style that Fordham favored in the 1920s and 1930s, the library was the most richly ornamented of all the new buildings erected in that era.

The main entrance was on the second floor through a stone porch and the vaulted vestibule of an 80-foot central tower that led to the main Reading Room or Great Hall in the center of the building. This was a spectacular chamber 47 feet high, 36 feet wide, and 79 feet long, with a ceiling of antique oak and timbered arches and walls with high mullioned glass windows. The west wall featured a mural of the missionary labors of St. Isaac Jogues in upstate New York. The interior walls were finished with natural

38. *FM*, June 1923, 591–92; *Ram*, January 16, 23, 1925. The gymnasium cost upward of $400,000. ARSJ, Keating to Ledóchowski, January 5, 1924.

Duane Library, which was opened in 1926 and was built in the collegiate Gothic style favored at Fordham in that era. It was named after Father William J. Duane, S.J., president of Fordham University, 1924–30.

limestone and nine-foot-high oak paneling. The whole structure was fireproof and contained sufficient room for 150,000 volumes. The north and south wings were deliberately designed in such a way that they could be expanded to meet future demands for more space. The additions were never built, but three tastefully designed metal galleries were later added to the side walls of the Great Hall. The library was later named in honor of Father Duane. It was extensively renovated after the opening of the Walsh Family Library in 1997. It now houses Tognino Hall, the Admissions Office, the Curran Center for American Catholic Studies, Butler Commons, and the offices of the Department of Theology.[39]

39. *FM*, November 1924, 153–54.

When the students returned from vacation in the fall of 1927, they found that the new Biology Building facing Fordham Road was ready for use. It has since been renamed in honor of Father John Larkin, Fordham's first Jesuit dean of studies and second Jesuit president. While the editors of the *Fordham Monthly* spared no superlatives in describing the spacious laboratories and the handsome exterior of the building that harmonized perfectly with the nearby library, what seemed to intrigue them the most about the new Biology Building was the space reserved for the live animals that were to be used in laboratory experiments. That summer a new fence was also erected along Fordham Road, between Third Avenue and Bathgate Avenue, and the stone pillars were dedicated to the Fordham alumni who had died in World War I.[40]

Four months after the completion of the Biology Building, in January 1928, the steam shovels were again at work on campus, this time excavating the site of the new Faculty Building, the future Loyola Hall, located north of the Administration Building. Like the library and the Biology Building, it was a stone building with limestone trim, five stories high with a center pavilion six stories high, flanked by two roof gardens. The interior contained fifty-five private bedrooms and three suites for the rector, minister, and an occasional episcopal guest. The building was fireproof and included a new-fangled push-button elevator and a spacious porch on the north side with ample room for rocking chairs. The lower floors contained a chapel, refectory, and separate community rooms for the priests, scholastics, and brothers. One missing amenity was private baths, which were still considered too luxurious for a mendicant order, as Father Robert I. Gannon liked to describe the Jesuits. By December 1928 the Jesuit faculty was busy moving to their new quarters from the west wing of Dealy Hall, leaving that space to be recycled as classrooms and private student residences.[41]

As work progressed on the new Faculty Building, Father Duane also undertook a major renovation and expansion of the University Church, which dated from 1846, when it served as the chapel for the adjacent diocesan seminary and also, after 1852, as the parish church of Our Lady of Mercy. Father Duane's renovations added two large transepts to the original structure and an apse containing the sanctuary and the main altar. The expansion added 75 feet to the length of the church for a total length of 180 feet, including the 75-foot-high belfry at the entrance to the church.

40. *FM*, October 1927, 60.
41. *FM*, January 1928, 323; *WL* 57 (1928): 305–30; *FM*, January 1929, 276.

The overall width of the two transepts was 110 feet and the interior width of each transept was 41 feet, the same as the width of the nave and the diameter of the dome.

The dome was perhaps the most original and impressive feature of the renovated church. Fifty-two feet high, it was surmounted by an octagonal "lantern" modeled after the one at Ely Cathedral in England. The dome was supported by four massive corner columns, which eliminated the need for additional interior columns and provided an unobstructed view of the sanctuary and main altar. The seating capacity was tripled to accommodate 1,150 people. The architect was Emile G. Perrot, who had also designed several of Father Duane's other new buildings, including the Biology Building and the library. The basement contained a chapel with nine altars, a necessity for a large community of priests in the pre–Vatican II era when concelebration at Mass was unknown. The church was re-dedicated by Cardinal Hayes on Sunday, April 7, 1929, at an elaborate ceremony in which the cardinal paid tribute to the contributions that Father Duane had made to Fordham as president.[42]

Father Duane's building program received enthusiastic endorsement and indispensable financial support from Father Joseph Keating, a native of Canada, who was the treasurer for thirty-eight years (1910–48), an era that spanned two world wars and the Great Depression. Even Father Charles J. Deane, the dean of Fordham College for many years, who rarely had a good word to say about his fellow Jesuits, regarded Keating as something of a financial genius. However, like St. Ignatius, Keating was more interested in souls than in money. He estimated that there were more than 8,000 Catholic students in non-Catholic colleges in the metropolitan area. "We must build to save the faith of these students," Keating said in 1926. "The opportunity is passing and the youth that we should be influencing fall under the influence of others." Keating had no hesitation in borrowing money to finance the expansion of the Rose Hill campus. "I am in favor of spending not only the reserve on hand," he told the father general, "but even to mortgage our property, which could easily carry a debt ten-fold our present liabilities."[43]

Keating politely declined compliments about his financial acumen and attributed his success to meticulous attention to detail and to prayer, espe-

42. *WL* 57 (1928): 303–4.; *FM*, May 1929, 592.

43. ARSJ, Keating to Ledóchowski, January 6, 1926; Deane to General, January 9, 1935. Duane assured the general that only the shortage of personnel prevented the Jesuits from attaining a virtual monopoly of Catholic higher education in the United States. ARSJ, Duane to Ledóchowski, August 6, 1926.

The End of the Little Liberal Arts College

Father Joseph T. Keating, S.J., the legendary treasurer of Fordham University, 1910–48, who gave the credit for his financial success during two world wars and the Depression to St. Joseph.

cially to his patron, St. Joseph, whose statue he kept on top of the safe in the vault. One of the few occasions when Keating lost his *sangfroid* was on Black Thursday, October 24, 1929, the day that the New York Stock Exchange began its disastrous collapse. That afternoon Keating spent several hours in prayer. Later that evening, when Keating entered the refectory for dinner, one of his fellow Jesuits greeted him with the cry, "Well, Joe, how much did you lose today?" Years later Keating admitted that he was torn between the desire to burst into tears and "the desire to do something terribly violent." He did neither.

Father Keating recommended that every Jesuit treasurer post a sign over the door of his office that read, "*In quantum possum et tu indiges*" [insofar as I am able and you are in need]. In 1935, when Father Duane's successor as president, Father Aloysius J. Hogan, erected the massive Gothic edifice at the crest of Rose Hill that was to become Fordham's signature building, he insisted on naming it in honor of Keating. Keating was grateful but said that "St. Joseph built it."[44]

The collapse of the stock market in October 1929 caused consternation on many college campuses. "The effects of the Depression affect everyone, not excepting Fordham," noted Father Keating. The Jesuits distributed

44. Kevin J. O'Brien, S.J., "Father Joseph T. Keating, 1871–1950," *WL* 81 (1952): 270–74.

food and even small sums of money every day to needy neighborhood people who came to the gates seeking help. However, by the end of 1930 Keating was able to say that "our situation is sound." In fact a year earlier Father Duane had announced plans for the construction of still another new building, the Physics Building, to be located on the south side of the ball field (today's Edwards Parade), and adjacent to the Science Building (today's Finlay Hall), which had been erected to house the Medical School in 1913. Named Freeman Hall in honor of Fordham's most famous nineteenth-century Jesuit science professor, it was ready for occupancy in the fall of 1930. The *Fordham Monthly* hailed it as "the beauty spot on the campus" and described it "another monument to Father Duane's work." A notable architectural feature was the spacious front porch or deck that was used for graduation ceremonies until the completion of Keating Hall some years later.[45]

The students were more generous in their appreciation of Father Duane's building program than Duane's second successor, Father Robert I. Gannon, who damned the new buildings with faint praise by saying that "from an architectural point of view, they were all acceptable though undistinguished, except for the remodeled church." Gannon even criticized Duane for such petty economies as using artificial limestone in the decoration of the Biology Building. The provincial, Father Lawrence Kelly, had been busy defending Duane from critics in Rome who criticized his new buildings as too ostentatious.[46]

Unfortunately, through no fault of his own, the decade of Father Duane's unprecedented building boom was also the occasion for two serious fires in the Administration Building. The first and more serious fire, a two-alarm blaze, occurred on December 30, 1924. It was discovered by Father Rush Rankin, who roused the other priests who were asleep in the building and then removed the Blessed Sacrament from the first-floor Sodality Chapel. Another Jesuit, Father Michael Jessup, attempted to rescue scholastic records from the record room, but, after forcing open a locked door, he was caught in a backdraft of flames that caused severe and painful burns to his hands and face. The fire caused extensive damage not only to the record room but also to several offices in the north wing of the building and to the roof and cupola. Insurance covered most of the cost of repairs,

45. ARSJ, Keating to General, January 6, 1931; *FM*, December 1929, 132, April 1930, 458, October 1930, 75.

46. Gannon, *Up to the Present*, 183–85. ARSJ, Kelly to Ledóchowski, January 25, 1928. Kelly described some of the older buildings at Rose Hill as so plain "that there was little to distinguish some of them from respectable looking factories."

but Father Jessup never fully recovered from his ordeal. The second fire, another two-alarm blaze, occurred on October 24, 1929, and caused extensive damage to Father Duane's office and to the office of the treasurer, Father Joseph Keating. It took the firefighters two hours to extinguish the blaze, which caused damages estimated at $25,000. Once again insurance covered most of the financial losses.[47]

The interwar years were the heyday of the so-called brick-and-mortar bishops in the American hierarchy, who presided over a vast expansion in the infrastructure of the American Catholic Church. Whether he would like it or not, Father Duane deserves honorable mention in their company. He should properly be credited with giving Fordham not just five but six new buildings, if one includes the smallest and nearly invisible addition to the campus in the 1920s, the seismic station or laboratory, which contains instruments to record the occurrence and severity of earthquakes.

The tiny building, whose innards lie deep underground, was constructed from stone acquired from a recent subway excavation and was blessed by Bishop John Collins, S.J., a retired president of Fordham, on October 24, 1924. He used a prayer recently composed by Pope Pius XI for the blessing of seismographs, which remains one of the lesser-tapped selections in the repertoire of papal blessings. Father Duane used the occasion in his address to emphasize the Church's encouragement of science. Like the Holy House of Loreto, but without angelic intervention, the seismic station experienced several changes of location within the next few years. In 1927 it was moved from the site of Loyola Hall to the top of Rose Hill, and it was moved again in 1931 to make way for Keating Hall, until it found a friendly resting place east of the newly constructed Freeman Hall.[48]

When Fordham celebrated its fiftieth anniversary in 1891, there were only a handful of modern buildings and a few hundred students on the campus of the little liberal arts college that was still called St. John's College. In 1930, when Father Duane handed the baton to his successor, Father Aloysius J. Hogan, Fordham was no longer a modest little Catholic liberal arts college but an ambitious and aspiring university that was seeking to establish its credentials in the rapidly evolving world of American Catholic higher education. Despite the impressive progress made in the early twentieth century, Fordham was striving too hard and too fast to attain the status of a bona fide university, and it led to the worst academic disaster in its history in the 1930s.

47. *FM*, February 1925, 370–71; December, 1929, 132.
48. *FM*, November 1924, 153; Schroth, *Fordham: A History and Memoir*, 142.

9

FROM COLLEGE TO UNIVERSITY

The Jesuits and Archbishop John Farley

At the commencement exercises on June 23, 1904, Father John J. Collins, S.J., the president of St. John's College, announced that the following September the college would become a university with the opening of both a medical school and a law school.[1] It quickly became obvious that this timetable was impractical, and the opening of the first two graduate schools was delayed until September 1905. The initiative for this transition from college to university did not come from Collins but from Father Thomas J. Gannon, the provincial of the Maryland–New York Province. "As far as I was concerned," Collins said, "the work was a work ordered by obedience."

A dozen years later Collins explained the unusual circumstances of Fordham's transition from college to university in a highly improbable and melodramatic tale that is reminiscent of a James Bond spy novel. According to Collins, at the annual meeting of the American Catholic archbishops in 1904 or 1905, they decided that every archdiocese in the United States should open a university as soon as possible. Archbishop Farley agreed and said that he was ready to start a Catholic university in New York City. One of the people present at the meeting was a Father Marquetti, an Italian priest who was a secretary at the Apostolic Delegation, the papal embassy to the U.S. bishops. As soon as the meeting was over, Marquetti rushed across town to Georgetown College to tell the news to Father John Conway. The two of them then sent a telegram in Latin to Gannon, who was in Boston, telling him of the decision of the archbishops. Gannon telephoned Collins and ordered him to forestall Farley by announcing that Fordham would open a university in the fall.

It is a wonderfully entertaining story, but of doubtful authenticity. There is no mention of such a decision by the American archbishops in their meetings in 1904 or 1905, and it is highly improbable that they would have called for the establishment of Catholic universities in such isolated places

---

1. New York *Catholic News*, June 25, 1904.

as Santa Fe and Oregon City. However, it is well documented that the Jesuits never informed Archbishop Farley of their intention to establish a university at Rose Hill. He first heard the news when he read it in the newspapers, and he was furious. Years later, Monsignor Michael Lavelle, the rector of St. Patrick's Cathedral and close friend of Farley's, told Dr. James J. Walsh, the former dean of the Medical School, that the Jesuits had spoiled Farley's plans to expand Cathedral College, his new minor seminary, into a university. According to Lavelle, Farley had even selected the faculty for the projected medical school and law school. Collins was caught between a rock and a hard place, his own superior and the archbishop. On three separate occasions he asked Gannon's permission to speak to Farley, and twice he was turned down. "You look after the charter," Gannon told Collins, "and leave the rest to me." Gannon finally agreed to let Collins call on Farley but ordered him to make clear that he was not asking Farley's permission but informing him of a *fait accompli*.

At a tense meeting with Farley on June 26, 1905, Collins tried to repair the damage. He never mentioned that he had been acting under orders from Gannon and shouldered the blame himself. Farley burst into an hour-long tirade against the Jesuits.

The usually placid archbishop seemed more hurt than angry. He told Collins that he had searched his conscience and said that he did "not know why the Jesuit Fathers had treated [him] with such discourtesy." He wondered if the Jesuits' hostility stemmed from his decision to establish Cathedral College in 1903, because he knew that the Jesuits at Xavier regarded the school as a rival to their own institution. Farley also raised another sensitive issue, the Jesuit opposition to the establishment of the Catholic University of America in 1887 and Father Robert Fulton's disparagement of the intellectual ability of the diocesan clergy.

Collins tried to placate Farley by inviting him to preside at the Fordham graduation the following year and at the dedication of the New Hall (present-day Collins Hall). Farley turned down both invitations on the grounds that he would be condoning the Jesuits' discourtesy to him. It was not an auspicious beginning for the transformation of St. John's College to Fordham University. However, it proved to be only a momentary squall. The Jesuits were fortunate that they were dealing with John Farley and not with John Hughes. Archbishop Farley was not a person to harbor grudges. Before Collins left, Farley embraced him, gave him his blessing, and said, "Anything I can do for Fordham University now that the matter is settled, I will gladly do." He was soon encouraging the Jesuits to expand their graduate program to include a School of Social

Service. The Jesuits were soon hailing him as their most distinguished alumnus.[2]

Although the initiative for the establishment of a university at Rose Hill did not come from Father Collins, he embraced the idea enthusiastically and soon regarded the Medical School and the Law School as only the first steps in creating a genuine university. At the annual alumni dinner at Delmonico's restaurant on February 6, 1905, he revealed that he also hoped to establish graduate schools of engineering, education, and theology in the near future. He realized that his expansionist plans would require donations on a scale never before achieved by Fordham. At a Memorial Day address in 1905 Collins noted that during the previous fifty years the Catholics of New York had donated less than $30,000 to Fordham. "I ask," he said boldly, "one million dollars." As he soon discovered, it was indeed a bold request. Thirty-five years later, when Father Robert I. Gannon tried to raise $1 million on the occasion of Fordham's centennial, all he got was $600,000.[3]

Father Collins had one of the shortest tenures of any Jesuit president of Fordham—only twenty-three months, between April 1904 and March 1906—but his abrupt departure was not due to dissatisfaction with his visionary plans for Fordham or his efforts to implement them. In 1906 the Holy See appointed him the apostolic administrator of the vicariate apostolic of Jamaica, British West Indies, where he had previously spent eight years as a missionary.[4]

On March 7, 1906, a year after Father Collins resigned as president to take up his new duties in Jamaica, the Board of Regents of the State

2. ARSJ, Collins to R. E. Noble, Kingston, Jamaica, December 1, 1919; FUA, Diary of Presidents, 1885–1906, Collins, September 26, 1905. There is no mention in the minutes of the meetings of the U.S. archbishops in 1904 or 1905 of any decision to open a Catholic university in every archdiocese. AAB, Minutes of the Meetings of the U.S. Archbishops. I am grateful to Dr. Tricia Pyne, the Director of the Archives at St. Mary's Seminary and University and Associated Archives in Baltimore, Maryland, for providing me with copies of the minutes.

3. *FM*, February 1905, 180; June 1905, 353; Robert I. Gannon, *Up to the Present: The Story of Fordham* (Garden City, N.Y.: Doubleday and Company, 1967), 231–32.

4. Collins was appointed vicar apostolic of Jamaica on October 13, 1907, and consecrated a bishop in the Church of St. Francis Xavier in New York City on October 28, 1907. He resigned in 1920 and returned to Fordham, where he lived until his death in 1934. "I think it can be said," he commented, "that during the fourteen years I have been Vicar Apostolic Jamaica has seen more natural disasters than in the four hundred years since its discovery." *WL* 64 (1935): 262–68. At Fordham, Collins wore the simple black cassock of a Jesuit priest. He left his episcopal regalia in Jamaica for his successor.

of New York amended the charter of St. John's College to reflect its new status as a university. The corporate name of the institution was officially changed to Fordham University and the name of the undergraduate department was changed to St. John's College of Fordham University. The regents also officially incorporated the two new graduate schools as the Fordham University School of Medicine and the Fordham University School of Law.[5]

The cordial relationship with the archdiocese was soon restored, but the shift from college to university created unprecedented challenges for the Jesuits on several different levels. They were surprised to discover how expensive it was to operate graduate schools, especially a medical school. For the first time they had to share authority with lay people who constituted the bulk of the graduate faculties and with the lay deans who were responsible for the day-to-day operation of the graduate schools. They also had to meet the academic requirements of the state educational authorities and professional accrediting agencies. This was to be a particularly difficult experience in the case of the Medical School. For the first time since they left Kentucky in the 1840s, they had to adjust to a situation wherein many of the students were not Catholics. Father Collins's successor as president from 1906 to 1911 was Father Daniel J. Quinn, an easygoing gentleman and an excellent preacher who found it increasingly difficult to preside over Fordham's transition from a college to a university.

The Fordham University School of Medicine

It was a bold and perhaps foolhardy venture for Fordham to establish a medical school at a time of increasing professionalization in medical education in the United States and the consequent disappearance of many small and inefficient medical schools throughout the country. There were about 150 medical schools in the United States in 1905 when the Fordham University School of Medicine was established. There were fewer than 100 medical schools a decade later, and Fordham's would soon be added to the growing list of casualties.[6] A key factor in the modernization of medical education in the United States was the publication in 1910 of the so-called Flexner Report, a comprehensive survey of the 155 medical schools in the United States compiled by Abraham Flexner under the auspices of the

5. Thomas J. Campbell, S.J., "Fordham University," *FM*, June 1916, 35. Campbell gives 1906 as the year in which the Board of Regents amended the charter from St. John's College, Fordham, to Fordham University.

6. William P. Healy, M.D., "The School of Medicine," *FM*, Diamond Jubilee Edition, June 1916, 134.

Carnegie Foundation. Despite howls of protest and at least one anonymous death threat, Flexner recommended that the number of American medical schools be reduced from 155 to 31.[7]

The origins of Fordham's Medical School may be traced to June 1, 1904, when St. John's College sold four acres of swampy ground at the corner of Southern Boulevard and Fordham Road to New York City for the erection of a municipal hospital. There was no explicit agreement between the city and the college that Fordham Hospital was to provide facilities for clinical practice for students at a future medical school at Fordham University. However, two weeks after the sale of the property, the administrators of the college met with twelve Fordham alumni who were physicians to consider the feasibility of opening a medical school. They selected a committee of six of their members to consider the question further. There is no record of their conclusions, but a week later it was announced that Fordham would establish a medical school.[8]

The Medical School began with six students in September 1905, the same number of students with which St. John's College had begun in 1841. The faculty consisted of seven professors, only four of whom were physicians. Two were Jesuits, one of whom, Father Thomas Freeman, was the professor of science. At first the Medical School occupied classrooms in the New Hall (now Collins Hall), where it shared quarters with the Law School until January of the following year when it moved to the Science Building (Thebaud Hall). Between 1907 and 1916 the number of medical students increased from 32 to 259 and the faculty grew to 110 professors, almost all of whom were adjuncts. The students received clinical experience at ten different local hospitals, especially at Fordham Hospital.

Originally applicants were required to have completed four years of high school and one year of college, including courses in biology, physics, and inorganic chemistry as well as either French or German, which was the standard minimum requirement in many American medical schools. In 1911 St. John's College established a pre-med program called the Collegiate Medical Department to enable undergraduates to meet these requirements. In order to comply with the demands of the New York State Examining Board, the entrance requirements were upgraded in 1918 to

7. Abraham Flexner, *Medical Education in the United States and Canada: A Report to the Carnegie Foundation for the Advancement of Teaching* (Boston: D. B. Updike/The Merrymount Press, 1910), 28, 151.

8. FUA, Diary of Presidents, 1885–1906, Collins, June, 18, 1904.

James J. Walsh, M.D., Ph.D., dean of Fordham University School of Medicine, 1906–12.

include two years of college, creating a six-year program that led to both the B.S. and M.D. degrees.[9]

The Medical School had a troubled existence throughout its brief sixteen-year existence. The first dean, James N. Butler, M.D., an alumnus of St. John's College, failed to keep his promise to give up his private practice and to devote his attention exclusively to the Medical School, leading to complaints from both faculty and students about his neglect of duty. Butler's successor as dean was James J. Walsh, M.D., a larger-than-life individual who had attended both high school and college at Fordham, from which he had been graduated as the head of his class in 1884 and remained for an additional year to earn the M.A. degree. He spent the following six years as a Jesuit novice and scholastic until he was forced to leave the Society of Jesus because of poor health.

He enrolled in the prestigious University of Pennsylvania Medical School in 1893 and received his M.D. degree two years later. He also did

9. Healy, "The School of Medicine," 133–35; *WL*, 34 (1905): 437; 36 (1907): 386–87; 42 (1913): 126–27.

postgraduate work in medical schools in Paris, Berlin, and Vienna. Walsh is best remembered today not as a physician or scientist but as a prolific historical writer whose best known work, *The Thirteenth: The Greatest of Centuries*, once enjoyed wide popularity among American Catholics. Significantly he was not only the dean of the Medical School but also professor of nervous diseases and the history of medicine.[10]

By temperament Walsh was a person who was inclined to operate on a grand scale. His model for the Fordham Medical School was nothing less than the Johns Hopkins School of Medicine in Baltimore, the best medical school in the United States. Johns Hopkins had introduced to America the so-called "Edinburgh system" of medical education, which emphasized hands-on clinical practice rather than classroom lectures. Walsh wanted to introduce the same system to Fordham and appointed as "pro-dean" or associate dean E. V. Sorapure, who was familiar with it. "In our system of training," said Sorapure, "we are guided by the general principle that *patients*, and not books, are the prime object of study." Walsh compared the "Edinburgh system" of medical education to the "case system" of legal training that Fordham Law School had adopted from Harvard Law School with great success between 1906 and 1909. "Nothing that I can see at the present time," said Walsh, "would do more to put Jesuit education where it ought to be in the estimation of the American public than [to] have a Medical School at Fordham attracting even more attention than the Law School."[11]

By 1911 discontent with the genial and easygoing Father Daniel Quinn as president of Fordham came to a head among some of his fellow Jesuits at Fordham. "Some are of the opinion that I am too indulgent," Quinn admitted, but he added that "the high standard of conduct maintained throughout the college is my defense." The provincial, Father Joseph Hanselman, thought otherwise. "Father Quinn has arrived at the end of his usefulness," Hanselman told the general, Father Franz Xavier Wernz. He cited a long

10. Harry W. Kirwin, "James J. Walsh: Medical Historian and Pathfinder," *CHR* 45 (1960): 410. Theodore Roosevelt was so intrigued with the book that he invited Walsh to lunch at the White House on April 21, 1908. The president asked Walsh why he put the challenge in the title of the book. "That's easy," Walsh replied; "I'm Irish and I go around with a chip on my shoulder." Ibid., 424–35. Walsh was the author of some 44 books and 500 articles and was awarded the prestigious Laetare Medal by the University of Notre Dame in 1916.

11. V. E. Sorapure, "A Needed Improvement in Medical Teaching in America," *FM*, February 1910, 269–73; James J. Walsh, "Reasons for a New Medical Building," *FM*, February 1910, 273–75.

list of complaints, such as Quinn's inability to handle the finances, reduce expenses, guide the establishment of the Medical School and Law School, consolidate Fordham with Xavier, retain the loyalty of the alumni, and arrange the projected transfer of the Jesuit scholasticate from Woodstock, Maryland, to Fordham. As a replacement for Quinn, Hanselman wanted and got another New Yorker, Father Thomas J. McCluskey, a capable administrator and strong-minded individual who soon locked horns with the equally strong-minded Dean Walsh.[12]

The year 1912 was the *annus horribilis* of the Fordham Medical School and the beginning of the end. The first crisis broke in May when Fordham applied to the State Board of Charities for a charter to establish a new hospital to be known as the Fordham University Hospital. The public hearings were a public relations disaster for the university. The four members of the Board of Charities questioned the need for a new hospital only a quarter-mile from the existing Fordham Hospital. Dean Walsh replied lamely that the new hospital would better serve the needs of poor Catholics in the neighborhood. "Our idea is not to rival Fordham Hospital in any way," he said. The Board also expressed concern about the presence on the faculty of the Fordham Medical School of Dr. Louis Anton Ewald, who had been expelled from the New York County Medical Society for falsifying records at Sydenham Hospital. The Board also questioned Dean Walsh about the relationship between Fordham University and a small maternity hospital in the South Bronx operated by Ewald that was called the Fordham University Hospital for Women. Walsh referred the matter to Ewald, who was present at the hearings.[13]

Six months later a bigger crisis erupted when the faculty of the Medical School split into two factions. Dean Walsh; the assistant dean, E. V. Sora-

12. ARSJ, Quinn to Wernz, February 7, 1908; Hanselman to Wernz, September 8, 1911. Seven months later McCluskey gave a horrifying portrait of what he found at Fordham. "The college and high school have been neglected for years," he told the general. "There is not a blackboard in the college or high school, only some black paint on the plaster walls; no desks, only old forms all cut and hacked by the boys . . . scarcely any maps in the classrooms, not a sacred picture on the walls." ARSJ, McCluskey to Wernz, April 3, 1912. Quinn was a New York diocesan seminarian before joining the Jesuits, and McCluskey was a New York diocesan priest for eight years before entering the Society in 1889. *WL*, 69 (1940); 369–70; 60 (1931): 161–62.

13. *New York Times*, May 17, 1912. One of the members of the Board was Thomas M. Mulry, an outstanding Catholic layman and for many years the leader of the St. Vincent de Paul Society in New York. Four of Mulry's brothers entered the Society of Jesus, but two died before ordination. Joseph A. Mulry, S.J, was president of Fordham University from 1915 to 1919. *WL* 51 (1922): 112–17.

pure; and Dr. William Maloney resigned from the faculty. The split was precipitated by an ongoing dispute among the faculty over the relationship of the Medical School with Fordham Hospital and complaints by Dean Walsh and others that the "Edinburgh system" was being undermined by sacrificing clinical practice to attendance at lectures. The immediate reason was the response of the university to the demands of the Council on Medical Education of the American Medical Association that Fordham Medical School would have to institute several changes in order to retain its classification as a Class A School. After an on-site inspection of the Fordham Medical School in May 1911, the AMA required the university to upgrade the Medical School by opening a clinic, employing at least six full-time professors instead of three professors, and setting aside $20,000 per annum to improve the quality of the teaching.

According to Dean Walsh's version of events, he, Sorapure, and Dr. Maloney formed a committee and informed the AMA that they had received written assurances from the newly appointed president of Fordham University, Father Thomas McCluskey, that Fordham would comply with the requirements. However, Walsh said that, in the fall of 1912, Father McCluskey dissolved the committee without opening a clinic or increasing the budget for teaching. Unable to fulfill their commitments to the AMA, Walsh, Sorapure, and Maloney resigned from the faculty in protest and were followed by a dozen other professors who also resigned from the faculty.[14]

Walsh was replaced as dean by Dr. William P. Healy, attending surgeon at Fordham Hospital and professor of clinical surgery at the Medical School, who gave a different version of the dispute. Healy claimed that the dissidents represented only a small faction of the faculty and said that they were unhappy because the Medical School was being reorganized on the model of the Medical School of St. Louis University, the best Jesuit medical school in the United States. Healy implied that Walsh and his friends felt threatened that the reorganization would end their quasi-dictatorial control of the Medical School. "After their influence had been practically supreme in the School of Medicine for the past five years," said Healy, "they found themselves out of control and took the step of resigning in consequence." Furthermore, Dean Healy denied that Father McCluskey

14. *New York Times,* November 9, 1912. Some of the dissident faculty members told the provincial, Father Anthony Maas, that they thought McCluskey had lost his mind, which brought a smile to Maas's lips. ARSJ, Maas to Wernz, November 18, 1912. Despite his disagreement with McCluskey, Walsh remained a loyal and enthusiastic supporter of Fordham and was soon teaching in the School of Social Service and Sociology.

had appointed Walsh, Sorapure, and Maloney to the committee that they had formed or that he had authorized the committee to make the commitments that it made to the AMA.[15]

Father McCluskey pointed out to the general that he had acted with the unanimous consent of the consultors and the provincial. "The medical men wish to push us out entirely from any supervision," he said, "except to give them all the money they wish to spend." He claimed that the Medical School was now in better condition than before the faculty revolt, although he admitted that he had gotten criticism from some Jesuits who were friends of Dean Walsh. The new provincial, Father Anthony Maas, took a more guarded view of the situation, which he described as some kind of a revolution. He criticized McCluskey for his vituperative language but admitted that he had successfully defended the Jesuit control of the Medical School.[16]

In January 1913 it was announced that the AMA had demoted the Fordham Medical School from Class A to Class B, which, as the *New York Times* noted, really reduced it to the level of a third-rate medical school. Dean Healy claimed that the action of the AMA had no connection with the resignation of Walsh as dean two months earlier and pointed out that the decision of the AMA was based on an on-site inspection of the Fordham Medical School in the summer of 1911. He said that the shortcomings noted by the AMA at that time had since been corrected. The Fordham Medical School recovered its Class A status by 1914 after constructing a new medical building (today's Finlay Hall, a student residence), which was opened in 1913 at a cost of more than $150,000. The university also established a clinic on campus, increased the number of full-time faculty to seven, and allocated even more money than the AMA required to improve the quality of medical education at Fordham. However, the basic problem still remained that the Fordham Medical School lacked an endowment.[17]

In 1916, when Fordham celebrated the seventy-fifth anniversary of its founding, Dean Healy publicly questioned whether the Jesuits had been aware of the financial commitment they would have to make when they decided to establish a medical school in 1905. "The Medical School was

15. *New York Times*, November 10, 1912.

16. ARSJ, McCluskey to Wernz, January 6, 1913; Maas to Wernz, November, 18, 1912.

17. ARSJ, McCluskey to Wernz, April 7, 1914. *New York Times*, January 20, 1913; *WL* 44 (1915): 133; 65 (1934): 31. The Flexner Report concluded that, among the medical schools in New York City, only Columbia's, Cornell's, and possibly New York University's had the potential financial resources to establish adequate endowments. Flexner, *Medical Education in the United States and Canada*, 276–77.

Finlay Hall, the last home of the Fordham School of Medicine from 1913 to 1921.
After the closure of the Medical School, it became the Chemistry Building ("Old Chem")
and was renamed Finlay Hall in 1990.

handicapped from the start by poor classroom facilities, and lack of equipment," he said. He faulted Fordham for failing to provide adequate laboratories, modern scientific equipment, library resources, hospital facilities, and full-time salaried teachers. Despite these shortcomings, Healy noted that the Fordham Medical School had recovered its Class A ranking from both the New York State Board of Regents and the American Medical Association, but he attributed this largely to the sacrifices of the faculty and the university, warning that this situation could not be expected to continue indefinitely.

Healy pleaded for the establishment of an endowment of at least $100,000 to be used exclusively for current expenses, "if Fordham is to continue to maintain a medical school of the highest class." And he added that "for Fordham to maintain a second- or third-rate school is out of the question." Healy's criticism of the precarious financial condition of the Fordham Medical School was directed primarily not at the university but at the Catholic community in New York City. "It is indeed a strange commentary on the lack of public interest in the professional schools of a great Catholic university," he said, "that the Fordham University School of Medicine, located in the greatest and wealthiest Catholic city in the world, finds itself after eleven years of existence still struggling along without one dollar of permanent endowment." Healy resigned shortly thereafter and was replaced as dean by Joseph Byrne, M.D., who was also professor of neurology.[18] The following year for the first time the Medical School showed a profit, but it was only a paltry $4,300 and it was made possible only by the donated services of the Jesuit faculty members. The red ink soon reappeared on the financial books when salaries had to be raised to prevent many of the faculty from quitting. The Jesuits noted that it was no longer possible to get professors to donate their services or to agree to accept a reduced salary. In view of the precarious financial condition of the Medical School and more rigorous standards imposed by the state educational authorities, the provincial, Father Maas, asked the Fordham Jesuits to consider whether the school should be closed.[19]

The Beginning of the End

In the spring of 1919 the new provincial, Father Joseph Rockwell, consulted with the father general, Father Wlodimir Ledóchowski, about the future of the Medical School, and they both decided that it should be closed. The board of consultors at Fordham were of the same opinion as was Dr. Joseph Byrne, the last dean of the Medical School, who was unhappy with the inferior quality of the faculty. The Board of Regents of the State of New York also recommended the closing of the Medical School. They reported that at the last convention of the AMA in Atlantic City, it was commonly said that the Fordham Medical School could not long retain its Class A status.[20]

The one person who was in favor of making a last-ditch effort to save the Medical School was the new president of Fordham University, Father

18. Healy, "The School of Medicine," 135–36. On the basis of its admission requirements, the Flexner Report placed Fordham Medical School in the second tier of medical schools along with those of the University of Virginia, Northwestern University, and the University of North Carolina. Flexner, *Medical Education in the United States and Canada*, 28.

19. FUA, Acta Consultorum, 1890–1938, November 8, 1917.

20. ARSJ, Rockwell to Ledóchowski, June 2, 1919.

Edward P. Tivnan, who fought strenuously to keep it open. He and the provincial met with the new archbishop, Patrick J. Hayes, and the board of diocesan consultors, the archbishop's principal advisory body, to try to persuade them to provide an endowment for the Medical School from diocesan funds. Archbishop Hayes replied that such a financial bailout was out of the question at a time when the archdiocese was conducting a major fundraising campaign on behalf of the newly founded Catholic Charities of the Archdiocese of New York.

Archbishop Hayes said that the more pressing need of the archdiocese was a School of Social Service, not a Catholic medical school. One of the diocesan consultors suggested that Fordham seek to affiliate its medical school with the Catholic University of America in Washington, D.C., but Monsignor Michael Lavelle said he was certain that the Catholic University would decline the offer. Another possibility was to appeal to the Knights of Columbus for financial assistance, but Father Tivnan ruled that out for fear that it would interfere with the archbishop's plans to have the Knights raise $300,000 for the Catholic Charities Appeal.[21]

On June 15, 1919, Father Tivnan announced that the Medical School would not reopen in September unless an appeal to establish an endowment of $1 million was successful. He explained that the Medical School still had no endowment at all and that for several years it had consumed the entire surplus of the university. After fifteen years the Medical School had awarded the M.D. degree to 377 graduates, and there were another 297 students enrolled. Most of the students were Jewish, who were attracted to Fordham because many U.S. medical schools restricted the number of Jewish students whom they would admit. The *New York Times* noted that the Fordham Medical School was a nonsectarian institution and commented that "all who knew and appreciated the quality of the instruction that was given there realized that a real misfortune [has] occurred" with the announcement of its closing.[22]

21. FUA, Acta Consultorum, 1890–1938, May 2, June 10, 1919; AANY, Minutes of the Meetings of the Diocesan Consultors, May 23, 1919.

22. *New York Times*, May 30, 191, July 17, 1919. According to Father Robert I. Gannon, in 1914 Dr. James Walsh, the former dean, offered to raise $500,000 for an endowment if Fordham could match the amount, but the university was unable to do so. Gannon, *Up to the Present*, 137. As late as 1953 the *New York Times* reported that a Protestant stood a better chance than a Catholic of being admitted to one of the nine medical schools in New York state, and a Catholic stood a better chance than a Jew. *New York Times*, July 10, 1953, in Will Herberg, *Protestant-Catholic-Jew* (Garden City, N.Y.: Doubleday, 1955), 43–44.

After 1919, no new students were admitted to the Medical School, but the two upper years were allowed to proceed to graduation and received their M.D. degrees in 1920 and 1921. There was a long list of expensive reforms that the AMA expected Fordham to implement if it was to retain its Class A standing, but it was impossible to do so without a substantial endowment. "We have some hope that someone will give us a big donation," the provincial, Father Joseph Rockwell, told the general, "but it is only a hope."[23]

The definitive end came on June 14, 1921, when Father Tivnan announced that the Medical School would close its doors permanently. By that date the Medical School had accumulated a deficit of $342,863, which the university could no longer sustain. "Had it not been for the fact that every dollar was carefully and skillfully applied," said Tivnan, "and that some of the professors were Jesuit Fathers who receive no compensation for their services save their board and clothing, the deficit would have mounted much higher."[24]

The closing of the Medical School was a major disappointment to Father Tivnan, who had struggled for two years to keep it open. In announcing the decision, Tivnan told Augustus Dowling, the assistant commissioner of the state Education Department and the director of professional education, "My purpose is the same as it was on the day that I went to Albany several years ago to consult you with regard to the school." "I said then," he reminded Dowling, "that I would close the school unless I secured an endowment sufficient to enable us to carry on our work according to the best methods of teaching. The endowment has not been forthcoming and so we shall close with the class that graduates this June."

Tivnan and Dowling became close friends in the course of the struggle to save Fordham Medical School. Tivnan told Dowling candidly, "It

23. Among other requirements from the AMA, the Fordham Medical School was expected to establish its own hospital and dispensary and to add a fifth year to the curriculum that students were to spend as interns at the university hospital under the supervision of the Medical School. AANY, O-9, "Report on Medical School." ARSJ, Rockwell to Ledóchowski, November 9, 1919.

24. *New York Times*, July 17, 20, 1919; June 14, 1921. Bennett Medical College, which was associated with Loyola University of Chicago, accused the AMA of anti-Catholic prejudice when it was forced to close because of the low ratings it received from the AMA. "In contrast," wrote Professor Kenneth Ludmerer, "Fordham, an underfinanced but honest Catholic medical school that closed gracefully in 1921, did not find any religious prejudice in the low rankings given it by the AMA." Kenneth M. Ludmerer, *Learning to Heal: The Development of American Medical Education* (New York: Basic Books, 1985), 243.

would have been possible for us to conduct the school on a lower plane, and I am sure that the public would not have been any wiser. But, if we had attempted anything of that kind, I would feel that I was a traitor to the sacred calling which I have adopted as an educator." Dowling congratulated Tivnan for his integrity and told him that "this was the magnet that attracted me to you at the very beginning of our acquaintance."[25]

The Afterlife of the Medical School

Fordham Medical School was like a corpse that had been buried in quicksand and periodically threatened to make an unwelcome appearance by bubbling to the surface.

In 1928 Father William J. Duane, the master builder among Fordham's early-twentieth-century presidents, suggested it was time to consider reopening the Fordham Medical School because of the difficulties Catholics were having in gaining admittance to Columbia, Cornell, and New York University medical schools. The father general of the Society, the Polish-born Wlodimir Ledóchowski, would not allow the reopening unless admission were restricted to Catholics. It is hard to believe that Ledóchowski feared an influx of Protestant students.[26]

In 1937, as the Nazis were making it impossible for German Jews to obtain a medical education in Germany, Father John M. Oesterreicher, a Jewish convert to Catholicism, and two German Jewish refugees called upon Father Robert I. Gannon, the president of Fordham University, and offered him $3,000,000 to reopen Fordham Medical School. Two conditions were attached to their offer. They wanted assurances that one-third of the faculty and one-third of the students would be Jewish. Father Gannon declined to accept either condition, and there was no follow-up to the offer.

Shortly thereafter Max Steuer, a well-known Jewish attorney in New York, invited Father Gannon to a dinner attended by perhaps twenty other guests. As coffee was being served at the end of the meal, Steuer brought

25. FUA, Tivnan Papers, Tivan to Dowling, April 11, 1921; Dowling to Tivnan, April 20, 1911. Although Tivnan did not accuse the AMA of anti-Catholic prejudice, he thought the AMA's efforts to reform medical education were high-handed and arbitrary. "If I could persuade myself that these men were really honest, I might be able to admire their effort. But I am far from believing that this is so. It is the old desire to control the whole field." FUA, Tivnan Papers, Tivnan to I. Maurice Wormser, a professor in the Fordham School of Law, December 17, 1920.

26. ARSJ, Duane to Provincial, July 5, 1928; Francis D. O'Laughlin, S.J., to Ledóchowski, January 6, 1919.

up the purpose of the dinner. According to Father Gannon, the following dialogue ensued.

Steuer asked, "Would you like to reopen the Medical School?"

Gannon replied, "Yes."

"How much would you need?

"Three million."

"I have clients who are willing to give ten."

"We could use ten."

"If we raised the money, how many Jews would you admit?"

"We have no quota at the university. We would take each year the seventy-five best applicants regardless of color, race or religion."

"Would you let us control the endowment?"

"Details of investment, yes; income, no."

"Would you let us appoint the entire faculty?"

"No."[27]

Steuer died a few months later and Gannon heard nothing more about the offer. Writing thirty years later, Gannon said, "That was the end of the ten million dollars and, up to the present, the end of our medical prospects." Gannon's memory was playing tricks on him. Four years after this incident, in 1941, a group of New York physicians inquired if Fordham would be willing to reopen its medical school. This time Gannon upped the ante and replied that it would require $4,000,000–$10,000,000 for a medical school building and an endowment of an additional $3,000,000 to generate a yearly income of $100,000. Once more nothing came of the proposal.[28]

Father Gannon found a silver lining in the closing of the Medical School. In his opinion it made possible the survival of the Graduate School, the future Graduate School of Arts and Science, because Fordham would never have been able to afford the heavy financial drain of supporting both the Medical School and the Graduate School. Another unexpected blessing of the closing of the Medical School led to the opening of the Graduate Department of Chemistry under the direction of Dr. Carl P. Sherwin, a former professor of biochemistry in the Medical School, who had received his doctorate at the University of Tübingen. Under the guidance of Dr. Sherwin and Father Tivnan, the Chemistry Department became the model for the other Fordham graduate programs in science.[29]

27. Gannon, *Up to the Present*, 158–59.

28. FUA, Gannon Papers, Box 13, Anthony Bassler, M.D., to Gannon, May 29, 1941; Gannon to Bassler, June 3, 1941.

29. Gannon, *Up to the Present*, 159.

One last tangential connection between Fordham University and its *ci-devant* Medical School occurred some years later in Father Robert Gannon's administration when the director of the Nursing School of Fordham Hospital inquired if the young women could use the Fordham athletic fields for their physical education classes. Father Gannon politely refused the request and delicately pointed out that the presence of scantily clad young women on an all-male campus "would attract a disproportionate amount of interest."[30]

Woodstock-on-the-Hudson

While the Jesuits at Rose Hill were preoccupied with transforming their little college into a university and coping with the problems of financing and administering a medical school, they also had to face the prospect that Fordham might become the site of another institution of higher learning as a result of forces beyond their control. For several years the superiors of the Maryland–New York Province debated the advantages and disadvantages of moving their theological seminary or *collegium maximum*, from Woodstock, Maryland, to the Rose Hill campus. The seminary had been established in 1869 at Woodstock on the banks of the Patapsco River, some thirty miles west of Baltimore, at a time when an isolated rural area was regarded as the ideal location for a seminary.

Twenty years later some Jesuits preferred a location closer to the resources of a Jesuit university, and a lively intramural debate ensued about the advantages of moving it either to Fordham University or to Georgetown University, which was the site favored by Father Joseph Havens Richards, the president of Georgetown, in the 1890s. Nothing came of the proposal, but the issue resurfaced after the appointment of Father Franz Xavier Wernz as the general of the Society in 1906. Wernz wanted Woodstock to be the nucleus of a great Jesuit university in the United States, and he wanted it located at Fordham rather than at Georgetown because he regarded New York City rather than Washington, D.C., as the intellectual and cultural capital of the United States. Wernz's choice of Fordham over Georgetown provoked considerable opposition from the Jesuits in the Maryland–New York Province who hailed from what Robert Emmett Curran called "the Chesapeake portion of the province."[31]

One snobbish Maryland Jesuit expressed vigorous opposition to relo-

---

30. FUA, Gannon Papers, Box 13, Gannon to Elsie Palmer, August 29, 1941.

31. Robert Emmett Curran, *Shaping American Catholicism: Maryland and New York City, 1805–1915* (Washington: The Catholic University of America Press, 2012), 274–77.

cating Woodstock to Fordham because of the working-class character of the surrounding neighborhood. For him the proximity of a municipal hospital a ("charity hospital," he called it) was sufficient proof of the unwelcome presence of large numbers of poor people. He also claimed that the nearby Bronx Zoo attracted so many lower-class visitors on weekends that it would be necessary to build a high wall around the seminary to shelter it from such undesirable elements. For good measure, he added that the area was infected with malaria. Father Thomas J. Gannon, former president of Fordham and former provincial, added his opposition to the move because of the proximity of the Botanical Garden and the lack of space compared with the extensive property at Woodstock. Other Jesuits were more specific about the "undesirable elements" in the neighborhood and identified them as Italian and Jewish immigrants.[32]

After listening to all these complaints about the proposed move to Rose Hill, in 1911 the provincial, Father Anthony Maas, confessed his perplexity at the widespread prejudice to the Fordham site in the Maryland–New York Province.[33] In that same year the president of Fordham, the usually easygoing Father Daniel Quinn, raised another complicating issue, the heavy debt that Fordham had incurred because of the Medical School. Several of Quinn's predecessors had indicated their receptivity to welcoming Woodstock to Rose Hill at minimum cost to the province, but Quinn informed the general that "conditions have changed since then and our debt has grown enormously." In view of its crippling financial situation, Fordham wanted $500,000 for the sale of twenty acres at Rose Hill to Woodstock, a price that the new provincial, Father Joseph Hanselman, considered exorbitant.[34]

One of the principal attractions of Fordham as the new site of the Woodstock seminary had been its bargain price. Once that was no longer the case, the Jesuits began to look elsewhere for a suitable site in New York. One possibility was an estate in Riverdale in the northeast Bronx, but they abandoned that quest when the property became entangled in legal squabbles among the heirs. Still another possibility was the Lillienthal property in North Yonkers, a fifty-two-acre estate overlooking the Hudson River, which the Jesuits bought for $750,000 in 1911. "It would be the loss of a

32. ARSJ, Joseph Himmel to Wernz, January 18, 1911; Thomas Gannon to Wernz, January 18, 1911.

33. ARSJ, Maas to Wernz, January 19, 1911. *In provincia viget nescio quod praejudicium contra situm Fordhamensem* [In the province an inexplicable prejudice prevails against the Fordham cite].

34. ARSJ, Quinn to Wernz, March 20, 1911; Hanselman to Wernz, January 20, 1911.

lifetime to miss this opportunity," Hanselman told Wernz.[35] Hanselman hoped to defray most of the cost by selling some of the property at Rose Hill. The irrepressible Father Wynne objected to the decision and emphasized the advantages of Rose Hill. He pointed out that the campus was three times the size of the Columbia University campus and claimed that there was room for fifty large buildings. "Fordham is ours," he said, "in the city, central, protected forever on all sides." Moreover, he warned that it would be difficult to attract benefactors for Fordham if the Jesuits began to sell off the property at Rose Hill.[36]

As usual, Wynne's complaints fell on deaf ears, although the Jesuits heeded his advice to the extent that they did not sell any property at Rose Hill. However, their grandiose plans to move Woodstock from the banks of the Patapsco to the banks of the Hudson never materialized. The closest they came to implementing the plan was to open a novitiate in Yonkers on the former Lillienthal estate in 1917, but it was in operation for only seven years, closing in 1924 after the opening the previous year of the novitiate at Shadowbrook, near Lenox, Massachusetts. It was not until forty-five years later, in 1969, that the Jesuits closed Woodstock and moved the institution to Manhattan. The second coming of Woodstock-on-the-Hudson proved to be even more short-lived than the first and lasted only five years.[37]

Back in 1907, when the Jesuits first gave serious consideration to moving Woodstock to New York, Father Hanselman called upon James Cardinal Gibbons, the archbishop of Baltimore, to inform him of their plans. The patriarch of the American Catholic Church expressed disappointment at the news, but he assured Hanselman that he would not interfere in an internal Jesuit matter. However, he said to Hanselman, "Tell the General from me that to sell Woodstock would be a very grave mistake." Today the building is a Job Corps Center and the former campus grounds are part of Patapsco Valley State Park.[38]

The Fordham School of Pharmacy

Although the Medical School lasted only sixteen years and a proposed Dental School never got beyond the discussion stage, one unexpected dividend of the short-lived Medical School was the School of Pharmacy. The initiative came from an unlikely source, Jacob Diner, a student in the Fordham Medical School, who persuaded both Father Daniel

35. ARSJ, Hanselman to Wernz, April 12, 1911.
36. ARSJ, Wynne to Wernz, December 1910.
37. *WL*, 40 (1911): 266; 76 (1947): 73; 53 (1924): 421.
38. ARSJ, Hanselman to Wernz, September 14, 1907.

Jacob Diner, M.D., dean of the Fordham University School of Pharmacy, 1912–32. Dr. Diner was the first Jewish dean in the history of Fordham University.

Quinn, the president of Fordham, and Dr. James Walsh, the dean of the Medical School, to establish a School of Pharmacy. Diner was joined by two other graduates of the Medical School, Dr. George Hohman and Dr. Gustave Horstman, and together they formed the faculty of the Pharmacy School, which was opened in September 1912 with eighteen students in the Science Building (Thebaud Hall). It conducted its first graduation in 1914, awarding certificates to seven students.[39]

From the very beginning Diner wanted high standards for the Pharmacy School, higher than those required by New York state. Initially he had to settle for a two-year, three-day-per-week, course of studies that led to a certificate of Graduate in Pharmacy. The students spent another three days a week gaining practical experience by working in a pharmacy. However, by 1928 Dean Diner had achieved his original goal of a four-year, five-day-per-week, curriculum, leading to a degree of Bachelor of Science in Pharmacy, which was later expanded to a five-year program.

Like many of Fordham's colleges and graduate schools, the Pharmacy School had a peripatetic existence during its early years. In 1916 it was moved to the basement of the new Medical Building (today's Finlay Hall), and in 1922 it returned to Thebaud Hall, where it occupied all three floors

39. *The Centurion, 1841–1941* (New York: Fordham University Press, 1941), 55–57. According to another version, the initiative came from Dean Walsh, who suggested the idea to Father Quinn as a way to utilize unused space for a profitable evening school. Gannon, *Up to the Present,* 133.

until it was closed in 1971. By 1923 the enrollment had grown from 18 to 600. The following year a philosophy course was introduced in the junior and senior years with special emphasis on the ethical issues associated with pharmacy. By 1939 the Pharmacy School was accredited by both the American Association of Colleges of Pharmacy and the American Council on Pharmaceutical Education.[40]

Dr. Diner was the first Jewish dean of a Fordham college or graduate school, and most of the students in the Pharmacy School were also Jewish. The presence of many Jewish students in the Medical School had already led to unfavorable comments from some of the Jesuit authorities in Rome and the United States, who questioned the wisdom of allocating Fordham's limited financial resources to a school that attracted so few Catholic students. In an official Jesuit visitation of Fordham in 1917, it was estimated that the number of Jewish students in the Medical School ranged between 20 and 50 percent, and the president of the university was told to reduce the number. The percentage of Jewish students in the Pharmacy School was even higher, 78 percent in 1925.

The presence of a Jewish dean was an especially neuralgic issue for the general, Wlodimir Ledóchowski, who wanted Diner fired. The son of a Polish count and the nephew of a cardinal, Ledóchowski was described by the German chancellor, Bernhard von Bülow, as having "the wrinkled and moulded features of a savant and the certainty of manner of a born aristocrat." Unfortunately, in the opinion of the American historian David I. Kertzer, Ledóchowski was also "a virulent anti-Semite."[41] At least one Jesuit administrator at Fordham, Father Charles J. Deane, who was the regent of the Pharmacy School from 1925 until 1952, agreed with Ledóchowski about Diner and warned Ledóchowski that the president of Fordham and the Jesuit consultors would attempt to evade his orders.[42]

However, the provincial and other Jesuits on the Fordham faculty successfully rallied to Dr. Diner's defense. The provincial, Father Lawrence Kelly, described Diner as an excellent and cultivated man who fully supported Fordham's religious identity and insisted on having courses in ethics taught by Jesuits in the Pharmacy School. Kelly also pointed out to the general that the proportion of Jewish students in the Pharmacy School was

40. FUA, Pharmacy School Files, Albert J. Sica, Historical Data, 1912–1962.

41. David I. Kertzer, *The Pope and Mussolini* (New York: Random House, 2014), xix, 233–34.

42. FUA, Memorialia R.P. Provincialium post Visitationes Inscripta, November 19, 1917. It is not clear who is the author of the memorandum. ARSJ, Lawrence Kelly to Ledóchowski, February 15, 1925; Deane to Ledóchowski, n.d. [1926].

no higher than in other Pharmacy Schools in New York City. The most eloquent defense of Dean Diner and the presence of Jewish students at Fordham came from Father Joseph T. Keating, the treasurer of the university for thirty-eight years. "The influence that Fordham has had upon the Jewish population has worked untold good," Keating told the general. He warned him to beware that "lying tongues and hypocritical sanctity have been disturbed because they are jealous of the manner in which Fordham has treated the Jews that [*sic*] have come under its influence and the manner in which Fordham has turned [many a Jewish student] from a scoffer of religion to an interested spectator and well-wisher."

With regard to Dean Diner himself, Keating told the general, "It appears that you want Dr. Diner dismissed, and the only reason assigned, as far as I know, is that Dr. Diner is a Jew." He urged the general to reconsider his decision. "There is no one man, either religious or lay, on the faculty of Fordham University, who has worked harder for, and shown more devotion to[,] Fordham than Dr. Diner," said Keating. "In season and out of season, early and late, night and day, he has worked for Fordham, defended it and made sacrifices for Fordham." As a punch line, Keating added, to dismiss him now, "without once having reprimanded him or accused him of fault, would be like a bolt from the blue and a cause of great wonderment."[43]

Another Fordham Jesuit, Father Rush Rankin, seconded Keating's defense of Diner and described him as a deeply religious man who tried to inculcate in the students respect for the Jesuits and Fordham. He mentioned that in the formative days of the Pharmacy School, Diner contributed not only his time but also his money to assure its success. Rather boldly for a lowly Jesuit professor in the 1920s, Rankin reminded the general pointedly that "our Father Ignatius told us always to be grateful to our benefactors." The Fordham Jesuits carried the day despite opposition from the general, and Diner remained dean of the Pharmacy School until 1932, when failing health forced him to resign and he was made dean emeritus. He died in 1937. Diner dedicated his whole life and his whole professional career to the Pharmacy School and to Fordham University. He was succeeded by Dr. James H. Kidder, a graduate of Fordham College and Cornell Medical School.[44]

Pharmacy students were not exempted from the draft during World War II, and as a result enrollment dropped to only 63 students in 1945, but the numbers quickly recovered in the postwar years and there were

43. ARSJ, Keating to Ledóchowski, January 6, 1926.
44. ARSJ. Rankin to Ledóchowski, January 12, 1926. *The Centurion*, 55–57.

412 students in 1950. Thereafter, the number was kept at 400 because of limited space on campus. In 1956 Dean Kidder resigned and was replaced by Albert J. Sica, the third and last dean of the Fordham Pharmacy School.

During the 1960s, declining enrollment and rising costs led to a two-year study of the feasibility and wisdom of continuing the Pharmacy School in view of Fordham's precarious financial condition and other academic commitments. Attempts to sell the Pharmacy School to the City University of New York and the State University of New York were both unsuccessful. However, Fordham concluded that the three pharmacy schools in the New York metropolitan area were capable of absorbing all the students in the Fordham School of Pharmacy. Consequently, on October 16, 1967, Father Leo McLaughlin, the president of Fordham, after obtaining the unanimous consent of the board of trustees, announced that the School of Pharmacy would accept no new students and would terminate operations no later than June 1972.[45]

The response from the public health authorities in New York City was swift and critical. Dr. Edward O'Rourke, the Commissioner of Health of the City of New York, expressed his "shock and dismay" at the announcement at a time when the city was about to implement the new Medicare and Medicaid programs of the federal government. He expressly mentioned that many of the most valued officials in the city's public health system were graduates of the Fordham School of Pharmacy. A spokesman for Mayor John V. Lindsay praised the high standards of the School of Pharmacy and offered unspecified help to enable the school to remain open. However, the obstacles to keeping the school open were overwhelming, and it ceased operations in June 1971, one year before the originally scheduled termination date.[46]

45. FUA, McLaughlin Papers, Box 6, McLaughlin to Pharmacy School, October 16, 1967; Sica to Parents, October 27, 1967.

46. FUA, McLaughlin Papers, Box 6, Edward O'Rourke to McLaughlin, December 6, 1967; Howard J. Brown to McLaughlin, November 30, 1967.

THE FORDHAM UNIVERSITY
SCHOOL OF LAW

IO

The Formative Years, 1905–23

Unlike the Medical School, the Fordham School of Law was to have a long and distinguished career. However, the establishment of the school in 1905 was a risky venture because there were already four law schools in New York City: Columbia University Law School, New York University Law School, the New York Law School, and Brooklyn Law School. Initially there was some discussion among the Fordham Jesuits of scaling back the plans for a law school and attempting to amalgamate it with the New York Law School. Some of the most prominent Fordham alumni who were lawyers favored this option, but Father Collins pushed aside their hesitations and insisted on establishing Fordham's own law school. He was fortunate in his selection of the first dean, Paul Fuller. Like James J. Walsh, M.D., the second dean of Fordham Medical School, Fuller was a larger-than-life figure with a remarkable pedigree who took no salary and assured the initial success of the new law school.[1]

Fuller's life had all the elements of a Horatio Alger success story. He was born on a clipper ship bound for San Francisco from New York City during the Gold Rush of 1849. Orphaned at an early age in California, Fuller made his way back to New York City, where he was befriended by Frederic R. Coudert, an attorney and a prominent figure in the closely knit local French Catholic community centered around the Church of St. Vincent de Paul that included such families as the Bouviers, Hoguets, Binsses, and Delmonicos.[2] Coudert gave Fuller a job at the age of twelve as an office boy in his law office. Fuller was an autodidact who taught himself law and became a partner in the Coudert Brothers law firm and an expert on international law. Although he had never spent a day in the classroom of a law school as either a student or as a professor, Fuller was an inspired choice to lead Fordham's fledgling law school in the opinion of Judge Wil-

1. FUA, Acta Consultorum March 28, 1905; ARSJ, Collins to R. E. Noble, December 1, 1919.

2. For Fuller's personal recollections of Coudert, see Paul Fuller, "Frederic R. Coudert," *HR&S* III: 2 (1905): 343–50.

Paul Fuller, dean of the Fordham University School of Law, 1905–13.

liam Hughes Mulligan, one of Fuller's most distinguished successors as the dean of the Fordham School of Law.[3]

Fordham had hoped to open the Law School in Manhattan at the College of St. Francis Xavier on West 16th Street, but these plans had to be scrapped because of a lack of space at the college. "The expected large increase in students of the high school there had perceptively lessened the warmth of our welcome to use of the lecture room," the Jesuit consultors at Fordham were told. Instead, on September 28, 1905, the School of Law began operations with nine or ten students at Rose Hill, where it shared space with the Medical School in the New Hall (present-day Collins Hall). The minimum requirement for admission was the completion of four years of high school, which was the standard practice in most law schools at that time. The tuition was $100 per annum, payable in advance. Classes were scheduled for the late afternoon and early evening to allow the students to work during the day as clerks in Manhattan law firms.

Within a few months it became obvious that commuting to Rose Hill from lower Manhattan each day was impractical, and in the spring of 1906 the Law School was moved to rented quarters at 42 Broadway. Dean Fuller said that the move was not only desirable but also necessary for the success

3. William Hughes Mulligan, "Fifty Years of Fordham Law School," *FLR* 24 (1955–1956): xi–xiii. On Fuller's scholarly reputation, see Robert J. Kaczorowski, *Fordham University School of Law: A History* (New York: Fordham University Press, 2012), 1–7.

of the school. Fordham Law School has remained ever since in Manhattan (except for a brief return of the evening division to Rose Hill between 1925 and 1938), but for its first fifty-five years it led a nomadic existence until finally finding a permanent home at the Lincoln Center campus in 1961.[4]

The first commencement exercises were held in 1908 in the theater of the College of St. Francis Xavier. Although there were only six graduates, the principal address was delivered by the governor of New York state, Charles Evans Hughes.[5] From its inception, the Law School required a three-year course of studies at a time when New York state and the state Bar Association required only two years. The original faculty consisted of three professors of law: Ralph H. Holland, H. Gerald Chapin, and Francis M. Pope, who was also the secretary of the Law School. Another valued member of the original faculty was Father Terence J. Shealy, S.J., a neo-Thomistic philosopher, who organized one of the first required courses in jurisprudence in any American law school.[6]

4. FUA, Acta Consultorum, September 8, 1905. "The School of Law," *FM*, October 1905, 25–28. In 1908, when there were 146 students, the Law School moved to 20 Vesey Street; in 1911 the Law School moved again, this time to 140 Nassau Street, where it occupied the entire ninth floor with space for 400 students; in search of more room in 1916, it rented the entire twenty-eighth floor of the Woolworth Building; in 1943, as a result of the drastic decline in enrollment during World War II, it moved to smaller quarters in the top five floors of the Vincent Building at 302 Broadway, where it remained until the relocation to Lincoln Center in 1961.

5. Twenty-five years later, when he was chief justice of the United States, Hughes said that he recalled the commencement exercises in 1908 vividly and, if the occasion arose, would gladly repeat his remarks on that occasion. FUA, Law School Papers, Box 2, Hughes to Vincent L. Leibell, May 22, 1933.

6. Father Shealy became the first Jesuit Regent of the Law School in 1919. FUA, Law School Papers, Box 10, Wilkinson to Father Rector, n.d. There were also two special lecturers, Alton B. Parker and Morgan J. O'Brien, both of whom had served as chief judge of the New York State Supreme Court, Appellate Division, First Department. Assisting them were John Joseph Lilly, the librarian and registrar, and Francis R. Stark, who had the quaint title of quiz master and whose function was to test the students about their mastery of the content of the lectures.

In 1906 the faculty was strengthened with the addition of another expert on jurisprudence, Ralph W. Gifford, a student of James B. Ames's at Harvard Law School, and later Kent Professor of Law at Columbia Law School. It was largely at the insistence of Gifford that the case system of legal education replaced the lecture-and-quiz system at Fordham between 1906 and 1909, leading to the unlamented demise of the office of the quiz master. In 1907 Frederic R. Coudert was appointed special lecturer in constitutional law and five other professors were added to the faculty, including Michael F. Dee, who served as pro-dean from 1912 until 1924.

In 1912 the faculty was further strengthened with the addition of three professors whom Dean Mulligan considered largely responsible for the early success of Fordham Law School. Two were young men who had graduated from Fordham School of Law *summa cum laude* the previous year, John T. Loughran and Ignatius M. Wilkinson.[7] Professor Loughran taught at the Fordham School of Law for eighteen years, wrote a highly regarded casebook on evidence, and in 1945 was appointed the chief judge of the New York State Supreme Court, Appellate Division, First Department, the highest judicial office in the state. Professor Wilkinson became dean of the Fordham Law School in 1923 and served in that position until his death in 1953 with a brief absence from 1943 to 1945 when he was the corporation counsel of the City of New York.

The third new member who was added to the faculty in 1912 was Professor William Kenner, who had been Story Professor at Harvard Law School and (like Professor Ralph Gifford at a later date) Kent Professor of Law at Columbia Law School. After his untimely death in 1913, Kenner was succeeded by a young professor from the University of Illinois, I. Maurice Wormser, a native New Yorker who was a graduate of Columbia Law School and the first Jewish professor at the Fordham School of Law. Wormser was to remain on the faculty for the next forty-two years, earning a national reputation for his expertise in contracts and corporation law. In addition to these three additions to the faculty, another graduate of class of 1911, Albert Conway, followed in the footsteps of his classmate John T. Loughran and was appointed the chief judge of the New York State Supreme Court, Appellate Division, First Department, in 1954. "After six years," said Judge Mulligan proudly, "the Law School was producing leaders in the legal profession."[8]

Mulligan, who entered the Law School in 1939, considered Professor Wormser the best teacher he'd ever had anywhere in his academic career despite the fact that Wormser was totally deaf. In class Worsmer put a black box on the desk with a connecting wire that he placed in his ear, which presumably allowed him to hear what the students were saying in their recitations. "It was, in fact," said Mulligan, "a complete fraud. The box was an empty shell and a mere prop for the consummate actor that

7. There was no problem with grade inflation in the Fordham School of Law. Loughran and Wilkinson were only two of 13 individuals among a total of 10,603 graduates who received their diplomas *summa cum laude* during the first sixty years of the Fordham School of Law. Kaczorowski, *Fordham University School of Law*, 11.

8. Mulligan, "Fifty Years of Fordham Law School," xi–xiii; Robert M. Hanlon, Jr., "A History of Fordham Law School," *FLR* 49 (1980–1981): xiv–xviii.

Wormser was." Once a student's lips stopped moving, he would question the student and explain the case with a clarity that would benefit even the most obtuse student in the class. "He had a brilliant mind, but was completely gentle and forbearing," said Mulligan. "I loved him."[9]

The president of Fordham, the feisty Father Thomas McCluskey, S.J., took as close an interest in the Law School as he did in the Medical School. In 1912 the question arose whether the Law School should conduct an evening school for part-time students. All of the administrators of the Law School, including Dean Fuller, Pro-Dean Michael Dee, Father Shealy, and Professors Gifford and Robert M. Hanlon Jr., opposed the evening school. Father McCluskey overruled them and prevailed, this time without the flurry of resignations that had accompanied his assertion of authority over the Medical School.

The graduates of the Law School in 1913 established an extraordinary record. In the bar examination at mid-term that year, there were 600 applicants from law schools all across the state. Only 70 applicants passed the examination, about 11 percent, compared with 88 percent of the Fordham graduates. The Fordham students did equally well in the examination at the end of the final term, when 85 percent of the graduates passed the exam compared with the statewide total of 48 percent. In 1920 Professor Wormser reported that "one of the most distinguished judges in the state" said he considered Fordham Law School the equal of any law school in New York.[10]

With the entry of the United States into World War I in the spring of 1917, enrollment dropped precipitously. The president, Father Joseph Mulry, S.J., feared that all the progress of the Law School during the previous decade was about to be undone unless some way could be found to finance it during this crisis. The situation was so serious that Father Edward P. Tivnan, S.J. (Mulry's immediate successor as president in 1919), suggested subletting the space occupied by the Law School in the Woolworth Building to the Fordham Medical School. Another solution was to admit women to the Law School, a proposal that was approved by all of the Jesuit consultors except those who thought it was hopeless even to try to continue the Law School. The more optimistic Jesuits prevailed, and in 1918 Fordham Law School admitted its first women students.[11]

9. William Hughes Mulligan, "A Former Dean Remembers," *FLR* 49 (1980–81): xxx–xxxi.

10. Hanlon, "A History of Fordham Law School," xvii. FUA, Tivnan Papers, Wormser to Tivnan, May 17, 1920.

11. FUA, Acta Consultorum, September 6, 1918. The first two African Americans

Enrollment bounded back quickly after the end of the war, jumping from 320 in 1918 to 1,462 in 1923.[12] The dean from 1919 to 1923 was Francis P. Garvan, the brother of Mrs. Genevieve Garvan Brady, whose wealthy husband, Nicholas Brady, was a generous contributor to Jesuit causes. Francis Garvan got the job of dean when he offered to make up all the deficits that the Law School might incur during the following five years. He promised to expand the faculty, introduce new courses, and make Fordham the premier law school in the United States. Garvan also pledged to donate more than $1 million to Fordham if it would move to New Haven and be supervised by Yale, his alma mater. "For some reason," said Father Robert I. Gannon, tongue in cheek, "this generous offer was not accepted."[13]

Early in the history of the Law School issues arose that would continue to plague the school for the next century, such as complaints about low faculty salaries, high ratio of students to professors, excessive involvement of faculty and administrators in outside legal work, and (until 1961) lack of space and inadequate library facilities. As Edmund Burke once remarked, great empires and little minds go ill together. In 1921 Father Tivnan initially balked at raising the salary of Pro-Dean Michael Dee because he took a full summer vacation. The following year Professor Loughran, one of Fordham's best law professors, was refused a $1,000 raise to defray the expenses of his weekly trip to Manhattan from his home in Kingston and his hotel bills in New York City.[14]

Dean Ignatius M. Wilkinson, 1923–53

Garvan's successor was Ignatius M. Wilkinson, an alumnus of the Fordham Law School, who joined the faculty immediately after graduation in 1911. Father Tivnan proved to be spectacularly wrong when he expressed reservations about the selection of Wilkinson because he was skeptical of his qualifications as an administrator. Judge Mulligan called the thirty years (1923–53) of Ignatius Wilkinson's tenure as dean the "the

---

to graduate from Fordham Law School were Ruth Whitehead Whaley and Oliver X. Williams in 1924. The following year Whaley became the first African American woman admitted to the bar in both New York and North Carolina. Kaczorowski, *Fordham University School of Law*, 46.

12. Ibid., 35.

13. Gannon, *Up to the Present*, 160.; FUA, Acta Consultorum, January 22, 1920. Professor Kaczorowski seems to think that Gannon's remark was meant seriously. Kaczorowski, *Fordham University School of Law*, 50.

14. FUA, Tivnan Papers; Tivnan to LeBuffe, October 11, 1921; LeBuffe, to Tivnan, May 16, 1922.

Ignatius M. Wilkinson, professor, 1911–53, dean of the Fordham University School of Law, 1923–53.

salad days of the law school" despite the fact they included the lean years of the Depression and World War II. Assistant Dean Robert M. Hanlon Jr. credited him with inaugurating "a new Fordham Law School."[15]

A patrician in appearance and style, and a WASP in all but religion, Wilkinson bore a certain physical resemblance to the young Franklin Delano Roosevelt (although he abhorred FDR's politics). He was independently wealthy from his law practice, lived on Park Avenue, attended the *bon ton* Jesuit Church of St. Ignatius Loyola, and ran the Law School as his personal fiefdom. His outspoken opposition to Roosevelt's attempt to "pack" the U.S. Supreme Court in 1937, especially his testimony before the Senate Judiciary Committee, doomed his chances of becoming a federal judge. Among his other accomplishments, Wilkinson expanded the size of the faculty, improved the library facilities, rewrote the statues, and revised the curriculum. Unfortunately, according to Judge Mulligan, Wilkinson then regarded the curriculum as immutable as the laws of the Medes and Persians. Two of his major accomplishments were raising admission standards and securing accreditation for the Law School from the American Bar Association and membership in the Association of American Law Schools.[16]

15. FUA, Tivnan Papers, Tivnan to Garvan, July 18, 1919; Hanlon, "A History of Fordham Law School," xx.

16. Wilkinson interrupted his service as dean to serve as corporation counsel of the City of New York from 1943 to 1945 at the request of Mayor Fiorello La Guardia despite

As was mentioned earlier, originally the only academic requirement for admission to Fordham Law School was the completion of four years of high school or its equivalent, which was common practice in many law schools. For example, John T. Loughran came to Fordham Law School fresh from Kingston High School. The lack of a college degree did not prevent him from later becoming the chief judge of New York state. In 1924 Dean Wilkinson raised the standard for admission by requiring at least one year of college, and after 1927 two years of college. By 1929, 53 percent of the entering class consisted of college graduates, who came from fifty-four colleges, of which thirty-one were Catholic institutions.[17] Curiously, Wilkinson never pushed for a college degree as a requirement for admission to the Law School because of his low opinion of college education in America.[18]

Professor Robert J. Kaczorowski, the historian of the Fordham School of Law, casts another light on the efforts of the American Bar Association and the Association of American Law Schools to raise admission standards in the American legal profession in the 1920s. To some extent, he believes, their efforts reflected the xenophobia among WASPs that was widespread even in professional circles. By contrast, he says, "Ignatius Wilkinson was dean of a part-time Catholic law school serving the very groups professional elites sought to exclude from the legal profession."[19]

In the 1920s finances were not a problem at the Law School. In fact, Father Joseph T. Keating, S.J., the capable treasurer of the university, valued both the College of Pharmacy and to a lesser extent the Law School

---

the fact they were polar opposites politically. "One of the oddest combinations of all time," Judge Mulligan called it. FUA, FOHP, William Hughes Mulligan, Interview with Michael Sheahan, September 20, 1988.

17. Kaczorowski, *Fordham University School of Law*, 98, Table 3-1.

18. "I am no believer in the value of a college education alone to guarantee character," Wilkinson told a colleague in 1934. "I am frank to say that much of what is taught in many of our so-called best colleges today is destructive of good character." FUA, Hogan Papers, Box 3, Wilkinson to Hollin W. Meeker, October 11, 1934.

The statistics cited by Wilkinson may give an exaggerated impression of the religious diversity of the student population. In fact, two-thirds of the college students came from Catholic colleges and a majority of the graduates of non-Catholic colleges were also Catholics. In 1934, 65.63 percent of the student body was Catholic, 19.91 percent was Jewish, and 14.4 percent was Protestant. FUA, Law School Papers, Box 11, Wilkinson to Duane, January 11, 1929; Wilkinson to Duane, n.d. [1930]; Wilkinson to Hogan, May 15, 1935.

19. Kaczorowski, *Fordham University School of Law*, 94.

as important sources of revenue for the university because he thought the newly founded Fordham Graduate School would never show a profit.[20]

Raising admission standards to the Law School was relatively easy. It was much more difficult to obtain the approval of the ABA and the AALS because of Fordham's extensive part-time program. Both of these professional organizations required law schools to spread out their part-time program over four years so that they were the equivalent of the full-time three-year program. However, Fordham Law School was unable to meet this requirement without first obtaining authorization from the New York Court of Appeals, which it obtained on January 16, 1931.[21] In all of his efforts to raise academic standards and win accreditation, Wilkinson had the complete support of the president of Fordham, Father Aloysius J. Hogan, S.J., even though it was anticipated that the rise in academic standards would lead to a decline in enrollment, which occurred in 1934–35, when enrollment declined by 11 percent in the Woolworth Building and by an alarming 48 percent at the Rose Hill campus.[22]

Unfortunately Father Hogan is remembered today largely for what his immediate successor, Father Robert I. Gannon, S.J., called "one of the darkest single days" in Fordham's history, the day in November 1935 when the university lost its membership in the Association of American Universities. Whatever his share of responsibility for that debacle, Hogan was unstinting in his support of Wilkinson's efforts to obtain accreditation for the Law School, and Gannon was quick to give him credit for that achievement. In November 1933, Hogan "authorized and directed" Wilkinson to apply for a change in the state rules governing part-time law programs so that Fordham Law School could apply for accreditation from the ABA.

Two years later Father Hogan told Wilkinson, "I am determined to obtain the recognition of our School of Law by the American Bar Association before the end of the present school year." Hogan announced that, beginning in 1936–37, Fordham Law School would limit its enrollment to 850 students to comply with the ABA's requirement of one full-time professor for every 100 students. He even urged Wilkinson to sever his outside legal work for fear of prejudicing Fordham's application before the

20. ARSJ, Keating to Father Wlodimir Ledóchowski, S.J., January 5, 1924. Ledóchowski was the general of the Society of Jesus.

21. Kaczorowski, *Fordham University School of Law*, 131.

22. Ibid., 132. As was mentioned earlier in this chapter, Fordham Law School made a brief return visit to its original home at Rose Hill in 1925 when it opened an evening division in three classrooms in Larkin Hall. The uptown evening school was closed in 1938.

ABA. Wilkinson himself played a crucial role by getting the ABA to accept Father John X. Pyne, S.J, professor of jurisprudence, as a full-time member of the faculty even though he was not a lawyer. Success came in 1936 when Fordham Law School received accreditation from the American Bar Association and membership in the prestigious Association of American Law Schools.[23] Professor Kaczorowski points out that "Fordham's victory was much greater than satisfying the ABA's numerical standard for full-time faculty. The ABA's acceptance of Father Pyne, a Jesuit who was not a lawyer, and his course in jurisprudence," says Kaczorowski, "was tantamount to the ABA's legitimization of the jurisprudence course and everything Catholic in the Law School."[24]

During his thirty years as dean, Wilkinson was more influential than any Jesuit in grounding the study of law at Fordham in neo-scholastic philosophy and in the Catholic natural law tradition in contrast to what he called the "philosophies of determinism and materialism" that prevailed in many of the most prestigious American law schools. However, Wilkinson did not achieve this goal by issuing *ukases* but by hiring like-minded professors (not all of them Catholic by any means). In 1949 he vigorously opposed efforts of Catholic "extremists" in the Jesuit Educational Association to establish restrictive religious norms for classroom teaching. "The faculty members have complete freedom in teaching their subjects," Wilkinson said proudly, and "problems of so-called academic freedom do not arise." "At Fordham we have taught the law against our background of Catholic philosophy," Wilkinson assured Father Robert I. Gannon, S.J., because the faculty "is made up predominantly of men who are Catholic both in faith and in culture." Likewise, Wilkinson discouraged the formation of an Association of American Catholic Law Schools because he did not want to isolate Catholic law schools from the mainstream of American legal education. "It seems to me," he said, "the place for debating the Catholic point of view is at the meetings of the Association of American Law Schools."[25]

23. ARSJ, Gannon to Ledóchowski, September 17, 1936; FUA, Hogan Papers, Box 3, Hogan to Wilkinson, November 17, 1933; November 19, 1935; November 20, 1935. In a follow-up inspection of Fordham Law School by the AALS many years later, one inspector had the temerity to question the propriety of a Catholic religious order's running a law school. Never one to suffer fools gladly, Wilkinson told the provost, Father Lawrence A. Walsh, S.J., "I determined to let him have both barrels right between the eyes." FUA, Law School Papers, Box 15, Wilkinson to Walsh, October 17, 1950.

24. Kaczorowski, *Fordham University School of Law*, 143–44.

25. FUA, Law School Papers, Box 10, Wilkinson to Gannon, January 5, 1949; Box 15, Wilkinson to Lawrence A. Walsh, July 20, 1950; Hogan Papers, Box 3, Wilkinson to Hogan, May 23, 1935.

Although the part-time evening program in the Law School was a complicating factor in obtaining accreditation from the ABA, its existence reflected Fordham's tradition of serving New York's working-class population, a tradition that stretched back to 1841, when Archbishop John Hughes established St. John's College at Rose Hill to meet the needs of New York's immigrant Catholic community. A century later Fordham Law School was still serving the children of immigrants, and not just Catholics, in ways that John Hughes could never have imagined.

In September 1922 the eighteen-year-old Louis J. Lefkowitz entered Fordham Law School. No one in New York City exemplified the immigrant work ethic better than Louis Lefkowitz. The son of Jewish immigrants who was raised in a tenement on the Lower East Side of Manhattan, Lefkowitz graduated from the High School of Commerce in January 1921 at the age of seventeen but had to wait until he was eighteen to be admitted to evening classes in Fordham Law School. In the meantime he worked as an assistant bookkeeper. During his three years at Fordham Law School, Lefkowitz held down a full-time job as a combination law clerk, stenographer, and typist for the princely salary of $8 a week. He supplemented his income by acting as a process server, delivering summons and subpoenas for a remuneration of $1 each, when he was successful in locating his prey. He said that he did most of his studying between 11:30 P.M. and 2:00 A.M. He later became a judge and the attorney general of the state of New York, holding the latter office for twenty-two years, longer than anyone else in the history of the state.[26]

During the Depression, enrollment declined from a peak of 1,200 to approximately 1,000. There was a further decline with the introduction of the four-year part-time course in 1934–35 and the increase in tuition in 1936–37. By the latter date the enrollment had fallen to 785 and did not return to pre-Depression numbers until the 1960s. One of the 60 students who enrolled in the short-lived revived Bronx campus of the Law School at Rose Hill in September 1933 was Malcolm Wilson, the future governor of New York. "With the exception of a retired Army officer who died during the first semester," said Wilson, "all my classmates had full-time employment. They were firemen, policemen, subway guards, teachers, bank tellers, and clerical employees in federal, state or city offices." As Wilson recalled years later, the library facilities at Rose Hill were so inadequate that students had to travel to the Woolworth Building to use the library

26. Louis J. Lefkowitz, "Evening Classes at Fordham Law School, 1922–1925," *FLR* 49 (1980–1981), xxxviii–xxxix.

and to take their examinations. "The sole amenities available to us," said Wilson, "were restrooms and a single coin-box telephone."[27]

In addition to Louis Lefkowitz and Malcolm Wilson, several other graduates of Fordham Law School also attained prominent positions in public life. Both Adrian P. Burke, '30, and John Scileppi, '25, became associate judges of the New York State Court of Appeals, while Irving R. Kaufman, '31, became chief judge of the U.S. Court of Appeals for the Second Circuit and David N. Edelstein, '34, became chief judge of the U.S. District Court for the Southern District of New York.

In the 1930s Fordham Law School became increasingly selective in accepting applications for admission. In 1939 Fordham admitted only 292 of the 450 applicants. By that date there was also a longstanding policy at Fordham Law School that it would not admit students who had been dismissed from other law schools. Wilkinson also refused to give letters of recommendation to students who had dropped out of Fordham Law School and had applied for admission to other law schools. However, he relented to the extent that he responded to personal inquiries from the deans of other law schools about the prospects of such students. They were not likely to get an easy pass from him. "Most students in my experience here who are excluded from law school," said Wilkinson, "are excluded not because of basic inability to do good work in the school, but because of lack of proper application to their studies."[28]

During World War II enrollment plummeted to 66 full-time students and 180 part-time students. Early in December 1941 (three days before the attack on Pearl Harbor), an anxious Wilkinson floated the idea of sending members of the Fordham Law School faculty to speak to the seniors at Catholic colleges in the hope of persuading them to come to Fordham Law School. It is curious that during the war most of the students were still men despite the impact of the Selective Service Act. At one point the full-time faculty was reduced to a total of four professors. Like many law schools, Fordham adopted an accelerated wartime program of three terms beginning in the summer of 1942. In 1944–45 Fordham was the "largest accredited under-graduate law school in America" with 300 students, but the following year the 317 students represented only 61 percent of the pre-war enrollment. The G.I. Bill led to an avalanche of applicants to law schools after the war, but Fordham was more selective than many other law

27. Malcolm Wilson, "Law School at Rose Hill," *FLR* 49 (1980–1981): xxxiv–xxxvi.
28. FUA, Law School Papers, Box 8, Wilkinson to Harold Shepherd, Secretary of AALS, February 15, 1939.

The Rose Hill campus in 1846, the year of the arrival of the first Jesuits from Kentucky.

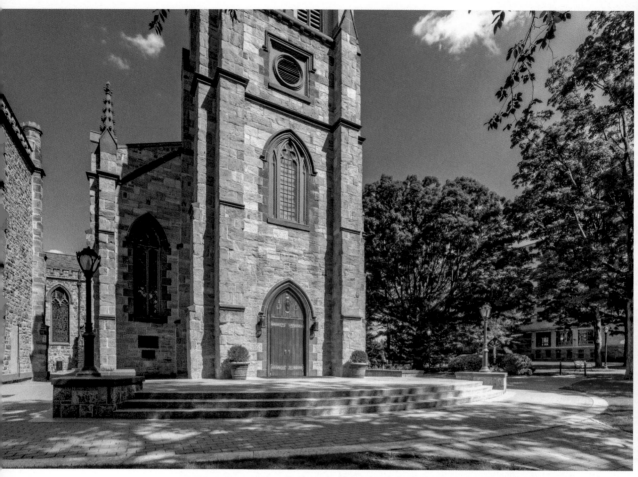

The University Church, erected in 1845, was expanded in 1929 and remodeled in 1990, 2003, and 2004. In 1970 it was declared a New York City landmark as one of the finest examples of Gothic architecture in the city.

The former Administration Building, which dates from 1838, was renamed Cunniffe House in 2013 in honor of alumnus and trustee emeritus Maurice J. Cunniffe.

Queen's Court includes three Halls: St. Robert's Hall (left, not visible in photo),
Bishop's Hall (center), and St. John's Hall (right). St. John's Hall served as
St. Joseph's Diocesan Seminary from 1845 to 1860.

The New York 69th Regiment leaves St. Patrick's Old Cathedral for service in the Civil War after the blessing of the colors by Archbishop John Hughes. (Courtesy Archives of the Archdiocese of New York)

The landscape of the rural Bronx in the mid–nineteenth century at Spuyten Duyvil, not far from Rose Hill. (Courtesy Archives of the Archdiocese of New York)

*Hughes Hall, erected in 1890, was completely renovated in 2012
and became the Rose Hill center of the Gabelli School of Business,
thanks to the generosity of alumnus Mario J. Gabelli.*

The Lion in Winter: portrait of founding father Archbishop John J. Hughes in his later years. (Courtesy Timothy Cardinal Dolan)

schools in accepting applicants if only because it did not have space at 302 Broadway to accommodate all of the applicants. Another factor in limiting the enrollment was the decision adopted by Fordham in 1946 to require a college degree for admission. However, Fordham made special provision for veterans, especially former law school students whose studies had been interrupted by the war.[29]

Dean William Hughes Mulligan: 1956–71

After Dean Wilkinson's death in 1953, he was succeeded by Professor George W. Bacon, who served for only one year as acting dean and was succeeded in turn by Professor John F.X. Finn. Upon Finn's resignation in 1956, the position went to William Hughes Mulligan, who had been a member of the faculty for the previous ten years. Mulligan's connection with Fordham was long and deep. He was baptized on St. Patrick's Day in 1918 in the Church of Our Lady of Mercy in the Bronx, which had been founded by Archbishop Hughes on the Rose Hill campus of St. John's College. The pastor, Monsignor Patrick Breslin, who was as much an autocrat as Dean Wilkinson or Archbishop Hughes, wanted to baptize the child as William Patrick Mulligan. However, Mulligan's father insisted on christening his son William Hughes Mulligan because he claimed to be a collateral descendant of John Hughes through the archbishop's sister Catherine. After attending Cathedral College, a combination high school and junior college that served as the diocesan minor seminary, young Mulligan graduated from Fordham College in 1939 and from Fordham Law School in 1942, just in time to be drafted into the army in World War II.

Mulligan's first encounter with Dean Wilkinson in 1946 was less than promising. After serving for three years in U.S. Army Counter Intelligence during World War II, Mulligan applied for a job at Fordham Law School and was interviewed by Wilkinson. Mulligan later claimed that he heard that the job was available through "professional sources" (the bar at the New York Athletic Club). The crusty and imperious Wilkinson was not impressed with Mulligan's wartime service and informed him curtly that he was running a law school, not a detective agency. Several months later, however, Wilkinson changed his mind and hired Mulligan. With his char-

29. FUA, Wilkinson to Gannon, December 4, 1941; McGinley Papers, Box 26, Wilkinson to McGinley, September 30, 1949. Only eight law schools in the nation required a college degree for admission in 1946. Acting Dean Walter B. Kennedy told Father Gannon that NYU Law School was the only serious competitor to Fordham as a part-time school and that Fordham was competitive with Columbia as a full-time law school. FUA, Law School Papers, Box 10, Kennedy to Gannon, November 21, 1945.

acteristically self-deprecating humor, Mulligan attributed Wilkinson's change of heart to the fact that he could not get anyone else to accept the starting salary of $4,000.

After serving as professor for ten years and as assistant dean for an additional two years, Mulligan was the overwhelming choice of the faculty for the job of dean in 1956 even though he was only thirty-eight years old. One of the most enthusiastic recommendations came from Professor Leonard F. Manning, a veteran member of the law faculty, who had proposed Mulligan for the post of dean three years earlier. He said that no other member of the faculty had the combination of qualifications that Mulligan possessed. Mulligan would be "sure, safe, and unanimously approved," Manning assured the president, Father Laurence McGinley. Father Lawrence A. Walsh, S.J, the provost of the university, was equally enthusiastic in his recommendation of Mulligan. Anticipating criticism that Mulligan lacked administrative experience, Manning said, "Administrative experience is a cowardly term." He explained, "I have observed too many politicos, businessmen and lawyers acquire administrative experience by sitting on their buttocks scribbling doodles."[30]

Even before his appointment as assistant dean, Mulligan gave voice to his vision for Fordham Law School when he told McGinley that "our objective is to make lawyers in the fullest sense and not legal dilettantes." In personality the genial and affable Mulligan was as different from the stiff and snobbish Wilkinson as chalk from cheese, but he shared Wilkinson's conviction that the study of law should be grounded in the classical Catholic philosophical and ethical tradition. "If we grant that moral leadership is to be sought at the Bar," he asked, "where better to seek it than at Fordham?" "This is by no means to suggest that we become a monastic or religious institution in any narrow sense," he explained. "We can obtain this objective generally within the framework of our present curriculum, but our philosophy should pervade our entire thinking in all courses and all our extra-curricular activities."[31]

30. FUA, McGinley Papers, Box 26, Manning to McGinley, July 24, 1953; Walsh to McGinley, July 16, 1953. Manning was surprised to discover that Mulligan had attended Cathedral College instead of a Jesuit prep school because he thought he had "the zeal and classical learning which characterizes a Jesuit." However, he admitted that the New York diocesan clergy "did a Jesuit-like job on him even in Latin and Greek." Mulligan's own choice for dean in 1953 was Professor Joseph W. McGovern. FUA, McGinley Papers, Box 26, Mulligan to McGinley, July 22, 1953. Mulligan was appointed dean on September 1, 1956.

31. FUA, McGinley Papers, Box 26, Mulligan to McGinley, July 22, 1953.

Assistant Dean Mulligan described Fordham Law School to a potential donor in 1954 as "a fine, conservatively run, yet progressive institution with a splendid faculty and an excellent student body."[32] The following year, when the Law School celebrated its golden jubilee, it could boast that it had produced 6,000 graduates, many of whom had gone on to distinguished careers at the bar and the bench. However, there were also serious problems to address, as was pointed out to Dean Finn by John G. Hervey of the ABA. Hervey, a Methodist layman, was a consistently good friend of Fordham Law School, and he warned Finn in a friendly fashion in 1954 before a periodic inspection by the ABA that Fordham Law School had serious problems. Its library acquisitions were inadequate, the salary scale was the lowest in the New York metropolitan area, and the student–full-time faculty ratio was the highest in the area. He also warned Finn, again in a friendly fashion, that the ABA would look unfavorably on the university's habit of siphoning off much of the profit of the Law School.[33]

Mulligan introduced a number of important innovations during his fifteen years as dean. Within three years he increased the number of full-time faculty from ten to nineteen, made the LSAT exams a requirement for admission, initiated major revisions in the curriculum, and broadened the recruitment of students from beyond Fordham College. Mulligan also hired a professional librarian (who was also a lawyer) for a library that still contained only 30,000 volumes. Mulligan said that for many years the principal asset of the law library was the view of the city that it offered from its windows on the upper floors of 302 Broadway. The previous librarian was a former law book salesman who never got beyond high school and did not believe in catalogues or indexes. As a result, said Mulligan, "You had to find the books on your own."[34]

32. FUA, Law School Papers, Box 2, Mulligan to Vincent Astor, July 6, 1954.

33. FUA, McGinley Papers, Box 26, September 13, 1954. Hervey's official title was advisor of the section of legal education and admission to the bar of the American Bar Association. The following year Father Edward A. Quain, S.J, the academic vice president, sounded a similar warning about the ratio of full-time to part-time professors. "There is no school of comparable size with so unfavorable a faculty ratio," he told McGinley. Fordham had nine full-time professors and fifteen part-time professors for a student body of approximately 675. St. Louis University Law School had exactly the same number of full-time and part-time professors for 259 students. FUA, McGinley Papers, Box 26, Quain to McGinley, February 17, 1955.

Both Finn and Mulligan were grateful to Hervey because they thought he could have been much more severe in his evaluation of Fordham Law School. FUA, McGinley Papers, Box 26, Quain to McGinley, March 1, 1955.

34. FUA, FOHP, Mulligan, Interview with Michael Sheahan, September 20, 1988.

Some of the criticisms made by the ABA, such as the inadequate library facilities and the high student–full-time faculty ratio, were impossible to correct because of the cramped quarters at 302 Broadway, where there was no room for expansion of the library or additional offices for new professors. "In my opinion," said Mulligan as late as 1959, "the greatest single factor in holding us back is the severe space limitations that we face in this building." In his own inimitable way he described 302 Broadway as better suited for opium dens or massage parlors than a law school.[35] Many full-time faculty members, including Mulligan, favored a relocation of the law school to a new building on the Bronx campus at Rose Hill. At Harvard, Yale, and Columbia the law schools were located on the university campuses, and Syracuse University and Boston College had recently relocated their law schools to the university campuses.

Dean Finn demurred and wanted the new location of the law school to be in Manhattan. Within a year of its establishment in 1905, Fordham Law School had moved from its original location on the Bronx campus to downtown Manhattan so that part-time law students could work in Manhattan law firms. Finn favored a continuation of that policy. "Our teachers note," he told the president, Father Laurence J. McGinley, S.J., "that the evening students are inevitably more mature, more serious, more thorough, and more effectively productive than the three-year day students. We have seen produced by the Fordham evening courses many very able lawyers who could not have made the grade financially in the day law school." "I have reached the considered conclusion," he added, "that Fordham should not desert the Abraham Lincoln who can competitively master his law books in one hand while mastering a trade in the other."[36]

Assistant Dean Mulligan agreed that Fordham should continue its policy of offering night courses for those students who could not afford to attend the day school. However, he deplored the division of the day school into morning and afternoon sessions because he thought it was an "occasion of sin" for the students (and faculty) and led them to spend an inordinate amount of time working in law firms. Dean Finn was a prime

35. Mulligan's sense of humor extended to matters great and small. As dean he once dismissed a student for poor grades. The student appealed his expulsion on the grounds that a ceiling fixture had fallen on his mother's head, causing a concussion and preventing him from studying properly. When the mother asked for a meeting with the president, Father Leo McLaughlin, S.J., Mulligan warned McLaughlin, "Make sure all the ceiling fixtures are firmly in place; otherwise we may have to let him back in." FUA, McLaughlin Papers, Box 6, Mulligan to McLaughlin, July 14, 1966.

36. FUA, Law School Papers, Box 2, Finn to McGinley, August 10, 1955.

The Fordham University School of Law

offender and it was one of the reasons for his being eased out of the dean's position in 1956.[37] Presumably this is what Mulligan meant when he described Fordham Law School as a "commercial school" or "trade school." He also thought the excessive involvement of the faculty in outside legal work accounted for their "abysmal record for scholarly publications." "I think the time is ripe to go forward," he told Father McGinley in the summer of 1955, "and not to stand still simply because we have been here for fifty years and have achieved a sort of middle class respectability, but not yet the eminence which we can attain."[38]

Three years later Fordham Law School received its first inspection from the ABA under Mulligan's tutelage as dean. As he had anticipated, the ABA found no major problems. Moreover, like Mulligan himself, the inspection team of the ABA attributed most of the shortcomings to the same cause as Mulligan, the lack of adequate space in the top five floors of 302 Broadway. However, in view of his own optimistic vision for the law school, he had to be disappointed at the critical verdict of the inspection team that Fordham Law School is "frankly a 'local' law school with no aspiration to compete on a national and international stage." Damning with faint praise, the inspection team credited Fordham with avoiding a "provincial point of view" but added that "in view of the sophisticated nature of the metropolitan practice, it could hardly be otherwise." Mulligan bit his tongue and described the report as "interesting."[39]

After wandering in the inhospitable terrain of lower Manhattan for fifty-five years, Fordham Law School finally caught sight of the promised land on May 3, 1960, with the blessing of the cornerstone of the new Law School building on West 62nd Street. It was the first building to be erected on the site of Fordham's new seven-and-a-half-acre Lincoln Center campus, and it contained three times as much space as the Law School quarters at

37. FUA, McGinley Papers, Box 26, Quain to McGinley, July 5, 1956. Finn had the cute practice of returning telephone calls from his law office as if he were in the dean's office at Fordham. Ibid.

38. FUA, McGinley Papers, Box 26, Quain to McGinley, March 1, 1955; Mulligan to McGinley, July 7, 1955. Mulligan described Professor Wormser as "our only legal writer with more than a local reputation and his work is not of recent date." Mulligan to McGinley, July 22, 1953.

39. FUA, McGinley Papers, Box 26, Inspection Report of the ABA, April 28–29, 1958; Mulligan to McGinley, July 1, 1958. Professor Kaczorowski says bluntly that "in the half-century of its existence Fordham Law School declined from an elite institution of legal education to a trade school." By 1950 New York University Law School replaced it as the second-most-important law school in New York City. Kaczorowski, *Fordham University School of Law*, 214, 205.

302 Broadway. The ceremony was preceded by a Mass at the neighboring Church of St. Paul the Apostle attended by 2,000 people. The celebrant was Father William A. Mitchell, C.S.P., the superior general of the Paulist Fathers. The presiding prelate was Francis Cardinal Spellman, the archbishop of New York and Fordham alumnus, class of 1911.

At the blessing of the cornerstone by Cardinal Spellman the principal address was delivered by Earl Warren, the chief justice of the United States. Also present was Governor Nelson Rockefeller, who noted that both Lieutenant Governor Malcolm Wilson and Attorney General Louis Lefkowitz (the two key players in his religiously balanced leadership team) were alumni of Fordham Law School. Mayor Robert Wagner Jr. was represented by Deputy Mayor, Paul O'Keefe, who claimed that there was now some confusion in local legal circles between the bench in the First Judicial District and the Fordham Law School Alumni Association.

Not to be overlooked at the ceremonies—and there was little chance that he would be overlooked—was Commissioner Robert Moses, who was responsible for the fact that Fordham University had received a new urban campus in the heart of the Lincoln Square renewal project. Moses hailed Father McGinley as a great priest and a great New Yorker and recalled how together they had pushed through the Lincoln Square project despite "the sensationalism, bias and bigotry, of which this town has more than its fair share."[40]

The following year, there was a two-day celebration of the dedication of the new law school building, which began on Friday, November 17, 1961, with a symposium featuring Bishop John J. Wright of Pittsburgh, Professor Arthur E. Sutherland of Harvard Law School, and Adlai E. Stevenson, the U.S. ambassador to the United Nations. The following day was the formal dedication, at which Robert F. Kennedy, the attorney general of the United States, received an honorary doctorate and delivered the principal address. After more than a half-century of waiting and three years of detailed planning by the dean and the faculty, Fordham Law School finally

40. New York *Catholic News*, May 7, 1960. Privately Moses told Father McGinley, "Who am I to tell Jesuits that education is a long process and to recall Vergil's phrase *forsan et haec olim meminisse juvabit*—in other words, that someday we shall look back over these trying times with genuine pleasure." At the time, Moses was preparing for the forthcoming World's Fair in New York City, and he told McGinley, "Some of us, like the old charger in the Bible, paw the ground, say 'ha ha' to the trumpet and smell the battle afar off. In fact, we are already girding for other frays, since no one has proven yet that life is other than a battle." FUA, McGinley Papers, Box 25, Moses to McGinley, November 1, 1961.

had a permanent home that was worthy of its ambition to become a first-class institution.

Six years later, John G. Hervey, Fordham's longtime friend at the ABA, called the building "one of the best law school buildings in the country—functional to the minutest detail." He added, "This is a building which other law schools have examined with profit over the past five years." Hervey also said that Fordham Law School had probably made the greatest progress of any multi-division, church-related law school in America during the previous twenty years. He was especially impressed with the improvement in the library, which had grown from 25,000 volumes in 1950 to 100,200 volumes in 1967. Perhaps the best measure of Fordham's success was that it was no longer in competition with St. John's Law School and Brooklyn Law School but with Columbia and New York University.

Hervey credited Dean Mulligan with much of the progress. Mulligan ended the inbreeding among the faculty by gently persuading a number of veteran full-time teachers to accept part-time status. By 1967 only five of the nineteen full-time faculty members were still alumni. Mulligan solved another longstanding problem by scheduling the classes in such a way that it was impossible for full-time students to take outside employment. He also raised considerable funds for scholarships, grants-in-aid, and loans, a necessity when the competition for promising students among Catholic law schools made the competition for athletes "look like a dress rehearsal." There was no longer any discussion of eliminating the part-time evening division. In Hervey's opinion the single biggest weakness at Fordham Law School was the precarious state of its finances. He believed that only additional funding would enable Fordham to raise faculty salaries, reduce class size, provide more student aid, and construct additional student housing, in order to reach its stated goal of becoming a top-flight A-1 law school. "Having advanced so far," Hervey predicted, "it appears unlikely that they will stop short of their goal." Unfortunately his prediction proved to be overly optimistic, at least in the short run.[41]

Crisis Mode

As Hervey perceptively pointed out, Fordham Law School's quest for excellence and national recognition was contingent on its receiving adequate funding from the university. However, this quest was complicated by the fact that it coincided in the late 1960s and early 1970s with the most serious financial crisis in the history of Fordham University. In

41. FUA, Walsh Papers, Box 6, Inspection Report of John C. Hervey, July 24, 1967.

an unprecedented development, in December 1968 the Roman authorities of the Society of Jesus forced the resignation of the president of Fordham University, Father Leo McLaughlin, S.J., because of fiscal mismanagement and replaced him with Father Michael Walsh, S.J., the former president of Boston College. Father Walsh spent the better part of the next two years struggling to restore Fordham's solvency. Moreover, his efforts were played out against the background of the widespread student protests against the Vietnam War that swept college campuses throughout the United States. At Fordham, campus unrest included several occupations of the Administration Building, the attempted torching of the Campus Center, and other disruptive activities.

The hagiographer Alban Butler said famously that church history is largely the story of quarrels between good men. The same observation could be made about the relationship between the leaders of Fordham Law School and the leaders of Fordham University in those years. Dean Mulligan's dream of upgrading Fordham Law School into a first-rate academic institution clashed with Father Walsh's more immediate priority of restoring the shattered finances of the university. The surface issue was the basis on which the yearly surplus generated by the Law School should be divided between the Law School and the university. The more fundamental issue was the degree of autonomy that the Law School should possess in its relationship to the university, a sensitive issue with many members of the Law School faculty, because many university-affiliated law schools in the United States enjoyed a greater degree of autonomy than did Fordham Law School.

Even before the onset of the financial crisis, Mulligan pleaded for an increase in the number of full-time faculty. Fordham's ratio was one full-time professor to 41 students, dangerously close to the AALS's minimum requirement of one full-time professor for every 50 students, and it placed Fordham at about 106 among the 135 law schools reporting. The average full-time faculty salary was $12,542, $8,000 less than the salary at some Ivy League law schools. Mulligan explained to the alumni in 1965 that Fordham Law School's ambition to compete on the national level rather than the local required substantially increased scholarship money and expanded dormitory facilities. In 1964 Mulligan had asked Father Vincent T. O'Keefe, S.J., the president of Fordham, for additional faculty, increased salaries, and more scholarships.[42]

42. FUA, O'Keefe Papers, Box 4, Mulligan to O'Keefe, January 8, 1964, Mulligan to O'Keefe, January 16, 1964; McLaughlin Papers, Box 6, Mulligan to McLaughlin, Janu-

The financial crisis of 1969–70 exacerbated the crisis and introduced a new element of antagonism and bitterness into the relationship between the Law School and the university. Early in 1969 Mulligan informed Father Walsh that he had a continuing problem in sustaining faculty morale "in light of the recent financial crises at the University which have had an adverse effect on our school which has been financially profitable and educationally sound." A month later Mulligan questioned whether the Law School was receiving a fair allocation of funds for full-time faculty salaries, and he warned Walsh that Fordham was lagging far behind comparable university law schools, leaving it in "a very poor competitive position." Walsh replied that he regretted that the university could not be more generous in view of the fact that it appeared that the financial situation would be even more critical the following year.[43]

The tension between the Law School and the university escalated in January 1970 when the Self-Study Committee of the Law School submitted its report to Father Walsh. The chairman of the Self-Study Committee, Professor Robert M. Byrn, summarized the main points in the report in a covering letter to Father Walsh. While recognizing the high quality of legal education at Fordham, the committee repeated longstanding demands for improvements in the library, the size and salaries of the faculty, funding for faculty research, curriculum revision, and additional secretarial help and student scholarships. The most provocative part of the report was the statement that "the experience of recent years demonstrates that the Law School must have internal control over its own quest for excellence if it is to survive." Specifically, the report declared that the Law School must be able to retain substantially all the income that it derived from tuition and student fees for the foreseeable future. "Mediocrity is unacceptable," declared Professor Byrn.[44]

Walsh waited a month before replying to Professor Byrn and then confessed that he was "terribly disappointed" with the failure of the report to place its conclusions and demands within the context of the financial crisis

ary 10, 1966; Mulligan to John J. Meng, December 13, 1966. O'Keefe Papers, Box 4. In 1964 O'Keefe had given Mulligan permission to hire two additional full-time professors. O'Keefe to Mulligan, February 11, 1964.

43. FUA, Walsh Papers, Box 6, Mulligan to Walsh, March 20, March 21, 1969; Walsh to Mulligan; Walsh to Mulligan, April 1, 1969.

44. FUA, Walsh Papers, Box 6, Robert M. Byrn to Walsh, January 9, 1970. The self-study committee was appointed in December 1968, the same month that Father Mc-Laughlin was forced to resign as president of Fordham University. The report of the self-study committee was approved by the faculty of the Law School a year later.

the university was experiencing. The heart of the report, said Walsh, was not a critical self-evaluation but a demand for academic and fiscal autonomy for the Law School. If the university acceded to this demand, Walsh painted a dire picture of the consequences. "In time," he said, "many of our most worthwhile academic programs would have to be phased out for lack of financial support, with the result that the university would become little more than a loose federation of autonomous, self-sustaining trade schools. But that hardly accords with the concept of a university."[45]

Unhappy with Walsh's response to the report of the Self-Study Committee, Byrn resigned as the chairman of the committee on February 16, 1970, but promised Dean Mulligan that he would continue his efforts to improve the quality of legal education at Fordham. He was as good as his word and a decade later served as the chairman of another important Law School committee.[46]

In his protracted tussle with the Law School and with the ABA (which encouraged the Law School's quest for greater fiscal autonomy), Walsh could count on strong support from two of the most effective vice presidents in the history of Fordham University, Dr. Paul Reiss, the academic vice president, and Dr. Joseph Cammarosano, the executive vice president. Dean Mulligan's successor at the Law School, Dean Joseph M. McLaughlin, had no doubts about Walsh's concern for the well-being of the Law School. He had an equally warm regard for Joseph Cammarosano. "I loved to deal with him," McLaughlin said, "because he never conned you. If he wasn't going to do something, he would tell you right up front. I loved him." An economist with a sense of history, Cammarosano warned Walsh that decentralization of the finances would transform Fordham University into "some kind of Hanseatic League, and then for not too long a period at that."[47]

On June 15, 1970, Mulligan submitted his resignation as dean. Ever the

45. FUA, Walsh Papers, Box 6, Walsh to Byrn, February 9, 1970. Walsh claimed that, at meetings the previous year, the faculty and students of the Law School proposed that "the Law School should be autonomous in every way." He claimed that Dean Mulligan made the same proposal more subtly. FUA, Walsh Papers, Box 6, Walsh to Cammarosano, October 20, 1969.

46. FUA, Walsh Papers, Box 6, Byrn to Mulligan, February 16, 1970. Professor Byrn's efforts on behalf of the pro-life movement won him a papal honor, the *Pro Ecclesia et Pontifice* medal, at the same time that he was jousting with Father Walsh. FUA, Walsh Papers, Box 6, Mulligan, Dean's Report to the Alumni, 1970.

47. FUA, FOHP, Joseph McLaughlin, Interview with Assistant Dean Robert Reilly, April 9, 1990, 42. FUA, Walsh Papers, Box 6, Cammarosano to Walsh, October 23, 1969.

The Fordham University School of Law

gentleman, Mulligan made no mention of his disagreements with Walsh. He cited only his desire to retire after a quarter-century of service to the Law School and the university. Walsh expressed polite regret at his decision to retire but did not twist his arm to remain as dean. Mulligan retained his chair at Fordham as the Wilkinson Professor of Law. Within months of his retirement as dean, however, Mulligan was appointed a judge of the United States Court of Appeals for the Second Circuit by President Richard M. Nixon. He was the first dean of Fordham Law School to receive this honor.[48] Like Dr. James J. Walsh, who resigned as dean of the Fordham Medical School almost sixty years earlier after a dispute with the president of Fordham, Mulligan, whose association with Fordham and the Jesuit community stretched over seven decades, remained a loyal and generous supporter of the university and the Society of Jesus.

Dean Joseph M. McLaughlin: 1971–81

The tug-of-war between President Walsh and Dean Mulligan over the relationship between the university and Fordham Law School continued under their respective successors, President James Finlay, S.J., and Dean Joseph M. McLaughlin, although in a less contentious manner. Finlay was the son of Irish immigrants who was able to attend college only because he won a scholarship to Fordham. Early in life he learned to appreciate the value of a dollar. Finlay's penchant for micromanagement reminded McLaughlin of President Jimmy Carter, who was famous for turning off light switches and lowering the thermostat in the White House. McLaughlin was a native of Brooklyn and a graduate of Fordham College and Fordham Law School and had been a professor at Fordham Law School at the time of his selection as dean in 1971. Like William Hughes Mulligan, McLaughlin had an infectious Irish sense of humor that he displayed even in the usually somber pages of the Annual Dean's Report. Assistant Dean Robert Reilly described "these fanciful reports with little drawings and special themes [as] probably the most unusual pieces of literature of their type in American legal jurisprudence."[49]

Neither President Finlay nor Dean McLaughlin was able to heal completely the rift between the university on the one hand and the Law School

48. FUA, Walsh Papers, Box 6, Mulligan to Walsh, June 15, 1970; Walsh to Mulligan, June 19, 1970. Mulligan resigned from the bench in 1981 and returned to private practice in New York City. He retired ten years later after suffering a stroke and died in 1996.

49. FUA FOHP, McLaughlin, Interview, April 9, 1990, 40. FUA, FOHP, December 9, 1991, Assistant Dean Robert Reilly, Interview with Robert Cooper Jr., December 9, 1991, 44.

and the ABA on the other hand in the 1970s. A partial détente took place only a decade later during the presidency of Father Joseph O'Hare, S.J., when John Feerick was dean of Fordham Law School. "I feel very proud of the developments that [took place] during the 1980s," said Dean Feerick in retrospect, because the university gave the Law School "greater autonomy with reference to its fiscal affairs and how its fiscal resources should be allocated among the priorities that the Law School identifies." Dean Feerick also noted that even earlier under Father Finlay the Law School gradually received greater control of its budget.[50]

While Finlay was engaged in his internal turf war with the Law School, he also became involved in a battle with the ABA when that organization made what seemed to him to be conflicting, if not contradictory, evaluations of the Fordham Law School. The ABA routinely praised Fordham Law School as a "good" or "very good" school but then demanded disclosures of the finances of the Law School that McGinley and Cammarosano regarded as unwarranted intrusions into the internal affairs of the university. Although Fordham Law School never lost its accreditation, it was not until the advent of Father O'Hare as president and John Feerick as dean in the 1980s that there was a noticeable amelioration in the prickly relationship between Fordham and the ABA.

Professor Kaczorowski credits Dean McLaughlin with building upon the efforts of Dean Mulligan but also making his own original contributions to enhance the reputation of Fordham School of Law. McLaughlin immediately increased the size of the full-time faculty by one-third and transformed the curriculum by reducing the number of required courses and increasing the number of electives. McLaughlin also took a different view of legal education from that of Dean Mulligan, who once announced that the purpose of a law school was "to prepare students for the bar exam and the rest was baloney." It was a surprising and disappointing comment from someone who had castigated his predecessor Dean Ignatius Wilkinson for conducting "a trade school."[51]

McLaughlin, who had a loftier and more humanistic concept of legal education, considered it a form of liberal arts education and wanted it to

50. FUA, FOHP, Interview with John D. Feerick by Assistant Dean Robert Reilly, September 20, 1991. Even earlier, during the waning days of the Walsh administration, the university made a major concession to the Law School when it allowed the Law School to conduct its own fundraising campaign, although the ultimate disposition of the funds remained in the hands of the president of the university. Kaczorowski, *Fordham University School of Law*, 267–68.

51. Cit. in Kaczorowski, ibid., 440n29.

be a cultural experience, not merely an exercise in vocational training. For that reason McLaughlin encouraged interdisciplinary courses such as "Law and Medicine" and "Law and Psychiatry." He welcomed the presence at the Law School of visiting professors from other Fordham graduate schools. McLaughlin was also responsible for the establishment of the first effective Placement Office, which, he thought, led to the discovery of Fordham Law School by major Wall Street legal firms. The revival of the moribund Alumni Association of the Law School also played an important role in raising the profile of the Law School, an achievement that McLaughlin credited largely to the efforts of John Feerick, the president of the association.[52]

McLaughlin also played an important role in increasing the size and quality of the *Fordham Law Review*, which had been established by students in November 1914 as one of the first dozen law reviews in the United States. It originally appeared as part of the *Fordham Monthly* and consisted of summaries of recent court decisions and a book review. The first article appeared in November 1915, and the *Fordham Law Review* appeared as a separate publication in January 1916. It suspended publication in June 1917 and did not resume publication until 1935.[53]

McLaughlin's successor as dean of Fordham Law School, John Feerick, gave McLaughlin much of the credit for making the *Review* "one of the nation's top legal publications." It was also during McLaughlin's tenure as dean that Fordham Law School established its second professional publication, the *Urban Law Journal*.[54] McLaughlin resigned as dean in 1981 when he was appointed to the U.S. District Court for the Eastern District of New York. At that point he had served Fordham Law School as a professor and dean for a total of twenty years.

Dean John Feerick: 1982–2002

Father Finlay was ecstatic when he informed the acting superior general of the Society of Jesus of the appointment of John Feerick. "We have a tradition of fine deans at the [Law] School," he informed Father Paolo Dezza, S.J., "but I suspect the new dean may prove even better than his predecessors." Finlay mentioned that Feerick "sacrificed a position as a senior partner in one of the largest law firms in New York to become dean." He explained that "people who are acquainted with the income he

52. Ibid., 275, 280–81, 283, 317.

53. Kaczorowski, *Fordham University School of Law*, 73–77.

54. John D. Feerick, "The Fordham Law Review and Dean Joseph M. McLaughlin: A Combined Tribute," *FLR* 50:1 (1981): v–vi.

John Feerick, dean of the Fordham University School of Law, 1982–2002; Leonard F. Manning Distinguished Professor, 2002–3; Sidney C. Morris Chair of Law, 2003–present.

had derived from his private practice are simply amazed that a relatively young man (45 years) with a large family (6 children) would make such a sacrifice." "His motives, I can assure you," added Finlay, "are the highest apostolic motives. He is simply an exceptional man."[55]

Finlay failed to mention that he had approached Feerick and asked him to consider accepting the position of dean, as had several senior members of the faculty of the Law School, including Professors Leonard Manning and John Calamari. However, Feerick said that the decisive reason for his accepting the invitation was the opportunity for public service. "There was something strong within me saying it was time to give something back to the world, at least a part [of the world] which meant a great deal to me and had done so much for me," said Feerick. "I always had a vision," he explained, "from the time that I graduated from Law School, that at some point in my life, I ought to be engaged in public service." The office of the dean of the Fordham School of Law seemed to offer that opportunity because, he said, "I associated much of what a law school dean has to do with service."[56]

Feerick was the son of Irish immigrants, a native of the South Bronx, and a graduate of a local Catholic elementary and high school, as well as

55. FUA, O'Hare Papers, Box 1, Finlay to Father Paolo Dezza, S.J., Delegate of the Holy Father to the Society of Jesus, December 17, 1981.

56. FUA, FOHP, Feerick, Interview, 28.

both Fordham College and Fordham Law School. He was to serve as dean of Fordham Law School for twenty years, longer than any other dean in the history of the Law School except Ignatius Wilkinson. Father Finlay's hopes that Feerick's achievements would prove to be even more impressive than those of his predecessors were not disappointed. At the time of Feerick's resignation as dean in 2002, his successor, Dean William M. Treanor, said, "No single individual in the history of the School has done more than John Feerick to advance our educational mission, to secure our future as a center of academic learning, and to create a place that is special for its scholarship, its ethical values, and its commitment to the public interest."[57]

The credibility that Feerick had acquired as the president of the Fordham Law School Alumni Association enabled him to establish a phenomenal record as dean as a fundraiser for the Law School, not only from the alumni but also from foundations. In 1984 the Annual Alumni Fund raised $288,000; in 1988, under the leadership of James Gill, the fund raised $1 million; and in 1995, under the leadership of Maureen Scannell Bateman, the fund raised $4 million. That same year, Louis Stein, one of the Law School's most generous alumni, donated another $1.1 million. During Feerick's tenure, Fordham Law School received other exceptionally generous gifts from Ned Doyle (a person who was an inspiration to Feerick), from the estate of Leo Kissam, and from the Norman and Rosita Winston Foundation. By 2002 Feerick had established an endowment of approximately $50 million for the Law School. In that year alone he raised more than $11 million in gifts and pledges.[58]

Previous inspections by the ABA had faulted the faculty for its inbreeding—what it called its "home-grown flavor"—and its lack of scholarly publications. Both shortcomings were addressed and corrected during the Feerick years. By 1994 no fewer than seventeen members of the Fordham faculty had received their initial law degrees from other law schools, and in that same year inspectors from the ABA complimented the Fordham Law School for the "immense progress" it had made in scholarly legal publications. Fordham Law School had also made considerable progress in the gender and ethnic diversification of the faculty. One-quarter of the faculty were women, and six were minorities (four African Americans, one Asian, and one Latino).[59]

57. Treanor, Dean's Annual Report to Alumni, 2001–2002, cit. in Kaczokowski, *Fordham University School of Law*, 367.

58. Kaczorowski, *Fordham University School of Law*, 328–29.

59. Ibid., 335–37. In 2001 the average salary of female graduates of Fordham Law

Feerick achieved comparable changes with the student body. He responded to a longstanding ABA complaint about the excessive student-to-faculty ratio by reducing the ratio at Fordham Law School to less than the ABA minimum standard of twenty students to each professor. Another noteworthy accomplishment (which the ABA was quick to notice) was his ability to raise admission standards at the same time that he was maintaining a high enrollment and diversifying the student body. In 1993 one-quarter of the entering class consisted of minority students, more than double the number in 1988.[60]

John Feerick said the primary motive that led to his decision to accept the invitation to become the dean of Fordham Law School was the opportunity it afforded him to repay the community that had enabled him, the son of Irish immigrants, to achieve such a prominent place in the New York academic and civic world. He sought to repay that debt through many forms of what he called "public service" but especially through promoting three centers or institutes at Fordham Law School. The first was the Stein Institute of Law and Ethics, which was established in 1982 during Feerick's first year as dean. It was the result of the generosity of Louis Stein, Law '26, and the warm relationship he had earlier established with Dean Mulligan. In 1973, while working closely with John Feerick, then president of the Fordham Law School Alumni Association, Stein had already established the Stein Prize to honor outstanding members of the legal profession. In the early 1990s Stein further increased his connection with Fordham Law School by creating both the Stein Center for Ethics and Public Interest Law as well as the Stein Scholars Program for students who were interested in pursuing a career in that specialty. In 1995 these two programs were combined with the Stein Institute of Law and Ethics to form the Louis Stein Center for Law and Ethics.[61]

Another example of Fordham Law School's involvement in public service is the Public Interest Resource Center, which acts as an umbrella organization for twenty-five student-run organizations, including Habitat for Humanity. It attracts annually the participation of some 500 law school students and in 2008 won the ABA's Pro Bono Publico Award, making Fordham Law School only the second university recipient of the award.

School was $105,295, compared with $97,151 for male graduates. *Fordham University Law School Student Bulletin*, 2002–2003, 99.

60. Ibid., 339, 348–50.

61. The recipients of the Stein Prize have included no fewer than seven justices of the U.S. Supreme Court, including Chief Justice Warren Burger and Chief Justice William Rehnquist. http://law.fordham./Louis-stein-center-for-law-and-ethics/1995.htm.

In the graduating class of 2015, no fewer than 67 percent of the graduates reported at least 100 hours of public service while at the Law School.[62]

Fordham Law School's commitment to public service became international in scope in 1997 with the establishment of the Joseph R. Crowley Program in International Human Rights, which brings human rights advocates from all over the world to speak at Fordham and enables Fordham Law students to spend part of their summer vacation working with human rights advocates abroad.[63]

Several other important developments took place at Fordham Law School during the Feerick years. One was the establishment of two LLM programs that attracted foreign lawyers to Fordham from across the globe. Another was the introduction of joint degree programs with the Business School and the School of Social Service. In addition, a joint program on International Political Economy and Development was introduced by the Law School and the Department of Political Science in the Graduate School of Arts and Sciences at Rose Hill, leading to a J.D./M.A. degree. Still another important development was the establishment of the Inter-Disciplinary Center with the School of Social Service that was originally focused on children. It was created by Professor Thomas Quinn of Fordham Law School and flourished for many years under his direction. Feerick said that Quinn "embodied our mission in the service of others." As far back as the 1960s Quinn urged every American law school to establish a course in poverty law.

Feerick was especially proud of two additional innovations that took place during his years as dean, although he was quick to give the credit for the success of the programs to others. One was a commitment on the part of the Law School to clinical legal education, teaching lawyers "lawyering skills." Introduced in 1990, it led to a "transformative" change in the Law School and became one of the best programs of its kind in the United States. Feerick gave the full credit for its success to Professor James Cohen, who directed the program for many years. Another innovation was the introduction of "problem-solving" courses in mediation, arbitration, and related processes, both on the domestic and international levels, under the leadership of Professor Jacqueline Nolan Hadley. Today it enjoys the highest specialty ranking of any program in the Law School.[64]

---

62. https://en.wikipedia.org/wiki/Fordham_University_School_of_Law. Feerick, personal communication to author.

63. Kaczorowski, *Fordham University School of Law*, 346.

64. Feerick, personal communication to author.

Retrospect

When John Feerick resigned as dean of the Fordham School of Law in 2002, the school was only three years short of celebrating its centenary. During its ninety-seven-year history, four deans had guided the school through three-quarters of its history: Ignatius Wilkinson (1923–53), William Hughes Mulligan (1956–71), Joseph M. McLaughlin (1971–81) and John D. Feerick (1982–2002). Each dean made his own contribution to the development of the school and built upon the achievements of his predecessors, but, as was previously mentioned, Dean William M. Treanor, Feerick's successor, said that no one had made a greater contribution to the development of the Fordham School of Law in the course of almost a century than John Feerick.

Not to be overlooked are the ancillary but vital roles played by Father John J. Collins, S.J., the president of Fordham University in 1905, who insisted on establishing the Law School despite the skepticism of his Jesuit confrères; Paul Fuller, the first dean, who served without pay and ensured the viability of the fledgling Law School; Father Aloysius J. Hogan, S.J., who successfully fought to obtain accreditation for the Law School from the ABA and membership in the AALS in the 1930s even as he was losing accreditation for the university; Dean John F.X. Finn, who, despite widespread opposition from the faculty, had the foresight in the 1950s to see that the future of the Fordham Law School was to be found in Manhattan rather than at Rose Hill; and last, but not least, Father Laurence McGinley, S.J., and Robert Moses, who together created a Manhattan campus for Fordham Law School at Lincoln Center.

When John Feerick stepped down as dean in 2002, the ABA was still voicing its two perennial complaints that Fordham Law School lacked sufficient space for its faculty and students, and that Fordham's accounting system made it difficult (at least for the ABA) to monitor the financial relationship between the Law School and the university.

Fordham University satisfied the ABA's complaint about the lack of space, at least for the foreseeable future, when it erected a new twenty-two-story Law School building at the Lincoln Center campus. The Law School occupied the lower nine floors of the building, while the upper thirteen floors served as a residential tower with rooms for 430 students. The dedication of the new building took place on September 18, 2014, in the presence of former Mayor Michael R. Bloomberg, who gave the keynote address, and U.S. Supreme Court Justice Sonia Sotomayor, who presided over the ribbon-cutting ceremony.

The ABA's other perennial complaint, that the university had failed to show sufficient transparency in its fiscal relationship with the Law School, proved to be more difficult to resolve. In 1976, when Father Finlay sought outside legal advice during his confrontation with the Law School over fundraising jurisdiction, he was advised that the ABA's position was "merely a facet of its interference with the university's affairs and as indefensible in principle as its insistence upon a diversion of the university resources to the Law School."[65] Two decades later, and a dozen years into the administration of Father Joseph O'Hare—who adopted a notably conciliatory stance toward the demands of the Law School and the ABA—O'Hare said, "I continue to have reservations about the intrusive nature of the ABA accreditation process, particularly in its monitoring of the financial relationships between the University and the Law School."[66]

This issue continues to be difficult to resolve because it involves not only financial matters but also the more basic issue of the relationship of the Fordham School of Law to Fordham University, but perhaps *solvitur ambulando*.

65. FUA, McGinley Papers, Leo A. Larkin to F. E. Larkin, November 15, 1976.
66. FUA, O'Hare Papers, O'Hare to Feerick, July 12. 1995.

THE GRADUATE SCHOOL
OF SOCIAL SERVICE

Origins

The initiative for the establishment of Fordham's first two graduate schools in 1905—Law and Medicine—came from the top down, from the decision of Father Thomas J. Gannon, the provincial of the Maryland–New York Province, a decision that was enthusiastically supported by Father John J. Collins, S.J., president of St. John's College. By contrast, the inspiration for the Graduate School of Social Service ten years later came from the bottom up. The person who is often credited with the establishment of the school was an Irish-born Jesuit, Father Terence J. Shealy, who was already deeply involved in the Fordham Law School as the first professor of jurisprudence. During the summer weekend of July 9, 1909, Shealy organized a "closed" retreat for eighteen Catholic laymen in the vacant dormitories of St. John's College at Rose Hill. The event is said to have been the genesis of the School of Social Service.

Annual retreats, short periods of intense prayer and spiritual reflection, had been an integral part of the lives of Catholic priests, brothers, and sisters for centuries. It was the genius of Father Shealy to recognize that many devout Catholic laymen would welcome and profit from a similar form of spiritual enrichment for themselves. Shealy's retreats for lay people became so popular that his superiors allowed him to establish a permanent center for his Laymen's League for Retreats in September 1911 at a rather run-down frame building located on twenty acres in the Fort Wadsworth area of Staten Island. He called it Mount Manresa. The following June Cardinal Farley blessed the center, the first retreat house exclusively for laymen in the United States, before a crowd of 2,000 people. By 1916 as many as 1,000 laymen (the retreats were limited to men) were making an annual retreat at Mount Manresa; four years later, Father Shealy estimated that their number had grown to 6,000.

The Laymen's League for Retreats is said to have been the catalyst for the foundation of the Fordham School of Social Service several years later because Shealy, who directed most of the retreats himself, emphasized not only personal prayer but also service to others. In October 1911 the

Laymen's League opened at Fordham a School of Social Studies, which was a nonaccredited program with the modest goal of training a corps of Catholic laymen to lecture in their parishes on the social issues of the day. There were no fees of any kind. Originally located on the premises of the Fordham Law School at 140 Nassau Street, the following year the school moved to Xavier High School, where it remained until 1916 when it moved again, this time to the downtown campus of Fordham University in the Woolworth Building.[1]

The apologetic thrust of the first lecture series was evident from the fact that the first twelve lectures in 1911, delivered by Father Shealy himself, were devoted to a criticism of socialism as irreligious and immoral. However, the program could hardly be called reactionary. The second lecturer was a young professor at the Catholic University of America, Father John A. Ryan, who was soon to earn a reputation as one of the most progressive social reformers in the American Catholic Church. *The Right Reverend New Dealer* was the title of a biography of Ryan by Francis Broderick, who emphasized Ryan's staunch support for the social reforms of President Franklin Delano Roosevelt.[2]

There is no doubt that the initiative for the foundation of the School of Social Service came from the bottom up, but there is an alternative narrative that gives the major credit not to Father Shealy and his Laymen's League but to two laymen, Thomas M. Mulry and Edmond J. Butler, who had long been active in the St. Vincent de Paul Society, the principal parish-based Catholic organization to assist the poor. Both men participated (Butler as a lecturer) in classes offered by the Summer School in Philanthropic Work that was sponsored by the nonsectarian Charity Organization Society in New York City. Their experience was so positive that they concluded there should be a similar school under Catholic auspices in New York City.[3]

They presented their proposal to Father Shealy, who seemed to be the

---

1. *WL* 41 (1912): 128–29; 52 (1923): 86–93. See also Joseph M. McShane, S.J., "A Survey of the Jesuit Labor Schools in New York: An American Social Gospel in Action," *RACHSP* 102:4 (1991): 37–43; and "'To Form an Elite Body of Laymen . . .' Terence J. Shealy, S.J., and the Laymen's League," *CHR* 78 (1992): 557–80.

2. *The School of Social Studies under the Auspices of the Laymen's League for Retreats and Social Studies, Session 1911–1912*, n.p. Francis Broderick, *Right Reverend New Dealer: John A. Ryan* (New York: Macmillan, 1963).

3. In 1904 the Summer School in Philanthropic Work evolved into a full-time institution as the New York School of Social Work and in 1940 became a graduate school of Columbia University.

logical person to approach at Fordham. Shealy initially expressed interest in the proposal but said he needed more time to consider it. A year later, after further prompting, he told Mulry and Butler, "I am too busy to give the matter any attention and do not wish to give it any further consideration." They then turned to the president of Manhattan College, Brother Edward, F.S.C., who agreed to locate the school at his institution. Here the plot thickens. Shortly thereafter, Father Joseph Mulry, S.J., the brother of Thomas Mulry, became president of Fordham University and was extremely disappointed to learn that Fordham had lost to Manhattan College. Butler was given the delicate task of appealing to Brother Edward to allow Fordham to sponsor the School of Social Service, which he graciously agreed to do.[4]

The Mulry family had long been associated with Catholic charitable activities in New York City through the work of the St. Vincent de Paul Society. For a quarter-century Thomas Mulry, the president of the Emigrant Savings Bank, had been one of the most prominent leaders of the St. Vincent de Paul Society, on both the local and national levels. He was also the first New York Catholic leader to collaborate with the Protestant and secular social reformers whom the local Catholic community had traditionally regarded with deep suspicion. In 1907 Governor Charles Evans Hughes recognized his prominence in the field when he appointed him a commissioner of the State Board of Charities. Two years later Mulry served as the convener and vice president of the White House Conference on the Care of Dependent Children.[5] In view of his family's long involvement in charitable activities, it is not surprising that Father Mulry jumped at the opportunity to establish a School of Social Service in the city that reputedly had the largest number of poor and disadvantaged Catholics in the United States.

4. FUA, Archivist's Files, Box 36, Butler to Father Matthew L. Fortier, S.J., Reminiscences, April 27, 1931. Father Robert I. Gannon accepted Butler's recollections of the origins of the School of Social Service as accurate. Robert I. Gannon, *Up to the Present: The Story of Fordham* (Garden City, N.Y.: Doubleday and Company, 1967), 146–47. As dean of the Fordham Graduate School in 1919, Fortier gave the credit for the establishment of the School of Sociology and Social Service to Thomas Mulry, Butler, and Cardinal Farley. He told the provincial without comment that "Father Shealy says the School is rather the outgrowth of the School of Social Studies conducted by the Laymen's League." FUA, Archivist's Files, Box 28, Fortier to Joseph Hanselman, S.J., July 27, 1919.

5. Dorothy M. Brown and Elizabeth McKeown, *The Poor Belong to Us: Catholic Charities and American Welfare* (Cambridge, Mass.: Harvard University Press, 1997), 40.

When Fordham University inaugurated the School of Sociology and Social Service on November 6, 1916, the title of dean or director was given to Father Shealy despite his original reluctance to start the school. It offered a two-year academic program covering all aspects of social service that included both classroom lectures and supervised field work. One casualty of the new School of Sociology and Social Service was Shealy's own School of Social Studies, which was hard-pressed for space in the Woolworth Building and seems to have quietly expired. Another casualty was Father Shealy himself, who died of overwork at the age of fifty-nine on September 5, 1922, after making significant contributions to the foundation of the Law School and to the School of Sociology and Social Service, where he served as dean from 1916 to 1917 and again from 1919 to 1920, until he was forced to resign because of ill health.[6]

By the 1920–21 academic year the School of Sociology and Social Service was slowly beginning to shed its bifurcated name, becoming the School of Social Service, and leaving the theoretical study of sociology to the Graduate School while it concentrated on the practical issues of social work in America's largest city. One of the strengths of the School of Social Service even in its earliest years was the high quality of its faculty despite the tiny enrollment. One of the adjunct professors who taught field work and supervised on-site inspections was Jane M. Hoey. During the Franklin D. Roosevelt administration she became one of the most influential women in Washington because of her position as director of the Bureau of Family Services in the Social Security Administration. Another faculty member was Father Joseph Husslein, S.J., who was soon to acquire a national reputation as an advocate of social justice and was the founder of the School of Social Service at St. Louis University in 1930. Two talented New York diocesan priests, who were graduates of the prestigious New York School of Social Service and gifted administrators, also enhanced the reputation of the faculty. One was Father Robert Fulton Keegan, a native of Nashua, New Hampshire, who organized the Catholic Charities of the Archdiocese of New York in 1920; the other was Father Bryan J. McEntegart, who later became president of the Catholic University of America and still later the bishop of Brooklyn, one of the largest dioceses in the United States.

6. FUA, Archivist's Files, Box 36, Fortier, Report of the Dean of Fordham University School of Sociology and Social Service, May 10, 1931. According to the unpublished capsule history compiled by the Fordham School of Social Service in 1952, it is the ninth-oldest such professional school in the United States. FUA, Archivist's Files, Box 37, "Historical Background of the Fordham University School of Social Service."

Still another member of the faculty was Brother Barnaby William, F.S.C., a graduate of Columbia and Cornell, who brought a unique perspective to his course on child welfare because he was director of the Boys' Division of the Catholic Protectory, one of the three largest Catholic child-caring institutions in the archdiocese of New York, which had well over 2,000 boys under its care. Two laymen contributed their own invaluable practical experience to the School of Social Service. Bernard J. Fagan, who taught a course on child welfare, was the chief probation officer of the Children's Court of New York City while Edwin J. Cooley, who taught a course on criminology, was the chief probation officer of the Magistrates' Courts of New York City. Neither of them needed any introduction to the real world of social service beyond the walls of academia.[7]

The Diocesan Connection

As was mentioned earlier, when the Fordham Medical School ran into serious financial difficulties and the university turned to the archdiocese for help, neither Cardinal Farley nor his successor, Cardinal Hayes, was willing to invest any archdiocesan money in a bailout. However, they both made plain to the Jesuits at Rose Hill that they would enthusiastically support the establishment of a Graduate School of Social Service. There was a longstanding Catholic tradition of providing help for the needy, but both prelates realized that in early-twentieth-century America such efforts could no longer be left to private charity and required the intervention of trained professional experts, the men and (especially) the women who were coming to be called "social workers."

Both Cardinals Farley and Hayes wanted a cadre of trained and dedicated Catholic social workers because of the unhappy experience of New York Catholics during the previous fifty years with social reformers whose efforts they regarded as insensitive to the well-being of poor Catholics in New York. A case in point was the policy of the Children's Aid Society under Charles Loring Brace, a Methodist minister, of dispatching "orphan trains" to distribute young Catholic children from broken homes in New York City to Protestant families in the rural Midwest. Another controversial issue was the state subsidies for the 20,000 children in the Catholic child-caring institutions in New York state. At the New York State Constitutional Convention of 1894 the Committee on Catholic Interests enlisted the services of both Democrats and Republicans to win a fiercely

---

7. Fordham University, School of Social Service, *Announcement 1920–1921*, 5–6.

contested battle to preserve these subsidies, but Catholics knew that their continued existence was always precarious.[8]

The opposition to state subsidies for private child-caring institutions did not stem exclusively or perhaps even primarily from anti-Catholic bias. A good example was Josephine Shaw Lowell, a Protestant socialite who was the first woman appointed to the New York State Board of Charities. Although she questioned the effectiveness of large child-caring institutions as a matter of principle, she gave a glowing report of the conditions she found when she conducted an official inspection of the New York Foundling Hospital, which had been founded and was operated by the Sisters of Charity. Nonetheless, she and many other social reformers contended that the placement of dependent children in foster homes offered them advantages that were difficult to duplicate in even the best-run institutions. One of the first Catholic leaders to recognize the force of this argument was Thomas Mulry, who was instrumental in establishing the Catholic Home Bureau in 1899, although he warned against the general public's succumbing to "institution-phobia."[9]

Both the growth of the Catholic child-caring institutions and the shift from institutionalization to foster care for dependent children created an urgent need for more professionally trained Catholic social workers in New York. What brought this need to public attention and turned it into a crisis for the archdiocese of New York was a series of city and state investigations of private child-caring institutions, many of them Catholic, that lasted from 1912 to 1916. The investigators reported numerous instances of fiscal mismanagement and mistreatment of children, such as the allegation (later disproved) that the children at the Mission of the Immaculate Conception on Staten Island were fed from the same pails as the pigs at the farm. "Orphans and Pigs Fed from the Same Bowl" was the inevitable headline in the newspapers the next day.

8. On the Constitutional Convention of 1894, see Samuel T. McSeveny, *The Politics of Depression: Political Behavior in the Northeast, 1893–1896* (New York: Oxford University Press, 1972), 69–79. The New York Foundling Hospital had its own "orphan trains" but placed the children with Catholic families.

9. Shortly before the new office of Commissioner of Charities of Manhattan and the Bronx was established in 1898, Shaw urged Archbishop Michael Corrigan to persuade Mulry to accept the position. She told the archbishop: "The ten thousand helpless and suffering men, women and children in our public institutions need the protection and care of a man of his character and capacity." AANY, G-14, Shaw to Corrigan, November 10, 1897. On Shaw, see Joan Waugh, *Unsentimental Reformer: The Life of Josephine Shaw Lowell* (Cambridge, Mass.: Harvard University Press, 1998).

Rightly or wrongly, with memories fresh in their mind of the orphan trains of the Children's Aid Society and the bitter fight at the Constitutional Convention of 1894, many Catholics accused the investigative commissions and Mayor John Purroy Mitchel (who was himself a Catholic) of anti-Catholic bias, an accusation that probably led to Mitchel's defeat when he ran for reelection in 1917. On a more positive note, Patrick J. Hayes, the newly appointed archbishop of New York, decided to respond to the crisis by launching a major overhaul of Catholic charitable services in New York.[10]

Archbishop Hayes approached the problem on a professional basis by engaging Dr. John A. Lapp of the National Catholic Welfare Conference to conduct a comprehensive survey of 175 Catholic charitable institutions and agencies in the archdiocese, which he did with the help of 42 assistants. The result was the incorporation on June 12, 1920, of the Catholic Charities of the Archdiocese of New York, a central coordinating and supervisory agency for the Catholic charitable network in New York. To head the agency Hayes appointed Father Robert F. Keegan, a well-credentialed social worker whose expertise and achievements led to his election in 1936 as president of the prestigious National Conference of Social Work. At his death in 1947 an official of that organization commented that "under the auspices of his archdiocese [Keegan] developed the social work program of Catholic Charities until its standards were second to none in that city."[11]

Catholic Charities and the Fordham School of Social Service quickly developed a symbiotic relationship and worked closely together for several decades. Catholic Charities looked to Fordham to supply its need for an ever-increasing number of social workers. Fordham relied on Catholic Charities to provide jobs for the graduates of the School of Social Service. For many years the Catalogue of the School of Social Service featured a letter of endorsement from Archbishop Hayes, dated July 18, 1919. Hayes also served as a member of the board of directors, as did Keegan and another New York diocesan priest associated with Catholic Charities, Father William A. Courtney. In addition, both Father Keegan and Father McEntegart served as faculty members of the School of Social Service. Archbishop Hayes, who was made a cardinal in 1924, even encouraged his

10. The best account of the Charities Controversy, as it came to be called, is Neil A. Kelly, "Orphans and Pigs Fed from the Same Bowl: The New York Charities Controversy," M.A. thesis, St. Joseph's Seminary, Dunwoodie, 1994.

11. For a survey and appraisal of the creation of the Catholic Charities of the Archdiocese of New York, see Brown and McKeown, *The Poor Belong to Us*, 13–50.

own clergy to take courses in social service at Fordham to improve their pastoral skills as parish priests.[12]

One of the minor mysteries connected with the early years of Fordham's School of Social Service was the close interest and warm support that it received from Monsignor Keegan (he was made a papal chamberlain in 1929) despite the fact that he was a notoriously autocratic and irascible character. Keegan was also the pastor of the Church of the Blessed Sacrament on West 71st Street. When he left the rectory each morning for the Catholic Charities Office on East 22nd Street, the sole elevator in that building was held at the ground floor until his arrival. One of Keegan's assistants, Father E. Roberts Moore (who also taught at the Fordham School of Social Service), said that when Keegan lost his temper, which was a daily if not an hourly occurrence, "all the neighbors and the neighbors' children took to the bomb shelters." Keegan's support, which reflected Cardinal Hayes's wishes, was invaluable in the early years of the school because Keegan enjoyed far more professional recognition in the field of social service than any of the Jesuits or lay members of the faculty of the School of Social Service at Fordham.[13]

Although there was never a religious test for admission to the School of Social Service and there was a sizeable increase in the number of Jewish students in the late 1930s, the Catholic orientation was obvious from the composition of the faculty, the content of the courses, and from what today would be called the mission statement of the school. "In the field of social work Catholics ought to be in the forefront," the catalogue announced in 1920, declaring that the Catholic Church "is the mother of private and organized Social Service." It traced the history of Christian social service from Jesus himself through the centuries to the pronouncements of Pope Leo XIII and the recent efforts of Archbishop Hayes to expand the work of Catholic charitable activities in the archdiocese of New York, which it characterized as "scientific charity charged with the spirit of Christ." The Fordham School of Social Service announced its readiness to contribute to that endeavor.

There was a two-year program for the diploma in Social Service. The first year consisted of twelve hours of classroom lectures and twelve hours of field work; in the second year the students were expected to concentrate in their area of specialization. They were warned that "lectures alone are

12. Fordham University, School of Social Service, *Announcement 1920–1921*, 1–6. Cardinal Hayes was often referred to as the Cardinal of Charities because of his role in establishing the Catholic Charities of the Archdiocese of New York.

13. There is no biography of Keegan, but see *DHGE*, 18: 1134–35.

not sufficient to make the student an efficient social worker . . . . Actual case work must be done by the student under careful and expert supervision." The School of Social Service held its first commencement exercises in 1918 with fifteen graduates, all but one of whom were women. The following year there were twenty graduates, and the men outnumbered the women by twelve to eight. The male predominance was a temporary aberration. During the academic year 1919–20 there were eighty-nine registered students. Only five were men, and three of them were priests. The women religious made their first appearance in 1919. A dozen of them were registered that year, the vanguard of many more to come.[14]

At the end of the school's first year in June 1917, Archbishop Hayes offered his congratulations, as did William McAdoo, the chief city magistrate, whose letter was more than a conventional expression of gratitude. "It would in my judgment have been a public misfortune," McAdoo told Father Mulry, "if [the Catholic Church] had remained aloof from the study of progressive, and, we might say, almost scientific philanthropy and sociology." McAdoo followed the progress of the school closely, and, a decade later, he asked the dean to consider offering special courses in criminology for the members of the police department.[15]

In 1924 Father Joseph T. Keating, the treasurer of the university, contrasted the healthy financial condition of the Law School, and especially the Pharmacy School ("splendid income producer"), with the failure of the School of Social Service to generate sufficient revenue to pay its own bills. Nevertheless, Keating justified the subsidy from the university to the Jesuit general in Rome and strongly recommended its continuation because of the good that it was doing in New York City.[16]

Father Matthew L. Fortier, S.J.

In addition to Father Shealy, three other Jesuits served as dean during the first eleven years—Richard R. Rankin; Francis J. Dore, M.D.; and Francis P. LeBuffe—but the School of Social Service came of age and established its professional reputation during the seven years (1927–34) that Father Matthew L. Fortier, S.J., served as dean. Although others had held the title of dean as far back as Father Shealy in 1916, the School of Social Service was really a department of the amorphous Graduate School

14. Fordham University, School of Social Service, *Announcement 1920–1921*, 8–10, 27–29.

15. FUA, Mulry Papers, Hayes to Mulry, August 20, 1917; McAdoo to Mulry, June 6, 1917. FUA, Duane Papers, McAdoo to Fortier, June 28, 1927.

16. ARSJ, Keating to Fr. Wlodimir Ledóchowski, S.J., January 5, 1924.

until the appointment of Father Fortier on May 1, 1927, when for the first time it became a distinct unit of the university. A native of Vergennes, Vermont, Fortier had no background in social service, but he had served as the first dean of the Graduate School of Fordham from 1917 to 1919 with responsibility for both the future Graduate School of Arts and Sciences and the School of Social Service. He was also responsible for inaugurating Fordham's first graduate summer school.

By 1927 the School of Social Service had an enrollment of approximately 695 students, and Fortier began a major overhaul of its operations with himself as dean, a new registrar (with a Ph.D.), new secretaries, an expanded board of directors, a new advisory council, and an expanded faculty. The school made no secret of its Catholic character. "Only a Catholic School can train the Catholic Social Worker in Catholic principle and practice, in true Philosophy of Life and Gospel Lessons of Charity," declared Fortier in the prospectus for the reorganized and expanded school.[17]

The school had already developed such a fine reputation that it had no difficulty in obtaining employment for its graduates. In 1927 they all found jobs as social workers within a week of receiving their diplomas. However, a major problem was the difficulty of recruiting more students for the full two-year program. The newly appointed registrar, Dr. Edward L. Curran, laid out the dimensions of the problem for the board of directors in the starkest terms. "The school has had to meet all the problems of a large institution without corresponding financial resources and the enthusiasm engendered by a large student body," he told them. Moreover, he pointed out the peculiar pitfalls of a career in social work. "We faced the difficulty of attracting properly qualified students for future labors in a field where the work is exacting, ofttimes [*sic*] depressing, where salaries are inadequate, where promotion is slow, and where standards are high."[18]

A second major difficulty was the perennial Fordham problem of the lack of money and the concomitant reluctance of wealthy New York Catholics to part with their cash for the purposes of Catholic higher education. In the fatal year 1929 a wildly optimistic Fortier hoped to raise an endowment of $500,000 over the course of five years. The campaign listed as patrons Cardinal Hayes, many members of the lay Catholic elite of New York, Governor Franklin D. Roosevelt, and Colonel Herbert H. Lehman. It got off to a rousing start with a concert at the Metropolitan Opera House

17. Fordham University, School of Sociology and Social Service, *The School of Sociology and Social Service of Fordham University Enlarged and Reorganized*, 1927.

18. FUA, Archivist's Files, Box 28, *Minutes of the Meeting of the Board of Directors, Fordham University School of Sociology and Social Service*, 1928, 6.

on April 15, 1929. Like Fordham University's ill-fated Million Dollar Campaign in 1921, the initial phase of obtaining pledges was to be limited to one week. Like the Million Dollar Campaign of 1921, which collected only $400,000, the fundraising campaign for the School of Sociology and Social Service, which was started only six months before the crash of the stock market, also appears to have quickly fizzled given that little more was heard of it.[19]

The concern about recruitment of students may seem surprising in view in the enrollment of almost 700, but that number was misleading. There were actually three groups of students. Only a small minority of them took the full two-year course leading to a diploma or, if they were academically qualified, to a degree issued in the name of one of the other units of the university. Many other students were practical nurses, teachers, probation officers, and attendance officers, who attended selective evening lectures at a cost of $15 for each thirty-hour course. A third group of students were preparing themselves to take civil service examinations and had an even more tenuous connection with the school.[20]

Desperate for new students in the summer of 1927, Father Fortier asked the members of the faculty and diocesan directors of Catholic Charities agencies in the metropolitan area to recruit students for Fordham. He complained that "mischievous agencies" had decimated the school by luring away students before they had completed the full course of studies. As a result he had only two or three qualified new candidates for the two-year course that fall. He also appealed to Cardinal Hayes for another public letter of support and commendation. The cardinal was happy to oblige, especially because he had now convinced himself that he was the real founder of the School of Social Service. He composed a broad-based appeal directed to the religious communities of men and women, to his own diocesan clergy, and to the laity, and he ordered the pastors to read it from the pulpit at Sunday Mass. In 1929 and again in 1930 the cardinal sent Fortier a check for $10,000 through Keegan.[21]

One reason for Father Fortier's success in attracting more students was that, within two years, he was able to make a dramatic improvement in

19. *New York Sun*, April 3, 1929.

20. In 1930–31, the total enrollment was 852, but only 62 were full-time students. FUA, Archivist's Files, Box 36, Fortier, Report of the Dean of the School of Sociology and Social Service, May 10, 1931.

21. FUA, Duane Papers, Hayes to Duane, July 11, 1927; Fortier to McEntegart, July 28, 1927; Hayes to Rev. Dear Father, August 25, 1927; Keegan to Fortier, February 4, 1929; July 3. 1930.

the academic reputation of the school. He received strong support and encouragement from Keegan, who assured him that "the School is a great necessity." Keegan also told Fortier not to be discouraged if progress came slowly because "in a field as this the building process will necessarily be slow." Keegan sounded an uncharacteristically paternalistic note when he added that "*we* are building solidly and on a firm foundation, and I have no fear for the future."[22]

Fordham's School of Social Service was not the only school of social service in the United States that experienced growing pains in the 1920s as the relatively new field of social service evolved into a full-fledged profession with increasingly rigorous academic standards. These internal tensions came to light at the annual convention of the National Conference of Social Work in San Francisco in the summer of 1929. At Father Fortier's request, Monsignor Keegan represented the Fordham School of Social Service at the convention. He reported to Fortier that there was constant mention at the convention of the need for social service to follow the example of the legal, medical, engineering, and nursing professions in raising standards. At the meeting of the American Association of Social Workers, Keegan said, there was an exceedingly bitter discussion between those who wanted higher standards and those who were satisfied with the status quo.

Keegan had no doubt that the future belonged to those who wanted higher standards. In practice that meant the Fordham School of Social Service would have to limit admission to those who had completed at least two years of college in order for the graduates to qualify for membership in the Association of Schools of Professional Social Work. Keegan's vision for the School of Social Service was very much like that of Father Tivnan for the Medical School fifteen years earlier. Tivnan closed the Medical School rather than run a second-rate operation. Keegan urged Fortier to maintain similarly high standards for the School of Social Service. "The school must send out workers comparable in technical training with any other school in the United States," Keegan told Fortier. "The church in her present-day development of charities must have this type of worker. The field of Catholic social work needs people who will rate professionally with the country's best."[23]

Keegan need not have worried. As he must have realized, Fortier shared his vision of excellence in social service, and he had been busy implement-

22. FUA, Duane Papers, Keegan to Fortier, February 4, 1929.
23. FUA, Duane Papers, Keegan to Fortier, July 23, 1929.

ing the kinds of changes that Keegan warned him would soon be mandatory in the profession. In the fall of 1929 Fortier had the satisfaction of receiving a letter from the Association of Schools of Professional Social Work informing him that Fordham had met all the requirements for membership in the association. Fortier was so delighted that he cabled the news to Hayes and Keegan, who were on a Cunard liner in the mid-Atlantic, and he received a cordial response from both of them. In 1932 admission to the full-time two-year program was limited to college graduates. Two years later the name of the school was officially changed to the School of Social Service, although the M.A. degree continued to be awarded through the Graduate School of Arts and Sciences until 1945, when the School of Social Service began to award the degree of Master of Science in Social Service. Five years later, following the directives of the state Education Department, the degree was changed to Master of Social Service.[24]

In 1930 Fortier expressed his disappointment to Keegan when he discovered that a New York diocesan priest, Father Patrick A. O'Boyle, was studying at the New York School of Social Service instead of at Fordham. Keegan reassured Fortier that he had not lost his confidence "in the Sons of St. Ignatius who throughout the centuries have pointed out the way in the field of Christian education." Father O'Boyle's presence at the New York School of Social Service was one more example of Keegan's professionalism. He explained to Fortier that he had sent the young priest there deliberately in order to keep abreast of the latest nonsectarian methodology. When Keegan resigned from the Fordham faculty later that year because of the pressure of other commitments, he recommended O'Boyle as his replacement as an expert on child welfare, a recommendation that Fortier was happy to follow. O'Boyle's expertise in social service later led to his appointment as the first cardinal archbishop of Washington.[25]

In 1931 Father Fortier represented both Fordham University and the archdiocese of New York at the celebration in Rome of the fortieth anniversary of *Rerum Novarum*, Pope Leo XIII's historic encyclical on the social question. He also made a personal report to the Jesuit general, Father Wlodimir Ledóchowski, and asked for a formal letter of approbation for the school from the Holy See, which Ledóchowski said he was

24. FUA, Duane Papers, Margaret Leal to Fortier, October 21, 1929; Archivist's Files, Box 37, Historical Background of Fordham University School of Social Service; McGinley Papers, McGinley to Deane, December 29, 1950.

25. FUA, Duane Papers, Keegan to Fortier, March 25, 1930; Fortier to Keegan, June 4. 1930.

The Graduate School of Social Service

happy to give him in view of the fact that it was *res maximi momenti*, "a matter of the greatest importance."[26] Three months later Fortier received a letter of commendation for the school from Pope Pius XI through his secretary of state, Eugenio Cardinal Pacelli, the future Pope Pius XII. It was especially welcome coming from a scholarly pontiff who had spent most of his life in academia. Only the year before, Pius XI had issued an apostolic constitution, *Deus Scientiarum Dominus*, in which he ordered an upgrading in academic standards in Catholic universities and seminaries in Rome and throughout the world.[27]

After 1932 a series of heart attacks forced Fortier to cut back on his activities and finally to resign as dean in June 1934. He died the following year after successfully transforming Fordham's fledgling School of Sociology and Social Service into a respected professional institution in New York City. Even more remarkable was the fact that he was able to do this with limited financial resources within three years of assuming the office of dean. "It is not for us Jesuits to go out on the housetops and publicly sing our own praises," Fortier told Father McEntegart, but he had good reason to be proud of what he had accomplished, not just for Fordham or for the Society of Jesus but for some of the poorest and most disadvantaged New Yorkers.[28]

The Great Depression, the New Deal, and World War II

"Unemployment is at peak proportions in this area, and the rapidly increasing demands made upon us for family care are straining our finances to the utmost," Monsignor Keegan told Father Fortier in the spring of 1930, explaining that Cardinal Hayes could not yet make his usual contribution to the School of Social Service because he was uncertain of the success of the annual Catholic Charities Appeal. Three months later Keegan told Fortier, "The heavy demands upon us for the elementary necessities of life this year surpass by far [those of] any other period in our history." At Rose Hill the Jesuits had started a bread line, distributing food to needy people who appeared every day at the gates of the university. That same year the thirty-nine-year-old Father Aloysius J. Hogan succeeded Father Duane as the president of Fordham. A native of Philadelphia with a doctorate from

26. FUA, Archivist's Files, Box 36, Ledóchowski to Fortier, January 21, 1932.

27. FUA, Archivist's Files, Box 36, Eugenio Pacelli to Aloysius Hogan, S.J., April 11, 1932.

28. *WL*, 64 (1935): 447–48, 456–57. FUA, Duane Papers, Fortier to McEntegart, July 28, 1927.

Cambridge University, Hogan quickly demonstrated his interest in social reform and his support for the School of Social Service.[29]

In 1932 the National Conference of Catholic Charities held its annual convention in New York City. As the president of the organization that year, Monsignor Keegan invited Hogan to be one of the principal speakers, along with Professor Parker T. Moon of Columbia University, Father John A. Ryan of the Catholic University of America, and Frances Perkins, the Secretary of Labor, a former social worker who was a close friend of Father Ryan's and the first woman to hold a federal cabinet post. Keegan asked Hogan to speak on the relevance of the papal social encyclicals to the situation in the United States. Hogan used the opportunity to praise President Roosevelt's New Deal for fostering the primacy of the common good, which he identified as one of the core principles of modern papal social teaching. "No president ever faced more colossal tasks," said Hogan before a crowded audience in the Grand Ballroom of the Waldorf Astoria Hotel, and he gave Roosevelt credit for averting a social revolution in the United States by his timely leadership.[30]

Keegan was delighted with Hogan's address, and Hogan did not have to worry about any adverse reaction from Cardinal Hayes because of the partisan nature of his remarks. As an auxiliary bishop in 1919 Hayes had been one of the four members of the Administrative Board of the National Catholic Welfare Conference to sign the Bishops' Program for Social Reconstruction, which was written by John A. Ryan and embodied many of the programs inaugurated during the New Deal. Although Hayes scrupulously avoided involvement in politics, even during the presidential campaign of 1928, he indicated his tacit approval of the New Deal through his support of Monsignor Keegan's endorsement of the progressive social welfare policies of the Roosevelt administration.

In the later years of Hogan's presidency the warm relationship between Fordham and the archdiocese cooled considerably, not only with Catholic Charities, but with Cardinal Hayes himself. Perhaps because of financial constraints during the Depression, Catholic Charities was now providing only a half-dozen openings for field work training. A bigger concern for Hogan and for Father Edward S. Pouthier, S.J., who succeeded Fortier as dean in 1934,[31] was the rumor that Keegan and O'Boyle were involved in

29. FUA, Duane Papers, Keegan to Fortier, March 25, 1930; Hogan Papers, Keegan to Fortier, July 8, 1930; ARSJ, Keating to Ledóchowski, January 6, 1931.

30. FUA, Hogan Papers, Hogan, "The Catholic Church and the Social Order," October 2, 1933; Keegan to Hogan, October 16, 1933.

31. Pouthier had a licentiate in social service from the Catholic University of Louvain

plans for the Catholic University of America to open a School of Social Service in New York City, which would have had a devastating effect on the enrollment at Fordham.

When the president of the National Conference of Catholic Charities, a diocesan priest from Cincinnati, failed to mention Fordham at the annual convention of the organization in 1935, Hogan lashed out at him in a letter dripping with sarcasm in which he claimed that it was "a signal honor" to be ignored in such circles. He boasted that the Fordham School of Social Service was making notable progress "despite the active opposition, both positive and negative, on the part of Catholic individuals, and Catholic institutions, and Catholic organizations."[32]

The paranoia was almost palpable, and the truculent tone adopted by Hogan on this and other occasions was partially responsible for the fact that later that year the Association of American Universities dropped Fordham from its list of approved institutions.[33] The disciplinary action of the AAU had no direct effect on the School of Social Service, because it did not compromise its membership in the Association of Schools of Professional Social Work, but it damaged Fordham's reputation in the academic world, especially on the graduate level. Nonetheless, Fordham's School of Social Service struggled on as the only Catholic School of Social Service in the New York metropolitan area, despite the fact that it had to operate in the shadow of the much larger and wealthier New York School of Social Service and that it had only three full-time faculty members and a modest budget of $40,000 per year.[34]

After replacing Hogan as the president of Fordham University in the summer of 1936, Father Robert I. Gannon gave the highest priority to regaining Fordham's membership in the Association of American Univer-

---

but failed to finish his dissertation and obtain his doctorate. He also was responsible for dropping "Sociology" from the name of the school. "We are not a School of Sociology nor should we pretend to be," he wrote. FUA Archivist's Files, Box 28, Pouthier, Memorandum, n.d.

32. FUA, Hogan Papers, Pouthier to Hogan, January 27, 1934; Hogan to Monsignor R. Marcellus Wagner, October 6, 1935.

33. On Fordham's loss of membership in the AAU, see Chapter 12.

34. FUA, Hogan Papers, Memorandum re School of Social Service, n.d. [September 20, 1935]. In 1938 there were thirty-eight schools of social service in the United States with a combined budget of between $1.5 million and $2 million. Three schools accounted for one-third of that sum. FUA, Gannon Papers, Marion Hathaway to Gannon, April 13, 1942. Hathaway was president of the American Association of Schools of Social Work.

Dr. Anna E. King, the first woman dean in the history of Fordham University, appointed dean of the Fordham School of Social Service in 1939 by Father Robert I. Gannon, S.J.

sities, but he did not neglect the School of Social Service. In 1939 Gannon appointed the first woman dean of the school, Anna E. King. She was not only the first woman dean at Fordham but also the first woman dean at any Jesuit college in the United States. Her appointment ruffled the feathers of some of the senior officials at the Jesuit headquarters in Rome, but Gannon did not seem especially upset when he received a letter of complaint about the appointment from the Jesuit general that began with the words "We are surprised" [*miramur*], the standard greeting in a letter of censure from the Jesuit Curia in Rome.[35]

Gannon felt vindicated in his selection of King when she was elected president of the American Association of Schools of Social Service in 1945. Like Keegan and Fortier earlier, she was an advocate of high standards. Even during the lean years of World War II, when Fordham experienced increased competition from the New York School of Social Service, New York University, and the New School, and she anticipated a decline of 15 percent in the number of full-time students, she urged the elimination of nongraduate, noncredit courses for part-time students on the grounds

35. I am indebted to Professor Emmett Curran for explaining to me this tidbit of Jesuit arcana.

36. FUA, Gannon Papers, King to Gannon, July 13, 1939; King to Raymond Schouten, S.J., April 27, 1942; Schouten to Gannon, April 29, 1942; Gannon to Spellman, February 3, 1945.

that Fordham's was the only Catholic school of social service in the locality and that it was one of the few strong Catholic social service schools in the entire country.[36]

A Home of Its Own

In 1942 Father Gannon was able to give the School of Social Service a home of its own when he purchased a five-story building at 134–136 East 39th Street between Lexington and Third avenues for $40,000 in the upscale Murray Hill section of Manhattan. It not only gave the school considerably more space than in the two rented floors in the Woolworth Building, but the relocation also saved $5,000 per annum in rent. An unexpected problem arose, however, when Gannon asked the archdiocese for permission to reserve the Blessed Sacrament in the chapel. It was a routine request that merited a perfunctory response and even a word of commendation from the archdiocese for the only Catholic school of social service between Washington, D.C., and Boston. Instead it led to a protracted correspondence between Gannon and the cantankerous chancellor of the archdiocese, auxiliary Bishop J. Francis A. McIntyre, over the custody of the key to the tabernacle in case of an emergency during the weekends when the school was closed. Both Gannon and McIntyre cited the Code of Canon Law and they quoted at length (in Latin) the opinions of learned canon lawyers in support of their respective positions.[37]

Gannon could be as charming and gracious as Hogan could be curt and abrasive, but it must have taxed even Gannon's patience to treat the obtuse McIntyre with the respect due his office, if not his person, over such a trivial matter. However, Gannon turned this minor twentieth-century investiture crisis on East 39th Street to the advantage of the School of Social Service by ingratiating himself with Monsignor Keegan, who loathed Bishop McIntyre with a passion and resented his constant interference in Catholic Charities. When the chapel was finished, Gannon invited Keegan, not McIntyre, to bless it, a gesture that Keegan deeply appreciated.[38]

In 1944 Father Gannon received a letter from a Jesuit priest in New York

37. FUA, Gannon Papers, Gannon to Mrs. Michael Gavin, July 13, 1942; Gannon to Pouthier, August 3, 1942; Gannon to McIntyre, August 11, 1942, March 2, March 4; McIntyre to Gannon, March 12, 1943.

38. FUA, Gannon Papers, Keegan to Gannon, January 19, 1943. McIntyre was appointed the archbishop of Los Angeles in 1948 and named a cardinal four years later. When Archbishop Paul J. Hallinan of Atlanta met McIntyre at the Second Vatican Council in 1962, he summed up his impression of him in two words, "absolutely stupid." Archives of the Diocese of Cleveland, Hallinan, Diary, October 16, 1962.

about a lay friend who was ready to establish an endowment of $650,000 for the School of Social Service. After receiving so many illusory assurances of an endowment to reestablish the Medical School, it must have been difficult for Gannon to suppress a yawn, but for a moment at least he dreamed of what he could do with such a princely gift. "The New York School of Social Work (Columbia U.) has a scholarship fund of more than a million dollars and endowment galore," he told his Jesuit confrère. "But, of course," he added, "we can always make a dollar go further than others can, and $650,000 would make us one of the finest Schools of Social Service in the country, not in a class with the Chicago or New York School in wealth and influence, but a greater force for real public good." Alas, like so many other pots of gold at the end of the rainbow in the history of Fordham, this one too failed to materialize.[39]

A year later, as World War II was coming to an end, instead of being able to dip into a nonexistent endowment to pay expenses, Father Gannon was stretching every available dollar and cutting faculty salaries to keep the university afloat. The School of Social Service was especially hard-hit because the salaries were already lower than in other graduate schools at Fordham and in many other universities. The School of Social Service did not even rank its professors as did the other graduate schools of the university. Nationally the recommended caseload for teachers in schools of social service was about twenty-one students; at Fordham it was closer to thirty students.

The Jesuit regent of the School of Social Service, Father Raymond Schouten, was so upset that he was threatening to quit and lapsing into ungrammatical English. "No one has to try to keep up that thing called morale like I do," he told Gannon. "And I can't see my way out. I don't know any more answers." Six months later Schouten got an answer when Gannon announced that the faculty of the School of Social Service would be included in the university's provisions for salary, rank, and tenure. The salary scale ranged from a minimum of $1,800 per year for an instructor with a bachelor's degree and a diploma in social service to a maximum of $4,500 for a full professor with a doctorate in a related field. Yearly increments in salary for most of the faculty were limited to $100.[40]

Somehow the Fordham School of Social Service survived under this ascetical regime and even thrived largely because of the dedication of the

39. FUA, Gannon Papers, Gannon to Rev. Patrick F. Quinnan, S.J., March 8, 1944.

40. FUA, Gannon Papers, Schouten to Gannon, August 7, 1945; Gannon to Schouten, November 17, 1945. The position of regent was created for the School of Social Service in 1939 at the time of the appointment of the first lay dean to assure overall Jesuit su-

The Graduate School of Social Service

faculty. At least, according to Fordham's own estimate, by 1952 it ranked second among schools of social service in the United States in total enrollment with 334 students; it ranked ninth in full-time enrollment with 129 students; and it ranked third in part-time enrollment with 124 students. By that time it had awarded approximately 1,100 master's degrees and had a faculty of 35, almost half of whom were full-time professors. Whether or not it was the best Catholic school of social service in the United States, as Father Gannon maintained, its track record was a creditable performance for a school that had survived and prospered on a shoestring budget for 36 years.[41]

Reality Check

In 1961, Father Laurence McGinley, the president of Fordham University, commissioned the most extensive and detailed self-study in the history of the university under the direction of Dr. Francis J. Donohue, a member of the Fordham faculty. The overall thrust of Dr. Donohue's report was positive and contained many practical suggestions for academic improvements, but Donohue was also brutally honest and perhaps overly critical in calling attention to the shortcomings he found in virtually all the units of the university. He was especially concerned that a high percentage of all the members of the Fordham faculty were natives of the New York metropolitan area and were graduates of local universities. As a result, he said, "We are not even a regional institution—we are a narrowly local one."

Donohue was far less positive in his evaluation of the School of Social Service than Father Gannon had been a decade earlier. Donohue made the devastating comment in the spring of 1961 that the full-time faculty of the School of Social Service "was the farthest [*sic*] from what a Fordham faculty should be." However, his comment itself also needs to be evaluated critically because Donohue based some of his criticisms on criteria that today would be regarded as offensively idiosyncratic, if not narrowly sectarian. For example, he deplored the fact that more than half of the faculty consisted of single women. "If we are to train people to advise others how to live," said Donohue, "let us use for their training a faculty which knows our beliefs and principles, and which is not untypical of normal society."

---

pervision of the school, although he was not supposed to interfere in routine scholastic matters. For a number of years there was also a Jesuit regent of the Law School and the Pharmacy School, where there were also lay deans. FUA, Gannon Papers, Schouten to Gannon, July 8, 1947.

41. FUA, Archivist's Files, Box 37, Historical Background of Fordham University School of Social Service.

Donohue was on firmer professional ground when he noted both the narrow geographical background of the faculty—the fact that most of them came from the New York metropolitan area—and also their academic in-breeding, given that 40 percent of them were graduates of the Fordham School of Social Service and another 10 percent had received their professional degrees from other Jesuit universities.[42] Only 20 percent of the full-time faculty (four out of twenty professors) had doctorates, and one of them was a psychiatrist with a private practice. The faculty of the School of Social Service ranked last among Fordham graduate schools in the publication of books and scholarly articles. Donohue also wondered about the Catholic identity of the School of Social Service because only a minority of the faculty were graduates of Catholic high schools or colleges.[43]

Donohue did balance his criticisms of the School of Social Service with several positive findings. The faculty ranked highest among all the units of Fordham University in their participation in civic and religious organizations (45 percent compared with 28 percent in the university as a whole). Their recruitment of new faculty reflected a careful selection process, comparable to that of the Fordham School of Law, given that all but one of the new faculty in the School of Social Service had been in professional practice at the time of their appointment to the faculty

The Fordham School of Social Service celebrated its fiftieth anniversary in 1966 in the middle of the most tumultuous decade in twentieth-century American history. By that date Fordham was one of six schools of social service in New York City, but it was still the only Catholic school of social service. Even as Dr. Donohue wondered about the continued commitment of the Fordham School of Social Service to its Catholic identity, the faculty members were convinced that they were paying a heavy price for their fidelity to Catholic principles as they were understood at that time. "[We] have been systematically discouraged in our own profession," the faculty of the School of Social Service declared in 1966, "because of our affiliation with a Catholic university." As an example, they mentioned that one of the largest family service agencies in New York City refused to accept students of the Fordham School of Social Service for their field work because they were considered "too identified with Catholic dogma to be able to use the

42. The Fordham School of Social Service conferred the M.S.S. degree until June 1962, when it changed it to the M.S.W. degree. In addition to the twenty full-time professors, there were fifteen part-time professors.

43. FUA, Self-Study, 1961–1963, Francis J. Donohue, Memorandum to the Other Members of the Self-Study Executive Committee, October 31, 1962,

psychoanalytic theory of personality which guided the agency's practice of casework."

By the mid-1960s the School of Social Service had outgrown its home on East 39th Street and had come to regret its physical separation from the rest of the university. The members of the faculty welcomed the relocation of the school from East 39th Street to the Lowenstein Building of the Lincoln Center campus because they desired to establish closer ties with both the School of Law and the School of Education and also with the departments of sociology, psychology, anthropology, and political science in the Graduate School of Arts and Sciences as they began a major overhaul of the masters program. Beyond that ambitious goal, they also envisioned the eventual creation of a doctoral program not only to train social workers along traditional lines but also "to produce leaders in the formulation of social policy and social work research."[44]

Dean James R. Dumpson, 1967–74

In 1967, while the Fordham School of Social Service was still located on East 39th Street, it achieved a new prominence outside the Catholic community with the appointment of Dr. James R. Dumpson as the dean. He came to Fordham with a distinguished background in both public service and academia. For six years he had been the commissioner of the Department of Welfare of the City of New York, only the second African American man to serve as a commissioner in New York City and the first African American in the United States to head a major social agency. After leaving public service in 1965, Dumpson became a professor and associate dean of Hunter College School of Social Work. In 1967 he was in line to become dean of the Hunter College School of Social Work when he received an invitation from Fordham to head its School of Social Service.[45]

Dumpson chose Fordham over Hunter for several reasons. He desired a change from the public sector to the private sector, but he said that the primary reason he chose Fordham was that he was a convert to the Catholic Church. "Even though I fuss and fight and fume about the Catholic Church and some of its positions," he said, "I am a practicing Catholic . . . . That's a

44. FUA, Archivist's Files, Box 37, Rita A. Maguire to McGinley, October 14, 1966, Fordham University School of Social Service: An Assessment of the Present and Some Proposals for the Future.

45. The two people who invited Dumpson to come to Fordham were Father Timothy Healy, S.J., the executive vice president, and Dr. John Meng, the academic vice president, who had known Dumpson when he was president of Hunter College.

stream that goes through who I am." He admired the liberalism and scholarship of the Society of Jesus, and he was confident that the Jesuits would support his desire to make the Fordham School of Social Service an agent of change in social welfare policies. "Here I was," he said, "a Black man, being asked by a major white university—Catholic to be sure—to come and be a dean .... This was an exciting offer to me and of course I accepted it." At that time only two schools of social service in the United States had African American deans, and both of them were primarily black institutions: Howard University and Atlanta University.

When Dumpson first met the faculty, he received a warm greeting from them but also noticed the apprehension in their faces and voices at the appointment of an outsider—a black man no less—to head a school with a closely knit, predominantly white female faculty. However, he quickly won their confidence and later said that one of the highlights of his professional career was that, within a year, the "faculty granted me the greatest amount of support that I think I have ever had in an administrative spot."[46]

As dean of the Fordham School of Social Service, Dumpson supervised the relocation of the school from East 39th Street to the Lowenstein Building at the Lincoln Center campus. In 1974 Dumpson resigned as dean to accept the position of commissioner of the New York City Department of Social Services at the request of Mayor Abraham Beame, one of five New York City mayors in whose administrations he served.

However, Dumpson retained his connection with the Fordham School of Social Service, returning in 1975 as an adjunct professor. Five years later Fordham University established an endowed chair in his name, the James R. Dumpson Chair in Child Welfare Research, to honor his passionate commitment to that particular field of social service. Dumpson was amused and perhaps flattered on one occasion when a Protestant minister, noting his concern for the poorest of the poor, told him, "You sound more like a clergyman than I do." Dumpson died on November 2, 2012, at the age of 103, the recipient of many awards and honors for his contributions to the field of social service and public policy.[47]

Dean Mary Ann Quaranta, 1975–2000

More than anyone else in the history of the Fordham Graduate School of Social Service, Mary Ann Quaranta was responsible for trans-

46. FUA, FOHP, James R. Dumpson, Interview with James Mullen, October 11, 1991, 3–7, 28. Dumpson's brother, Father Roland Dumpson, was a priest of the archdiocese of New York.

47. *New York Times*, November 9, 2012.

The Graduate School of Social Service

forming the school from a small local Catholic school into a highly respected institution that has continued to be ranked among the dozen most prestigious graduate schools of social service in the United States and the highest-ranked graduate school in Fordham University. Her connection with Fordham went back to 1948, when, fresh from graduation at the College of Mount St. Vincent in Riverdale, she applied for admission as a student in the School of Social Service. She showed up wearing a floral dress and a large hat. The no-nonsense dean who interviewed her, Dr. Anna King, was not impressed with her appearance. She asked Quaranta, "Do you expect to dress like that as a social worker?" "Well, I hope so," replied Quaranta. "That's kind of a metaphor of my life," Quaranta said years later.

After earning her M.S.W. degree in 1950, Quaranta spent ten years working as a guidance counselor and field instructor for Catholic Charities, the principal social service agency of the archdiocese of New York. She also earned a D.S.W. degree from Columbia University. She accepted an invitation to return to Fordham, where she became the chair of Casework and director of Field Instruction in the Graduate School of Social Service. By 1975 she was dean of the school. Her early hands-on experience of social work left a lasting impression on her policies as dean. Although she was not opposed to innovations in the training of social workers, she insisted on the necessity of actual clinical experience rather than reliance solely on classroom instruction.

As dean for a quarter-century Quaranta presided over a major transformation in what she called "the character of the school." When she assumed the reins as dean in 1975, she said that "we had been a large 'C' Catholic school," by which she meant that both the faculty and the students were mostly Catholic and the school served largely the needs of the local Catholic community. Sixteen years into her tenure as dean she noted that the faculty and student body had become much more diverse in their ethnic origins, geographical backgrounds, religious affiliations, and philosophical outlooks. She welcomed these changes because she thought they made the school more representative of the community that it attempted to serve. She also welcomed the fact that Fordham was now attracting older students who already had experience in the field of social service instead of young people like herself who had come to graduate school directly from college. "I think of how green and naïve we were to do this," she said.[48]

48. FUA, FOHP, Interview with Mary Ann Quaranta by Helen Dermody, June 21, 1991, 1–5.

Dr. Mary Ann Quaranta, dean of the Fordham School of Social Service, 1975–2000.

Diversity was a high priority for Quaranta, and she was proud that more than one-third of the students at the Fordham Graduate School of Social Service represented minority populations of many different kinds. Quaranta thought this provided the faculty with a golden opportunity to promote the virtues of diversity in the classroom. "You can teach about diversity and you can have literature on it," she said, "but unless you actually experience it, it's very hard for it to become integrated."

By the 1990s Quaranta may have seemed rather old-fashioned to some of her colleagues in the field of social service education because she insisted on promoting the importance of the field work experience of working personally with individuals and families rather than concentrating on community organization. At Fordham under Quaranta's leadership field work remained an integral part of the curriculum, and she was vociferous in the Council on Social Work Education in asserting its importance in the face of increasing indifference. She cited the example of the positive experiences Fordham students had when they witnessed the work done on the Upper East Side of Manhattan by the supervisor of a program for mentally ill homeless people. "Students love to go to her," she said, "and see the wonderful things she does with these homeless people."[49]

49. Ibid., 11–18.

During her twenty-five years as dean, Dr. Quaranta also revived the moribund doctoral program in the School of Social Service. She insisted that the emphasis in the doctoral program be on research, but she remained true to her convictions that experience of field work should be an integral element in the education of every social worker. For that reason she refused to admit students from the masters program into the doctoral program until they had acquired practical field experience of social work. She applied the same standard to the faculty. She deplored professors "who taught from books." "This really isn't possible anymore," she said. "For the faculty to maintain credibility among their peers, they've got to be doing something that is relevant to the field."[50]

Dr. Quaranta received national recognition when she was elected president of the National Association of Social Workers and was elected to numerous other leadership positions in NASW and in other professional organizations. She was instrumental in winning for Fordham the prestigious National Institute of Mental Health research grant with a concentration on Hispanic mental health. Fordham's was only the eighth school of social service in the United States to win the award and the only one without an affiliated medical school. A hallmark of her leadership of the Fordham Graduate School of Social Service was her readiness to form partnerships with local community social service agencies.[51]

One of Dr. Quaranta's goals was to achieve parity with the other Fordham graduate schools because she thought that the Graduate School of Social Service was regarded as "a step-child discipline or school." Before she retired she had the satisfaction of seeing the Graduate School of Social Service become the recipient of more outside money than any other school in the university. She was equally successful in attaining her other goal of winning national recognition for Fordham's Graduate School of Social Service. During her tenure as dean, the school was ranked among the dozen best graduate schools of social service in the United States, a position that it has since retained.[52]

50. Ibid., 18–22, 24–25. Dr. Quaranta was instrumental in establishing at Fordham the Children and Families Institute for Research, Support and Training, the Ravazzin Center for Social Work Research on Aging, the Institute for Managed Care and Social Work, the Interdisciplinary Center for Family and Child Advocacy (in collaboration with the Fordham School of Law), and the National Center for Schools and Communities (in collaboration with the Graduate School of Education). http://www.fordham.edu/Campus_Resources/enewsroom/topstories_1740.asp.

51. http://www.nasw foundation.org/pioneers/q/quaranta.html.

52. FUA, FOHP, Quaranta, Interview, 24, 28.

After retiring from Fordham in 2000, Dr. Quaranta served for four years as the provost of Marymount College, which was affiliated with Fordham University at that time, and then served as special assistant to the president for community and diocesan affairs. At her death on December 16, 2009, Father Joseph M. McShane, S.J., the president of Fordham University, said, "Mary Ann Quaranta was the most elegant person I ever met. She had the ability," said Father McShane, "to figure out a program on the way to work." More important, added McShane, "she possessed eyes that enabled her to look on the poor and see in them God's greatest riches. We at Fordham were blessed to have her as colleague, mother superior, visionary dean and friend." In her honor Fordham University established the Mary Ann Quaranta Chair for Social Justice for Children.[53]

53. http://www.fordham.edu/Campus_Resources/enewsroom/topstories_1953.asp.

12

THE GRADUATE SCHOOL
OF ARTS AND SCIENCES

The Woolworth Building

The Graduate School of Arts and Sciences had a modest and informal beginning in the fall of 1916 under the name of the Graduate School on the twenty-eighth floor of the Woolworth Building with four graduate courses and eight students. The original faculty consisted of three Jesuits—Fathers Michael J. Mahony, J.F.X. Murphy, and Terence J. Shealy—and one layman, Condé B. Pallen. The Graduate School was formally inaugurated the following November when the curriculum was expanded to twenty-nine courses and three seminars that included scholastic philosophy, literature, history, economics, jurisprudence, Latin, Greek, Spanish, and Italian, although it is impossible to verify how many of the courses were actually taught.

The faculty was also increased from four to sixteen, all but three of whom were Jesuits. They were self-described as "some of the most eminent members of the Society of Jesus." Several of them, like Fathers Husslein and Fortier, also taught in other units of the university (and Fortier did double duty as dean) while three other Jesuits were on the staff of *America*, including the editor, Father Richard H. Tierney. Two of the laymen, Thomas F. Reilly and the ubiquitous James J. Walsh, were medical doctors who taught sociology. As the number of students and courses proliferated, the Jesuits increasingly employed public school teachers and administrators as adjunct faculty, a development that did little to improve the academic reputation of the Graduate School. The number of advertised courses sometimes outstripped the pool of potential students. As early as 1917 the university warned that courses would be canceled without a sufficient enrollment. Father Hogan later set the minimum number of students at ten.[1]

---

1. FUA, Gannon Papers, Gannon to James J. Walsh, November 24, 1936. The Jesuits were Fathers William Clark, John J. Wynne, Owen A. Hill, Edmund J. Burke, John C. Reville, Michael J. Mahoney, Joseph Husslein, Richard H. Tierney, Matthew L. Fortier, J.F.X. Murphy, John J. O'Connor, John H. Fisher, and Paul V. O'Rourke.

The Woolworth Building, the tallest building in the world for a brief period, served as the home of "Fordham Downtown" from 1916 to 1943.

The Graduate School of Arts and Sciences

The courses were one hour in length and were scheduled between 6:00 P.M. and 10:00 P.M. five evenings a week to accommodate part-time students who, in the quaint words of the catalogue, were thought to be seeking "mental diversion from ministerial occupation and business routine." In fact the motives of most of those who applied for admission were more mundane and practical. Many were public school teachers seeking tenure and promotion from the New York City Board of Education, and others were teaching sisters, brothers, and priests in the local Catholic schools who were sent to get advanced degrees by their religious superiors. In view of the professional needs of many of the students it seemed logical for Fordham to maintain a close connection between the graduate school and Fordham's Teachers' College, which had been established at the same time as the Graduate School in the Woolworth Building. The name, Teachers' College, was misleading. It was a full-fledged liberal arts college that became the undergraduate division of the School of Education in 1938. (For a fuller treatment, see Chapter 13.)

Despite their limited resources in money and personnel, the founders of the Graduate School did not suffer from self-doubt. A year after its founding the Graduate School was offering no fewer than five graduate degrees: Master of Arts, Master of Science, Master of Philosophy, Licentiate of Philosophy, and Doctor of Philosophy. Fordham also awarded its first six master's degrees that year. The graduate students were expected to spend a minimum of one year in residence for the master's degree and to complete the doctorate within three or four years. The residential requirement was a euphemistic reference to course work, because there was no provision for university housing for the graduate students and little opportunity for them even to mingle with one another outside of class. The Fordham Graduate School had little physical resemblance to Oxford or Cambridge or even to Harvard or Yale, because the original campus was confined to just a small area of one floor in the tower of the Woolworth Building.[2]

The graduate students were also required to demonstrate a reading knowledge of French or German or another modern language related to their field of interest upon entrance into the program, but it is not clear how rigorously their proficiency in foreign languages was tested. In the Fordham Teachers' College, which was closely connected with the Graduate School until 1932, students were permitted to satisfy the language requirement by presenting evidence that they had studied a foreign language

2. Fordham University, *Bulletin of Information, Graduate School, 1917–1918*, 5–15.

for three years in high school or by writing a paper on "some phase of education" in a non-English-speaking country.[3]

The mandatory dissertations for both the master's degree and the doctorate also raise questions of quality control. Doctoral candidates were required to submit 100 copies of their dissertation to the library, but "for reasons of weight," the dean could waive this requirement if the dissertation were to be published in a reputable scholarly journal, which gives some indication of the modest size of the early doctoral dissertations. It was specified that the masters theses (they were also called dissertations) had to consist of at least 6,000 words, which in practice meant no more than two dozen doubled-spaced typed pages, if the student set generous margins in the typewriter.

A notable absence in the early curriculum was any mention of science courses. That deficiency was remedied in 1919 with the addition of a science department offering courses in chemistry, bacteriology, physiology, and biology. There was no space available in the Woolworth Building for this expansion of the Graduate School, but classrooms and laboratories unexpectedly became available at the Rose Hill campus that year when the university announced that it was phasing out the Medical School. The Science Department of the Graduate School found a home in the new building at the Bathgate Avenue entrance to the campus that had originally been erected to house the Medical School. It was renamed the Science Building and still later renamed Finlay Hall. Sixteen years later, under Father Robert I. Gannon, the rest of the Graduate School followed the example of the Science Department and moved to the newly constructed Keating Hall at Rose Hill despite dire predictions of a precipitous decline in the number of students because of the distance from Manhattan.[4]

For the first decade-and-a-half of its existence the administration of the Graduate School was a hand-to-mouth operation because the dean was also more or less responsible for the supervision of the Fordham Teachers' College, the downtown college, and the School of Sociology and Social Service. As one anonymous Jesuit described the situation, "one secretary and one registrar sufficed for all. The records of the Graduate School, speaking figuratively, could be carried in a portfolio under the arm; those of individual departments could be carried in the head." By 1932 the Graduate School had grown to such an extent that it was separated administra-

3. FUA, Duane Papers, Memorandum of the Meeting of the Faculty of the Teachers College, March 9, 1929.

4. FUA, Archivist's Files, Box 27, Father Joseph F. Mulligan, S.J., Address to the Faculty of the Graduate School of Arts and Sciences, September 16, 1964.

The Graduate School of Arts and Sciences

tively from the Teachers' College and other units of the university in the Woolworth Building and given its own dean with his own administrative offices.[5]

That same year, writing in *Commonweal*, Dr. Roy J. Deferrari, dean of the Graduate School at the Catholic University of America and a leading Catholic educational reformer, called for an upgrading in standards for master's degrees in American universities. Father Aloysius J. Hogan, the president of Fordham, congratulated Deferrari on his article and expressed his wholehearted approval. He pointed out that the Graduate School at Fordham had already implemented many of his proposals, such as requiring both comprehensive examinations and a dissertation and refusing to accept extension courses or correspondence courses in fulfillment of regular course requirements.[6]

Too Much Too Soon

Hogan was proud of the masters program at Fordham, but the doctoral program left much to be desired. In the 1920s, Fordham's Graduate School had developed one of the largest doctoral programs in the United States despite scandalously inadequate library facilities and science laboratories and a dearth of full-time students and full-time faculty. Father Joseph F. Mulligan, S.J., who was dean of the Graduate School of Arts and Sciences in the 1960s, calculated that between 1920 and 1929 Fordham awarded 240 doctorates and ranked sixteenth or seventeenth among all American universities granting the Ph.D. degree.[7] Even in the brief period between 1922–23 and 1926–27 Fordham awarded 325 master's degrees and 108 doctorates, exceeding those awarded by any other American Catholic university.[8]

The increase in enrollment at Fordham was a reflection of the vast expansion of American Catholic higher education in the 1920s on both the

5. FUA, Archivist's Files, Box 27, The Graduate School of Arts and Sciences, n.d. [1941], 2.

6. Roy J. Deferrari, "Rehabilitating the Master's Degree," *Commonweal*, June 29, 1932, 233–35. FUA, Hogan Papers, Hogan to Deferrari, June 28, 1932; Deferrari pointed out to Hogan that the Catholic University accepted without question graduate work done at Fordham. Deferrari to Hogan, July 5, 1932.

7. FUA, Archivist's Files, Box 27, Mulligan, Address to Faculty of GSAS, September 16, 1964.

8. *Bulletin of the National Catholic Educational Association* 25:1 (November 1928): 107. The comparable figures for the runner-up, the Catholic University of America, were 274 master's degrees and 64 doctorates.

undergraduate and graduate levels, but the sheer number of the graduate degrees awarded by Fordham led Professor Philip Gleason, a leading authority on twentieth-century American Catholic higher education, to question their value, especially given that so many of the students who received them were part-timers. In the 1930s there was a sharp drop in the number of Fordham doctorates, either because of the Depression or because of the tightening of academic standards, or both. Fordham awarded only twenty-four doctorates between 1931 and 1933, but that number still placed Fordham second only to the Catholic University of America (which produced fifty-six doctorates) among the thirty-three leading American Catholic colleges and universities.[9]

Other statistics also raised questions about the nature of Fordham's graduate program. In 1931–32 only 25 of the 684 graduate students were full-time students; there was a slight improvement in 1932–33 when 67 of the 753 graduate students were full-time students. The comparable figures for the faculty were even more lopsided. Only 13 of the 88 instructors were full-time in 1931–32; the statistics were even worse for 1932–33, when only 15 of the 96 instructors were full-time.[10] The situation attracted critical notice from the Association of American Universities as early as 1930 when one official of the organization, Professor Adam Leroy Jones, sent a friendly personal note to the dean of the Graduate School, Father Miles J. O'Mailia, warning him that major changes were needed to assure Fordham's continued membership in the organization. "The general spirit and effectiveness of a school are made to a considerable degree by the full time faculty and full time student body," Jones said.[11]

Many of the AAU's criticisms of Fordham's questionable academic standards were shared by Father Charles J. Deane, the dean of Fordham College from 1925 to 1937. In 1931 he complained that not a single Jesuit was teaching at the downtown college and that students who had been dismissed from the college at Rose Hill had been admitted to the downtown

9. *Bulletin of the National Catholic Educational Association* 30:1 (November 1933), 96. In those two academic years Fordham ranked fifth among American Catholic universities in the number of master's degrees it awarded (128), behind the Catholic University of America (280), St. Louis University (212), Boston College (183), and the University of Detroit (142). Philip Gleason, *Contending with Modernity: Catholic Higher Education in the Twentieth Century* (New York: Oxford University Press, 1995), 175.

10. *Bulletin of the National Catholic Educational Association* 30:1 (November 1933): 114, 116.

11. FUA, Hogan Papers, Jones to O'Mailia, October 10, 1930; Jones to Hogan, October 16, 1933.

college and given B.S. degrees. He also complained of the poor quality of the teaching in the Graduate School and said that many courses "have no academic value." Three years later he saw little improvement and claimed that, except for the Law School, the standards in Fordham's graduate schools did not measure up to the standards in comparable universities. He was especially critical of the situation in the Graduate School, where the two previous deans had been appointed to that office without any professional background. "That is educational suicide," he informed the Jesuit general in 1933, "simply giving the [AAU] the opportunity they seek of dropping us from the approved list. All this makes our education a laughing stock in the eyes of educated men."[12]

As a gadfly in the Maryland–New York Province of the Society of Jesus, Deane was a worthy successor to Father John J. Wynne, S.J., although not nearly as creative or productive as Wynne. In 1934 Deane complained to his friend Father Wilfrid Parsons, S.J., the editor of *America*, about the alleged intellectual indolence of his Jesuit confrères at Fordham. "I have given their names and paid their dues to educational societies with very little result," he told Parsons. "With the exception of two or three here, Ours read very little that is not in line with their work, have no opinion on matters of the day, do not keep up even with the names of new worthwhile books." As a result, said Deane, "they do not inspire their classes to read and to form habits which will last them after college days are over." Deane saved the cruelest blow for last. "I might add that they are not even interested in *America*."[13]

The Day of Reckoning

Although Fordham made some progress in increasing the number of full-time faculty in the graduate schools, Hogan himself was pessimistic about the outcome of an inspection by the AAU that was scheduled for the fall of 1935. He had good reasons for his apprehensions. Hogan was eager not only to maintain Fordham College's approval by the AAU but also to secure membership for the whole university in the AAU's coveted list of Universities of Complex Organization. His enthusiasm was not entirely sincere or spontaneous. In the spring of 1935 Hogan was ordered to do so by Father Daniel M. O'Connell of Loyola University in

12. ARSJ, Deane to Ledóchowski, January 13, 1931, January 24, 1934, January 16, 1933.
13. Archives of the Georgetown University Library, Deane to Parsons, November 15, 1934. I am grateful to Fr. Anthony Andreassi, C.O., for providing me with a copy of this letter.

Chicago, who had been appointed the secretary of the newly founded National Jesuit Educational Association in the United States the year before. The general, Father Wlodimir Ledóchowski, had also appointed O'Connell commissarius for education in the American Assistancy of the Society of Jesus with a mandate to implement his *Instructio* of August 15, 1934, which called for a revision of Jesuit higher education in the United States.[14]

O'Connell and Hogan resembled each other in the sense that they were both strong-minded and abrasive individuals, but in their educational philosophies they were as different as chalk from cheese and they personified the growing divergence between the Jesuit universities in the Midwest and the Northeast. Father O'Connell represented the new breed of progressive Jesuit educators in the Midwest who were reshaping and modernizing Jesuit higher education in the United States because they recognized the necessity of cooperating with the regional accrediting associations if they were to preserve and enhance the academic reputation of their colleges and universities. It was no accident that by 1933 the only two American Catholic universities that had achieved inclusion in the AAU's list of Universities of Complex Organization were both Jesuit institutions in the Midwest, St. Louis University and Marquette University. They had achieved this distinction by satisfying the exacting standards of the North Central Association of Colleges and Secondary Schools.[15]

By contrast, Father Hogan was openly contemptuous of the academic standards of the regional accrediting association for the northeastern United States, the Middle States Association of Colleges and Secondary Schools, whose requirements were considerably more flexible and less demanding than those of the North Central Association. "We refuse to be stampeded into following the pseudo-educational vagaries of experimentalists," he announced at the Faculty Convocation of 1934. His point of view was shared by other Jesuits at Fordham. At the same Faculty Convocation, Father Ignatius W. Cox, professor of ethics, threw down the gauntlet to the Middle States Association when he declared, "I would say to the standardizing agency: we are developing a type and culture not your own, but still a culture not inferior to yours, but to our minds infinitely superior." He was of course referring to the Jesuit *ratio studiorum*. Still another

14. Thomas E. Curley Jr., "Robert I. Gannon, President of Fordham University, 1936–1949: A Jesuit Educator," Ph.D. diss., New York University, 1973, 78–79.

15. *Bulletin of the National Catholic Educational Association* 30:1 (November 1933): 109.

Fordham Jesuit, Father Francis P. Donnelly, accused his midwestern confrères of surrendering to "[Harvard President Charles] Eliot's heresy that anything can educate."[16]

After a visit to Fordham, O'Connell sent Hogan a lengthy list of recommendations through the provincial of the Maryland–New York Province, Father Edward C. Phillips. Hogan discussed the recommendations thoroughly with his consultors on February 26 and March 4, 1935. They welcomed many of the recommendations and pointed out that they had already begun to implement some of them, such as improving the library of the graduate school and hiring more full-time professors. They agreed to separate the graduate courses from the undergraduate courses and to publish separate catalogues for the Graduate School and the Teachers' College. However, with regard to O'Connell's recommendation to offer more scholarships, they replied that many of the scholarships went begging because potential students were too poor to accept them in the middle of the Depression. The consultors strenuously resisted some of O'Connell's other recommendations, such as closing the School of Pharmacy and introducing the departmental system in the college, which, they said, smacked of "electivism." They also flatly rejected as impossible O'Connell's order to move the Graduate School to Rose Hill. In his covering letter to Hogan, Phillips added another order that must have been especially displeasing to him. He told Hogan to suspend all building projects, including the completion of his beloved Keating Hall, and "to devote practically all the revenues of the university for several years to come to the improvement of the graduate and professional schools."[17]

Nine months later, on November 26, 1935, Hogan's worst fears about accreditation were confirmed when he received a devastating letter from Dr. Fernandus Payne, the chairman of the Committee on the Classification of Colleges and Universities of the AAU. Payne informed Hogan that, as a result of both the on-site inspection and the reports submitted by Fordham, the AAU had voted to drop Fordham from its list of accredited institutions. The exclusion applied not only to the Graduate School but also to the college, which had been on the approved list for ten years. It was "a humiliation," said Father Robert I. Gannon, "that could come to the atten-

16. Robert I. Gannon, *Up to the Present: The Story of Fordham* (Garden City, N.Y.: Doubleday and Company, 1967), 197–98.

17. FUA, Hogan Papers, Excerpts from the Minutes of the Consultors' Meetings, February 26 and March 4, 1945. The *procès-verbaux* of these two meetings were never recorded in the Minutes of the Meetings of the Consultors. Phillips to Hogan, February 24, 1935.

tion of every educator in the country." As a result, he added, "It was one of the darkest single days in 125 years."[18]

The AAU gave two reasons for its decision. The first was that the library facilities were inadequate, especially the downtown library in the Woolworth Building where most of the graduate courses were taught. The library at Rose Hill was somewhat better stocked, but (as the dean of the Graduate School, Father Lawrence A. Walsh, admitted privately to the general), the librarian was so fearful of theft that he intimidated both faculty and students from using the library. The AAU inspectors found many of the reference books in locked cases or inaccessible rooms. The second reason the AAU dropped Fordham from membership was the allegedly poor performance of Fordham alumni in graduate and professional schools. This criticism was more problematic, because the secretary of the AAU inadvertently failed to include in his calculations a list of more than one hundred of Fordham College's most successful alumni. For the previous five years he included only the graduates of the downtown college and the Teachers' College but not the graduates of the college at Rose Hill, where academic standards were considerably higher.[19]

Still another but more intangible factor in Fordham's loss of membership in the AAU was the undeniably belligerent attitude of Father Hogan. Father Gannon said that he "almost provoked [the AAU] to a fight," and Father Walsh faulted him for his "impolitic" statements even before the arrival of the inspection committee. The ever-critical Father Deane complained in 1935 that "the government of this house is at present a one-man rule. The rector has taken upon himself not only the direction, but the execution of everything from seeing that the floors are clean to the outlining of the graduate courses."[20]

Hogan's truculent attitude was not limited to his dealings with the AAU. It was characteristic of his *modus operandi* in the face of any opposition, real or imagined. He seemed totally indifferent in 1933 when Fordham lost its membership in the American Council of Education solely because he refused to comply with a request for the number of books published by the faculty. Hogan even faced down the general of the Society, Father Ledóchowski, when he ordered him to suspend the construction of Keating Hall during the depths of the Depression and to use the money instead

18. FUA, Hogan Papers, Payne to Hogan, November 26, 1935. Gannon, *Up to the Present*, 206–7.

19. ARSJ, Walsh to Ledóchowski, January 18, 1937.

20. ARSJ, Gannon to Ledóchowski, September 11, 1936; Walsh to Ledóchowski, n.d.; Deane to Ledóchowski, January 9, 1935.

for the Graduate School and the college. Hogan won a reprieve from the general when he claimed that Keating Hall had cost only $65,532 and that the university would lose $265,000 if it suspended construction on the building. The provincial of the Maryland–New York Province, Father Phillips, told Hogan that he did not believe him. "This is more than 50% of the total contract price," Phillips pointed out to Hogan, "and no such penalty could be imposed for cancellation or postponement of contracts."[21]

Keating Hall was ultimately completed six months after Hogan left office at the astronomical sum of $1,343,000, which was somewhere between two and three times the originally projected cost. From one perspective it may be the most expensive building ever erected on the Rose Hill campus because it temporarily cost Fordham its approval by the AAU. However, in the long run, future generations of Fordham students can be grateful to Father Hogan for insisting on erecting the splendid tower of Keating Hall, which has ever since made Keating Hall Fordham's signature building. He succeeded by persuading both the general and the provincial that it was not a luxury, but an essential feature of the building, because it was the only suitable location on the campus for a water tank! Besides, he assured them, it would cost only an additional $25,000. The real bill came to $343,000.[22]

The contentious Hogan even managed to tangle with the easygoing archbishop of New York, Patrick Cardinal Hayes, alienating him over a number of issues. One issue was the St. Patrick's Day parade, an annual demonstration of the Catholic—and especially the Irish Catholic—presence in New York City. In 1936 Cardinal Hayes asked all the Catholic colleges in New York City to send a delegation of students to march in the parade in order to enhance its prestige and to offset the unruly behavior of some of the participants. For some unexplained reason Fordham was the only Catholic college that declined to honor the cardinal's request, and Hogan's rebuff deeply offended Hayes.

Another source of friction with the archdiocese was Fordham's abrupt termination of its participation in the Catholic Summer School of America in Plattsburg, New York, which offered extension courses in imitation of the highly successful Chautauqua Summer School established by the Methodists in upstate New York in the 1870s. Hogan may have thought that Fordham's participation diminished its academic reputation or that the Catholic Summer School was in competition with Fordham's own summer school, but he seems to have overlooked the fact that the Cath-

21. FUA, Hogan Papers, Phillips to Hogan, February 24, 1935.
22. Gannon, *Up to the Present*, 202–7.

olic Summer School of America was a special favorite of Monsignor Michael Lavelle, the rector of St. Patrick's Cathedral and a close confidant of Hayes's. In an unprecedented snub, the cardinal indicated his displeasure with Hogan when he declined to preside at the commencement exercises in 1936 even though it was the occasion for the blessing of the cornerstone of Keating Hall. Hogan also blamed Lavelle for preventing him from moving Fordham Preparatory School from Rose Hill to Riverdale because Lavelle claimed that the location was too close to Manhattan College, Hayes's alma mater.[23]

"Making Something Fine out of Fordham"

By 1936 Father Hogan had become a liability both academically and ecclesiastically. His Jesuit superiors replaced him on June 25 of that year with Father Robert I. Gannon, the forty-three-year-old president of St. Peter's College in Jersey City. A native New Yorker, Gannon was the youngest of nine children, the son of a railroad executive, and an alumnus of Loyola School in New York City and Georgetown College. As a young Jesuit, he spent some time at Oxford and Cambridge acquiring not only first-hand experience of English higher education but also a carefully modulated hint of an English accent that Father Raymond Schroth memorably described as "plumy." Gannon had reopened St. Peter's College in 1930 after it had been closed during World War I, raised the enrollment from 80 to 416 in the space of six years, and erected a modern facility to house the college. He also excelled at public relations. No stranger to Fordham, Gannon had spent four years at Rose Hill as a scholastic teaching a variety of subjects at both Fordham Preparatory School and at Fordham College, although he was never given the opportunity to teach history, the subject that was dearest to his heart. One of Gannon's first decisions as president of Fordham was to hire a public relations firm to repair the university's damaged image.[24]

While Gannon politely praised Hogan's administration as "admirable," he immediately served notice that he planned to take Fordham in a different direction. "Having a registration of 7,500 is nothing to boast about," he said. After seventeen years of constant expansion, Gannon wanted to concentrate on quality rather than quantity, particularly in the college and the Graduate School. He promised to freeze the enrollment in both schools at their existing levels for the next six years. "We see our responsibility to

23. ARSJ, Gannon to Ledóchowskl, September 17, 1936.
24. Curley, "Robert I. Gannon," 5–20.

Father Robert I. Gannon, S.J., president of Fordham University, 1936–49.

save those two schools from becoming machines in which candidates take a series of courses and earn a degree without having broadened mentally or socially the slightest bit."[25]

Gannon's highest priority was to regain Fordham's accreditation. Within two weeks of taking office, he wrote a conciliatory letter to Dr. Fernandus Payne of the AAU, outlining the changes that had already been made in the libraries and gently reminding Payne that his (Payne's) secretary was partially responsible for Fordham's loss of accreditation because he had inadvertently omitted the names of more than one hundred of Fordham's most successful graduate students. Rather than belabor the point, as Hogan would almost certainly have done, Gannon magnanimously offered to excuse the error as "just one of those unfortunate things that can happen in the most efficient organization." He invited Payne to send another inspection team to Fordham to see for himself the progress that had been made. "We are very eager to make something fine out of Fordham," he assured Payne, "and loss of prestige at this time is a very serious handicap."[26]

25. *New York Herald-Tribune*, June 26, 1936.

26. FUA, Gannon Papers, Gannon to Payne, July 6, 1936. That same day the librarian at Rose Hill submitted his resignation, which was promptly accepted.

By the fall of 1936 Fordham had added 15,850 books to the university libraries and Gannon had decided to move the Graduate School from the Woolworth Building to Keating Hall at Rose Hill, a transition that he hoped would be completed within two years. He was willing to accept an anticipated decline in both registration and income for the Graduate School as a result of the move (which did not happen), but he counted on an increase in the number of full-time students that would improve academic standards. "We have a wonderful opportunity, ambitious plans and high hopes," Gannon told Payne in an unusually personal letter, "but these are to a great extent dependent on preserving our reputation, so I am asking you to trust me . . . . If we are branded as incompetent, it will take years to win back the confidence that is necessary for a Graduate School, but if the Association of American Universities does the friendly thing—results will be much more rapid."[27]

Evidently Payne and the Committee on the Classification of Colleges and Universities of the AAU did trust Gannon and they responded, as he had hoped, by doing "the friendly thing." On November 6, 1936, the AAU restored Fordham College to its approved list and eventually admitted the university to its prestigious list of Universities of Complex Organization.[28] By December 1936 Fordham Law School had been accredited by the American Association of Law Schools, and in May 1937 it received the final approval of the American Bar Association. Shortly thereafter the Pharmacy School, the Business School, and the Teachers' College (now renamed the School of Education) all obtained the approval of their respective professional associations. Gannon did not claim exclusive credit for these major advances in the professionalization of Fordham. He readily admitted that they would not have been possible without the inspired and creative bookkeeping of the university treasurer, Father Joseph Keating. Although Gannon did not mention it, Hogan also deserved credit for his constant support of the efforts of Dean Wilkinson to win full accreditation for the Law School.[29]

At the dedication of Keating Hall, the new home of the Graduate School, on December 8, 1936, Gannon described it as a "$1,200,000 gift" to the educated Catholics of New York, especially the teachers in the Catholic schools of New York. He estimated that the Graduate School would require an annual subsidy of $100,000 from the university, but he prom-

27. FUA, Gannon Papers, Gannon to Payne, October 30, 1936.
28. Curley, "Robert I. Gannon," 124.
29. Gannon, *Up to the Present*, 213–14.

The Graduate School of Arts and Sciences

ised to provide it "until the well runs dry." Despite dire predictions of a loss of graduate students because of the relocation of the Graduate School to Rose Hill, there was actually a modest increase in enrollment from 836 students in 1935–36 to 972 students in 1938–39. There was a slight drop to 916 students in 1939–40 after the graduate degrees in education were switched to the School of Education. Nevertheless, in 1940 Fordham was still awarding more graduate degrees than any other American Catholic university except the Catholic University of America. Perhaps the most impressive change in the Graduate School was the increase in the number of full-time students. In 1935–36 only 141 of the 836 students were full-time; by 1939–40 one-third of the graduate students (301 out of 916) were full-time students.[30]

Gannon's conciliatory efforts as president of Fordham were not limited to his dealings with the officials of the AAU. He also made several overtures to repair Fordham's strained relations with Cardinal Hayes because he recognized that a close connection with the archdiocese was crucial to Fordham's success as a Catholic institution. Hayes was a shy and kindly gentleman who avoided public controversies, but, as the New York priest-historian Harry Browne once pointed out, "[O]bservers sometimes missed the angle of his jutting jaw, which betrayed another aspect of his personality." Unlike Hogan, Gannon did not make the mistake of considering Hayes a cipher. The difference was evident at the dedication of Keating Hall, when both Hayes and Lavelle were present, and the atmosphere could not have been more cordial as a result of the charm and affability of Fordham's president.[31]

New Blood

One of Gannon's major contributions to the Graduate School was the recruitment of distinguished faculty members, many of them foreign-born scholars who were fleeing the Nazis in their homeland. The most famous was Victor Hess, the Austrian-born physicist whose research on radiation earned him an international reputation and the Nobel Prize in physics in 1936. He remains Fordham's sole Nobel Lau-

---

30. *Bulletin of the National Catholic Educational Association*, 1938, 159; 1941, 128.

31. Gannon would have been a successful *éminence grise* under the *ancien régime*. In 1938 he established the Cardinal Hayes Jubilee Scholarship in the GSAS, a scholarship that was reserved for a Christian brother, the community that ran Manhattan College, Hayes's alma mater. When Gannon received an honorary doctorate from Manhattan College, Hayes noted with satisfaction, "It is another bond between us." FUA, Gannon Papers, Hayes to Gannon, May 11, 1938.

Dr. Victor Hess, professor of physics for twenty-five years and Fordham's sole Nobel Laureate. He received his Nobel Prize in 1936 for his research on the cosmic ray.

reate. After the Nazi occupation of Austria in 1938, he emigrated to the United States with his Jewish wife and taught at Fordham until his retirement in 1956. Another German-speaking scientist who sought refuge in the United States was Dr. Friedrich Nord, a professor at the University of Berlin who came to America after the rise of Hitler and taught chemistry at Fordham. Still another refugee from Nazi Germany was Father Rudolph Arbesmann, O.S.A., a cavalry officer in World War I who was awarded the Iron Cross, First Class, for his service in the kaiser's army. He became an Augustinian friar after the war and taught classics at the University of Wurzburg. In 1936 he found himself stranded in New York, and the following year he joined the Fordham faculty as professor of classics, where he quickly established a reputation as an outstanding teacher. He was also a prolific writer, publishing numerous books and articles in both German and English.

The Philosophy Department at Fordham profited from the addition of Dietrich von Hildebrand from the University of Göttingen. Gannon offered him a teaching position on the recommendation of Jacques Maritain, who described him as one of the three best Catholic philosophers in Europe. A convert to Catholicism and an early and outspoken critic of the Nazis, Hildebrand and his wife left Germany for Italy in March 1933 with $15 in his pocket and eventually reached America after a lengthy and

The Graduate School of Arts and Sciences

circuitous odyssey through Austria, Czechoslovakia, Switzerland, France, Portugal, and Brazil, arriving in New York in December 1940.

In the 1930s Hildebrand was an influential figure in a small circle of German-speaking Catholics—almost all of them converts—who helped to reshape Catholic attitudes to the Jews and paved the way for *Nostra Aetate*, the declaration at Vatican II that called the Jewish people "beloved of God" and made no mention of a call to conversion of Jews to Christianity. While in Austria Hildebrand edited an anti-Nazi weekly, *Der Christliche Ständestadt*, which has been described as "the most sophisticated Catholic platform for criticizing Nazism."[32]

In February 1941 Hildebrand began teaching at Fordham, where he remained until his retirement nineteen years later. In his later years he was a fierce critic of many aspects of the post–Vatican II Catholic Church, especially the liturgical changes. Fordham had an opportunity to add Maritain himself to the faculty, but the possibility evaporated when Gannon told Maritain that he would not allow him to criticize the wartime policies of Pope Pius XII in his class.[33]

Oscar Halecki was still another refugee from the Nazis who found a home at Fordham. A professor and dean at the University of Warsaw, Halecki escaped from Poland after the German invasion of his country in 1939 and taught eastern European history at Fordham from 1944 until 1961. Gannon marveled at his ability to lecture without notes and field questions in five languages. Still another political refugee, in this instance from the communists rather than from the Nazis, was Nicholas Timasheff, whose father had been a cabinet minister under Czar Nicholas II. A professor at the University of St. Petersburg, he left Russia in 1920 and came to Fordham by way of Harvard, where he was a pioneer in the development of the study of the sociology of law.[34]

Not all of new additions to the faculty proved to be successful. At the dedication of Keating Hall, Gannon teased the guests by announcing that, only the night before, "the most famous man in English Catholic letters"

32. In 1935 Cardinal Eugene Pacelli, the Vatican secretary of state and future Pope Pius XII, told Hildebrand that he hoped moderate strains in Nazism might win out. Hildebrand replied that moderate Nazism did not exist. John Connelly, *From Enemy to Brother: The Revolution in Catholic Teaching on the Jews, 1933–1965* (Cambridge, Mass.: Harvard University Press, 2012), 58, 95. Hildebrand figures prominently throughout Connelly's book.

33. Curley, "Robert I. Gannon," 123. The information is based on Curley's interview with Gannon on June 27, 1973.

34. *FM*, January 1937, 253–54; Gannon, *Up to the Present*, 212–13.

had cabled his acceptance of an invitation to teach at Fordham the following semester. Shortly thereafter it was revealed that the person in question was Hilaire Belloc, who taught at Fordham as a visiting professor in 1937. Belloc, who once described himself as a publicist rather than a historian, would have been chagrined to know that Gannon agreed with his self-characterization. Gannon did not think that Belloc's classroom lectures were sufficiently scholarly for a graduate school, but he welcomed the publicity that Belloc's presence gave Fordham, at least in Catholic circles. "If the old gentleman's purposes were less frankly commercial," Gannon confided to a friend, "he could have put [in] a great deal more time on the Fordham work and less time on everything else." As a follow-up to Belloc, Gannon hoped to entice Christopher Dawson, the English Catholic historian, to come to Fordham as a visiting professor, but at a lesser salary than Belloc's. Unfortunately, Fordham failed to attract Dawson, and he came to America only many years later, as the first Chauncey Stillman Professor of Catholic Studies at Harvard University.[35]

The History Department of the Graduate School especially profited from Gannon's hiring practices. A valuable addition was Ross J.S. Hoffman, who brought strength to the teaching of modern European history at Fordham. A descendant of a colonial Pennsylvania family and a convert to the Catholic Church, Hoffman was a forerunner of the conservative movement associated with William F. Buckley Jr. that blossomed in the United States in 1950s. One of the icons of that movement was Edmund Burke, the eighteenth-century Anglo-Irish political philosopher, and in 1945 Hoffmann founded the Edmund Burke Society at Fordham to promote Burke's philosophy of conservatism in postwar America.[36]

Hoffman also urged his fellow Catholic historians to strive for the highest scholarly standards in their research and writing. He warned them especially not to succumb to the apologetic approach to historiography associated with James J. Walsh and his glorification of the Middle Ages as the apex of civilization. In his later years the imperious Hoffman was a stately and even intimidating presence on campus, resembling in his mannerisms the eighteenth-century Whig aristocrats who were the subject of much of his later scholarly research. He never regretted his move from New York

35. FUA, Gannon Papers, Gannon to Demetrius Zema, S.J., April 21, 1937.

36. Patrick Allitt, *Catholic Intellectuals and Conservative Politics in America, 1950–1985* (Ithaca, N.Y.: Cornell University Press, 1993), 49–58. Together with Paul Levack, a Harvard Ph.D. and a colleague in the History Department of Fordham, Hoffman edited *Burke's Politics: Selected Writings and Speeches of Edmund Burke on Reform, Revolution and War* (New York: Knopf, 1949).

University to Fordham and told Gannon in 1949, "It was your inspiring presence, above all else, that convinced me more than ten years ago that it would be good to come to Fordham."[37]

Another distinguished member of the History Department was Professor Jeremiah F. O'Sullivan, a professor of medieval history, who admired Gannon for the respect he showed to lay teachers in a university that was still a largely clerical institution. A devout Catholic layman himself, O'Sullivan told Gannon, "You gave the layman stability at Fordham and so begot in him a sense of loyalty to the university." A shy and modest individual in contrast to the gregarious Ross Hoffman, O'Sullivan never sought much personal contact with Gannon, but he told him that, after one conversation, "I felt, if need so demanded, that I could go to you, talk things with you, and be understood when I did." He added, "It's a great comfort to have that feeling."[38]

Coming of Age

During World War II the Graduate School of Arts and Sciences, as it was officially called in the catalogue for the first time in 1938–39, experienced a decline in enrollment, as did colleges and graduate schools throughout the United States. However, enrollment in the GSAS rebounded after the end of the war as a result of the G.I. Bill and the large-scale expansion in the number of Catholic secondary schools and colleges with teachers seeking graduate degrees. In his address to the faculty of the GSAS in September 1953, Father Arthur A. North, S.J., the newly appointed dean, boasted that Fordham was the largest Catholic graduate school in the eastern United States.

North also noted that the visitation team of the Middle States Association of Colleges and Secondary Schools had recently inspected Fordham and praised the faculty of the GSAS for the high quality of their teaching, but they also chided the faculty for their failure to publish scholarly books and articles and regretted that they saw little evidence of a Fordham community of scholars. North was somewhat sheepish in bringing this criticism to the attention of the faculty, because he candidly admitted that he himself had published relatively little. "Today, as we well know," he told the faculty, "good teaching, excellent teaching, while important and essential[,] is not sufficient. We professors of the Graduate School must turn our efforts more and more toward research and publications."

37. FUA, Gannon Papers, Hoffman to Gannon, January 7, 1949.
38. FUA, Gannon Papers, O'Sullivan to Gannon, January 18, 1949.

North's encouragement of research and publishing represented a major advance in the ethos of the leadership of the GSAS. Only fifteen years earlier one of his predecessors as dean of the GSAS, Father George Bull, S.J., had deplored the fact that research had become a "fetish" in American graduate schools. He declared that research could not become the major function of a Catholic graduate school because it was antithetical to the "Catholic life of the mind" that prized contemplation, not research, as the most important intellectual activity. For Bull there were no new worlds to be discovered, only old worlds to be better explored.[39]

North emphasized the need for research from the faculty not only because American academic accrediting agencies considered it an essential element in evaluating the faculty of a graduate school but also because the general of the Society, Father Louis Janssens, had strongly encouraged young Jesuit scholars to pursue graduate degrees at the best secular universities. "And let them not be drawn away from [scholarship]," Janssens added, "by the illusion that they can serve God better by work that seems to be more immediately priestly and apostolic." In citing the example of the Jesuits as a model for the lay faculty, North's implicit assumption was that they shared the same sense of vocation as the Jesuits. "Publishers must know we exist," said North. "Books bearing your name," he told the faculty, "purveying the sound Christian tradition in the various fields of learning, must appear in the market place and on the shelves of other universities' libraries."[40]

North also made a comprehensive survey of the graduate degrees given by Fordham between 1917 and 1953. He was unable to guarantee the accuracy of the statistics for the first ten years because the records had been so poorly preserved, but he was certain that the records after 1927 were accurate. He concluded that Fordham had probably granted 545 master's degrees between 1917 and 1927 and had certainly granted 3,818 master's degrees between 1927 and 1953.

The master's degree was offered in fifteen departments. The most popular degrees were in education (478), English (435), history (383), psychology (252), and chemistry (245). Approximately two-thirds of the graduates of the masters program were lay students (2,090 out of 3,226). Among the third who were priests and religious, more than half were sisters (629), followed by Jesuits (180), other priests (169), and brothers (168). Almost

39. George Bull, S.J., "The Future of the Catholic Graduate School," *Thought* 13 (September 1938), 364, 372, 378.

40. FUA, McGinley Papers, Arthur North, Address to the Faculty of the GSAS, September 11, 1953.

all of the graduates were destined to serve as teachers and administrators in the Catholic schools in metropolitan New York City, except for the priests and religious, who were members of international orders like the Society of Jesus who were likely to be sent to any part of the world by their superiors.[41]

A decade later Father North's successor as dean of the GSAS, Father Joseph F. Mulligan, S.J., indicated that little had changed at Fordham during the previous ten years. He described the GSAS as "a Catholic graduate school in New York City with a faculty consisting of excellent teachers instructing predominantly part-time students, who in turn seem more interested in teaching than in research." As a result, said Mulligan, Fordham had acquired a reputation of producing many excellent college teachers and administrators but few scholars who made notable contributions to their area of expertise. Mulligan was echoing the complaints made in the mid-1950s by Monsignor John Tracy Ellis, professor of church history at the Catholic University of America, about the shortcomings of Catholic higher education throughout the United States. Ellis attributed the problem largely to a lack of "a love of learning for its own sake" on the part of American Catholics.

At Fordham, Mulligan identified three specific problems that hobbled the GSAS and prevented it, in his view, from achieving excellence in the academic world. One was the lack of adequate library facilities, another was the dearth of full-time students, and the third was Fordham's inability to provide sufficient scholarship money to attract full-time graduate students. In 1963–64 there were 386 full-time students and 975 part-time students enrolled in the GSAS, an improvement over previous years' enrollments but still an unacceptably lopsided ratio. "We must face the brutal fact," said Mulligan, "that any really first-rate graduate student today does not have to pay for his graduate education, and that Fordham does not have the financial resources to award a large number of generous Graduate Fellowships." Mulligan also thought it was virtually impossible for even the best teacher to communicate a love of learning to his students when he met them only once a week in a crowded classroom.[42]

In 1970 the American Council on Education issued a critical evaluation of Fordham's graduate program. Both Father Michael Walsh, S.J., the president of Fordham, and Dr. Paul J. Reiss, the vice president for Ac-

41. FUA, McGinley Papers, North, A Study of the Enrollment of the Graduate School of Arts and Sciences, 1917–1953, 3, 34.

42. FUA. AF, Box 27, Rev. Joseph F. Mulligan, S.J., The Fordham Graduate School—Yesterday, Today, and Tomorrow, September, 16, 1964.

ademic Affairs, had serious reservations about the methodology used in the evaluation. Dr. Reiss drew up his own evaluation, which, however, was equally critical in some respects. He rated the fourteen departments in GSAS according to five categories: distinguished (none); strong (philosophy and psychology); good (history, sociology, theology, chemistry, English, classics); adequate (biology, French, physics, and mathematics); and marginal (economics and political science).[43]

In subsequent years Fordham made considerable strides in addressing the problems that Father Mulligan pointed out in 1964. The opening of the Walsh Family Library in 1997 finally gave Fordham a library worthy of a research university. During the presidency of both Father Finlay and Father O'Hare—and later that of Father McShane—Fordham drew upon a wide variety of sources to increase substantially the financial aid to full-time graduate students, because there was no prospect that the GSAS would ever be financially viable on its own. Father O'Hare also encouraged the expansion of the policy of giving larger stipends to fewer graduate students in order to compete more successfully with other universities for the best applicants. Nonetheless, despite the progress made by Fordham in improving the graduate program, in 1995 the GSAS received a disappointingly critical evaluation from the NRC that included the familiar complaint of the lack of scholarly publications by the faculty.[44]

Back in 1964, in his extensive critique of the GSAS, Father Mulligan raised the issue of what unique contribution the GSAS could cite to justify its existence when it was a constant drain on the meager financial resources of a poorly endowed university like Fordham. In 1980 Father Finlay noted with dismay the decline "in size and strength" of the GSAS during the previous years. Except for philosophy, psychology, and theology, he thought the future of the GSAS was problematic. He could think of only one compelling reason to justify Fordham's continued financial support of the GSAS. As he pointed out to Father Pedro Arrupe, the father general, the academic world was perhaps the most secularized element in American society. "As long as Fordham preserves quality doctoral programs," Finlay told Arrupe, "there is at least one university in this region at which future university professors can receive scholarly training that respects religious values."[45]

43. FUA, Walsh Papers, Walsh to Cammarosano, December 28, 1970; Reiss to Walsh, January 11, 1971.

44. FUA, O'Hare Papers, Himmelberg to Faculty in Graduate Departments, October 31, 1995. O'Hare to Dr. Nancy Busch, dean of the GSAS, September 3, 2002.

45. FUA, O'Hare Papers, Finlay to Arrupe, January 4, 1980; January 7, 1981.

FORDHAM DOWNTOWN, UPTOWN, ALL AROUND THE TOWN

13

Downtown

When the Law School, the Graduate School, and the School of Sociology and Social Service all took up residence in the Woolworth Building in 1916, it was the beginning of a major expansion of Fordham in downtown Manhattan. Within a decade "Fordham Downtown" would also include a teachers' college, business school, graduate school, Fordham College (Manhattan Division), summer school, the short-lived School of Irish Studies, and a dozen university centers. "University centers" was a euphemism for satellite campuses located as far away as Passaic, New Jersey.

The Woolworth Building, only three years old in 1916 and the tallest building in the world at the time, was an ideal location for the home of a commuter school in New York City. It was located at the hub of a dense network of transportation facilities that included five elevated lines (including one on the Brooklyn Bridge) and the East Side IRT subway. Together these mass transit facilities provided easy access to upper Manhattan, the Bronx, Queens, and Brooklyn for the price of the sacrosanct nickel fare that no politician dared to disturb. In addition, within walking distance of the Woolworth Building were the Hudson Tubes to Hoboken and Newark (today's PATH lines), the Staten Island ferry, and five Hudson River railroad ferries that deposited passengers on the New Jersey shore at the terminals of their respective companies as far north as Weehawken.

Father Gannon gave much of the credit for the rapid expansion of the schools at Fordham Downtown to three talented and energetic Jesuits: Father Matthew L. Fortier (who originally served as dean of both the Graduate School and the School of Sociology and Social Service) and Father Michael Jessup and Father R. Rush Rankin, both of whom returned to Fordham in 1919 after service as chaplains in World War I. In Gannon's words, Rush Rankin was "dean of everything" at Fordham Downtown except the Law School and the School of Social Service from 1920 to 1926. A lay faculty member described him tellingly as "a peppery and dynamic leader" but also "a man of limited patience but boundless energy." Another significant figure in the development of Fordham Downtown was Father Miles J. O'Mailia, who succeeded Rankin as dean from 1926 until 1931.[1]

The School of Education

Fordham's School of Education began in 1916 under the name of Teachers' College (the apostrophe was soon dropped) on the seventh floor of the Woolworth Building. It was intended not only to train future teachers and school administrators but also to imbue them with the traditional Catholic and Jesuit educational philosophy for service in a field that was increasingly dominated by secular philosophical currents. Coincidentally the year that Fordham's Teachers' College opened was also the year that John Dewey published his *Democracy and Education*, a seminal work that would soon make Dewey, a professor at Columbia University's Teachers College, an iconic figure in American education and the *bête noire* of American Catholic educators.

Fordham's Teachers College also served the practical purpose of enabling public school teachers to advance their careers in the New York City public school system. Many of these teachers had received their professional education at the state Normal Schools (the state teacher training schools), but they lacked the B.A. degree they needed in order to compete for promotion to principal or assistant principal. The courses in the Teachers College were deliberately designed to remedy that deficiency in their education. By 1927 Fordham offered seven supervisor training courses specifically designed for teachers seeking promotion in the New York City public school system. The classes were scheduled for the late afternoon or early evening to enable public school teachers to attend them at the end of the school day. One of the instructors was William Jansen, who became superintendent of schools in New York City twenty years later.

In contrast to the state Normal Schools, which emphasized practical pedagogical methods, the undergraduate program at Teachers College offered a fully rounded liberal arts education that included no fewer than eleven courses in philosophy as well as courses in history, English, and mathematics. In addition, a prerequisite for admission was the require-

1. Joseph F.X. McCarthy, *Learning in the City: The Graduate School of Education Reviews Its Seventy-Five Years in New York, 1916–1992* (New York: Fordham University Graduate School of Education, 1992), 23; Robert I. Gannon, *Up to the Present: The Story of Fordham* (Garden City, N.Y.: Doubleday and Company, 1967), 160, 178–79.

ment that candidates had studied at least three years of Latin in high school. There were even specialized courses in the teaching of business subjects such as accounting and stenography as well as the administration of vocational high schools.[2]

The close connection between Teachers College and the Graduate School (located in the same building and founded in the same year) enabled Fordham to offer graduate degrees as well as undergraduate degrees in education. In 1919 a separate Department of Education was established in the Graduate School, with six required core courses: history of education, principles of education, school administration, educational psychology, educational hygiene, and school methods. From the very beginning both Teachers College and the Graduate School were coeducational institutions, a rare if not unique distinction at that time in American Catholic higher education and Jesuit education worldwide. By 1919 Teachers College could even boast of a woman faculty member, Marietta Riley, who earned a doctorate at Fordham the following year. Three years later five of the twenty-three members of the faculty of Teachers College were women.

During the first decade of its existence Teachers College suffered from two of the same weaknesses as the Graduate School. The enrollment consisted largely of part-time students who paid $10 for a one-unit course and $20 for a two-unit course. The faculty was also largely part-time—not only the instructors, but even the administrators. In the late 1920s two of the three most important supervisors of the undergraduate program were full-time public school administrators, who were responsible for the direction and evaluation of even full-time instructors in Teachers College. There was not even a real campus for Teachers College. Although the Woolworth Building was its official home, classes were also taught at Rose Hill and at a number of satellite campuses.[3]

In the summer of 1927 Father O'Mailia faced a major challenge from his Jesuit superiors that threatened the future of many of the programs at Fordham Downtown. Without any warning and only a few weeks before the beginning of the summer session, Father F. J. Connell, the regional director of the Association of Jesuit Colleges and Universities in the Maryland–New York Province, writing at the behest of the provincial, Father Lawrence J. Kelly, told O'Mailia to limit admission to Teachers College and the summer school to priests, brothers, and sisters. He also ordered him to increase the required credit hours to bring them into conformity with

2. McCarthy, *Learning in the City*, 20, 29.
3. Ibid., 10, 24.

the bloated credit requirements at the "uptown college," Fordham College at Rose Hill.[4]

O'Mailia was furious and fought back vigorously. He told Father Duane, the president of Fordham, "Someone has just awakened to the fact that we have in all essentials a downtown college and is trying to kill it." He also warned Duane that "these decisions will kill all hope for a real university graduate school and will put an end [to] the aspirations of many public school men and women for our philosophy, and will also end our high aspirations for an ever greater and better Fordham University."

O'Mailia defended his stewardship of Fordham Downtown by pointing out that during the previous seven years nearly 350 men and women, lay and religious, including "many public school teachers," had received B.A. or B.S. degrees at Fordham Downtown through the Teachers College or the summer school. Moreover, he added that he had received the most flattering compliments both from Cardinal Hayes and from the state Education Department in Albany. In his appeal to the provincial, O'Mailia said, "Father Connell's action is to me inexplicable as well as unfair in its suddenness and finality." O'Mailia won his battle with Connell and Kelly, but he paid a high price personally for his victory. While the outcome was still in doubt, he told Father Duane, "I have been knocked down and trampled on, so I feel. My rest has been ruined; I am tired now from disappointment and discouragement, and I'll have to start Tuesday morning with I know not what confusion ahead of me."[5]

Several major changes occurred at Fordham Downtown in the 1930s. In 1932, during the administration of Father Aloysius Hogan, Teachers College, the Graduate School, and Fordham College (Manhattan Division), and the Business School were each assigned a separate dean. Father Joseph Lennon, S.J., became dean of Teachers College and held that position for the next six years.[6] In 1937 Father Robert I. Gannon recruited Dr. Francis M. Crowley, the first lay dean of the School of Education at St. Louis University, to make a comprehensive survey of the educational programs at Fordham. The following year Gannon accepted most of the

4. FUA, Duane Papers, Connell to O'Mailia, June 21, 1927.

5. FUA, Duane Papers, O'Malia to Duane, June 26, 27, 1927; O'Mailia to William Tallon, June 23, 1927. Fordham College at Rose Hill required 170 credit hours for the bachelor's degree; Fordham Downtown and Georgetown University required 128 credit hours; Columbia University required only 120 credit hours for a comparable degree.

6. Father Lawrence A. Walsh, S.J., was appointed dean of the Graduate School, and Father Thomas C. Hughes was appointed dean of the Business School and Fordham College (Manhattan Division). Gannon, *Up to the Present*, 201.

recommendations in Crowley's report and completely reorganized the educational programs on both the graduate and undergraduate levels. The stated purpose of the changes was to provide for better integration and coordination of the teacher training program and to place both graduate and undergraduate work under one administration.[7]

On the graduate level, in 1938 the Department of Education in the Graduate School was separated from the Graduate School and became the School of Education with Crowley as dean. On the undergraduate level Teachers College disappeared from the university catalogue and became the undergraduate division of the School of Education. At the same time, Father Lennon was appointed regent of the School of Education to assure a continued Jesuit presence in the administration of the school, a practice that already existed at Fordham in the Law School and the School of Pharmacy, which also had lay deans.[8]

By the mid-1930s Fordham was beginning to make its mark on public education in the New York metropolitan area. Both the president of Hunter College, Eugene A. Colligan, and the president of Brooklyn College, William A. Boylan, were alumni of the Graduate School and Teachers College, as was the associate superintendent of the New York City public schools, and the superintendent and associate superintendent of the public schools in Jersey City. In addition, Fordham counted among its alumni eight high school principals and twenty-seven elementary school principals in New York City and the suburbs.[9]

---

7. FUA, Gannon Papers, Box 6, Gannon to Crowley, August 17, 1938. CFU, Fordham College, 1938–1939, 19. Before going to St. Louis University, the Irish-born Crowley had served as director of the Bureau of Education of the National Catholic Welfare Conference, the national organization of the U.S. hierarchy. McCarthy, *Learning in the City*, 30. When Crowley composed a list of the twenty-one leading scholars in the field of education in Catholic colleges and universities in the United States in 1932, he included only one Fordham professor. Dr. Pierre Marique, a Belgian-born scholar with a doctorate from New York University. Francis M. Crowley, "Only One Graduate School?" *America*, June 11, 1932, 235.

8. Gannon, *Up to the Present*, 217. Ibid., 30. Although the School of Education was authorized to confer master's and doctoral degrees in education, the degrees continued to be conferred by the Graduate School of Arts and Sciences. As far back as 1919 the university catalogue occasionally referred to Teachers College as the School of Education. When Crowley asked Gannon to clarify the role of the regent, he replied that the regent was the rector's personal representative and was in charge of the budget, but the dean had authority over all scholastic matters. FUA, Gannon Papers, Crowley to Gannon, August 19, 1938.

9. FUA, Hogan Papers, Graduates of the Graduate School and Teachers College, n.d.

In Boston, where the Catholic presence, especially the Irish Catholic presence, was much more pervasive than in New York City, Catholics dominated the public school system by 1920 through the large number of Catholic teachers and administrators. Boston College established a school of education in 1919, three years after Fordham had established its Teachers College. The high-water mark of the symbiotic relationship between public and Catholic education in Boston occurred in the following decade when Father James Mellyn, S.J., was the director of teacher education at Boston College, and his sister, Mary Mellyn, was the assistant superintendent in charge of teacher development for the public schools. As James W. Sanders pointed out, "James provided the course work for the students, while Mary supervised their practice teaching." "The relationship could hardly have been closer," said Sanders; it "was literally all in the family."[10]

Despite the name, the undergraduate division of the School of Education was a full-fledged liberal arts college even though the science courses had to be taken at Rose Hill, where the laboratories were located. Moreover, many of the students in the School of Education had no intention of becoming teachers. They were interested in fulfilling the undergraduate requirements at a convenient location in downtown Manhattan to prepare for a business career or to apply for admission to law school or medical school. The dean of the School of Education was kept busy assuring the admission officers of law schools and medical schools that Fordham's School of Education was in fact a bona fide college of arts and sciences with laboratory-based science courses.[11]

The university authorities were explicit in asserting the liberal arts character of the undergraduate department of the School of Education despite the fact that the only degrees they offered were both science degrees, a B.S. and a B.S. in education. "The liberal ideal of breadth and depth of knowledge, in keeping with the Jesuit tradition, is accorded an eminent place," proclaimed the university catalogue in 1938–39. "Thus,

10. James W. Sanders, "Catholics and the School Question in Boston: The Cardinal O'Connell Years," in *Catholic Boston: Studies in Religion and Community, 1870–1970*, ed. Robert E. Sullivan and James M. O'Toole (Boston: The Roman Catholic Archdiocese of Boston, 1985), 143–48. I am grateful to Professor Gleason for calling this reference to my attention.

11. McCarthy, *Learning in the City*, 37–38. Because the School of Education was coeducational and science majors had to travel to Rose Hill to use the science laboratories, undergraduate women made their first furtive appearance on the Rose Hill campus several decades before the establishment of Thomas More College in the 1960s. Ibid., 43–44.

approximately seven-tenths of the courses included in the teacher training curricula of the School of Education may be readily classified as cultural in content and purpose. The student must know *what* to teach as well as *how* to teach."[12]

In the 1930s the archdiocese of New York made a major effort to promote higher educational requirements for the men and women religious who constituted the bulk of the teachers in the parochial schools. In 1934 the superiors of the seven largest communities of teaching sisters in the archdiocese voted unanimously that all teaching sisters should be certified by the archdiocese and that they should have a minimum of two years of college before they could teach. Cardinal Hayes approved the resolution, which was to go into effect in September 1939 with a grandfather clause exempting teachers who already had fifteen years' experience in the classroom. The archdiocese turned to Fordham and other local Catholic colleges for assistance in implementing this new rule. By 1939 more than a thousand sisters and brothers were enrolled in teacher training programs in the School of Education at Fordham.[13]

In 1943 all of the units of Fordham Downtown, including the School of Education, moved out of the Woolworth Building after twenty-seven years because of the need to economize in view of the increased rent and the declining student enrollment during World War II. Fordham's principal Manhattan home for the next twenty-six years was the Vincent Building at 302 Broadway, at the intersection of Duane Street, one block north of Chambers Street, midway between City Hall and Foley Square. It became common thereafter to speak of the Vincent Building as the home of the City Hall Division of Fordham, although the Woolworth Building was closer to City Hall than the Vincent Building. The School of Education as well as the Law School and (to a lesser extent) the Business School remained there until their relocation to the new Lincoln Center campus between 1961 and 1969.

As Father Gannon was quick to point out, the acquisition of the Vincent Building was an unusual bargain. It had been built by William Waldorf Astor in 1899 at the cost of $900,000. Gannon bought it for $122,000. He had to spend another $138,000 in renovations, but the added expense was well worth it because it doubled the floor space that Fordham had occupied in the Woolworth Building. Moreover, it saved Fordham $50,000 per

12. CFU, Fordham College, School of Education, 1938–1939, 20.

13. William R. Kelly and John J. Voight, "Parish Schools in New York, 1800–1939." New York *Catholic News*, June 17, 1939.

The Vincent Building at 302 Broadway, which replaced the Woolworth Building as the Manhattan home of "Fordham Downtown" from 1943 until the completion of the Lincoln Center campus in 1969.

Fordham Downtown, Uptown, All Around the Town

year in rent, a savings that paid for the whole transaction during the course of the next five years.[14]

The School of Education suffered fewer losses in students during World War II than the college and the graduate schools because of the high percentage of women students. Nonetheless, the curriculum was compressed and the program was accelerated so that full-time students who entered the program in September 1942 were graduated in June 1945.

As expected, the School of Education experienced a postwar boom. Between 1945 and 1950 the graduate enrollment grew from 190 to 460 and the undergraduate enrollment grew from 1,130 to 2,220. However, in 1950 only 10 percent of the graduate students and 40 percent of the undergraduate students were full-time students.[15]

When Leo Met Harry

During its early years the Fordham School of Education had a closer connection with the public schools than with the parochial schools in New York City. As mentioned earlier, that situation changed in the 1930s when the archdiocese of New York and many religious communities looked to Fordham (and other Catholic colleges) to enable teaching brothers and sisters to obtain bachelor's and master's degrees. For several decades it was a familiar sight to see the classrooms of Fordham's School of Education filled with brothers and sisters, especially on Saturday mornings.

In the 1960s that scenario changed again as the number of men and women religious suffered a catastrophic decline after Vatican II with devastating effects on the size of the Catholic school system. Thereafter fewer and fewer sisters and brothers were enrolled in the Fordham School of Education. In that same decade a heightened sense of social justice led many Catholic educators to wonder about the Church's obligation to public education, especially on the elementary level in urban areas where there were widespread complaints about the failure of public schools to provide an adequate education for minority children. One Catholic educator who entertained these questions and sought answers to them was Father Leo McLaughlin, S.J., the dynamic and adventuresome president of Fordham University in the 1960s.

In his report to the faculty in 1967, McLaughlin pointed out that Fordham's location in New York City "imposes a strict obligation to serve the

14. Gannon, *Up to the Present*, 240.

15. McCarthy, *Learning in the City*, 39–40. FUA, AF, Box 35, Brief History and Current Status of the Graduate School of Education, n.d. [April 1987].

city at a time when people wonder if the city can survive." McLaughlin was also unhappy with the academic reputation of the School of Education and told the faculty that he was determined to close it unless they could improve the situation. Because McLaughlin had already announced the closing of Fordham's College of Pharmacy, his threat was taken seriously, especially by the faculty. When the opportunity arose to appoint a new dean of the School of Education in 1966, the first choice of the faculty was Dr. Harry N. Rivlin, the dean of teacher education at the City University of New York, but they doubted they could lure him from the City University to Fordham.

However, after a conversation with Father McLaughlin and Father Timothy Healy, S.J., the executive vice president of Fordham, Rivlin accepted the offer to become the new dean of the Fordham School of Education. The deciding factor was Father McLaughlin's assurance of Fordham's commitment to improving the quality of urban public education. "I take it that Fordham did not hire me for my ability to train parochial school teachers," said Rivlin with a smile, who was only the second Jewish dean in the history of Fordham University. "The fact that they asked me to become dean indicates that Fordham believes that the future of the School of Education lies with working closely with the public schools."[16]

During his six years as dean Dr. Rivlin developed pre-service field-centered programs designed specifically to train future teachers in urban schools. He was especially proud of the Instructional Administrators Program (IAP), funded by the Ford Foundation, which prepared sixty black and Hispanic teachers to qualify for certification as public school principals. In 1969 Rivlin also initiated a program called Training Teacher Trainers (TTT), which established a close working relationship between the School of Education and local community associations on the Upper West Side of Manhattan.

It was during Rivlin's tenure as dean in 1967 that the School of Education became exclusively the Graduate School of Education when the undergraduate courses were dropped and integrated into the curriculum of the new undergraduate college at Lincoln Center. In the three decades since the resignation of Dr. Rivlin as dean, the Graduate School of Education has continued the close association with urban public education

16. FUA, FOHP, Interview with Dr. Harry N. Rivlin, by Dr. Regis Bernhardt, June 29, 1988, 3–10. *New York Times*, March 6, 1966. At City University Rivlin was responsible for the training of 38,800 students at four undergraduate colleges. At the Fordham School of Education the enrollment was 2,580.

that he pioneered. Father James C. Finlay, S.J., the president of Fordham, claimed in 1980 that the first black and Hispanic principals in the New York City public schools had been trained at the Graduate School of Education, as had been many of the administrators of the Catholic schools in the archdiocese of New York and surrounding dioceses.[17]

The School of Business

The School of Business owes its origin to a layman, Dr. Hugh S. O'Reilly, who persuaded Father Edward Tivnan, the president of Fordham, to establish a business school in September 1920. Located on the seventh floor of the Woolworth Building, it was originally known as a School of Accounting because the two-year academic program consisted of noncredit evening courses in accounting, business law, and business English that were designed to prepare young men to take the New York State CPA examination. Economics was added to the curriculum in 1922 when a three-year certificate program was introduced. The following year there were 93 students, not only in Manhattan but also in satellite centers in Hoboken and Jersey City with tentative plans (never implemented) to open another satellite center in Brooklyn. By 1926 it was officially designated the School of Business with a four-year full-time day program and a six-year part-time evening program leading to a B.S. degree. Admittance was limited to men. Three years later there were 3,000 students in the Business School, Teachers College, and Graduate School.[18]

The name School of Business Administration was in use by the mid-1930s. The courses were evenly divided between liberal arts and business economics, and both programs led to the degree of Bachelor of Science with a major in accounting, which met the state requirements for admission to the CPA examination. Originally the only major was accounting, but, in the mid-1930s other areas of specialization were added, including banking and finance, general business administration, management, and marketing. Students took the required liberal arts courses in the downtown college, which occupied the same floor of the Woolworth Building as the College of Business Administration and had introduced a four-year B.S. course in 1928.

Fordham was not apologetic about the unusually heavy emphasis on the liberal arts in a business school. In 1931 almost two-thirds of the 2,000 can-

17. FUA, AF, Box 35, Brief History and Current Status of the Graduate School of Education, n.d. [April 1987]. FUA, O'Hare Papers, Finlay to Arrupe, January 4, 1980.

18. *WL* 58 (1929): 262. FUA, AF, Box 34, The History of the College of Business Administration.

didates who took the CPA examination in New York state failed the exam. Father O'Mailia blamed the dismal showing on the lack of a liberal arts education in many business schools. "The business world today demands that the successful business man be also a man of culture," the university catalogue declared in the depths of the Great Depression, more as an aspiration than as a statement of fact.[19]

In 1939 the College of Business Administration was admitted to both the prestigious American Association of Collegiate Schools of Business and to the Zeta New York chapter of Beta Gamma Sigma, the leading honors society for business students. No unit of Fordham University has led a more peripatetic existence than the College of Business Administration, especially during World War II. In August 1942 the CBA moved from the Woolworth Building to the Rose Hill campus, where it used Collins Hall for classroom space. A year later the day program was suspended because of the dearth of male applicants during the wartime draft. In April 1944 the CBA moved back to Manhattan, this time to the newly acquired Vincent Building at 302 Broadway. By that date the enrollment had slipped to approximately 75 students, and the decision was made to make the school coeducational. The first four women were admitted that year and graduated four years later.

After the war the CBA experienced a rapid increase in enrollment with many veterans taking advantage of the G.I. Bill. In 1947 the CBA established a campus division at Rose Hill while retaining its presence in the Vincent Building. Its campus home was hardly palatial. It was a former army barracks that was purchased from the Surplus Property Administration and named Reidy Hall in honor of Sgt. Daniel Claude Reidy, an alumnus who was killed at the Anzio beachhead during the Italian campaign. Somehow or other 400 students were able to squeeze into the building. Enrollment peaked in 1949–50 with 1,943 full-time students and leveled off to 1,336 in 1957–58.[20]

The campus division of the CBA continued its nomadic but upwardly mobile existence at Rose Hill. In 1955 it moved to the renovated Dealy Hall and ten years later to Faculty Memorial Hall, a renovated commercial building adjacent to the campus on Belmont Avenue. In 1968 it was decided to phase out the classes at 302 Broadway. The following year, when

19. FUA, Hogan Papers, O'Mailia, Meeting of Representatives of Schools of Business in New York State, Albany, April 29, 1932. CFU, School of Business, 1938–1939, 9–10; 1935–1936, 5.

20. FUA, AF 27, James J. McGinley, S.J., "For the Record" . . . Aileen Hughes and Robert Vitarelli, "Expansion over the Years," *Maroon Quill*, December 5, 1955.

the new campus opened at Lincoln Center, the CBA maintained a residual presence in the Lowenstein Building until June 1972, when the last CBA students graduated. A decade later there were 1,250 students enrolled in the CBA at Rose Hill.[21]

Meanwhile, in 1969 Fordham University launched a Graduate School of Business Administration with its own dean that was located in the Lowenstein Building at the new Lincoln Center campus. It was a bold venture because New York City already possessed two top-notch business schools at Columbia University and New York University. A dozen years later the GBA was still struggling financially, although it was attracting good students and developing a strong faculty. "We intend to make this School one of the best in this area," Father Finlay assured the general of the Society of Jesus, Father Pedro Arrupe.[22] In 1986, however, Arthur R. Taylor, dean of the GBA, admitted candidly that "nobody maintains that Fordham is in the first rank of business schools." Taylor attempted to establish a niche for Fordham in the highly competitive world of business schools that were turning out 60,000 new M.B.A.s every year by establishing a Center for Communications to train M.B.A.s to introduce corporate America to the new world of the computer and the Internet.

Dr. Taylor played to Fordham's strengths by emphasizing the university's commitment to the inculcation of ethical values in the business world at a time when he said, "The perception is that business schools are turning out bright little assassins." Another objective of Dean Taylor's was to increase the number of full-time students, who numbered only one-quarter of the student population in the 1980s. His objective met with strenuous opposition from some successful graduates of the GBA's part-time program. "I hope that Fordham never loses its affinity for the part-time students," said one graduate of the GBA, Ed Neff Jr., the president of the Computer Equity Corporation. "For people who have been out of school for a while, who have kicked around, and who have reached the point in their lives when they know it is time to do something with themselves," he said, "Fordham has always offered a healthy balance between the reality of working during the day and attending class at night."[23] Thirty years later, in the days of its newfound prosperity, Fordham Business School

21. FUA, AF Box 34, The History of the College of Business Administration. FUA, AF Box 34, Annual Report: Schools of Business, 1981–1982. The offices of CBA at Rose Hill were moved three times between 1973 and 1996, from Hughes Hall to Thebaud Hall to Faber Hall.

22. FUA, O'Hare Papers, Finlay to Arrupe, January 7, 1981.

23. *New York Times*, September 21, 1986.

remained faithful to its more modest past by continuing to offer a part-time M.B.A. degree.

Father Finlay's patience paid off between 1987 and 1992, when the GBA experienced a 40 percent increase in enrollment. By 1992 the enrollment in the GBA was almost twice as large as the undergraduate enrollment in the CBA: 1,846 versus 1,100. The full-time faculty in the GBA also increased by 40 percent in those five years, to 83 professors.[24]

The single most important development in the history of Fordham's two business schools took place two decades later, beginning in 2012 when the university began the gradual process of combining both the undergraduate and graduate schools into the Gabelli School of Business. The school was named after Mario Gabelli, CBA '65, whose gift of $25 million—the largest gift in the history of Fordham University—made possible the transformation of the venerable nineteenth-century Hughes Hall on the Rose Hill campus into the state-of-the-art Gabelli School of Business, the successor of the College of Business Administration. Hughes Hall had been the site of Fordham Preparatory School when Gabelli was a student there in the 1950s. At the ribbon-cutting ceremony at the site of his high school alma mater on September 27, 2012, Gabelli said, "I cobbled my way through the Prep and to college and through graduate school through scholarships, and so we have to find a way to give back and keep the flame burning."[25]

In 2012 the Gabelli School of Business maintained a presence not only at Rose Hill but also at Lincoln Center. The Graduate School of Business Administration, located at Lincoln Center, offered three variants of the M.B.A. degree (including one part-time program) as well as a master of science degree in fourteen specialized programs. In 2012 Fordham University began a lengthy process of unifying the Gabelli School of Business with the Graduate School of Business Administration under the direction of Dr. Donna Rapaccioli, GBA '83, the dean of the Gabelli School of Business and dean of the business faculty. Plans were also under way to introduce the Gabelli Ph.D. Program in Business in August 2015.[26]

Fordham College, Manhattan Division

The downtown college (Fordham College, Manhattan Division) had a brief life span of only nineteen years as a separate unit of the uni-

24. FUA, O'Hare Papers, Dean of the Business Faculty and Graduate School of Business Administration, Criteria Statement, n.d.

25. http://legacy.fordham.edu/campus_resources/enewsroom/archives/archive_2529.asp.

26. http://business.fordham.edu/about/.

versity. It owed its origins to a new state law in 1923 requiring one year of college for admittance to law school. Fordham Law School immediately established a one-year extension school for high school graduates on the same floor of the Woolworth Building as the Law School with courses specifically designed to satisfy the state requirement. The classes were scheduled from 6:00 P.M. to 9:00 P.M. In 1925 the program of the Extension School was increased to two years in order to meet the new state requirement of two years of college for admittance to law school that was to take effect the following year.[27]

In 1928, only a year after Father O'Mailia's confrontation with the provincial over Teachers College and the summer school, the two-year prelaw program was expanded into a four-year college offering a B.S. degree under the title of Fordham College, Manhattan Division. The school was designed to attract not only pre-law students but also those young men (the school was not coeducational) who wanted a Jesuit education and diploma but could not afford to be full-time students. Students in Teachers College were also able to cross-register for courses in Fordham College, Downtown Division. Identical courses were scheduled at the downtown college from 9:15 A.M. to 1:00 P.M. and again from 6:05 P.M. to 9:40 P.M. to enable part-time students to work before or after school. It was anticipated that many students would remain for only two years before applying for admission to law school, and they were assured that the curriculum of the freshman and sophomore years met all of the state requirements for admission to law school.[28]

Fordham College, Manhattan Division, ceased to exist in August 1942, during the darkest days of World War II, when enrollments in men's colleges plummeted everywhere in the United States. Full-time students were transferred to either the Business School or to Fordham College at Rose Hill. However, over the course of the following seventy years, Fordham College, Manhattan Division, has preserved a long if somewhat tenuous afterlife as a school for part-time students. Its immediate successor was Fordham Evening College, which was founded in 1942 with a four-year curriculum that led to a B.S. degree in science with a major in social science.[29]

27. CFU, 1923, School of Law, 9.

28. CFU, 1938–1939, Fordham College, Manhattan Division, 7–9. A few women had been admitted to the pre-legal extension courses, but in 1930 the provincial, Father Phillips, told O'Mailia to allow the five or six women students to remain only until the end of the year and then to drop them. ARSJ, Phillips to Ledóchowski, November 12, 1930.

29. CFU, 1942–1943, Fordham Evening College, 111–12.

In 1944 Fordham Evening College gave way to the School of Adult Education, which was especially geared to meet the needs of returning servicemen who wished to take advantage of the G.I. Bill enacted by Congress that year. The dean of the school, Father Edward J. Baxter, S.J., was also the chairman of the Veterans' Committee of Fordham University. The program was extremely flexible. Prospective students could take as little as one course per semester or a full academic schedule; they could enroll for classes without credit or work for college credits or even matriculate for a degree. The classes consisted of double periods starting at 5:15, 6:15, and 8:05 P.M. and on Saturday morning and early afternoon. Fees ranged from $10 to $14.[30]

After the war the School of Adult Education was renamed the School of General Studies and featured both a basic course program for students who wished to take only one or two courses, and a certificate course in general studies with a curriculum that approximated a basic liberal arts program. In 1955 a branch of the school was opened at Rose Hill, and by 1967, on the eve of the transition to the new Lincoln Center campus, the school could boast of an enrollment of 1,100 students with credit courses leading to degrees in education, liberal arts, and business administration.[31]

In 2015, ninety-three years after its founding and several additional changes in name and curriculum, the ghost of Fordham College, Manhattan Division, remains an integral part of Fordham University as one of Fordham's four undergraduate schools, the School of Professional and Continuing Studies. It offers courses on three campuses (Lincoln Center, Rose Hill, and West Harrison) and remains an enduring symbol of Fordham's commitment to its past and the education of part-time students.

School of Irish Studies

One of the most unusual of Fordham's many past and present schools was the School of Irish Studies, founded by Joseph Campbell. A native of Belfast, Campbell was a poet, an ardent Irish nationalist, and a promoter of the Irish language. He supported the Easter Rising of 1916, was interned by the Free State government in 1922–23 during the Irish Civil War, and emigrated to the United States in 1925. Campbell founded the school as a tiny independent enterprise in December 1925 on East 12th Street in the hope that it would develop into an Irish cultural center.

30. CFU, 1944–1945, School of Adult Education, 91–92.
31. CFU, 1953–1954, School of General Studies, 113–14; Gannon, *Up to the Present*, 240–41.

One of his admirers and supporters, Father John P. Monaghan, an Irish-born New York diocesan priest well known for his work with organized labor, suggested that the school should affiliate with one of the city's universities. In 1927 Campbell consulted Father O'Mailia, who welcomed the suggestion, and the following year the school was incorporated into Fordham University as the School of Irish Studies with O'Mailia as the dean and Campbell as the director. The first classes were offered in the spring of 1928, and within a year more than 200 students had enrolled in courses in the Irish language, literature, drama, and history.[32]

Campbell had a grandiose vision for the school as a means of promoting interest in Irish culture among Irish Americans by endowing scholarships in Gaelic research, publishing an Irish literary magazine, creating an Irish reference library, and establishing an Irish social center. "Other American universities have chairs of Celtology," he announced, "but this will have the distinction of being the first school of its kind devoted to the study [of] the Irish arts as a whole." The reality was rather different. In 1929 the School of Irish Studies offered fifteen courses (which were cross-listed with the English Department), and the enrollment peaked in 1930–31 with 374 students, but Campbell himself admitted that many of the students were of only high school caliber.[33]

Father Gannon damned the school with faint praise as "colorful and sentimental," but another Fordham University administrator, evaluating the curriculum of the school eighty years later, took a considerably more favorable view. Dr. John P. Harrington, professor of English and dean of the Faculty of Arts and Sciences, was struck by the cosmopolitan approach that Campbell took to the study of Irish culture, and he attributed it to Campbell's admiration for John Henry Newman.

Little of Campbell's ambitious agenda was ever achieved partly because of the unfortunate timing. With the beginning of the Great Depression in 1929, economic problems became the primary concern of most Irish

32. *WL* 58 (1919): 264; CFU, School of Irish Studies, 1930–1931, 36–37. New York Catholicism still had a heavily Irish flavor in the early twentieth century. In 1911, when the archdiocese of New York issued a new curriculum for the parochial schools, it included three pages on Irish history. "As the majority of the children attending the parochial schools of this diocese are of Irish birth or descent," declared the authors of the curriculum, "they should not be left in ignorance of the glorious deeds of their brave forefathers." *Course of Study and Syllabus for the Elementary Schools of the Archdiocese of New York* (New York: New York Catholic School Board, 1911), 53.

33. Thomas C. Hennessy, S.J., "Joseph Campbell and the School of Irish Studies at Fordham University, 1928–1932," *New York Irish History* 10 (1996): 24–30.

Americans rather than their cultural heritage. Campbell himself felt the pinch of the Depression and complained privately of "miserly ecclesiastics" like Father Joseph Keating, the treasurer of Fordham, who failed to pay him the salary he thought he deserved, although he had no academic degree and was only an adjunct professor. The school was closed in 1932 and absorbed into the English Department. Campbell continued to teach at Fordham until 1938 and a year later returned to Ireland, where he died in 1944.[34]

All Around the Town

As dean of most of the units at Fordham Downtown, Father O'Mailia was eager to establish "university centers" (satellite campuses) for students who found it difficult to travel to the Woolworth Building for classes. As mentioned already, as far back as 1923 the Business School had opened extension centers in Hoboken and Jersey City. When Father O'Mailia wished to expand the program in 1928, he received enthusiastic support from Father Duane, but he ran into opposition from his old nemesis, the provincial, Father Lawrence J. Kelly, who was skeptical about the feasibility of O'Mailia's plans and fearful that the extension courses in New Jersey would hamper the growth of St. Peter's College in Jersey City. He also said that the plans would require the approval of the father general.[35]

O'Mailia must have obtained the approval of the general because in 1931 Fordham was operating no fewer than ten university extension centers in New York City, New Jersey, Staten Island, and Westchester County. They were located in either Catholic or public schools, and the courses were taught in the evening after regular school hours. Some of the programs were quite modest, such as the four courses offered at Good Counsel College in White Plains and the four courses at the Institute of the Holy Angels in Fort Lee, New Jersey, but a total of thirty-eight courses (all but three of them education courses) were offered in 1930–31 at the Textile High School Center in New York City, where the principal, William H. Dooley, had a doctorate in education from Fordham. The tuition was quite reasonable: a $3 registration fee and a tuition of $15 for each two-credit, thirty-

34. John P. Harrington, "Voyager to the West: Joseph Campbell and Irish Studies," *Times Literary Supplement*, January 13, 2012, 14–15.

35. ARSJ, O'Mailia to Ledóchowski, n.d. [1928 or 1929]; FUA, Duane Papers, Kelly to O'Mailia, April 28, 1928. At the request of Kelly, Duane provided assurances that Fordham would discontinue the extension courses in New Jersey as soon as St. Peter's College was able to conduct them. FUA, Hogan Papers, Memo on Extension Courses in New Jersey, September 18, 1928.

hour course. There were also extension centers at the mother houses of at least five local communities of sisters. In addition there were classes at the Woolworth Building on Saturdays.[36]

Summer Sessions

Even more extensive than the network of satellite campuses was the summer school program, which apparently dates from 1917. The first catalogue for the summer session did not appear until 1926. Whatever the uncertainty about the origin of the summer sessions, there is no doubt about their popularity among teaching sisters, brothers, and priests and among lay teachers in both parochial and public schools. In 1919, 260 registered for the summer sessions, and 229 took the examinations. Many of them were nuns, some from local colleges but others from as far away as the Midwest.[37]

The summer sessions took place at the Rose Hill campus every year between the first week of July and the second week of August. It was a very genteel operation. Women from out of state who had arranged for rooms through the Catholic Room Registry were met at the railroad station, if so desired, and conducted to their destination. There were escorted tours of the Botanical Garden six days a week and plentiful opportunities for religious services. Four Masses were "read" each morning (in the words of the catalogue) beginning at 6:30, confessions were available on Thursday afternoon, and on Friday afternoon a sermon was preached in the University Church followed by benediction of the Blessed Sacrament. Provision was even made for serving lunch to those who were reluctant to contend with the noonday crowds in the cafeteria. All this came at the modest price of a one-time registration fee of $5, tuition of $7.50 per credit, and an additional fee of $5 for those who wished to use the tennis courts, for which there was not a heavy demand on the part of the women religious who were still arrayed in full religious habits.[38]

In 1926 no fewer than 181 courses were listed in the catalogue of the summer session, although it is impossible to know how many of the courses were actually given. The most popular subject was education, followed by English, science, history, and philosophy. There were no courses in theology or religion, because Catholics in those days confined the teaching of

36. FUA, Hogan Papers, Fordham University Extension Centers, 1930–1931; McCarthy, *Learning in the City*, 18.

37. FUA, AF 30, The Fordham University Summer Session, May 3, 1972; *WL* 48 (1919): 441.

38. CFU, Summer Session, 1928, 8–9.

the sacred sciences to seminary classrooms. One-third of 70 members of the faculty were Jesuits, and among the lay faculty there were two women, one of them a nun. In the absence of theology courses, there was a philosophy course on Mariology, which included a treatment of the doctrine of the Immaculate Conception and the Assumption of the Virgin Mary. Father Moorhouse F.X. Millar took a bulldog approach to his course on historical research, claiming that "non-Catholics habitually misrepresent or overlook [it] because of the lack of proper comprehension."[39]

Neither the Depression nor (initially) World War II diminished the popularity of the summer sessions. In 1934 Fordham announced plans for more than 200 courses in 20 subjects, including religion (although not theology). In the summer of 1941, six months before the attack on Pearl Harbor, with the country already embarking on a rearmament program, Fordham offered 143 courses in the summer sessions, 116 at Rose Hill and 27 in the Woolworth Building.[40]

In the meantime, as was mentioned already, in 1933, Father Hogan severed Fordham's ties with the Catholic Summer School of America, located at Cliff Haven near Plattsburg. It may have been a wise decision academically, but it was a bad move politically because the school was a favorite of Monsignor Michael Lavelle, the rector of St. Patrick's Cathedral and a close friend of Cardinal Hayes's. The following year, when Hogan made plans to move Fordham Preparatory School from the Rose Hill campus to an estate in Riverdale, he was surprised to receive a letter from Lavelle informing him that the Christian Brothers at Manhattan College objected to the move because of the proximity of the site to their own institution. Lavelle added that both he and Cardinal Hayes (both "Brothers' Boys" and alumni of Manhattan College) found the brothers' objection reasonable. Fordham Prep remained at Rose Hill.[41]

Uptown

Despite the proliferation and popularity of new schools on both the undergraduate and graduate levels, in many respects the heart and soul of the Fordham remained its oldest unit, St. John's College, Rose Hill, whose name was officially changed to Fordham College in 1931. Much had changed at Rose Hill since the arrival of the French Jesuits from Kentucky

39. CFU, Summer Session, 1926, passim.

40. *The [Brooklyn] Tablet*, June 30, 1934; FUA, Gannon Papers, n.d.; Hogan Papers, Hogan to Lennon, November 22, 1933.

41. ARSJ, Hogan to Ledóchowski, February 1934.

in 1846, but at Fordham College, more than in any other school in the university, the Society of Jesus was able to maintain its centuries-old tradition of providing young men with an education that combined a broad immersion in the liberal arts with a detailed knowledge of the Christian faith and personal spiritual and moral formation. "Learning is an element of education, not its end," the college catalogue explained in 1935. "The end is culture, and mental and moral development."[42]

The cost of an education at Rose Hill in 1930 was $200 for tuition, the same as it had been a century earlier for both room and board. However, the latter expense for resident students had risen to an additional $450 (not including laundry). The sparsely furnished open dormitories of an earlier era had given way to a variety of accommodations that ranged from a room without running water for two students at a cost of $135 to a more-or-less palatial suite of three rooms for two students in St. John's Hall (restricted to upperclassmen) at a cost of $250. Like colleges everywhere, by 1930 Fordham had discovered the financial advantages of adding a variety of additional fees to the basic tuition. Although there were no mandatory purchases of chocolate bars, as in many Catholic elementary schools, the total cost of additional fees would have amounted to the astronomical sum of $299.50 in the unlikely eventuality that any student incurred all of them. One of the lesser fees was a charge of $2 per day for a stay in the infirmary.

The *ratio studiorum* of the Society of Jesus still shaped the basic curriculum of Fordham College, but the Jesuits assured its viability in twentieth-century America by adapting it to changing needs and circumstances. The Latin program, with its emphasis on the Greek and Roman classics leading to the A.B. degree, retained pride of place and was the most popular of the three academic programs. There were also two science programs leading to the B.S. degree; both required only one year of a modern language. There were 260 graduates in the class of 1930. Only 68 students opted for the B.S. degree, while 192 chose the A.B. degree.

The commercial course, so much deplored by many Jesuit educators in the nineteenth century, disappeared from the curriculum and was replaced by the College of Business Administration. Despite the decades-long Jesuit opposition to "electivism" in American higher education (and no one railed against it more than Father Gannon), elective courses had crept into the program of studies at Fordham College, one elective in junior year and two in senior year. In junior and senior year all three programs placed a heavy emphasis on scholastic philosophy, which included not only Aqui-

42. CFU, Fordham College, 1935–1936, 26.

nas, Bonaventure, and Duns Scotus but also, as a testament to institutional filial piety, the Spanish Jesuit Francisco Suárez.

Although theology as such did not figure in the curriculum, the aggregate content of the four years of mandatory religion classes, in contrast to contemporary amorphous "religious studies" programs, amounted to a well-rounded presentation of the Christian faith. The classes, all taught by Jesuits, met twice weekly and included such topics as revelation, soteriology, ecclesiology, the sacraments, and Christian ethics (which was still called morality). The prominent role of religion in the curriculum at Rose Hill could not have come as a surprise to any student who had read the college catalogue, which asserted unambiguously that "religious truth, being definite and certain, may be taught with as much exactness as language and philosophy."[43]

The pervasive religious atmosphere at the Rose Hill campus in the early twentieth century was due to many other factors in addition to the religion classes. The overwhelmingly Catholic complexion of both the faculty and the student body created and maintained a distinctly Catholic ethos on the campus. Almost a third of the faculty were Jesuits, who were represented in virtually every department and whose expertise in such areas as chemistry and physics could not have gone unnoticed by skeptical young men wondering about the compatibility of religion and science. Many, if not most, of the lay faculty were Catholic laymen, often alumni of Fordham or of other Jesuit colleges, who welcomed the opportunity to teach in a Catholic college. Moreover, in both the History and English departments the course offerings reflected the importance the professors placed on the influence of Christianity in the shaping of Western culture.

The Jesuit commitment to the *cura personalis* of their students meant that they placed a high priority on not only their acquisition of religious knowledge but also on their religious practice. This became more a matter of encouragement than of obligation as Fordham College shifted from a predominantly residential school to a predominantly commuter school. Such nineteenth-century rules as mandatory attendance at morning and evening prayers, as well as at daily Mass, became impractical and were quietly dropped. However, the annual student retreat remained a staple of campus life until after World War II. The Jesuits also continued to promote the student sodalities that for centuries had proven to be so successful in their colleges as a means of attracting interested young men to a deeper appreciation of their faith.

43. CFU, Fordham College, 1930–1931, 24–25.

The Parthenian Sodality, which the French Jesuits had established in Kentucky before their arrival in New York, was the premier sodality, whose membership was limited to resident students, but there were two other sodalities for the day students, one for freshmen and sophomores and the other for juniors and seniors. Another link with the past at Rose Hill was the local branch ("conference") of the St. Vincent de Paul Society, the most important Catholic voluntary charitable organization in New York. The Fordham Vincentians, as the members of the Society were called, visited the sick in the hospitals and provided basic religious instruction for "poor Christian children whether free or imprisoned." The latter phrase is an allusion to their work at the House of Refuge on Randalls Island, where they assisted the Jesuit chaplain in his pastoral care for the young people confined in that institution, a tradition that went back almost fifty years.[44]

After Fordham lost its endorsement by the Association of American Universities in 1935, Father Gannon deliberately tightened admission standards in a successful effort to restore Fordham's scholastic reputation and regain professional accreditation. He said famously that he never thought an increased enrollment was necessarily a sign of academic success or good Ignatian pedagogy. In 1937 he announced that he would cut the incoming freshman class by 150 in order to reduce the enrollment in Fordham College to 1,200. "The financial temptation is to open the gates, let down the bars and water the soup," he said, "but we are determined year by year to be more exacting and more exclusive in the candidates we accept for the freshmen [*sic*] class." He made no secret of his model for Fordham College. "In New York City we are surrounded by mass production in education as in everything else," he explained, "and we feel there is a crying need for a select and conservative college." He read the tea leaves correctly. In 1939 only one of three applicants was accepted, and the student body of the college represented 165 high schools from 15 states.[45]

From 1925 until 1938 the dean of Fordham College was Father Charles J. Deane, whose connection with Fordham lasted more than sixty years. A stern-faced but kindly man, he was described by one alumnus as "a canny Irish New Englander." As dean of Fordham College he kept up a constant stream of criticism to the father general in Rome, complaining about virtually every aspect of the operation of the university except the financial management of the treasurer, Father Joseph Keating, for whom he expressed

44. CFU, St. John's College of Arts and Sciences, 1930–1931; Fordham College, 1935–1936.

45. *New York Times*, June 17, 1937, September 13, 1939.

the highest admiration. Deane reserved some of his most scathing criticism for the role of his fellow Jesuits at Fordham College. Like many a veteran administrator before and since, Deane complained that the younger generation of Jesuits failed to measure up to the standards of his generation. He claimed that they were indolent, wanted only minimal teaching responsibilities, and took little personal interest in their students.[46]

Deane was a zealous advocate of higher academic standards, and he faulted Jesuit superiors for failing to encourage scholarship among the younger members of the Society. "Why are there so few writers?" he asked and offered as his explanation that "*gubernatio fortasse est nimis suavis, non fortis*" [the direction is perhaps too mild, not strong]. However, for him the path to educational excellence was not to imitate the innovative methods of the Jesuits in the Midwest but to return to traditional Jesuit pedagogy. "We Jesuits have the very best system of education," he told the general in 1928. "We should be very, very slow about sacrificing what has been our boast for something that even its supporters find to be unsatisfactory." It never dawned on Deane that perhaps one reason for the lack of scholarly activity on the part of both the Jesuits and the lay faculty was the heavy undergraduate teaching load that was demanded of them. In fact he did not think that any member of the college faculty was overburdened with work.[47]

Father O'Mailia had his own misgivings about the future prospects of Fordham. Because the number of Jesuits failed to keep pace with the growing enrollment, he regretted that it was necessary to depend more and more on the lay faculty to teach courses traditionally entrusted to the Jesuits, such as philosophy, history, and ancient and modern languages. He thought the Society was making poor use of its manpower. "Ours are often wasted in small colleges and high schools," he said, "and after many years despite their labors little remains." He also deplored the lack of interest in research and scholarship among the lay faculty. Gannon was critical not only of the academic standards at Fordham College but even more so those at Teachers College, which he seems to have regarded as the weakest unit of the university. "More an extension school than a college," he said publicly in 1938.[48]

46. FUA, RP, Deane File, Maurice L. Ahern to Ed Sullivan, October 11, 1954; ARSJ, Deane to Ledóchowski, January 13, 1931.

47. ARSJ, Deane to Ledóchowski, January 6, 1928, January 1, 1929, January 10, 1933.

48. ARSJ, O'Mailia to Ledóchowski, January 20, 1928. *New York Times*, May 16, 1938. The ever-censorious Charles Deane claimed that the downtown schools sometimes awarded B.S. degrees to students whom Fordham College at Rose Hill had refused to admit. ARSJ, Deane to Ledóchowski, January 13, 1931.

After the First One Hundred Years

When Fordham celebrated its centennial in 1941, Father Gannon could take pride in the progress that Fordham had made since 1841, when John Hughes founded the college, especially the progress made since 1907, when the original charter was changed and St. John's College officially became Fordham University. When Francis J. Spellman, a boy from Whitman, Massachusetts, entered the college that year, the total enrollment of the college was 105 and the entire teaching staff consisted of ten Jesuit priests and two scholastics. The only two graduate schools, the Medical School and the Law School, had begun operation two years earlier. Two additional graduate schools, the Graduate School and the School of Sociology and Social Service, were founded in 1916 as well as Teachers College. They in turn were followed by the Business School in 1920 and the downtown college in 1928.

By 1921 the total enrollment in the university reached 2,157 and more than doubled four years later to 4,466. By 1937 the enrollment was 7,500, including 1,961 women. In fact, the School of Social Service was overwhelmingly female, with some 400 women and fewer than 100 men. In 1940 Fordham had 7,649 students and a faculty of 450, only 50 of whom were Jesuits. The Graduate School had the highest enrollment in its history with 900 students despite the transfer of 150 students to the Graduate School of Education. That spring Fordham registered 1,650 students for its summer session, which featured 194 courses. With the war in Europe (as the American press still called World War II) entering its second year, half of the 1,200 students in Fordham College were enrolled in the ROTC.[49]

By his own admission, as soon as Gannon arrived at Fordham as president he was conscious of the need for Fordham to project a more positive public image. One of his first major decisions was to hire a prominent public relations firm to enhance the university's reputation. He got a golden opportunity to focus attention on Fordham in the fall of 1936 when it was announced that Eugenio Cardinal Pacelli, the papal secretary of state, would spend three weeks as a guest at the Long Island estate of Mrs. Nicholas Brady, a wealthy widow and a papal duchess. Although Gannon never explained how he did it, before Pacelli boarded his ship in Naples he had agreed to accept an honorary degree from Fordham during his stay in New York.

49. CFU, University Register of Students, 1920–1921, 1–51; University Register of Students, 1924–1925, 1–78; *New York Times*, March 7, 1937, March 24, July 6, October 4, October 20, 1940.

Eugenio Cardinal Pacelli, the papal secretary of state and later Pope Pius XII, received an honorary doctorate on the occasion of his visit to Fordham on November 1, 1936. To Pacelli's right is Auxiliary Bishop Francis J. Spellman of Boston (the future cardinal archbishop of New York), and to Pacelli's left is Bishop James E. Kearney of Rochester.

The reception for Pacelli took place on November 1, 1936, on the steps of Keating Hall in the presence of numerous civic and ecclesiastical dignitaries and 5,000 spectators gathered on Edwards Parade. After the initial ceremonies Pacelli was escorted to the gymnasium, where he received his honorary degree in the presence of 3,000 invited guests. Gannon choreographed the whole event from beginning to end. When Pacelli insisted on speaking in English, Gannon reluctantly deferred to his wishes despite the fact that the cardinal's accent was very pronounced. When Pacelli objected to the presence of photographers from the major wire services, Gannon mollified him by telling him that he would censor their work, adding under his breath, "as far as circumstances allow." Three years later, when Pacelli was elected pope, Gannon noted with delight that many of the pictures that appeared in the American press had been taken at Fordham.[50]

50. Gannon, *Up to the Present*, 208–9.

The Depression and World War II prevented Gannon from attempting to match the impressive building program of his two immediate predecessors, Father Duane and Father Hogan. However, Gannon did make his own more modest contribution to the expansion of the campus in 1939–40 with the construction of two new dormitories, St. Robert's Hall and Bishop's Hall. They were extensions of St. John's Hall and together formed Our Lady's Court (today Queen's Court), adjacent to the University Church. The exterior walls of the two new buildings came from the old Lenox Library and were a perfect match for St. John's Hall, which Bishop John Hughes had erected in 1845 as the diocesan seminary. The funding came from a wealthy woman whom Gannon charmed at a dinner party. As he was leaving her home, she presented him with a check for $160,000 and later added another $50,000.[51]

Four years after Cardinal Pacelli's visit to Fordham, Gannon's now-legendary charm was put to the test by the unexpected visit of another dignitary whom Gannon could hardly fail to welcome to the campus, the president of the United States, Franklin D. Roosevelt. Gannon was a self-styled third-generation Republican who made no secret of his dislike of FDR's New Deal. The president was campaigning for an unprecedented third term against the Republican candidate, Wendell Willkie, and Gannon had no desire to enhance Roosevelt's chance of success. The president's visit to Fordham was "contrived," as Gannon admitted, partly because he (Gannon) was outfoxed by the White House and the powerful Democratic leader of the Bronx, Edward J. Flynn, an alumnus of Fordham Law School, whom he dared not alienate.

The initiative for FDR's visit to Fordham actually originated with Willkie's campaign managers, who asked for an honorary degree for him. Gannon politely declined the request with a suggestion that both Willkie and Roosevelt should address the youth of the nation via a coast-to-coast radio broadcast from the steps of Keating Hall. The White House quickly rejected the suggestion, and Willkie had to settle for an appearance at the Fordham–St. Mary's football game on Saturday, October 26. However, the reaction to Willkie's presence on campus did not sit well with the overwhelmingly Democratic Fordham alumni, and Gannon scrambled to re-

51. Ibid., 230. Bishop's Hall contains features not usually associated with college dormitories. It includes a richly paneled lounge with leaded windows displaying the crests of bishops associated with the history of Fordham University. The focal point of the room is a large fireplace where logs were to be kept blazing after dinner on cold winter nights. Gannon complained that his successors failed to keep the home fires burning.

President Franklin D. Roosevelt was greeted by Father Gannon on the occasion of his widely publicized visit to Fordham on October 28, 1940, a week before Election Day, ostensibly to review the Fordham ROTC as commander-in-chief.

cover from his *faux pas*. Acting through Ed Flynn as an intermediary, Gannon immediately extended an invitation to FDR to review the Fordham ROTC as the commander-in-chief, and the president appeared at Rose Hill two days after Willkie.[52]

Gannon was in top form when he greeted Roosevelt on Monday, October 28, as an honorary alumnus who had received an LL.D. degree as governor of New York in 1929. He broke the ice by recalling the visit to Fordham the previous year of the president's mother, the formidable Sara Delano Roosevelt, whom Gannon described as "the most charming of all the Roosevelts." The occasion for Mrs. Roosevelt's visit had been the ded-

---

52. Willkie came to Rose Hill on a Saturday and Roosevelt came on the following Monday. The sophomores told the freshmen that Earl Browder, the head of the U.S. Communist Party, was expected to attend Benediction in the University Church on Sunday. "Reverend Gannon Recalls Fordham's Past," *Ram*, February 7, 1968.

ication of a plaque to her distant cousin Archbishop James Roosevelt Bayley, the fourth president of the university. It was a rainy day that left all the guests thoroughly drenched. Ever the gentleman, after the ceremony, Gannon invited Mrs. Roosevelt to his office for a glass of sherry. She replied, "For one awful moment I thought you were going to suggest a cup of tea."

As for the guest of honor, Gannon asked the students if they could tell him of a single event that took place during the presidency of another New Yorker, Chester A. Arthur. "Not one!" he answered triumphantly. Then, turning to the president, he said to the students and guests, "Today you stand before a man whose imprint is forever fixed on our national history. Our country has been reshaped in the last eight years and will never again be just what it was before." Gannon thought that the president was much flattered by his words, but perhaps, if FDR reflected on them later, he may have come to the conclusion that they were more enigmatic than he first thought.[53]

In 1940 Fordham had only sixteen fewer students than Harvard, but Robert I. Gannon would not have appreciated the comparison. In an interview with the *New York Times* the following year to commemorate Fordham's centennial, he excoriated Harvard as the home of that "Pied Piper" (President Charles W. Eliot) "who fifty years ago had all the mice and men of American universities trailing behind him as he played his tune of electivism." As a result, Gannon claimed, most American universities were permeated with socialism, pragmatism, and exaggerated "experimentationalism." Although Gannon never advocated the simplistic return to the past advocated by traditionalists like Charles Deane (whom he replaced as dean of Fordham College in 1938), Gannon left no doubt about the direction in which he wished to lead Fordham. "We are too devoted to eternal principles to be entirely pragmatic, and we are too impressed by all the wisdom of the human race ever to have our school ignore the past," he declared. "Any civilization is ninety per cent heirlooms, lessons and memories. We need the past; we need it terribly."[54]

The highlight of Fordham's one-hundredth anniversary was supposed to be the Fordham Centenary Fund Appeal, which was launched on Alumni Day, September 28, 1940, at a rally in the university gymnasium. The goal was $1,000,000. Unfortunately, like many previous Fordham fundraising campaigns, it fell far short of its goal. It had collected only around $600,000 by the time Archbishop Spellman asked Father Gannon

53. Gannon, *Up to the Present*, 232–33.
54. S. J. Woolf, "Fordham's 100 Years," *New York Times*, September 14, 1941.

to suspend the campaign because he was conducting his own fundraising drive to erect Cardinal Hayes High School in the South Bronx. The total number of alumni and alumnae who responded to the Centenary Fund Appeal came to only 2,635, and the average pledge was a mere $52.03. The per capita contribution at Fordham College was $125. Former Governor Alfred E. Smith commiserated with Father Gannon by telling him that "Catholics in this town are not interested in higher education. You have to show them a starving baby." Gannon thought Smith's remarks were an exaggeration but that they also provided food for thought.[55]

55. Gannon, *Up to the Present*, 230–31.

Fordham Downtown, Uptown, All Around the Town

WORLD WAR II AND AFTER

14

A Wartime Campus

In October 1940, thirteen months after the outbreak of the war in Europe, there were still 8,100 students registered at Fordham. Even a year later, two months before the attack on Pearl Harbor and the entry of the United States into the conflict, the enrollment had declined by only 654, or 7 percent. Immediately after Pearl Harbor, Gannon announced that he anticipated no major changes in the functioning of the university. However, within a month, Father Lawrence A. Walsh, the dean of Fordham College, revealed plans for an accelerated three-year college course. In 1942 the enrollment slipped by 20 percent, which meant a loss of $600,000 in tuition. Shortly thereafter the draft age was lowered to 18 years, and by October 1944 the enrollment hit rock bottom with only 3,086 students, little more than a third of the pre-war enrollment.

As in most American colleges, the great majority of students at Fordham were now either women, young men under 18 years of age, or "4Fs," men who had obtained a deferment from the draft for medical or other reasons. Some of the professional schools, such as the Law School, Pharmacy School, and Day Business School, were especially hard hit, as was Fordham College, where there were only 24 graduates in 1944 in an accelerated freshman class that had numbered almost 400. It was the smallest graduation class since World War I. A third of all the students in the university were enrolled in the School of Education, and most of them were women.[1]

Prior to Pearl Harbor, like many Republicans in the late 1930s, Father Gannon had been a staunch isolationist, accusing President Roosevelt of spoiling for a fight and dragging the country into war. However, at the Annual Mass of the Holy Spirit that opened the new school year on September 7, 1942, Gannon publicly admitted that he and his fellow isolationists had been wrong and that the president had been right. "If he had listened

---

1. *Ram*, December 12, 1941, January 16, 1942, October 20, 1944. Robert I. Gannon, *Up to the Present: The Story of Fordham* (Garden City, N.Y.: Doubleday and Company, 1967), 234–38.

to us," Gannon declared, "China, Russia and Great Britain would now be prostrate, and we should be facing our zero hour alone and unprepared." Gannon's remarks received much favorable comment in the press, especially in the *New York Herald-Tribune*, a leading interventionist Republican newspaper.[2]

Gannon spent three months in England in 1943 at the invitation of Arthur Cardinal Hinsley, the archbishop of Westminster. He flew to England in a B-24 Liberator Bomber (wearing an oxygen mask for most of the trip) and returned home in relative luxury as the ad hoc Catholic chaplain on the *Queen Elizabeth*, which had been converted into a troopship. Gannon spent most of his time in London at the Jesuit church on Farm Street, but he also traveled extensively, complaining about the crowded trains and lack of dining cars. He even managed to celebrate St. Patrick's Day as the dinner guest of the Duke of Norfolk, England's premier peer and leading Catholic layman.[3]

The impact of the war was felt on the Rose Hill campus in many ways. Both undergraduates and graduate students rallied to the colors, serving in every branch of the armed forces. Keating Hall was designated an air raid shelter and the tower became the official lookout post for the northeast Bronx; the first blackout drills were organized complete with volunteer air raid wardens; two Masses were offered every day for the safety of Fordham men and women in uniform; Father John W. Tynan, S.J. ("Black Jack," the students called him), a former prefect of discipline and now an army chaplain, lectured the sophomore sodality on life in the military. On January 21, 1943, members of Fordham's first accelerated graduation class received their diplomas. Most of them quickly joined sixty-six other young men of the Class of 1943 who had already left Fordham for military service. Jack Coffey, the graduate manager of athletics, announced that, for the first time since 1920, Fordham would not have a football team. "There's nothing we can do about it," he admitted. "We just haven't enough material to field a team." There were light moments on the campus even in wartime. A mischievous freshman interrupted a practice drill of the ROTC, yelled "Forward, March," and led a contingent of docile cadets off somewhere in the direction of the Botanical Garden. Fordham's "Lost Patrol," the students called it.[4]

The War Department selected Fordham as a site for two units of the

2. *Ram*, September 18, 1942.
3. *Ram*, August 6, 1943.
4. *Ram*, January 16, April 24, 1942, January 22, February 12, August 6, 1943.

ASTP (the Army Specialized Training Program). In June 1943 the gymnasium was converted into a dormitory for the troops who at their peak numbered 788. No sooner was this program phased out in April 1944 than the army requisitioned the gymnasium, Dealy Hall (which was virtually vacant), and part of Keating Hall to house 900 men of the Army Postal Service. They remained on campus until January 1945. One young soldier who had a brief experience of Fordham through the ASTP was a future mayor of New York, Edward I. Koch. At one point a cafeteria in Keating Hall was serving 2,750 meals a day, beginning at 4:00 A.M. and lasting until midnight. In the meantime, on December 8, 1943, the military service flags were blessed at a Solemn High Mass in the University Church. There were 4,730 stars on the flags, each star representing a Fordham alumnus or alumna in uniform. Forty-three of them were gold stars commemorating those who had been killed in action, two of them at Pearl Harbor. By October 1944 it was estimated that one-quarter of Fordham's 25,000 alumni and alumnae were serving in the armed forces. By the end of the war there were 229 gold stars on the service flags, which were dedicated to Our Lady of Fordham. One was hung in the University Church and a larger one was flown from the tower of Keating Hall.[5]

Despite the war, the university was able to make a number of improvements in the physical plant at Rose Hill, such as remodeling the theater in Collins Hall and installing the old main altar of St. Patrick's Cathedral in the University Church, which was a gift from Archbishop Spellman to Father Gannon, who had deftly courted the new archbishop, now that he was Fordham's most illustrious alumnus. Gannon was a master of the hyperbolic compliments so much appreciated and expected by high-ranking Catholic ecclesiastics. Upon the announcement of Spellman's appointment as archbishop of New York, Gannon told him, "Faculty, Alumni and Students are all in high glee—bragging shamelessly." Father Raymond Schroth noted that Spellman's picture (always the same picture) appeared in the *Ram* almost as often as in the diocesan newspaper.[6]

As was already mentioned, Fordham transferred its downtown campus from the Woolworth Building to the newly acquired Vincent Building at 302 Broadway and purchased a building on East 39th Street to house the School of Social Service. The perennial search to find a new location for Fordham Prep was unsuccessful despite promising possibilities in Westchester County, on Long Island, and in Riverdale. An unexpected windfall for Fordham and other colleges was a government-sponsored program to provide space on college campuses for the anticipated influx of veterans after the war by relocating temporary wartime buildings from military bases to college campuses. As a result Fordham acquired eight additional frame buildings: four dormitories, two classroom buildings, an annex to the chemistry building, and a service building. The total cost was approximately $600,000, but Fordham had to pay only about $20,000.[7]

A far more significant development than the relocation of surplus buildings to college campuses was the Servicemen's Readjustment Act, better known as the G.I. Bill, signed into law by President Roosevelt on June

5. *Ram*, February 12, October 22, December 17, 1943, May 5, September 8, October 20, 1944. Gannon, *Up to the Present*, 241–243. On Ed Koch, see Philip Gleason, *Contending with Modernity: Catholic Higher Education in the Twentieth Century* (New York: Oxford University Press, 1995), 213.

6. FUA, Gannon Papers, Gannon to Spellman, April 25, 1939. Raymond A. Schroth, *Fordham: A History and Memoir* (Chicago: Loyola University Press, 2002), 168. Years later, as pastor of the Church of St. Ignatius Loyola in Manhattan, Gannon sent Spellman a check for $100,000 for one of his innumerable anniversaries.

7. Gannon, *Up to the Present*, 238–39, 243–44.

22, 1944. By 1952 it had enabled 7,600,000 veterans to obtain a college education with the help of some form of government financial assistance. Many of the beneficiaries were Catholics, often the first members of their families to attend college. Forty years later, a prominent historian of American Catholicism, Father James Hennesey, S.J., called the G.I. Bill "one of the great leveling processes in American history" and he claimed that "its impact on the American Catholic community has been permanent." With the advantage of hindsight, however, Hennesey was ambivalent about the long-term benefits of the G.I. Bill on Catholic higher education. While it made possible a massive expansion in the enrollment in Catholic colleges and universities, Hennesey also thought that in many instances "reckless expansion" led to a diminution of academic standards and a dilution of a distinctive Catholic identity. "[B]y the mid-sixties," wrote Hennesey, "the [C]hurch's educational establishment had awakened to find that it had, in varying degrees and with some exceptions, secularized American Catholic education in return for government subsidy."[8]

On V-E Day (Victory in Europe, May 8, 1945) Fordham celebrated the Allied victory in Europe with Benediction of the Blessed Sacrament and a *Te Deum* in the University Church at a ceremony presided over by Father Gannon. That evening, for the first time since the beginning of the war, the lights in the tower of Keating Hall were illuminated. The war in the Pacific dragged on for another three months, but one sign that that conflict was also drawing to a close was the arrival on campus of sixty-five Jesuit priests, scholastics, and brothers of the New York Province who had been liberated from Japanese internment camps in the Philippines. They were housed temporarily in Dealy Hall while they recovered from their wartime ordeal.[9]

As Father Gannon contemplated the contours of the postwar world at Fordham, he had no worries about preserving the university's Catholic identity, which seemed securely established. However, he did worry that a too-hasty expansion would threaten the academic standards that he had painfully rebuilt in the late 1930s in the wake of the university's loss of accreditation. Between 1945 and 1947 the enrollment increased four-fold, from 3,086 to 13,200, an all-time high up to that point. "Dangerous expansion became a patriotic duty," Gannon commented dryly as he received almost daily requests from the governor and the state commissioner of ed-

---

8. James Hennesey, S.J., *American Catholics: A History of the Roman Catholic Community in the United States* (New York: Oxford University Press, 1981), 283.

9. *Ram*, June 8, 1945.

ucation to accept more students with the promise of additional temporary buildings to house them.

As early as December 1944 more than 100 veterans were enrolled in various schools of the university. It was only the tip of the iceberg. In one year alone 4,800 veterans were admitted to Fordham. Gannon was honest enough to admit afterward that his fears about the negative impact of large numbers of veterans at Fordham had proved groundless. "Fordham was fortunate enough to get the top of the barrel," he said, "and her veterans took the lead in maturity, application and scholarship." Never a fan of what he would have called the Gadarene rush to total equality in American higher education, Gannon did not believe that every American was capable of benefiting from a college education, certainly not the kind of liberal arts education that he envisioned as the model. For that reason he deplored the recommendation of a Commission on Higher Education appointed by President Harry S. Truman that urged the expansion of college facilities, because Gannon thought it was a missed opportunity to "squeeze out the watered stock." Under pressure in September 1947 Fordham accepted 800 applicants into the freshman class, but Gannon hoped to reduce the number in future years to 450. There were now 740 boarders (compared with 130 in 1936) representing 28 states, including 200 students from foreign countries.[10]

Two Centennial Celebrations

Fordham had celebrated its centennial in 1941 with a three-day program that culminated in a ceremony at Rose Hill on September 17 attended by representatives of 446 colleges and universities (92 of them presidents), 69 more guests than Harvard had attracted to its tercentenary in 1936. Gannon informed his guests unapologetically that Fordham was dedicated to restoring wisdom to a world in possession of "a glut of facts that it cannot yet assimilate." Gannon could sometimes be his own worst enemy. On this occasion there was the same kind of "numbing smugness" in his rhetoric that Eamon Duffy deplored in some papal encyclicals that attributed all progress in society to the influence of the Church. "It is the voice of a man who has worn a cassock and lived among clerics all his life," said Duffy. Gannon must have gulped hard when he heard that President Roosevelt had dispatched Vice President Henry A. Wallace to represent him at the dinner in the Waldorf Astoria. The political views of the genial

---

10. *Ram,* December 7, 1944. Gannon, *Up to the Present,* 245–46.

but politically naive vice president were as far to the left as Gannon's views were to the right.[11]

After the war Gannon was looking for an occasion to stage a reprise of Fordham's centennial celebration. He found a suitable occasion with the hundredth anniversary of the acquisition of Fordham's state charter, which Bishop Hughes had obtained for St. John's College on April 26, 1846, when it was still a diocesan institution. There were a half-dozen lectures and symposia, but the highlight of the celebration was the visit to the campus on April 26, 1946, of President Truman, the second president to visit Fordham in six years. The original plans called for honorary degrees to be conferred on the mayor, the governor, and the president as symbolic gestures of Fordham's service to the city, state, and nation, but the White House insisted that protocol demanded the president alone should be the recipient of the degree. An embarrassed Father Gannon had to rescind the invitation that he had already extended to Governor Thomas E. Dewey, who was not pleased with Gannon's explanation, "Protocol?" said Dewey. "Hell! It's politics."[12]

As was his wont, Gannon carefully choreographed the whole ceremony down to the last detail. As Gannon escorted the president from his office across Edwards Parade to the terrace in front of Keating Hall, Truman paused to ring for the first time the Victory Bell that had been presented to the university by Admiral Chester W. Nimitz, one of the heroes of the war in the Pacific. Some 6,000 spectators witnessed Gannon confer a Doctorate of Laws degree on Truman, who then delivered an address that was both broadcast and televised. Afterward the president spent an hour in private conversation with Gannon in his office. That evening 2,000 guests attended a dinner at the Waldorf Astoria where they heard Gannon and William J. Wallin, the chancellor of the New York State Board of Regents, exchange compliments.

Sports and the End of Big-Time Football

One of the casualties of World War II at Rose Hill was Big-Time Football. The modest origins of the sport at Fordham can be traced to December 26, 1883, when St. John's College faced off against the College of St. Francis Xavier. Xavier was ahead by two touchdowns when the game

---

11. Eamon Duffy, *Saints and Sinners: A History of the Popes* (New Haven, Conn.: Yale University Press, 1997), 242. *Ram*, October 3, 1941.

12. Gannon, *Up to the Present*, 251–53. Dewey was correct. The White House made no objection to Truman's sharing the platform with Bernard Cardinal Griffin, the archbishop of Westminster, who also received an honorary degree.

was called at dusk, but that did not prevent St. John's from boasting that its country-bred athletes were superior to the city slickers from Xavier in weight and muscle. The Fordham student magazine decried the lack of interest in football on the part of the undergraduates, but twenty years later 800 spectators turned out to witness St. John's whip Yale by 6 to 3. The students celebrated by bolting from the campus without permission in defiance of the rules and marching in procession to Tremont and back waving the Fordham flag with drums beating and horns blaring while the college authorities turned a blind eye to their misbehavior.[13]

In the 1920s and especially in the 1930s, the Fordham Rams attained a national reputation in the world of American collegiate football despite the modest size of Fordham College, its spartan athletic facilities and limited financial resources. The Rams even lacked a stadium where the varsity could play its home games. Fordham's brief prominence in Big-Time Football began at the end of World War I under Coach Frank Gargan and continued after 1927 under the Iron Major, Frank Cavanaugh. Tens of thousands of fans flocked to Yankee Stadium and the Polo Grounds to see the Rams play each weekend. In 1929 they had an undefeated season, and they failed to receive an invitation to the Rose Bowl only because two games had ended in a tie. Fordham also profited from the fact that the Rams became a favorite with New York sportswriters at a time when the city had a dozen daily newspapers with such outstanding sports columnists as Grantland Rice of the *Herald-Tribune* and Arthur Daley (a Fordham alumnus) of the *New York Times*.

Fordham reached the peak of its football fame in the late 1930s under Coach "Sleepy Jim" Crowley, whom Fordham had lured from Michigan State in 1933. During his nine years as head coach Fordham's record was 58 wins, 13 losses, and seven ties. As a halfback at Notre Dame he had earlier achieved fame as one of the legendary "Four Horsemen" immortalized by Grantland Rice. After 1936, when the Associated Press began to rank the top 20 football teams in the country, Fordham always made the list, and in 1937 it was ranked third in the nation, despite the fact that the Rams played a grueling schedule that included some of the best football teams in the country, such as those of Pittsburgh, Purdue, Alabama, and Michigan State. The 1936 and 1937 seasons were especially memorable, with the Rams achieving a 12–1–3 record.

Much of Fordham's success was due to the seven linemen who, on de-

13. *The Fordham College Monthly*, December 1883, 134–35; November 1884, 6. FUA, Fordham History, Box 2, Diary, March 26, 1904.

fense in the course of the 1936 and 1937 seasons, held every opponent to no more than seven points per game and shut out no fewer than seven teams. One of the linemen was a small but scrappy youngster and former high school seminarian from Sheepshead Bay, Brooklyn, named Vince Lombardi, who would later achieve fame as the coach of the Green Bay Packers. A Fordham publicist, Timothy Cohane, dubbed the line the "Seven Blocks of Granite" in 1936. The name stuck and became part of football legend like Grantland Rice's "Four Horsemen."

Cohane readily admitted that the name "Seven Blocks of Granite" had not originated with him. It first appeared as a caption in a wire service photo of the Fordham line in action against Holy Cross in 1930. To this day no one knows who invented the name. In 1930 the nickname did not catch on, but it was revived and became famous when the 1936 team reminded fans of the original "Seven Blocks of Granite." A memorial at the entrance to Coffey Field honors the memory of both the 1929–30 and the 1936–37 Seven Blocks of Granite.[14]

14. Thomas Riley, FCO '81, "Willing Hearts and Hands," *Fordham*, Fall 1986, 16–18. The original 1929–30 Blocks of Granite were Adam Elcewicz, John Conroy, "Whitey"

The Seven Blocks of Granite of the 1936 line in the front row (left to right): John Druze, Al Barbarsky, Vince Lombardi, Alex Wojciechowiez, Nat Pierce, Ed Franko, Leo Paquin. Center row: Andy Palou. Back row (left to right): Frank Mautte, John Locke, Al Gurske.

Fordham lost another opportunity to appear in the Rose Bowl in 1936 when the Rams suffered a heartbreaking loss in the final game of the season to archrival NYU 6–7 before 81,000 fans at the Polo Grounds. The Rams subsequently appeared in two bowl games: the Cotton Bowl in 1941, when they lost to Texas A&M 12–13, and a year later in the Sugar Bowl, when they beat Missouri 2–0.[15]

The attitude of the Fordham administration to Big-Time Football was considerably more ambivalent than that of the fans. While the Jesuits wel-

---

Miskinis, "Pat" Foley, Walt Tracey, Peter Wisniewski, and Tony Siano. During two seasons Fordham piled up 291 points, limited the opposition to 48 points, and finished with a combined record of 15–1–2. Craig Mysliwiec, "The Blocks of Granite: Significant Seven," *Ram*, February 7, 1968.

15. The other Blocks of Granite of the 1936 line were Vince Lombardi, Leo Paquin, Johnny Druze, Alex Wojciechowicz, Ed Franco, Al Babartsky, and Natty Pierce. "I feel at home with this squad because they are big and I can't pronounce their names," Crowley told James Reston, who was then a young sportswriter for the Associated Press. David Maraniss, *When Pride Still Mattered: A Life of Vince Lombardi* (New York: Simon & Schuster, 1999), 48.

comed the favorable publicity that the Rams brought to the university, they were also keenly aware that the professionalization of college football had been a corrupting influence on other campuses, including Catholic campuses. From as far away as Jesuit headquarters in Rome came orders in January 1932 to all Jesuit colleges in the United States not to award sports scholarships or use improper inducements to attract athletes or offer them special privileges. Father Hogan, who was an avid sports fan, assured the father general that "every athlete is a bona fide student" and that many of them were members and officers of the sodalities, a claim that his successor, Father Gannon, noted without comment. Hogan took such a close interest in both football and baseball that on Monday afternoons in season he regularly conducted postmortems with both Sleepy Jim Crowley and Jack Coffey, the baseball coach. Both Crowley and Coffey would have agreed with Father Charles Deane, the dean of Fordham College, who told the general that Hogan "would not allow people to do their work." Deane also complained that Hogan was so interested in athletics that he was seen selling tickets to the football games.[16]

Father Gannon, who succeeded Hogan in 1936, took far less interest in football than Hogan and barely concealed his distaste for the game. He dutifully showed up at each game, sitting on the fifty-yard line, but by his own admission he was never able to banish the thought that he was attending a rodeo. Gannon was more interested in enhancing Fordham's academic reputation than in maintaining its fame as a football powerhouse, especially after the crowds began to dwindle and the deficits grew larger. The net profit of $34,369.32 for the 1937–38 season shrank to a profit of only $4,658.07 the following year and to a deficit of $9,946.46 in 1939–40. Additional income from the Cotton Bowl and the Sugar Bowl resulted in modest profits the following two years, but in 1942–43 the deficit was a whopping $36,998.85. At that point, because of both the deficit and the loss of so many football players to the wartime draft, Fordham suspended its Big-Time Football program for the duration of the war, never to return to it.[17]

Wojciechowicz played professional football for thirteen years and was inducted into the Football Hall of Fame in 1968. Vince Lombardi was inducted posthumously three years later. Another Fordham alumnus, although not a football player, Wellington Mara, the owner of the New York Giants, was inducted in 1997. Jack Clary, "125 Years of Fordham Football," *Fordham* (Summer 2007).

16. Gannon, *Up to the Present*, 193–94; Marannis, *When Pride Still Mattered*, 44. ARSJ, Deane to Ledóchowski, January 9, 1935.

17. Gannon, *Up to the Present*, 253–54.

After the war Gannon was determined to prevent a revival of Big-Time Football, but he underestimated the tenacity of some of the alumni who were eager to see Fordham return to the salad days of the late 1930s on the gridiron. Gannon called their bluff when he informed them that they would have to raise $50,000 for each of the following three years. The alumni came up empty-handed, and Gannon proceeded to downsize Fordham's football program to a Class B team that posted a desultory record for nine years until football was completely dropped in 1954 under the administration of his successor, Father Laurence J. McGinley.[18]

Gannon's jousting with Fordham's football fans brought him nationwide notoriety in the fall of 1947 because of some unguarded remarks he made at a Communion breakfast of Fordham alumni in New Jersey. Gannon should have known better because he had made the same mistake at another Communion breakfast in New Jersey ten years earlier. On that first occasion he had declared that "football has no place in an educational institution which has Phi Beta Kappa ambitions." Fortunately for him, his remarks did not circulate further than the *Jersey Journal*.[19]

Unaware that there was a reporter present at the breakfast in 1947, he managed to offend a half-dozen different groups in the space of a few minutes. He declared that Fordham "does not ever again want a football team rated among the nation's ten heaviest." He added that "we are not interested in providing business for the gambling fraternity." He lashed out at the baseball Giants, calling them extortionists for the fees they charged Fordham to play at the Polo Grounds. "They have gotten more than a million and a half of our money," he claimed. Gannon also took a swipe at the sportswriters, calling them "tyrants of tyrants" and accusing them of thinking that "a university's main purpose is to provide them with an income." As if that were not enough damage for one morning's address, Gannon also caused deep resentment in the Jewish community when he announced that Fordham was interested in playing football only for the pleasure of its students and alumni and "those on the subway circuit who cross themselves."[20]

18. Ibid., 254. Clary, "125 Years of Fordham Football." In 1964 a group of students revived football at Fordham on the club level with the assistance and encouragement of Father George McMahon, S.J., the dean of Fordham College. In 1970 Fordham football moved up a notch when the Rams became a Division III team, the NCAA's lowest varsity ranking. The Rams moved up still another notch in 1990 when they were admitted to the NCAA's Division I-AA as a member of the newly formed Patriot League. Clary, ibid.

19. *Jersey Journal*, October 25, 1937.

20. *New York Times*, October 20, 1937.

Gannon's remarks provoked a torrent of criticism from sportswriters across the country, and the Giants even threatened to evict the Rams from the Polo Grounds. Among his gentler critics was the Anti-Defamation League of B'nai B'rith, which politely asked him for a word of explanation. Gannon's lame response was to lay the blame on an "unscrupulous reporter" and to insist that he had said nothing offensive. Although Gannon did not apologize for his remarks, at least not publicly, the university issued a statement a few days later announcing that Fordham planned to erect its own stadium in the near future. The university also listed three requirements to play on any Fordham team. Players would have to be capable athletes, satisfactory students, and "young men of excellent character."[21]

Gannon could find only five sportswriters in the whole country who agreed with his criticism of Big-Time College Football, but one of them was Arthur Daley of the *New York Times*, one of the most respected sportswriters in America. Writing a few months after the storm had subsided, Daley conceded that he had originally disagreed with Gannon's desire to deemphasize sports at Fordham but that he had come to appreciate the wisdom of his remarks. "[W]ith evidences of growing hypocrisy and increasing departure from pure amateur ideals," said Daley, "the thought finally has penetrated here that the president of Fordham has been on the right track all along. The college presidents can purify college sports overnight, if they so desire. And here is one educator who has been pursuing a sound policy all along, receiving only criticism for his efforts, not that that would deter him one iota."[22]

Sleepy Jim Crowley resigned as head football coach in 1942 to join the navy and eventually serve in the South Pacific. His nickname belied the fact that he had a keen intelligence and quick wit. When he was a student at Notre Dame an angry Knute Rockne once belittled him for some mistake by asking him if there was anything dumber than a dumb Irishman. "Yes," said Crowley, "a smart Swede." Gannon told one fan that he valued Crowley because "in addition to being a good coach, he has a good influence on the boys and is an excellent representative of Fordham on the outside." In view of Gannon's decision to deemphasize football, Crowley did not return to Fordham after the war, in contrast to his colleague Jack Coffey,

21. FUA, Gannon Papers, Benjamin Epstein to Gannon, October 22, 1947; Gannon to Epstein, October 24, 1937. *New York Times*, October 23, 1947.

22. *New York Times*, December 15, 1947.

who was to remain at Rose Hill as head baseball coach and later as athletic director for a record thirty-three years.[23]

Jack Coffey

A native of the Bronx who had been born only a few miles from Rose Hill, Coffey was a student at Fordham from 1905 to 1910, then played for and/or managed professional baseball teams in twelve cities in eight leagues—"a prolonged series of peregrinations to points provincial," the erudite Coffey called his professional career. In 1925 he returned to Fordham full-time as head baseball coach and the following year succeeded Frank Gargan as graduate manager of athletics (athletic director). Under Coffey, Fordham's baseball team won fourteen Metropolitan Conference titles and five Eastern Collegiate Conference championships.[24]

Coffey was an immensely likeable person, genial and charming, who became Fordham's ambassador of good will. An autodidact, he taught himself French, German, Italian, and Spanish and earned a law degree while head baseball coach at Fordham. He liked to regale friends with detailed descriptions of his home runs as a pro, because he freely admitted that he had hit only two of them in fifteen years. He was also famous for his ability to remember the birthday of virtually every player and colleague, no fewer than 3,000 of them by one count. Arthur Daley admired him enormously: "Mr. Chips with muscles," he called him and said that he became as much a campus fixture as the statue of Archbishop Hughes in front of the Administration Building. "Every undergraduate who played for him or even came in contact with him came away a little bit better because of his association with this true molder of character," said Daley.[25]

Unfortunately Coffey's career at Fordham did not coincide with the years that Frankie Frisch, Fordham's greatest baseball player and all-round athlete, was a student at Fordham College (1915–19). A native of the Bronx and a graduate of Fordham Prep, Frisch was elected captain of the college baseball, football, and basketball teams and excelled at track as well. Immediately upon graduation in 1919 he was offered a job as second baseman with the New York Giants under manager John McGraw, where he remained until 1926, when he was traded to the St. Louis Cardinals. He habitually called his new team the "Cawd'nals" in his pronounced Bronx

23. Maraniss, *When Pride Still Mattered*, 34. FUA, Gannon Papers, Gannon to Monsignor Aloysius C. Dineen, November 29, 1938.

24. Maurice Bouchard, "Jack Coffey," http://sabr.org/bioproj/person/ab1d19fc.

25. Arthur Daley, "Sports of the Times," *New York Times*, May 12, 1958; February 15, 1966.

Frankie Frisch '20 ("The Fordham Flash"), outstanding baseball, football, and basketball player at Fordham and later Hall of Fame second baseman with the New York Giants and St. Louis Cardinals.

accent. In 1921 he led the National League in stolen bases; hence his nickname, "the Fordham Flash." He also managed the Cardinals, Pittsburgh Pirates, and Chicago Cubs before retiring in 1951. He was inducted into the Baseball Hall of Fame as a player in 1947.[26]

Arthur Daley left a memorable portrait of the impression that Frankie Frisch made on him as a freshman at Fordham Prep. "The university was so small and compact that everyone knew everyone else, at least by sight. And the most god-like creature on campus was Frisch, brilliant half-back on the football team . . . a dazzling basketball player and a baseball shortstop of such skills that the Giants snatched him off the campus." "When I would see him walking toward me," said Daley, "my heart would flutter and I would wonder if I would ever screw up enough courage to say hello to him (I never did)." "No man in baseball was faster than Frisch," said Daley. On one occasion Yankee manger Joe McCarthy said to Daley, "Was there ever anything that Frisch could not do?"[27]

26. http://sabr.org/bioproj/person/0bbf3136.
27. Arthur Daley, *Ram*, February 7, 1968.

The Gannon Legacy

Not the least of Gannon's contributions to Fordham was the key role he played in the racial integration of the university. African Americans had been admitted to some of the graduate schools as early as the 1920s, but an especially shameful incident occurred in 1924 when a black woman, Ruth Whitehead Whaley, won the top prize in the Law School and the donor of the prize withdrew it when he discovered that it was to go to an African American woman. In 1932 the School of Education awarded its first doctorate to an African American, Willis Nathaniel Huggins. However, the student body at Fordham College remained entirely white. When a black graduate of Xavier High School, Hudson J. Oliver Jr., was refused admission to the college in 1934, Father John LaFarge, the founder of the Catholic Interracial Council in New York, blamed it on the alleged bigotry of Father Hogan and the dean, Father Charles Deane, and appealed the decision all the way up the Jesuit chain of command to the general. "There seems nothing left but prayer," LaFarge told the provincial, "but I know that serious trouble will sooner or later come from Fordham's attitude."[28]

Two years after the Oliver incident Gannon welcomed the members of the Catholic Interracial Conference to Fordham for their annual meeting and assured them that every school in the university would be open to African Americans. Nonetheless, African American students were slow to come to Rose Hill. According to the researches of Father Schroth, Fordham's first black undergraduate was Matthew Ebenezer Adams, who entered an accelerated wartime class in February 1943 and, after service in the navy, returned to Rose Hill, where he was graduated in 1947.[29]

That same year Gannon was contacted by Mrs. Caroline J. Putnam, the treasurer of the Catholic Scholarships for Negroes, Inc., whose patron was Archbishop Richard J. Cushing of Boston. Gannon assured her that every school and department of the university was open to African Americans. "Our colored students are taken for granted by the others," he assured her, "and seem happy and adjusted." Gannon pointed with pride to the ethnic diversity of the student body, which included Chinese, Indians, Filipinos, Iraqis, and Egyptians. As a consequence, he told her,

28. Ibid., 172–74. ARSJ, LaFarge to Phillips, May 20, 1934. LaFarge may have been too quick to accuse Hogan and Deane of racial prejudice. Under pressure from the provincial, Father Edward Phillips, S.J., St. Peter's College reluctantly admitted Oliver, but he proved to be a poor student, twice flunking out of the college. St. Peter's ultimately gave him a degree in 1946. Schroth, *Fordham: A History and Memoir*, 179.

29. Ibid., 178.

"When we say 'colored people' we mean a very large group and not all [American] negro."[30]

While Gannon's charm was legendary, he could also react with razor-sharp invective to what he considered unfair criticism of Fordham or himself. When *Time* described Fordham in 1939 as "rough, tough and commercial," Gannon dashed off a letter to the publisher, Henry Luce, complaining that such a description denied that Fordham possessed any of the ideals of an institution of higher learning. "If you are interested in the trustworthiness of your subordinates," he told Luce, "you can check their estimate of Fordham with the enclosed report." When a Bronx resident complained about a newspaper report of a symposium sponsored by the Fordham alumni in support of General Francisco Franco and the Nationalist cause in the Spanish Civil War, Gannon replied, "Your letter makes me regret exceedingly that you were unable to attend the symposium on Spain, as you then could have corrected almost every statement made in your letter."[31]

One of the few personal letters that Gannon saved from his copious official correspondence came from a Jewish alumnus who had become a successful lawyer. "I am one of the innumerable Jewish students who [have] found [their] way to the portals of Fordham," this alumnus told Gannon. "I remember well the constituents of my class. Their ancestors must have emanated from all the far corners of the earth. Russia, Ireland, Italy, Spain, even the Philippine Islands were represented. There we were," this alumnus told Gannon, "Catholic, Protestant and Jew, all seated within the confines of a small room on the seventh floor of a New York skyscraper. There we were learning, learning in an environment that led to tolerance and a true spirit of the brotherhood of man."[32]

Like American Catholic bishops, university presidents in the Gannon era were often judged by their success with brick-and-mortar, the number of the new buildings that they erected. Gannon cut a modest but creditable figure in that regard in view of the fact that most of his thirteen-year tenure

---

30. FUA, Gannon Papers, Gannon to Putnam, July 19, 1947. In 1947 Fordham had 102 African American students, second only to St. Louis University (which had 150 African American students) among the 26 Jesuit colleges and universities in the United States. Francis K. Drolet, S.J., "Negro Students in Jesuit Schools and Colleges, 1946–1947," *WL* 76 (1947): 301–2. There were 456 black students in a total enrollment of 105,288 in the 64 Jesuit schools and colleges in the United States.

31. FUA, Gannon Papers, Gannon to Henry Luce, June 10, 1929; Gannon to A. Robert Albert, May 16, 1938.

32. FUA, Gannon Papers, Marcus Werther to Gannon, January 25, 1939.

coincided with the Depression and World War II. Downtown he moved the "campus" from the Woolworth Building to larger and less expensive accommodations in the Vincent Building at 302 Broadway and acquired property on East 39th Street for the School of Social Service.

At Rose Hill he added two wings to St. John's Hall, St. Robert Bellarmine Hall, and Bishop's Hall to form Queen's Court. He also was responsible for the erection in 1947 of Cardinal Spellman Hall, which was originally designed to be a residence for Jesuits and graduate students. Today it is the principal residence of the Jesuit faculty at the university. Thanks to a major benefaction from Mrs. Patrick McGovern, who paid the entire cost of the building, he erected St. Mary's Hall, a residence for sisters studying at Fordham, on the grounds of the nearby Academy of Mount St. Ursula. It was deeded to the Ursuline nuns with the proviso that it would revert to the university if the nuns ever gave up supervision of the facility.

On December 8, 1948, Gannon was present at the dedication of the Fordham War Memorial in the University Church. One of the guests was the new provincial, Father John J. McMahon, who was shocked at Gannon's haggard appearance. Only a few months earlier at the age of fifty-five Gannon had been appointed to an unprecedented fifth three-year term as president of Fordham. However, in January 1949, McMahon informed Gannon that he was to step down as president at the end of the month and become the superior of the Mount Manresa Retreat House on Staten Island. By his own admission, Gannon was stunned by the change. McMahon was not dissatisfied with Gannon's leadership of Fordham but concerned about his health. Gannon realized only months later how much his health had been impaired. As to the change itself, he told an interviewer, "No man seeks a job in the Society. He accepts what is assigned him and does the best he can."[33]

Peter McDonough's portrait of Gannon in his study of twentieth-century American Jesuits concentrates on Gannon's bromides against liberalism, communism, and secular humanism on American college campuses. He leaves the impression that Gannon's biggest impact on New York Catholicism was his witty speeches before boozy and sympathetic Irish American audiences. "Tabloid conservatism," McDonough condescendingly called Gannon's talks, which he thought were aimed at the "Runyonesque" common man. He virtually ignores Gannon's role as pres-

---

33. Schroth, *Fordham: A History and Memoir*, 381. Gannon, *Up to the Present*, 260–61; Thomas E. Curley, "Robert I. Gannon, S.J., President of Fordham University, 1936–1949, A Jesuit Educator." Ph.D. diss., New York University, 1973," 194.

ident of Fordham, the reforms he made in the university, and his contribution to the city through the university.[34]

Father Schroth provides a far more informative and even-handed appraisal of Gannon's stewardship of Fordham than McDonough despite the fact that Schroth candidly admits that as a young man he took an instant dislike to Gannon. "[H]is wit was often at the expense of ideas and persons I had admired all my life such as Franklin Delano Roosevelt," explained Schroth. Despite his political and philosophical differences with Gannon, Schroth believes Gannon's most important contribution to the university was his ability to change the public perception of Fordham. He recovered Fordham's accreditation and guided the university through the lean years of the Depression, the crisis of World War II, and the challenges of rapid postwar expansion. Schroth is generous in his praise of Gannon for upgrading the intellectual caliber of the faculty, raising academic standards for the students, modernizing the norms for tenure and promotion, and giving Fordham an expanded theater program, a communication arts department, and its own FM radio station.[35]

Philip Gleason, in his comprehensive study of American Catholic higher education in the twentieth century, places Gannon's achievements in the context of the unprecedented crisis he faced upon assuming the presidency of Fordham. The university had just suffered a double humiliation when the Association of American Universities not only denied Fordham's application for admission to the charmed circle of Universities of Complex Organization but also dropped Fordham College from its list of approved colleges. Gleason notes that Gannon was able to reverse both setbacks within a few years by improving the quality of both graduate and undergraduate education at Fordham even though it meant the deliberate downsizing of the enrollment in the college.[36]

Gannon brought other improvements to Fordham. He placed the university on a secure financial foundation by requiring each school to adhere to a budget. In the opinion of Thomas E. Curley, his greatest achievement was the recovery of accreditation without loss of the Jesuit ethos of education. His influence was especially noticeable in Fordham College. He told Curley that, if he had more time, he would have made it even smaller, which was consistent with his philosophy that the college should not expand beyond the point where it could continue to provide a thoroughly

34. Peter McDonough, *Men Astutely Trained* (New York: The Free Press, 1992), 322–32.

35. Schroth, *Fordham: A History and Memoir*, 157–66.

36. Gleason, *Contending with Modernity*, 198–99.

Catholic and Jesuit education for its students. The year Gannon left Fordham for Staten Island, an inspection team of the Middle States Association of Colleges and Secondary Schools reported that "the Catholic and Jesuit point of view of the university is clearly expressed, is thoroughly understood and accepted by its administration and faculty and appears to be respected . . . . The controlling position of the Jesuit Order in the administration, their singleness of purpose and their prestige in the faculty guarantee its continuity."[37]

The President and the Rector

Gannon made a farsighted recommendation to his Jesuit superiors in 1940 when he told them that Fordham had become so large that the office of president had to be separated from the office of the rector of the Jesuit community. Ultimately his recommendation for the separation of the two positions was adopted not only at Fordham but also at other large Jesuit universities in the United States. However, the immediate consequences of Gannon's recommendation were nine years of pain and grief for him personally. The root of the problem was the unsatisfactory way in which the offices of president and rector were separated at Fordham.

As Gannon explained to the president of Creighton University in 1949, "[I]t all began when I asked to be relieved from my office of rector in 1940. The job here at Fordham had killed my predecessor and I felt I was coasting into a nervous breakdown."

Gannon wanted a rector-president to be the head of the university and a subordinate superior to govern the religious community of Jesuits. Instead, the opposite happened. On August 5, 1940, the American assistant of the Society of Jesus, Father Zacheus Maher, appointed a rector at Fordham with authority over the whole university, including the president.[38]

It took Gannon nine years to convince his superiors that this arrangement would not work. He was fighting an uphill battle against two powerful officials in the Society, Maher and Father Edward B. Rooney, the

37. Gannon, Interview with Thomas E. Curley, June 27, 1973, cit. in Curley, "Gannon," 194, 196.

38. FUA, Gannon Papers, Gannon to William H. McCabe, S.J., January 17, 1949. Maher was implementing the norms promulgated by Ledóchowski in 1934 that required the president to administer the institution "*sub alto ductu Rectoris*" [under the supreme command of the rector]. The "mysterious *altus ductus*," Gannon called it. FUA, Gannon Papers, Gannon, Memorandum on Rector-President Normae, 1932. Paul A. Fitzgerald, S.J., *The Governance of Jesuit Colleges in the United States, 1920–1970* (Notre Dame, Ind.: University of Notre Dame Press, 1984), 111.

influential executive director of the Jesuit Educational Association of the United States. Unknown to the general public, this internal quarrel within the Society over the extent of his authority as president took a heavy toll on Gannon's health. He found it humiliating when journalists, politicians, and leaders of secular universities realized that he did not have ultimate authority over the university, because the rector, not the president, was the legal head of the university and *ex officio* the chairman of the board of trustees.

The first rector appointed under this arrangement, Father J. Harding Fisher, was a former novice master with limited experience in Jesuit universities, who complained that Gannon habitually infringed on his authority. News of the continual friction between Gannon and Harding spread throughout the Jesuit communities in the United States, earning Gannon a stinging rebuke from Maher, who could not persuade any other American Jesuit college to adopt the system in effect at Fordham. The second rector, Joseph A. Murphy, appointed in 1947, was a former provincial of the Maryland–New York Province and considerably more assertive than Harding. Gannon claimed that Murphy intended "to let the public know that he is running the university through me." Ever the showman, Gannon threatened to resign as president and assume "the most inconspicuous status" in the province, although not at Fordham for fear that it might be disedifying.[39]

Gannon finally got a sympathetic response from his superiors with the appointment of Father John J. McMahon as the new provincial of the New York Province in 1948. McMahon asked Gannon for his advice about a new administrative arrangement at Fordham that envisioned a rector-president with full authority over both the university and the Jesuit community. The plan also involved the appointment of a superior for the Jesuit community who would act as the delegate of the rector-president. It was essentially the administrative structure that Gannon had been advocating in vain for nine years. He must have been especially pleased with the provision that, in case of conflict between the superior and the rector-president, the decision of the latter would be final. Gannon graciously told McMahon that

39. FUA, Gannon Papers, Maher to Gannon, February 29, 1944; Gannon to Maher, January 25, 1947; Gannon to F. A. McQuade, February 12, 1947. Later there were similar complaints about the difficulties involving dual leadership of president and rector when the system was introduced at Loyola University, Chicago, and at the University of San Francisco. As Paul Fitzgerald commented, the arrangement "attempted to accomplish the impossible, that is, to separate and, at the same time, to reconcile the two offices." Ibid., 111, 114.

his plan was even better than the one that he had been advocating, because he had been willing to leave the superior under the direct jurisdiction of the general.[40]

The new order made its debut at Fordham on February 2, 1949, when Father Laurence J. McGinley was appointed rector-president of the university without any mention of a religious superior for the Jesuit community. The same procedure was followed during the next few years at Georgetown University and Boston College with the appointment of rector-presidents and still later at St. Louis University and Marquette University. Religious superiors were subsequently appointed who were subject to the jurisdiction of the rector-president.[41]

Even Father Edward Rooney, who once claimed that the abandonment of the dual leadership of rector and president would be a disaster for Jesuit education in the United States, reversed his position. In a conversation with the general, Father John Baptist Janssens, in September 1954, Rooney told him that the old system whereby the rector was superior to the president in American Jesuit colleges was not working and could not work. He now favored governance by a rector-president and a subordinate religious superior.[42]

Father Vincent McCormick, Maher's successor as the American assistant, had come to the same conclusion seven years earlier. He was not impressed with Rooney's argument that the system of dual leadership had been the personal command of Ledóchowski. Writing from Rome, he told Rooney, "Perhaps our proximity to infallibility makes us so keenly aware of human fallibility." While the outcome of the disagreement over the governance of Jesuit colleges in the United States was still in doubt in 1947, McCormick urged Gannon to continue his struggle for unified direction of Jesuit universities and colleges under the leadership of the president. "It is something new in the Society," he admitted. "Of course," he said, "so is a university like Fordham."[43]

The change in the administrative structure at Fordham came too late to be of much benefit to Gannon, but he could take pride in the fact that his persistent complaints about the inadequacy of the system of dual lead-

40. FUA, Gannon Papers, McMahon to Gannon, November 9, 1948; Gannon to McMahon, November 14, 1948.

41. Fitzgerald, *Governance of Jesuit Colleges*, 118–20.

42. FUA, Gannon Papers, Rooney to McCormick, March 27, 1945. Fitzgerald, *Governance of Jesuit Colleges*, 119.

43. FUA, Gannon Papers, McCormick to Rooney, May 20, 1945; McCormick to Gannon, March 14, 1947.

ership of rector and president was a major factor in bringing about the change that clearly delineated the leadership role of the president in the governance of American Jesuit universities and colleges. It proved to be a boon not only for Fordham but also for Jesuit higher education throughout the United States.

15

THE HALCYON YEARS

Avant le Déluge

The 1950s are remembered nostalgically today by a rapidly dwindling number of elderly Americans as a quiet and peaceful interlude between the dislocations of the immediate postwar period and the turmoil of the late 1960s and early 1970s. A booming economy, helped by successful entrepreneurs, robust labor unions, and the lack of foreign competition, enabled many working-class Americans to boost themselves into the middle class and attain a degree of security and comfort that would have been unthinkable for their parents. Numerous young families were able to move from cramped tenements in disintegrating urban neighborhoods to modest starter homes in the booming suburbs. "In the suburbs," said Andrew Greeley, the priest-sociologist, in 1959, "the Catholic is regarded at last as a full-fledged American."[1] One indication of increasing middle-class prosperity was that more Americans owned automobiles than ever before and used them during the summer for paid family vacations on the new interstate highways that were one of the major domestic accomplishments of the Eisenhower administration.

Historians and social scientists have been quick to point out that the prosperity of the 1950s was unevenly distributed and that it did little to improve the economic and social condition of many minorities, most noticeably women and African Americans. In the face of such regrettable shortcomings, Alan Ehrenhalt had the temerity to wonder if there ever was a society that assured perfect equality for all of its citizens. "In drawing up our balance sheet for 1950s America," Ehrenhalt admitted that "we need to examine the holes in the assumptions of contentment." Nonetheless, added Ehrenhalt, the fact that "the contentment was real—and widespread—is a truth that needs to be remembered as well."[2]

1. Andrew M. Greeley, *The Church and the Suburbs* (New York: Sheed and Ward, 1959), 56, cit. in Jay P. Dolan, *In Search of an American Catholicism* (New York: Oxford University Press, 2002), 185.

2. Alan Ehrenhalt, *The Lost City: The Forgotten Virtues of Community in America* (New York: Basic Books, 1995), 110.

The sense of contentment was unmistakable even among the traditionally restive students in American colleges and universities. The result was that an almost preternatural calm descended on many campuses. In 1957 Dr. Philip Jacob of the University of Pennsylvania conducted a survey of fifty colleges across the country and reported that "students are gloriously contented both with regard with present day-to-day activity and their outlook for the future." Far from being pleased with the results of his own research, Dr. Jacob was alarmed at the degree of contentment on college campuses because he claimed that many of the students were self-centered and oblivious to the problems of the world. From a more ethereal vantage point the Protestant theologian Paul Tillich voiced the same misgivings at the apathy on college campuses in 1957 when he told a graduating class, "We hope for non-conformists among you, for your sake, for the sake of the nation, and for the sake of humanity." The president of Yale, A. Whitney Griswold, feared that America's colleges were producing "a whole nation of yes-men." A decade later no one would be complaining of apathy on college campuses, but there was little hint in the placid early 1950s that such a dramatic change was in the offing.[3]

At Fordham, Father Laurence McGinley shared the same misgivings as other college presidents about student apathy, but, unlike many of them, he traced the causes to a lack of spiritual and moral values. In October 1949, at the Mass of the Holy Spirit, the liturgical event that traditionally inaugurated the liturgical year, McGinley told the students with uncharacteristic bluntness: "To any student who leaves these walls where loyalty and sacrifice and loving responsibility of man for man are held precious, and goes out into the world uncaring, indifferent, unloving for all but self—I say, 'Brother, when they ask you where your alma mater is, tell them it's south of Fordham Road.'"[4]

Fordham undergraduates in the 1950s displayed many of the same characteristics that disturbed and disappointed America's more activist academics. In a poll taken in 1951, 65 percent of the students said that they had no definite plans for the future; 29 percent never participated in any extracurricular activities; only 34 percent said they would volunteer for military service in wartime; only 25 percent frequently asked instructors to explain points they did not understand; and only 11 percent frequently argued with instructors when they disagreed with them. Politically the drift to the right was evident in their assessment of the Truman administration. Only

3. Ibid., 60–62.
4. *Ram*, October 14, 1949.

26 percent approved of his domestic policies; only 20 percent approved of his foreign policy, and 55 percent wanted Secretary of State Dean Acheson removed from office.

When asked to name their favorite public person, 29.1 percent of Fordham undergraduates chose General Douglas MacArthur (nine months after President Truman had dismissed him as commander of the UN forces in the Korean War); 11.5 percent chose General Dwight D. Eisenhower; 11.4 percent chose Senator Robert A. Taft of Ohio, "Mr. Republican"; and 8.1 percent chose Senator Joseph McCarthy of Wisconsin. In the popularity poll Winston Churchill edged out Pope Pius XII (4.7 percent to 4.5 percent) and Cardinal Spellman finished second from last (with a mere 2.8 percent of the vote), trailing both President Truman and New York Governor Thomas E. Dewey. Thirty percent of the students had no favorite public person at all.[5]

The poll was never published in the *Ram*, which had conducted the survey, although it was already set in type when the staff of the *Ram* asked Father Thurston Davis, the dean of Fordham College, to obtain a comment from Father McGinley that they could publish together with the poll. The poll expired in the "President's Room," the folksy designation that McGinley used for his office. The docile editors announced that they would not publish the poll because its validity was open to question. However, they promised to replace it with a more rigorous poll to be conducted with the help of the Psychology and Sociology departments of the university, but that poll never saw the light of day either.[6]

The following year, during the run-up to the 1952 presidential election, a poll in the *Ram* revealed that Fordham undergraduates favored General Eisenhower over Illinois Governor Adlai E. Stevenson by a margin of two to one. The student president of the Fordham Republican Club gave much of the credit to Father McGinley for his speech at the Mass on the Holy Spirit a few weeks earlier at which he had lambasted liberals "for whom no good thing exists in heaven or upon earth that can transcend themselves." The poll also revealed that the Fordham students supported the controversial tactics of Senator McCarthy by a margin of four-and-a-half to one. Father McGinley made no effort to suppress the results of this poll.[7]

At least among the undergraduates Republican sentiment remained strong at Fordham throughout the Eisenhower years. In October 1960,

5. FUA, McGinley Papers, Thurston Davis to McGinley, December 1951.
6. *Ram*, December 13, 1951.
7. *Ram*, October 2, 24, 1952.

when Vice President Richard M. Nixon visited the campus one month before the presidential election that pitted him again Massachusetts Senator John F. Kennedy, an estimated 6,000 students jammed the auditorium to hear him. They screamed and shouted their approval so loudly that they almost drowned out the attempt of the college band to greet him by playing "California, Here I Come." Afterward the audience gave Nixon a four-and-a-half-minute standing ovation.[8]

The Civil Rights Movement

An exception to the pervasively conservative mood on campus was a concern on the part of at least a few students for racial justice as the civil rights movement began to gather momentum in the United States in the late 1950s. This development was all the more surprising because of the small number of African American undergraduates at Rose Hill, who made their first appearance on campus only after World War II. Much of the credit for the growing sensitivity to racial injustice can be traced to the small but zealous Campus Interracial Council, an offshoot of the Catholic Interracial Council of New York, which was founded in 1934 by Father John LaFarge, S.J., a pioneering figure in promoting Catholic interest in interracial justice. Beginning in 1952, the Campus Interracial Council of Fordham sponsored an annual Interracial Justice Sunday Mass as well as numerous lectures and panel discussions on race relations.

When Jackie Robinson, the star second basemen for the Brooklyn Dodgers (who broke the color barrier in major league baseball in 1947), spoke at Keating Hall in October 1958 after his retirement, he praised the Catholic Interracial Council for its "fine work in promoting better relations between the races." In a hilarious spoof of the self-advertised tolerance of white liberals for interracial marriages, Robinson deadpanned: "I would not want my son to marry a white girl, but, if he falls in love with one, and the girl with him, I would not stop him."[9]

It is difficult to estimate the extent of the sympathy for racial integration among the undergraduates at Rose Hill in the 1950s, but only a reckless gambler would have placed a heavy wager that enthusiasm ran very high. To be fair, a week before Robinson delivered his address at Rose Hill, an editorial in the *Ram* praised Archbishop Joseph Rummel of New Orleans for his courage in beginning to desegregate the parochial schools in his Deep South archdiocese and called upon the federal government to force

8. *Ram*, October 6, 1960.
9. *Ram*, October 23, 1958.

southern states to integrate their public schools. "The only way to prove to the decent people of the South that the Negro is not inferior," said the editorial writer, "is to give him equal opportunity from his childhood."[10] However, it is not clear to what extent the forthright editor was expressing the *vox populi* on campus.

A year later another editor of the *Ram*, an outstanding athlete and a graduate of a Jesuit high school, expressed a more ambivalent opinion of the progress of the civil rights movement that may have been a more accurate reflection of student attitudes. He recognized and apparently approved the role of the National Association for the Advancement of Colored People in the litigation that led to *Brown v. Board of Education*, the landmark decision of the U.S. Supreme Court in 1954 that outlawed racial segregation of public schools. However, he went on to excoriate the NAACP as an organization of extremists and agitators that had become the black equivalent of the notorious White Citizens Councils in the South. He warned that the NAACP's declared objective of achieving complete integration as soon as possible was a threat to "the Southern way of life" and raised the incendiary specter that the NAACP would soon push for the repeal of state laws barring interracial marriages and miscegenation (in the South, segregationists called it "mixing the races").[11]

For a brief period in the early 1960s the leading edge of the civil rights movement shifted to a series of well-publicized peaceful sit-ins at segregated lunch counters throughout the South that attracted national attention. The reaction at Fordham was mixed, at best. A panel discussion that included James Farmer, the program director of the NAACP; Father Donald Campion, S.J., associate editor of *America*; and Richard J. Regan, S.J., a Jesuit scholastic, offered strong support for the sit-ins. However, a better index of the student reaction may have been a decision of the Fordham College Student Congress, as the student government was known at that time. After a contentious discussion, it passed a resolution applauding the efforts of the "Negro" students to secure their civil rights, but it also affirmed the obligation of all to obey the law.[12]

The exasperated editor of the *Ram*, more sympathetic to the civil rights movement than his immediate predecessor, commented bitterly but correctly that "in effect the resolution cancelled itself." It is not clear how many Fordham students would have agreed with him when he complained

10. *Ram*, October 16, 1958.
11. *Ram*, November 5, 1959.
12. *Ram*, April 7, 1960

that it was "hard to understand the attitude of those who reject all forms of discrimination as undemocratic and un-Christian and then refuse fully to support the southern Negroes honorably and courageously resisting such discrimination."[13] A week earlier the Campus Interracial Council decided to stage a more straightforward endorsement of the sit-ins. For an hour on March 30 twenty-one Fordham students picketed the Woolworth's Five-and-Ten-Cents store at the corner of Fordham Road and Valentine Avenue. They chose this site because many of the sit-ins in the South took place at the lunch counters of the ubiquitous local Woolworths. The police on duty said that it was the most peaceful demonstration they had ever witnessed.

Many passers-by seemed unacquainted with the issue. "What do these kids know about injustice?" asked one woman shopper. As news of the demonstration spread on campus, many Fordham students skipped classes and trekked up the steep hill to Valentine Avenue to watch the picketing. Most of them laughed at the demonstrators and expressed their disapproval in various ways. One student leader called it a fad and compared it to the popular stunt of jamming students into a phone booth. Despite the disapproval and mockery of their peers, the spirit of the student demonstrators remained high. "We may evoke an awareness of injustice against Negroes by our actions," said one of them. "That's all we are asking for." The demonstrators achieved their aim. The picketing was no fad, declared the *Ram*. "Such action, both here and elsewhere, has smashed the label of 'the silent generation' which many so-called experts have attached to the present college generation."[14]

Indian Summer at Rose Hill

While the Fordham undergraduates were hardly the "yes-men" who Yale President Griswold feared were populating the nation's campuses, they did seem content with the status quo. The closest thing to a conflict was a two-year dispute over a new charter for the student government, but it involved disputes among the students themselves, not conflict between the students and the administration. The two most popular causes were the fate of the football team and the activities of the Reserve Officers Training Program, the ROTC, which included some 1,800 students by 1953. Two of the highlights of the school year were the annual Military Ball in February when a young woman was elected Sweetheart of the Regiment

13. *Ram*, April 7, 1960
14. *Ram*, March 31, 1960.

and made an honorary colonel, and the annual Demonstration Day in the spring when the rector reviewed the cadets on Edwards Parade.

No one could complain that Fordham men (and, of course, all the undergraduates were men) were neglecting their patriotic obligations during the Cold War. In 1950 the Fordham Air Force ROTC team outranked 145 other colleges to win a national championship. Thanks to the Pharmacy School, Fordham also became the first university in the nation to offer a first-aid course to assist victims of a potential nuclear attack by the Soviet Union. That same year both the Democratic and Republican clubs at Fordham joined forces to try to prevent the reelection in East Harlem of Congressman Vito Marcantonio, who, in the political jargon of the day, was widely regarded as a communist "fellow-traveler." Eschewing such relatively polite euphemisms, the *Ram* called Marcantonio "Stalin's last-ditch fighter in the U.S. Congress."[15]

A more scholarly contribution to winning the Cold War was the establishment on the Rose Hill campus in 1952 of the Institute of Contemporary Russian Studies, which offered courses in the Russian language, culture, and history. The initiative came from Father Thurston Davis, S.J., the dean of Fordham College. The director from 1952 until the closing of the Institute in 1969 was Father Walter C. Jaskievicz, S.J., who joked that the Soviet propaganda machine may have helped to publicize the Institute when in its usual ham-handed way it accused Fordham of operating a spy school. An article in a Soviet magazine claimed that Fordham was the pride of the U.S. government because it "converted blockheads into diploma-ed [*sic*] spies and certified murderers."[16]

The 1950s were boom years for religion, as the historian Jay Dolan has noted, with 63 percent of Americans affiliated with a church by the end of the decade. Catholics now accounted for almost one-quarter of the nation's population. The religious atmosphere that permeated American society was evident in many ways on the Fordham campus. In the unpublished *Ram* poll conducted in December 1951, 59 percent of the respondents said they considered themselves good Catholics; 61 percent received the sacraments regularly; and 91 percent said they attended Mass every Sunday. If the last statistic was accurate, attendance at Sunday Mass at Rose Hill rivaled that of rural Ireland or Québec. Although the requirement of mandatory daily Mass had long been discontinued, there was a

15. *Ram*, May 12, 1949; March 16, September 28, October 5, October 26, 1950.

16. FUA, McGinley Papers, McGinley to Janssens, February 8, 1953; *Ram*, October 24, 1952; Walter C. Jaskievicz, S.J., *As I Remember Fordham: Selections from the Sesquicentennial Oral History Project* (New York: Fordham University Press, 1991), 99–101.

*The Leon Lowenstein Center: the educational and
social center of the Lincoln Center campus.*

The newest residence halls at Rose Hill, dedicated in August 2010: Campbell Hall, the gift of Robert E. Campbell and his wife, Joan M. Campbell; and Salice and Conley halls, the gift of Thomas P. Salice and his wife, Susan Conley Salice.

Opened in 1959, the McGinley Center is named in honor of Father Laurence J. McGinley, S.J., president of Fordham University, 1949–63.

Named after New York City's master power broker and city planner, Robert Moses Plaza provides an oasis of greenery in the heart of the Lincoln Center campus.

Coffey Field, the home of Fordham's football and soccer teams, is named in honor of John Francis ("Jack") Coffey, the legendary father of Fordham athletics.

Opened in 1997, the William D. Walsh Family Library, one of the largest university libraries in the United States, in named in honor of the late Fordham alumnus and benefactor William D. Walsh and his wife, Jane.

Watercolor of the Carolyn Dursi Cunniffe Fountain, located between Dealy Hall and Hughes Hall, named for the wife of Maurice J. Cunniffe.

His Eminence Avery Cardinal Dulles, S.J. (1918–2008),
the first American theologian appointed to the College of Cardinals
(on February 21, 2001). (Courtesy Dr. Anne-Marie Kirmse, O.P.)

continual round of voluntary religious observances throughout the year, such as Marian devotions in October and May and penance services during Lent. Not only were the religious services well attended, but student leaders, especially members of the sodalities, often played a prominent role in conducting them. The editors of the *Ram* were not shy about urging their fellow students to discover the value of asceticism during Lent and to combine patriotism with religious devotion by promoting Marian devotions in May as a response to the communist celebration of May Day.[17]

The annual pilgrimage to the Shrine of the North American Martyrs in Auriesville, New York, commemorating the martyrdom of the Jesuit Saints Isaac Jogues, René Goupil, and Jean De Lalande in the seventeenth century, always drew several hundred participants. In 1949 almost 400 Fordham students and their friends made the 200-mile trip by train. During the height of the Cold War in 1949, the egregious "show trial" of József Cardinal Mindszenty, the Hungarian primate, by the communist regime in Budapest led to widespread protests by American Catholics. At Fordham the Student Council took the initiative by sending a sternly worded protest to President Truman and organizing a mass meeting on Edwards Parade. When Pope Pius XII observed the golden jubilee of his priestly ordination later that year, Fordham joined every Jesuit school throughout the world in scheduling a Mass in his honor. At Rose Hill the Mass was a command performance celebrated by Father McGinley in the gymnasium and attended by the whole university without a whimper of protest.[18]

State of the University

Under Father Gannon the size of the student population had been deliberately reduced during the late 1940s to 9,780. After consulting the deans in the spring of 1949 shortly after his appointment as president-rector, Father McGinley decided to reduce the student population still further. He intended to shed 1,280 students within a few semesters to arrive at a permanent student population of 8,500, which he thought was the maximum number that Fordham could effectively educate if it were to establish its reputation as the leading Catholic university in the country. That was not the only reason why McGinley wanted to cap the student population at 8,500. He also wished to erect a new dormitory to increase

17. Dolan, *In Search of an American Catholicism*, 180–82. *Ram*, October 19, 1950, February 8, April 26, 1951.

18. *Ram*, September 29, February 10, March 31, 1949.

the resident student population and erase the reputation of Fordham as primarily a part-time commuter university.

In 1949 only 738 of the 9,780 students were residents, and the great majority of them were not in Fordham College, but in other schools of the university. However, the father general, Jean-Baptiste Janssens, who had already indicated that he wanted a reduction in the size of Fordham, would not give McGinley permission to build the new dormitory until he set a ceiling for the student population. Janssens feared that otherwise McGinley would seek permission to erect another building in eight or ten years. "*Sed sic itur ad astra!*" [This is shooting for the stars!], Janssens said caustically, quoting Vergil about McGinley's plans for a new dormitory.[19]

McGinley wanted the college to be the heart of the university, and for that reason he was willing to increase the enrollment beyond the number envisioned by Gannon. In September 1949 Fordham College enrolled 503 students, of whom 348 came from the New York metropolitan area, another 37 came from upstate New York, and 85 came from New Jersey, Connecticut, Pennsylvania, and Massachusetts. The other 43 states contributed a grand total of 25 students, and eight students came from other countries. In other words, five northeastern states accounted for 93.4 percent of the population of Fordham College. More dormitory space was obviously essential if Fordham were to establish a national reputation on the undergraduate as well as the graduate level. McGinley, a native New Yorker, saw another advantage to increasing the number of out-of-state and foreign students. "We have found that their presence at the university has done much to eliminate a certain narrowness of view, typical of New York boys," he said privately to another New York Jesuit from the West Side of Manhattan, the provincial, Father John McMahon.[20]

During McGinley's second year as rector (as he was always called instead of president in keeping with long-established Jesuit tradition), he had to contend with a major financial crisis that was occasioned at least in part by the Korean War, which began on June 25, 1950. There was a 6 percent decrease in enrollment from 9,426 the previous year to 8,876. Fordham College was especially hard hit with a loss of 325 students in the

19. FUA, McGinley Papers, McGinley to John McMahon, May 19, 1949; Janssens to McMahon, May 5, 1949; McMahon to McGinley, May 12, 1949. McGinley relied on the experienced and astute American assistant in Rome, Father Vincent A. McCormick, to obtain Janssens's approval, which he succeeded in getting. FUA, McGinley Papers, McGinley to McMahon, May 16, 1949.

20. FUA, McGinley Papers, Dean of Freshmen to McGinley, October 5, 1949; McGinley to McMahon, May 19, 1949.

ROTC program who were called to active duty. The result was a decline in income of $250,000 and the first deficit since the end of World War II. "Prosperity is not just around the corner," McGinley warned the faculty, although he assured them that he would not rescind the increase in salaries they had recently received.[21]

The heavy expenses of maintaining a football team remained a serious financial problem throughout the early 1950s. "The pressures and public relations aspects of this problem are unbelievable to anyone who has not attempted to meet the difficulty," McGinley told the father general in 1953. McGinley tackled the problem by forming a committee of select alumni and informing them that Fordham could not continue its football program unless they could guarantee an income of $100,000 per year. The vociferous complaints from the alumni against eliminating football rang hollow when it became apparent that they would not support football with their wallets. In 1954 less than 5 percent of the more than 20,000 alumni heeded a plea to purchase season's tickets. "And so, at long last," McGinley told them, "our head must rule our heart." He discontinued Fordham's participation in intercollegiate football, a tradition that went back almost a century.[22]

There were other extraordinary expenses as well. By the mid-1950s Fordham was providing about $350,000 in scholarships through a variety of programs. Some 342 students received approximately $134,000 in direct financial aid. Another $115,000 went to 118 student athletes for room, board, and tuition. Fordham granted an additional $100,000 in scholarship assistance to 784 religious brothers and sisters who were taking courses at Fordham. Father Lawrence A. Walsh, Fordham's first provost, was especially eager to maintain this program so that Fordham could help to improve the quality of education in the local Catholic elementary and secondary schools. Fordham had already received some financial help for this program when Cardinal Spellman made Fordham the official teacher training school for the archdiocese of New York. Fordham agreed to pay a third of the tuition and the archdiocese agreed to pay three-fifths of the remainder. McGinley hailed this as a splendid example of real cooperation between the university and the archdiocese.[23]

21. *New York Times*, December 3, 1951.

22. FUA, McGinley Papers, McGinley to Janssens, February 8, 1953; McGinley to Alumni, Students, Faculty and Friends, December 15, 1954.

23. FUA, McGinley Papers, Lawrence Walsh to McGinley, March 12, 1955; McGinley to Janssens, February 8, 1953.

When McGinley took command of Fordham in 1949, he had a faculty of 112 Jesuits distributed among the eight schools of the university and Fordham Preparatory School. The Jesuits constituted slightly less than one-quarter of the total faculty of the university. Like every president of Fordham since Father Thomas Gannon a century earlier, McGinley insisted that he needed more Jesuits to do an adequate job, especially because he identified the chief weakness in the university as the poor quality of the teaching of religion. "It will take time," he said about the problem, "but it simply must be solved."

However, philosophy, not religion, was queen of the undergraduate sciences in Jesuit colleges. Only Jesuits were permitted to teach philosophy courses, and they were in increasingly short supply at Fordham by the mid-1950s. Senior philosophy professors complained about the burden of teaching 190 students in each class. McGinley received little solace from John McMahon, the provincial, who agreed that the number of Jesuits at Fordham was inadequate, but McMahon saw little hope of increasing the size of the Jesuit faculty over the following ten years. However, in a refreshing and admirable departure from the handwringing of some of his predecessors about the shortage of Jesuits, McGinley acknowledged that he shared the blame because he had failed to make wise strategic decisions for the best utilization of the available Jesuit personnel.[24]

As McGinley gained more information about the operation of the university, he concluded that two least satisfactory units were the Department of Communication Arts, which had been the brainchild and pride-and-joy of Father Gannon, and the School of Business. In the case of the Communication Arts Department, McGinley regretfully concluded that the talented young Jesuit who headed the department, Father Alfred J. Barrett, had been unable to end the bitter internal divisions in the faculty of the department. The situation in the School of Business was more serious because it was one of the largest schools in the university and its shortcomings placed at risk the whole reputation of the university. In this case also McGinley placed the blame on a Jesuit, the dean, Father William Griffiths. McGinley faulted him for failure to provide adequate leadership with the result that there had been a decline in academic standards.[25]

In the face of such serious problems, McGinley explained to the provincial that, in a university as large as Fordham, it was impossible for the

24. FUA, McGinley Papers, McGinley to McMahon, March 26, 1949; McGinley to Janssens, July 23, 1952; McMahon to McGinley, December 3, 1952; McGinley to Janssens, February 8, 1953; McMahon to McGinley, December 1, 1953.

25. FUA, McGinley Papers, McGinley to Janssens, July 23, 1952.

president to provide leadership for every aspect of the operations and that he had to rely on the deans for adequate supervision of the individual schools. As a general principle, this observation made eminently good sense. However, in the case of the School of Business in 1954, it would appear that McGinley was selling himself short because in fact he took effective control of the situation himself. After familiarizing himself with the inner workings of the school, he identified several specific problems that needed immediate attention and announced in October 1954 that major changes would be forthcoming in the spring semester. He wanted a new catalogue for the School of Business, a search committee to recruit new professors, the strengthening of the weaker departments in the school, and more productive work from the older faculty.[26]

Father Laurence J. McGinley, S.J.

Father Raymond Schroth once observed, "If it helps a university president to look like a president, Laurence J. McGinley was singularly blessed." "Distinguished in appearance and accomplishments" was the lapidary phrase that another highly regarded contemporary Jesuit educator, Paul A. Fitzgerald, used to sum up his impression of McGinley.[27] Jim Farley, former postmaster general under FDR and senior Democratic strategist, described McGinley as "an ideal Jesuit." His gravitas, charm, competence, and self-confidence conveyed the reassuring image of a seasoned Jesuit educator, although McGinley was only forty-three years old when he became president of Fordham in 1949, the same age as Father Gannon when he had become president in 1936.

McGinley did not seem the least bit intimidated by the reputation of his predecessor, who had become an iconic figure in the history of Fordham. McGinley was to serve as president for fourteen years, surpassing Gannon's record by a year. Together their presidencies spanned more than a fifth of Fordham's history up to that point. After four years as president of Fordham, McGinley offered to resign and make way for someone with "far greater spiritual and intellectual and even physical qualities." It is not clear how serious he was, but, in any event, his offer was not accepted by Father Janssens, the Jesuit general.[28]

26. FUA, McGinley Papers, McGinley to Provincial, October 21, 1954.

27. Raymond A. Schroth, S.J., *Fordham: A History and Memoir* (Chicago: Loyola University Press, 2002), 217; Paul A. Fitzgerald, S.J., *The Governance of Jesuit Colleges in the United States, 1920–1970* (Notre Dame, Ind.: University of Notre Dame Press, 1984), 119.

28. FUA, McGinley Papers, McGinley to Janssens, February 8, 1953.

Like Gannon, McGinley was a native New Yorker, born on the Upper West Side of Manhattan. Gannon and McGinley had different gifts and each of them used their gifts for the betterment of Fordham in different ways. Gannon not only rescued Fordham from the disastrous loss of accreditation in 1935, but he also used his charm and bonhomie on the lecture circuit to make himself and Fordham a well-known presence in New York City not only as a football powerhouse but also as a serious academic institution. McGinley did not try to emulate Gannon's success as an after-dinner speaker. Instead he established a national reputation as an educator in both Catholic and in secular circles.

The prominence that McGinley attained in the highly competitive world of American higher education was especially impressive because, prior to his appointment as president of Fordham, he had spent his entire life in Jesuit institutions except for his elementary school education in New York City public schools. McGinley was a graduate of Xavier High School in Manhattan, Woodstock College, and the Pontifical Biblical Institute and the Pontifical Gregorian University in Rome, where he received a doctorate in theology in 1939. At the time of his appointment as president and rector of Fordham ten years later, McGinley was regent and prefect of studies in the sheltered world of the theologate of the Maryland–New York Province of the Society of Jesus in rural Woodstock, Maryland.[29]

Unlike many Catholic educators of that era, especially in the northeastern United States, McGinley took an active interest in the regional and national college and university accrediting associations. In 1953 he hosted a meeting at Fordham of the Association of Colleges and Universities of the State of New York. At the end of the meeting he was elected secretary-treasurer of the Association. He also served as the vice president of the Middle States Association of Colleges and Secondary Schools, the regional accrediting agency; and as a member of the Regents State Examination Board and the Commission on Institutions of Higher Education. In 1960 he was elected president of the Association of Urban Universities.

He told the general that he often regretted the time he was forced to devote to these organizations, but he thought it was time well spent because of the recognition and prestige his participation brought to Fordham. In the course of his membership in these associations McGinley established a warm personal relationship with Ewald B. Nyquist, who was not only the secretary of the Middle States Association of Colleges and Secondary Schools but also the secretary of the New York State Education Depart-

29. *Ram*, January 13, 1949.

ment. They corresponded on a first-name basis. When McGinley considered resigning from the Commission on Institutions of Higher Education in 1953, Nyquist successfully pleaded with him not to do so because he valued his participation so highly.[30]

Ironically McGinley was less successful in an effort to secure a greater policymaking role for the presidents of Jesuit universities and colleges within the Society of Jesus. In 1959 he was one of six Jesuit university presidents who asked the Jesuit provincials (who *ex officio* constituted a board of governors of Jesuit colleges and universities) to establish a Council of Presidents of Jesuit Colleges and Universities within the framework of the Jesuit Educational Association. Their request was strongly resisted by Father Edward B. Rooney, the longtime executive director of the JEA, who viewed this request as a threat to his own authority. After some hesitation the provincials sided with Rooney and agreed to establish only a toothless Conference of Presidents. The following year the Jesuit presidents made a second attempt to obtain more influence in the JEA, but they met with similarly disappointing results.[31]

Although Gannon and McGinley differed markedly in style and personality, as Jesuits they shared the same basic approach to Catholic education. They both wanted to give top priority to the liberal arts in Fordham's program of undergraduate education. Like Gannon, McGinley was a benign elitist who feared that indiscriminate access to higher education would erode academic standards and result in what he called "assembly-line schools." McGinley also decried what he discerned as a growing materialism on the part of college students who valued a college degree largely as a means of obtaining more lucrative jobs and neglected the opportunity of

30. FUA, McGinley Papers, McGinley to Janssens, July 23, 1952; February 8, 1953; Nyquist to McGinley, January 19, 1953. *Ram*, December 10, 1953, November 17, 1960. McGinley also served on the board of the Higher Education Assistance Corporation (which annually disbursed $100 million in college loans), the Lincoln Center for the Performing Arts, the New York State Commission on Educational Leadership, and the executive committee of the World's Fair. He accepted the last position as a favor to Robert Moses in gratitude to Moses for his assistance in securing the site of the Lincoln Center campus for Fordham. FUA, McGinley Papers, McGinley to John J. McGinty, January 9, 1964.

31. The other Jesuit university presidents who were part of this unsuccessful *coup d'état* were Paul C. Reinert of St. Louis University, Michael P. Walsh of Boston College, Charles S. Casassa of Loyola University in Los Angeles, Albert A. Lemieux of Seattle University, and W. Patrick Donnelly of Loyola University in New Orleans. Paul Fitzgerald regarded Father Reinert as the ringleader of the rebels. Fitzgerald, *Governance of Jesuit Colleges*, 124–30.

enhancing their own cultural enrichment. He also shared Gannon's detestation of unnamed and undefined liberals, "for whom no good thing exists in heaven or upon earth that can transcend themselves."[32]

Although McGinley could be charming in dealing with students, he valued his privacy and chose to live in a special apartment he created for himself at the south end of the second floor of the Administration Building rather than in Loyola Hall, the main Jesuit residence. The provincial chided him gently for his aloofness from the rest of the Jesuit community after receiving complaints that he failed to meet with some of them for more than a year. Another source of irritation was McGinley's habit of prolonging dinner because no one was permitted to leave the table in the Jesuit refectory until the father rector finished his dessert.[33]

McGinley was an accomplished and successful player in the arcane world of ecclesiastical politics, which flourished even in a mendicant order like the Society of Jesus, as Father Robert I. Gannon liked to call the Jesuits. When Father McGinley sent the father general a new typewriter, he attached to it a small metal plaque to remind Father Janssens where it came from every time he used it. At the centennial celebration of the Pontifical Gregorian University in Rome in 1953, Fordham was the only American Jesuit university represented, much to the amazement of the astute American assistant, Father Vincent A. McCormick, who told McGinley, "Too bad Ours over there do not understand the propriety of such acts of courtesy." One of the ten cardinals present at the celebration in Rome was Fordham's most illustrious alumnus, Francis Cardinal Spellman, whom McGinley sedulously cultivated, although he never achieved the same close personal relationship with Spellman as had Robert I. Gannon.[34]

32. *Ram*, February 10, 1949, October 2, 1952, November 24, 1954.

33. FUA, McGinley Papers, McMahon to McGinley, December 1, 1953; Schroth, *Fordham: A History and Memoir*, 217–18.

34. FUA, McGinley Papers, Brother James Kenny, S.J., to Vincent A. McCormick, October 29, 1953; McCormick to McGinley, October 19, 1953.

16

SLOUCHING TOWARD
THE SIXTIES

The Lincoln Center Campus

Without a doubt the single most important contribution that Father McGinley made to Fordham University was the establishment of the Lincoln Center campus in Manhattan. For many years both the faculty and students had complained about the cramped quarters in the two Fordham facilities located in Manhattan: the Vincent Building at 302 Broadway that housed the Law School, the School of Education, and the downtown Business School; and the two converted townhouses on East 39th Street that housed the School of Social Service. Father McGinley tells the story of how Fordham acquired the Lincoln Center campus with a disarming modesty that minimizes the crucial role that he played in the process. When McGinley heard that Robert Moses, one of the most powerful men in New York as the city's master planner and quintessential power broker, was about to erect the Coliseum Building at Columbus Circle, he asked for an appointment to see him. Moses invited McGinley to his home on Long Island, where McGinley asked him if Fordham could rent five floors in the new Coliseum building for classrooms.

"I was kind of scared," McGinley admitted, but the response of Moses to this request swept McGinley off his feet. "No, you don't want that," Moses said about the space in the Coliseum. "It's not built for that purpose. It's built for offices." Instead Moses offered to bring McGinley in on the urban renewal project that he was planning in the run-down area one block west of the Coliseum. McGinley naïvely asked what an urban renewal project was. Moses explained it to him and then asked, "How much room would you need, ten acres?" "When he mentioned acres, I couldn't believe it," said McGinley. "I never heard anyone talk about New York real estate in terms of acres. I gulped." Moses showed McGinley a map of the neighborhood. "Look," he said, "maybe a couple of these blocks; that would be about ten acres or something like it."

McGinley was content to settle for most of the two blocks between Columbus and Amsterdam avenues from 60th Street to 62nd Street, which amounted to about seven-and-a-half acres. Fordham acquired this prime

Father Laurence J. McGinley, S.J., president of Fordham University, 1949–63.

real estate at the bargain price of $2,242,610. McGinley chose the site because it was close to the IRT and IND subway lines at Columbus Circle and it was adjacent to the spacious Paulist Church of St. Paul the Apostle, which he hoped to use for special religious ceremonies. Moses's gift to Fordham was only a small part of the Lincoln Square Renewal Project, which was to become the Lincoln Center for the Performing Arts and would include the new home of the Metropolitan Opera, the New York Philharmonic Orchestra, the New York City Ballet, and the Julliard School of Music.

Fordham's acquisition of the Lincoln Center site provoked a lawsuit from an attorney who claimed that it was a violation of the separation of church and state. This determined gentleman waged a protracted legal battle against Fordham with the support of Protestants and Other Americans United for the Separation of Church and State, an aggressively secularistic organization that later revealed its true colors when it dropped "Protestant" from its name. McGinley was advised that the easiest way to contest the lawsuit from POAU was to claim that Fordham University was not a Catholic institution. McGinley adamantly refused to fight the case on those grounds and ultimately was vindicated when he won the case after two appeals to the U.S. Supreme Court. The provincial advised McGinley to clear the Lincoln Square project with Cardinal Spellman, who was a personal friend of Moses's. Spellman congratulated McGinley on his success and told him, "This is the greatest thing that has happened to Fordham since my predecessor Archbishop Hughes built the university up at Rose Hill."[1]

Father McGinley displayed imagination and boldness in making his plans for developing Fordham's new Lincoln Center campus. He hoped to double the enrollment in Fordham's downtown schools from 4,000 to 8,000 by raising $25,500,000 for new facilities over the course of the next few years. He could not have been unaware that only twenty years earlier his predecessor Father Robert I. Gannon had been unsuccessful in his efforts to raise even $1 million for Fordham's centennial campaign.

McGinley envisioned a building program that was to take place in three stages, which quickly fell behind schedule. The first phase was the construction of the new Law School. The unveiling of the cornerstone took place on May 3, 1960, in the presence of 4,000 guests at a ceremony that could not have pleased POAU because it illustrated the amicable relationship between church and state in the United States. The principal address was delivered by Earl Warren, the chief justice of the United States, and Cardinal Spellman offered a dedicatory prayer. The new four-story premises of the Law School and its adjacent library were ready for occupancy the following October with 700 students, a year behind schedule.

The second stage of Father McGinley's plans for the Lincoln Center campus proved to be even more difficult to accomplish on time. He wanted a building to provide classrooms, faculty offices, and improved library facilities for a new downtown college and for the Schools of Business, Education, Social Service, and General Studies. It was scheduled to open in 1962 but was not finished until 1969. Named the Leon Lowenstein

1. McGinley, *As I Remember Fordham: Selections from the Sesquicentennial Oral History Project* (New York: Fordham University Press, 1991), 1–3. McGinley diplomatically omitted mentioning that Moses was furious when he showed him the galleys of an article that *America* was about to publish indirectly criticizing the methods that Moses had employed to acquire the Lincoln Square real estate because it had allegedly resulted in the dislocation of many poor residents. At McGinley's insistence, *America* quashed the article. According to Father Schroth, only three of the 2,805 residential and commercial tenants displaced by the entire Lincoln Square Renewal Project were evicted. Raymond A. Schroth, S.J., *Fordham: A History and Memoir* (Chicago: Loyola University Press, 2002), 244.

Father McGinley inspects the progress of the
construction of the campus at Lincoln Center.

Slouching Toward the Sixties

Building in honor of a prominent benefactor, the fourteen-story building soon proved to be inadequate to meet the needs of the rapidly expanding enrollment. As so often in the history of Fordham, the basic problem was the lack of an adequate endowment and the parsimonious response of the alumni for financial support.[2]

Unfortunately the third phase of McGinley's plans for Lincoln Center never got beyond the planning stage. He hoped to erect another building on the campus that would provide additional space for classrooms and laboratories as well as a student union building and an ornamental campanile. However, financial constraints prevented any further major expansion of the physical plant at Lincoln Center for more than forty years, except for the construction in 1993 of a twenty-story residence building, which was later called McMahon Hall, in honor of Father George McMahon, S.J., a popular dean and administrative vice president.[3]

The Evolving Jesuit Faculty

Father Raymond Schroth singled out Father Thurston Noble Davis, the dean of Fordham College, as "the prime reforming force" at Fordham in the 1950s, One of Davis's major contributions at Fordham College was the organization of the Honors Program. The program was first introduced by Father Gannon in the late 1930s as part of his effort to restore Fordham's academic luster, but it was Thurston Davis who really devised a challenging and well-coordinated program of studies for the Honors Program. It consisted of a three-year sequence beginning with a probationary period in sophomore year, when candidates for the program were assigned a mentor to help them in the composition of four substantial papers on literary topics. The students were also required to attend weekly seminars at which they discussed their assigned readings. Those who were accepted into the program were expected to spend their junior and senior years examining the philosophical issues associated with their area of concentration in keeping with the longstanding Jesuit tradition of emphasis on

2. *Ram*, April 17, 1959. The first occupant of the Lowenstein Building was the new downtown college. Originally called the Liberal Arts College, it was later renamed the College at Lincoln Center and in 1996 Fordham College at Lincoln Center. John D. Rockefeller III, the chairman of the board of the Lincoln Center for the Performing Arts, generously allowed Fordham to use the coveted name of Lincoln Center for its new downtown college. He also supported Father McGinley throughout his legal battle with POAU. Schroth, *Fordham: A History and Memoir*, 244–45.

3. Father Schroth described Father McMahon as "one of those 'Mr. Fordham's' who knit generations together." Schroth, *Fordham: A History and Memoir*, 253.

the importance of philosophy. The Honors Program culminated in senior year with the submission of a senior thesis of at least fifty pages that the candidates were required to defend in a one-hour oral examination.[4]

A spinoff of the Honors Program was the opportunity for honor students to spend their junior year in France, studying at either the Sorbonne or the Institut Catholique in Paris. It was inaugurated in 1951 with nine students. Thurston Davis made sure that the time spent in France would not be a vacation from serious academic work. He established detailed rules that only the most highly motivated students were likely to follow. They were required to obtain prior approval from him for the courses they intended to take in Paris and then to submit monthly progress reports, certification of the successful completion of their courses, and letters of commendation from their professors. In addition they were expected to demonstrate fluency in French upon their return to Rose Hill for their senior year.[5]

The decision of the American Jesuit superiors after World War II to send their most talented young men for advanced degrees to the best American and European universities began to pay handsome dividends for Fordham in the 1950s as Father Schroth has noted. Father Davis was just one of three young Jesuits who arrived at Rose Hill in that decade with doctorates from Harvard. Davis had studied under one of the leading classical scholars of that day, Werner Jaeger. Father Joseph Frese, a specialist in American colonial history who later became academic vice president, was a disciple of Samuel Eliot Morison and Arthur Schlesinger Sr. Father Joseph Fitzpatrick, who virtually founded the Sociology Department at Fordham, had studied under Oscar Handlin, an expert in American immigration history. Handlin was "a Jew who taught Fitzpatrick what it meant to be Irish," in Schroth's memorable phrase.[6]

Father Fitzpatrick was to devote his whole life, both professionally and pastorally, to the social and spiritual well-being of the Puerto Rican community in New York City during the peak period of the Puerto Rican migration. He first became interested in the Puerto Ricans in 1944 while serving as a chaplain in a city hospital in New York City, where he had occasion one day to administer the sacrament of the sick to a pregnant young Puerto Rican woman who was about to undergo a Caesarian section. Eight hours later he was summoned to the operating room to give the last rites to

4. FUA, McGinley Papers, Davis to McGinley, September 10, 1952.
5. FUA, McGinley Papers, Davis to Roger, November 15, 1951.
6. Schroth, *Fordham: A History and Memoir*, 219.

this woman, who died while he was there. The head nurse in the maternity ward told Fitzpatrick afterward that her death was the fault of an incompetent resident doctor who wanted to gain experience performing Caesarian sections. "This was the beginning of my insight that there were people called Puerto Ricans in New York," said Fitzpatrick, "and that they often suffered as helpless victims."[7]

Fitzpatrick made the first of his many trips to Puerto Rico in 1952 and received strong support from both Father McGinley and the provincial, Father John McMahon, for his efforts on behalf of the Puerto Ricans. He was also influential in shaping the response of the archdiocese of New York to this pastoral challenge and helped to establish a center at the Catholic University in Ponce, Puerto Rico, which trained hundreds of priests and religious for work in Hispanic parishes in New York. Although he was an innately humble man, he was intensely proud of the fact that he was the only person named Fitzpatrick who was ever named Puerto Rican Man of the Year by the grateful Puerto Rican community in New York.[8]

In the early years of his apostolate to the Puerto Rican immigrants, Fitzpatrick collaborated closely with another Harvard-trained Jesuit on the Fordham faculty, the anthropologist Father J. Franklin Ewing, who helped him with his research. Ewing devoted many summers to his pet project of excavating the remains of the Indian village of Ossernenon, the site of the death of the North American Martyrs. A survivor of a Japanese internment camp as a missionary in the Philippines during World War II, Ewing was never one to shy away from controversy, boldly defending the compatibility of evolution and Christian faith at a time when it was not politically (or theologically) correct to do so in the pre–Vatican II Catholic Church. Ewing once startled the guests at a Fordham symposium on the Ignatian philosophy of education by rising from his place in the audience to decry the "hyper-reverence" of the Catholic laity for their clergy. "There is nothing in the ordination ceremony," he declared, "that endows the priest with the charism of an educator."[9]

Harvard was not the only source of the academic revitalization of Fordham's Jesuit faculty. Father Leo McLaughlin and Father J. Quentin Lauer,

7. Joseph Fitzpatrick, S.J., *The Stranger Is Our Own: Reflections on the Journey of Puerto Rican Migrants* (Kansas City: Sheed & Ward, 1996), 4–6.

8. FUA, McGinley Papers, Fitzpatrick to McGinley, May 30, 1952; McGinley to McMahon, June 4, 1952. Joseph Fitzpatrick, S.J., Lecture at St. Joseph's Seminary, Dunwoodie, March 3, 1989.

9. FUA, McGinley Papers, Fitzpatrick to McGinley, May 30, 1952. *Ram*, September 15, 1952, April 26, 1956.

both graduates of the University of Paris, brought to the Fordham campus the intellectual ferment of the European universities. McLaughlin was to become president of Fordham during one of the most troubled periods of the university's history. Lauer was to play a major role in broadening the scope and interests of Fordham's Philosophy Department from the rigid neo-Thomism that characterized it in the pre-war years.[10] According to another talented Jesuit member of Fordham's philosophy department, Father Gerald McCool, the popularity of neo-scholasticism or neo-Thomism reached its peak in the 1950s. The decline was so rapid and so complete that Professor Philip Gleason believes it is no exaggeration to refer to it as a collapse.[11]

Perhaps the most influential figure in the professionalization of Fordham's Philosophy Department was Father Joseph Donceel, a Belgian Jesuit of the Flemish Province, who found himself trapped in the United States by the outbreak of World War II and became a U.S. citizen. Donceel introduced to Fordham the "Transcendental Thomism" of his fellow Jesuits Joseph Maréchal and Karl Rahner, which was a bold and innovative attempt to "reconcile" Thomism with modern philosophy, especially the philosophy of Immanuel Kant. In the opinion of at least one well-informed historian of American Catholic higher education, Professor Philip Gleason, Fordham became the leading center for the promotion and transmission of Transcendental Thomism in the United States.[12]

Donceel himself also gave generous credit for the modernization of the Philosophy Department at Fordham to such colleagues as Father Robert Roth, a future dean of Fordham College; Dr. Anton Pegis, later the director of the Pontifical Institute of Medieval Studies in Toronto; Dr. Robert Pollock; Dr. Dietrich von Hildebrand; and Dr. Elizabeth Salmon. They were reinforced by the arrival of other European-trained Jesuits, not only Father Lauer, but also W. Norris Clarke and Robert O'Connell. "Their Thomism had weakened and died in France," said Donceel dryly, who had a particularly high regard for Norris Clarke as "one of the leading Catholic philosophers of this country." At Donceel's instigation, Clarke served for twenty-five years as the American editor-in-chief of the *International Philosophical Quarterly*, published by the Flemish Province of the Belgian Jesuits.[13]

10. Schroth, *Fordham: A History and Memoir*, 219.

11. McCool wrote extensively on the rise and fall of neo-Thomism in American Catholic colleges. See Philip Gleason, *Contending with Modernity: Catholic Higher Education in the Twentieth Century* (New York: Oxford University Press, 1995), 297, 407.

12. Ibid., 302.

13. Joseph Donceel, S.J., W. Norris Clarke, S.J., *As I Remember Fordham*, 37–39, 52–54.

Still other impressive Jesuit scholars on the Fordham faculty included William F. Lynch, a brilliant English teacher who lectured and wrote extensively on the relationship between faith and the theater. He is best remembered for *Christ and Apollo: The Dimensions of the Literary Imagination* (1960). Father Robert W. Gleason, S.J., was the author of some dozen books and was instrumental in establishing the graduate program in the Department of Theology. Lay professors who added to Fordham's academic reputation included the historian Robert Remini and the sociologist Thomas O'Dea, although they both spent most of their academic careers at other institutions.

Fordham could boast of two scholarly publications. One was *Thought*, founded in 1926 as "A Quarterly of the Sciences and Letters." The first editor was Wilfrid Parsons, S.J., who also continued to serve as the editor of *America*. Professor Emmett Curran considered *Thought* the most visible manifestation of Fordham's commitment to Catholic scholarship. It ceased publication in 1992.

Fordham's other scholarly journal was *Traditio*, an annual that published learned articles on ancient and medieval history and religion of the same high caliber as the best European scholarly journals. It was founded by two German émigré scholars at the Catholic University of America: Johannes Quasten, a patrologist, and Stephen Kuttner, a specialist in the history of canon law. *Traditio* was originally published by a small scholarly press in New York City between 1943 and 1949 but was discontinued in 1949 after the death of the publisher. Father Rudolf Arbesmann, O.S.A., another émigré scholar from Nazi Germany and chair of the Classics Department at Fordham, persuaded Father Edward A. Quain, S.J., the academic vice president to bring the journal to Fordham. In 1951 volume seven of *Traditio* appeared for the first time under the imprint of Fordham University Press.

By the 1950s and 1960s Fordham had come a long way from the obscurantist mentality of Father George Bull, S.J., the dean of the Graduate School in the 1930s. By the 1960s, said Professor Emmett Curran, "the clear *perception* was that, among Jesuit colleges and universities in the East, Fordham was far and away the institution with the most scholarly production from its faculty."[14]

In the 1950s and 1960s intellectually rambunctious American Jesuits like Donceel, Ewing, and John Courtney Murray could count on little support from their Jesuit superiors, but Father Donceel was the only Fordham

14. Emmett Curran, personal communication to the author.

Father McGinley presents an honorary degree to Senator John F. Kennedy in 1958.

professor who was directly caught up in the aftermath of Pope Pius XII's 1950 encyclical *Humani Generis*, condemning the *nouvelle théologie* of such scholars as Henri de Lubac, S.J., and Yves Congar, O.P. At the behest of two censors in Rome, Father Janssens objected to Donceel's treatment of evolution in his textbook *Philosophical Psychology* (Fordham University Press, 1952) and forbade its sale or use in the classroom. Janssens complained that Donceel had not given sufficient attention to the "mind of the teaching authority of the contemporary church" (*mens magisterii Ecclesiae hodiernae*) on the topic of evolution, which meant *Humani Generis*. Father John McMahon conveyed Janssens's criticism to Donceel with a gentle and fatherly admonition to comply with the general's directives in the spirit of Jesuit obedience. Donceel did do so, and like Henri de Lubac and others, he lived to see a better day.[15]

15. FUA, McGinley Papers, Janssens to McMahon, March 25, 1954; McMahon to Donceel, April 2, 1954. De Lubac was made a cardinal in 1983 at eighty-seven, well past the age when he was likely to write anything that would be offensive to pious ears in Rome.

Brick-and-Mortar at Rose Hill

Although Father McGinley is especially remembered for his role in the creation of Fordham's Lincoln Center campus, he also made several important physical improvements at the Rose Hill campus. First, despite initial opposition from the father general, he greatly expanded the dormitory space with the construction of Martyrs' Court in 1950–51, enabling Fordham to begin to shed the unwelcome reputation of a commuter college. The building was named after three Jesuit missionaries who were martyred in upstate New York in the seventeenth century: Saints Isaac Jogues, René Goupil, and Jean de Lalande.

The state-of-the-art design of the sprawling four-story brick building represented a welcome departure from the sterile architectural features of many college dormitories. Martyrs' Court consisted of seven sections, each with a separate entrance, eliminating the need for long corridors. Each section contained two apartments on each floor with four double bedrooms, a common study area and a bathroom with shower facilities. The new building had accommodations for 400 students as well as for 25 Jesuit faculty members.[16]

McGinley's second building project at Rose Hill was forced upon him because of the deteriorating condition of Dealy Hall, which was centrally located on the campus and was, in McGinley's words, "one of the great traditional buildings of Fordham." However, its massive granite exterior walls concealed the fact that the four-story building was a firetrap because of the extensive use of wood in the construction of the interior of the east wing, which dated from 1867. McGinley estimated that it would cost $1 million to demolish the building and that it would be prohibitively expensive to replace it with a comparable stone building.

His solution was to leave the exterior walls intact, but to gut the interior of the building, replacing the wooden rafters with steel beams. The renovations were done in two stages in the mid-1950s, first in the older east wing and later in the west wing, which dated from the 1890s. McGinley used the opportunity to eliminate the remaining dormitories and dining hall from Dealy, transforming it into an exclusively academic building with classrooms and offices, except for a chapel on the ground floor. He hoped to create no fewer than fifty new classrooms in the two wings of Dealy, which proved to be a wildly optimistic prediction. By 1956 twenty-eight new classrooms were in operation in the east wing of Dealy Hall.[17]

16. *Ram*, October 27, 1949.
17. *Ram*, January 16, 1956.

Unfortunately, in renovating Dealy Hall, McGinley's architect also decided to remove the handsome mansard roof with its attractive cupola and replace it with an ugly concrete structure on the top floor that had all the grace and charm of an air raid bunker in the sky. Students were puzzled about the function of the structure. A reporter for the *Ram* hazarded the guess that it contained the machinery for the supply and removal of air (perhaps cool air and hot air respectively) from the classrooms on the lower floors. One need only compare Dealy Hall today with the recently renovated Hughes Hall with its modernistic version of a mansard roof and its stylish windows to regret that Father McGinley did not entrust the renovation of Dealy Hall to a more talented architect.[18]

Father McGinley's third major building project at Rose Hill was the construction of a much-needed Student Center adjacent to the gymnasium, which was built at a cost of $3.5 million, half of it a loan from the federal government. It was dedicated by Cardinal Spellman in February 1960 and opened in May of that year, just as the new Lincoln Center campus was beginning to take shape. The spacious three-story Campus Center (which was later named in honor of Father McGinley) included a cafeteria for 1,000 students, a faculty dining room (originally restricted to religious faculty), lounges for the students and lay faculty, meeting rooms for lectures and social events, a Rathskeller, and even a U.S. Post Office substation in the basement. The new student cafeteria enabled Father McGinley to close the cafeteria in Keating Hall as he had already done with the dining room in Dealy Hall and to consolidate all of Fordham's student dining facilities in one place. A side benefit of this consolidation was that it freed valuable space in Keating Hall for classrooms and other academic purposes. The utilitarian new Campus Center brought many needed amenities to the Rose Hill campus for the students, but its design failed to impress architectural critics who were skeptical about the architect's claim that his inspiration for the building was the soaring interior space of Grand Central Terminal.[19]

A fourth building project, completed shortly before Father McGinley's departure in 1963, was the construction of Faber Hall, a seven-story addition to Loyola Hall, the main Jesuit residence on the campus. It provided living quarters and dining facilities for some one hundred Jesuits and benefited not only the members of the Jesuit faculty but also the wider

18. FUA, McGinley to Thomas E. Henneberry, November 29, 1954. *Ram*, January 16, 1956.

19. *Ram*, October 11, 1956, June 12, 1963.

Fordham community because it made more residential space available to students as Jesuit professors moved to their new quarters in Faber Hall from student dormitories, especially Martyrs' Court.

Father McGinley's contributions to Fordham were not limited to brick-and-mortar. In 1961 he secured Fordham's membership in one of the most prestigious national scholastic honor societies, Phi Beta Kappa, an achievement that had eluded Father Gannon as far back as 1938. Fordham was only the third Catholic college to achieve this distinction and the first Catholic men's college to do so.[20] McGinley also broke new ground in May 1959 when he announced the establishment of a board of lay trustees for Fordham, a decision with momentous implications for the future. In addition to his responsibilities at Fordham, McGinley was also deeply involved in the plans of the New York Province of the Society of Jesus to build a new seminary in Shrub Oak, near Peekskill, New York. The estimated cost was $5 million, and Fordham was assigned a quota of $400,000. McGinley dutifully dispatched a series of begging letters to alumni to meet the quota.[21]

When it was announced on April 25, 1963, that McGinley would step down as the president of Fordham on June 30, one of the most generous tributes he received came from the *New York Times*, in an era when its editorial page still expressed appreciation to religious institutions for their contribution to American education and public life. The *Times* praised him especially for his role in the development of the Lincoln Square project. "He has made an invaluable intellectual and educational contribution to his city and to his country," said the *Times*. "He has won our admiration and gratitude."[22]

Storm Clouds on the Horizon

Scholars have questioned the claim that the 1950s were a monolithically placid and conformist era. Jay Dolan contends that, for American Catholics, it would be more accurate to describe the 1950s as a Janus-like decade when many of them looked both to the past and to the future. The older generation of American Catholics looked back with pride and self-confidence on the achievements of their immigrant forbears, who had created a thriving American Catholic subculture, especially in the working-

20. The other two institutions were the College of St. Catherine in St. Paul, Minnesota, and the Catholic University of America. *Ram*, October 5, 1961.

21. *Ram*, November 7, 1952. At the time there were 1,500 Jesuits in the New York province.

22. *New York Times*, April 26, 1963.

class neighborhoods of the industrial cities of the Midwest and Northeast. However, as the younger generation of American Catholics, who were better educated than their parents or grandparents, looked to the future, they faced the new challenge of preserving their distinctive cultural and religious identity as they moved into upscale middle-class suburbs and sought professional and social acceptance in an increasingly secular American society. Fordham graduates exemplified Dolan's comment that "Catholics seemed to sit at the top of the world."[23] Many, if not most of them, were the sons of working-class parents, and they ended their days as successful retired lawyers, doctors, bankers, brokers, and businessmen living in comfortable surroundings in Westchester, Fairfield, Nassau, or Bergen counties.

One area where the dichotomy between the past and the future was most apparent for American Catholics in the 1950s was in the field of education. As Sister Patricia Byrne, C.S.J., has pointed out, by the 1950s American Catholics had literally created the largest private school system in the history of the world with more than 4 million students without a penny of government money, an achievement that was made possible by the generosity of the Catholic laity and the contributed services of the men and women religious and the often-underpaid lay teachers.

However, in 1955, Monsignor John Tracy Ellis, who was a grateful recipient of his own education in small Catholic schools in rural Illinois, detonated a bomb in the sedate world of American Catholic education when he questioned the quality of this educational system on the college and university levels. Ellis commanded attention and respect because he was professor of church history at the Catholic University of America in Washington, D.C., and the preeminent Catholic church historian of his generation. He accused American Catholics of intellectual indolence and accused American Catholic educators of perpetuating academic mediocrity.

Ellis raised the hackles of many Catholic educators when he said that American Catholics could no longer excuse their unimpressive intellectual performance by attributing it exclusively to anti-Catholic bias and to their relative poverty as a working-class community. He asked American Catholics to confront the embarrassing question of whether their basic problem might be a lack of a love of learning for its own sake, which had been a hallmark of Catholic culture for many centuries. Ellis also decried the proliferation of academically and financially weak Catholic colleges in

23. Jay P. Dolan, *In Search of an American Catholicism* (New York: Oxford University Press, 2002), 182, 189.

the United States. Privately he often said that the best friend of Catholic higher education was the sheriff who periodically padlocked the doors of these institutions when they could no longer pay their bills.[24]

Some members of the male religious order that operated the largest number of Catholic colleges and universities in the United States took umbrage at Ellis's remarks because they thought they were directed at them. However, at Fordham, Ellis's criticisms were welcomed by the editors of the *Ram*, if not by the administration and the faculty. One student expressed his gratitude to Ellis by saying, "Let us hope that this smug attitude which we radiate of being self-professedly the elect or chosen with the keys to the deposit of truth will be dispelled."[25]

Ellis's critique, "American Catholics and the Intellectual Life," was originally an address that he delivered at the annual convention of the Catholic Commission on Intellectual and Cultural Affairs in St. Louis on May 14, 1955. It received much wider circulation when an expanded version was published in *Thought*, the scholarly Fordham periodical, in August 1955. The editor of *Thought*, Father John Courtney Murray, S.J., told Ellis: "I count it as the one single achievement during my term as editor." "Your article was splendid both in content and in tone," Murray assured Ellis. "You said all the things that badly needed to be said, and with such balance and urbanity that no one but a churl could possibly take offense. It only remains to be seen if the churls are still around."[26]

Ellis was astonished by the "extent and persistence" of the favorable reaction that he received. "Some, needless to say, would like to poison me," he speculated, "but one must expect that reaction from plain talking such as I indulged in." He told a close priest friend and fellow educator, "I am not interested in gilding the lily but rather in the truth, and the record, as you will readily presume, is really shameful."[27] As Father John Courtney Murray had anticipated, the churls were quick to express their

24. John Tracy Ellis, "American Catholics and the Intellectual Life," *Thought* 30 (August 1955): 351–88. It was later reprinted as a monograph, *American Catholics and the Intellectual Life* (Chicago: Heritage Foundation, 1956). For a perceptive analysis of the importance of Ellis's critique in precipitating a "grand debate" on American Catholic higher education, see Gleason, *Contending with Modernity*, 287–91. "Among the factors contributing to the impact of Ellis's critique," said Gleason, "his personal stature cannot be overlooked."

25. *Ram*, January 16, 1956.

26. Archives of the Catholic University of America: John Tracy Ellis Papers (hereafter ACUA: JTEP), Murray to Ellis, October 11, 1955.

27. ACUA: JTEP: Ellis to Rev. Edward Cardinal, C.S.V., July 26, 1955; November 14, 1955; December 25, 1956.

dissent. More than one American bishop intimated to Ellis privately that it was a disservice to the church for him to wash dirty linen in public. One of the most articulate and witty churls to register his public displeasure with Ellis's critique was a former president of Fordham University, Father Robert I. Gannon, who took the opportunity of an address at a Manhattan College Alumni Dinner in 1958 to dispute many of Ellis's allegations of the shortcomings of American Catholic higher education.

Gannon called Ellis's critique "a little spiritual sputnik of our own," a disparaging reference to the Soviet space satellite launched the previous October that shocked Americans into recognizing the deficiencies of their science education programs. "Monsignor Ellis wanted to prove that there were not enough Monsignor Ellises in the Catholic Church," said Gannon waspishly, although he softened his tone by adding, "and [on] that we are in agreement." He faulted Ellis for making exorbitant demands on an American Catholic community that was just emerging from its immigrant and working-class origins. Gannon also complained that Ellis had not given sufficient credit to Catholic universities for the progress they had recently made in creating bona fide research centers. However, in the opinion of some, Gannon weakened his own argument and unwittingly confirmed Ellis's thesis by stating that the primary purpose of Catholic colleges and universities should be to produce good teachers like the fictional Mr. Chips rather than exceptional scholars like the Einsteins and the Oppenheimers.[28]

It would be gratifying to think that both Ellis and Gannon were equally pleased when, a dozen years after Ellis dropped his bombshell, thirteen Fordham seniors received Woodrow Wilson Fellowships, surpassing Fordham's previous record of nine fellowships awarded in 1959. Fordham's performance in 1966 was exceeded only by that of Yale and Columbia in their geographical division. In that same year two of the Fordham

28. *New York Catholic News*, March 1, 1958. Gannon also used his address to criticize Father Gustave Weigel, S.J., professor of ecclesiology at Woodstock College, and Father John J. Cavanaugh, C.S.C., the former president of the University of Notre Dame, for echoing much of what Ellis had said. Gannon could not resist adding that Cavanaugh had suggested that "amidst all this Catholic ignorance and decadence one beacon of hope was shining somewhere in the Middle West."

Gannon ignored another critic of American Catholic higher education, Thomas O'Dea, whose *American Catholic Dilemma: An Inquiry into the Intellectual Life* (New York: Mentor Paperback, 1958) was considered by Professor Philip Gleason as second in importance only to Ellis's critique. Gleason, *Contending with Modernity*, 292. In his acknowledgments O'Dea said that Father Laurence J. McGinley was the first one to suggest that he publish his book after reading a preliminary draft.

recipients of the Woodrow Wilson Fellowships also received Danforth Fellowships and seven other Fordham seniors received honorable mention from the Wilson Foundation.[29]

Even as Fordham gained national prominence as an academic institution, there were signs of the student restlessness and discontent that were to become a common phenomenon in American colleges and universities in the late 1950s and 1960s. The administration at Fordham viewed at least three short-lived student publications as so objectionable that they either removed the editors or shut down the publications entirely. Even students who were unsympathetic to the tone of these publications complained about the high-handed way that the decisions were made to censor them. In the case of one publication, a humor magazine called *The Thorn of Rose Hill*, the faculty advisor, Father J. Franklin Ewing, who did not suffer fools gladly, was informed of the decision in a curt memo. Meanwhile, outside the campus gates on Fordham Road, for several years beginning in 1956, students were offered free copies of an underground newspaper called *Mar* or *The Mar*, which the *Ram* described as an example of "illiterate, gutter journalism."[30]

A more ominous and unsettling development than rambunctious student editors or even underground newspapers was the unsubstantiated rumors that circulated on the Rose Hill campus that a small cadre of radical students were plotting a campus uprising. In the spring of 1959 they were reported to have burned a block "F" on the lawn and to be staging "practice riots" by tossing light bulbs, firecrackers, and (even more improbably) Molotov cocktails at night from the windows of their dormitory rooms. None of these alleged activities ever made their way to a police blotter, which is good reason for questioning their accuracy, but Father McGinley seemed to believe that the best response to revolution—either real or imagined—was preventive reforms. Consequently he responded positively to student requests that Fordham follow the example of St. Louis University, which had recently established a Student Advisory Council.[31]

In late October 1959 McGinley announced a three-point program for better communications between the administration and the students. First, he promised that he would direct senior administrators to attend periodically the monthly meetings of the University Student Council. Second, he pledged to convene an annual convocation of the entire undergraduate

29. *Ram*, March 18, 1966. The other two publications were the *Month* and the *Scrivener*.

30. *Ram*, October 9, 1958, October 1, 1959.

31. *Ram*, April 16, 1959.

student body at which he would deliver a report on the state of the university similar to the annual reports he made to the board of trustees and the faculty. Third, he assured the students that he would continue to meet with them every six months and invited them to submit an agenda for the meetings.[32]

The *Ram* pronounced Father McGinley's proposals a good start, but student dissatisfaction flared up over other issues like prohibitions against allowing controversial public figures such as Governor George C. Wallace of Alabama, a prominent segregationist, to speak on campus. Many students who abhorred Wallace's racist views were offended that they were prevented from hearing him by what they considered the paternalistic decision of administrators who paid lip service to the principle of freedom of expression.

The situation was more complicated than many students realized. During the summer of 1963 a Fordham student invited Wallace to speak at Rose Hill as part of Fordham's New Age lecture series. Shortly thereafter, on Sunday, September 15, 1963, the Ku Klux Klan set off an explosion in the 16th Street Baptist Church, a black church in Birmingham, killing four little girls and injuring twenty-two other people. Dr. Martin Luther King Jr. called it "one of the most vicious and tragic crimes ever perpetrated against humanity."

The NYPD told McGinley they would need every policeman in New York to preserve the peace if Wallace showed up on campus. "I thought this would have represented a great risk to the whole community," said McGinley, and he canceled the invitation to Wallace. "We were sacked in the press," recalled McGinley years later, but, he insisted, "if I had to do it again today, I would do the same thing."[33]

Faculty Discontents

The polarization among the undergraduates was paralleled by similar disagreements among the faculty about the purpose and direction of Fordham. These basic differences came to light in 1961 when a Self-Study Committee appointed by Father McGinley attempted to define the objectives of Fordham University and its constituent schools. The Self-Study Committee, acting in conjunction with the University Academic Advisory Council, achieved a sufficient consensus to assert that Fordham

32. *Ram*, November 5, 1959.

33. McGinley, *As I Remember Fordham*, 5–6. McGinley got the date wrong. The bombing occurred in 1963, not 1964.

University was a "Catholic university in the Jesuit tradition" and to declare that the objectives of Fordham College were to promote "an intelligent appreciation of religious, philosophical and moral values."[34]

Three months earlier a draft of the statement of the university's objectives had been circulated among the 353 full-time members of the faculty, but only 193 of them replied. Those who did reply voiced a wide variety of opinions. One Jesuit faculty member expressed concern that the religious mission of the university was emphasized to the detriment of the intellectual mission, while another Jesuit was grateful to references to Fordham as a Catholic and Jesuit institution, because he had scarcely heard those attributes mentioned in the committee meetings he had attended. "If Fordham is not a Catholic and Jesuit institution," he asked, "why are we running the school?"

One layman thought that the reference to the Jesuit tradition was meaningless because there was such a wide disparity of academic standards among American Jesuit colleges and universities. "Some were advancing vigorously," this professor thought, "but others were just proliferating." Another faculty member, who may have been reading Ellis; Father Gustave Weigel, S.J.; and O'Dea, faulted the statement of objectives for failing to mention that one of the goals of Fordham should be to produce scholars and leaders. "As one who has been connected with Jesuit education as a student and teacher since 1909," he said, "I consider the statement, as it stands, hopelessly inadequate." One dyspeptic professor opined that the proposed statement of objectives would be more appropriate for a third-rate Catholic girls' college, which drew a tart comment from the director of the Self-Study Committee, Dr. Francis J. Donohue, that "even a third-rate Catholic girls' college must have some worthwhile function."[35]

After the release of the report of the Self-Study Committee, as Father McGinley neared the end of his presidency at Fordham, he reflected privately on the difficulty of administering a modern American university while remaining faithful to the spiritual inspiration of St. Ignatius Loyola. "There are, as you know," he told his friend and provincial, Father John McGinty, "those who do not find this possible. I have never agreed," he

34. FUA, AF #29, Francis J. Donohue, The Fordham University Self-Study: Extracts from the Annual Report of the Executive Director, June 1961.

35. FUA, AF #29, Francis J. Donohue, The Fordham University Self-Study, The Objectives of the University: A Preliminary Report to the Executive Committee of the Self-Study, March 1961.

told McGinty, "and remain convinced that the Society can retain all the fullness of the spirit of obedience and still conduct universities."[36]

In retrospect, if not at the time of his departure from Fordham then perhaps a short time later, Father McGinley may have felt fortunate that he left Fordham when he did. He had been president for fourteen years. During the next ten years, Fordham was to have no fewer than three presidents. Each of them had a different background, different talents, and different philosophies of education, as well as different conceptions of the role of the president of an American Jesuit university. However, they all had one thing in common. They were to face challenges that no other president of Fordham had to face in the course of the previous 122 years. As Father McGinley was packing his bags at Rose Hill in 1963, the tumultuous 1960s were announcing their arrival in full force, and nowhere was the impact of 1960s to be felt more keenly than on American college campuses.

36. FUA, McGinley Papers, McGinley to McGinty, December 11, 1961. At the University of Notre Dame, Father Theodore Hesburgh, C.S.C., was as committed as Father McGinley was at Fordham to maintaining the Catholic character of his institution while operating a first-rate university. Like Father McGinley, Father Hesburgh also initiated a self-study of Notre Dame in 1961. The result revealed how difficult it was to reconcile and preserve the dual commitment to academic excellence and Catholic identity. Gleason, *Contending with Modernity*, 296.

FORDHAM'S DECADE
OF THREE PRESIDENTS

17

A Society and Church in Turmoil

Friday, November 22, 1963, is a date that remains so deeply embedded in the memory of every American who was alive on that day that many can recall the exact time and place when they first heard the news of the assassination of President John F. Kennedy in Dallas, Texas. The tragedy was a shock to all Americans, but especially to American Catholics, because Kennedy's election three years earlier symbolized their acceptance as full-fledged members of American society. From another perspective, it marked "the end of Protestant America," according to Professor Martin Marty, a distinguished Lutheran historian of American religion who is not much given to exaggeration.[1]

Many Americans, not just Catholics, found the year 1963 an unexpectedly disappointing and discouraging turning point in the history of their country. The decade had begun on an optimistic and positive note symbolized by the presence in the White House of a handsome and charismatic president who was the youngest person ever elected to that office. His assassination ushered in an era of unprecedented discord and violence in modern American history that was punctuated by the assassination of Dr. Martin Luther King Jr. on April 4, 1968, and the assassination of President Kennedy's forty-two-year-old younger brother, Senator Robert F. Kennedy, two months later.

By that date the country was convulsed in the upheavals of the civil rights movement and polarized by the Vietnam War. Popular discontent, especially among younger Americans, reached such a dangerous boiling point that President Kennedy's successor, President Lyndon B. Johnson,

---

1. Cit. in Jay P. Dolan, *In Search of an American Catholicism* (New York: Oxford University Press, 2002), 192. There were exceptions to the general outpouring of grief over the death of President Kennedy. On the day of the assassination, a history professor in the Graduate School of Arts and Sciences at Fordham, who was well known for his conservative political views, refused a request from a student to cancel the class. "It is too bad that it happened," he said, "but many people will be glad that he is dead." The author was a student in that class.

could not appear in public without precipitating violent protests. A year earlier, in December 1967, when Johnson attended the funeral Mass in New York City of Cardinal Spellman, one of the staunchest supporters of the Vietnam War, he traveled from the airport to Central Park by helicopter and had to be virtually smuggled in and out of the back door of St. Patrick's Cathedral for his own safety.

The year of President Kennedy's assassination was also a seminal date for American Catholics and for Catholics throughout the world because of the death of Pope John XXIII six months earlier. In 1958 this pope had inaugurated a new era in the modern history of the Catholic Church with his cordial reference to the contemporary world and his openness to dialogue with non-Catholic and even non-Christian religions. He was elected pope at the age of seventy-five in the confident expectation that he would be a caretaker pontiff who would preserve the status quo in the Church until the selection of a younger successor.

However, this devout and deeply conservative man shocked many of the cardinals who had elected him when he proved to be one of the great reforming pontiffs in modern Church history. A year before his death John XXIII set in motion many far-reaching changes in the Church (not all of which he would have welcomed or approved) when he convened the Second Vatican Council. He set the tone for the council when he distanced himself from the "prophets who are always forecasting doom as if the end of the world were at hand" and reminded the council fathers that the "deposit of faith, the truths contained in our venerable doctrine, are one thing; the fashion in which they are expressed but with the same meaning and the same judgment is another thing."

As both an American and a Catholic university, by the mid-1960s Fordham could hardly have remained immune to the winds of change swirling around Rose Hill and Lincoln Center from both American society and the Catholic Church. By an odd coincidence, the year 1963, so fateful for Americans of every religious persuasion and none, and for Catholics throughout the world, also proved to be a turning point in the coming-of-age of Fordham as a modern American and Catholic university. In that year the administration and faculty of the university began to grapple with the findings and recommendations of a comprehensive two-and-a-half-year self-study of the operation of the university.

The Self-Study of 1960–63

The Self-Study of 1960–63 was the most comprehensive and thoroughly researched evaluation of Fordham University that the administration and faculty had ever undertaken up to that date, far more extensive than the self-study that the university had undertaken ten years earlier. The final report, which was submitted in January 1963 to the Commission on Institutions of Higher Education of the Middle States Association of Colleges and Secondary Schools, was a meticulously documented appraisal of selected aspects of the university's operation. It was supplemented by eight highly informative mimeographed volumes containing the minutes of the meetings of the various faculty committees involved in the self-study and their criticisms and recommendations.

The unusual and innovative nature of the self-study of 1960–63 owed its origins in 1958 to the friendly relationship that had developed between Dr. F. Taylor Jones, the executive secretary of the Commission on Institutions of Higher Education of the Middle States, and Father McGinley, who was a member of the commission. Because Fordham was due for a routine reevaluation of its accreditation in 1960, both Dr. Jones and Father McGinley agreed to replace the usual routine reevaluation process with an innovative pilot project at Fordham that would concentrate on a close analysis of perhaps a half-dozen aspects of the university's operation. Dr. Jones allowed Father McGinley to select the aspects to be examined because he had complete confidence in Fordham's ability to carry out this self-study with both competence and integrity. If it proved to be successful, Dr. Jones intended to use it as a model for the evaluation of other large universities.[2]

The self-study got under way in the spring of 1960 when Father Edward F. Clark, S.J., the academic vice president of Fordham, appointed Dr. Francis J. Donohue the executive director of the self-study. In June 1960 Father Clark was appointed the president of St. Peter's College in Jersey City and was replaced as academic vice president by Father Vincent T. O'Keefe, S.J. Dr. Donohue proved to be an excellent choice as executive director of the self-study. As both a former undergraduate and graduate student at Fordham, Donohue had a much closer acquaintance with the university than Father O'Keefe, whose experience at Fordham had been limited to teaching a class in the summer session. Over the course of the following two-and-a-half years Donohue amassed vital statistical information about the state of the university and conducted extensive consultations with the faculty about Fordham's strengths and weaknesses.

2. FUA, The Self-Study of Fordham University: A Report Presented for the Consideration of the Commission on Institutions of Higher Education of the Middle States Association of Colleges and Secondary Schools, January 1963, 1–4.

Dr. Donohue performed an invaluable service to the university as the executive director of the self-study whose conclusions remain a tribute to his thoroughness and honesty. He was also a professional educator who preferred the clarity of the king's English to the opacity of educational jargon in expressing his opinions. His candor and efforts to raise academic standards profited the university in many ways, but they also caused him considerable grief because he ruffled the feathers of some university administrators and upset some ensconced professors, one of whom had been born in 1883 and another who published his first book the year that he retired.

One Fordham administrator who admired Donohue's integrity and tenacity commented that, "as the Self-Study project developed, his numerous reports were increasingly censored and his own thoughts and opinions became more entrenched." It is not surprising that almost immediately after the completion of the self-study Donohue left Fordham to accept a position with the New York State Department of Education in Albany. Unfortunately he died shortly thereafter.[3]

Student Body

The self-study revealed that in the 1961–62 fall semester Fordham University had a total enrollment of 9,864 students. Approximately half of them, 5,810 students, were undergraduates in six separate schools: Fordham College, School of Business (in three separate units: Campus Division at Rose Hill, Downtown Day Division, Downtown Evening Division), School of Pharmacy, School of Education, and the two affiliated Jesuit seminaries at Shrub Oak and Poughkeepsie. There were also 2,913 graduate students in the Graduate School of Arts and Sciences, Graduate School of Education, Law School, School of Social Service, and Loyola Seminary.

In addition there were 1,141 part-time students in the School of General Studies, as it was known in its most recent reincarnation, a school whose purpose was to enable older students to obtain a college degree while engaged in full-time employment. Perhaps the most surprising statistic was the number of women students, 3,148, almost one-third of the student body, a major change in an institution that had once been a bastion of male exclusiveness. By 1962 women were admitted to all the schools of the university, except two of the undergraduate schools, Fordham College and

3. George L. Haag, Fordham University Self-Study, 1960–1963, Supplementary Materials, Vol. I. Haag was the university registrar.

the Rose Hill division of the School of Business. They constituted the majority of the students in both the Graduate and Undergraduate divisions of the School of Education, and in the School of Social Service and the School of General Studies. In the Undergraduate School of Education, the single largest unit in the university, women outnumbered men by a margin of almost three to one, 1,445 to 566.[4]

A socioeconomic analysis of the members of the senior class in the six undergraduate units of the university in 1961 underscored the "blue collar" background of the majority of the student body. The parents of the Fordham seniors had less formal education than the national average. Only 18 percent of the fathers of the seniors were college graduates, compared with a national average of 25 percent, and only half of the fathers were high school graduates. Less than a third of the seniors came from families with an annual income of $10,000 or more, and only 10 percent came from families with an annual income of $15,000 or more. The percentage of Fordham seniors employed either full-time or part-time was higher than the national average, in some schools as high as 84 percent of the students.[5]

The average Fordham graduate in 1961 in the six undergraduate units of the university was American-born and almost exclusively white. Only three of 412 respondents identified themselves as nonwhite. Most were men despite the fact that four of the six undergraduate units were coeducational, and 82 percent of the seniors were the first members of their family to be graduated from college. More than a third of the seniors listed financial obstacles as at least one reason for not going on immediately to graduate or professional school.[6]

Fordham could hardly match the prestige or the financial resources of the Ivy League schools or the great state universities of the Midwest. Nonetheless, on the basis of the statistics compiled by Dr. Donohue, Fordham could make a convincing claim that it was serving the needs of the local Catholic community, which was the primary purpose that Bishop John Hughes had had in mind for Fordham when he founded the institution in

4. FUA, Fordham University, Self-Study, 1960–1963, Supplementary Materials, Vol. I. There were also 831 students, all male, in Fordham Preparatory School.

5. The comparison between the Fordham seniors and the national averages was based on a nationwide survey of 33,982 seniors conducted in 1961 by the National Opinion Research Center of the University of Chicago.

6. FUA, Fordham University Self-Study, 1960–1963, Fordham University Seniors: A Survey of the June 1961 Class in Six Units of the University, Supplementary Materials, Vol. III.

1841. One of the major objectives of the self-study was to enable Fordham to continue and to improve this service to the local Catholic community and also to broaden Fordham's appeal to a wider national constituency by raising its academic standards.

Faculty

If the student body was largely local, so was the faculty. Almost half (47 percent) of the full-time faculty and 60 percent of the part-time faculty had been born in New York City. Slightly more than half of their doctoral degrees came from New York City institutions. It was a relatively elderly faculty with full professors averaging fifty-six years of age, and one part-time professor still teaching at the age of seventy-eight despite a mandatory retirement age of seventy. The faculty was also overwhelmingly male. Ninety percent of the fulltime faculty were men, except in Education (where women made up 25 percent of the faculty) and in Social Service (where women made up 60 percent of the faculty). Of the 291 full-time faculty members, 52 percent had a doctoral degree or its equivalent and another 46 percent had either the master's degree or an appropriate professional degree.

As might be expected, the faculty was predominantly Catholic, with only 7 percent indicating a non-Catholic religious preference and 3 percent failing to indicate any religious preference at all. Because several Jesuits listed themselves in the latter category, the wording of the questionnaire may have been unclear. More than half of the faculty (58 percent) were graduates of a Catholic high school, and a third of them were graduates of a Jesuit high school. The percentage of full-time faculty who were graduates of Catholic colleges ranged between 69 and 81 percent for every unit of the university, except in the School of Social Service, where it was only 45 percent. Almost one-quarter of the full-time faculty (23 percent) had received their bachelor's degree from Fordham.

Faculty publication was not impressive for a university with aspirations of becoming a research institution. Over the course of a five-year period 52 of the 291 full-time faculty published a total of 77 books, an average of 0.3 books apiece. The faculty fared better in producing scholarly articles, 621 over a five-year period, but 56 percent of the full-time faculty produced no scholarly articles at all. Among the part-time faculty the production of scholarly articles was virtually nonexistent. Twelve of them published a total of 30 books, but 17 of these books were the work of a single individual. The faculty of the Law School ranked first in the production of books, with 38 percent of the professors publishing one or more books, while the

School of Social Service ranked last with only 5 percent of the professors publishing one or more books.

Dr. Donohue noted, but did not attempt to explain, a curious phenomenon in the process of promoting faculty through the ranks from instructor to assistant professor to associate professor to professor. Faculty with doctorates from Catholic universities (including Fordham and other Jesuit universities) fared poorly in gaining promotion in comparison with faculty with doctorates from non-Catholic universities. Thus only 21 percent of the full professors at Fordham had doctorates from Catholic universities, compared with 51 to 63 percent of the faculty in the three lower academic ranks. Donohue carefully refrained from offering a possible explanation for the disparity, which may have been due to the fact that perhaps the graduates of non-Catholic universities were better trained and motivated, or more gifted teachers, or more productive scholars than their counterparts from Catholic graduate schools.

However, Donohue pulled no punches when he criticized the promotion process at Fordham, because he thought it showed evidence of favoritism toward female faculty members and discrimination against Jesuit faculty members. He cited two statistics to make his point. Among the full-time faculty 50 percent of the women, but only 40 percent of the laymen and 22 percent of the Jesuits, held tenured positions. Two-thirds of the Jesuits were only untenured assistant professors compared with only 45 percent of the laymen and 40 percent of the lay women in that category.

Donohue emphasized the contribution made to Fordham by the eighty-eight Jesuit members of the faculty. Most of them (seventy out of eighty-eight) were graduates of Woodstock College, which, Donohue claimed, numbered a higher percentage of its alumni as college professors than any other college in the United States. Some of the Jesuits had earned as many as four degrees at Woodstock and afterward proceeded to acquire one or more additional graduate degrees at non-Catholic universities in the United States and Europe. Among the many Jesuit contributions to Fordham, Donohue credited them with reducing the inbreeding that was a disturbing feature of the profile of the lay faculty. The Jesuits were unevenly distributed among the schools of the university, constituting 40 percent of the full-time faculty of the Graduate School and Fordham College, approximately 25 percent in three of the other undergraduate schools, but only 8 percent of the faculty in the Law School and 5 percent in the School of Social Service.[7]

7. FUA, Fordham University Self-Study, 1960–1963, Supplementary Materials, Vols. III and IV.

The self-study also included a survey of the attitudes and opinions of the faculty with regard to many aspects of the university. One of the areas canvassed was faculty opinions about the sensitive topic of academic freedom. Their response was overwhelmingly positive. More than 90 percent of the faculty felt free to discuss controversial topics in the classroom and to participate actively in community political organizations. A whopping 95 percent of the lay faculty felt free to select any books and other educational material they wished to use in their courses. They also indicated satisfaction with the relationship between the Jesuit and lay faculty. By lopsided majorities the lay faculty agreed that the Jesuits met the same academic requirements and handled the same workload as the lay faculty. Seventy percent of the lay faculty even thought it was easier for the lay faculty to secure academic promotions than the Jesuits.

There were two areas in which the lay faculty expressed dissatisfaction with the administration. One was the role of the department chairs in the structure of the university. Seventy percent of the lay faculty commended their own department chairs for representing their concerns to the administration, but only 47 percent thought the administration gave the chairs adequate recognition. The other area where the lay faculty found fault with the administration was in the lack of programs to improve the quality of teaching.

One of the more puzzling results of the survey of the lay faculty was their ambivalent attitude to the role of Catholic universities in American society. Ninety-three percent of the lay faculty thought the graduates of Fordham received due recognition in professional and business circles in New York, but 85 percent complained that the accomplishments of Catholic universities and colleges were not well known to the general public. They offered a possible answer to this conundrum when they criticized themselves and the faculties of other Catholic universities and colleges for their failure to participate and assume leadership roles in professional and academic organizations.[8]

Recommendations

As the self-study wound down in the fall of 1962, Dr. Donohue made a number of extremely critical observations about the faculty that must have confirmed Dr. Jones's confidence that Fordham could be trusted to conduct the self-study with rigor and integrity, but Donohue's candid

8. FUA, James W. Fogarty, Study of Faculty Opinions and Attitudes, Fordham University Self-Study, 1960–1963, Supplementary Materials, Vol. VI.

observations could hardly have pleased the Fordham administration. He complained that Fordham was not even a regional school, only a narrowly local one, because so many of the faculty had been born and educated in the New York metropolitan area. He called the academic inbreeding among the faculty so extensive that it was difficult to believe and, among the part-time faculty in business, law, and education, "a positive disgrace." The major exception to this inbreeding were the Jesuit members of the faculty because of the diversity of the universities where they had earned their doctorates. As mentioned earlier, Donohue complained that Jesuits often failed to receive promotion even though they were equally qualified as or better qualified than their lay colleagues.

He also thought there was a need to hire more women faculty, except in the School of Social Service, where Donohue complained that there were far too many women professors. In fact he singled out the faculty of the School of Social Service for especially severe criticism as "the farthest [*sic*] from what a Fordham faculty should be" because of the shallow grounding of so many of the faculty in Catholic beliefs and principles.

Two other major criticisms of the faculty voiced by Donohue were the lack of scholarly publications by the full-time faculty and the poor academic qualifications of many of the part-time faculty. With regard to scholarly publications, the problem was not the relatively small number of books produced but the fact that many faculty produced nothing at all. What caught Donohue's eye about the part-time faculty was not only their unimpressive academic background but also their inflated academic ranks and salaries, "as if it were first determined what the stipend would be, and then the academic rank was set to fit the stipend."

Father Vincent T. O'Keefe, S.J.

Although the massive self-study of Fordham was begun and conducted during the administration of Father McGinley, the burden of implementing its recommendations became the responsibility of Father Vincent T. O'Keefe, who succeeded McGinley as president of Fordham in June 1963. McGinley's 14-year presidency, which ended on June 23, 1963, was the longest in the 122-year history of Fordham to that date. By contrast, O'Keefe's tenure as president was to be one of the shortest in Fordham's history because at the 31st General Congregation of the Society of Jesus in Rome he was elected assistant *ad providentiam* to the newly elected general, Father Pedro Arrupe. A genial individual and noted raconteur with an endless fund of humorous stories, Father O'Keefe was highly respected by his Jesuit confrères. He was "a man of vision, integrity and humor," said

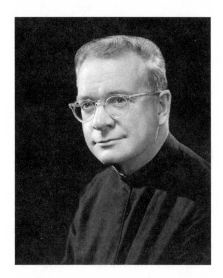

Father Vincent T. O'Keefe, S.J., president of Fordham University, 1963–65.

one of his successors as president of Fordham, Father Joseph M. McShane, at the time of Father O'Keefe's death at the age of 92 in 2012. "Though his tenure as President was relatively short," added Father McShane, "Fordham would not be the university it is today without his influence."

A native of Jersey City, Father O'Keefe came to Fordham in 1960 as academic vice president and was promoted to the newly established office of executive vice president in June 1962. One year later he was appointed president of Fordham. He was only forty-three years old, a relatively young age for such an important position in a Church accustomed to geriatric leadership, but not unusual in the Society of Jesus. Both of Father O'Keefe's immediate predecessors, Father Gannon and Father McGinley, had been appointed president of Fordham at the age of forty-three.[9]

Father O'Keefe's background also reflected the policy of the American Jesuits after World War II of giving their most promising young members an international education. Fluent in English, French, German, Italian, and Spanish, O'Keefe had the opportunity to study at Münster, Germany; at the Jesuit theologate at Eigenhoven-Louvain, Belgium, where he earned a licentiate in theology; and at Rome, where he received his doctorate in theology from the Pontifical Gregorian University. He taught at Regis High School in Manhattan and at Woodstock College before his appointment to Fordham in 1960 to fill the newly created position of academic vice president.

O'Keefe envisioned the office of a university president as having a twofold purpose. Ideally he (or she) should be the face of the university to

9. *Ram*, October 4, 1962, April 25, June 12, 1963.

the outside world, and also the leader responsible for the internal educational direction of the university. O'Keefe sharply disagreed with those who thought that fundraising was beneath the dignity of a university president. "There is a crying need for money," he explained, and prospective donors, whether individuals or organizations or government agencies or foundations, "want to see the president." O'Keefe retained the newly created office of executive vice president, which he had just vacated and was now in the hands of Father Joseph Frese, because it relieved him of the routine burden of dealing with the other vice presidents. O'Keefe candidly announced that he had no ambition to make Fordham the largest Catholic university in the United States, because he thought that indiscriminate expansion was incompatible with the traditional Jesuit ideal of the *cura personalis*, the dedication of the faculty to the intellectual and spiritual well-being of every student.[10]

Faculty Senate

One of the recommendations of the now famous self-study was that Fordham should unify the university by providing some structure for the faculty to participate in policy decisions. Father O'Keefe responded positively to the recommendation by establishing the Faculty Senate, which he regarded as one of his major accomplishments as president. "We wanted it to be the Fordham faculty, not the Jesuit faculty," he explained. Fortunately for Fordham, the first president of the Faculty Senate was Dr. Joseph Cammarosano, an economist and gifted teacher who was a devout Catholic totally dedicated to the well-being of Fordham. As the executive vice president a few years later, during the worst period of the student upheavals and campus violence, Cammarosano was to provide decisive and courageous leadership in guiding Fordham through some of the most challenging years in its history.[11]

Father O'Keefe's receptivity to the establishment of an elected Faculty Senate was indicative of his attitude to the role the lay faculty in a Catholic university. Shortly after assuming the reins at Fordham, O'Keefe told his counterpart at Loyola University in Chicago, "My own views on the ideal role of the layman in Jesuit higher education are that the layman should be a full partner in our total educational process. We are far from the day

10. *Ram*, June 12, 1963.

11. O'Keefe, *As I Remember Fordham: Selections from the Sesquicentennial Oral History Project* (New York: Fordham University Press, 1991), 5; Raymond A. Schroth, S.J., *Fordham: A History and Memoir* (Chicago: Loyola University Press, 2002), 295, 304.

when the layman was considered as someone filling a position where no religious was available." Father Schroth credits O'Keefe with initiating a "quiet revolution" in the status of the lay faculty at Fordham, which paid handsome dividends for his successors as president, especially Father Michael Walsh, who could usually rely on lay support when he sought a consensus for some of his more controversial decisions.[12]

There were few more famous or divisive Jesuit scholars in the 1960s than Pierre Teilhard de Chardin, the French paleontologist, philosopher, and theologian, whose teaching and writings had been censored since the mid-1920s by his religious superiors and by the Holy See, culminating in a *monitum* from the Holy Office (the present-day Congregation for the Doctrine of the Faith) on June 30, 1962, warning Catholics against the alleged errors and ambiguities in his writings. Fifteen months later, Father James M. Somerville, S.J., the chair of the Philosophy Department, and Father James A. Sadowsky, S.J., the acting chair of the Theology Department, asked Father O'Keefe for permission to organize a symposium or institute at Fordham on Teilhard's thought that would be coordinated by Father Robert J. O'Donnell, S.J. "Certain quarters," they admitted, "regard his thought as dangerous; if that is the case, then his attraction makes responsible evaluation of his ideas an urgent need." O'Keefe gave his enthusiastic support to the project.[13] It is not clear if the symposium ever took place on the scale originally contemplated.

Graduate Programs and Fordham College

In 1963 the Middle States Association recommended greater coordination among the various units of the university. One way that Father O'Keefe implemented this recommendation was to appoint Father Joseph F. Mulligan, S.J., the dean of the Graduate School of Arts and Sciences, to be the dean of the faculty with special responsibility for the supervision of the various liberal arts programs at Fordham on both the graduate and undergraduate levels.[14] "The graduate programs at Fordham are in good hands," the assistant commissioner for higher education in New York state assured Father O'Keefe a year later. He commended

12. FUA, O'Keefe Papers, O'Keefe to James F. Maguire, S.J., June 3, 1964. Schroth, *Fordham: A History and Memoir*, 296.

13. FUA, O'Keefe Papers, Somerville and Sadowsky to O'Keefe, October 1, 1963; O'Keefe to O'Connell, October 7, 1963. Teilhard's later admirers included Cardinal Henri de Lubac, S.J., Pope John Paul II, and Pope Benedict XVI.

14. FUA, O'Keefe Papers, Frese to Father George J. McMahon, S.J., July 20, 1964.

Fordham both for the reasonable teaching load of three courses per semester and the policy of expecting professors in the graduate school also to teach on the undergraduate level.

Fordham had recently introduced new doctoral programs in mathematics and theology. The state educational officials were so impressed with the careful process of devising and implementing both of these two doctoral programs that they waived the usual requirement for an additional on-site visitation. Their one major criticism of Fordham's graduate programs was the predominance of part-time students, which they attributed largely to the scarcity of scholarships and the lack of fellowships for full-time students. No one at Fordham could quarrel with their accurate and well-intentioned observation that "the whole question of institutional support for graduate students remains, therefore, one of the great unresolved problems for Fordham." It would remain an unresolved problem for many years to come because of financial constraints.[15]

The early 1960s were also an era of steady academic progress at Fordham's premier undergraduate school, Fordham College, despite a decrease of several hundred students in the enrollment (or perhaps because of the decrease). "I have never had belief in the concept of the 'good old days,'" said Father Charles P. Loughran, S.J., the dean of Fordham College. "The days of true glory for Fordham College are still in the future," and he pronounced the freshman class of 1962–63 the best class in the history of the college. He also predicted that within two years the college would set new records.[16]

Despite efforts to recruit students from across the nation, the stellar performance of the students at Fordham College was due largely to local talent from Catholic high schools. In the 1962–63 academic year 15.2 percent of the students (288 out of 1,886) qualified for the Dean's List with a grade of B+ or an index of 3.5. Of that number 78.1 percent (225) were graduates of high schools in the New York metropolitan area. An even higher percentage (86.1 percent, 248 students) were graduates of Catholic high schools in the New York metropolitan area and elsewhere. Four local Jesuit high schools—Regis, Fordham Preparatory, Brooklyn Preparatory, and Xavier—accounted for a total of 101 students or 35 percent of the students on the Dean's List. An interesting change in the ethnic background of the students (judging from their surnames) was the significant num-

15. FUA, O'Keefe Papers, Allan A. Kuusisto to O'Keefe, January 11, 1965.
16. FUA, O'Keefe Papers, Loughran to O'Keefe, July 25, 1963.

ber of Italian names, 25.3 percent compared with 30.9 percent with Irish surnames.[17]

Father O'Keefe is best remembered for taking a major step in the transformation of Fordham University into a completely coeducational institution by establishing Thomas More College for women on the Rose Hill campus. As mentioned earlier, ten of the twelve units of the university were already coeducational—some of them had been for several decades—but Fordham College was different and remained an exclusively male preserve in accordance with longstanding Jesuit tradition. Fordham College was not alone in this respect. Relatively few Catholic men's colleges in the United States admitted women in 1963.

There was considerable resistance among the Jesuit faculty to making Fordham College coeducational. "In the eyes of many people, especially the Jesuits," said O'Keefe, "Fordham University really was Fordham College." Another reason for preserving Fordham College as an all-male school was that, despite a decrease of several hundred students in the enrollment (or perhaps because of the decrease), in the early 1960s the academic performance of the students was never higher. As a result Father O'Keefe and Father Frese devised a compromise by establishing on the Rose Hill campus a women's college that lasted from 1964 until 1974, when it was deemed to have served its purpose and was folded into Fordham College, finally making Fordham College a completely coeducational institution.[18]

Thomas More College

The establishment of Thomas More College was a direct result of the self-study of the university in 1960–63. One of the recommendations of the self-study was that Fordham prepare itself for the massive expansion in the number of college students that was expected to occur during the following decade, especially the increase in the number of women students, who already outnumbered men among high school graduates. Thomas More College opened its doors in September 1964 as a liberal arts college for women with programs leading to a B.A. or B.S. degree. Father O'Keefe limited the freshman class to 200 with the ultimate goal of no more than 800 students.[19]

The first dean was the scholarly Father John W. Donohue, S.J., the chair of Division I in the Graduate School of Education and a 1939 grad-

17. FUA, O'Keefe Papers, Fordham College Students of High Scholastic Standing for the Year Ending June 1963.

18. O'Keefe, *As I Remember Fordham*, 5.

19. FUA, O'Keefe Papers, O'Keefe to F. Taylor Jones, May 8, 1964.

uate of Fordham College. Father Donohue explained the appropriateness of the name of the new college by pointing out that St. Thomas More, the noted sixteenth-century lord chancellor of England, Christian humanist, and Catholic martyr, gave his three daughters the same education at home as he gave his son. A modest man who was a favorite of O'Keefe's, Donohue joked that he got the job of dean because it was thought that his resemblance to Cardinal Spellman would reassure parents who were fearful of sending their daughters to a predominantly male campus. Donohue did not think he was a particularly effective dean and harbored no grudges when he was fired as dean in 1966 by Father O'Keefe's successor, Father Leo McLaughlin, and replaced by Dr. Patricia Plante, whom Donohue had hired as assistant dean.[20]

When the father general gave permission for the establishment of Thomas More College, the Jesuit vicar general expressed concern that it would prove to be a "second rate" part of the university. The opposite proved to be true. Ninety-five percent of the freshmen in Thomas More College in 1964 were in the top 10 percent of their high school classes, and their median verbal test scores were one hundred points higher than those of the freshmen in the School of Business and the College of Pharmacy. The young women even outperformed the freshmen in Fordham College, although by a lesser margin, despite the fact that, according to Father Frese, the all-male 1964 freshman class in Fordham College was "one of the smartest classes we have ever had." He warned the parents of the Fordham College freshmen that "perhaps your sons will be introduced to some healthy academic competition." Another welcome feature of the creation of the new college was that it reversed the decline in the total freshman enrollment that had fallen from 750 in 1958 to 404 in 1962. With the opening of Thomas More College the freshman enrollment shot up to 690 in 1964.[21]

After a brief on-site inspection, the New York state educational authorities expressed approval and even admiration for the new college, using the word "remarkable" several times in their report, although they added

20. Donohue, *As I Remember Fordham*, 58–60.

21. FUA, O'Keefe Papers, O'Keefe to McGinty, February 19, 1965; Frese to O'Keefe, April 8, 1964. Father Charles F. Loughran, S.J., the dean of Fordham College, shared Frese's high opinion of the Fordham freshmen in the early 1960s. Loughran to O'Keefe, July 25, 1963. Frese, Address at Freshmen Parents' Day, Fordham College, April 26, 1964. Tongue-in-cheek, Frese told the parents of the Fordham College freshmen that their sons were so smart that he had ordered the teachers either to give more difficult tests or to teach less clearly.

a gentle reminder that Fordham might consider introducing more flexibility (they called it "maneuverability") into the curriculum. At the same time that Thomas More College was receiving lavish praise from the state educational authorities, it encountered severe criticism from within the Society of Jesus on several levels. There was considerable opposition from Jesuits in the Fordham community; from Father Edward Rooney, the director of the Jesuit Educational Association; and, most ominously, from the Jesuit authorities in Rome, who complained that Father O'Keefe had exceeded his mandate in establishing Thomas More College.[22]

As the provincial, Father John J. McGinty, discovered on a visit to Rome either in late 1964 or early in 1965, the vicar general and father assistant of the Society were not pleased with Thomas More College. They had two basic objections to the structure and operation of the college. First, they complained that permission had been given only for a coeducational college, not for an exclusively women's college. Second, the expectation in Rome had been that the women students would take some basic liberal arts courses in Thomas More College and then be funneled into the undergraduate professional schools of education, business, and pharmacy.[23]

Father Donohue was stunned at the reaction in Rome and warned Father O'Keefe that "we now have a de facto situation from which we cannot retreat without immeasurable damage to the university's professional reputation." He admitted that Thomas More College had evolved in a different direction from what had been originally envisioned, but he attributed this difference not to "fraud on our part" but to the natural process of development to be expected when a general concept is spelled out in detail. He suspected that the real reason for the unhappiness with Thomas More College in the Jesuit Curia in Rome was that they could not reconcile themselves to the notion of Jesuits' operating a women's college.

Father Donohue formulated two responses to the criticism from Rome. One was more convincing than the other. First he made the rather questionable claim that "in theory" there was only one single coeducational liberal arts institution at Rose Hill, composed of two units of unequal size: Fordham College and Thomas More College. He based this claim on the fact that the two units shared the same curriculum and the same faculty and had achieved a "high degree of integration in their classes." Because there were no men enrolled in Thomas More College, and Donohue himself said that it was too late to enroll men for the 1965–66 academic year,

22. FUA, O'Keefe Papers, Allan A. Kuusisto to O'Keefe, December 30, 1964.
23. FUA, O'Keefe Papers, McGinty to O'Keefe, February 3, 1965.

he seemed to be saying that coeducational integration meant that men and women took the same courses in separate classrooms.

Donohue's second argument was more plausible. He expressed confidence that the theoretical existence of coeducation at Thomas More College would become an empirical reality when the new coeducational liberal arts college at Lincoln Center was made the in-town division of Thomas More College. Father O'Keefe used these two arguments in replying to the Jesuit critics in Rome and apparently satisfied them, because Thomas More College not only survived but thrived until 1974, when the Fordham administration under President Father James C. Finlay merged Thomas More College with Fordham College largely for financial reasons.[24]

Ironically, in 1972, when the administration under President Finlay announced the decision to merge the two colleges, much of the opposition came from the students and alumnae of Thomas More College, who had come to appreciate the advantages of a separate women's college because of the advantages it gave them as a distinct community on an overwhelmingly male campus. The Thomas More students also feared that the lower admissions standards at Fordham College would jeopardize their academic reputation and questioned whether they would suffer from fewer opportunities in extracurricular activities and student leadership positions. Financial considerations decided the issue and made the merger inevitable. "In its ten years," said Father Raymond Schroth, evaluating the significance of the college, "Thomas More had radically transformed Fordham College by forcing Fordham men—faculty and students—to rethink the role of women in Catholic education and in their own lives."[25]

Postscript

After leaving Fordham, O'Keefe spent eighteen years in Rome in the Jesuit Curia establishing a close working relationship with the Jesuit general, Father Pedro Arrupe, and rising to a more prominent and influential position in the central headquarters of the Society of Jesus than any American Jesuit before or since. In 1975 he was elected general assistant and general counselor to Father Arrupe, and, after Arrupe suffered a de-

24. FUA, O'Keefe Papers, Donohue to O'Keefe, February 8, 9, 1965; O'Keefe to McGinty, February 19, 1965.

25. Raymond A. Schroth, S.J., "How Women Came to Fordham: The Life and Death of Thomas More College," *Conversations on Jesuit Higher Education*: Vol. 29, Article 12, 33–34. Father Schroth says O'Keefe told McGinty in 1965 that he would have to look for a new president of Fordham, if he forced him to close Thomas More College.

bilitating stroke in 1981, Arrupe appointed O'Keefe the vicar general of the Society.

Pope John Paul II, who was unhappy with O'Keefe's appointment and suspicious of the Jesuits in general because of their alleged disobedience, effectively undermined O'Keefe's authority in an unprecedented move two months later by appointing an eighty-year-old Italian Jesuit, Father Paolo Dezza, as his "personal delegate" to the Society. It was an exercise of papal authority that was deeply resented by many Jesuits throughout the world because they thought it was disrespectful to both Arrupe and O'Keefe. O'Keefe urged his Jesuit confrères to accept the pope's decision in the spirit of Jesuit obedience and remained in Rome assisting Dezza until the election of the new general, Peter-Hans Kolvenbach, in September 1983. O'Keefe returned to the United States the following year to serve as rector of the Jesuit community at Fordham.[26]

26. James Martin, S.J., "Vincent O'Keefe," *America,* July 24, 2012.

18

QUASI-REVOLUTION
ON CAMPUS

The Roaring Sixties

The 1960s ushered in a decade of changes in American society whose impact merits comparison with the changes that occurred a century earlier as a result of the Civil War and the era of Reconstruction. In 1960 America was still largely a racially segregated society, legally so in the South (even in the nation's capital) and informally but pervasively so in the North. The growing Latino presence was hardly noticed and had little political impact nationally. The role of women in the highest echelons of politics, academia, the professions and the business world was minuscule. Margaret Chase Smith, Republican senator from Maine, was often mentioned in the press because at that time she was one of the few female U.S. senators in American history. Unfortunately, a more representative figure of American women in the workplace, at least during World War II, was Rosie the Riveter, the temporary female substitute for male workers in the defense industries. Patriotism ran strong and deep in the wake of both World War II and the Korean War, and the leaders of the armed forces enjoyed widespread respect among the American public. Few noticed President Dwight D. Eisenhower's warning about the questionable influence of the "military-industrial complex" in postwar American society.

By the mid-1970s the political and social landscape in America had been changed—"changed utterly," as Yeats said about the Easter Rising of 1916 in Ireland, although he was unlikely to have added that "a terrible beauty is born." The civil rights movement achieved major victories with the enactment of the Civil Rights Act of 1964 and the Voting Rights Act of 1965. As a result African Americans finally if only incrementally secured the civil rights theoretically guaranteed to them a century earlier. Women made notable gains in public and professional life, although economically they still lagged behind their male counterparts in the business world. The painful experience of the Vietnam War led many Americans to take a more critical and skeptical view of the decisions and pronouncements of their political and military leaders. Even the most neglected of all American minorities—Native Americans—began to receive belated recognition. A satirical cartoon in *The New Yorker* captured the domino effect of the spirit of the times. It featured an African American spokesman in the pulpit of a posh WASP church presenting a series of compensatory demands to a dutifully contrite white congregation while an eager Native American chief in full Indian headdress was racing up the center aisle flaunting his own list of anticipated reparations.

There were many reasons for the changes in American society in the late 1960s and early 1970s, but an influential factor in shaping public opinion and eventually public policy was the ferment that took place on America's college campuses. However, revolutions, even of the amateur student variety, tend to be many-splendored things, and the campus protests that engulfed many American colleges and universities proved to be a two-edged sword. They not only led to a number of beneficial changes in American society, but they also provoked a conservative political backlash that became evident in the presidential election of 1968 when former Vice President Richard M. Nixon narrowly defeated Vice President Hubert H. Humphrey. Four years later the backlash was even more evident when Nixon was reelected by an overwhelming majority over the hapless Senator George S. McGovern of South Dakota, an erstwhile history professor who was a favorite of campus radicals.

The University of California at Berkeley, the home of the Free Speech Movement made famous by Mario Savio and others, became the most prominent center of the college protest movement as early as 1964. Closer to home, at Columbia University students occupied five buildings on campus until the president of the university, braving faculty wrath at the violation of academic cloister, summoned the NYPD to eject the intruders in the early hours of April 30, 1968. The most tragic event in the wave of student protests that swept the nation occurred on May 4, 1970, at Kent State University when panicky and inexperienced soldiers of the Ohio National Guard opened fire on unarmed protesters, killing four of them and wounding nine others.

Like Berkeley, Columbia, Kent State, and hundreds of other American universities and colleges across the country, Fordham College experienced its own era of student unrest, which included acts of vandalism and even arson that replicated similar incidents on other campuses. Perhaps the most surprising feature of *les évènements* at Rose Hill was that they occurred at all at a politically conservative Catholic campus in the Bronx.

Ferment at Rose Hill

Three weeks before the presidential election of 1964, 53.6 percent of the students who responded to a straw poll said that they favored Senator Barry Goldwater of Arizona over President Lyndon Johnson. A week later the *Ram* noted the death of former President Herbert Hoover by declaring that "his passing is a great sorrow to us all."[1] In the aftermath of the student demonstrations at Berkeley in 1965, two Fordham undergraduates were asked for their reaction. One student criticized the demonstrations while the other defended them, but both students gave the same reason why they believed there was no possibility that such demonstrations might take place at Fordham. "Nobody gives a damn," they both said disgustedly. However, as an afterthought, the more liberal of the two students left open the possibility that one issue might provoke student demonstrations at Rose Hill, and that was the threat to raise tuition. "Anything that involves money arouses the passions of Fordham students," he said.[2] Both students were soon proved wrong. It remains questionable, however, whether the disruptive protests that followed hard on the heels of the expression of these sentiments reflected a sudden change in the attitude of most students or the successful efforts of a determined and resourceful radical minority to attempt to manipulate student opinion to their own advantage.

The two principal causes of unrest in American society and especially on college campuses were the civil rights movement and the opposition to American involvement in the Vietnam War. A common feature of both the civil rights movement and the anti-war movement was the wide range of objectives and tactics. For example, Dr. Martin Luther King Jr. and other civil rights leaders advocated peaceful demonstrations and passive resistance to obtain their goal of political and social equality for all Americans. The violence they often encountered in the South was not due to them but to their opponents, who utilized all the political power at their command, including the nightsticks and attack dogs of the state troopers, in a vain effort to preserve a segregated society that most Americans had come to regard as an embarrassing anachronism.

However, both the mainstream civil rights movement and the anti-war movement had to contend with unwelcome revolutionary splinter groups in their own ranks. Small but well-publicized fringe groups like the Black Panther Party and the so-called Weathermen, who made no secret of their commitment to the violent overthrow of the government, frightened many

1. *Ram*, October 16, 23, 1964.
2. *Ram*, February 25, 1965.

Americans and intensified their suspicion of both the civil rights movement and the opposition to the war.

At Rose Hill, students reacted much more positively to the civil rights movement than to the anti-war movement, especially after March 1965, when civil rights activists in Alabama attempted to march from Selma to the state capitol in Montgomery to present a voting rights petition to Governor George Wallace. The brutal mistreatment of the peaceful marchers by the state police was a turning point in the history of the civil rights movement in the United States, mobilizing public opinion on behalf of the marchers. Two faculty members from Fordham were among the 25,000 participants in the third march, Father Herbert Rogers, S.J., of the Theology Department, and Assistant Dean James R. Kelly, S.J.[3]

At Rose Hill some 1,000 students gathered in front of the gym to express their support for the marchers and to hear Father James Finlay, S.J., a future president of Fordham, declare that "there are times when silence shouts approval. For too long we have been silent and our silence has been interpreted as an approval of oppression."[4] If Selma was a turning point in the history of the civil rights movement, the gathering of some 1,000 Fordham students and faculty in front of the university gym was a turning point in Fordham's own involvement in the civil rights movement. Only five years earlier, when twenty-one members of Fordham's Campus Interracial Council had staged a sit-in at the Woolworth's store on Fordham Road because of Woolworth's segregated lunch counters in the South, they had drawn sneers and jeers from a crowd of hostile Fordham students who came to watch them.[5]

Not everyone on campus was satisfied that the outpouring of sympathy for the civil rights marchers in the South evinced sufficient commitment to racial equality on the part of Fordham University. Taking advantage of the climate of rising expectations and galloping entitlement, in 1969 the leaders of the Society for African-American Advancement demanded that Fordham College immediately guarantee that 20 percent of the student

3. *Ram*, April 1, 1965. Rogers noticed that there was no American flag visible at the Alabama Capitol, only the Confederate battle flag and the Alabama state flag. Two weeks later Rogers spoke at the Community Church in New York City and presented the minister with a memorial book with 1,000 names in honor of the Reverend James Reeb, a courageous Unitarian Universalist minister who had been shot and killed by white racists during the second Selma march. *Ram*, April 13, 1965.

4. *Ram*, March 24, 1965.

5. *Ram*, March 31, 1960.

body would henceforth be composed of African Americans. In fact 15 percent of the freshman class at Fordham College that year consisted of blacks and Hispanics.[6]

The anti-war movement was a much more polarizing force on campus than the civil rights movement, causing bitter divisions among the students as it did at many other American colleges and among the American public. By late 1967 there were more than 500,000 American troops in Vietnam. An increasing number of Americans began to question the wisdom of a war whose evil side effects seemed to outweigh the positive results, calling into question the traditional Catholic "just war" theory. Rightly or wrongly, Pope Paul VI was thought to share that opinion.

An important factor in the student discontent at Fordham was the students' unhappiness with the quality of the teaching and the lack of personal contact with members of the faculty.[7] However, student opposition to the Vietnam War soon replaced their unhappiness with their classroom experiences. Their opposition to the Vietnam War was not altogether altruistic, because the U.S. military depended heavily on the draft to fill the ranks of the armed forces. An editorial writer in the *Ram* unintentionally revealed his own elitist sense of entitlement when he declared that "we find it unfortunate that any student may be required to interrupt his education, especially since we oppose the war which will cause this."[8] More persuasively, John Kerry, a twenty-seven-year-old decorated Vietnam veteran—a volunteer, it should be noted—remarked before a subcommittee of the U.S. Senate Foreign Relations Committee on April 23, 1971, "How do you ask a man to be the last man to die for a mistake?"[9]

For American Catholics, the Vietnam War was a watershed in their involvement in political life. Hitherto American Catholics had unquestionably identified their Catholic faith with their American patriotism. During World War I, for example, there were only two Catholic conscientious objectors in the whole country. The reaction to the Vietnam War was different. The division among American Catholics, as among most Americans, took place largely along generational lines. An older generation of

6. *Ram*, September 9, 1969.

7. Dr. Joseph Cammarosano, FUA, FOHP, #77, Interview with Michael J. Sheahan, September 18 and 25, 1990. Cammarosano has been a faculty member for sixty years and served as both the first president of the Faculty Senate and executive vice president on two different occasions, 46.

8. *Ram*, March 3, 1966.

9. As a U.S. senator from Massachusetts, Kerry would later serve as chair of the Foreign Relations Committee and later as U.S. secretary of state.

American Catholics, typified by Francis Cardinal Spellman, identified the Vietnam War with World War II and was genuinely puzzled by the lack of popular support.

However, a younger generation of American Catholics hesitated to make the same equivalence between World War II and the Vietnam War. For the first time in American history Catholic clerics like the two Berrigan brothers, Daniel, a Jesuit priest, and Philip, a Josephite priest, openly defied the law to protest what they regarded as an immoral American foreign policy. Only a minority of American Catholics probably approved their tactics, but the widespread publicity that the Berrigans and other Catholic protesters received provoked considerable soul-searching in the American Catholic community.[10]

The most prominent anti-war organization in American colleges was the Students for a Democratic Society, a national organization that was founded in 1960 at the Ann Arbor campus of the University of Michigan. For a brief period in the 1960s the SDS was a power in the land through its influence in shaping student and faculty attitudes in the susceptible world of American academia. At the Rose Hill campus the local branch of the SDS was the leading force in mobilizing opposition to the existence of the ROTC (Reserve Officers Training Corps) and the presence on campus of recruiters for the armed forces. In May 1966 protesters interrupted a review of ROTC cadets by hurling tomatoes and eggs and shouting obscenities at them. The following fall protesters forcibly prevented students from having access to military recruiters on campus. Afterward, when the students were polled about their reaction to the event, they disavowed the demonstrators by voting by a margin of 1,912 to 392 to continue the practice of allowing military recruiters on campus.[11]

In late 1968 anti-war sentiment on American college campuses escalated (to use a favorite Vietnam-era expression) as the United States became more deeply involved in the conflict. Speaking at Rose Hill in the fall of 1968, Mark Rudd, a leader of the SDS at Columbia University, announced that "the whole revolution is just beginning." That same month the president of the United Student Government at Fordham told the incoming

10. In February 1966 Philip Berrigan spoke at a symposium at Rose Hill sponsored by the Catholic Peace Fellowship on the topic of "The Moral Challenge of Vietnam in Light of Vatican II." *Ram*, February 25, 1966.

11. *Ram*, May 6, 1966, November 16, 1967. In 1969, after several years of anti-ROTC demonstrations, more than 300 students were still enrolled in the four-year noncredit military science courses sponsored by the ROTC. *Ram*, September 9, 1969.

freshman class that Fordham is "a basically undemocratic and dictatorial institution" and he urged them "to fight for yourselves."[12]

Some older students hardly needed such incitement. Taking advantage of the general breakdown of respect for authority that was one of the side effects of the Vietnam War, they had already formulated their own list of antinomian demands that transcended ideology. They demanded the end to such "barnacles of tradition" as the dress code, the midnight curfew, "cult observances" like the recitation of the Hail Mary before class, and the prohibition of alcohol in the dormitories. Although they railed against mandatory English courses, they had evidently profited sufficiently from their exposure to them to display a Swiftian sense of invective irony when they pleaded that the presence of women visitors in their rooms would lend an atmosphere of sophistication to the campus and "should work to make the Fordham student a man of character."

Jonathan Swift would also have enjoyed an editorial in the *Ram* urging the public to "Keep Off the Grass." It was not a plea for ecological sensitivity but a demand for the legalization of the sale and use of marijuana. The students registered an ecumenical note when they called attention to the unfortunate Protestant students who could not get bacon and eggs in the cafeteria on Friday mornings. The core curriculum was a particular *bête noire*. "Why should a sophomore be required to take English Prose?" they asked. "Why should a senior take anything required?"[13]

It became common practice for harried college administrators to attempt to defuse volatile situations by making concessions to student demands, a practice that yielded mixed results at best. Fordham was no exception to the general pattern. When seventeen members of the AAAAF, the African American society, barricaded the dean of students, Dr. Martin J. Meade, in his office for two-and-a-half hours, he promised that Fordham would take no punitive action against black students who engaged in peaceful demonstrations, which may or may not have included barricading him in his office. If the report in the *Ram* was accurate, Meade said that he had not been coerced to make this concession. It was a sign of the deteriorating civility on campus that, when Meade reportedly suffered a heart attack the next day, some students greeted the announcement with skepticism rather than sympathy.[14]

Discontent was not confined to Rose Hill. The new Liberal Arts Col-

12. *Ram*, September 11, 1968.
13. *Ram*, October 28, 1966, January 30, December 5, December 6, 1968.
14. *Ram*, December 5, 6, 1968. In fact Meade had not suffered a heart attack.

lege at Lincoln Center opened in September 1968 with an experimental curriculum that proved to be unworkable three months after its inauguration. The administration's suspension of the program led to protests by half of the faculty and many of the 300 freshman students. The administration responded by rescinding its decision and reinstating the experimental curriculum. The usually critical editors of the *Ram* offered praise of questionable value when they declared that "the administration, and President McLaughlin in particular, have [*sic*] bent over backwards to meet the demands of the [student and faculty] groups."[15]

Not everyone was as complimentary as the *Ram* about the conciliatory leadership style of Father Leo F. McLaughlin, S.J., who had become president of Fordham in 1965. He received widespread criticism for his reversal of positions about the experimental curriculum at Lincoln Center and denied that he had capitulated to student demands. "None of these recommendations can be so represented," he insisted, "nor do they violate the proper competence of faculty and students in university decision making."[16]

The person who rescued the Liberal Arts College at Lincoln Center from its chaotic beginnings and placed it on a solid academic foundation was a young sociology professor, Dr. Paul Reiss, whom Father Joseph Fitzpatrick had recruited from Marquette University. Three senior professors at Lincoln Center with long experience in other universities with multiple campuses—Margaret Mead, Harry L. Levy, and Livingston L. Biddle Jr.—strongly recommended that Reiss (who was the acting academic vice president of the university) be appointed to the defunct position of executive vice president for Lincoln Center while retaining his position as dean of the Liberal Arts College at Lincoln Center.

"In an age when young administrators are in frantic demand," Reiss's admirers told Dr. Joseph Cammarosano, the executive vice president of the university, "Fordham University is almost incredibly fortunate in having in its service an administrator, scholar and teacher of the first rank under the age of forty." They praised Reiss for the rare ability of "combining practical administration with academic *savoir faire* which is nothing short of surprising." Father McLaughlin's successor as president of Fordham, Father Michael P. Walsh, had already come to the same conclusion about Reiss. In the spirit that no good deed goes unpunished, Walsh promoted Reiss to academic vice president of the university while retaining him in

15. *Ram*, December 13, 1968.
16. *Ram*, December 11, 1968.

his position as dean of the Liberal Arts College at Lincoln Center. "It was quite a job to handle both of them at the same time," said Reiss modestly.[17]

Riding the Whirlwind

Talleyrand once said that no one can imagine how pleasant life can be unless he happened to have the good fortune to be born as an aristocrat before the French Revolution. Likewise no one can imagine how unpleasant life can be unless he had the misfortune to be a university president in the United States during the tumultuous 1960s and 1970s. That was the fate that befell both Father McLaughlin (1965–69) and his immediate successor, Father Michael P. Walsh (1969–72), who together guided Fordham University through the most challenging years in its history.

Father Leo McLaughlin had deep roots in New York City and in the Society of Jesus. His paternal grandfather was born in New York City in 1825 and had fourteen children, one of whom, a lawyer, was the father of Leo, and he had sufficient means to send his son to Loyola School in New York City and then to Georgetown College.[18] As a Jesuit, Leo was one of a number of young American members of the Society of Jesus who were sent to Europe after World War II to earn degrees at the leading secular universities in order to enhance the academic standards of the faculties of American Jesuit universities.

After his return to the United States from Paris with a doctorate in philosophy from the Sorbonne, McLaughlin rapidly scaled the ladder of the American Jesuit university hierarchy, beginning as a professor in the Communication Arts Department at Fordham in 1950 and moving up to dean of Fordham College three years later. In 1959 he became the dean of St. Peter's College in Jersey City, and finally in 1965 he was appointed president of Fordham to replace Father Vincent O'Keefe, who had been unexpectedly called to Rome to serve as an assistant to the general. According to one unverifiable source, McLaughlin was the overwhelming choice of the New York Jesuits to succeed O'Keefe as president of Fordham.[19]

Father McLaughlin appreciated the wisdom of Cardinal Newman's remark that "to live is to change and to be perfect is to have changed often." He recognized the acute need for American Catholic higher education to

17. FUA, AF 29, Meade, Levy, and Biddle to Cammarosano, October 17, 1969. Paul J. Reiss, FUA, FOHP, Self-Interview, #70, September 1969, 19.

18. FUA, McLaughlin Papers, McLaughlin to Joseph Jacubec, October 31, 1967.

19. Thomas J. Fleming, "Fordham Is Trying to Be catholic with a Small 'c.'" *New York Times Magazine*, December 10, 1967. Fleming was a 1950 graduate of Fordham College.

change in the late 1960s if it was to compete successfully with the best private and public American universities and to refute the caustic comment of George Bernard Shaw that a Catholic university was a contradiction in terms. He was not a Lone Ranger in his reading of the signs of the times. He was one of several dozen Catholic university educators (including a bishop, an archbishop, and a future cardinal, Monsignor Theodore McCarrick, a Fordham graduate), who signed the Land O' Lakes Statement of 1967 advocating greater autonomy for American Catholic universities.[20]

At Fordham, McLaughlin raised admission standards for students, facilitated the transfer of the legal ownership of the university from the Jesuit board of trustees to a predominantly lay board of trustees, and welcomed the addition of non-Catholic faculty and administrators. Two of his trademark expressions became emblematic of his educational philosophy. He said that he "would pay any price, break any mold, in order to achieve [Fordham's] true function as a university" and that he wanted Fordham to be Catholic with both a large "C" and a small "c."

Two years after McLaughlin became president of Fordham, the scores of the incoming freshman class on the College Board examinations had risen one hundred points, and three-quarters of the graduates went on to graduate school. Father George McMahon, S.J., the dean of Fordham College, said, "They have no trouble getting into the best schools in the country—Stanford, Harvard." Faculty salaries were increased to the level where they equaled those of the best universities in the country according to the standards of the American Association of University Professors. One prestigious national college-rating agency evaluated Fordham College and Thomas More College as only one notch below their top category. Likewise, another university-rating agency singled out four departments at Fordham—Philosophy, Classics, English, and French—as only one level below their highest category.[21]

Father McLaughlin also made important improvements for the faculty, giving individual departments increased autonomy from the deans, raising faculty salaries, introducing a major medical program largely funded by

20. Both Father Vincent O'Keefe, S.J., and Father Michael Walsh, S.J., respectively McLaughlin's predecessor and successor as president of Fordham, also signed the statement, as did Father Paul C. Reinert, S.J., the widely respected president of St. Louis University, and Father Theodore M. Hesburgh, C.S.C., the president of the University of Notre Dame.

21. Fleming, "Fordham Is Trying to Be catholic with a Small 'c.'" To be fair, as Fleming noted, the College Board scores of the incoming freshmen had been rising for the previous fifteen years.

Father Leo P. McLaughlin, S.J., president of Fordham University, 1965–69.

the university, and bringing to Fordham the widely popular TIAA-CREF university retirement plan. When McLaughlin heard that some elderly retirees were in serious financial difficulties, he gave them a raise. He also overhauled Fordham's archaic tenure process, effectively providing tenure for any professor who had been a member of the faculty for more than seven years. Both Michael Sheahan, the longtime university secretary, and Dr. Cammarosano agreed that McLaughlin never received due credit for these innovations.[22]

At the same time that McLaughlin was making these impressive changes at Fordham, its academic rival across the East River, St. John's University in Queens, embarked on a campaign to become the largest Catholic university in the United States. It soon found itself involved in a messy eighteen-month faculty strike after dismissing thirty-one professors in the fall of 1965. "I guess it is one of our sister universities," McLaughlin confided dryly to a friend "in so far in a broad sense it may be called Catholic and a university, but I sincerely hope that we do not have much else in common."[23]

22. FUA, FOHP, #77, Interview with Cammarosano, 11–16.
23. FUA, AF 29, McLaughlin to Dean Alfred H. Buford of Villanova University.

Impressive as McLaughlin's initial achievements were, his full program for Fordham would have been difficult to implement even under the best of circumstances, because his brief tenure as president coincided with the most divisive era in recent American history and he was constrained by the perennial problem of Fordham's limited financial resources. McLaughlin encountered opposition from both sides of the political spectrum, both from students and faculty on the left who demanded more radical changes, and also from those on the right who resisted any changes at all.

When an ad hoc group that called itself the Student–Faculty Coalition for a Restructured University urged students to withhold their tuition until their demands were met, Father Francis Canavan, a professor of political science and a Jesuit of the old school, who combined deep-seated conservatism with a lively sense of humor, told McLaughlin, "Whom the gods would destroy, they first make mad. I believe the Coalition are [*sic*] showing the first unmistakable signs of madness with this proposal. I sincerely hope that you will take full advantage of it." McLaughlin politely declined to follow Father Canavan's advice. Instead he used his Irish gift for the soft answer that turns away wrath to disarm less implacable critics than Father Canavan. When a group of students complained that Fordham had failed to proclaim a day of mourning at the death of Cardinal Spellman (who was not one of McLaughlin's favorite prelates), he replied that it would be inappropriate, "since our Christian faith should comfort us all that Cardinal Spellman is rejoicing with God in heaven."[24]

When a woman of a certain age deplored the decision of some Jesuits professors to abandon their religious habit for secular garb, McLaughlin told her that he agreed with her but hoped that he would not "have to die for a tie." On a more serious note, when an alumnus complained that McLaughlin seemed to disparage the achievements of Fordham prior to the 1960s, he was quick to offer an apology. "Fordham without its past is absolutely nothing," he told the alumnus. "I truly glory in that past and I am sorry that anything that I really said or was quoted as saying gave you the impression that I thought otherwise." He then invited the individual to meet with him personally. When the mother of five girls asked McLaughlin to make Fordham Prep a coeducational school, he replied, "Good Lord,

24. FUA, McLaughlin Papers, Canavan to McLaughlin, December 11, 1968; McLaughlin to Mr. Tony Martin, December 6, 1967. McLaughlin also pointed out to the student representative that he would be the principal celebrant at a memorial Mass for Spellman at which the homilist would be Bishop Edwin Broderick, a Fordham alumnus and Spellman's former secretary. "This would hardly qualify as indicating a lack of respect for our most esteemed and outstanding alumnus," he added.

Lady! You are driving me out of what I optimistically think of as my mind." Instead of offering to meet with her, he said that he would pray for her.[25]

In addition to myriad problems on campus, McLaughlin also had to contend with the unsettling aftermath of Vatican Council II on American Catholics in general and especially on the clergy and members of religious orders, including the Society of Jesus. Last but not least, the location of the Rose Hill campus became a geographical liability as the Bronx became nationally famous or infamous as a symbol of urban decay when a wave of crime, arson, and abandonment of residential buildings spread from the South Bronx five miles north to the front gates of the Rose Hill campus.

McLaughlin quickly discovered that a major responsibility of his job was fundraising. During his first six months as president, he averaged about five dinners a week.[26] Despite this hectic schedule, he spent an inordinate amount of time meeting with critics or corresponding with them, especially with confused and upset alumni, rather than leave this unwelcome task to subordinates. Defending his claim that Fordham must strive for greatness, McLaughlin told one concerned Catholic layman, "I am beginning to put the whole position this way: if we can't achieve greatness, we better stop being." He added prophetically, "Strangely enough, I am finding many people to agree with me. And in the theoretical order, it doesn't sound too bad. In the real order," however, he added, "it is going to involve a tremendous amount of suffering."[27]

McLaughlin was more candid and less gentle in dealing with the bureaucracy of the National Catholic Educational Association. He predicted correctly that many small Catholic colleges would go out of existence in the following twenty-five years, but he thought the greater danger was that many of those that would survive would be only nominally Catholic. "A Catholic educational institution does not deserve to continue to exist," he said, "if it does not have a strong department of theology." Never one to mince words, McLaughlin told the officials of the NCEA, "I think that it is important to face the fact that some Catholic institutions do not deserve to continue to exist." Radical as his evaluation sounded, McLaughlin was only echoing and reinforcing the comments made a decade earlier

25. FUA, McLaughlin Papers, McLaughlin to Margaret O'Brien, November 3, 1967; McLaughlin to Albert G. McCarthy III, February 28, 1968; McLaughlin to Mrs. Michael J. Grimes, June 13, 1966.

26. Six months into his presidency, McLaughlin received his first letter of thanks for his dedication to the banquet circuit. "Really, I had not expected to be thanked," he said. FUA, McLaughlin Papers, McLaughlin to David G. Baird, April 12, 1966.

27. FUA, McLaughlin Papers, McLaughlin to Charles J. McCarthy, March 8, 1967.

by Monsignor John Tracy Ellis, the most prominent American Catholic Church historian of that era.[28]

One of McLaughlin's most perceptive and polite critics was Martin Quigley, a devout Catholic layman and a graduate of Georgetown, who was the publisher of several highly successful motion picture trade journals and a key figure in the establishment of the Legion of Decency, the most successful grassroots Catholic pressure group in American history. He told McLaughlin that "stressing a small 'c' rather than a capital 'C' may be a good slogan, but it cannot serve as a road map to the goal." No matter how catholic Fordham and every other Catholic college becomes, Quigley thought that they should do two things: offer excellent courses in theology and philosophy and provide a climate "that will nourish the Christian living of the Catholic leaders and opinion makers of future years." "If Fordham becomes a Harvard," he asked, "why not go to Harvard?"[29]

Father McLaughlin took Quigley's two criticisms to heart and offered him a surprisingly candid self-evaluation of his successes and failures in addressing both issues. When he became dean of Fordham College in 1953, McLaughlin said that he found that the Philosophy Department showed "signs of strength," but that the recently founded Theology Department was described by the students as consisting of "the deaf, the dumb and the blind." He explained that the students' description referred to the "physical and mental abilities of the faculty." He blamed the situation on the common perception in Catholic colleges that it was taken for granted that "a priest who couldn't do anything else could teach theology, or, if he could do nothing, he could teach theology." However, McLaughlin thought the Theology Department was gradually becoming the strongest department on campus.

As for Quigley's second criticism, about the failure to establish a climate on campus that would foster the development of Christian leaders, McLaughlin admitted that it was a valid complaint, but he also explained that it was a difficult problem to solve. Reflecting on his own experience as an undergraduate at Georgetown, he thought that many of the regulations under which he lived were foolish, but he admitted that "it was at least a climate." Unlike some of the faculty and the alumni, McLaughlin realized that it was impossible to turn back the clock to a less critical and more deferential age. "All I can say in this regard," he pleaded, "is that we are really trying."[30]

28. FUA, McLaughlin Papers, McLaughlin to Rev. C. W. Friedman, May 26, 1966.

29. FUA, McLaughlin Papers, Quigley to McLaughlin, February 3, 1967.

30. FUA, McLaughlin Papers, McLaughlin to Martin Quigley Jr,. February 8, 1967.

The Gellhorn Report

One of the most significant initiatives undertaken during Father McLaughlin's administration was the decision of the executive committee of the university board of trustees (all of whom were Jesuits) to authorize a comprehensive legal study of the structure of Fordham University. The primary purpose was to determine what changes Fordham needed to make in its structure and operation in order to achieve legal parity with other private universities in the state and become equally eligible for state financial aid. The immediate occasion for the study was the decision of the New York state attorney general, Louis Lefkowitz—an alumnus of Fordham Law School—that Fordham was ineligible for such assistance because it was a "sectarian" institution and as such was barred from receiving state financial aid by the so-called Blaine Amendment to the state constitution.[31]

Fordham entrusted the study to two professors at Columbia Law School, Walter Gellhorn and R. Kent Greenwalt, in the summer of 1967. They completed their 265-page report the following summer, and it was released to the public on October 17, 1968. At that time 90 percent of the student body at Fordham were Catholics despite extensive efforts to recruit non-Catholic students, and there were 85 Jesuits among the 500 full-time members of the faculty.[32]

Some of the Gellhorn Report's less crucial observations—such as those involving the presence of the crucifix in the classroom, the recitation of prayers before and after class, and the religious garb of the professors—received the most publicity, and they were not always reported accurately. The two authors of the Gellhorn Report raised no red flags about Jesuits' wearing their religious habit or a Roman collar in the classroom, although they mercifully refrained from commenting on the sartorial taste of those

---

31. The background to Lefkowitz's decision was the attempt by Fordham to secure a grant of $100,000 from New York state for the Albert Schweitzer Chair in the Humanities for Marshall McLuhan, the Canadian expert on communications, who was at the height of his ephemeral fame. Not all the students shared Father McLaughlin's enthusiasm for McLuhan. "Oracle, Genius or Carnival Pitchman?" asked the *Ram*. While Fordham was embroiled in litigation to obtain state funding for his chair, McLuhan commented blithely, "It rolls off my back like a duck." *Ram*, January 6, September 19, 1967. Fordham never received any financial aid from New York state for McLuhan's chair because the voters rejected a referendum to repeal the Blaine Amendment in November 1967. When McLuhan returned to Canada the following spring, he sniffed that Canada had long since resolved the church–state controversy over education. *Ram*, March 1, 1968.

32. *The Chronicle of Higher Education*, October 28, 1968.

Jesuits, beginning with Father Quentin Lauer of the Philosophy Department, who had opted for secular garb.

Nor did the authors of the Gellhorn Report object to the retention of the university seal with its rich religious symbolism, but they did so for reasons that were unintentionally offensive to many Catholics, because they dismissed it as an inoperative antiquarian relic like the presence of the English crown in the seal of Columbia University in recognition of its colonial charter. They also seriously underestimated the importance that generations of American Catholics attached to the presence of a crucifix in the classroom of a Catholic school. They were probably correct when they said that respect for the increasingly religious diversity of the student population made the presence of crucifixes in the classrooms problematic, but they seemed to trivialize their own argument when they suggested that the crucifixes could be removed more or less surreptitiously whenever the classrooms were scheduled to be repainted.

They suggested that the University Church might become an ecumenical chapel, like St. Paul's Chapel on the campus of Columbia University, or, more palatably, that it might be sold to the Society of Jesus to assure its continuation as a Catholic church. Their recommendation to relocate Fordham Prep from the university campus was, as they noted, only a reaffirmation of a proposal that had been made repeatedly by the Jesuit authorities themselves both locally and in Rome for at least thirty years, but they failed to mention that, unlike them, the Jesuits had not made the recommendation because they did not want a professedly Catholic high school associated too closely with Fordham University.[33]

The heart of the Gellhorn Report was the question of how Fordham could qualify for state aid, since the Blaine Amendment to the state constitution specifically prohibited the state from giving financial assistance to an educational institution under the control of a religious denomination. In a surprising finding, Messrs. Gellhorn and Greenwalt concluded that the legal owner of Fordham University, according to the charter that Bishop John Hughes had obtained from the state of New York in 1846 (when it was still a diocesan institution), was not the Society of Jesus, but the nine trustees of St. John's College at Rose Hill specified in the charter.[34] For more than a century after the Jesuits bought the college from

33. FUA, AF, Box 17, Walter Gellhorn and R. Kent Greenwalt, "An Independent Fordham? A Choice for Catholic Higher Education," 1968, 81–83, 88–91, 172–89.

34. The original trustees were Bishop Hughes, four diocesan priests, three Catholic laymen, and a Protestant layman. Ibid., 103n38.

the diocese in 1846, the successors of those nine trustees had been Jesuits closely associated with the college and its successor institution, Fordham University. According to Gellhorn and Greenwalt, those nine Jesuit trustees, not the Society of Jesus, were the legal owners of Fordham University in 1968.

The Jesuits had recently reorganized the board of trustees so that it was composed exclusively of nine Jesuits who had no institutional connection with Fordham, except for the president of the university. However, Gellhorn and Greenwalt doubted that this reorganization would survive a civil suit alleging that Fordham was still controlled by a religious denomination. "To end debate on that score," they said, "the Jesuit Board's present monopoly of legal power would have to end." They contended that only a predominantly lay board of trustees would convince the courts that Fordham was an "independent" Catholic university.[35]

McLaughlin and the Jesuit trustees accepted the validity of the argument. Even before the release of the Gellhorn Report, they had petitioned the state legislature to issue a new charter for Fordham University providing for as many as thirty-one members. By the end of 1968 the Fordham board of trustees consisted of twenty-six people—fifteen laymen and eleven Jesuits—and the board was headed by a lay chair, Joseph A. Kaiser, an alumnus of the class of 1926 and the president of the Williamsburg Savings Bank in Brooklyn.[36]

Quo Vadis?

Three weeks before the release of the Gellhorn Report, the legal trustees of the university (all of whom were still Jesuits) and Kaiser, the chair of the lay board of trustees, met for two days at Rose Hill to assess the anticipated reaction to the release of the report. They were joined by Professor Gellhorn, who assured them that his study of Fordham had enhanced his respect for the institution. With regard to the question of Fordham's eligibility for government financial assistance, Gellhorn said that both he and Professor Greeenwalt did not think that Fordham would have any problem qualifying for federal aid, but that they thought that Fordham would have difficulty obtaining aid from New York state "as long as the

---

35. Ibid., p. 11l. The Fordham Board of Lay Trustees established by Father McGinley in 1958 had grown to thirty-three members, two of them women. "It is a great deal more than a paper tiger," Gellhorn and Greenwalt conceded, but they also concluded that it had no legal authority. Ibid., 107–8.

36. *Ram*, November 1, 1968; *The Catholic News*, December 19, 1968.

flavor of the institution is as it is" because of the Blaine Amendment to the state constitution.[37]

The financial stakes were high for an institution like Fordham struggling to meet its expenses. In 1968 the New York state legislature voted to allocate a total of $24 million in financial assistance to eligible private institutions. The legislation was based on the recommendation of a select committee appointed jointly by Governor Nelson A. Rockefeller and the New York State Board of Regents, which was headed by McGeorge Bundy, the president of the Ford Foundation. Hence the financial aid recommended by his committee quickly became known as Bundy Money.[38] Despite the allure of the Bundy Money, several of the Jesuit trustees raised serious concerns about the implications of the Gellhorn Report.

Father Robert A. Mitchell, the provincial of the New York Province of the Society, said that he had encountered "a lot of trouble" with Archbishop Terence J. Cooke of New York on the last occasion that he saw him, and that rumors were rife that Fordham no longer wanted to be a Jesuit institution. Father Donald R. Campion feared that giving a copy of the Gellhorn Report to the New York State Education Department would be "like giving a man a gun with which he is going to shoot me." Even Father McLaughlin, who had commissioned the Gellhorn Report and welcomed many of its recommendations, despaired of gaining approval from the Jesuit authorities in Rome. "An autonomous university is impossible for Dezza," he said, referring to Father Paolo Dezza, the former rector of the Pontifical Gregorian University and an influential figure in the Jesuit Curia in Rome. Father Edmund G. Ryan agreed with this bleak assessment. "His university is a seminary," he said.

The person who took command of the situation at the meeting by clarifying the issues was the acting chair of the board of trustees, Father Michael P. Walsh, the former president of Boston College. "I commend you very highly," he told Professor Gellhorn. "You have shown great respect for the Fordham man and the traditions of Fordham." And he told his fellow Jesuits, "He [Gellhorn] admits that we should always keep our traditions and heritage. There is a very positive approach about a lot of things

37. The so-called Blaine Amendment (Article XI, Section 3, of the state constitution) prohibited the expenditure of state funds on "any school or institution of learning wholly or in part under the control or direction of any religious denomination, or in which any denominational tenet or doctrine is taught." *New York Times*, January 6, 1970.

38. Ibid. The Bundy Money was to be distributed to the colleges and universities on the basis of $400 for each bachelor's and master's degree, and $2,400 for each doctorate conferred during the twelve-month period that would end on June 30, 1969.

in the text." He also pointed out that Fordham had already been in the process of implementing many of the recommendations made in the Gellhorn Report. On the other hand, Walsh raised objections to the Gellhorn Report's suggestion that Fordham sever its ties with the Jesuit Educational Association and with the National Catholic Educational Association. "I'm not so sure that is important," he said.

Walsh was under no illusions about the critical reaction the Gellhorn Report would receive in the secular media. "*The [New York] Times* will report: Fordham is secular," he said. He also urged his fellow Jesuits to face squarely the tradeoff that Fordham (and other Catholic colleges) was seeking to negotiate. "We pit getting money out of the State against the terrible reaction from traditional publics." He predicted that the alumni would answer the question whether Fordham was still a Catholic and Jesuit institution. If they were confused, Walsh attributed their uncertainty partially at least to Fordham's own failure to define clearly its identity. "Sometimes it's Catholic," he said, "sometimes it's purely educational."[39]

As anticipated at Fordham, the release of the Gellhorn Report caused a firestorm in many Catholic quarters, where it was suspected of being a blueprint and justification for the transformation of Fordham into a secular university despite the assurances of the Fordham administration that it would examine the report critically. In releasing the report, Father McLaughlin and the board of trustees stressed that Fordham "has no intention of divesting itself of its character as an independent, Catholic and Jesuit institution of higher education; it proposes to remain true to itself and to continue the untrammeled pursuit of academic excellence."[40]

Predictably, critics included conservative spokesmen like Patrick Scanlan, the editor of the *Brooklyn Tablet*, one of the most widely circulated diocesan newspapers in the United States, who expressed the hope that Fordham would not abandon its Catholic identity "in a shortsighted attempt to obtain the assistance of government funding."[41]

However, some senior Jesuit members of the Fordham faculty who did not often find themselves in the same ideological camp as Scanlan shared his misgivings about the Gellhorn Report. Father Quentin Lauer, the chair

39. FUA, AF, Box 6, Notes of the Meeting of the Board of Trustees, September 24–25, 1968.

40. FUA, AF, Box 6, Statement by Leo McLaughlin, S.J., President of Fordham University, October 16, 1968; Fordham Trustees State Policy on Study, October 30, 1968. The cost of the study was underwritten by a grant of $45,000 from the P&P Gerli Foundation, which appreciated its significance for all of American higher education.

41. *The Tablet*, October 24, 1968.

of the Philosophy Department, warned that a "secular" Fordham would "a denial of all Fordham has been for 128 years." Father Joseph Fitzpatrick insisted that the Theology Department must define the values of the university, while the chair of the Theology Department, Father Christopher Mooney, objected to the Gellhorn Report's criticism of the heavy preponderance of Catholic clerics and laity in his department.[42]

Despite the skeptical reaction to many of the implications of the Gellhorn Report, the doubts expressed by Professors Gellhorn and Greenwalt over Fordham's eligibility for Bundy Money were quickly confirmed by the state education commissioner, Ewald B. Nyquist. An old friend of Fordham's former president Father Laurence J. McGinley's, Nyquist announced that he had been legally compelled to rule that Fordham and twenty other New York state colleges with religious affiliations were ineligible for Bundy Money. "I regret that the [state] Constitution still precludes such support," he added.[43]

Less than two months later, however, Commissioner Nyquist reversed his decision and announced that Fordham and two other Catholic colleges (Manhattanville College of the Sacred Heart in Purchase and St. John Fisher College in Rochester) were eligible to receive Bundy Money. He reached his decision only two days after Fordham announced the composition of its newly expanded board of trustees with a majority of lay members. "While each of these three institutions were [sic] founded under Roman Catholic auspices," Nyquist explained, "I have concluded after an extensive and careful review that none of them is now under the control or direction of a religious denomination or teaches denominational tenets or doctrines." As a result of Nyquist's decision, Fordham immediately became eligible for an estimated $1,077,600 in state aid that year.[44]

Nyquist's good intentions were beyond question because he had braved considerable secularist opposition to reverse his previous decision. Unfortunately, however, the awkward ambiguity of his statement that Fordham had ceased to teach "denominational tenets or doctrines" provided fuel for Catholic critics who claimed that Fordham had ceased to be a Catholic institution. On the contrary, it seems a reasonable and more benign interpretation of Nyquist's remarks to say that he was declaring that Fordham was eligible for state aid because it had transformed "religion classes" into

42. *Ram*, November 26, 1968.

43. *New York Times*, January 6, 1970.

44. *Ram*, February 18, 1969. New York State Education Department, press release, February 19, 1970.

the teaching of theology as a scholarly academic discipline rather than a form of catechetical instruction.

Catholic critics of Fordham's decision to accept Bundy Money sometimes contrasted Fordham with St. John's University in Queens as a "more Catholic university" because it had declined to apply for Bundy Money for fear of compromising its Catholic identity. Dr. Paul Reiss, who played a key role in obtaining the Bundy Money for Fordham, vigorously disagreed. Two decades after Fordham received its first installment of Bundy Money, Reiss said, "I challenge anyone to be able to demonstrate that in some way St. John's has been able in actual practice to be more Catholic than Fordham . . . because it has not been receiving Bundy Aid. I don't believe that Fordham has had to compromise its principles, had to compromise its Catholic character." In fact in the past forty years the New York State Department of Education has never objected to Fordham's ample offerings of courses in Catholic theology on both the undergraduate and graduate levels.[45]

"Nice Guys Don't Win Pennants"

The famous comment of dubious accuracy—"Nice guys don't win pennants"—attributed to Leo Durocher, the hard-nosed and pugnacious manager of the Brooklyn Dodgers in 1946, about the failures of baseball managers who were "nice guys" might well be applied to Father Leo McLaughlin. Whatever McLaughlin's shortcomings as president of Fordham, he was never accused of being hard-nosed or pugnacious. On the contrary, Father Schroth has described poignantly how deeply hurt McLaughlin was by the intemperate reaction of some of his confrères in the Fordham Jesuit community. "It must have been excruciating for him to live with them," said Schroth.[46] "He was a role model for me as Dean of Fordham College when I was a student, 1954–1958," said John Feerick, the future dean of Fordham Law School, "and I tried to follow in his footsteps in relating to the students."[47]

McLaughlin's Jesuit critics feared that he was betraying Fordham's Catholic identity by succumbing to the siren calls of people like Jacque-

45. Reiss faulted Nyquist for saying that Fordham had become eligible for state aid because it had become "sufficiently secular." He thought that it would have been more accurate for Nyquist to say that "indoctrination was not the object of our academic program in religion and theology." Reiss, FUA, FOHP, 33–34.

46. Raymond A. Schroth, S.J., *Fordham: A History and Memoir* (Chicago: Loyola University Press, 2002), 264.

47. Personal communication to author.

line Grennan, a former sister of Loreto and president of Webster College in Webster Groves, Missouri, who achieved a brief moment of fame as an innovative educator when she presided over the secularization of the Catholic college she headed. At a speech on the Rose Hill campus in the spring of 1968, Grennan urged Fordham to imitate her example and predicted that "Fordham has the chance to become the greatest university to come out of the Catholic tradition."[48] Grennan's fame proved to be even more evanescent than that of Marshall McLuhan.

However, the issue that led Father McLaughlin to offer his resignation as president of Fordham to the board of trustees on December 14, 1968, was not the wave of student protests on campus nor the critical reaction of many to the Gellhorn Report nor the polarization of the faculty and the student body over the Vietnam War, but the more mundane issue of the precarious state of the university's finances. At the Mass of the Holy Spirit in September 1967 inaugurating the new academic year, McLaughlin announced that "Fordham is faced with the greatest crisis in her long history of crises" and called it a "matter of life and death."

Six months later, in March 1968, he said that "we have reached a moment of truth" and revealed that Fordham would have to raise a minimum of $3.5 million by June 30, 1969. Robert A. Kidera, vice president for university relations and development, stressed the gravity of the situation when he added that "the university has critical need for immediate financial support in amounts never before obtained by this institution."[49] At the meeting of the Jesuit board of trustees in October 1968, McLaughlin told Brother James M. Kenny, S.J., financial vice president and treasurer, "Jim, I'm busted," and he added for the benefit of the rest of the Board, "We are coming to a screeching halt."[50]

Rightly or wrongly, McLaughlin suspected that he was not well served by his financial advisors. He told the general, Father Pedro Arrupe, in the summer of 1967 that "I have been trying in vain to obtain a clear, concise and accurate picture of the financial situation. It seems quite sure that we must obtain better methods of keeping our books and reporting upon our financial situation. I shall ask experts to help in this." Six months later the situation had not improved, and McLaughlin told Arrupe, "I am quite

48. *Ram*, March 26, 1968. In 1970 Grennan became president of Hunter College, where she soon found herself barricaded in her own office by student protesters. *New York Times*, January 25, 2012.

49. *Ram*, October 3, 1967, March 26, 1968.

50. FUA, AF, Box 6, Meeting of the Fordham University Board of Trustees, October 15–16, 1968.

convinced that one reason why [the financial problems at Fordham] are so overwhelming is because of the outdated and poor methods used by our Treasurer's Office. After two years of failing to correct this situation, I am convinced that major changes in personnel must be made in that department."[51]

McLaughlin did not identify the people whom he wished to replace in the Finance Office, but the problem may have been not bad advice from them but McLaughlin's reluctance to accept sound but unwelcome advice from them, including Brother Kenny and Father Gib O'Neill, S.J., the university treasurer. "I did gradually conclude that [McLaughlin] was not on top of the financial situation," said Father James J. Hennesey, S.J., the superior of the Jesuit community at Fordham. "One week we were headed for disaster; the next everything was all right . . . . He had no one who could make him face the hard financial facts."

On Thanksgiving Eve in 1968 Father Arrupe summoned Hennesey to Rome. He left that evening for Rome, where he met with Arrupe; the American assistant Father Small; Father Andrew Varga, a general assistant and former philosophy professor at Fordham; and Father Walsh, who was in Rome on business in connection with the Gregorian University. Hennesey was told that it was Arrupe's wish that McLaughlin resign as president of Fordham. Back in New York, when Hennesey informed McLaughlin of Arrupe's decision, he replied, "Tell him I'll do it, and I'll never tell anyone why." He submitted his resignation to the board of trustees in a terse one-sentence statement on December 14, 1968.[52]

Fordham tried to ease the pain of McLaughlin's resignation as president by creating a new position for him as chancellor of the university, a post whose main responsibility was fundraising from wealthy potential donors, which had little appeal for him.[53] He resigned in 1970 to take a teaching position at a predominantly black college in North Carolina. Two years later he joined the faculty of Ramapo College in New Jersey, where he taught

51. FUA, McLaughlin Papers, McLaughlin to Arrupe, August 21, 1967, January 16, 1968.

52. FUA, FOHP, #89, Self-Interview of Father James J. Hennesey, S.J., October 31, 1990, 4–5. A short time later the board of trustees also decided that McLaughlin should resign. Two Jesuits were tasked with breaking the news to him at a dinner in a restaurant. McLaughlin said to them, "I know what you have to tell me. I'll resign, so let's have a pleasant meal." Ibid., 6.

53. McLaughlin's efforts were directed at obtaining donations of $50,000 to $200,000 from the notoriously parsimonious Fordham alumni. "If he gets one out of fifteen, we'll be lucky," said Father Walsh. *Ram*, June 7, 1969.

until he suffered a series of strokes in the 1980s. Meanwhile, in 1974, at the age of sixty, he married a twenty-five-year-old woman without waiting for a response to his request from the ecclesiastical authorities for a dispensation from his vows. "I'm not young," he said in justification of his decision, "and a year is a long time to wait."[54]

McLaughlin was increasingly incapacitated by a series of strokes after the death of his wife in 1994, and he gratefully accepted a generous offer from the provincial, Father Joseph Parkes, to spend his last months at Murray-Weigel Hall, the Jesuit infirmary on the Rose Hill campus, where he died in August 1996 at the age of eighty-four. Thus a Fordham presidency characterized by bitter controversy and intramural recrimination ended at least within the Jesuit community with a peaceful reconciliation symbolized by the large number of Jesuit concelebrants at Father McLaughlin's funeral Mass.[55]

"Father McLaughlin caught my imagination like few people have done in my life," said Father James Hennesey. "I genuinely like[d] him, wanted him to succeed. The Fordham that he and Father [Timothy] Healy created, even if briefly, had great appeal." However, Hennesey added, "Leo McLaughlin was a genuine romantic who dreamed great dreams. So it had to end, but it was a wonderful experience while it lasted."[56]

54. *New York Times*, August 18, 1996.
55. Schroth, *Fordham: A History and Memoir*, 290.
56. FUA, FOHP, Hennesey, Self-Interview, 3, 7.

WAR AND PEACE

19

The Most Important Man on Campus

When Father McLaughlin resigned as president of Fordham in December 1968, few Jesuits were vying to take his place. The person who volunteered for the challenging task was Father Michael P. Walsh, who had been the acting chair and later the chair of Fordham's board of trustees for the previous six months. A native of Boston, Walsh was a graduate of Boston College and had earned a doctorate in biology from Fordham before returning to BC as a professor and then as chair of the Biology Department. In 1958, at the age of forty-six, he became the president of Boston College, where he expanded the physical plant with ten new residence halls and made notable strides in establishing BC's reputation as a national rather than a local college. Early in his academic career he had said that his model as a university president was Father Robert I. Gannon, a prophetically appropriate choice given that Fordham in 1968 was facing the greatest crisis in its history since the university had suffered the loss of accreditation in the 1930s, leading to the appointment of Father Gannon as president in 1936.[1]

Walsh was to be the last president of Fordham appointed by the nine-man Jesuit board of trustees. He deflected criticism of the manner of his appointment by pointing out that there was insufficient time for a wider consultation. Walsh's selection as president of Fordham personified the incisive comment of the Anglican historian A. G. Dickens that a major reason for the success of the Society of Jesus as far back as the sixteenth century had been the uncanny ability of the Jesuits to recognize the talents of their members in times of crisis and to place them in key positions of responsibility. Walsh further illustrated that same ability in the selection of two of his most important administrators. Neither was a Jesuit, but they were dedicated Catholic laymen: Dr. Joseph Cammarosano and Dr. Paul Reiss. Walsh made Cammarosano, who was the chair of the Economics Department, executive vice president, and, as was already mentioned, he

1. *The Catholic News*, December 19, 1968.

Father Michael P. Walsh, S.J., president of Fordham University, 1969–72.

persuaded Reiss, who had been the chair of the Sociology Department, to become the academic vice president while retaining his position as dean of the College at Lincoln Center. The two other key figures in his administration were a Jesuit brother, James M. Kenny, whom Walsh retained in his position as financial vice president and treasurer, and a third layman, Dr. Martin J. Meade, vice president for student affairs.

Cammarosano, Reiss, and Meade were especially valuable in helping Walsh to cope with the campus unrest and violence that reached its peak in the early 1970s. In the spring of 1970, when the dust had yet to settle after the most recent student demonstrations, an irate but unusually well-informed student paid Walsh a backhanded and perceptive compliment when he said that "Father Walsh is not only the most powerful, but the most influential person on the campus. Certainly [he is] the most skillful and brilliant politician I have ever met. Father Walsh knows how to manipulate every single power bloc on campus." The student could not resist adding that "[Walsh] has pulled a series of fast ones this year, earning his place with blood, sweat and tears" as the most important person on campus. It was an assessment with which many more sympathetic administrators, professors, and students would have agreed.[2]

2. *Ram*, April 10, 1970.

Joseph Cammarosano has said that, despite all the heartaches and humiliations associated with the campus turmoil of the early 1970s, he considered his three years with Father Walsh the high point of his sixty years of service to Fordham. "He was a great man, a great leader, and a first-rate administrator in every way," said Cammarosano. In dealing with the financial crisis, Walsh and Cammarosano complemented each other by playing the classic game of good cop and bad cop in negotiating the annual budget with the deans and other administrators. As Cammarosano explained, "I would take a hard line and try to take as much money off the table as I could. Father Walsh, on the other hand, was low key and quite conciliatory. But, in the end, he would succeed in picking up whatever loose change was left and he did this in his own subtle way."[3]

Paul Reiss shared Joseph Cammarosano's high opinion of Walsh both professionally and personally. He described him as a hard-driving person who expected equally hard work from his administrators, but he noted that Walsh softened his demands by presenting them as suggestions rather than as orders. Reiss's predecessor as academic vice president, Dr. Arthur Brown, resigned when he returned from vacation to find a pile of memoranda from Walsh on his desk. "I just can't take it," said Brown, "I can't handle it." However, when Reiss looked at the memoranda himself, what impressed him was the kind and conciliatory tone of Walsh's communications. "That was Father Walsh's style," said Reiss; "he got a lot done by using that gentle but very firm hand in his administrative style." On a more personal note, Reiss said that his wife, Rosemary, always knew when he had spent time at a meeting with the chain-smoking Father Walsh because he reeked of cigarette smoke when he came home in the evening.[4]

Father Walsh was often described, not always with admiration, as a "Boston Irishman." Father James Hennesey added a further specification to that characterization when he described Walsh as a "canny South Boston Irishman." Walsh once said to Hennesey, "Jim, you and I understand

3. FUA, FOHP, Cammarosano, Interview, 36–37. Even in his role as the bad cop, Cammarosano displayed a gift for turning down requests for more money without creating ill will. On one occasion, at a meeting at Rose Hill, Cammarosano refused a request for additional funding from Dr. Joseph Mulholland, an administrator at Lincoln Center. As Mulholland was driving back to Lincoln Center on the West Side Highway, he was congratulating himself on his successful performance at the meeting. "And then," he said, "I stopped and realized that, at that meeting, I didn't get a single thing that I wanted, yet somehow or other, I still felt good after I came out." FUA, FOHP, Paul Reiss, Self-Interview, 51.

4. FUA, FOHP, Reiss, Interview, 49–50.

one another because I'm from South Boston and you're from Jersey City. These New Yorkers are different." Despite this intimation of a special bond between them, Walsh kept Hennesey at a distance and seemed to be wary of him. Perhaps that is why Hennesey called him "a canny Southie." Nonetheless, Hennesey respected Walsh as a tough pragmatic administrator who was not afraid to make unpopular decisions, and he admitted that Walsh was enormously popular in the Jesuit community because the Jesuits correctly gave him credit for saving the university from disaster.[5]

High Noon at Rose Hill

The peak period of American campus protests, at least at Fordham, coincided with the three years of Father Walsh's administration between 1969 and 1972. However, unlike the denouement in Fred Zinnemann's classic 1952 American Western *High Noon*, which lasted for only a few minutes and ended in the violent death of the outlaws, the confrontation at Fordham between student radicals and the administration extended over several years, punctuated by two major occupations of the Administration Building and the torching of the Campus Center, and gradually petered out in an undeclared truce, which was in fact a victory for the restraint of the administration.

Upon assuming the reins at Fordham, however, Father Walsh's first priority was not to come to grips with the campus unrest but to restore the solvency of the university. He relied heavily on Joseph Cammarosano for advice and direction, and together they made rapid progress. The severity of the financial crisis became evident in June 1968 at the end of the fiscal year, when the deficit ballooned to about $2 million compared with $617,000 the previous year. Characteristically, Cammarosano gave much of the credit for the resolution of the financial crisis to others, specifically Father Walsh, the University Budget Committee appointed by Father McLaughlin, and to McLaughlin himself, who drastically cut back on spending in the spring of 1968 but not soon enough to save his own job. Despite his modest disclaimers, Cammarosano himself also played a vital and indispensable role second only to that of Father Walsh.

In the space of a single year Fordham's financial crisis was resolved, and within two years a deficit of $2 million was turned into a surplus of $2 million, a turnaround of $4 million. "That was no mean feat," as Joseph Cammarosano pointed out. However, Father Walsh would not allow the figures on the income statement to be called a surplus for fear that the pub-

5. FUA, FOHP, Hennesey, Interview, 7–8.

licity would create a false sense of euphoria and lead to renewed demands for bloated budgets from faculty and administrators with short memories. Officially the surplus had to be euphemistically disguised as excess of revenues over expenditures.

The contribution of $1 million in Bundy Money from New York state was an important factor in Fordham's fiscal recovery, but the main reason was Fordham's own ability to limit discretionary spending until income gradually exceeded expenditures. The temporary austerity measures included the prohibition of the purchase of electric typewriters and even requirements to use carbon paper instead of copy machines. Cammarosano was quick to admit that the purpose of such petty regulations was more psychological than economic. They were meant to convey to the faculty and the staff the gravity of the situation and to instill in them a sense of fiscal discipline. However, said Cammarosano proudly, "at no time did we reduce the size of the faculty or curtail essential academic outlays."

Cammarosano had no illusions about the gravity of the financial crisis that Fordham was facing in 1969. "We were fighting for survival," he said, "and I don't mean survival for survival's sake alone. Fordham was and is an institution that is worthy of continued life. And so we did what had to be done. The alternative would have been Chapter 11." Cammarosano acknowledged the important roles played by Paul Reiss, Brother James Kenny, and himself in rescuing Fordham from the threat of bankruptcy in 1969, but he gave most of the credit to Father Walsh. "Without his leadership," said Cammarosano, "our efforts would have gone for naught." He never ceased to marvel at how a former biology professor at Boston College became a financial expert during his "too brief" tenure at Fordham. He also respected Walsh's total dedication to Fordham. "Missed lunches and cold dinners were not unusual for him," noted Cammarosano, and he said that Father Walsh's idea of a good weekend was to gather up all the university catalogues and to read "the damn things" line-by-line in an effort to make Fordham a better university.[6]

The main object of the student protests was the presence on campus of the ROTC and its four-year program of noncredit courses, which enrolled some 300 students in 1969. The previous May, the Faculty Senate had voted to continue the ROTC program by a vote of 16–0–1. Nonetheless, the annual review of the ROTC, when the cadets marched in uniform on Edwards Parade, was a golden opportunity for the Students for a Democratic Society to fan opposition to the Vietnam War. The first pro-

6. FUA, FOHP, Cammarosano, Interview, pp. 23–41.

test occurred in 1965 when one brave soul staged a lonely vigil outside the Campus Center. Over the course of the next few years, demonstrations grew larger and provoked counter-demonstrations. In 1966, a hundred protesters marched around the sidewalk surrounding Edwards Parade at the annual ROTC review while an equal number of students marched in the opposite direction to show their support for the ROTC. In both the spring and fall of 1969 students staged brief but peaceful occupations of the Administration Building.

However, by the fall of 1969, there were indications that the anti-war movement at Fordham had reached its peak and had begun to decline. In October a rally against the ROTC drew only forty students who met with Father Walsh, who refused their demand to end the presence of the ROTC on campus. Later that month 53 percent of the students who voted in a student poll approved the presence of the ROTC on campus and 72 percent approved the practice of allowing the armed forces to recruit on campus. The self-styled Committee to Abolish the ROTC, which had been organized by the local chapter of the SDS, attempted to explain the repudiation of its agenda by noting that only 24 percent of the students had participated in the poll. The SDS failed to mention that it had urged the students to boycott the poll.[7]

Perhaps in an effort to stem the declining interest in anti-war activism, the Committee to Abolish ROTC organized a major escalation of the campus turmoil on November 12, 1969, when its members broke into the Administration Building and occupied the ground floor of the south wing, which included the president's office. It was estimated that as many as seventy-five students were involved in the break-in. Unlike those of previous demonstrations against the ROTC, the tactics of the student radicals on this occasion could hardly be described as peaceful, since they smashed windows and forced open locked doors that had been secured in anticipation of such an event. Even the usually sympathetic editors of the *Ram* described the activities of the protesters as "almost anarchistic from the start" and criticized their tactics as the opposite of "a rational means to evict ROTC from the campus."[8]

At the time of the break-in, Father Walsh, Vice President Cammarosano, and Dean Meade happened to be holding a conference in Walsh's office. The demonstrators subjected Walsh to verbal abuse, scuffled briefly with Cammarosano and Meade, and ordered them to leave the premises.

7. *Ram*, October 21, 31, 1969.
8. *Ram*, November 19, 1969.

Initially they refused to do so but then withdrew to the north wing of the Administration Building to formulate their response to the student barricade of the south wing. Over the course of the next seven hours Walsh, Cammarosano, and Meade met with the executive committee of the Faculty Senate, with other administrators and faculty members, and with leaders of the student government.

Meanwhile, newspaper photographers and television camera crews descended on the campus in search of a good story as some 200 people assembled on the south lawn in front of the Administration Building to offer encouragement to the protesters inside. Not all of the spectators were Fordham students; many were students from other colleges who flocked to Rose Hill as a result of radio reports of the disturbances. Fearful of a counter-demonstration by Fordham students that would end in a violent confrontation, Meade asked Father Robert McNamara, S.J., the chair of the Sociology Department, to visit the residence halls and urge the students to remain in their dorm rooms.

On four occasions Dean Meade assured the demonstrators that they would be subject only to academic disciplinary measures if they withdrew peacefully from the Administration Building and that their safety would be guaranteed by the campus security guards. More than a dozen students took advantage of this implicit offer and left the building. However, when Meade repeated this offer for the fifth time, the security guards were attacked (and six were injured) when they attempted to remove the barricades and escort other students from the building.

At this point Father Walsh decided to appeal to the NYPD for help. He was informed that it might take as long as three hours for New York's Finest to respond to his plea to restore law and order on the Rose Hill campus. As Father Walsh was waiting for the arrival of the NYPD, sounds of police sirens were heard on East Fordham Road. Suspecting that perhaps the patrol cars might be headed for the Fordham campus, the student protesters scurried to end their occupation of the Administration Building. In the process of their rapid exodus, they injured six security guards, who filed charges of criminal assault against them. When the police finally arrived on campus, they were greeted with cries of "Off the Pigs." They arrested thirteen students in addition to the six who had already been arrested when the security guards filed charges against them. They were all charged with criminal trespass and criminal mischief.[9]

9. FUA, Walsh Papers, Box 2, Report of Demonstration against ROTC, November 12, 1969, n.d., 3–31. FUA, FOHP, Cammarosano, Interview, 48.

At a hearing on January 21, 1970, the Bronx district attorney, Burton Roberts, offered to reduce the charges against the arrested students from criminal liability to the obligation to take youth counseling treatment for a period of six months. Eventually fourteen of them accepted the generous offer, but five others opted instead for a trial on the original charge of criminal trespass.[10] When their request was granted, the defendants attempted to gain maximum publicity from their trial in the massive Art Deco Bronx County Court House at the Grand Concourse and East 161st Street by presenting themselves as innocent victims of political oppression.

They called themselves the "Fordham Five" in an allusion to the "Chicago Seven," who had turned their trial in 1969 into a well-publicized political circus when they were indicted for attempting to disrupt the Democratic National Convention in Chicago the previous year. Unfortunately for the "Fordham Five," however, except for their tiresome proclivity to shout obscenities in the courtroom, they seemed pale imitations of the more talented Yippie activists in the Chicago trial like Abbie Hoffman and Jerry Rubin and their defense attorney, William Kunstler. Even the New York tabloids quickly lost interest in the fate of the "Fordham Five" after they were convicted and received suspended sentences in the spring of 1970. Father Walsh did not help their case when he explained calmly under cross-examination why he had summoned the NYPD to expel the students who were occupying the Administration Building. "Because they did not belong there," he said. "They were occupying the building against our rules and regulations."[11]

Walsh was personally disappointed with the leniency of the court, the district attorney, and even the police commissioner. He told a lawyer friend, "We of the administration have become so discouraged by the Bronx Courts that we almost begin to wonder whether or not we should bother arresting students as we have done in the past." However, he added, "I can assure you that we are giving our utmost efforts to preserve the freedom necessary for peaceful dissent but to move in rapidly on anarchy or disruption or violence." Although Father Walsh was disappointed with the adjudication of the cases of the nineteen arrested Fordham students, his own handling of the occupation of the Administration Building received support from both the faculty and the student government. The executive

10. FUA, Walsh Papers, Box 2, Meade to Walsh, February 25, 1970. The *New York Post* claimed that fifteen students accepted Burton Roberts's offer. *New York Post*, February 25, 1970.

11. FUA, Walsh Papers, Box 2, Walsh to Fordham Community, n.d. *Ram*, April 10, September 15, 1970.

council of the Faculty Senate endorsed his actions by a margin of 20–0–1, and even the leaders of the student government rejected a proposal to stage a second ("non-violent") occupation of the Administration Building by a margin of 7–9–2.[12]

Nonetheless, a second occupation of the Administration Building took place in the spring of 1970. It lasted two days, from April 13 to April 15, and involved as many as 400 students, according to one estimate. Both the circumstances and the outcome of the second occupation were different from those of the first occupation five months earlier. The cause of the second occupation was not the presence of the ROTC on campus or a further escalation of the Vietnam War (President Nixon did not announce the extension of the war into Cambodia until the end of the month) but a routine academic issue, the denial of tenure to a popular young assistant professor in the English Department, Dr. Ronald Friedland.[13]

The second occupation of the Administration Building began at 11:00 P.M. on April 12, when Robert Reger, the former executive vice president of the United Student Government, "peacefully" broke a window in the president's office and led 250 students into the building. Unlike the first occupation of the Administration Building, this sit-in ended without violence when the university obtained a temporary restraining order, the first step in securing a permanent injunction against the occupiers. Reger claimed that the students had left the premises "the way we found it" in contrast to the extensive damage that had occurred during the first occupation. Reger's statement was not quite accurate, since a window had been broken and that one of the student occupiers, Bill Arnone, admitted that he had taken advantage of the opportunity to rifle through Father Walsh's files and to publish one of his letters in the *Ram*.[14]

The end of the second occupation of the Administration Building was followed by a short-lived student strike and an invitation to sympathetic professors to establish what proved to be an even shorter-lived Free Uni-

12. FUA, Walsh Papers, Box 2, Walsh to Paul W. Lynch, May 11, 1970. *Ram*, November 19, 25, 1969.

13. The grounds for the denial of tenure to Friedland was his failure to publish a sufficient number of scholarly articles or books, one of the three standard criteria for receiving tenure in a research university. *Ram*, March 13, 1970.

14. *Ram*, April 15, 17, 1970. Raymond A. Schroth, S.J., *Fordham: A History and Memoir* (Chicago: Loyola University Press, 2002), 300–3. The estimated cost of repairing the damage caused by the first occupation of the Administration Building in November 1969 came to $9,067.35. FUA, Walsh Papers, Box 2, Ralph J. Pacifico to Brother James Kenny, S.J., December 8, 1969.

versity in the Student Center. Although it was claimed that at one point three-quarters of the students were boycotting classes, the *Ram* noted unsympathetically that there was a lower absentee rate in the classes where the professors were strict in taking attendance. The original issue of the denial of tenure to Dr. Friedland led to a more radical student demand for equal representation of the students with the faculty in the governance of the university departments. Walsh addressed both issues at a faculty convocation in Keating Hall on April 20 that was attended by more than 300 professors. As usual, after three hours of discussion, Mike Walsh got what he wanted. The faculty endorsed his decision to deny tenure to Professor Friedland and approved an anodyne proposal that there be greater but unspecified student participation in the departmental structure of the university.[15]

Early in May, at a meeting of a radical fringe group of the SDS, Father Schroth heard one of the participants say, "The only way to get attention here is to burn a building." A week later, on May 7, Schroth was awakened in the middle of the night in his room on campus by the sight of flames coming from the Campus Center and the sounds of the firefighters struggling to contain the blaze. The three-alarm fire began around 1:00 A.M. in the basement bookstore of the building, where it was likely to cause maximum damage, and it burned out of control for four-and-a-half hours. The cause of the fire was never determined, nor was it ever linked to any Fordham student.[16]

The torching of the Campus Center was only one of hundreds of demonstrations that occurred on college campuses all across the country in the days and weeks following the most tragic of all the anti-war demonstrations of that era, the killing of four unarmed students and the wounding of nine others at Kent State University by units of the Ohio National Guard on May 4.

At Fordham the fire in the Campus Center was followed by the burning of the American flag, which had been snatched from the campus flagpole, and the vandalism of several buildings, including the library, where some of the card catalogues were trashed. The situation became so threatening that the chief of the campus security force asked Vice President Cammarosano to summon the NYPD to help restore order. Fearful of intensifying

15. *Ram*, April 15, 21, 1970.

16. Schroth, *Fordham: A History and Memoir*, 304. Walsh doubted that any Fordham student was responsible for the fire. FUA, Walsh Papers, Box 2, Walsh to John Tarpey, May 20, 1970.

the violence, Cammarosano declined to accede to the request and decided to "tough it out," as he put it. Nonetheless, disturbances continued on a daily basis, culminating in an effort to force the cancelation of final exams by blocking the entrances to Keating Hall. With the assistance of the maintenance staff, Cammarosano and Dean Meade broke open the entrances to Keating Hall, and the final examinations took place on schedule.[17]

The Turn of the Tide

The campus disturbances at Fordham reached their peak in the fall of 1969 and the spring of 1970 but then gradually subsided as the United States accelerated its disengagement from the Vietnam War. Throughout this period, Father Walsh was under pressure from outraged alumni and the more conservative students to take swifter and more aggressive action against the small minority of disruptive students. A particular object of their ire was Walsh's tolerance on campus of the Fordham chapter of the SDS. Although Walsh may have been tempted to follow their advice at times, he prudently refrained from doing so for fear of playing into the hands of student radicals by resorting to coercive measures that might alienate a much larger segment of the faculty and student body.

He told one concerned alumnus, "I can assure you that we have been as firm and strong as possible [but] still mindful that peaceful dissent and demonstration should be allowed on campus today. We have moved, however, whenever the action has been disruptive or bordering on the violent." In a response to another alumnus, who urged Walsh to suppress the SDS immediately, he said, "I still do not feel that this is the proper time to remove the SDS. It is so important for us to allow people to dissent" but, he added, "[If] I become convinced in the near future that the SDS can only use violence to further their aims, obviously I will move quickly for their suppression."[18]

Such carefully calibrated responses to both radical provocations and conservative complaints enabled Walsh to create a leadership style based on consensus rather than on unilateral decisions. At the same time, Walsh was able to project the equally important impression of strength rather than weakness or indecision, because he made plain that he was not attempting to shirk personal responsibility for university policies but seeking faculty approval for the reasonableness of decisions that he had formulated with

17. FUA, FOHP, Cammarosano, Interview, 49–52.

18. FUA, Walsh Papers, Box 2, Walsh to Edward Hiross, May 14, 1970; Walsh to James W. Fogarty, November 17, 1969.

the assistance of his closest administrative advisors. His *modus operandi* inspired confidence in his judgment, led to the pacification of the campus, and ultimately assured the successful outcome of his presidency.

A curious sidelight on Fordham's history during these troubled times was the lack of support the administration received from most of the faculty. "It was notable by its absence," Dr. Cammarosano commented years later. "For the most part the faculty kept out of it," he said. "We were all alone." In fact the administration found its closest allies in the maintenance staff, who showed deep concern not only for the protection of university property but also for the personal safety of the administrators. There were a few notable exceptions to the lack of faculty involvement. Two young history professors, Dr. Robert Himmelberg and Dr. Roger Wines, enjoyed the confidence of both the students and faculty and often acted as mediators between them, as did two veteran Jesuit members of the faculty, Father Joseph Fitzpatrick of the Sociology Department and Father George McMahon, the dean of Fordham College.[19]

In the fall of 1970, the new academic year opened in an atmosphere that was remarkably peaceful in comparison with the disturbances of the previous year, as was true also in many campuses across the country. An attempt by the SDS early in September to test the mood on campus by picketing the ROTC registration booth backfired when its members discovered that they could muster only thirty supporters. They quickly canceled their planned demonstration when they realized that the paucity of their numbers left them vulnerable to disciplinary action. Cammarosano warned them that he would suspend any student who violated the university code of conduct. The SDS took him at his word. "They called the cops in the past," said one alarmed SDS leader. "They'll do it in the future." In October another anti-ROTC demonstration also fizzled. Later that month a resolution of support for the ROTC failed to win the support of the United Student Government by only one vote. In the spring of 1971, a year after the trial of the "Fordham Five" in the Bronx County Courthouse, a headline appeared in the *Ram*, "What Ever Happened to SDS?" "The Campus Center lobby is deserted these days," lamented the author of the article.[20]

19. FUA, FOHP, Cammarosano, Interview, 54. Richard Ouzounian, "Question: Who Are the 10 Most Influential People at Fordham?" *Ram*, April 10, 1970. In the opinion of the author, Dr. Himmelberg was "probably the most influential and powerful lay faculty member."

20. *Ram*, September 15, October 20, October 27, 1970; February 19, 1971.

The waning of anti-war sentiment was not the only change on campus. The financial situation had improved to the point that Walsh could announce in the fall of 1970 that he was setting aside a half-million dollars in the budget to provide a 6 percent increase in faculty salaries and that the university would assume the full cost of medical insurance for full-time faculty. No doubt the generous offer contributed to another development the following year that Walsh regarded as one of his major contributions to Fordham, the defeat of an attempt to establish a faculty union.[21]

Even more than Walsh, Cammarosano feared the introduction of a union because he believed that it would destroy faculty collegiality, diminish Fordham's academic reputation, and drastically alter the culture of the university. It was an uphill struggle to prevent the faculty from voting in favor of a union. Early polls indicated that three-fourths of the faculty were prepared to vote in favor of it. "We were the clear underdogs," said Cammarosano, but "Father Mike Walsh, Paul Reiss and I gave no quarter and fought with a single-minded purpose to turn back the challenge." "In my judgment," he added, "that victory represented the single most important contribution by Father Walsh and his administration."[22]

The turn of the tide at Fordham was signaled and symbolized by the resignation within five weeks of one another of two of the people who had been mainly responsible for successfully guiding Fordham through the conflicts that the Irish might have euphemistically described as "The Troubles." On December 20, 1971, Father Walsh submitted his resignation as president to the board of trustees, to take effect the following June. On January 27, 1972, Dr. Cammarosano announced his resignation as executive vice president, to take effect that September.

Both men were confident that their successors would not face any major problems. After serving as president of two of the nation's largest Jesuit universities, the sixty-year-old Walsh said, "I like new challenges and do not want to get tied down to one institution." Cammarosano was eager to return to teaching economics and to "live the life of a normal professor," although he was to give up his normal life a second time in the 1980s to guide Fordham through another fiscal crisis.[23]

21. *Ram*, October 27, 1970; November 12, 1971.

22. FUA, FOHP, Cammarosano, Interview, 61–67. The proposal to establish a faculty labor union was defeated by the narrow margin of 226–207. *Ram*, November 12, 1971.

23. *Ram*, January 25, 28, 1972. Walsh said that he would have remained longer if the faculty had voted in favor of a union because he did not think that it would be fair to leave a new president with the challenge of dealing with a union. FUA, FOHP, Cammarosano, Interview, 93.

"A Traveling Curse"

As the Vietnam War wound down with the withdrawal of the last American troops in 1973 and came to an end with the communist victory two years later, anti-war agitation shriveled up and disappeared on U.S. campuses. Unlike many other American colleges, however, Fordham found itself facing a new challenge on the site of its main campus because of the rapidly deteriorating economic and social conditions in the Bronx. "The South Bronx" had once been a bland geographical designation for a one-square-mile section of Mott Haven. However, in the late 1960s and early 1970s, "the South Bronx" became "a Traveling Curse" in the words of one observer as a wave of arson, crime, drugs, street gangs, and the wholesale abandonment of residential buildings spread north to Fordham Road, engulfing 20 square miles of the borough, leading to the flight of 200,000 residents.

A visitor to the area in 1968 found it "a place beyond description [where] wild dogs roamed the streets, tearing in and out of buildings, and through the trash that covered the sidewalks and the buildings." She conjured up Dickensian images of London's Victorian slums when she said, "People scarcely recognizable as human were prey and predator to one another. Fires burned everywhere."[24]

The rhetoric was not entirely overblown. In 1960 there were 11,185 fires in the Bronx; in 1974, there were 33,465 fires. New York's Senator Daniel Patrick Moynihan noted the resemblance between the South Bronx in 1970 and Berlin in 1945. So did schoolchildren in the South Bronx as they looked at the photos of postwar Germany in their history books. One police station was popularly known as Fort Apache until most of the surrounding buildings were burned to the ground. It was then renamed the Little House on the Prairie. An especially blighted area on Charlotte Street located a few miles south of Rose Hill received national attention after it became an obligatory photo-op for politicians following the visit of President Jimmy Carter in 1977.

Like Senator Moynihan, Jill Jonnes, the historian of the Bronx's ordeal by fire in the 1960s and 1970s, gave major credit to the Catholic Church for the survival and revival of the South Bronx. "The Catholic Church quietly emerged as the institution most committed to preserving and resurrecting the benighted South Bronx," she said. "Not one Catholic church

---

24. Adele Chatfield-Taylor, cit. by Daniel Patrick Moynihan, in Jill Jonnes, *We're Still Here: The Rise, Fall, and Resurrection of the South Bronx* (Boston: Atlantic Monthly Press, 1986), xxi.

[or] school was closed." These Catholic parishes—there were sixty-nine of them in the Bronx—served as local anchors to help stabilize faltering neighborhoods. For example, one former parishioner of Sacred Heart parish in Highbridge was shocked at what he saw on a visit to his old neighborhood. "Apartment houses on Woodycrest Avenue that used to sing with the life of bustling families had become burnt-out tombs," he discovered. The one bright spot he found was Sacred Heart School, as spotless and well organized as it had been forty years earlier.[25]

Because of its very size, Fordham University also became an important anchor in the stabilization and revival of the Bronx as a result of its commitment to maintain the Rose Hill campus as the principal site of the university despite rumors that it was planning to leave the Bronx for a location in the suburbs. New York University abandoned its University Heights campus in the West Bronx in 1973 and sold it to Bronx Community College. Skeptics wondered if Fordham was planning to do the same when they noticed that the entrance to the new student dormitory building (now Walsh Hall) faced not the campus but East 191st Street, which enhanced its potential resale value as an apartment building. Their fears proved to be groundless.

The person who became Fordham's point man in its relationship with the local community during this crisis was not a Jesuit priest or a member of the Fordham faculty but a young Jesuit scholastic, Paul Brant, who was studying philosophy at Fordham and residing off-campus with several other scholastics in a dilapidated apartment building on garbage-strewn Marion Avenue, where he had first-hand experience of the deteriorating housing in the neighborhood. Brant persuaded Father Walsh to appoint him director of community relations with an office in the Administration Building. "The relationship of university and community is important to both parties," Brant said, pointing out that they needed each other to survive.[26]

Brant was a "firebrand," according to Jill Jonnes, who liked and admired him, but Brant managed to form an unlikely alliance with a mild-mannered local Catholic pastor, Monsignor John McCarthy, who shared Brant's con-

25. Ibid., 317. Michael Scanlon, "Return to Highbridge," *Catholic New York*, October 7, 1993. As the Bronx began to recover, Senator Moynihan commented, "After much travail, and much failure, and much avoidance of the obvious, the people of the South Bronx and the Catholic church got together and have set to work. And the Lord's work it is." Cit. in Jonnes, *We're Still Here*, xxiv.

26. Jim White, "Paul Brant: providing as a link to the community," *Ram*, November 20, 1970.

cern over the plight of his displaced parishioners. McCarthy introduced Brant to the Northwest Bronx Clergy Conference, an ineffective group of sixteen Catholic pastors who had been struggling for years with limited success to represent the interests of their parishioners in the face of opposition from landlords and the indifference of city officials. Brant suggested a new approach and persuaded the priests to transform their association into a nonprofit ecumenical organization, the Northwest Bronx Community and Clergy Coalition.

The name of the new organization was a bit of a misnomer, because it actually encompassed one-quarter of the neighborhoods of the Bronx, everything from the city line in the north to the notorious Cross Bronx Expressway in the south. The Coalition hired six full-time organizers, one of them a veteran of similar efforts in Chicago inspired by the tactics of Saul Alinsky. The Coalition also enlisted the services of numerous Fordham students as volunteers. The Coalition scored a major success when it won the endorsement of Auxiliary Bishop Patrick V. Ahern, the ranking Catholic cleric in the borough and a close friend of Cardinal Terence Cooke, the archbishop of New York. Bishop Ahern agreed to speak at all the Sunday Masses in the local Catholic parishes over a period of several months, repeating the same message: "If the Bronx dies, then the hopes of a million-and-a-half people for justice and a decent life, here and now, will die with it. We're trying to stop that from happening."

Bishop Ahern's sponsorship of the Coalition was invaluable. He not only raised more than $40,000 in donations to get the Coalition up and running, and much more money later from corporate and Church sources, but on at least one occasion he joined Monsignor McCarthy on a picket line to protest the mortgage policies of a local bank. The impact of two elderly Catholic clergymen in Roman collars on a picket line was electric. Moreover, Bishop Ahern's name on the letterhead of the Coalition was a reassurance to bankers and businessmen—and a warning to politicians—that the Northwest Bronx Community and Clergy Coalition was a responsible professional organization, not a ragtag collection of rabble-rousers. Fordham's direct involvement in the Coalition diminished after the parish clergy and laity assumed a larger role and Brant was reassigned to Chicago in 1975, but Fordham played a crucial role in the establishment of the Coalition in 1970 thanks to a "brash" young Jesuit scholastic with a thirst for social justice.[27]

27. Jonnes, *We're Still Here*, 344–62.

Bensalem

Father James Hennesey once noted with both respect and regret that Father Leo McLaughlin was an incurable romantic, which goes far in explaining McLaughlin's most quixotic initiative as president of Fordham, the establishment of an experimental college called Bensalem, a bold venture even in the radical American academic world of the 1960s. Bensalem grew out of a conversation between McLaughlin and Dr. Elizabeth Sewell, who had taught briefly at Rose Hill when McLaughlin was the dean of Fordham College. Sewell was a poet and author who had been born in India of English parents and had impeccable academic credentials, with a doctorate from Cambridge University. She opined in 1968 that "almost everything we have come to take for granted as constituting education in this country may be on the way out."

Sewell's iconoclastic approach to higher education struck a responsive chord with McLaughlin, who was looking for a way of appealing to bright but disaffected high school students who he feared would reject the opportunity for a college education altogether because they loathed traditional college academic programs. He also thought that an elite unit in the university like Bensalem College would further his plans to enhance Fordham's reputation as a first-rate university. With the best of intentions but also with an innocence that even Rousseau might have found naïve, McLaughlin and Sewell envisioned Bensalem as a college where faculty and students would live together sharing authority and responsibility as equal partners without such awkward constraints as core courses, examinations, term papers, or grades.

Dr. Sewell hoped that Bensalem would become an alternative to what she called "the inherent bookishness" of colleges like "Big Fordham" with its "pretty well dug-in system of education." The name of the new college was inspired by the mythical island where lost mariners found refuge in Francis Bacon's utopian novel *The New Atlantis*. The loose administrative and flexible academic structure of Bensalem was designed by a group of enthusiastic students whom Sewell recruited and called "a lovely organic Revolutionary Committee." In keeping with the ethos of equality, the only requirement for graduation was the obligation of the students to keep a portfolio listing their activities on and off campus, which faculty members were obliged to endorse upon request of the students.

Shortly before the new school opened, at Father McLaughlin's suggestion Dr. Sewell made a guest appearance before the Faculty Senate to describe Bensalem's purpose and plan of opertation. "If it's to be an experimental college," Vice President Cammarosano asked her, "on what basis are you going to judge whether or not this experiment is a success?" She smiled, waved her hand in the air, and replied, "Ha, we haven't even defined the term 'success' yet." After that answer Cammarosano thought it was useless to pursue the issue further.[28]

Bensalem College began its existence in July 1967 in a building at 558 East 191st Street directly across from the Walsh Student Residence on the Fordham campus. The first class consisted of thirty students—seventeen men and thirteen women—most of whom were freshmen. Four or perhaps as many as six full-time resident faculty also made up the Bensalem community. Bensalem featured a three-year program with emphasis on the humanities leading to a B.A. degree. In a departure from the general spirit of permissiveness at Bensalem, however, Sewell wanted both faculty and students to study an Eastern language in order to liberate their minds from what she considered to be Western cultural domination. "This year we are learning Urdu," she announced proudly in February 1968. "This seemed a good place to begin," she explained, because a Pakistani consultant had suggested it, although he was now back in Lahore and contemplating a move to Kathmandu. Sewell's announcement about the popularity of Urdu at Bensalem proved to be premature, however, because the students promptly took advantage of the egalitarian governance of the college to reject it.[29]

Bensalem got off to a good start given that the first students were bright and well motivated, and they even started a tutoring program for disadvantaged schoolchildren. The experimental nature of the college also attracted considerable media attention because of its departure from the standard profile of an American Jesuit college. The seventeen students in the first graduating class in 1970 enhanced Bensalem's reputation when they won six Woodrow Wilson Fellowships and three Danforth Scholarships, and most of them easily gained admission to prestigious graduate schools. However, the departure from Fordham of both Father McLaughlin and especially Dr. Sewell after 1970, and Father Walsh's preoccupation with more pressing problems, accelerated a steep decline in virtually every aspect of the Bensalem experiment.[30] "When Elizabeth Sewell left Bensalem," said one observer, "what remained was a group of young faculty uncloaked of the mantle of Sewell's academic reputation."[31]

28. FUA, FOHP, Cammarosano, Interview, 90.

29. Elizabeth Sewell, "Bensalem: education becomes relevant," *Ram*, February 7, 1968. FUA, AF, Box 5, Sewell to unidentified correspondent, n.d.

30. [James McCabe], "A Radical Departure: College in the 60s," *Inside Fordham Libraries* 21 (Fall 2005), 3.

31. FUA, AF, Box 5, Bensalem College at Fordham University—1967. Dean Reiss

Sewell herself said that, prior to the Bensalem experiment, she had no idea how destructive unlimited freedom could be for college students. In the course of its seven-year history, Bensalem had six deans; most faculty left after one or two years; student attrition averaged around 50 percent. A sympathetic visitor in May 1971 was shocked at what he saw. "The building could easily have qualified as a slum," he said. "It was dark and dingy, needing paint and plaster. There was no common eating space, no classrooms, no seminar area, and only a tiny lounge with a few broken pieces of furniture and a vivid arrangement of obscenities on the walls. Furniture in the apartments consisted of bare mattresses usually strewn on the floors."[32]

When Dr. Cammarosano visited Bensalem, he was pleasantly surprised to find that the students were growing their own tomatoes on the roof of the building until he realized upon closer inspection that they were marijuana plants. The impressive academic achievements of the first three years were not duplicated after the admissions committee, which was dominated by the students, neglected academic credentials in order to recruit likeminded ideologues. As a result, said one critic, the academically oriented student of the early years was replaced by a new breed of escape-oriented student.[33]

In light of the widespread criticism of Bensalem, Fordham commissioned an outside evaluation of the college in 1970 by Dr. Joseph Finkelstein, professor of history and economics at Union College in Schenectady, New York, who responded with an assessment that must rank as one of the most scathing evaluations any American college has ever received. "Bensalem in November 1970 is less an educational experience than an intellectual and physical shambles," he reported. Although Professor Finkelstein liked the students he met, he said that "it is inconceivable that anyone could have designed a physical structure more ill-suited to the life of the mind. Bensalem is ugly and dirty."

Finkelstein described his own experience sitting in the common room in an overstuffed armchair with only three legs. "Each time I made a point or bent forward to listen to a student," he said, "the chair collapsed." He

considered this unpublished analysis of the rise and fall of Bensalem by an anonymous author as "quite accurate" except for his claim that the opposition of the Fordham faculty played a major role in its demise. "By and large," said Dean Reiss, "the faculty knew little about Bensalem and also cared little." FUA, AF, Box 5, Reiss to President James F. Finlay, S.J., December 7, 1976.

32. John Coyne, "Bensalem: When the Dream Died," *Change* 4:8 (October 1972): 40.

33. FUA, FOHP, Cammarosano, Interview, 92. FUA, Box 5, Bensalem College at Fordham University–1967, n.d.

seemed especially grateful that he did not have the opportunity to meet any of the dogs or cats that the students had recently invited to take up residence in the building. "[T]he physical facilities are so bad," he said, "that it seemed virtually impossible for any student to do any kind of intellectual work." His devastating conclusion was that "Bensalem is not now an experimental college. It doesn't know whether it is reformist or revolutionary [and] most Bensalemites don't care."[34]

A year after Professor Finkelstein's report, the Faculty Senate voted to close Bensalem by 1974, when all of its students would have graduated. The board of trustees gave their approval and no additional students were admitted. The last dean of Bensalem, Dr. Roger Wines, offered a measured judgment of Dr. Elizabeth Sewell's experimental college. "A lot of people made very good use of the freedom," he said, and "a lot of people should have gone somewhere else." Father Schroth described Bensalem wistfully as "an experiment in the powers and limitation of friendship."[35]

The Fordham Jesuit Community After Vatican II

The Second Vatican Council (1962–65) was arguably the single most important event in the history of the Catholic Church in the twentieth century, when the bishops of the world met in Rome to examine virtually every aspect of Catholic belief and practice. From one perspective it has been described as major surgery performed without anesthesia on a patient who had no idea that he was ill. Others have explained the many unanticipated disruptive consequences of the council by invoking Alexis de Tocqueville's comment about the French Revolution that the most dangerous time for a bad government is when it begins to make changes, especially when the changes do not keep pace with the wave of rising expectations.

The unsettling effects of the council were especially noticeable in the impact they had on the clergy and religious orders. In the United States, at least, the number of diocesan priests and of both men and women religious peaked immediately after the council and then suffered an abrupt

34. FUA, AF, Box 5, Joseph Finkelstein, Evaluation and Report on Bensalem College, Fordham University, November 1970.

35. Cit. in [James McCabe], "A Radical Departure," 4. Raymond A. Schroth, S.J., "College as Camelot," *The Saturday Review*, December 1972, 52–57. I am grateful to Father Schroth for sending me a copy of the article. The vote of the Faculty Senate to discontinue Bensalem was surprisingly close, 25–17–2, a confirmation perhaps of Dean Reiss's observation that most of the faculty had little knowledge of conditions at Bensalem. *Ram*, November 10, 1971.

and unexpected decline that has continued virtually without interruption to the present day. Not only did large numbers of priests and religious resign from the active ministry or their religious communities, but a once-plentiful supply of new vocations slowed to a trickle for reasons that have been endlessly debated for the past fifty years with few agreed-upon conclusions.

Nowhere in the United States was the decline in religious vocations more evident than in the case of the teaching sisters, who had been mainly responsible for the creation and success of the American Catholic school system, which has been described without exaggeration as the largest private school system in the history of the world.[36] At its zenith at the time of Vatican II the system reached its peak enrollment with 5.5 million students and then began an apparently irreversible decline. One matter-of-fact statistic dramatizes the magnitude of the change. In 1967 there were 7,314 teaching sisters in the archdiocese of New York and the diocese of Brooklyn. In 2008 there were only 5,718 teaching sisters in the entire United States.[37]

Even the Society of Jesus, the largest religious order in the Catholic Church, was not immune from these worrisome ripple effects of Vatican II, although they did not manifest themselves at Fordham as quickly as in some other Jesuit houses and other religious communities. When an article appeared in the *New York Times* in October 1967 claiming that fifteen priests at Fordham University had left the priesthood, Father Leo McLaughlin replied that only one Jesuit priest had applied for and received laicization. "In view of the fact that there are 214 priests at Fordham," he added, "this record is rather extraordinary."[38]

When Father James M. Somerville, the provincial for higher education in the New York Province, made a visitation of Fordham the following January, he was so pleased with what he found that he hoped that Fordham would become a paradigm for other Jesuit communities in coping with the challenges of Vatican II. "The religious and academic superiors of Fordham University have approached their task with a degree of creativity that

36. Patricia Byrne, C.S.J., in *Creative Fidelity: American Catholic Intellectual Traditions*, ed. R. Scott Appleby, Patricia Byrne, and William L. Portier (Maryknoll: Orbis Books, 2004), 55.

37. *The Official Catholic Directory*, 2008, 167, 877.

38. FUA, McLaughlin Papers, William Restivo to McLaughlin, October 14, 1967; McLaughlin to Restivo, October 18, 1967. It is not clear where McLaughlin got the figure of 214 priests at Fordham. They were certainly not all Jesuit members of the faculty of Fordham University.

may be unique in the Society today," he told the Fordham Jesuit community. Reflecting both the widespread uncertainty and euphoria that were characteristic of the Catholic Church in the immediate aftermath of the council, Somerville said that "there is no absolutely 'safe' course in the explosive climate of the hour." He confronted the Fordham Jesuits with a stark choice. "One has the option of dying quietly on the vine," he said, "or of taking the initiative which could make Fordham a great Catholic university." He had no doubt which of those two options the Fordham Jesuits would choose.

Two years after Father Somerville's optimistic appraisal of Fordham's future, Father James Hennesey expressed a demurrer. As both a historian of American Catholicism and the religious superior of the Fordham Jesuit community, Hennesey possessed a unique background to evaluate the changes that were taking place around him. He was not pleased with what he saw. He told his old friend and mentor, John Tracy Ellis, "Like yourself, I cannot understand just what is happening." He added, "This year alone we lost eight men from this community, every one of them topflight." "It becomes clearer and clearer," Hennesey told Ellis, that "we have to find ways of living in the modern world that will differ from those we have known," but, he explained, "the polarities are so fierce that it is hard to get a community even to discuss the issues."

Reflecting on his own experience as superior, he said that his biggest challenge came not from the impatience of younger Jesuits but from older Jesuits whom he had described to the father general as the "secularized"— not in a technical canonical sense, but in their way of life and outlook. "Their values are secular," he said; "their time is spent in secular pursuits. They seem to have lost all apostolic zeal." He cited the example of one Jesuit in his mid-fifties who defended his lifestyle by pleading that he was too old to leave the Society. "No one had suggested it," said Hennesey, "but he knows that his life as a priest has little meaning left in it. Those are the ones I find really sad," he told Ellis.[39]

The "fierce polarities" that Hennesey deplored in the Fordham Jesuit community surfaced the following June in an especially embarrassing way at the Jesuit ordination ceremonies that took place as usual in the University Church on the Rose Hill campus. As usual also, the ordaining prelate was the archbishop of New York, on this occasion Terence Cardinal Cooke, who also happened to be the military vicar for the armed forces. Toward the end of the Mass two of the newly ordained Jesuit priests refused to ex-

39. ACUA, John Tracy Ellis Papers, Hennesey to Ellis, June 2, 1970.

change the traditional liturgical kiss of peace with Cardinal Cooke. One of them grabbed the microphone and launched into a denunciation of Cooke as a warmonger. The Jesuit provincial made an effort to intervene, but Cooke waved him away and calmly took charge of the situation himself. The cardinal explained that he too was an advocate of peace, because his role as military vicar made him acutely aware of his responsibility for the spiritual welfare of all the members of the armed forces. After his remarks, Cooke again invited the two young dissident Jesuits to exchange the kiss of peace with him. One of them rather grudgingly accepted the invitation, but the other still refused. Cooke had the better of the exchange. To him the cardinal said softly, "Peace especially to you, my friend."[40]

James Hennesey and John Tracy Ellis were not the only Catholic clerics who were puzzled and upset by the disarray in the postconciliar Catholic Church. "Unless we are blind," said Father Louis Bouyer, C.O., the French Catholic scholar, in a book published in 1968, the same year as Pope Paul VI's controversial encyclical *Humanae Vitae*, "we must state bluntly that what we see looks less like the hoped-for regeneration of Catholicism than its accelerated decomposition." When James Hennesey heard that one of his Jesuit classmates had asked U.S. Attorney General John N. Mitchell (a Fordham alumnus) to order the FBI to investigate the supposedly subversive activities of the leaders of the New England Province of the Society of Jesus, he exclaimed, "It's becoming a Mad Hatter's Ball!!!!"[41]

When Father Somerville made his visitation of Fordham in January 1968, he reminded his fellow Jesuits that the Society of Jesus had been born in an age of crisis and transition, from which he drew the conclusion that the "imperative is to move with the times." This facile optimism begged the question of how to move with the times. The council fathers had coupled the imperative of *aggiornamento* with the imperative of *ressourcement*, the need to modernize the Church, not by uncritically embracing every contemporary fad but by recovering and appropriating the teachings of Jesus and the Church's own authentic tradition, a connection that was often overlooked in the dysfunctional atmosphere that followed the close of the council.

40. ACUA, John Tracy Ellis Papers, Hennesey to Ellis, June 28, 1971. One of the altar servers, an alert Jesuit scholastic, Nicholas Lombardi, anticipating trouble when the saw the dissident young Jesuit snatch the microphone from Cardinal Cooke, temporarily turned off the public address system, depriving him of most of his potential audience. I am grateful for this information from Father Joseph Lienhard, S.J., who was one of the Jesuit priests ordained on that occasion.

41. ACUA, John Tracy Ellis Papers, Hennesey to Ellis, June 28, 1971.

Like Louis Bouyer, John Tracy Ellis was disappointed by the immediate aftermath of Vatican II. However, he told a friend in 1968, "*Mater Ecclesia* has been here before and has seen and endured worse." "It is not the most positive of arguments for the *aggiornamento*," he added wryly, "but it helps to steady one's nerves." During the spate of mutual recriminations that filled the columns of Catholic newspapers and periodicals as liberals and conservatives blamed one another for the unfulfilled expectations of the council, the self-appointed watchdogs of orthodoxy sometimes mistook their best friends for enemies, as James Hennesey, a self-described reactionary, discovered when he was warned that he was suspected of radicalism in Rome. After returning from a disappointing institute on Jesuit apostolic community, filled with liturgical gimmickery and the need for personal emotional satisfaction, Hennesey longed for a return to basics. "I think that perhaps we had better begin talking rather loudly about faith," he told Ellis, "and a theological basis for what we are about."[42]

42. ACUA, John Tracy Ellis Papers, Ellis to George Kelly, April 27, 1968; Hennesey to Ellis, June 28, 1971. Hennesey was neither a radical nor a reactionary. He might best be described as "that most progressive of conservatives," a phrase he once used to describe Bernard McQuaid, the first bishop of Rochester.

THE NEW "NORMALCY" 20

Après le Déluge

In 1815, after the collapse of the Napoleonic Empire and the rush to restore the *ancien régime*, Pope Pius VII's sagacious secretary of state, Ercole Cardinal Consalvi, sounded a perceptive warning that it was impossible to restore the status quo as it had existed before the French Revolution. He regarded the attempt as an exercise in futility because of the radical transformation that had taken place in the young people of Europe during the course of the previous twenty-five years. "If the older generation does not realize this," he added, "they misread the situation."

The context of Consalvi's cautionary remarks was his effort to prevent the *zelanti* in the Roman Curia from implementing a full-blown restoration of the pre-revolutionary clerical government in the Papal States where, he said, "the young people have not known the pontifical government, and they have formed a bad impression of it." Consalvi's words were also good advice 160 years later as a plea for moderation on the part of American college presidents who were struggling to restore some degree of "normalcy" on their campuses in the aftermath of the upheavals of the late 1960s and early 1970s.[1]

Although protests and demonstrations ceased to be daily events in academia during the course of the 1970s, the college students of that era—even those who eschewed the violent tactics of the dwindling breed of campus radicals—were different from their immediate predecessors. Many remained deeply concerned about political, economic, and social issues and expected to have a greater role in the shaping of their own college education. In Catholic institutions the winds of change unleashed by Vatican II were an additional reason to believe that the attempt to restore the *ancien régime* was not only inadvisable but probably impossible.

In the fall of 1972 Fordham's newly elected president, Father James J. Finlay, S.J., a self-styled New Deal Democrat, quickly indicated that he

---

1. Consalvi to Cardinal Pacca, June 12, 1815, in Jean Leflon, *La Crise Révolutionnaire, 1789–1846* (Paris: Bloud & Gay, 1951), 310.

harbored no dreams of attempting to impose a Bourbon restoration at Rose Hill or at Lincoln Center. "Confrontation politics are here and will remain with us for some time to come," he said somewhat ambiguously, but he welcomed the fact that student activists now seemed committed to working through the American political system rather than seeking to subvert it. He also endorsed the expanded role that the university had given to students in the governance of the university, a concession that he thought had been a major factor in addressing their grievances. "I would also like to provide challenges for young people," he said. "What bothers me most," he added, "is not so much the useful protests on campus, but the bright kid who is somehow apathetic." Finlay's remarks were an omen for the future of Fordham that Cardinal Consalvi would have found encouraging.[2]

Father George J. McMahon, S.J., who had been at the epicenter of Fordham's era of *Sturm und Drang* for a dozen years as the dean of Fordham College at Rose Hill, was in a unique position to assess the changed mood on campus by the mid-1970s. He ignored superficial irritants like the long hair and bizarre clothes favored by some students, but he welcomed the fact that Fordham had become a less authoritarian institution and insisted that Fordham's basic values were alive and well. "Inside the classroom," McMahon said, "Fordham has not changed much." "In the late 1960s," he explained, "imagination became indignation with demonstrations and sit-ins." Now, he said, "the kids are inquisitive but not indignant. They keep pressing you for an answer, but they don't do it with a chip on their shoulder."[3]

Father James J. Finlay, S.J.

The prematurely gray forty-nine-year-old Father Finlay was the thirtieth president of Fordham, but the first president in 131 years who was elected by the predominantly lay board of trustees. Born in Ireland in 1923, he came to the United States at the age of eight with his parents, who settled on the Upper West Side of Manhattan. As the son of a publican in the old country, Finlay freely admitted that he was not to the manor born,

2. FUA, Finlay Papers, Finlay, draft of remarks for the faculty convocation, n.d. [Fall 1972]. Anthony Mancini, *New York Post*, June 1, 1972.

3. "And Still Very Much In," *Fordham*, Spring 1974, 9–10. McMahon, who was widely respected by both students and faculty and was an excellent basketball player even in advanced middle age, admitted that during the height of "The Troubles" on campus, he sometimes hid students in his office to protect them from the dean of students. "Should you print that?" he asked a student who interviewed him. "I guess so," McMahon answered.

unlike some pretentious English Jesuits of his generation. After graduation from Regis High School, the only tuition-free Jesuit high school in the United States, Finlay was able to afford a college education only because he won a scholarship to Fordham College. He entered the Society of Jesus in 1942 about two weeks before his twentieth birthday, when he would have become eligible for the draft. "So," he said, "I have always considered myself one of the earliest draft dodgers." On a more serious note, Finlay said that he never entered the Fordham University Church without looking at the roster of the Fordham servicemen who had died in the service of their country. "I knew quite a number of them," he said, and "it was always a moving experience to reflect on the sacrifices made by those young men, and made so generously."

Because World War II made it impossible to send Jesuit seminarians to Europe, Finlay finished his theological studies at a now-defunct French-language Jesuit theologate in Montréal where the *ancien régime* had been restored in painstaking detail. He compared the experience to a plunge into the sixteenth century, especially after witnessing the Jesuit scholastics play hockey in their cassocks. After completing graduate studies at Georgetown University and Duke University (where he earned a doctorate in political science), Finlay returned to Fordham in 1960 to join the Political Science Department, quickly becoming the department's chair. At the time of his election as president of Fordham, he had been dean of the Graduate School of Arts and Sciences for the previous four years.[4]

Fordham alumni who feared that their alma mater was destined to become a secular university in 1972 because of its predominantly lay board of trustees misjudged the situation. They underestimated the tenacity and resourcefulness of the chairman of the board, Felix Larkin, a dedicated Catholic layman who was an alumnus of Fordham College, a lawyer, and president of W. R. Grace and Company. Larkin was determined to ensure that Father Walsh's successor would be a Jesuit. He solicited candidates for the presidency of Fordham from all twenty-eight Jesuit colleges in the United States, receiving more than sixty replies. Larkin winnowed down

4. *Catholic News*, June 1, 1972; *Ram*, February 26, 1976. FUA, FOHP, Self-Interview of Rev. James C. Finlay, S.J., January 29, February 4, 1989, 8. Finlay's birthplace was Roscommon in County Roscommon, the only town in the west of Ireland, he said, that could boast of an Italian neighborhood. Finlay told a local Italian American civic association, "If you meet a man or woman with an obvious Italian name but who speaks English with an Irish brogue, you can be sure he or she comes from a town called Roscommon and that they [*sic*] are in the mosaic business." FUA, Finlay Papers, Finlay, Address to the [Mount Vernon] Italian Civic Association, Inc., June 5, 1974.

Father James C. Finlay, S.J., president of Fordham University, 1972–83.

the applicants to two people, both of them Jesuits, Father Finlay and Father Donald Monan, a professor of philosophy at Le Moyne College in Syracuse. Finlay was a reluctant applicant for the job who had submitted his name only because of pressure from Larkin. Both candidates made impressive oral presentations to the trustees.

Meanwhile Larkin deflected anticipated objections from Fordham trustees who wanted a lay president by engaging in what he called "a little sneaky thing." He consulted the presidents of Columbia University and Pace University—both Fordham alumni—who assured him that the next president of Fordham should be a Jesuit. The meeting of the trustees to elect a new president of Fordham lasted all day. "It was like electing the pope," said Larkin. Larkin was particularly exasperated with Father Michael Walsh, a member of the board, who kept switching his vote from Finlay to Monan and back again on each successive ballot. "You're messing up the whole thing," Larkin told Walsh. "No, no," replied Walsh mischievously, "I just want to keep it alive." Finally, after six ballots, the trustees chose Finlay over Monan. Larkin had difficulty in communicating the result to Finlay because he was at Lawrence Hospital in Bronxville visiting his secretary, who was dying of cancer.[5]

Continuity and Change

In Father Finlay's first address to the faculty, he drew upon what he called the "historico-social triangulation" of Fordham's history as a private, urban, and religious university to map out his vision of Fordham's future. "A university is not a welfare agency," he said. "It is not a church. It is not a political instrument." He warned that "there is a temptation for universities to become each of these things, even to become a business enterprise." "We must resist these siren calls," he declared emphatically.

After distancing himself from some of the popular contemporary models of an American university, Finlay laid out his own model for Fordham. "I do not envision Fordham as a quiet backwater pool where the frightened and the foolish can bask in the warm sun of piety, protected from the excitement of a tumultuous world and from the risks of personal initiative," he said. On a more positive note, he explained, "What I do envision is a university where men and women are alive to the ideas, the issues, the movements of our times; where they have the courage to challenge and to be challenged; where there is a constant, imaginative, intelligent effort to make the learning experience exciting as well as effective."[6]

When Father Finlay became president of Fordham in the fall of 1972, the university had an enrollment of 13,898 students, 8,079 full-time and 5,819 part-time. The "book value" of Fordham's real estate and buildings was approaching $100 million, a considerable change from 1841, when Bishop John Hughes was hard-pressed to raise $30,000 to establish St. John's College. The registration in all the graduate and undergraduate schools was booming, except in the School of Liberal Arts at Lincoln Center (which had been established for older part-time students), where there had been a significant drop in numbers from 350 to 219 because Fordham had deliberately raised admission standards. In the case of the other eight schools, however, the tightening of admission standards led not only to an increase in numbers but also to an increase in the qualifications of the applicants.

5. FUA, FOHP, Interview with Felix Larkin by Fr. Gerald Reedy, S.J., May 11, 1988, 28–32. Shortly after the selection of Finlay as president of Fordham, the presidency of Boston College became vacant. The search committee in Boston asked Larkin if he would care to recommend a candidate. "Oh boy, would I ever," said Larkin. "Get Don Monan." As president of Boston College, Monan rescued the institution from the brink of bankruptcy and transformed it into one of the leading American Catholic universities.

6. FUA, Finlay Papers, Finlay, Address at the Faculty Convocation, October 22, 1972.

For example, in 1972 the median SAT scores for the incoming freshman class at both Fordham College Rose Hill and Thomas More College (1150 and 1120, respectively) were 200 points above the national average. A year later, Fordham posted a 37 percent increase in enrollment over the previous five years due largely to the expansion of graduate programs in education, social service, law, and business administration at the Lincoln Center campus. Most remarkably, although the student population had increased by one-third in recent years, the full-time faculty had increased by only 7 percent, a disparity that must have pleased the financial officers of the university. Finlay was particularly proud of the fact that Fordham did not rely on poorly paid graduate students or adjunct faculty to teach the undergraduate courses. "Eighty-five percent of our full-time faculty are engaged in undergraduate instruction," he boasted. According to data compiled by the American Association of University Professors, the salaries of the Fordham faculty were higher than those in 60 percent of both private and public U.S. universities with doctoral programs.[7]

However, the financial condition of the university was less reassuring than its academic reputation, a familiar story in Fordham's history. In 1972 Fordham had been debt-free for the previous four years, thanks to careful management of the finances by Father Walsh, Dr. Cammarosano, and Brother Kenny, but it was hardly rich or even comfortably well-off. "So how do I propose to move Fordham into the future?" asked Father Finlay. He answered his own question by saying that he intended to use "every method short of larceny to build up our financial resources."[8] Fordham was the smallest of the so-called "Big Six," the six largest private doctoral-granting universities in New York state. Father Finlay admitted that, when he met periodically with the presidents of the other five institutions, he became covetous of his neighbors' goods. Rochester University had an endowment of $550 million; Columbia, $425 million; NYU, a cushion of $100 million; Cornell, $53 million. "Jim Finlay of Fordham would be ecstatic," he said, "if he could have for endowment the amounts these gentlemen receive in interest."

Fordham's endowment in 1972 was only $9,160,000, but the budget for that year was almost three times as large, $24,100,000, which meant that 90 percent of the income came from tuition. Another 5 percent came from public funds and the rest from gifts and a variety of other sources. "The

7. FUA, Finlay Papers, Finlay, Draft of a Press Release, October 22, 1973. Finlay, Address at the Meeting of the Faculty Senate, April 1, 1974, Press Release to the *Ram*.

8. FUA, Finlay Papers, Finlay, Address at Faculty Convocation, October 22, 1972.

so-called 'Bundy Money' is not large," said Finlay, "but it represents our margin of survival." At the suggestion of Robert M. Brown, the director of university relations, Finlay made a point to thank publicly Governor Nelson A. Rockefeller, the state legislature, and the taxpayers of New York for the Bundy Money. "Private philanthropy, in the pattern we have witnessed for too long at Fordham, would not have saved us from disaster," he explained. Finlay was confirmed in his impressions of the limitations of private philanthropy at Fordham as he surveyed the Rose Hill campus and noted that every building had been made possible largely as a result of the contributed services that the Society of Jesus had made to the university for more than a century. The only exception was the recently erected John Mulcahy Chemistry Building, which was the gift of one exceptionally generous Catholic alumnus and philanthropist.

Thanks to careful financial management, Fordham ended the fiscal year 1972 with a modest surplus of $162,384. Despite its limited monetary resources, in that year Fordham dispensed $2.4 million in financial aid to needy students and an additional $600,000 to minority students. The university continued to operate in the black, but the margin of error to avoid insolvency was always perilously close for an institution that aspired to be a major research university. "We have achieved a lot and we have done it the hard way," Finlay asserted. "No other university, I would say, has achieved so much with so little."[9] Four years later Finlay noted that only 200 of the several thousand independent colleges and universities in the United States possessed an endowment of more than $5 million. "Fordham is one of these," he said, "but just barely." He warned that "with our annual budget of $33 million, two or three years of injudicious or careless management could wipe out that endowment completely and probably force us to close."[10]

Despite efforts stretching back several decades to make Fordham more than a regional university, in the early 1970s approximately 85 percent of the student body still came from the New York metropolitan area and fully one-third of them came specifically from the Bronx. One notable change, however, was the shift in the ethnic background of the students. When Finlay left Fordham as an undergraduate in 1942 to enter the Society of

9. FUA, Finlay Papers, Fordham Council, Some Statistics for Father Finlay, October 11, 1972. Finlay, Notes for an address to the Board of Trustees, June 1972. Finlay, Address to the Washington, D.C., Alumni of Fordham University, September 28, 1972. Finlay, Address at Faculty Convocation, October 22, 1972. Finlay, President's Report to the Board of Trustees, December 19, 1972. Finlay, Draft of a press release, October 22, 1973.

10. FUA, Finlay Papers, Finlay, Address to Faculty Convocation, October 24, 1976.

Jesus, it was still an overwhelmingly Irish American institution, and most of the undergraduates came from Catholic high schools. By 1974 Finlay estimated that approximately 40 percent of the student body was Italian American. Two years later about one-half of the freshmen came from public schools, and six of the top twenty feeder schools for Fordham's undergraduates colleges were New York City public schools.[11]

Another notable change was the increase in the minority population to 26.5 percent among the undergraduates, higher than the proportion of minority students in any of the four-year colleges in the state university system and higher than the proportion of minority students at both Brooklyn College and Queens College in the city university system. Moreover, by the end of the decade, Fordham was operating one of the most successful HEOP (Higher Education Opportunity Programs) in New York state for 400 economically and academically disadvantaged students at both Rose Hill and Lincoln Center. Fordham's participation in the HEOP program was part of a larger commitment to make a college education available to a broad spectrum of students who, like young James Finlay thirty years earlier, could not afford to attend a private college like Fordham. In the 1978–79 academic year Fordham provided $3.3 million in unfunded student aid to needy students, one-third of whom were minority students. Finlay wanted the Law School to make a more aggressive effort to attract African American and Hispanic students, but he was pleased that in 1974 some 20 percent of the freshmen class consisted of women.[12]

Finlay was quick to admit that much of his success as president of Fordham was due to the fact that he could rely upon the advice and support of three capable and seasoned administrators who had served Fordham under both Father McLaughlin and Father Walsh. One of Finlay's first decisions as president was to reappoint Dr. Joseph Cammarosano executive vice president, Dr. Paul Reiss academic vice president, and Brother James Kenny, S.J., university treasurer and vice president for finances. He never had reason to regret any of those three decisions.

Three years later, when Dr. Cammarosano resigned as executive vice president to return to the classroom, Finlay told the general, Father Pedro

11. FUA, Finlay Papers, Finlay, Address to [Mount Vernon] Italian Civic Association, June 5, 1974. Finlay, Address at the New York Academy of Public Education Dinner Meeting, October 26, 1976.

12. FUA, Finlay Papers, Finlay, Address to new faculty members, September 12, 1973. Finlay, Address to the Bronx Rotary Club, January 29, 1974. Finlay to Mr. Frederick O'Neal, April 27, 1979. Finlay to Vincent O'Keefe, S.J., October 24, 1974. Finlay preferred to call Fordham an independent university rather than a private university.

Dr. Joseph Cammarosano ("Dr. C") '47, RCRH '56, GSAS, characteristically takes personal charge of the restoration of Edwards Parade in the spring of 1973.

Arrupe, that Cammarosano was the person mainly responsible for Fordham's success in weathering both a severe financial crisis and the wave of violent student protests. "I know no one so devout, so profoundly Christian," Finlay told Arrupe. "The Society of Jesus and this university owe him a debt of gratitude that we can never repay." He added, "When you meet such a man as Dr. Cammarosano, you are proud that the Society could educate him as it did here at Fordham and somehow inspired in him a loyalty we scarcely merit."[13]

Finlay's installation as president was decidedly informal. At the commencement ceremonies in the spring of 1972 it was mentioned in passing that Finlay was to become the new president in the fall. However, the closest Finlay came to enjoying a formal inauguration occurred late that sum-

13. FUA, O'Hare Papers, Box 1, Finlay to Arrupe, September 30, 1975. At the same time Finlay told the provincial, "If Fordham is alive and flourishing today, it is due to no one more than to Joe [Cammarosano]." FUA, Finlay Papers, Finlay to Eamon Taylor, S.J., September 30, 1975. Cammarosano, the consummate professional economist, had the highest regard for Brother Kenny, who was self-taught without a degree in economics, accounting or finances. "But he really did not need one," said Cammarosano. When Brother Kenny fell ill in the summer of 1984 and Father Joseph O'Hare, the new university president, asked Cammarosano to replace Kenny on temporary basis, Cammarosano said: "My God, there is no way of filling this man's shoes." FUA, FOHP, Cammarosano, Interview, 93–94.

mer when he accompanied Father Walsh to the airport for his flight back to Boston. Walsh said farewell and offered Finlay his best wishes while handing him the keys to the house car and perhaps lighting up another cigarette.

The Waning of the Jesuit Presence

Jesuits still constituted approximately one-fifth of the faculty of Fordham when Finlay took over the reins in 1972. The Jesuits were especially concerned about the answer to the question that was asked of every president of Fordham after Vatican II: "Is Fordham still a Catholic university?" In Finlay's case, it was an especially poignant question because it was put to him not only by many of the Fordham alumni and alumnae, and by his Jesuit confrères but even by his own elderly mother, who had been asked that question by her neighbors on the park benches in Parkchester, the large private housing complex located not far from Fordham in the Bronx. Finlay confessed that he was shocked to hear that question from his mother, because he realized that she was unwittingly acting as the *vox populi* in expressing the uncertainty that many people had about Fordham's religious identity. "My look of anger and despair cut off that discussion," he added.

With regard to the Jesuit community at Fordham, Finlay attempted to find a *via media* between those who hankered for a return to the "good old days" and those who were eager to plunge into unchartered waters. "This is not a time for lamentation or regret," Finlay told the conservatives, and he warned the liberals that "structures are terribly important and cannot be ignored." "We have a great opportunity here," he told the Fordham Jesuits, "the opportunity to give a contemporary definition of what it means to be a Catholic in the intellectual environment that is a university." Finlay frankly admitted that he could not meet this challenge without the support of his religious confrères. "Surely," he said, "there is in this group of Jesuits enough love, enough hope and enough faith, plus all the natural gifts of mind and personality, not to allow the opportunity of this moment to slip by without responding to the challenge."[14]

By the early 1970s it was obvious that the Society of Jesus would find it increasingly difficult to maintain the number of Jesuits it provided for the Fordham faculty and for the faculties of the other twenty-seven Jesuit colleges and universities in the United States. At Fordham, as the faculty

14. FUA, Finlay Papers, Finlay, Notes for an Address to the Board of Trustees, June 1972. Finlay, An Address to the Jesuit Community. September 20, 1973.

grew, the percentage of Jesuits declined. By the early 1980s there were still seventy-one Jesuits employed full-time in the university—twenty-one administrators and fifty faculty members—but during the previous decade the percentage of Jesuits in the full-time faculty had shrunk from approximately 20 percent to only 10 percent. They ranged in age from thirty-seven (Father John Dzieglewicz) to ninety-one (Father Harold Mulqueen), but most were in their late fifties and only a handful were under forty-five.[15]

The problem of maintaining a Jesuit presence at Jesuit universities was due not only to the unprecedented number of departures from the Society and the widespread decline in vocations to the priesthood and religious life but also to the decision of an increasing number of Jesuits to devote their lives to the social apostolate rather than to education. It was a trend that accelerated after the 32nd General Congregation of the Society of Jesus encouraged Jesuits throughout the world to discern how they could best serve the needs of the Church and humanity in a rapidly changing world. Finlay, who might be described ideologically as an extreme centrist, hesitated to join the rush to social activism. "I do not say this to denigrate social action," he explained in a confidential letter to the vice provincial, "but simply to keep things in focus." "If education follows Jesuit traditions," he insisted, "it is social action in the most profound sense."[16]

Alarmed at the problem of maintaining a Jesuit presence at Fordham, the provincial of the New York Province, Father Eamon G. Taylor, sought the advice of two of the most experienced and respected lay administrators at Fordham, Cammarosano and Reiss. He received thoughtful responses from both of them.

Cammarosano told Taylor that, on the basis of his limited contact with young Jesuits who had opted for a more activist calling, "I fail to discern any really significant accomplishments." In fact, he added, "A number of them, I find, have no moorings and are drifting rather aimlessly in a sea of uncertainty and indecision." He told the provincial, "I feel that the Society can do far more to alleviate present-day social, political, ecological and economic problems by placing its human and material resources in teaching and research than in direct, practical political and social action." With regard to the governance of Jesuit universities, Cammarosano set a

15. Jerry Buckley, "The Jesuit Presence," *Fordham*, Fall 1985, 20–25.

16. FUA, Finlay Papers, Finlay to John J. Canavan, S.J., April 1, 1982. "Like many another who read the proceedings of the General Congregation as well as the decrees," Finlay told Father Vincent O'Keefe, "I was fearful that that there might be an excessive emphasis placed on social activism." FUA, Finlay Papers, Finlay to O'Keefe, September 9, 1975.

high bar when he warned Taylor, "If Jesuit institutions of higher learning are not to lose their identity, it is absolutely essential that their presidents be Jesuits." For good measure he added, "It is equally important that other senior administrative positions be filled by Jesuits."[17]

Dr. Reiss agreed with Cammarosano that the "corporative presence" of the Society of Jesus was necessary to preserve a Jesuit and Christian ethos in Jesuit institutions, although he was not as insistent as Cammarosano that the principal administrative offices must remain in Jesuit hands. Reiss urged the Jesuits to face the fact that, if they expected to maintain a significant Jesuit presence in their own universities, their corporative commitments might have to take precedence over the career choices of individual Jesuits. In view of their diminishing numbers, he also prodded them to consider how many universities and colleges they could reasonably hope to maintain as authentically Jesuit institutions. He complained that the Jesuits seemed to be drifting and had failed to take decisive action to meet this problem. He warned Taylor, "The consequence could well be that there will be within another decade no Jesuit institutions at all."[18]

Shortly before Father Finlay's election as president, at the time the Jesuits transferred the ownership of the university to a predominantly lay board of trustees, they also secured the legal rights and assets of the Jesuit community by incorporating the Jesuit community as The Jesuits of Fordham, Inc. Even as the Fordham Jesuits witnessed their numbers diminish with a corresponding decline in their influence in the university, they continued to support Fordham financially by donating to the university each year a substantial portion of their salaries. In 1977 they donated $243,545 to the university, but the sum decreased thereafter because of their need to increase their contributions to their own retirement funds.[19]

Town and Gown

Despite the rapid growth of the Lincoln Center campus, Rose Hill remained the historic and symbolic home of Fordham University, but

17. FUA, Finlay Papers, Cammarosano to Taylor, August 6, 1973.

18. FUA, Finlay Papers, Reiss to Finlay, July 26, 1973. Reiss's warning echoes a remark made 140 years earlier by the Jesuit General, Father Jan Roothan, who told an American bishop that "the great plague of the Society in your part of the world is that we undertake too many things." Roothaan to Bishop Martin J. Spalding, n.d., in Gilbert J. Garraghan, S.J., *The Jesuits of the Middle United States* (New York: America Press, 1938), III, 274.

19. FUA, Finlay Papers, Vincent Potter, S.J., to the Fordham Jesuit Community, April 18, 1978.

Fordham's Bronx campus also became a beleaguered oasis as the wave of arson, crime, and wholesale abandonment of commercial and residential buildings described in the previous chapter continued unabated throughout the 1970s and traveled north to the gates of Fordham University. As was already mentioned, the historian Jill Jonnes aptly characterized this process of local urban decomposition when she said that the term "South Bronx," which had already achieved national notoriety, ceased to be a geographic designation and became "a traveling curse."

More than any of his predecessors as president of Fordham, Father Finlay involved himself in the Bronx's ordeal by arson and crime and attempted to work with local political and civic leaders to reverse the downward spiral. His motivation was both professional and personal. He was well aware that the South Bronx's toxic reputation put at risk the survival of Fordham's largest undergraduate college. Parents who wanted a Jesuit education for their sons or daughters but were concerned about their safety were more likely to send them to Fairfield University or Scranton University rather than to Fordham. However, there was also a deeply personal dimension to Finlay's concern for the future of the Bronx.

As a professor of political science, Finlay had introduced his students to the changing demographics of the Bronx by showing them the census returns of 1960 for certain areas of the borough and then directing them to make on-site inspections to see for themselves the changes that had subsequently taken place in those neighborhoods. On one summer evening, as he was driving up the Major Deegan Expressway from Lincoln Center to Rose Hill, Finlay made the kind of risky detour through the crime-infested local streets immortalized by Tom Wolfe in *The Bonfire of the Vanities* because he wanted to see for himself the former site of NYU's Bronx campus on University Heights in the West Bronx. Finlay was deeply upset at what he found: block after block of abandoned and burned-out apartment buildings on garbage-strewn streets. It was an experience that strengthened his determination to prevent a similar fate from engulfing the environs of Fordham University's Rose Hill campus. On an even more personal note, he mentioned that he remembered how impressed he was as a child to see the park benches in the Bronx adorned with the logo "Borough of Universities and Colleges." Because Fordham was the borough's only remaining university, Finlay wanted it to remain a Bronx university.[20]

Fordham was not the only urban American university that had to cope

20. FUA, Finlay Papers, Finlay, Remarks at the Big Apple College Fair Reception, Fordham University, September 28, 1983.

with the deterioration of its surrounding neighborhood in the 1970s. The University of Chicago, Yale University, Columbia University, and other urban American universities all had to contend with similar problems. The high-handed and insensitive approach of some universities to the process of urban renewal often provoked a backlash of heated criticism from the residents of the local communities. Finlay was determined to learn from the experience of those institutions to avoid making the same mistakes. As he became more deeply involved in the problems of the Bronx, Finlay said that his guiding principle was "to be supportive of local initiatives and local people but not to impose our view on them." As a result, he said, "I was much happier cooperating with them than trying to tell them what the solutions should be."[21]

One of Finlay's first overtures to the Bronx business community was to deny rumors that Fordham was planning to move north from the brick and concrete of the Bronx to the lush green swards of Westchester County. "We have been part of the Bronx since 1841," he told the Bronx Rotary Club in January 1972. "We have grown with this borough; we have benefited from this borough; we have made a contribution to this borough." In a Sherman-like statement, he declared, "We are here to stay." His audience hardly needed to be reminded that only six months earlier NYU, the largest private university in New York state, had sold its Bronx campus to City University to stave off the threat of bankruptcy. Finlay also mentioned that financial problems had forced twenty-three private colleges in New York state to close their doors in the previous nine years. He promised that Fordham University would cooperate closely with local political and business leaders not only for the sake of Fordham but also to support their efforts to stabilize and revitalize the Bronx.[22]

From the very beginning of his presidency, Finlay's principal involvement in social activism was to address the sad state of Fordham Road, a major east–west artery in the borough that had once been a thriving shopping district but had degenerated into the urban equivalent of a low-class suburban strip mall lined on both sides of the street with seedy discount stores and fast-food eateries. The south side of Fordham Road directly opposite the Third Avenue entrance to Fordham University contained a six-acre site of dilapidated commercial buildings that had been condemned as uninhabitable by the city as far back as the early 1960s. For the following

21. FOHP, Finlay, Self-Interview of the Reverend James C. Finlay, S.J., January 29 and February 4. 1989, 20–21.

22. FUA, Finlay Papers, Finlay, Address to the Bronx Rotary Club, January 29, 1974.

twenty-five years nothing was done to improve the site except for the demolition of some of the buildings and the proliferation of vacant lots.

Around 1969 a few local civic and business leaders, who were alarmed at the deterioration of the neighborhood, established the Fordham Road Area Development Corporation under the chairmanship of Henry Waltemade, the president of the Dollar Savings Bank and one of the leading businessmen in the Bronx. Finlay described Waltemade as a crotchety old gentleman, but one of the very few Bronx businessmen who showed a willingness to take positive steps to arrest the decline of the borough. Four years later the City Planning Commission endorsed the efforts of these local leaders to transform the six acres at the intersection of Fordham Road and Third Avenue into an urban renewal project that was to be called Fordham Plaza and was to include a new General Post Office and a discount department store. However, their efforts suffered a setback shortly thereafter when the department store chain (E. J. Korvette) filed for bankruptcy, and the U.S. Postal Service demanded an exorbitant sum for the property it owned.

When Father Finlay entered upon the scene as the president of Fordham, he reacted with a determination and finesse that would have won the admiration of a seasoned South Boston politician like his predecessor as president of Fordham, Father Michael Walsh. First Finlay joined forces with Waltemade, and the two of them sent a joint letter of complaint about the languishing state of the Fordham Plaza project to New York's two U.S. senators, Jacob Javits and James Buckley, and to Congressman Jonathan Bingham. They then released their letter to the press. Second, Finlay threatened to resort to the equivalent of the nuclear option. Only two years after Finlay had pledged that Fordham University would never abandon the Bronx, he declared that the indifference of the city, state, and federal government to the needs of the borough had reached such proportions that the university was seriously considering relocating to Westchester County.[23]

"Are we really ready to move?" Finlay asked the Fordham faculty at the Faculty Convocation in the fall of 1974. He answered that question by referring the faculty to the response of Vice President Cammarosano when the story first broke in the press. On that occasion Cammarosano parried

23. *Ram*, October 16, 1974. Finlay said that Fordham pumped between $10.5 million and $12 million into the economy of the Bronx every year, which represented between 35 percent and 40 percent of the university's operating budget. Fordham University owned the Calder Center, a 114-acre site in Armonk, and the Society of Jesus owned a 337-acre site in Shrub Oak near Peekskill.

reporters' questions by invoking the name of the Santini Brothers, a well-known Bronx moving company. "We haven't called in the Santini Brothers . . . yet," Cammarosano said teasingly, "but, if it takes a salvo to get things off dead center, then we've just fired it." (Cammarosano later admitted that he was bluffing.) Finlay assured the jittery faculty that he knew that the many fine private upstate New York universities and colleges did not need another neighbor even if its name was Fordham, but he warned the local politicians pointedly that the Bronx could not afford the loss of another university two years after the departure of NYU from the borough. "We intend to say so," he told the faculty, "and long before we seriously consider dialing Santini Brothers, we will make our presence and concern felt."

In a borough whose citizens were used to being suspicious of and cynical about the hidden agendas of public figures from long experience of dashed hopes, Finlay appealed to the public to trust the motives for his involvement in urban renewal. "We have no proprietary interest in the land across the street from our gates," he assured them, but "we do have an intense interest in the state of life in the Bronx." The day is long past, said Finlay, "when a university can raise the drawbridge, deepen the moat, and ignore devastation taking place around and about it." At the time a fatuous proposal was floated to erect a skyscraper in the Bronx to symbolize its anticipated rebirth. Finlay dismissed the proposal out-of-hand. "I care far more what is happening to the million-and-a-half lives of those who are trying to build a decent existence for themselves under the present skyline of the Bronx," he said, "than I do about seeing another addition to that skyline."[24]

Even after Finlay's threat to relocate the Rose Hill campus from the Bronx to Westchester County, more than a decade elapsed before Fordham Plaza became a reality. The delay was due partly to the severe financial crisis that New York City experienced in the 1970s and also to the unforeseen complications in relocating the few remaining residential and commercial tenants. One of the last commercial tenants to move away was the Eldorado Bar, which may have had a closer connection with Fordham University than any of the other establishments, because it was a favorite watering hole for Fordham students and perhaps some of the faculty.[25]

Father Finlay had ceased to be president of Fordham University by the time Fordham Plaza was finally dedicated in the early 1980s after its

24. FUA, Finlay Papers, Finlay, Address at the Faculty Convocation, October 20, 1974.

25. *Ram*, September 18, 1974. The editors of the *Ram* also claimed that Bronx Congressman Herman Badillo delayed the construction of Fordham Plaza by attempting

protracted gestation. At the groundbreaking ceremonies, both Mayor Ed Koch and Father Joseph O'Hare, S.J., Finlay's successor as president of Fordham, paid tribute to Finlay for his contributions to the creation of Fordham Plaza. The result, however, could hardly have been what Finlay or any longtime resident of the Bronx envisioned. Fordham Plaza evoked few comparisons with Manhattan's Grand Army Plaza as a center of civic pride. The pretentiously named plaza was basically an outdoor bus terminal located over the tracks of the Metro North Railroad with kiosks selling one-dollar slices of pizza, fruit and vegetables, and inexpensive clothing. The other component of Fordham Plaza was an unimpressive thirteen-story circular office building that Father Schroth generously described as a "sort of cylindrical ziggurat with wings."

The long-range plans for the revitalization of the Bronx anticipated that Fordham Plaza would spark a renaissance of the Fordham Road commercial corridor from Third Avenue to the Grand Concourse and would include a department store, shopping mall, parking garage for 500 cars, and, even more improbably, a cultural center. Paul Brant, the Fordham Jesuit scholastic and community activist, warned in 1974 that "unless something is done in the near future, the Bronx will go down the drain." Fortunately, Brant's apocalyptic alarms proved to be exaggerated.

Although the Bronx remains the poorest of the five boroughs of New York City and one of the poorest counties in New York state, in the past forty years it has made an astonishing comeback as crime subsided and massive infusions of government money led to the rebuilding or replacement of much of the borough's burned-out housing stock. Fordham Road fared less well in the process of renewal and has yet to recover its reputation as the borough's premier shopping district. Like the store owners in many downtown main streets throughout the United States, the merchants on Fordham Road struggle to survive in the face of stiff competition from both urban and suburban malls. Nonetheless, the habitable state of the Bronx has improved to the point that no president of Fordham has again felt the need to threaten to leave the Bronx for a more hospitable environment north of the city line.[26]

---

to divert federal funding from Fordham Plaza to his own congressional district in the South Bronx. If the allegation was true, it would have been doubly disappointing even by the flexible ethical standards of Bronx politics, because at the time Badillo was an adjunct professor in the Fordham University Graduate School of Education. *Ram*, September 15, 1983.

26. *Ram*, October 30, 1974.

In contrast to the frustrations that Finlay experienced in dealing with politicians and government bureaucrats, he quickly developed a high regard for the work of the Northwest Bronx Community and Clergy Coalition, an organization of sixteen Catholic parishes whose origins were traced in the preceding chapter. As the coalition became more sophisticated in its *modus operandi*, it became increasingly effective in obtaining several million dollars from insurance companies and banks to combat the physical deterioration of the Bronx. Paul Brant, the thirty-three-year-old campus minister and later an adjunct professor at Fordham, continued to play an important role in the operation of the coalition. He identified its principal goals as guaranteeing decent housing for low-income families (especially those on welfare), making politicians accountable to the electorate, building a new Fordham Hospital to replace underfunded Medicaid mills, and urging the Catholic Church to use its considerable political clout to improve the quality of life for all Bronx residents.[27]

With Finlay's encouragement, both the university and the Fordham Jesuit community offered strong support to the coalition. Finlay even tried to persuade the New York Province of the Society to provide financial assistance for the coalition, which, he said, is "becoming a very powerful force for good in the Bronx." In 1983 Finlay publicly associated Fordham with the coalition in an unconventional way when he awarded an honorary doctorate to Ms. Anne Devenney, a feisty sixty-four-year-old grandmother and neighborhood resident who was the president of the coalition. Devenney, a native New Yorker who grew up during the Great Depression and never had the opportunity to attend college, appreciated the honorary Fordham doctorate as an endorsement of the work of the coalition, but she also demonstrated her New York grit when she added, "I learned all that I needed to know from my father and from the school of hard knocks." One happy side effect of Fordham's support of the coalition was the mutually advantageous relationship that developed between the university and the Bronx parish priests. In fact, Finlay told Father Vincent O'Keefe, now an influential figure in the Jesuit Curia in Rome, "I don't think that there has ever been such close cooperation between the university and the local clergy at any time in the past."[28]

27. Ibid. Although the Catholic clergy was instrumental in founding the coalition, at the urging of Paul Brant it expanded its membership to become an ecumenical organization. On Paul Brant, see "Impact in the Bronx," *Fordham*, Spring 1974, 10–14.

28. FUA, Finlay Papers, Finlay to Vincent O'Keefe, S.J., October 24, 1974; Finlay to Vincent M. Cooke, S.J., August 30, 1982; Patrick Ahern to Finlay, December 30, 1983. "Anne Devenney, Mother Courage of the NWBCCC," *Fordham*, Summer 1984, 21.

Dr. Joseph Cammarosano, once again happily professor of economics after stepping down as executive vice president, made his own contribution to the assessments of the future prospects of the South Bronx with two thoughtful studies of the area that not only documented the well-known blight but also offered rarely voiced economic reasons for optimism about the future. One was entitled "A Profile of the Bronx Economy" sponsored by the Federal Office of Economic Opportunity (Washington, D.C., 1967). The other was "Industrial Activity in the Inner City: A Case Study of the South Bronx," which Cammarosano wrote in 1981 at the request of the New York City Public Development Corporation. In both studies Dr. Cammarosano drew attention to often-overlooked positive factors such as the strategic location of the area, the tenacity of the companies that had remained in the South Bronx, the large labor pool, the availability of vacant land for industrial use, and many other factors that made it premature to abandon hope for the revival of the South Bronx.[29]

Protecting the Patrimony

Finlay's enthusiastic embrace of the Northwest Bronx Community and Clergy Coalition was all the more impressive because he carefully evaluated requests for financial assistance from many other organizations and bluntly rejected those that he feared would compromise Fordham's reputation or put a dent in its finances. Finlay did not hesitate to tangle with the widely esteemed Catholic Interracial Council, which he suspected was living off the reputation of its founder, the saintly Father John LaFarge, S.J. After consulting with Father Joseph Fitzpatrick, a Fordham Jesuit sociologist with impeccable credentials in the minority community, Finlay demanded that the Catholic Interracial Council remove the endorsement of Fordham University from its letterhead. "Evidence of genuine labor in the vineyard on the part of the Catholic Interracial Council has simply not surfaced," explained Finlay curtly.[30]

Finlay was equally skeptical when he turned down an invitation from his friend Father Timothy S. Healy, S.J., the president of Georgetown University, who urged him to join the board of the recently founded Association of Urban Universities. "What is the track record of the Association?" asked Finlay. After receiving an unsatisfactory answer, Finlay refused to contribute $3,000 to an association that seemed to offer few tangible ben-

29. See also Joseph Cammarosano, "Write Off the South Bronx? Not by a Long Shot!" *Fordham*, Fall 1981, 3–4.

30. FUA, Finlay Papers, Finlay to Frederick O'Neal, April 27, 1979.

efits to Fordham. Closer to home, Finlay even declined an invitation to introduce U.S. Senators Howard H. Baker of Tennessee and Sam J. Ervin of North Carolina when they arrived at Coffey Field by helicopter to speak at Rose Hill about the Watergate scandal at a student-sponsored event attended by 3,000 students and faculty members. Finlay's objections were not political but financial. He was outraged at the hefty fees that the two senators demanded for their services. In fact Finlay did not even attend their lectures, to show his displeasure.[31]

Although Finlay was skeptical about spending university funds on dubious causes, he was generous in devoting his time to serving on the board of an organization that he respected, the Association of Colleges and Universities of New York State. The respect was reciprocal and he was elected president of the organization in 1980. Finlay always preferred to speak of Fordham as an independent university rather than a private university. Thus he took a close interest in every proposal that came before the state legislature to enable parents and students to select the colleges of their choice. "Father Finlay was a very effective advocate for independent higher education in New York state and on the national level," said Father Joseph O'Hare, his immediate successor as president of Fordham, a comment that was echoed by Dr. Joseph Cammarosano.[32]

Finlay's prudent safeguarding of Fordham's endorsements and finances was balanced by his deep involvement in the world outside the gates of the Rose Hill campus, which was not limited to his involvement in the creation of Fordham Plaza. For example, immediately adjacent to the athletic field of Fordham Preparatory School on Southern Boulevard was a vacant lot that had been abandoned by the New York Botanical Garden. With the assistance of Congressman Mario Biaggi, Fordham was able to obtain funding from the federal government through the Department of Housing and Urban Development to use the site to erect the Rose Hill Apartments, a residential facility for the elderly and disabled. Monsignor Charles Fahey, a faculty member at Fordham, was instrumental in suggesting the project, but Finlay gave the major credit for managing the complicated planning and construction of the Rose Hill Apartments to Brian J. Byrne, a Fordham graduate student and a veteran volunteer at the Northwest Bronx

31. FUA, Finlay Papers, Finlay to Healy, August 18, 1983. FOHP, Finlay, Self-Interview, 47. The fee of $2,500 paid to the two senators seems unbelievably abstemious by present-day standards. In response to criticism from a student, Senator Baker defended the size of his stipend as small compensation for working twenty hours a week. "Two Senators Drop In," *Fordham*, Winter 1974, 8.

32. FUA RP, Box 2, Press Release, December 5, 1992.

Community and Clergy Coalition, whom Finlay later made his executive assistant. Still later Byrne became vice president for Lincoln Center. When Finlay retired as president of Fordham in 1984, a local Bronx newspaper paid him a handsome compliment when it said that "Father Finlay in a sense made a large part of the Bronx his campus."[33]

Academics

Throughout the dozen years of Father Finlay's presidency, the enrollment at Fordham remained stable at approximately 13,000 students, an impressive achievement at a time of declining enrollments in many American universities and colleges.

Two important changes took place in Fordham's undergraduate program during Finlay's administration. One was the decision to merge Thomas More College—Fordham's women's college—with Fordham College at Rose Hill. Although Thomas More College was only ten years old, it had established a high academic reputation and could already boast of a fiercely loyal alumnae, as Finlay discovered to his cost when they vigorously protested the decision to merge their nascent alma mater with Fordham College. When Finlay attempted to explain the reasons for the merger to the alumnae, many of whom were his former students, he received such a hostile reception that he walked out of the meeting.[34]

The second major change on the undergraduate level was the introduction of the Presidential and Jesuit Community Scholarship programs. The scholarships were not awarded on the basis of financial need but were designed to attract bright students to Fordham from throughout the country in an effort to broaden the demographic base of the student body and reverse slipping academic standards. The program succeeded in drawing applicants from as far away as Texas, California, and Hawaii. Finlay called it "one of things of which I am proudest."[35]

On the graduate level Finlay created Fordham's first new graduate school in many years, the Graduate School of Religion and Religious Education. The background to the establishment of the new graduate school was the ferment that took place after Vatican II as Catholic educators recognized the pedagogical inadequacy of attempting to hand on the faith to a

33. FUA, FOHP. Finlay, Self-Interview, 64–66. Finlay also noted the involvement in the project of George Doty, a Fordham trustee and one of its most generous benefactors, as well as his wife, Marie, who had a particular concern for the problems of the elderly. *Bronx Press Review*, March 22, 1984.

34. FUA, FOHP, Finlay, Self-Interview, 45.

35. Ibid., 40.

generation of more sophisticated young people by the traditional method of rote memorization of questions and answers from the catechism.

A graduate program to explore new methods of religious education had been established at Fordham as early as 1964 in the Graduate School of Education with the cooperation of the Theology Department, but there was considerable hesitation about expanding this program into a full-fledged graduate program in religious education for fear that it would compromise Fordham's eligibility for Bundy Money. However, when a program in religious education at NYU passed muster from the state educational authorities, Fordham interpreted it as a green light to establish its own graduate program as the Graduate School of Religion and Religious Education in 1975.

Eight years later, enrollment in the GSRRE had grown from a few dozen students to 150, three-quarters of them women. The school also attracted many priests and religious from all parts of the English-speaking world. The first dean of the GSRRE was Father Vincent M. Novak, S.J., whose graduate degrees included the prestigious S.T.D. Diplôme de Lumen Vitae, from the world-famous Catholic catechetical institute in Brussels. Novak was to remain dean of the school for the following forty years. Finlay credited him with carefully developing the programs of the GSRRE and earning an international reputation for the school. From its inception, the GSRRE required a subsidy from the university because of its limited enrollment. Finlay, who was always protective of the university's bottom line to the verge of parsimony, made an exception for the GSRRE. He thought the subsidy was money well spent because it enabled Fordham to preserve its fidelity to its Catholic and Jesuit traditions.[36]

Another innovative academic program introduced by Finlay was the Third Age Center, which grew out of the All-University Center on Gerontology established in 1978 with an initial grant from the Department of Health, Education and Welfare. The status of the Center was enhanced two years later thanks to a gift of $1 million from the family of George E. Doty, which enabled Fordham to create the Marie Ward Doty Chair of Gerontology Studies. The first occupant of the chair, Monsignor Charles Fahey, was also the director of the Third Age Center, whose purpose was to encourage research and training throughout the university on both the undergraduate and graduate levels, especially in connection

36. Ibid., 54. See also *Fordham*, Spring 1982, 24. Together with his brother, Father Joseph Novak, S.J., and John Nelson, Novak wrote a series of high school religion textbooks that were a considerable improvement over the venerable Baltimore catechism.

with the doctoral program in gerontology in the Graduate School of Social Services.[37]

Fordham University at Age 140

When Fordham University celebrated its 140th anniversary in 1981—nine years into Father Finlay's presidency—it was a low-key affair rather like Father Walsh's passing the baton (or more accurately the keys of the house car) to Father Finlay a decade earlier in the parking lot at John F. Kennedy International Airport. Finlay was content to publish a list of statistics that indicated the progress Fordham had made during his tenure, although he was quick to give much of the credit for that progress to the faculty and his administrative staff.

In 1981 Fordham University had slightly more than 14,000 students— 8,002 in the four undergraduate schools and 6,126 in the six graduate and professional schools. The most surprising development on the undergraduate level was the rapid growth of the College at Lincoln Center with 3,003 students compared with 3,015 students at Fordham College (as the two colleges were then called). There were an additional 1,305 students in the College of Business Administration and another 679 in the School of General Studies.

Among the graduate schools, the School of Education had the largest enrollment (1,892), followed by the Graduate School of Arts and Sciences (1,216), Fordham Law School (1,168), Graduate School of Business Administration (965), Graduate School of Social Service (734), and the Graduate School of Religion and Religious Education (151).

The most impressive addition to the physical plant at the Rose Hill campus during Finlay's administration was the erection of a new two-and-a-half-acre athletic facility, the Vincent T. Lombardi Memorial Athletic Center, which was dedicated on October 30, 1976. The completion of the center, which cost $5 million, was delayed because fundraising for the new facility proved to be more difficult than anticipated after Lombardi's death in 1970. Finlay also faced opposition from those who wanted the new facility to be restricted to varsity sports and create a high-profile Madison Square Garden North at Rose Hill. Finlay prevailed when he vetoed that proposal and insisted that the Lombardi Center should serve the interests of all Fordham students. At Lincoln

---

37. FUA, AF, Box 39, Aging Studies and Related Topics: Courses of Instruction and Related Topics, Spring 1982. Fahey to Board of Trustees, March 11, 1986. Fahey had served as the head of the Federal Council on Aging under President Jimmy Carter.

Center the Law School was expanded under Father Finlay with a new addition that cost $8 million.

With less fanfare than that which accompanied the erection of the Lombardi Center, Finlay spent $8.3 million renovating the older buildings at Rose Hill, because he was especially concerned about the condition of their antiquated electrical wiring. In addition, Larkin Hall received a new biological research laboratory for the pre-med students and biology majors at a cost of almost $2 million, and "Old Chem" (once the Medical School and today's Finlay Hall) was transformed into a dormitory for 331 students at a cost of $5.5 million, a decision that was part of Finlay's ongoing effort to promote Fordham as a residential college. "I think that every year while I was president," said Finlay, "we had some housing crisis." The lack of sufficient campus housing stymied Finlay's efforts to shake Fordham's reputation as primarily a commuter college.[38]

In 1979 a proposal was made to relieve the student housing problem by converting Loyola-Faber Hall, the principal Jesuit residence, into a student residence hall. In return the university was to be asked to build an entirely new residence for the Jesuit community. The estimated cost for the total project was $13,205,000, a budget-breaking sum that made the proposal dead on arrival. Three years later, Finlay sent a panic-stricken letter to the Jesuit community at the beginning of the summer, warning them that Fordham faced the loss of $1 million in tuition the following September because the university could not provide housing for more than 200 incoming freshmen. As an emergency measure, Finlay converted three floors of Hughes Hall (the former site of Fordham Prep) into student housing, but he admitted that it was only a stopgap solution. A more permanent solution was to be the work of his two successors.[39]

Finlay's concern for the future of Catholic higher education was not limited to Fordham. The 1970s were a crucial decade for many small Catholic women's colleges throughout the United States as they faced the problems of shrinking enrollments and mounting financial problems. Because

38. Finlay, "The President's Report," *Fordham*, Winter 1981, 3–16. FUA, FOHP, Finlay, Self-Interview, 36–37.

39. FUA, Finlay Papers, A Proposal: A New Residence for Fordham's Jesuit Community, June 9, 1979; Ralph G. Heiman to Brother James Kenny, S.J., October 3, 1979; Finlay to the Loyola/Faber Community, June 28, 1982. Finlay told the Fordham Jesuits that Hughes Hall could remain a student residence only temporarily because he needed the space for classrooms, because he intended to transform Keating Hall into the university library.

Fordham was the only Catholic university in the archdiocese of New York, Finlay offered his support to three local Catholic women's colleges that faced those difficulties.

He received different responses from each of them. In the case of Good Counsel College in White Plains, a small college run by a diocesan community of sisters, the Religious of the Divine Compassion, it quickly became obvious to him that his efforts of support were superfluous because the sisters had already decided to sell their college to Pace University. He might have expected a more positive response from Manhattanville College in Purchase, New York, because the Religious of the Sacred Heart, who had founded the college, had a century-old relationship with the Society of Jesus both in Europe and in the United States. However, as Finlay quickly realized, the nuns, in a hasty embrace of *aggiornamento*, had surrendered control of their college to a lay board that, in Finlay's euphemistic words, "seemed to be moving out of the orbit of the Catholic educational system." Predictably the lay board of trustees at Manhattanville declined an association with Fordham. However, Fordham received a more positive response from Marymount College, where Finlay was able to work out a mutually satisfactory agreement that enabled Fordham to offer graduate courses in education, business administration, and social work at Marymount's Tarrytown campus.[40]

Finlay liked to quote a prediction that Father Robert I. Gannon made on the occasion of Fordham's centennial in 1941, that only two kinds of American universities would continue to exist, those that were very rich and those that were indispensable. Neither Gannon nor Finlay ever thought that Fordham would fit into the first category, but both of them made determined efforts to prove that Fordham was becoming an indispensable presence in the world of American higher education on both the local and national scenes.[41]

Fifty years after Father Gannon made his prediction, Fordham could boast of approximately 70,000 living alumni and alumnae from all parts of the United States. More than half of them had received their diplomas during Finlay's tenure. Fordham ranked among the top 10 percent of American universities and colleges whose graduates were chief executives in the Fortune 500 list of major U.S. corporations. The undergraduate student retention rate was 20 percent higher than the national average, and Fordham graduates were in demand in the business world, as was evident from

40. FUA, FOHP, Finlay, Self-Interview, 54–57.
41. FUA, RP, Box 2, Finlay, Address at the Faculty Convocation, October 23, 1977.

the fact that representatives from 150 corporations now conducted job interviews at Fordham every year.

The Fordham faculty was also instrumental in enhancing the university's standing. Father Joseph Fitzpatrick, S.J., established a national reputation as a sociologist as a result of his studies of Puerto Rican immigration to the mainland United States. As was mentioned earlier, the Belgian-born Jesuit philosopher Father Joseph Donceel made Fordham the leading center of Transcendental Thomism in the United States, while his Jesuit confrère Father Gerald McCool was a pioneer in introducing Americans to the thought of the German Jesuit theologian Father Karl Rahner. Mary Ann Quaranta, the dean of the School of Social Service, received the highest professional accolade in her field when she was elected president of the National Association of Social Workers, a prestigious organization with 85,000 members. Father Finlay was especially proud that he selected John Feerick to be the dean of Fordham Law School in 1982. Feerick was not only a graduate of Fordham College and Fordham Law School but also a native son and loyal champion of the South Bronx. He served as dean of Fordham Law School with distinction for two decades, quickly establishing such an outstanding reputation for integrity that he was twice selected by governors of New York to head state investigative commissions.[42]

When Father Finlay retired as president of Fordham in 1984, he commented with a sigh of relief that "there is just so much one person can do." Finlay moved to Le Moyne College in Syracuse, New York, where he held several administrative positions, including that of interim president in 1988. After his health began to fail, he returned to Fordham to take up residence in Murray-Weigel Hall, the infirmary for retired Jesuits, where he died in December 1992.

42. Finlay, "The President's Report," *Fordham*, Winter 1981, 3–16. When Governor Eliot Spitzer appointed Feerick to head a new Commission on Public Integrity in 2007, he described him as "the one individual who is pre-eminent among all New Yorkers in standing for the principles of integrity in government." *New York Times*, April 17, 2007. Feerick validated Spitzer's praise a year later when he resigned from the commission.

21

APPROACHING THE SESQUICENTENNIAL

Fordham's cantankerous founding father, Archbishop John Hughes, was in a particularly irritable mood in the spring of 1858 because he was in failing health and fearful that Pope Pius IX would appoint a co-adjutor archbishop to govern his diocese. In a report to Rome that year filled with complaints both real and imagined, Hughes lashed out at the Society of Jesus among many others in New York because he claimed that St. John's College had "retrograded" since he had sold it to the Jesuits in 1845. The Jesuits had incurred his displeasure because the enrollment had declined during the previous dozen years and Hughes claimed that the college had suffered a loss of prestige since its ceasing to be a diocesan college. "The number [of students] at present hardly exceeds one hundred," said Hughes in 1858, "and the institution has unfortunately become comparatively obscure."[1]

When Fordham celebrated its sesquicentennial in 1991, perhaps even John Hughes would have been pleased with its resurrection from alleged obscurity (and quick to claim credit for it). The total enrollment on both the graduate and undergraduate levels was more than 13,000. Two other changes would have been impossible for John Hughes to fathom. First, more than half the students (56 percent) were women. Second, almost one-third of the students were members of minorities: 16 percent Hispanic, 11 percent African American, and 2 percent Asian. The student body, once overwhelmingly New Yorkers of Irish and Italian background, now came from more than forty states and fifty-five foreign countries.

The transformation of Fordham from a local to a national university, especially on the undergraduate level, was made possible by the addition of dormitory rooms for 2,800 students at Rose Hill during the previous seven years, and plans were also under way to provide a residence hall at the Lincoln Center campus. One area where a relatively slow pace of

1. Hughes to Abbot Bernard Smith, O.S.B., March 23, 1858, published as "The Archdiocese of New York a Century Ago: A Memoir of Archbishop Hughes, 1838–1858," ed. Henry J. Browne, *HR&S* 39–40 (1952), 145.

change was a blessing for Fordham and helped to maintain its Catholic heritage was the continued presence of a sizeable number of Jesuits on campus. In 1991 there were still forty-two Jesuits on the faculty and eighteen in administration. By one calculation it was a larger number of Jesuits than in any other Jesuit educational institution in the United States.[2]

Father Joseph A. O'Hare, S.J.

The fifty-three-year-old Father Joseph Aloysius O'Hare, the tall, silver-haired priest who succeeded Father Finlay in 1984, brought a unique background to the office of president of Fordham. He was the first native of the Bronx to become president, and he was to remain as president for a record-setting nineteen years.[3]

2. *Fordham Sesquicentennial History*, n.p.

3. Whether O'Hare is the only native of the Bronx to become president of Fordham is a matter of some dispute and depends upon the political status of Marble Hill, the "Bronx" neighborhood that is the birthplace of Father Joseph M. McShane, S.J., O'Hare's successor as president. Marble Hill has been separated physically from Manhattan Island since the construction of the Harlem River Ship Canal in 1895, but in 1984 the New York state legislature declared that Marble Hill was still part of Manhattan.

Ms. Anne Devenney, the longtime president of the Northwest Bronx Community and Clergy Coalition. At his inauguration, Father O'Hare hailed her as "one of Fordham's most respected honorary alumnae."

O'Hare's inauguration as the thirty-first president on September 30, 1984, was only the second formal inauguration of a new president of Fordham in 134 years. The sole exception was the inauguration of Father Aloysius Hogan, S.J., in 1930. Father George McMahon, S.J., the master of ceremonies on the occasion of O'Hare's inauguration, commented: "Only a university with a wondrous sense of its history, identity and vision for the future could take the first step in establishing a custom, and then not take the second step until 54 years later." Among the 2,000 guests were 260 presidents and delegates from universities throughout the country; John J. O'Connor, the newly appointed archbishop of New York; and Father O'Hare's mother, Mrs. Marie O'Hare. Another invited guest was an elderly Bronx resident, Ms. Anne Devenney, the longtime president of the Northwest Bronx Community and Clergy Coalition. O'Hare hailed her as one of Fordham's most respected honorary alumnae and quoted her comment about the prospects for the Bronx: "We're not moving," she said. "We're improving."

Father O'Hare used his inaugural address to lay out a two-fold vision for the future of Fordham. With regard to the internal life of the university, he insisted that Fordham remained committed to pursuing what he called "the dialectical relationship of faith and intelligence" in an atmosphere that avoided the extremes of both narrow religious indoctrination and moral skepticism. The second part of O'Hare's vision for Fordham was its responsibility for the world and the people outside the gates of the campus, a concern that he traced back to *Spiritual Exercises* of St. Ignatius Loyola. He promised that Fordham would continue "to awaken in its students a concern for others, a great-hearted response, a commitment that goes beyond calculation."[4]

O'Hare's educational background was different from that of any of his Jesuit predecessors, many of whom had received their higher education in Europe. Unlike them, O'Hare spent a total of eleven years in the Philippines, where the New York Province of the Society had a long-established presence. First as a seminarian and later as a priest, O'Hare taught at two Jesuit institutions there, Berchmans College in Cebu City and the Ateneo de Manila University. At both institutions he was impressed with the high caliber of the students. He also left the Philippines with the lasting impression that the attempt to preserve the common worldwide identity of Catholic universities must respect the reality of sharp cultural differences. "Standardization may be cost-effective for a multi-national corporation like IBM," he said years later, but, "for the life of a university, standardization imposed by Rome could be fatal for the life of Catholic universities around the world."[5]

Between several assignments in the Philippines, O'Hare also received a theology degree from Woodstock College in Maryland, spent two years in graduate studies at the Institut Catholique in Paris, and earned a doctorate in philosophy from Fordham in 1968. His arrival at Fordham was as an "outsider" because he was not a tenured member of the faculty and had spent the previous nine years as the editor-in-chief of *America*, the national Jesuit weekly. However, in addition to his Fordham doctorate, he had other ties to Fordham, because he had been ordained a priest in the Fordham University Church in 1961 and had taught as an adjunct professor in the Excel Program at the Lincoln Center campus from 1975 to 1978. As editor-in-chief of *America*, O'Hare had been an outspoken commentator on contemporary events. When he was asked if he planned to continue the same policy as president of Fordham, O'Hare replied, "I have taken three vows—poverty, chastity and obedience—and I have had enough difficulty

4. "Local Boy Makes Good," *Fordham*, Winter 1985, 2–5.

5. FUA, O'Hare Papers, O'Hare, "Places in the Heart," an address at the Ateneo de Manila University, July 24, 1990. The occasion was the conferral of an honorary doctorate by the Ateneo.

trying to observe those. I don't intend to take a vow of silence because I am sure that I would not observe it."[6]

Reimagining Two Campuses

Like every president of a large American university with a growing student population, O'Hare faced the two-fold problem of providing more classroom and dormitory space and then finding the money to pay for it. The need for more student housing on the undergraduate level was especially acute at Fordham, if Fordham College were to attain its coveted goal of achieving national recognition and shedding its reputation as primarily a local commuter school. Several presidents of Fordham dating back to Father Gannon in the 1930s had made progress in providing additional undergraduate residential housing. However, as has already been mentioned, even as recently as the early 1970s approximately 85 percent of the students still came from the New York metropolitan area, and fully one-third of them came from the Bronx. In retrospect Father James Finlay, president of Fordham from 1972 to 1983, regretted that he had not done more to build additional residential housing.[7]

The big change came under Father Finlay's successor, Father O'Hare, who was ultimately responsible for providing additional space for more than 3,500 students at both Rose Hill and Lincoln Center. His building program involved the construction and renovation of no fewer than six buildings. At Rose Hill, the three-story Sesquicentennial Hall was opened in September 1986 for 150 students. It was renamed Tierney Hall after the tragic death of William Tierney of the class of 1998, a popular football player who collapsed shortly before the homecoming game at Coffey Field in 1996. The opening of Alumni Court South and Alumni Court North in 1987 provided space for approximately 540 additional students. In 2009 Alumni Court North was renamed Loschert Hall in honor of a generous benefactor, William J. Loschert, CBA '61, a retired businessman living in London, who had given Fordham more than $5 million in gifts.

In 1994, after Fordham Preparatory School vacated Hughes Hall for its new building, it temporarily became a Fordham College freshman residence. That same year Queen's Court (whose oldest building dates from 1845, when it was St. Joseph's New York Diocesan Seminary) was completely renovated and designated a New York City landmark. The most

6. Eileen Hughes, "A Conversation with Fordham's New President," *Fordham*, Summer 1984, 11.

7. FUA, Finlay Papers, Finlay, Address to New Faculty Members, September 12, 1973. Interview with Father Joseph M. McShane, S.J., August 28, 2014.

impressive of O'Hare's residential building projects at Rose Hill was the erection of Millennium Hall, a $40 million five-story innovative residence hall that provided space for 560 students. Appropriately, it was renamed O'Hare Hall after Father O'Hare's retirement as president in 2003, and the Great Room on the ground floor (with meeting space for 350 people) was renamed the O'Keefe Commons after another former Fordham president, Father Vincent O'Keefe, S.J.

O'Hare's boldest building project for providing student housing was to erect a residence in the heart of Manhattan at the Lincoln Center campus, which met a crying need that had gone unanswered for thirty years. The Lincoln Center Residence Hall, which was opened in 1993 (and was re-named the Father George J. McMahon, S.J., Hall four years later), was a 20-story building located at 155 West 60th Street, adjacent to the Lowenstein Building on the Lincoln Center Campus. It provided accommodations for some 850 students. Unlike the exclusively undergraduate residence halls at Rose Hill, McMahon Hall provided housing for both undergraduate and graduate students and was especially popular with students in Fordham Law School.[8]

At Lincoln Center in the spring of 1984 the $9 million wing and atrium of Fordham Law School was dedicated at a ceremony during which U.S. Supreme Court Justice Sandra Day O'Connor received an honorary degree. Governor Mario Cuomo, Senator Alfonse D'Amato, and Mayor Ed Koch were also in attendance. The proliferation of new residence halls was complemented by the ongoing beautification of both the Manhattan and Bronx campuses. The completion of the renovations of the Robert Moses Plaza at Lincoln Center coincided with the opening of the new Lincoln Center Residence Hall in 1993.

Fordham's athletic programs received a major boost in the fall of 1990, when $3 million was invested in the construction of a new 7,000-seat grandstand at Coffey Field as well as the refurbishment of the football and baseball fields. In 1997 the newly renovated Murphy Field was re-dedicated to Connie Murphy of the class of 1932. The 14-month renovation of the University Church was completed in October 2004, a project made possible in part by a gift of $1.5 million from George Doty, FCO '38, and his wife, Marie. At the re-dedication ceremonies on October 13, Edward Cardinal Egan, the archbishop of New York, thanked Fordham for being "a beacon here on a hill" in an age of increasing secularism.[9]

8. "155 West 60th Street," *Fordham*, Fall–Winter 1993–94, 14.

9. Built in 1845, expanded in 1929, and remodeled in 1990, 2003, and 2004, the Uni-

While new buildings were sprouting like mushrooms on the Rose Hill campus, two faculty members, Roger Wines, professor of history, and Allan S. Gilbert, associate professor of archaeology, were engaged in the lonely task of diligently burrowing beneath the surface of the Rose Hill campus in the fall of 1985 in search of the remains of the Rose Hill Manor House, a pre–Revolutionary War building that had been demolished in 1896. It was the first professional archaeological dig in the Bronx in a century and was sponsored by the Bronx Historical Society as well as by several departments of the university.[10]

Edwards Parade, a lawn almost as large as a football field in the center of the Rose Hill campus, had once been a showcase of Fordham's rustic greenery in the heart of the urban Bronx, but years of neglect had allowed it to deteriorate by the 1960s into what Father O'Hare called "a pathetic dust bowl." Dr. Joseph Cammarosano, a veteran of combating crabgrass on his own suburban front lawn for forty years, took it upon himself to remedy the situation. Characteristically it was a hands-on operation. In his office Dr. Cammarosano proudly preserves a photo of himself driving a tractor across Edwards Parade to begin the process of restoring it to its former glory. "Between the students who kept walking on the ground," he said, "and the birds [that] kept feeding on the seed, it was not easy." Nonetheless, he succeeded beyond expectations, and Edwards Parade re-emerged as a lush green carpet in front of Keating Hall. It was not the least of Dr. Joseph Cammarosano's many contributions to Fordham.[11]

Fordham's commitment to providing more undergraduate housing was so successful that, within twenty years, the university had reversed the proportion of residential and commuter students. In 1972, 70 percent of Fordham undergraduates were commuters; in 1992, 70 percent of Fordham undergraduates lived on campus. However, the success of Fordham's transformation into a predominantly residential college raised a moral dilemma for many faculty members, including members of the Fordham Jesuit community at the Rose Hill campus.

The population of the Bronx in 1992 was 74 percent African American and Hispanic. It was the poorest of the five boroughs of New York City,

versity Church was declared a New York City landmark in 1970. http://www.fordham .edu/campus_resources/enewsroom/archives/archive_395.asp.

10. O'Hare, "The President's 15-Year Report," *Fordham* 33:3 (1999), 3–39.

11. Interview with Dr. Joseph Cammarosano, September 28, 2014. O'Hare, "The President's File," *Fordham*, Summer 1998. Interview with Father McShane, August 28, 2014.

and Rose Hill was located in the congressional district that was contiguous to the poorest congressional district in the United States. Although minority students constituted a record one-quarter of the incoming freshman class at Fordham in the fall of 1992, 81 percent of the total undergraduate enrollment was still white. Few minority parents in the Bronx could afford the annual Fordham tuition of $16,800.[12]

In the spring of 1997 Father O'Hare announced that Fordham would offer a $4,000 tuition discount to all freshmen who continued to live with their families at home. It was an impressive reaffirmation of Fordham's commitment to the local community at the time when the freshman class came from thirty-five states and ten foreign countries. "The president is a local Bronx boy," explained Father Joseph M. McShane, dean of Fordham College at Rose Hill, "and he really feels this is a moral imperative for a place with our heritage and our location in the Bronx and New York." O'Hare's tuition discount and the continuing success of Fordham's Higher Education Opportunity Program (HEOP) made a difference in attracting more minority students. At least one professor at the Rose Hill campus who arrived early for his college classes often noticed a cluster of students in the classroom speaking to one another softly in Spanish, a small but striking indication that Fordham was succeeding in its efforts to provide the same educational opportunities for Hispanic students (and for other minority students as well) that it had earlier provided for the children of Irish, German, and Italian immigrants.[13]

Academics and Finance

Two major changes occurred in the academic structure of Fordham during the O'Hare years. Both involved the closer integration of the Rose Hill and Lincoln Center campuses in the academic structure of the university. On the undergraduate level this meant the adoption of an identical common core curriculum at both campuses. On both the undergraduate and graduate levels it meant the consolidation of both faculty and course offerings in departments that offered identical or similar courses on both campuses.

The original version of an undergraduate core curriculum dated from 1980 at Rose Hill and had last been revised in 1990. Two years later O'Hare proposed the adoption of the common core curriculum at both Rose Hill

12. Ian Fisher, "Fordham's Evolving Role at the Heart of the Bronx," *New York Times*, November 6, 1992.

13. Karen Anderson, "Fordham Offers a Discount for Commuters," *New York Times*, October 22, 1997.

and Lincoln Center. It was implemented on both campuses in November 1995 following a mandate from the board of trustees in May 1994 and eighteen months of discussion by the faculty. The new core curriculum consisted of eighteen courses spread over four years that included English, history, philosophy, theology, physical and social sciences, fine arts, and foreign languages as well as a senior seminar in values and moral choices.[14]

One of the more hotly contested issues that surfaced during the process of campus integration and the adoption of the common core curriculum was the future of the study of theology or religious studies at Fordham. Rose Hill had a department of theology while Lincoln Center had a department of religious studies. The underlying issue was more than a question of nomenclature, as one faculty member pointed out when he said, "I take [religious studies] to mean religion as a social science or sociological phenomenon whereas religious study in the Jesuit tradition ought to be a critical confrontation between religious traditions and human reason."

Those who favored the replacement of theology with religious studies claimed that only about one-half of the students at Lincoln Center were Catholics. They weakened their argument, however, and perhaps tipped their hand, when they asserted that a department of religious studies would "de-stigmatize theology in the minds of many non-Catholics and non-Christians." The internal faculty debate had national implications, because Fordham was one of only five Catholic universities in the United States that offered a full range of doctoral studies in theology. "Fordham University without a department of theology is unthinkable," said one of the participants in the faculty debate. He (or perhaps she, as the participants were anonymous) carried the day, and Fordham continued to contain one of the stronger theology departments of any Catholic university in the United States.[15]

Father O'Hare regarded these two related changes—the integration of the arts and sciences faculties at Rose Hill and Lincoln Center and the establishment of a common core undergraduate curriculum—as "the most ambitious and far-reaching academic changes" that took place during his first fifteen years as president of Fordham. Three different academic vice

14. Fordham University, *Undergraduate Bulletin*, 1998–2000, 23–27.

15. FUA, O'Hare Papers, James M. Loughran to Faculty Integration Committee, February 10, 1995, 3–6.

The Department of Religious Studies at Lincoln Center was discontinued, but students at both Lincoln Center and Rose Hill (as well as students in the Fordham College of Liberal Studies) were able to pursue a major or minor in either theology or religious studies in all three schools.

presidents were responsible for managing the sometimes contentious negotiations between 1992 and 1995 that finally secured faculty approval of these changes: Father Gerard Reedy, S.J.; Dr. Robert W. Carrubba; and especially Father James M. Loughran, S.J., who was "a master at making it happen," according to Dorothy Marinucci, Father O'Hare's secretary, who was a close observer of the process.[16]

O'Hare thought that the new unified curriculum was more faithful than its predecessor to traditional Jesuit educational pedagogy and that it also enhanced the value of Fordham's undergraduate degrees because it ensured more consistent standards throughout the undergraduate programs. His one regret was that the process came to be known as "restructuring" because that term had become a code word for downsizing in corporate America. In fact the size of the Fordham faculty grew significantly during this period of restructuring. Between 1985 and 1999 the size of the full-time faculty grew from 670 to 902, and the number of degrees and advanced certificates conferred (both undergraduate and graduate) increased from 2,784 to 3,519.[17]

Academic standards on the undergraduate level received a major boost in the fall of 1986 with the establishment of the Matteo Ricci Society. Named after the sixteenth-century Italian Jesuit missionary to China, the Matteo Ricci Society assisted undergraduates in obtaining prestigious fellowships. Over the following ten years Fordham produced more than sixty prestigious scholarship recipients, including more than fifteen Fulbright Fellowships. O'Hare was especially grateful for the efforts of Dr. Harry Nasuti, the program advisor. What impressed Dean McShane was the ripple effect of the success of the seniors and juniors on the freshmen and sophomores. "They see that Fordham students can and should enter into competition with students from the Ivies," he said, "and do so with a real hope of winning."[18]

In 1996 *U.S. News & World Report* ranked Fordham second only to Notre Dame in value among American Catholic universities. The fol-

16. Ms. Dorothy Marinucci to author, October 24, 2024.

17. O'Hare, "A Foundation for the Future: The President's 15-Year Report," *Fordham* (2000): 3–6. Father Reedy left Fordham in June 1994 to become president of the College of the Holy Cross, and Father Loughran left Fordham the following year to become president of St. Peter's College in Jersey City and later president of Loyola Marymount in Los Angeles. They were two of eight Fordham administrators to become presidents of other institutions between 1985 and 2000, beginning with Dr. Paul Reiss, who became president of St. Michael's College in Winooski, Vermont, in the fall of 1985.

18. O'Hare, "Students Take Top Scholarships," *Fordham*, Summer–Fall 1996.

lowing year it ranked Fordham number one in value among all Catholic universities and among the top 50 schools in value among all American universities. That same year *U.S. News & World Report* ranked Fordham Law School 28 out of 179 law schools nationwide, and it ranked the Graduate School of Social Service eleventh out of 127 such programs across the country.

The achievements of several Fordham faculty members added to the university's reputation. Dr. Anne Anastasi served as president of the American Psychological Society, 1965–67, and as emerita professor of psychology in 1987 received the National Medal of Science, the nation's highest award for scientific achievement, from President Ronald Reagan. She was the first woman to receive this medal for work in the behavioral sciences. Dr. Mary Ann Quaranta, the dean of the Graduate School of Social Service for twenty-five years, was president of the National Association of Social Workers, 1981–83, and was invited to deliver an address to Pope John Paul II during his visit to the United States in September 1987.

Father O'Hare raised the profile of the Theology Department in 1988 when he persuaded Father Avery Dulles, S.J., to leave the Catholic University of America and accept the Laurence J. McGinley Chair of Religion and Society, which he held for twenty years. While retaining the McGinley Chair, Dulles was appointed a cardinal by Pope John Paul II on February 21, 2001. He declined the offer from the pope to be ordained a bishop because of his age (83 at the time). Father O'Hare led the Fordham delegation of more than 200 alumni and friends who attended the consistory in Rome.

In 1995 Dr. Elizabeth Johnson, C.S.J., was the first person elected president of the Catholic Theological Society of America while a member of the Fordham faculty, and ten years later she was elected president of the American Theological Society.[19] Father Joseph T. Lienhard, S.J., was elected president of the North American Patristics Society in 2000 and president of the Academy of Catholic Theology in 2011, and since 1997 he has served as editor of *Traditio*, Fordham's one remaining scholarly journal since the demise of *Thought* in 1992. Dr. Maureen Tilley was elected president of NAPS in 2005.

Fortunately or unfortunately, fundraising had become a major responsibility of every American university president by the 1980s. Fordham

19. Father Avery Dulles was elected president of the CTSA in 1975 while a professor at the Catholic University of America. Dr. Terrence Tilley was elected president of the CTSA while chairman of the Theology Department of Fordham in 2008, and Dr. Bradford Hinze became president-elect in 2014 and president in 2015.

alumni had a notoriously poor record in supporting their alma mater, which must have given Father O'Hare pause when he launched a $150 million campaign as part of Fordham's celebration of its 150th anniversary. However, in November 1997, one month after the dedication of the Walsh Family Library, he was able to report that the campaign had exceeded its goal by raising $155.6 million. It was by far the most successful fundraising campaign in Fordham's history and the most ambitious fundraising campaign undertaken by any American Jesuit university or college to that date.

Despite the successful fundraising campaign, tuition and fees, which represented 68 percent of the operating revenue, continued to be Fordham's main source of income. Fordham's endowment and reserve funds in 1999 amounted to $256 million, a mere pittance compared with the multi-billion-dollar endowments of Harvard and Yale, but an impressive improvement over Fordham's endowment of only $40.6 million as recently as 1984.[20]

The William D. Walsh Family Library

By far the most important building project undertaken by O'Hare in his nineteen years as president was the erection of the William D. Walsh Family Library, which was dedicated by John Cardinal O'Connor on October 17, 1997. The $54 million library was named after the family of William D. Walsh, FCO '51, a California businessman whose donation of $10.5 million was the largest single gift that Fordham had ever received to that date.[21] Another $9 million came from New York state and more than $17 million came from the alumni. The handsome four-story stone building located just inside the Third Avenue entrance was clearly visible to pedestrians walking down Fordham Road from the Grand Concourse and invited comparison with the iconic image of Keating Hall looming in the background.

The Walsh Library was an absolute necessity if Fordham were to achieve recognition as a bona fide research university and had a long gestation period. Sesquicentennial (later Tierney) Hall had a gestation period of exactly nine months from design to completion of construction; by contrast, Walsh Library was literally a work in progress for almost a half-century. When young Father Joseph Fitzpatrick arrived at Rose Hill in 1949 with

20. O'Hare, "The President's 15-Year Report," *Fordham* 33:3 (1999), 13, 38–39.

21. Walsh asked that $1 million be used as a permanent endowment to maintain the library and that another $1 million be used to name the Archives and Special Collections room in honor of Father O'Hare. *Fordham*, Summer 1997, 5.

his new doctorate in sociology from Harvard, the president of Fordham, Father Laurence J. McGinley, appointed him to a committee charged with planning a new university library. Forty-five years later, in October 1994, the eighty-one-year-old Father Fitzpatrick, then professor emeritus, delivered the invocation at the blessing of the cornerstone of the Walsh Library. Father O'Hare, who had handpicked Fitzpatrick to offer the invocation, observed dryly, "One might say that long-range planning takes on a different dimension at Fordham University."[22]

Duane Library, built in the 1920s, was a charming and beautiful building, as Dr. James P. McCabe, the director of Fordham University libraries, admitted, but he said that "we did not have enough space for either the material or the people." Duane was built to house 150,000 volumes, and in the 1940s triple-tiered stacks were added on both sides of the Great Room to provide shelving for an additional 50,000 volumes. By the 1990s some 400,000 books were crammed into Duane, and another 300,000 books were stored in the basement of Keating Hall. Space was so tight that no new book could be added to the Duane collection unless another book was transferred to the basement of Keating. Until 1991 there was not even an accurate way to determine what books were in Duane or in Keating, or what books had been lost or stolen.[23]

Before building the Walsh Family Library, Fordham conducted an extensive search for an architectural firm that could meet its expectations. The search led to the selection of the Boston firm of Shipley Bulfinch, one of the best-known specialists in library architecture in the United States.[24] When the Walsh Library was opened in the fall of 1997, Dr. McCabe, who had played a major advisory role in designing the building, said that both faculty and students were "awed by [it]." What impressed them especially was the spaciousness of the 240,000-square-foot structure after their experience of the cramped quarters in Duane Library. "It's bigger on the inside than it is on the outside," said Professor Roger Wines. Everybody knew what he meant. The new library was not only spacious, but it was also bright and airy, because it was designed around a soaring four-story central atrium and featured large windows that illuminated the interior spaces

22. O'Hare, "A Groundbreaking Event," *Fordham*, Fall 1994. Unfortunately Father Fitzpatrick died a few months before the dedication of the Walsh Library. On the construction of Sesquicentennial Hall, see FOHP, Interview with Joseph Cammarosano, 104.

23. James P. McCabe, "Looking Ahead: The New University Library," *Fordham Libraries*, vol. 12, 1996.

24. Ms. Dorothy Marinucci to author, October 23, 2014.

with sunlight. Creature comforts included not only carpeting throughout and upholstered chairs but also numerous study carrels, many of them equipped for use with laptop computers.

Patrice Kane, the university archivist and the director of the special collections, was especially pleased with the Walsh Library. "This is the first time that we've had everything all together," she said, mentioning, among other valuable holdings, the library's collection of Jesuit history and Irish-language books that had languished for years in cardboard boxes and were now stored in climate-controlled rooms and were available to qualified researchers. While Patrice Kane and her assistant, Vivian Shen, the preservation and conservation librarian, were diligently preserving the written legacy of the past, Michael Considine, the head of Walsh Library's Electronic Information Center, was busy introducing both faculty and students to the unfolding information revolution made possible by the computer and the Internet. The Electronic Information Center in the Walsh Library was linked to the Regional Educational Technology Center for the training of high school teachers in the Bronx and lower Westchester County.

Father McShane reassured traditionalists that the advent of the electronic age did not portend the end of the printed book. "The book and the technology of the Web," he insisted, "are not opposed to one another. One grows out of the other." "Whenever you hear about the death of the book," Dr. McCabe noted with amusement, "it's usually printed in a book." Roger Wines expressed the sentiments of many veteran faculty members at the dedication of the Walsh Library when he said, "Duane Library was a great college library, but this is a university library." In addition to the volumes in the Walsh Library, another 900,000 volumes were at Fordham's Lincoln Center and Marymount campuses, giving Fordham a total of 1.6 million volumes and making Fordham's libraries the seventh-largest academic library system in New York state.[25]

Public Service

The first president of Fordham University to become a public figure in New York City was Father Robert I. Gannon in the 1930s and 1940s through his witty performances on the banquet circuit and at university fundraising events. Father O'Hare achieved even greater recognition for himself and for Fordham in the 1980s and 1990s, not only through his

25. Bill Schmitt, FCO '78, "Cathedral for the Curious," *Fordham*, Fall 1997, 31–35. Michael Gates, "BiblioTech," *Fordham*, Spring–Summer 1994, 16–18.

speeches at Fordham fundraising events but also through his service on three city commissions. In March 1986 Mayor Ed Koch appointed O'Hare to a three-year term on the New York City Mayor's Committee on Appointments, a five-member board that screened prospective appointees to various city commissions. Later that year Mayor Koch appointed O'Hare to the New York City Charter Revision Commission, whose recommendations led to the adoption of a new city charter in 1989.

Mayor Koch was so pleased with O'Hare's contribution to the two commissions that in 1988 he appointed O'Hare chair of the newly established New York City Campaign Finance Board with the responsibility of monitoring voluntary public financing of municipal elections, a position that he continued to hold for the following dozen years. Not even the ACLU objected to O'Hare's chairmanship of the Campaign Finance Board, and Mayor Koch was especially pleased with his performance. "He had a wonderful manner," said Koch. "You felt that he was listening." And the irrepressible Ed Koch added good-naturedly, as only he could do without giving offense, "I guess that he gets that from hearing confessions."[26]

The following year the Campaign Finance Board demonstrated its mettle when it withheld approximately $120,000 from David Dinkins, the Democratic mayoral candidate, because of his sloppy campaign records. In 1989 Dinkins narrowly won election as the city's first black mayor but

26. Frank Lynn, "Private Lives, Public Service," *Fordham*, Spring 1990, 8.

lost his bid for reelection in 1993. During his reelection campaign Dinkins once again had trouble with arithmetic and was fined $320,000 for irregularities in reporting financial contributions to this campaign. On December 31, 1993, hours before he left office after losing the election to Rudolph Giuliani, Dinkins fired O'Hare as the chair of the Campaign Finance Board. The dismissal was widely interpreted as an act of political retribution and was criticized by all four major New York City newspapers.

Dinkins's midnight replacement for O'Hare lasted only one week before he resigned in the face of widespread public criticism. Three days later Mayor Giuliani reappointed O'Hare to another five-year term. Noting that Dinkins had yet to explain $1 million in questionable financial spending, the *New York Daily News* commented, "Only O'Hare has the credibility to finish that task." In 1997 *The Village Voice* remarked that Father O'Hare's role as chair "has come to symbolize the integrity of the Campaign Finance Board." Reflecting on his twelve years in that office, O'Hare said he had learned that "municipal politics is not a non-contact sport."[27]

Father O'Hare was not the only Fordham administrator to make an important contribution to public service. Dr. John Feerick, the dean of Fordham Law School, made an equally important contribution when he reluctantly agreed to accept a request from Governor Mario Cuomo to chair the new State Commission on Government Integrity in April 1987. Cuomo was so eager to have Feerick head the commission that he dispatched three of his top aides from Albany to New York City by helicopter to plead with Feerick to accept the position. Feerick finally agreed to accede to Cuomo's request because he regarded it as a way to promote the cause of public service that he had been emphasizing at Fordham Law School.

As Frank Lynn pointed out in a perceptive article in *Fordham*, both Feerick and O'Hare focused on the corrupting influence of large contributors on political campaigns and government policies. What O'Hare had done on the city level, Feerick did on the state level. Neither Koch nor Cuomo escaped Feerick's scrutiny. Feerick uncovered a patronage operation known as the Talent Bank in the basement of City Hall, leading to the firing and indictment of the manager of the operation. Like the suave French police inspector played by Claude Rains in the classic movie *Casablanca* who claimed ignorance of gambling taking place under his nose, Koch professed to have no knowledge of what was taking place in the cel-

27. *New York Newsday*, January 8, 11, 1984; *New York Daily News*, January 8, 1984; *The Village Voice*, September 30, 1997. FUA, O'Hare Papers, O'Hare, Draft of Address at Loyola University, Chicago, March 28, 2000.

Approaching the Sesquicentennial

lar of his office. Likewise, when Dean Feerick confronted the usually glib Cuomo at a public hearing in Albany about the tactics of his fundraisers, Cuomo disclaimed any knowledge of their tactics even after Feerick produced detailed reports to Cuomo from his fundraisers.

Commenting on his role as chair of the State Commission on Government Integrity, Feerick said, "I don't think there's anything more important than shoring up confidence in our government." Governor Cuomo dutifully thanked Dean Feerick's commission for doing "an excellent and superb job." However, nothing really changed in Albany, because the political leaders of both parties, in a familiar display of unenlightened self-interest and selfish bipartisanship, successfully combined to resist the changes recommended by the commission. "The commission succeeded," said Cuomo. "We have failed."[28]

Social Justice and Human Rights

Father James Finlay often insisted that an essential element in Jesuit education was a concern for social justice. By the 1980s many Fordham students were spending parts of their summer vacations in such places as India, Mexico, Ecuador, Jamaica, Guatemala, and Mississippi, where they were engaged in building houses and providing assistance to impoverished families through Global Outreach projects. Closer to home, during the school year more than 700 undergraduates were involved each semester in a wide variety of local community service projects that included staffing neighborhood shelters and soup kitchens, delivering meals to homebound AIDS patients, and tutoring children of recent immigrants from Third World countries and eastern Europe. Fordham students also volunteered their services to Amnesty International, while still other Fordham students acted as mentors to minority children in inner-city schools. Fordham University Law School established the Death Penalty Defense Project to assist defense attorneys in ensuring equal justice for all citizens, especially minorities, in case of the implementation of the death penalty in New York.

While Fordham students were active both at home and abroad in promoting social justice, Father Finlay was one of several presidents of Fordham who publicly indentified the university with the cause of human rights. At the commencement ceremonies in 1984 Fordham awarded an honorary doctorate to "the man from Gdansk," Lech Wałęsa, the embattled leader of the Solidarity movement in communist Poland. When Dr. Paul Reiss, the academic vice president, announced the award, the 8,000

28. Lynn, "Private Lives, Public Service," 6–9.

people assembled on Edwards Parade jumped to their feet and broke into prolonged applause. It was only the second time since 1846 that Fordham had awarded an honorary doctorate in absentia.[29]

In a letter to Father Finlay and the faculty, Wałęsa explained why he was unable to accept the award in person. "When my friends and comrades are sitting in prisons and undertaking hunger strikes to achieve humane living conditions," he said, "I am unable to leave the country." This self-educated labor union leader, whose courage thrilled people throughout the world, added, "In Poland today, the search for values that are more lasting than ideological doctrines" is universal. "Working people find these values in Christianity and in the teachings of John Paul II," said this machinist from a shipyard in Gdansk.[30]

The linguist and political critic Noam Chomsky once contrasted the widespread support in the United States for political dissidents in eastern Europe with the sparse attention given by the United States to opponents of right-wing dictatorial regimes in Latin America. One could hardly include Fordham in that criticism. Five years after Fordham awarded an honorary doctorate to Lech Wałęsa, Father O'Hare used his position as president of Fordham as a bully pulpit to condemn the murder on November 16, 1989, of six Spanish Jesuits and their housekeeper and her daughter by government-sponsored death squads in El Salvador. The Jesuits included the rector and vice rector of the Central American University in San Salvador, whose political views incurred the wrath of the right-wing regime, which enjoyed strong support from the U.S. government. Six days after the murders in El Salvador, at a Mass for the victims in the Church of St. Ignatius Loyola in Manhattan that was attended by 1,000 people, including John Cardinal O'Connor and Archbishop Renato Martino, the Holy See's representative to the United Nations, O'Hare publicly implicated the U.S. government in the murder of the victims of the El Salvador death squads. "They were not men of violence," said Father O'Hare of the slain Jesuits; "they were men of peace and reason. Yet they died violently." "Can we hand weapons to butchers and remain unstained by the blood of their innocent victims?" he asked from the pulpit.

O'Hare noted that the slain Jesuits were not only murdered, but their brains were spilled out on the ground to demonstrate the power of the

29. Ironically the only other occasion on which Fordham awarded an honorary doctorate in absentia occurred during the presidency of Father Robert I. Gannon in 1943 during World War II when Fordham awarded a doctorate to Władysław Raczkiewicz, the president of the Polish government-in-exile in London.

30. "Commencement '84," *Fordham*, Summer 1984, 8–9.

bullet over the brain. "It represents the contempt of men of violence for the power of the truth," he said. O'Hare also used the horrific circumstances of the deaths to clarify his understanding of the role of a Catholic university in the modern world. Responding to critics who claimed that the slain Jesuits in El Salvador had "meddled in politics," O'Hare replied that "no university can be insulated from the agonies of the society in which it lives." Moreover, he said, "No university which identifies itself as Catholic can be indifferent to the call of the Church to promote the dignity of the human person." Anticipating the criticism that his candid remarks were likely to provoke in some Catholic quarters, O'Hare invoked the authority of Pope John Paul II, "a man from the university world," who, said O'Hare, "has often challenged Catholic universities to confront the crucial issues of peace and justice in our world today."[31]

The following year the commencement speaker at Fordham was William P. Ford, the brother of Sister Ita Ford, a Maryknoll missionary who was murdered in El Salvador on December 2, 1980, together with two other American women religious and a lay woman missionary.[32] The murderers were agents of the same Salvadoran regime that was later responsible for the death of the six Jesuits in 1989. Ford was to spend more than twenty-five years in an unsuccessful attempt to bring to justice the officials in El Salvador who had been responsible for the murder of his sister and the three other women missionaries. In his address at the Fordham commencement, Ford made a moving plea to the graduates and their guests "to work to correct our country's moral compass and bring it back to the ideals that made it great."[33]

Sometimes Fordham advertised its support of human rights and social justice by a policy of calculated omission. A case in point was the Philippines, where Fordham had a close connection because of the longstanding mission of the New York Province of the Society of Jesus in that country. After the Philippines secured its independence from the United States in 1946, it became customary for Fordham to award an honorary doctorate to the president of the Philippines. No fewer than six presidents of the Philippines have been recipients of honorary doctorates from Fordham, and their names are inscribed on the steps leading to the Terrace of Presidents in front of Keating Hall. A notable exception is the name of President Fer-

---

31. FUA, O'Hare Papers, O'Hare, Mass in Honor of Slain Jesuits and their Associates, St. Ignatius Church, New York City, November 22, 1989.

32. The three other murdered women were Sr. Maura Clarke, M.M.; Sr. Dorothy Kazel, O.S.U.; and Ms. Jean Donovan.

33. "The President's Fifteen-Year Report," *Fordham*, 33:3 (1999), 19.

dinand Marcos (1965–86), whose dictatorial regime aroused widespread disapproval both at home and abroad and whom the Catholic Church in the Philippines played a major role in removing from office.

9/11: The Terrorist Attack on America

On the morning of September 11, 2001, the United States suffered the worst terrorist attack in its history when Al Qaeda terrorists seized control of four commercial airplanes. They crashed two of the planes into the Twin Towers of the World Trade Center in downtown Manhattan, crashed another plane into the Pentagon in Virginia, and the fourth plane (which perhaps was intended for the White House or the Capitol) crashed in southwestern Pennsylvania when heroic passengers overpowered their terrorist captors. The total death toll was 2,977, of whom 2,753 perished in the collapse of the Twin Towers between 8:56 A.M. and 10:28 A.M. One city official said, "New York City took a hit for America on September 11." The hero of the hour was Mayor Rudy Giuliani, who seemed to be everywhere and was nearly killed himself.

New York City came to a temporary standstill as a result of the terrorist attack, especially after the suspension of subway service. At Rose Hill, the campus was shut down, and only those traveling north were allowed to leave. All other faculty, students, and employees were provided with emergency sleeping facilities in the McGinley Center, Lombardi Center, and the Walsh Library. John Carroll, the director of security, said: "We haven't even begun to realize how deeply this will impact our community." Carroll was gratified with the cooperation he received from the whole Fordham community. "We have had no incident on or off campus," he reported.

During the course of the day, as faculty, students, and staff scrambled to hear the latest news reports, many of them also turned to prayer. More than 500 people assembled on Edwards Parade for a prayer service led by the United Student Government president, Paul Casey, CBA '02. Many others attended one of the three Masses that were offered on the campus that day. One of the celebrants, Cardinal Dulles, a World War II veteran, compared the terrorist attack to the attack on Pearl Harbor; Father O'Hare compared it to the assassination of President John F. Kennedy; while Father Gerard Blaszczak, the campus minister, compared it to his experiences as a Jesuit missionary in Zimbabwe and Rwanda. "We still must hope," said Father Blaszczak, "because without hope we die."[34]

At Lincoln Center, Father Robert Grimes, S.J., the dean of Fordham Col-

34. *Ram*, September 13, 2001; Ms. Dorothy Marinucci to author, October 23, 2014.

lege at Lincoln Center, presided at a packed prayer service in the Generoso Pope Auditorium that was attended by some 600 people. Like many other prayer services in the United States that day, it concluded with the singing of "Amazing Grace." At least three alarmed parents came long distances (one from Russia) to bring their children home from Lincoln Center. One freshman had the horrible experience of watching the collapse of the Twin Towers from the top floor of the Lowenstein Building knowing that his mother had been on board one of the planes that had crashed into the building.

One of Father Grimes's strongest memories of 9/11 is of the generosity of the students. Resident students were quick to share their rooms with commuters who were unable to get home. They were equally generous when neighboring Roosevelt Hospital asked for donations of men's clothing for burn victims. "Within a half-hour," said Father Grimes, "students were rolling huge containers of men's clothing given by the residents of McMahon Hall." Two days after 9/11 the winds shifted in Manhattan and the acrid smell emanating from Ground Zero drifted north, "a smell that I will never forget," said Grimes. As at Rose Hill, a memorial plaque to the thirty-nine Fordham alumni who perished on 9/11 was placed at the Lincoln Center campus.[35]

Father O'Hare was the homilist at the Church of St. Ignatius Loyola on October 29, 2001, for the Fordham University Mass of Hope and Remembrance for the victims of the terrorist attacks. It must have been one of the most difficult homilies he had ever been called upon to deliver, because New Yorkers of all faiths and none were still reeling from the wholesale murder of so many innocent people. The Mass was offered for all of them, including thirty-nine alumni of Fordham.

Father O'Hare called the attack on the World Trade Center "an act of blasphemy" on the part of individuals who believed that "paradise awaits those who destroy the innocent." He captured the mood of the congregation that evening when he said that "we stand numb before the wanton cruelty that human beings can inflict on the innocent, when they are blinded by hate." However, O'Hare issued not a call for vengeance but an appeal for hope and trust in the Lord even when He seems silent and absent. "Faithful to Him," said O'Hare, and "faithful to one another, we will not only restore our world and our city and ourselves, but we can inherit a new heaven and a new earth."[36]

35. Reverend Robert Grimes, S.J., to author. I am grateful to Father Grimes for this information.

36. FUA, O'Hare Papers, O'Hare, Homily from the Fordham University Mass of Remembrance and Hope, Church of St. Ignatius Loyola, New York City, October 29,

Catholic Identity

In 1990 Peter Steinfels, the well-known Catholic journalist, editor of *Commonweal*, and religion editor of the *New York Times*, interviewed many Catholic university presidents about the Catholic identity of their institutions. What surprised and disappointed him was the reaction of many of these Catholic educators, who responded to his questions, Steinfels said, with "a mood of avoidance, passivity and defensiveness." While virtually all of them admitted the importance of the issue, it appeared to him that most of them seemed to have avoided grappling directly with it and regarded it like "an unwelcome guest at a dinner party." "I was surprised and dismayed by this apparent resignation to drift," said Steinfels.

Six years later Steinfels thought there had been a significant change as Catholic educators began to come to grips with the problem. He gave Father O'Hare credit for helping to reverse this drift by initiating a series of Catholic Identity Symposia at Fordham. O'Hare also addressed the issue publicly on a number of other occasions, most notably during his address at the meeting of the Catholic Commission on Intellectual and Cultural Affairs in 1987 at Fordham.[37]

O'Hare was well aware that discussions had been under way in Rome for several decades about formulating new canonical legislation to govern Catholic universities. O'Hare made no secret of his views on the matter. Echoing John Henry Newman's comments of a century earlier, O'Hare insisted that a university "is not a catechetical center or a retreat house; it is not a seminary or a parish." "The purpose of a university," said O'Hare, "is the discovery and sharing of truth, not indoctrination or proselytizing." For good measure, he added, "For the Catholic university to fulfill this special mission as a place of dialogue between faith and reason, between religion and culture, it must enjoy the institutional autonomy and academic freedom that allows it to be a university."[38]

As far back as 1975 Father Finlay sensed that the Roman authorities were unhappy with recent developments in American Catholic higher ed-

---

2001. Father O'Hare pledged that the children of the Fordham alumni who perished at the World Trade Center would receive scholarships to Fordham when it came time for them to begin college. The class of 2002 created a memorial garden on the Rose Hill campus for the victims of 9/11 that contains the names of thirty-nine alumni. *President's Report*, 2001–2002, 1.

37. Peter Steinfels, "Sacred Ties: Re-examining Fordham's Catholic Identity," *Fordham*, Winter 1995–1996, 15.

38. Joseph A. O'Hare, "The American Catholic University: Pluralism and Diversity," Catholic Commission on Intellectual and Cultural Affairs, *Annual 1987*, 1–10.

ucation. On a visit to Rome that year he was surprised by the "obsession" of many of the Roman authorities with the issue of the role of laity in the direction of many American Catholic universities. Finlay said that even Pope Paul VI "seemed to me and to others to express a desire that we turn back the clock." A decade later, Father Vincent O'Keefe tried to explain the situation to a Fordham student on the basis of his long experience in Rome. "The Roman Curia still does not seem to fully understand the role and function of private Catholic education in the United States," he said. "At the curial office that deals with Catholic education," he explained, "most of the staff came out of seminaries, not universities."[39]

The long-anticipated Roman document on Catholic universities finally saw the light of day with the promulgation of *Ex Corde Ecclesiae*, an apostolic constitution issued by Pope John Paul II on August 15, 1990, that became operative in the United States only eleven years later on May 3, 2001, after extensive and largely desultory discussions between the U.S. hierarchy and the Roman Curia. The document was welcomed in principle by the Fellowship of Catholic Scholars, but strong reservations were voiced by the Catholic Biblical Association, the Catholic Theological Society of America, the College Theological Society, and the Canon Law Society of America.[40]

Two of the most controversial provisions of *Ex Corde Ecclesiae* were the requirements that "to the extent possible" a majority of the trustees and faculty in Catholic universities should be Catholics, and that Catholic professors of theology should obtain a *mandatum* from the local bishop. The *mandatum* was defined in the document as "an acknowledgment by church authority that a Catholic professor of a theological discipline is a teacher within the full communion of the Catholic Church."[41] To the relief of some American Catholics and to the chagrin of some others, these two provisions remained largely a dead letter. Most American Catholic bishops decided that the implementation of the requirement that the ma-

39. FUA, Finlay Papers, Finlay to O'Keefe, September 9, 1975. "An Interview with Father Vincent O'Keefe, S.J.," *Fordham*, Spring 1985, 7.

40. Alice Gallin, O.S.U., ed., *"Ex Corde Ecclesiae": Documents Concerning Reception and Implementation* (Notre Dame, Ind.: University of Notre Dame Press, 2006), 297–442. For the background to *Ex Corde Ecclesiae*, see Philip Gleason, "The American Background to *Ex Corde Ecclesiae*: A Historical Perspective," in John P. Langhan, S.J., ed., *Catholic Universities in Church and Society* (Washington: Georgetown University Press, 1993), 1–34.

41. *The Application for "Ex Corde Ecclesiae" for the United States* (Washington: United States Conference of Catholic Bishops, 2014), Art. 4. 2b, 4a, 4e, pp. 7–8.

jority of the trustees and faculty be Catholics should be left in the hands of the local Catholic colleges and universities. In the case of the *mandatum*, they said that the obligation to seek a *mandatum* was the private obligation of the individual faculty member. Few bishops pushed the issue further.[42]

Father O'Hare welcomed this less juridical interpretation that was adopted by virtually the entire U.S. hierarchy. He pointed out that the text of *Ex Corde Ecclesiae* asserted that "Catholic identity does not require ecclesiastical control." He pledged to pursue a delicate balancing act of preserving both Fordham's commitment to its Catholic identity as well as its commitment to academic freedom. O'Hare was especially pleased that the U.S. bishops did not insist on a *numerus clausus* of non-Catholics on the faculty or the board of trustees. "Over the years," he said, "among the most staunch supporters of Fordham's Catholic identity have been men and women of other religious traditions, and those who, while still seeking faith, nonetheless find the goals of Jesuit education worthy of the gamble of a lifetime."[43]

Father O'Hare's balancing act between Catholic identity and academic freedom was tested by two student groups as far back as the spring and fall of 1990, when they applied for official recognition and university funding as bona fide clubs, FLAG (Fordham Lesbians and Gays) and Fordham Students for Choice. FLAG had existed for eleven years at Fordham; the pro-choice group was a more recent organization. In the case of both groups, O'Hare scrupulously followed established university procedures for processing applications for the recognition of a new student club. He referred both requests to the United Student Government, which in turn referred the applications to the Student Activities Council, which granted probationary status to both clubs.

O'Hare's balancing act in the case of these two student groups resembled the nimble gyrations of a skilled tightrope walker. By processing the applications through the student government, he deflected accusations of censorship. At the same time, he publicly declared his belief that abortion was a moral and social evil, and he reaffirmed his commitment to Catholic teaching on homosexuality. However, he nuanced his position with regard to both student groups by stating that it was his understanding that the members of Fordham Students for Choice were concerned about public policy on abortion. Likewise, with regard to FLAG, he noted that the

42. http://ajcunet/edu.ECE.
43. O'Hare, "Fordham's Catholic Mission," *Fordham*, Winter 1995–1996, 36.

stated objective of the group was the "promotion of a more enlightened understanding of homosexuality." Because both of those objectives could be reconciled with Catholic teaching, O'Hare seized upon these statements (which he later admitted were "admittedly ambiguous") to announce that he saw no reason why he should interfere with the normal process of club approval by the student government.[44]

O'Hare's trust in the processes of the student government proved justified when it rejected the application of both groups for recognition as clubs. The rejection had nothing to do with academic freedom. It was based on the technical grounds that, during their eighteen-month probationary period, both groups had been largely inactive.[45] Unfortunately, through no fault of his own, O'Hare was not as successful in deflecting criticism of his leadership outside of Fordham as he was within the confines of the university. Much of the criticism was ill informed and even vicious, based on distorted reports of what was taking place on campus.

A week before the sesquicentennial commencement ceremonies in 1991, which were attended by Father Peter-Hans Kolvenbach, S.J., the father general of the Society of Jesus, a letter was circulated to the families of the graduates alleging that Fordham had a policy of referring young women to Planned Parenthood for abortions and also had endorsed student groups that advocated "abortion, fornication and sodomy." Such accusations had been made several times during the previous two years. O'Hare rejected them as "outright falsehoods" and "reckless slander."[46]

The author of the letter also criticized the commencement speaker, Marian Wright Edelman, president of the Children's Defense Fund, on the grounds that her organization was an advocate of abortion, a charge that O'Hare rejected as untrue. He quoted Father Joseph Fitzpatrick, S.J., who commented that "it would be hard to imagine a more pro-life or pro-family commencement address." Six months later O'Hare felt compelled to repudiate similar accusations from an organization that called itself Fordham Lovers Advocating Responsibility in Education.[47]

44. FUA, O'Hare Papers, O'Hare to Fordham Community, May 11, 1990; Statement from Fordham University: FLAG at Fordham, November 1990. O'Hare to Cardinal John O'Connor, January 10, 1991.

45. FUA, O'Hare Papers, O'Hare to Alumni and Friends of Fordham, December 10, 1991.

46. FUA, O'Hare Papers, O'Hare to the Families and Members of the Class of 1991, May 31, 1991.

47. FUA, O'Hare Papers, O'Hare to Alumni and Friends of Fordham, December 10, 1991.

While O'Hare was attempting to demonstrate Fordham's commitment to academic freedom, he became increasingly concerned about the other half of the equation, Fordham's Catholic identity. A cursory review of the content of student publications disturbed him because it led him to fear that "very few of the voices that we hear have a clear grasp of what Catholic tradition really is." He was chagrined that one student accused him of espousing Christian rather than Catholic values, but he was particularly concerned about FLAG. "I can certainly support the need for 'a more enlightened understanding of homosexuality' on campus," he told several of the Jesuit undergraduate deans, "but I would not like this to be interpreted as a surrender of traditional Catholic teaching on homosexuality."[48]

The result of O'Hare's uneasiness was an unsigned position paper, "FLAG at Fordham," issued in November 1990. It showed telltale signs of perhaps having originated as the work of a committee whose members were searching unsuccessfully for agreement among themselves. In the position paper Fordham affirmed its commitment to presenting Catholic teaching on sexuality in "as clear and compelling a manner as possible," but it also seemed to leave open the possibility that "a more enlightened understanding of homosexuality" might result in an even more "clear and compelling" presentation of this teaching. Perhaps, in the light of future developments, the most intriguing contribution of this position paper was the suggestion that the ongoing dialogue between Catholic tradition and academic freedom in a university setting would be greatly enhanced by "the cultivation of the art of disagreement."[49]

Gay and lesbian students were more successful in establishing an organization in the Law School. By the mid-1980s they had received approval from both Dean Feerick and Father O'Hare for their own organization, which was one of the first gay and lesbian student organizations in any Catholic law school in the United States. Its successor organization is OUTLaws: Fordham's GLBT Law Student Association, which provides support for gay, lesbian, bisexual, and transgender students in Fordham School of Law.

48. FUA, O'Hare Papers, O'Hare to John Shea, S.J., and Gerard Reedy, S.J., November 19, 1990.

49. FUA, O'Hare Papers, Statement from Fordham University, FLAG at Fordham, November 1990.

The President and the Cardinal

On January 26, 1984, six months after Father O'Hare's appointment as the president of Fordham, Pope John Paul II appointed a new archbishop of New York, John J. O'Connor, who was made a cardinal the following May. The two of them were to share an uneasy relationship for the following sixteen years. O'Connor's predecessor as archbishop of New York, Terence Cardinal Cooke, was an almost compulsive optimist who was a master of the soft answer that turns away wrath while conceding nothing of substance. Cardinal O'Connor deliberately adopted a more confrontational style of leadership that was reminiscent of that of Fordham's founding father, Archbishop John Hughes, although O'Connor, a native of Philadelphia and former rear admiral in the U.S. navy and chief of chaplains, admitted privately that he had never heard of Hughes until he came to New York.

The tension between the president and the cardinal often surfaced in the spring of the year when O'Hare dutifully invited O'Connor to attend the Fordham commencement exercises and O'Connor predictably declined the invitation on the grounds of a previous commitment. In 1994 O'Connor's priest-secretary noted that this was the ninth time in ten years that O'Connor had declined the invitation to the commencement ceremonies on that basis. In 1991, however, as Fordham prepared to celebrate its sesquicentennial in the presence of the father general, Father Peter-Hans Kolvenbach, O'Connor dropped the pretense and announced that "integrity" forced him to boycott the ceremonies because Fordham had given financial support to two student groups advocating positions opposing Church teaching in two crucial areas. O'Connor was obviously alluding to FLAG and Fordham Students for Choice. He asked O'Hare to inform Kolvenbach of the reasons for his absence.[50]

O'Connor's broadside was hardly an invitation to dialogue, but O'Hare tried to set the record straight by assuring O'Connor that the two groups were probationary clubs that received no funds from the university and that their activities would be carefully monitored. Apparently his efforts were successful, at least temporarily, because O'Connor was the principal celebrant and homilist at the Mass in St. Patrick's Cathedral some months later at the close of the celebrations of Fordham's sesquicentennial year. On other occasions also O'Connor displayed a conciliatory attitude to Fordham. He congratulated O'Hare in 1993 when he read in the local

---

50. FUA, O'Hare Papers, James F. McCarthy to O'Hare, March 22, 1990; O'Connor to O'Hare, December 27, 1990.

Catholic press that Fordham ranked first in the nation by graduating 93 percent of its black athletes and ranked third in graduating all athletes. He also accepted an invitation to dedicate the Walsh Family Library on October 17, 1997.[51]

The Mass in the cathedral on September 29, 1991, proved to be a truce, not a permanent peace treaty, and it was breached on several occasions by O'Connor, who was on the offensive again when he heard rumors that O'Hare had extended an invitation to President Bill Clinton to be the commencement speaker at the 1996 graduation. O'Hare explained that the invitation had been extended before Clinton vetoed the partial-birth abortion ban by Congress. In 1999 O'Connor objected to the selection of former Senator George Mitchell of Maine because of his voting record on the issue of abortion. "There may be a reason for this selection that has eluded me," he said tartly. O'Hare replied that the reason for Mitchell's selection was his prominent and well-publicized role in the Good Friday 1998 Peace Agreement in Northern Ireland and that O'Hare was unaware of his voting record in the Senate.[52]

The jousting between O'Hare and O'Connor resembled the confrontation between Archbishop John Hughes and Father John Larkin, S.J., in the 1840s, although the issues were totally different. Like that earlier confrontation between an overbearing archbishop of New York and a feisty president of St. John's College, the disputes between O'Connor and O'Hare did not take place on a level playing field. On more than one occasion, however, O'Hare's Irish wit was more than a match for that of O'Connor. When the cardinal heard that Betty Friedan, the aging *grande dame* of the feminist movement, had been invited to speak at the Lincoln Center campus, he raised objections because of her views on birth control and abortion. He said to O'Hare, "May I ask you for some information on this?" O'Hare replied that he had not been consulted by the Graduate School of Social Service when it extended the invitation to Friedan, but he assured O'Connor that, because the focus of her talk was to be largely her own reflections on aging, "the issues of abortion and birth control are not expected to be part of this discussion."[53]

Fordham was drawn into the political arena in 1994 when former Con-

51. FUA, O'Hare Papers, O'Hare to O'Connor, October 10, 1991; O'Connor to O'Hare, September 2, 1993.

52. FUA, O'Hare Papers, O'Connor to O'Hare, April 30, 1996; O'Hare to O'Connor, May 6, 1996; O'Connor to O'Hare, May 27, 1999; O'Hare to O'Connor, June 7, 1999.

53. FUA, O'Hare Papers, O'Connor to O'Hare, March 10, 1995; O'Hare to O'Connor, March 29, 1995.

gresswoman Geraldine Ferraro, a practicing Catholic, an alumna of Fordham Law School, and an unsuccessful vice-presidential candidate in 1984, was the featured speaker at the diploma ceremony on May 17, when the graduates of Fordham Law School received their diplomas. The graduates of the Law School traditionally recommended the speaker for their diploma ceremony, and neither Father O'Hare nor Dean Feerick saw any reason to veto their choice in 1994, especially because the graduating class wanted to honor a woman who had made a significant contribution to public life.

However, the selection of Ferraro as the speaker at the diploma ceremony touched off a firestorm of criticism among many Fordham alumni and alumnae as well as among many of the local diocesan clergy. Both O'Hare and Dean Feerick received hundreds of written objections. Dean Feerick received almost a thousand letters of complaint. They both responded to their critics with a polite form letter in which they explained that it had long been the policy of Fordham University to allow the administration, faculty, and students the greatest latitude in choosing speakers for the diploma ceremony. It was one of the rare occasions when Father O'Hare lost his composure. He may have had someone else in mind when he told one especially irate and persistent Catholic layman: "I suggest that you get your facts straight before you bluster on in pontifical fashion."

Passing the Baton

Father O'Hare passed the baton to Father McShane, dean of Fordham College at Rose Hill, on June 30, 2003. He left Fordham with the largest endowment, budget, student enrollment, and faculty in the history of the university. The market value of Fordham's long-term investments on the day of Father O'Hare's departure was $242.2 million. Operating revenues for the fiscal year totaled $305.6 million while operating expenditures totaled $288.4 million. It was the thirty-fourth consecutive year in which the university achieved an operating surplus. The consolidation of Marymount College in Tarrytown with Fordham had been completed the previous July. Tuition and fees, which accounted for 71 percent of operating revenue, continued to be the university's main source of revenue.

Despite Fordham's modest endowment, during the previous year the university increased student financial aid from $64.2 million to $74.2 million, a 15.6 percent increase that demonstrated the university's commitment to providing financial aid to students who otherwise could not afford to attend Fordham. One of the sources of this financial aid was a dinner in Grand Ballroom of the Waldorf Astoria Hotel on March 31, 2003, to honor

Father O'Hare that was attended by 900 guests, who contributed nearly $2 million to the Fordham Founder's Presidential Scholarship Fund.

The total student enrollment for the year ending June 3, 2003, was 15,814, an increase of almost 2,000 students over the previous year. Undergraduates slightly outnumbered graduate students by a margin of 8,846 to 7,328. Also significant was the diversification of the base of the student population with students from several foreign countries and 42 states. There was a notable increase in students from the Southwest and the Pacific Northwest, areas from which Fordham had never been able to recruit many students in the past. This geographical diversification of the student body would not have been possible without O'Hare's determined effort to build additional residence halls, and it was indispensable for the success of Fordham's effort to establish a national reputation.[54]

As was mentioned earlier, O'Hare considered that his two most ambitious academic achievements as president of Fordham were the integration of the arts and science faculties at Rose Hill and Lincoln Center and the implementation of a common core undergraduate curriculum at both campuses. He was also proud of the fact that he had encouraged the expansion of interdisciplinary programs on both the undergraduate and graduate levels as well as a major development of university centers and institutes to study various aspects of legal, social, ethical, and business issues. These centers and institutes numbered more than thirty by the time O'Hare left office, and many were designed to provide an assortment of services to the communities adjacent to Fordham's two campuses.[55]

Father O'Hare's round of farewell appearances was something of a bittersweet experience that he accepted with good humor. As O'Hare was about to step off for the last time with the Fordham contingent marching up Fifth Avenue in the St. Patrick's Day Parade, an elderly alumnus approached him, introduced himself, and, as O'Hare said, he "warmed my heart." He said to O'Hare: "Thank you for all you've done for Fordham—Father McGinley."[56]

At his final faculty convocation at Lincoln Center on March 30, 2003, O'Hare noted that, even after nineteen years as president of Fordham, he was not eligible for the *Bene Merenti* medal that Fordham confers upon veteran faculty members after twenty years of service to the university.

54. Joseph M. McShane, S.J., "President's Report, 2002–2003," *Fordham*, 2002–2003, 1–5.

55. O'Hare, "The President's Fifteen-Year Report," *Fordham* 33:3 (1999): 15.

56. O'Hare, "The President's File: Stepping Out," *Fordham*, Summer 2003, 1.

However, said O'Hare, "Father McShane is exactly the same age that I was when I first became president in 1984. If he stays in office for nineteen years, as I have done, I will be 91 when he steps down. I expect to be fully rested and prepared to assume the responsibilities of president once again in order to gain my own *Bene Merenti* medal the following year."[57]

Many friends of Fordham will say to both of them: *Ad Multos Annos*.

57. FUA, O'Hare Papers, O'Hare, Fordham University Convocation, Lincoln Center, March 30, 2003.

PRESIDENTS OF ST. JOHN'S COLLEGE
AND FORDHAM UNIVERSITY

DIOCESE OF NEW YORK

1841–1843	Rev. John McCloskey[1]
1843	Rev. Ambrose Manahan
1843–1845	Rev. John Harley
1845–1846	Rev. James Roosevelt Bayley[2]

SOCIETY OF JESUS

1846–1851	Rev. Augustus J. Thébaud, S.J.
1851–1854	Rev. John Larkin, S.J.
1854–1859	Rev. Remigius Tellier, S.J.
1859–1863	Rev. Augustus J. Thébaud, S.J.
1863–1865	Rev. Edward Doucet, S.J.
1865–1868	Rev. William Moylan, S.J.
1868–1874	Rev. Joseph Shea, S.J.
1874–1882	Rev. William Gockeln, S.J.
1882–1885	Rev. Patrick Dealy, S.J.
1885–1888	Rev. Thomas J. Campbell, S.J.
1888–1891	Rev. John Scully, S.J.
1891–1896	Rev. Thomas Gannon, S.J.
1896–1900	Rev. Thomas J. Campbell, S.J.
1900–1904	Rev. John A. Petit, S.J.
1904–1906	Rev. John J. Collins, S.J.[3]
1906–1911	Rev. Daniel J. Quinn, S.J.
1911–1915	Rev. Thomas J. McCluskey, S.J.
1915–1919	Rev. Joseph A. Mulry, S.J.
1919–1924	Rev. Edward P. Tivnan, S.J.
1924–1930	Rev. William A. Duane, S.J.
1930–1936	Rev. Aloysius J. Hogan, S.J.
1936–1949	Rev. Robert I. Gannon, S.J.
1949–1963	Rev. Laurence J. McGinley, S.J.
1963–1965	Rev. Vincent T. O'Keefe, S.J.
1965–1969	Rev. Leo P. McLaughlin, S.J.
1969–1972	Rev. Michael P. Walsh, S.J.
1972–1983	Rev. James C. Finlay, S.J.
1984–2003	Rev. Joseph A. O'Hare, S.J.
2003–	Rev. Joseph M. McShane, S.J.

1. Bishop of Albany 1847–64; archbishop of New York 1864–85; first American cardinal 1875
2. Bishop of Newark 1853–72; archbishop of Baltimore 1872–77
3. Vicar Apostolic of Jamaica, British West Indies, 1907–20

ACKNOWLEDGMENTS

First of all, I wish to thank my cousin, Father Joseph M. McShane, S.J., for inviting me to write a history of Fordham that was to conclude in 2003 with the end of the presidency of his predecessor, Father Joseph O'Hare, S.J. I deeply appreciate Father McShane's kindness not only for offering me the opportunity to write this history but also for his unfailing patience and encouragement during the inordinately long time that it took me to complete the book. I am also grateful to him for granting me a sabbatical when I was still a member of the Fordham faculty so that I could begin work on this project and for a travel grant from the university that enabled me to consult the Roman archives of the Society of Jesus.

Many present and former members of the faculty of Fordham University gave me invaluable assistance. There are three former colleagues in particular to whom I owe a great debt of gratitude. One is Father Joseph T. Lienhard, S.J., professor of theology at Fordham, who read every page of the manuscript with his eagle eye as the longtime editor of *Traditio*. He saved me from many blunders and explained numerous aspects of Fordham history of which I was unaware. Another person who was extremely helpful was Father Raymond A. Schroth, S.J., the most recent historian of Fordham and presently the literary editor of *America*. Father Schroth was not only generous with his advice, but he also graciously placed at my disposal all the materials he had accumulated for his own history of Fordham and had deposited in the Fordham University archives. John Feerick, J.D., the former dean of the Fordham University School of Law and my classmate from St. Angela Merici parochial school in the South Bronx, not only corrected and clarified many aspects of Fordham history, but he also offered me his invaluable insights from his long association with Fordham.

Two other scholars who read the entire manuscript and gave me the benefit of their deep and discerning knowledge of American Catholic higher education were Philip Gleason, emeritus professor of history at the University of Notre Dame, and Robert Emmett Curran, emeritus professor of history at Georgetown University. I deeply appreciate their generosity in sharing with me their unrivaled mastery of this field and the time and effort they expended on my behalf to make this a much better book.

Others to whom I am indebted for advice and assistance include Father Anthony D. Andreassi, C.O.; Ms. Margaret Ball; Father Dean Bechard, S.J.; the late Henry Bertels, S.J.; Father Gerard Blaszczak, S.J.; Dr. Joseph Cammarosano; Father Robert Grimes, S.J.; the late Thomas C. Hennessy, S.J.; the late Robert H. Hinkle; Mr. Robert Howe; the late George Hunt, S.J.; Dr. Elizabeth Johnson, C.S.J.; Dr. Anne-Marie Kirmse, O.P.; Ms. Elizabeth Manigan; Ms. Dorothy Marinucci; Dr. James McCabe; Ms. Joyce O'Leary; Father Thomas McCoog, S.J.; Father Joseph Parkes, S.J.; Monsignor Joseph Quinn; Father Patrick Ryan, S.J.; Father Thomas Schirgi, S.J.; Ms. Catherine Spencer; Father James van Dyke, S.J.; and Ms. Anne-Marie Sweeney.

Every historian is dependent on the expertise and good will of the gatekeepers who control access to the treasures he wishes to use. It is said that the motto of one nineteenth-century archivist at the Vatican archives was: "No one comes in and nothing goes out." Unlike one of my previous forays into one diocesan archive, at Fordham I was spared the experience of dealing with archivists of that ilk in the research for this book. Ms. Patrice Kane, the Fordham University archivist and director of special collections in the Walsh Family Library, and her assistant, Ms. Vivian Shen, the preservation and conservation librarian, could not have been more helpful or more gracious in facilitating my use of the university archives. I am deeply grateful to both of them. Ms. Kane and Ms. Shen also drew upon their unique familiarity with Fordham's pictorial history to furnish most of the illustrations and photographs that enhance the text.

Father Peter Schineller, S.J., the former archivist of the New York Province of the Society of Jesus, gave me access to indispensable sources for the history of the earliest years of the Fordham Jesuits both in Kentucky and in New York. Mr. Joseph Gorski, the vice president for advancement at Xavier High School, allowed me to use the Xavier archives, which contain much valuable material about Jesuit education in nineteenth-century New York City. Dr. Tricia Pyne, the director of the archives at St. Mary's Seminary and University and Associated Archives in Baltimore, Maryland, was characteristically gracious in responding to my request for assistance. Father Michael Morris, the archivist of the Archdiocese of New York, and his assistant, Ms. Kate Feighery, the archival manager, and Ms. Elizabeth Alleva, the assistant archivist, offered me their full cooperation.

Likewise, at the Roman archives of the Society of Jesus, the director, Father Brian MacCuarta, S.J., and his assistant, Father James F.X. Pratt, S.J., guided me through the labyrinthine ways of Italian archival procedures. If I may interject a purely personal note, after scribbling away furiously at the Jesuit archives in Rome at Borgo Santo Spirito 4, I nearly lost my notebook with the fruit of my labors during the chaos that passed for airport security at Rome's Fiumicino Airport. I will always be grateful to Father Anthony Andreassi for having the presence of mind to retrieve it for me.

I am grateful to Mr. Fredric Nachbaur, director of Fordham University Press; Mr. Eric Newman, the managing editor of the Press; Mr. William Cerbone, editorial associate and assistant to the director of the Press; and Ms. Ann-Christine Racette, the production manager of the Press, for their professional expertise and personal dedication, which has made it possible for Fordham University to have such a handsome volume to commemorate its 175th anniversary.

Finally, I wish to record my heartfelt gratitude to my two sisters, Helen and Mary, for their never-failing encouragement and ever-practical assistance. Without them this book would have gotten started, but it would never have been completed.

Thomas J. Shelley
St. John's Day
June 24, 2015

BIBLIOGRAPHY

ARCHIVAL SOURCES

Archives of the American Irish Historical Society

Archives of the Archdiocese of Baltimore

Archives of the Archdiocese of New York

Archives of the Archdiocese of St. Louis

Archives of the Catholic University of America

Archives of the College of St. Francis Xavier

Archives of the Curia Generalizia della Missione

Archives of Mount St. Mary's College and Seminary, Emmitsburg

Archives of the New York Province of the Society of Jesus

Archives of St. Joseph's Seminary, Dunwoodie

Archives of the University of Notre Dame

Archivum Romanum Societatis Jesu

Fordham University Archives

PERIODICALS AND MAGAZINES

Fordham

Fordham Law Review

Fordham Monthly

Woodstock Letters

BOOKS

Ahlstrom, Sydney. *A Religious History of the American People*. New Haven, Conn.:
  Yale University Press, 1972.

Albion, Robert Greenhalgh. *The Rise of New York Port, 1815–1860*. New York:
  Scribner's, 1939, repr. 1984.

Allitt, Patrick. *Catholic Intellectuals and Conservative Politics in America, 1950–1985*.
  Ithaca, N.Y.: Cornell University Press, 1993.

Andreassi, Anthony D., C.O. *Teach Me to Be Generous: The First Century of Regis
  High School in New York City*. New York: Fordham University Press, 2014.

The Application for "Ex Corde Ecclesiae" for the United States. Washington: United
  States Conference of Catholic Bishops, 2014.

As I Remember Fordham: Selections from the Sesquicentennial Oral History Project.
  New York: Fordham University Press, 1991.

Baker, George E. *The Works of William Seward*. New York: J. S. Redfield, 1853. Vol. II.

Bayley, James Roosevelt. *A Brief Sketch of the Early History of the Catholic Church on
  the Island of Manhattan*. New York: The Catholic Publication Society, 1870.

Billington, Ray Allen. *The Protestant Crusade: A Study of the Origins of American
  Nativism*. New York: Macmillan, 1938.

Bonner, Jeremy, Christopher D. Denny, and Mary Beth Fraser Connelly, eds.
  Empowering the People of God: Catholic Action before and after Vatican II.
  New York: Fordham University Press, 2014.

Broderick, Francis. *Right Reverend New Dealer: John A. Ryan.* New York: Macmillan, 1963.

Brown, Dorothy M., and Elizabeth McKeon. *The Poor Belong to Us: Catholic Charities and American Welfare.* Cambridge, Mass.: Harvard University Press, 1997.

Buckley, Cornelius M., S.J. *Nicolas Point, S.J.: His Life and Northwest Indian Chronicles.* Chicago: Loyola University Press, 1989.

Burnichon, Joseph, S.J. *La Compagnie de Jésus en France: Histoire d'un Siècle.* Paris: Beauchesne: 1914–1922. 4 vols.

Byrne, Patricia, C.S.J., R. Scott Appleby, and William L. Portier, eds. *Creative Fidelity: American Catholic Intellectual Tradition.* Maryknoll, N.Y.: Orbis Books, 2006.

Carey, Patrick W. *People, Priests and Prelates: Ecclesiastical Democracy and the Tensions of Trusteeism.* Notre Dame, Ind.: University of Notre Dame Press, 1987.

The Centurion, 1841–1941. New York: Fordham University Press, 1941.

The College of St. Francis Xavier: A Memorial and a Retrospect. New York: The Meany Printing Company, 1897.

Connelly, John. *From Enemy to Brother: The Revolution in Catholic Teaching on the Jews, 1933–1965.* Cambridge, Mass.: Harvard University Press, 2012.

Course of Study and Syllabus for Elementary Schools of the Archdiocese of New York. New York: New York Catholic School Board, 1911.

Curran, Francis X. *The Return of the Jesuits.* Chicago: Loyola University Press, 1966.

Curran, Robert Emmett. *The Bicentennial History of Georgetown University.* Washington: Georgetown University Press, 1993. Vol. 1.

———. *Shaping American Catholicism: Maryland and New York, 1805–1915.* Washington: The Catholic University of America Press, 2012.

Dansette, Adrien. *Histoire Religieuse de la France Contemporaine.* Paris: Flammarion, 1948. 2 vols.

Dimnet, Ernest. *My Old World.* New York: Simon & Schuster, 1935.

Dolan, Jay P. *In Search of an American Catholicism.* New York: Oxford University Press, 2002.

Duffy, Eamon. *Saints and Sinners: A History of the Popes.* New Haven, Conn.: Yale University Press, 1997.

Ehrenhalt, Alan. *The Lost City: The Forgotten Virtues of Community in America.* New York: Basic Books, 1995.

Farley, John Cardinal. *The Life of John Cardinal McCloskey.* New York: Longmans, Green and Company, 1918.

Farrell, Allan P., S.J. *The Jesuit Code of Liberal Education: The Development and Scope of the "Ratio Studiorum."* Milwaukee: The Bruce Publishing Company, 1938.

Fitzgerald, Paul A., S.J. *The Governance of Jesuit Colleges in the United States, 1920–1970.* Notre Dame, Ind.: University of Notre Dame Press, 1984.

Fitzpatrick, Joseph, S.J. *The Stranger Is Our Own: Reflections on the Journey of Puerto Rican Migrants.* Kansas City: Sheed & Ward, 1996.

Flexner, Abraham. *Medical Education in the United States and Canada: A Report to the Carnegie Foundation for the Advancement of Teaching.* Boston: D. B. Updike / The Merrymount Press, 1910.

Fogarty, Gerald P., S.J. *American Catholic Biblical Scholarship.* San Francisco: Harper & Row, 1989.

Gallin, Alice, O.S.U., ed. *"Ex Corde Ecclesiae": Documents Concerning Reception and Implementation.* Notre Dame, Ind.: University of Notre Dame Press, 2006.

Gannon, Robert I., S.J. *The Cardinal Spellman Story.* Garden City, N.Y.: Doubleday and Company, 1962.

———. *Up to the Present: The Story of Fordham.* Garden City, N.Y.: Doubleday and Company, 1967.

Garraghan, Gilbert J., S.J. *The Jesuits of the Middle United States.* New York: America Press, 1938. 3 vols.

Gibson, Ralph. *A Social History of French Catholicism.* London: Routledge, 1989.

Glazier, Michael, and Thomas J. Shelley, eds. *The Encyclopedia of American Catholicism.* Collegeville, Minn.: The Liturgical Press, 1983.

Gleason, Philip. *Contending with Modernity: Catholic Higher Education in the Twentieth Century.* New York: Oxford University Press, 1995.

Greeley, Andrew M. *The Church and the Suburbs.* New York: Sheed & Ward, 1959.

Hanley, Thomas O'Brien, S.J. *The John Carroll Papers.* Notre Dame, Ind.: University of Notre Dame Press, 1976. 3 vols.

Hassard, John. *Life of the Most Reverend John Hughes, D.D., First Archbishop of New York.* New York: D. Appleton and Company, 1866.

Hennesey, James, S.J. *American Catholics: A History of the Roman Catholic Community in the United States.* New York: Oxford University Press, 1981.

Hennessy, Thomas C., S.J., ed. *Fordham: The Early Years.* New York: Something More Publications, 1998.

———. *How the Jesuits Settled in New York: A Documentary Account.* New York: Something More Publications, 2003.

Herberg, Will. *Protestant-Catholic-Jew.* Garden City, N.Y.: Doubleday and Company, 1955.

Hughes, Thomas J., S.J. *History of the Society of Jesus in North America.* New York: Longmans, Green and Company, 1908–1917. 4 vols.

Jackson, Kenneth T. *Encyclopedia of the City of New York.* Second Edition. New Haven and New York: Yale University Press and the New-York Historical Society, 2010.

Jonnes, Jill. *We're Still Here: The Rise, Fall and Resurrection of the South Bronx.* Boston: Atlantic Monthly Press, 1986.

Kaczorowski, Robert J. *Fordham University School of Law: A History.* New York: Fordham University Press, 2012.

Kehoe, Lawrence, ed. *Complete Works of the Most Reverend John Hughes.* New York: Lawrence Kehoe, 1866. 2 vols.

Kertzer, David I. *The Pope and Mussolini.* New York: Random House, 2014.

Klein, Felix. *In the Land of the Strenuous Life.* Chicago: A. C. McClurg, 1905.

Langhan, John P. *Catholic Universities in Church and Society.* Washington: Georgetown University Press, 1993.

Lannie, Vincent P. *Public Money and Parochial Education: Bishop Hughes, Governor Seward and the New York School Controversy.* Cleveland: The Press of Case Western Reserve University, 1968.

Lee, Joseph, and Marion Casey, eds. *Making the Irish American: History and Heritage of the Irish in America.* New York: New York University Press, 2006.

Leflon, Jean. *La Crise Révolutionnaire, 1789–1846*. Paris: Bloud & Gay, 1951.

Lord, Robert, John Sexton, and Edward Harrington. *The History of the Archdiocese of Boston*. Boston: Boston Pilot Publishing Company, 1944. 3 vols.

Ludmerer, Kenneth. *Learning to Heal: The Development of American Medical Education*. New York: Basic Books, 1985.

Mahoney, Kathleen. *Catholic Higher Education in Protestant America: The Jesuits and Harvard in the Age of the University*. Baltimore: Johns Hopkins University Press, 2003.

Maraniss, David. *When Pride Still Mattered: A Life of Vince Lombardi*. New York: Simon & Schuster, 1999.

Marrone, Debra Caruso. *Fordham University and the United States: A History*. New York: E-LIT Books, 2013.

McCarthy, Joseph F.X. *Learning in the City: The Graduate School of Education Reviews Its Seventy-Five Years in New York City, 1916–1992*. New York: Fordham University Graduate School of Education, 1992.

McDonough, Peter. *Men Astutely Trained*. New York: The Free Press, 1992.

McKeown, Elizabeth. *War and Welfare: American Catholics and World War I*. New York: Garland Publishing Company, 1988.

McSeveny, Samuel T. *The Politics of Depression: Political Behavior in the Northeast, 1893–1896*. New York: Oxford University Press, 1972.

The Metropolitan Catholic Almanac and Laity's Directory for the Year of Our Lord 1841. Baltimore: Fielding Lucas Jr., 1841.

Miller, Randall, and Jon L. Wakelyn, eds. *Catholics in the Old South*. Macon, Ga.: Mercer University Press, 1983.

Morris, Charles R. *American Catholic*. New York: Times Books / Random House, 1997.

O'Dea, Thomas. *The American Catholic Dilemma: An Inquiry into the Intellectual Life*. New York: Mentor Books, 1958.

Padberg, John W., S.J. *Colleges in Controversy: The Jesuit Schools in France from Revival to Suppression*. Cambridge, Mass.: Harvard University Press, 1969.

Ratner, Sidney, ed. *New Light on the History of Great American Fortunes: American Millionaires of 1892 and 1902*. New York: Augustus M. Kelly, Inc., 1953.

Roche, Richard J. *Catholic Colleges and the Negro Student*. Washington: The Catholic University of America Press, 1948.

Rosenwaike, Ira. *Population History of New York City*. Syracuse, N.Y.: Syracuse University Press, 1972.

Rybolt, John C., C.M., ed. *The American Vincentians: A Popular History of the Congregation of the Mission in the United States, 1815–1987*. Brooklyn, N.Y.: New City Press, 1988.

Schroth, Raymond A., S.J. *Fordham: A History and Memoir*. Chicago: Loyola University Press, 2002.

Shelley, Thomas J. *Dunwoodie: The History of St. Joseph's Seminary*. Westminster, Md.: Christian Classics, 1993.

Smith, John Talbot. *The Catholic Church in New York*. New York: Hall & Locke, 1908. 2 vols.

Spalding, Thomas W. *Martin John Spalding: American Churchman*. Washington: The Catholic University of America Press, 1973.

Spann, Edward. *The New Metropolis*. New York: Columbia University Press, 1981.

Sullivan, Robert E., and James M. O'Toole, eds. *Catholic Boston: Studies in Religion and Community, 1870–1970*. Boston: The Roman Catholic Archdiocese of Boston, 1985.

Taaffe, Thomas Gaffney. *A History of St. John's College, Fordham*. New York: The Catholic Publication Society, 1891.

Thébaud, Augustus J., S.J. *Forty Years in the United States of America*. New York: United States Catholic Historical Society, 1904.

Waugh, Joan. *Unsentimental Reformer: The Life of Josephine Shaw Lowell*. Cambridge, Mass.: Harvard University Press, 1998.

Webb, Ben J. *The Centenary of Catholicity in Kentucky*. Louisville, Ky.: Charles A. Rogers, 1884.

Wilentz, Sean. *Chants Democratic: New York City and the Rise of the American Working Class, 1788–1850*. New York: Oxford University Press, 1984.

ARTICLES

Binsse, Henry. "The Church of St. Vincent de Paul (The French Church)." *HR&S* 12 (1918): 102–14.

"Bishop John J. Collins, S.J." *WL* 64 (1935): 262–68.

Bull, George, S.J. "The Future of the Catholic Graduate School." *Thought* 13 (September 1938): 364–80.

Cammarosano, Joseph. "Write Off the South Bronx? Not by a Long Shot!" *Fordham*, fall 1981: 3–4.

Cassily, Francis B., S.J. "Catholic Students at State Universities." *AER* 34 (1906): 113–20.

Clarke, W. Norris, S.J., *As I Remember Fordham: Selections from the Sesquicentennial Oral History Project*. New York: Fordham University Press, 1991: 52–54.

Clary, Jack, FCRH '54. "125 Years of Fordham Football." *Fordham*, summer 2007: 20–23.

Cornell, Thomas C. "Catholic Beginnings in Yonkers." *HR&S* 36 (1947): 68–96.

Crowley, Francis M. "Only One Graduate School?" *America*, June 11, 1932.

Curran, Francis X., S.J. "Archbishop Hughes and the Jesuits." *WL* 97 (1968): 5–56. Reprinted as "Archbishop Hughes and the Jesuits: An Anatomy of Their Quarrels" in Thomas C. Hennessy, S.J., ed., *Fordham: The Early Years* (New York: Something More Publications, 1998), 177–221.

———. "The Founding of Fordham University and the New York Mission." *Archivum Historicum Societatis Jesu* 26 (1957): 285–94.

———. "The Jesuits in Kentucky, 1831–1846." *Mid-America* 35 (1953): 223–46.

Deferrari, Roy J. "Rehabilitating the Master's Degree." *Commonweal*, June 29, 1932: 233–35.

Donceel, Joseph, S.J., *As I Remember Fordham: Selections from the Sesquicentennial Oral History Project*. New York: Fordham University Press, 1991: 37–39.

Donohue, John W., S.J., *As I Remember Fordham: Selections from the Sesquicentennial Oral History Project*. New York: Fordham University Press, 1991: 58–60.

Drolet, Francis K., S.J. "Negro Students in Catholic Schools and Colleges." *WL* 76 (1947): 299–309.

Ellis, John Tracy. "American Catholics and the Intellectual Life." *Thought* 30 (August 1955): 351–88.

"Father Thomas Ouellet: A Sketch." *WL* 24 (1895): 375–80.

Feerick, John D. "*The Fordham Law Review* and Dean Joseph M. McLaughlin: A Combined Tribute." *FLR* 50:1 (1981): v–vi.

Fleming, Thomas J. "Fordham Is Trying to Be catholic with a Small 'c.'" *New York Times Magazine*, December 10, 1967.

Fuller, Paul. "Frederic R. Coudert." *HR&S* 3 (1904): 343–50.

Garraghan, Gilbert J., S.J. "Fordham's Jesuit Beginnings." *Thought* 16 (March 1941): 17–39.

Gleason, Philip. "From an Indefinite Homogeneity: Catholic Colleges in Antebellum America." *CHR* 94:1 (2008): 45–74.

———. "The Main Sheet Anchor: John Carroll and Catholic Higher Education." *Review of Politics* 38:4 (October 1976): 576–613.

Hanlon, Robert M., Jr. "A History of Fordham Law School." *FLR* 49 (1980–81): xiv–xviii.

Harrington, John P. "Voyager to the West: Joseph Campbell and Irish Studies." *The Times Literary Supplement*, January 13, 2012: 14–15.

Hennessy, Thomas C., S.J. "Joseph Campbell and the School of Irish Studies at Fordham University, 1928–1932." *New York Irish History* 10 (1996): 24–30.

Hill, Walter H., S.J. "Some Facts and Incidents Relating to St. Joseph's College, Bardstown, 1861–1868." *WL* 26 (1897): 90–108.

———. "Some Reminiscences of St. Mary's College, Kentucky." *WL* 20 (1891): 25–38.

Jaskievicz, Walter C., S.J., *As I Remember Fordham: Selections from the Sesquicentennial Oral History Project*. New York: Fordham University Press, 1991: 99–101.

Kelly, William R., and John J. Voight. "Parish Schools in New York, 1800–1939." *New York Catholic News*, June 17, 1939.

Kirwin, Harry W. "James J. Walsh: Medical Historian and Pathfinder." *CHR* 45 (1960): 410–35.

Lefkowitz, Louis J. "Evening Classes at Fordham Law School, 1922–1925." *FLR* 49 (1980–81): xxxviii–xxxix.

Loomie, Albert J., S.J. "Father John Wynne, S.J." *WL* 80 (1951): 61–66.

Martin, James, S.J. "Vincent O'Keefe." *America*, July 24, 2012.

McGinley, Laurence J., S.J., *As I Remember Fordham: Selections from the Sesquicentennial Oral History Project*. New York: Fordham University Press, 1991: 1–3, 5–6.

McQuaid, Bernard. "Our American Seminaries." *AER* 16 (1897): 472–73.

McShane, Joseph, S.J. "'To Form an Elite Body of Laymen . . .' Father Terence J. Shealy, S.J., and The Laymen's League." *CHR* 78 (1992): 557–80.

———. "A Survey of the Jesuit Labor Schools in New York: An American Social Gospel in Action." *RACHSP* 102:4 (1991): 37–43.

Mulligan, William Hughes. "Forty Years of Fordham Law School." *FLR* 24 (1955–56): xi–xiii.

———. "A Former Dean Remembers." *FLR* 49 (1980–81): xxx–xxxi.

Nelligan, Francis J., S.J. "Father John Larkin, 1801–1858." *The Canadian Messenger of the Sacred Heart*, 1957: 33–41, 105–10.

O'Brien, Kevin J., S.J. "Father Joseph T. Keating, S.J., 1871–1950." *WL* 81 (1952): 270–74.

O'Keefe, Vincent T., S.J., *As I Remember Fordham: Selections from the Sesquicentennial Oral History Project*. New York: Fordham University Press, 1991: 5.

O'Malley, Austin. "Catholic Collegiate Education in the United States." *Catholic World* 67 (1898): 293–304.

Power, Edward J. "The Formative Years of Catholic Colleges Founded before 1850 and Still in Existence as Colleges and Universities." *RACHSP* 65 (1954): 24–39, 230–39; 66 (1955): 19–34.

"Reminiscences of Father Michael Nash, S.J." *WL* 26 (1897): 257–83.

Scanlon, Michael. "Return to Highbridge." *Catholic New York*, October 7, 1993.

Schroth, Raymond A., S.J. "College as Camelot." *The Saturday Review*, 1972: 52–57.

———. "How Women Came to Fordham: Life and Death of Thomas More College." *Conversations on Jesuit Higher Education*, vol. 29, art. 12: 33–34.

Shelley, Thomas J. "John Cardinal Farley and Modernism in New York." *CH* 61 (1992): 350–61.

Taaffe, Thomas Gaffney. "Rev. Peter Tissot, S.J." *HR&S* 3:1 (1903): 38–41.

Wilson, Malcolm. "Law School at Rose Hill." *FLR* 49 (1980–81): xxxiv–xxvvii.

Wines, Roger, and Allan S. Gilbert. "St. John's College at Fordham and Its Pioneering Electrification in the Bronx." *The Bronx County Historical Journal* 51, 1 & 2 (spring & fall 2014): 28–46.

"A Year with the Army of the Potomac: Diary of the Rev. Father Peter Tissot, S.J., Military Chaplain." *HR&S* 3:1 (1903): 42–87.

NEWSPAPERS

The Catholic Advocate
The Goose-Quill
New York Catholic News
New York Catholic Register
New York Evening Post
New York Freeman's Journal
New York Herald
New York Herald-Tribune
New York Mercantile Advertiser
New York Post
New York Sun
New York Times
New York Tribune
Ram
Tablet (Brooklyn)
Truth Teller

DISSERTATIONS AND THESES

Curley, Thomas E., Jr. "Robert I. Gannon, S.J., President of Fordham University, 1936–1949, A Jesuit Educator." Ph.D. diss., New York University, 1973.

Kelly, Neil A. "Orphans and Pigs Fed from the Same Bowl: The New York Charities Controversy." M.A. thesis, St. Joseph's Seminary, Dunwoodie, Yonkers, New York, 1994.

Klein, Christa. "The Jesuits and Catholic Boyhood in Nineteenth-Century New York City: A Study of St. John's College and the College of St. Francis Xavier, 1846–1912." Ph.D. diss., University of Pennsylvania, 1976.

Lannie, Vincent P. "Archbishop Hughes and the Common School Controversy, 1840–1842." Ph.D. diss., Teachers College, Columbia University, 1963.

Nolan, David E. "The Catholic Club of New York City: A Study of Lay Involvement in New York City, 1888–1960." M.A. thesis, St. Joseph's Seminary, Dunwoodie, Yonkers, New York, 1995.

INDEX

9/11 terrorist attacks, 480–81

140th anniversary, 457

1920s, 168–77

1950s: American Catholics and, 334–35, 361–66; civil rights movement, 337–39; Cold War, ROTC cadets and, 340; Eisenhower years, 334–35; faculty discontent, 366–68; finances, 342–43; Korean War, 342–43; population reduction, 341–43; religion boom, 340–41; student restlessness, 365–66; students' favorite public person, 336

1960s: campus revolutions, 388–89. *See also* self-study of 1960–63

1970s: Jesuit presence, 444–46; turmoil, Walsh and, 412–13

AAU (Association of American Universities): 1935 inspection, 265–66; Gannon and, 271–72; graduate program, 264; Graduate School inspection, 265–66; membership loss, 169, 209, 247, 267–68; restoration to list, 272

ABA (American Bar Association): Feerick years at Law School, 227–28; Law School accreditation, 210; Law School conflicts, 224; Pro Bono Publico Award to Law School, 228–29; Wilkinson and, 207–10

Abell, Rev. Robert A., 32

abortion public policy, rumors surrounding, 485

accreditation, McGinley and, 346–47

Act Against Jesuits and Popish Priests, 28

Adams, Matthew Ebenezer, 326

admission requirements: Gilded Age, 126–27; Law School, 208–10; Teachers College, 282–83

Admissions Office, 172

Agar, John G., 166

Ahern, Bishop Patrick V., South Bronx revival and, 426

All-University Center on Gerontology, 456–57

alumni: AAU decision and, 268; Civil War and, 91–96; clergy among, 82–83; early, 81–84; Gannon's prediction, 459; victims of 9/11 attacks, 481; WWI service, 162

Alumni Court North/South, 465

America, 357; O'Hare as editor-in-chief, 464–65

American Association of Law Schools accreditation, 272

American Bar Association. *See* ABA (American Bar Association)

American Catholics: 1950s, 361–66; education and, 154, 279; immigration and growth, 52–53; Kennedy assassination, 369–70; in Kentucky, 31; New York mayors, 123; Pope John XXIII death, 370; population growth, 123; private school system, 362; Vietnam War and, 391–92; WWI and, 158–60

American Council on Education, GSAS evaluation, 279–80

American Holy Land (Kentucky), 31

Anastasi, Anne, 471

anti-war movement: building occupations in protest, 418–20; faculty involvement, 422; Fordham Five, 418; Kerry, John, before subcommittee, 391; ROTC, protests and, 415–17; slowing, 423; Students for a Democratic Society, 392–93, 416, 420–21; vandalism, 420–21

Arbesmann, Rev. Rudolph, O.S.A., 274

archaeological dig for Rose Hill Manor, 467

Arrupe, Rev. Pedro, S.J.: McLaughlin resignation, 409; O'Keefe and, 385–86

Association of Colleges and Universities of New York State, Finlay and, 454

Association of Urban Universities, 453–54

athletic programs: baseball, 324–25; Big-Time Football, 317–19; Coffey, John, 324–25; early years, 68; under O'Hare, 466; WWII years, 312

bachelors degrees, 72–73

Bacon, George W., 213

Baker, Howard H. (Senator), visit to Fordham, 454

Barbarsky, Al, *320*

Barrett, Rev. Alfred J., S.J., 344

baseball team, 324–25

lege at Lincoln Center, 394–95; Rose Hill, 389–95

campus unrest of 1970s, 412–14

Carnegie, Andrew (Mrs.), 167

Carrigan, Andrew, 9, 9n7, 9n8; son at St. John's, 82

Carroll, John, security during 9/11 attacks, 480

Carroll, Archbishop John, 5–6

Carrubba, Robert W., integration approval, 470

Catholic Charities, School of Social Service and, 237–39

Catholic Club, 116–17

Catholic colleges: Land O'Lakes Statement, 396; surviving, 20

Catholic communities. *See* American Catholics

Catholic education: American Catholic colleges, 20; "American Catholics and the Intellectual Life" (Ellis), 363–64; critics, 154–57; critique by Msgr. Ellis, 362–63; *Ex Corde Ecclesiae* (Pope John Paul II), 483–84; higher education requirements in 1930s, 287; McClay bill, 16; Pius XI recommendation for standards upgrade, 245; private school system size, 362; Public School Society and, 15–16; public schools and, 286; students at secular schools, 151–54

Catholic Halls at secular colleges, 153–54

Catholic identity: and academic freedom, 484–85; Steinfels interviews, 482. *See also* American Catholics

Catholic Identity Symposia, 482

Catholic Interracial Conference, 326; Bronx and, 453–54

Catholic Summer School of America, 269–70

Cavanaugh, Frank (Iron Major), 318

centennial, 305; Connolly, Francis, on, 149; post-war celebration, 316–17

Center for Communications, M.B.A.s, 293

Chabrat, Bishop Guy: clashes with Jesuits, 42–43; sabotage of Jesuits' plans, 43–44

Chapin, H. Gerald, 203

Chardin, Pierre Teilhard de, planned symposium, 380

Chazelle, Rev. Peter, S.J., 34–35; instructions from Father Renault, 35–36

Christ and Apollo: The Dimensions of the Literary Imagination (Lynch), 357

Church of St. Lawrence O'Toole, 113–14

Church of the Holy Name of Jesus, 97–99

civil rights movement, 337–39; Rose Hill, 389–90; Selma, Alabama, 390; Society for African-American Advancement, 390–91

Civil War years, 90–96

Clark, Rev. Edward F., S.J., Donohue and self-study, 371–72

Clarke, Rev. W. Norris, S.J., 356

classical course, *versus* commercial, 132

Clinton, President Bill, commencement speaker invitation, 488

coeducation resistance, 382; Thomas More College, 384

Coffey, John F. (Jack), 312–*13, 105*; 324–25

Cold War: Institute of Contemporary Russian Studies, 340; ROTC cadets and, 340

Coler, Bird S., 167

College of Business Administration, 291; American Association of Collegiate Schools of Business, 292; Beta Gamma Sigma, 292; liberal arts education and, 291–92; Rose Hill, 292–93

College of St. Francis Xavier, 102, *105*; alumni sodality, 114–17; Americanization, 104; archbishops, future, 109; bishops, future, 109; classical course, 132; classical education, 107–8; curriculum, 105–6; graduates' vocation choices, 108–9; growth, 102–3; Herbermann, Charles George, 109–10; independence from St. John's, 104–5; Jesuit alumni, 109; philosophy courses, 106; *ratio studiorum,* 107–8, 132; St. John's consolidation, 117–20, 147; state charter, 105–6; tuition, 103; Xavier Union, 115–17. *See also* Xavier University

College of the Holy Cross, 20

College of the Holy Name, 100; Larkin resignation, 100; Ryan, Rev. John, S.J., 100–1. *See also* College of St. Francis Xavier

college-seminary model, 9–10

Colligan, Eugene A., 285

Collins, Bishop John J., S.J., 177; on discipline, 67; graduate schools, 147; Law School establishment, 201, 230; university establishment, 178–81; vicar apostolic of appointment, 180–81

Colton, Bishop Charles H., 108

commencement: Clinton, Bill, speaker invitation, 488; Ford, William P., address, 479;

program, 455; retirement, 460; Rose Hill
Apartments, 454–55; students and gov-
ernance, 436; Third Age Center, 456–57;
Thomas More College merge, 455; vision
for future, 439; youth, 436–37
Finlay Hall, 176, 262; Medical School, *188*
Finn, John F.X., 37–38, 213, 230
fires on campus, 176–77
Fisher, Rev. J. Harding, 331
Fitzpatrick, Rev. Joseph, S.J.: anti-war move-
ment and, 422; Gellhorn Report, 406; li-
brary planning committee, 472–73; Puerto
Rican community and, 354–55, 460
FLAG (Fordham Lesbians and Gays), 484–85
FLAG at Fordham position paper, 486
Flaget, Bishop Benedict Joseph, 31; as coad-
jutor, 48; sabotage of Jesuits' plans, 44; St.
Joseph's and, 32–33, 43–44, 45, 48
Foch, Marshal Ferdinand, honorary degree,
162–64, *164*
football: discontinuation, 343. *See also* Big-
Time Football
Ford, Sister Ita, 479
Ford, William P., commencement address, 479
Fordham Centenary Fund Appeal, 309–10
Fordham College: O'Mailia on, 304; transition
to, 300–4
Fordham College, Manhattan Division, 294–
95; School of Professional and Continuing
Studies, 296
Fordham Downtown, 281–82; separate deans
for schools, 284; Vincent Building, 287,
288, 289
Fordham Evening College. *See* School of
Adult Education
Fordham Five, 418
Fordham Founder's Presidential Scholarship
Fund, 489–90
Fordham Law Review, McLaughlin and, 225
Fordham Manor, 8–9
Fordham Monthly: Dealy and, 138–39; fiftieth
anniversary graduate list, 142–44
Fordham Plaza, Finlay and, 450–51
Fordham Station, *134*
Fordham Students for Choice, 484
Fordham University, WWI years, 157–64
Fordham University Hospital, 185
Fordham University Press, 170
foreign language proficiency, 261–62
Fortier, Rev. Matthew L., S.J., 240–45; expan-

sion and, 281; Graduate School of Arts
and Sciences, 259; letter of commendation
from Pope Pius XI, 244–45; *Rerum No-
varum,* 244–45
Fouché, Rev. Simon, S.J., 35
Franko, Ed, *320*
Free Speech Movement, 388
Freeman, Rev. Thomas J. A.: Medical School,
182; Parthenian Sodality, 137–38; science
instruction, 133
Freeman Hall, 176
French Jesuits, 29–32; American citizenship,
36
Frese, Rev. Joseph, S.J., 354
Friedan, Betty, speaking invitation, 488
Friedland, Ronald, denial of tenure, 419
Frisbee, Rev. Samuel H., S.J., Xavier, 107–8
Frisch, Frankie, 324, *325*
Fuller, Paul, *202, 230*; dean of Law School,
201–2

Gabelli, Mario, 294
Gabelli School of Business, 294. *See
also* Graduate School of Business
Administration
Gage, Rev. William, S.J., 28
Gannon, Rev. Robert I., S.J., 271; AAU and,
271–72; Association of American Universities membership, 247–48; Bishop's
Hall, 328; on construction expansion, 176;
expansion post–WWII, 315–16; expansion
under, 270–71; faculty recruitment, 273–77;
FDR visit, 307–9, *308*; financial steward-
ship, 329–30; football, 321–23; Fordham
War Memorial, 328; Keating Hall dedication, 272–73; McIntyre and, 249–50; on
Msgr. Ellis's critique, 364; as public figure,
474; Queen's Court, 328; racial integration
and, 326–30; St. Robert Bellarmine Hall,
328; Walsh's role model, 411; war dead,
162, 164–65
Gannon, Rev. Thomas J., S.J., 145–47, 344
Gargan, Frank, 318
Garvan, Francis P., 166, 206
Gellhorn, Walter, 401; trustees and, 403–4
Gellhorn Report, 401–3; reception, 405–6;
secular media, fears concerning, 405; trustees and, 403–4
geographical distribution of students, 73–74
Georgetown University, 20

Schools, 266; National Conference of Catholic Charities, 246–47

Hohman, George, 197

Holland, Ralph H., 203

homosexuality teachings, 486

honorary degrees: Devenney, Anne, 452; Duffy, Rev. Francis P., 162; Foch, Ferdinand, 162–64; Kennedy, John F., *358*; O'Connor, Sandra Day, 466; Pacelli, Eugenio Cardinal, 305–6; president of the Philippines, 479–80; Walesa, Lech, 477–78

Honors Program: Davis, Rev. Thurston, 353–54; study in France, 354

Horstman, Gustave, 197

Huckleberry Line (horsecar), *134, 135*

Huggins, Willis Nathaniel, 326

Hughes, Archbishop John, 2–3, *6*; Civil War, 91; College of St. Francis Xavier, 102; emigration, 5; faculty, 11–14; faculty, Jesuit recruiting, 23–25; funding for College of the Holy Name, 101; fundraising, initial, 11–14; funds for Church of the Holy Name of Jesus, 98–99; Lafargeville purchase, 8; lay trusteeism and, 14–15; leadership style, 99–100; naming of new college, 101; Nativism and, 17; obscurity fears for St. John's, 461; ordination, 5; plans for Rose Hill, 9–11; Public School Society and, 15–16; retrograde of St. John's, 125–26; Rose Hill purchase, 7; St. John's 1845 commencement, 1–2; St. John's fiftieth anniversary, 141–42; St. Joseph's Seminary, 86–88; statue, 142, *143*

Hughes Hall, Gabelli School of Business, 294

Husslein, Rev. Joseph, S.J.: Graduate School of Arts and Sciences, 259; School of Social Service, 235

IAP (Instructional Administrators Program), 290

immigration, growth of Catholic community and, 52–53

"Industrial Activity in the Inner City: A Case Study of the South Bronx" (Cammarosano), 453

Institut Catholique, Honors students and, 354

Institute of Contemporary Russian Studies, 340

Interracial Justice Sunday Mass, 337

Irish Catholics, politics, 122–23

Iron Major (Frank Cavanaugh), 318

Jaffré, Rev. John, S.J., 112

Jansen, William, 282

Janssens, Rev. Jean-Baptiste, S.J.: building expansion under McGinley, 342; graduate degrees, 278; on *Philosophical Psychology* (Donceel), 358

Jarry, Michael, S.J., 39

Jaskievicz, Rev. Walter C., S.J., Russian Studies, 340

Jessup, Rev. Michael, S.J.: expansion and, 281; fire and, 176

Jesuit Curia: Dezza, 404; O'Keefe, 385–86

Jesuit education: AAU inclusion, 266; Brann, Rev. Henry, on, 152; Campbell, Father Thomas, on, 152; criticism, 150; criticism by Charles Eliot, 150–51; dual leadership, effects on, 332; Harvard Law School and, 150–52; Murphy and, 40; O'Hare on, 470, 484; Petit, Rev., George, on, 152; primary objective, 62; progressives, 266; School of Education and, 282; social justice and, 477; Thébaud on, 37; Walsh, James, on, 184

Jesuit Educational Association: Conference of Presidents, 347; Gellhorn report recommendation, 405; O'Connell, Rev. Daniel, 265–66; Rooney, Rev. Edward, S.J., 330–31; Wilkinson, Ignatius, 210

Jesuits: 1950s faculty recruitment, 344–45; early New York presence, 28–29; early recruiting, 23–25; French, 29–32; French, American citizenship, 36; Jogues, Isaac (Saint), S.J., 28; leaving Kentucky, 44; missionaries in Kentucky, 31; Mount St. Mary's Seminary, 33–36; murdered in El Salvadore, 478–79; pastoral ministry of, 111–14; secular clothes, 81; self-study of 1960–63, 374–75; St. Joseph's, 32–33. *See also* Society of Jesus

Jewish faculty, fleeing Nazism, 273–75

Jewish students: Pharmacy School, 196–200; School of Social Service, 239

Jogues, Isaac (Saint), S.J., 28; Martyr's Court, 359; pilgrimmage, 341

John XXIII (Pope), death, American Catholics and, 370

John Paul II (Pope): *Ex Corde Ecclesiae*, 483; O'Keefe and, 386

Center fire, 420–21; Committee to Abolish the ROTC, 416; Rudd, Mark, 392–93; Walsh's tolerance, 421; waning support, 422–23

seal of the university, Gellhorn Report and, 402

secular clothes for clergy, 81; Gellhorn report, 401–2; McLaughlin on, 398

seismic station, 177

Self-Study Committee, 366–68

self-study of 1960–63, 370–72; faculty, 374–76; Faculty Senate, 379–80; Jesuit faculty, 374–75; O'Keefe's responsibilities, 377–78; recommendations, 376–77; student body and, 372–74; Thomas More College, 382–85

Séné, James, S.J., 40

Seniors' Hall (Rose Hill), 129; Dealy Hall, 136; fundraising, 130

Servicemen's Readjustment Act, 314–15

sesquicentennial (1991), enrollment, 461

Sesquicentennial Hall, 472–73

Seven Blocks of Granite, 319, *320*

Seward, William H., Catholic school establishment, 15–16

Sewell, Elizabeth, Bensalem College and, 426–27

Shaw, Robert Gould, 81

Shea, Rev. Joseph, S.J.: dissatisfaction among students, 131–32; Freeman, Rev. Thomas J.A., S.J., and, 133; modernization and, 130–31; renovations, 130–31

Shealy, Rev. Terence J., S.J., 203, 259; Graduate School of Social Science, 232; School of Social Service, 233; School of Sociology and Social Service, 235

Shen, Vivian, Walsh Library and, 474

Sherwin, Carl P., 193

Shrine of the North American Martyrs pilgrimage, 341

sit-ins during civil rights movement, 338–39

Smith, Governor Alfred E., and Fordham Centenary Fund Appeal, 310

Smith, Alfred H., 167

smoking on campus, early years, 70–71

social justice at Fordham, 477–80

Society for African-American Advancement, 390–91

Society for the Propagation of the Faith, 12

Society of Jesus: return to New York, 29–32; St. John's College, 3–4. *See also* Jesuits

sodalities, 136–38; Legoüais and, 80–81; Parthenian Sodality, 137, 303; *Prima Primaria,* 138; Xavier, 114–17

Somerville, Rev. James M., S.J.: de Chardin symposium plans, 380; post–Vatican II visit, 431–32

Sopranis, Rev. Félix, S.J., philosphy teaching and, 106

Sorapure, E. V., Medical School faculty dispute, 185–86

Sorbonne, Honors students and, 354

South Bronx: Cammarosano's studies, 453; Catholic Church and, 424–25; neighborhood blight, 424–25; revival, 424–26. *See also* Fordham Plaza; Bronx, the

Spalding, Archbishop Martin, 34

Spellman, Francis Cardinal: admission to St. John's, 126–27; diocesan newspaper pictures, 314; enrollment at Fordham, 305; interview by Father Quinn, 126–27; President Lyndon B. Johnson at funeral Mass, 370; Law School cornerstone, 218; University Church altar, 314

sports and recreation. *See* athletic programs

Spring Hill College, 20

Squires, Lt. Herbert G. U.S.A., cadet corps, 139

St. John's College, 20; admission requirements, 126–27; alumni, early, 81–84; alumni vocations (fiftieth anniversary), 142–44; American changes to nomenclature, 126; Campbell, Rev. Thomas, S.J., 49–50; change to Fordham College, 300–4; Civil War years, 90–96; classical education, 126–27; College of St. Francis Xavier consolidation, 147; commencement 1845, 1–4; core curriculum, first, 21; Dealy Hall, 55; enrollment (1845), 144; enrollment records, 72–73; faculty at opening, 18–20; faculty in early years, 75; fiftieth anniversary, 141–44; graduate schools, first, 147; Hughes Hall, 55; initial curriculum, 60–62; opening day, 17–18; philosophy courses, 106; projected plans, *125*; rules, 21; rural character, 124–28; Society of Jesus and, 3–4; student life in early years, 62–68; Thebaud Hall, *55*; Tivnan's expansion plans, 165–68; transformation to Fordham University, 147; tuition, first, 21; university establishment,

178–79; Xavier consolidation, 117–20. *See also* Rose Hill

St. John's Hall (St. Joseph's Diocesan Seminary), *83*

St. Joseph, Father Keating and, 175

St. Joseph's College, 31, 32–33; Civil War years, 49; current usage, 49; Flaget and, 43, 45–46; Jesuits' arrival, 32–33; sale offer, 46

St. Joseph's Seminary, 84–90; cornerstone festivities, cadets and, 139–40

St. Louis University, 20

St. Mary's. *See* Mount St. Mary's College and Seminary

St. Patrick's Cathedral, 29; dedication, 122–23

St. Vincent's College, 20

state aid: Blaine Amendment, 402, 404; Gellhorn Report and, 402–3; Lefkowitz and, 401; rulings, 406

statement of university objectives, 367

steam heat installation, 133–34

Steinfels, Peter, Catholic identity, interviews, 482–83

Steinmeyer, Rev. Ferdinand, S.J. (Father Farmer), 28–29

Steuer, Max, Medical School reopening, 193

Stevenson, Adlai E., 218

student athletes, 320–21

student body: background in 1970s, 441–42; minority population in 1970s, 442; restlessness of 1950s and 1960s, 365–66; self-study of 1960–63 and, 372–74

student demonstrations of 1970s, Walsh and, 412–14

student life: early years, 62–71; sodalities, 136–38

student publications, censored, 365–66

Student-Faculty Coalition for a Restructured University, 398

summer sessions, 299–300

Sutherland, Arthur E., 218

Taaffe, Thomas Gaffney, rural character of Fordham, 124

Talley, Alfred J., 110

Tartar, Helen, 170

Taylor, Arthur R., 293

Taylor, Rev. Eamon G., S.J., Jesuit presence at Fordham, 445

Teachers College, 261; admission requirements, 282–83; B.A. degrees for career advancement, 282; Graduate School and, 283; liberal arts education, 282–83; limits on admission, 283–84; women on faculty, 283. *See also* School of Education

Thébaud, Rev. Augustus, S.J., 40; curriculum at Rose Hill, 60–62; Harvard and Yale visits, 58–59; Jesuit education for Protestants, 37–38; on New York, 52; smoking on campus, 70–71; St. Mary's College, 57

Thebaud Hall, 133

Theology Department, under Father O'Hare, 471

Third Age Center, 456–57

The Thirteenth: The Greatest of Centuries (Walsh), 184

Thomas More College: Donohue as dean, 382–83; establishment, 382; merge with Fordham College, 385, 455; opposition, 384–85; Plate, Patricia, 383

Thomism in Philosophy Department, 356

The Thorn of Rose Hill (humor magazine), 365

Thought, 357; "American Catholics and the Intellectual Life" (Ellis), 363–64

Tierney Hall, 465; Sesquicentennial Hall, 472–73

Tilley, Maureen, 471

Tilley, Terrence, 471n19

Timasheff, Nicholas, 275

Tissot, Rev. Peter, S.J., 94–95

Tivnan, Rev. Edward P., S.J., *164*, 165; fundraising, 165–68; graduate programs, 193; Medical School and, 189–90; Memorial Gateway and, 162

Tognino Hall, 172

Traditio, 357; Lienhard, 471

trustees: Gellhorn Report and, 403–4; lay president preference, 437–38; state aid and, 403; Walsh appointment last, 411

TTT (Training Teacher Trainers), 290

tuition discount for freshman living at home, 468

underground student publications, 365–66

university centers (satellite campuses), 298–99

University Church: as ecumenical chapel, Gellhorn Report and, 402; expansion, 173–74

university establishment, 178; Farley, Rev. John Murphy, and, 179–80

President Franklin D. Roosevelt being greeted by Father Robert I. Gannon, S.J., on the occasion of his visit to Fordham University on October 28, 1940